REGULATING DISPUTE RESOLUTION

This book proposes a principled approach to the regulation of dispute resolution. It covers dispute resolution mechanisms in all their varieties, including negotiation, mediation, conciliation, expert opinion, mini-trial, ombudsman procedure, arbitration and court adjudication. The authors present a transnational Guide for Regulating Dispute Resolution (GRDR). The regulatory principles contained in this Guide are based on a functional taxonomy of dispute resolution mechanisms, an open normative framework and a modular structure of regulatory topics. The Guide for Regulating Dispute Resolution is formulated and commented upon in a concise manner to assist legislators, policy-makers, professional associations, practitioners and academics in thinking about which solutions best suit local and regional circumstances.

The aim of this book is to contribute to the understanding and development of the legal framework governing national and international dispute resolution. Theory, empirical research and regulatory models have been taken from the wealth of experience in 12 jurisdictions: Austria, Belgium, Denmark, England and Wales, France, Germany, Italy, Japan, the Netherlands, Norway, Switzerland and the United States. Experts with a background in academia, practice and law-making describe and analyse the regulatory framework and social reality of dispute resolution in these countries. On this basis the authors draw conclusions about policy choices, regulatory strategies and the practice of conflict resolution.

Regulating Dispute Resolution

ADR and Access to Justice at the Crossroads

Edited by
Felix Steffek and Hannes Unberath
in cooperation with
Hazel Genn, Reinhard Greger
and Carrie Menkel-Meadow

•HART•
PUBLISHING

OXFORD AND PORTLAND, OREGON
2013

First printed in 2013 and reprinted in 2014
Published in the United Kingdom by Hart Publishing Ltd
16C Worcester Place, Oxford, OX1 2JW
Telephone: +44 (0)1865 517530
Fax: +44 (0)1865 510710
E-mail: mail@hartpub.co.uk
Website: http://www.hartpub.co.uk

Published in North America (US and Canada) by
Hart Publishing
c/o International Specialized Book Services
920 NE 58th Avenue, Suite 300
Portland, OR 97213-3786
USA
Tel: +1 503 287 3093 or toll-free: (1) 800 944 6190
Fax: +1 503 280 8832
E-mail: orders@isbs.com
Website: http://www.isbs.com

British Library Cataloguing in Publication Data

Data Available

ISBN: 978-1-84946-258-7

Typeset by Forewords, Oxon
Printed and bound by
CPI Group (UK) Ltd, Croydon, CR0 4YY

In Memoriam

Hannes Unberath

Preface

This book proposes a principled approach to the regulation of dispute resolution. It covers dispute resolution mechanisms in all their varieties, including negotiation, mediation, conciliation, expert opinion, mini-trial, ombudsman procedure, arbitration and court adjudication. The authors present a transnational Guide for Regulating Dispute Resolution (GRDR). The regulatory principles contained in this Guide are based on a functional taxonomy of dispute resolution mechanisms, an open normative framework and a modular structure of regulatory topics. The Guide for Regulating Dispute Resolution is formulated and commented upon in a concise manner to assist legislators, policy-makers, professional associations, practitioners and academics in thinking about what solutions best suit local and regional circumstances. The discussion of transnational principles for regulating dispute resolution has just started. The aim of this book is to contribute to the understanding and development of the legal framework governing national and international dispute resolution.

Theory, empirical research and regulatory models have been taken from the wealth of experience in 12 jurisdictions: Austria, Belgium, Denmark, England and Wales, France, Germany, Italy, Japan, the Netherlands, Norway, Switzerland and the United States of America. Experts with a background in academia, practice and law-making describe and analyse the regulatory framework and social reality of dispute resolution in these countries. On this basis, the authors draw conclusions regarding policy choices, regulatory strategies and the practice of conflict resolution. The method employed is comparative, interdisciplinary and oriented towards an integration of theory and practice. All texts are up-to-date as of 1 March 2013 and often even later.

The content of this book is the result of a team effort and enthusiasm at many levels. In 2009 the editors and authors began to develop the goal, subject and analytical framework of this project and agreed to meet in Bayreuth from 13 to 16 September 2012. There they were joined by a selected group of law-makers, professionals and academics, and discussed structures and principles of dispute resolution. All participating experts deserve our gratitude for their reliable commitment, openness to dialogue and analytical inspiration. While this book often focuses on the individual and his or her conflict, the ideas presented here are based on a collective effort.

This project was very generously funded by the Fritz Thyssen Foundation. The meeting in Bayreuth was kindly hosted by the University of Bayreuth and its Faculty of Law and Economics. Additional funding was kindly provided by the Alumni Network of the Faculty of Law and Economics Bayreuth as well as the Bayreuth University Society. We would like to thank all our supporters for their generosity and kind encouragement.

In addition to this financial support, the organisation of the project and the publication of the book benefited greatly from support emanating from the respective academic homes of Hannes Unberath and Felix Steffek, namely the Chair for Civil and Procedural Law at the University of Bayreuth and the Max Planck Institute for Comparative and International Private Law in Hamburg. In Bayreuth the reliability and diligence of Jana Härtling has carried this project. The work's publication and overall organisation was also excellently taken care of by Birgit Heining, Corinna Hereth, Gordon Kardos, Martin Koch, Martina Kössler, Sven Lauritzen, Ricarda Lotte and Felix Wilke. In Hamburg, Gill Mertens and in particular Michael Friedman have thoroughly nurtured the language in this book as native speakers with helpful guidance from Christian Eckl. At Hart Publishing Richard Hart, Rachel Turner, Melanie Hamill, Tom Adams and Joanne Ledger have skilfully guided this text towards publication.

Hannes Unberath, who initiated and inspired the research on principles for regulating dispute resolution, passed away on Monday, 28 January 2013. When asked whether the project should be stopped due to his illness, he replied with the adage 'Even if I knew the world was coming to an end tomorrow, I would still plant a little apple tree today'. Hannes Unberath's efforts in organising the project, performing the underlying research and conducting the meeting in Bayreuth were undertaken with unparalleled energy, and he was pleased with the discussion and results. In January 2013 he reviewed the principles we are presenting here and proposed their name: Guide for Regulating Dispute Resolution. This work is part of his legacy and this book is dedicated to his memory.

The Editors
August 2013

Contents Summary

Detailed Contents

Contributors

Lin Adrian

Dr Lin Adrian is an Assistant Professor at the Law Faculty at the University of Copenhagen. She teaches mediation for law students and for students in a post-graduate executive mediation programme. Lin Adrian also conducts training for mediation professionals. She has been a mediator since 1988 and has published articles and books on mediation. In 2011 she received her PhD on an empirical study of court-connected mediation. Her current research focuses on mediation in institutionalised settings and the use of ADR in general.

Aldo De Matteis

Professor Aldo De Matteis started his career as a magistrate in labour and welfare law. From 1998 to 2008 he was Councillor at the Italian Supreme Court of Appeal and at the Labour Department, as well as a Member of the Civil United Sections of the Court. After retiring, he became a mediator at the JAMS International ADR Center in Rome, Italy. Professor de Matteis is Professor of Procedural Labour Law at the University of Siena and has spoken at several conferences focused on welfare and labour law. He is a member of the Association of European Labour Court Judges.

Giuseppe De Palo

Professor Giuseppe De Palo is President of the ADR Center and a Director of London-based JAMS International. A full-time mediator since 1998, he has contributed to the resolution of over 500 complex commercial disputes. An international Professor of alternative dispute resolution law and practice at Hamline University School of Law in St Paul (USA), he is the editor, author and co-author of several books and articles in the field of ADR. Professor De Palo has spoken on mediation before the Italian and European Parliaments and has been the team leader of projects—funded by the World Bank, the European Commission and the Inter-American Development Bank—aiming to promote ADR.

Frédérique Ferrand

Professor Dr Frédérique Ferrand is a Professor at the University Jean Moulin Lyon 3 (since 1991). Her professional affiliations include the Institut Universitaire de France, the Organising Committee of the Commission on European Family Law, the Scientific Board of the Max Planck Institute Hamburg, the Scientific Council of the Ecole Nationale de Procédure, Paris, the International Institute of Enforcement Law of the International Bailiffs' Association, the Conseil National des Universities and the

Scientific Council of the law review *Droit et Procédures*. She serves as French correspondent for UNIDROIT as well as for German and English law reviews.

Hazel Genn

Professor Dame Hazel Genn DBE, QC (Hon), FBA, BA, LLB, LLD is Dean of Laws, Professor of socio-legal studies and Co-director of the Judicial Institute at University College London, where she is also an Honorary Fellow. She has widely published on civil justice, including several evaluations of court-linked mediation schemes for the Ministry of Justice. Professor Genn was one of the team leading the Nuffield Foundation's inquiry on empirical legal research and is one of the authors of the final report. Her work focuses on the experiences of citizens caught up in legal problems and the responsiveness of the justice system to their needs.

Reinhard Greger

Professor Reinhard Greger held initial positions as a Judge and Prosecutor before becoming Division Head at the Bavarian Ministry of Justice. He later served as a Judge at the Federal Court of Justice before becoming a Professor at the University of Erlangen-Nuremberg. There he was a Member of the Board of Directors of the Institute for Lawyer's Law and Practice and later retired in 2011. Professor Greger has completed several research studies commissioned by justice ministries concerning alternative dispute resolution, in particular relating to mandatory conciliation, mediation and conciliation procedures by judges (*Güterichter*). He has furthermore trained lawyers and judges and instructed *Güterichter* for the Bavarian and Thuringian Ministries of Justice.

Jana Härtling

Jana Härtling has been a Research Fellow and Lecturer at the University of Bayreuth since 2010. She studied law in Jena and Montpellier, specialising in international law, and interned at the Office of the United Nations High Commissioner for Refugees (UNHCR) in Geneva. After passing her first state examination in 2008, she completed her legal clerkship in Thuringia, Berlin and Paris, passing the second state examination in 2010. She is currently writing her doctoral thesis on mediation settlement agreements.

Burkhard Hess

Professor Dr Burkhard Hess, RiOLG, is Professor of civil law, civil procedural law, international private law and international procedural law and Director of the Institute for Private International Law at the University of Heidelberg, Germany. He is Executive Director of the Max Planck Institute for International, European and Regulatory Procedural Law, Luxembourg, and a Judge at the Higher Regional Court (OLG) Karlsruhe. Professor Hess worked as an expert for the European Commission and serves as a court expert for foreign law, private international law and international procedural law. He is Co-editor of the law review *Practice of international private and procedural law* (*IPrax*).

Ulrike Janzen

Ulrike Janzen is Head of the Unit responsible for mediation, conciliation and international conflicts in parent and child cases in the Federal Ministry of Justice (Germany). She has been working as an expert in family law, private international law and European Union law in the Ministry of Justice since 2000. From 2003 to 2007, she served as Legal Secretary at the Court of First Instance (now the General Court) in Luxembourg and as expert at the General Secretariat of the Council of the European Union in Brussels in the unit responsible for judicial cooperation in civil law matters, where her activities included work on the Mediation Directive.

Shusuke Kakiuchi

Professor Shusuke Kakiuchi is Professor of Law at the graduate schools for law and politics of the University of Tokyo (since 1999). He is a member of the Executive Board of the Japan Association of the Law of Arbitration and Alternative Dispute Resolution, the Conférence Internationale de Médiation pour la Justice, the Japanese Association of the Law of Civil Procedure, the Japan Association of Private Law, the Société franco-japonaise de science juridique and the Japanese Association of Sociology of Law. In 2011–2012 he was Chairman of the Working Group on the Reform of ADR Law of the Japan ADR Association.

Lars Kirchhoff

Professor Lars Kirchhoff, practicing mediator and international lawyer, is a Co-director of both the Institute for Conflict Management and the Center for Peace Mediation at the European University Viadrina. He is also one of the founders of the Master's Program in Mediation offered at the European University Viadrina, a partner of the Berlin-based mediation firm TGKS and an instructor of mediation and ADR skills at the German Academy of Judges, the United Nations, the European Union and the Training Academy for International Diplomats at the German Federal Foreign Office. In 2007 he was awarded a doctoral degree for his thesis on *Constructive Interventions—Paradigms, Process and Practice of International Mediation.*

Peter G Mayr

Professor Dr Peter G Mayr is Head of the civil procedural law department of the University of Innsbruck, having earlier been Assistant Professor (from 1989) and Extraordinary Professor (from 1997). He has been a Visiting Scholar at the Universities of Mainz, Strasbourg, Paris and Athens. Professor Mayr has been awarded several prizes for his research achievements.

Isaak Meier

Professor Dr Meier is Professor of civil procedural law, debt collection and bankruptcy law as well as private law at the University of Zurich and has been a legal advisor for the law firm Peyer und Partner since 1991; since 2004 he has been Vice-Dean of resources at the faculty of law. Since 1992 he has served as President of the Institute for Civil Court Procedure in Zurich. Professor Meier received a degree in mediation in business and administration in 2001/2002 and received the *venia legendi* for mediation in 2004. In 2003, the Swiss government appointed him as member of the revision commission Swiss Insolvency Law.

Carrie Menkel-Meadow

Professor Carrie Menkel-Meadow is Chancellor's Professor of Law at the University of California, Irvine, and the AB Chettle, Jr Professor of Dispute Resolution and Civil Procedure and Director of the Georgetown-Hewlett Program in Conflict Resolution and Legal Problem Solving at Georgetown University Law Center. Her research focuses on alternative dispute resolution, the legal profession, legal ethics, clinical legal education, feminist legal theory and women in the legal profession. She sits on numerous boards of public interest organisations and the editorial boards of journals in dispute resolution, law and social science and feminism. Professor Menkel-Meadow is the author of more than 10 books and 200 articles on dispute resolution and other subjects, including *Complex Dispute Resolution* (Foundational Processes, Multi-Party Dispute Resolution and International Dispute Resolution, Ashgate Press, 2012). In addition to her academic work, she has served as a mediator and arbitrator in hundreds of private and public disputes, and trains mediators on several continents.

Kristin Nemeth

Assistant Professor Dr Kristin Nemeth was appointed as Assistant Professor at the Department of Civil Law at the University of Innsbruck in 2008. She is a member of the Association of Austrian Jurists (Österreichischer Juristentag) and a founding member of the Association of European Consumer Law.

Ashley E Oleson

Ashley E Oleson has been a Fellow at ADR Center with the International Projects Unit since the start of 2013. She is currently completing a graduate program at the New York (USA) based college, St John's University, via their Rome (Italy) campus. In 2014 she will earn her master's degree in government and politics with a concentration in international relations, as well as a certification in international law and diplomacy. Prior to her graduate studies she spent time serving as both a criminal and civil litigation paralegal in the United States.

Machteld Pel

Machteld Pel has been a mediator since 1998. She has been working for the Netherlands judiciary for 30 years as a Judge at the Arnhem District Court and was Vice-President at the Arnhem Court of Appeal until 2010. Additionally, from 1999 until the beginning of 2010 Machteld Pel was the director the Netherlands court-connected mediation agency. In this capacity she took the lead in implementing referrals to mediation within the Netherlands judiciary. Since April 2010 she has acted as a Substitute Justice at the Arnhem Court of Appeal. She is a member of the Independent Standards Commission of the International Mediation Institute.

Nils Pelzer

Nils Pelzer is a Research Fellow at the Max Planck Institute for International, European and Regulatory Procedural Law, Luxembourg. He studied both law and East Asian studies with a major in Chinese studies at the University of Heidelberg, earning a BA in 2010. In July 2012 he passed his first state examination. In his ongoing PhD project he examines the operating principles of the mediation system in the People's Republic of China.

Katherine Pleming

Katherine Pleming (BA, LLB) studied Human Geography at University College London. She then did her Graduate Diploma in Law at the College of Law, Bloomsbury and went on to do her Legal Practice Course at the College of Law, Moorgate. She is currently working for the Home Office in London as a Presenting Officer in the Immigration and Appeals Tribunal.

Shiva Riahi

Shiva Riahi is a research assistant for the UCL Judicial Institute and Centre for Access to Justice. She holds a degree in Law (LLB) from UCL, as well as obtaining cum laude honours in Philosophy and International Relations (BA) from Tufts University.

Anneken K Sperr

Dr Anneken K Sperr is an Associate Professor at the Faculty of Law, University of Bergen, and was a postdoctoral Research Fellow at the same faculty from 2009 to 2012. Previously she lectured at the University of Hamburg. From 2005 to 2009 Dr Sperr worked as a Senior Research Fellow at the Max Planck Institute for Comparative and International Private Law, Hamburg, and was responsible for the Unit for Northern European Legal Systems. She studied law, political science and Scandinavian studies in Bergen, Greifswald and Copenhagen. After completing her legal clerkship in Hamburg in 2008, Dr Sperr became a member of the Hanseatic Bar Association, Hamburg. Her research interests include national and European administrative law, comparative private and public law (including procedural law), family law and international private law.

Felix Steffek

Dr Felix Steffek LLM (Cambridge) is a Senior Research Fellow at the Max Planck Institute for Comparative and International Private Law in Hamburg. Past and present teaching positions include posts at the Universities of Hamburg, Cambridge, Warsaw and Beijing (CUPL). He has conducted research at Harvard Law School (Visiting Researcher), the University of Cambridge (Visiting Fellow) and the University of Oxford

(Academic Visitor). He has acted, inter alia, as an expert for the German Ministry of Justice, the German Parliament and the European Commission. His research interests encompass private law, company and commercial law, insolvency and procedural law.

Hannes Unberath

Professor Hannes Unberath studied law in Erlangen and Oxford (Rhodes Scholar, MJur and DPhil). After completing his legal clerkship in Nuremberg he worked as a Lecturer at the University of Erlangen-Nuremberg and at the Institute for International Law of the University of Munich. In 2006 he was appointed Professor at the University of Jena, and in 2007 he was seated as a Judge at the Thuringian Court of Appeal. From September 2009 Professor Unberath held the Chair for private law and civil procedural law at the University of Bayreuth. His research focused on alternative dispute resolution, comparative private law, civil procedure and philosophy of law.

Ivan Verougstraete

Professor Ivan Verougstraete, Honorary President of the Belgian Court of Cassation and the Benelux Court, is an accredited mediator with the Belgian Federal Commission on Mediation and CEDR, JAM's panelist and a member of B-mediation Brussels and the Belgian Union of Professional Mediators. He concentrates on commercial mediation. From 1989 to 2010 Professor Verougstraete was Judge and, later, President of the Belgian Court of Cassation. He was President of the Belgian Competition Authority (1992–2002) and from 2000 to 2010 (Vice-)President of the Benelux Court of Justice. From 2005 to 2009 Professor Verougstraete was President of the European Association of Judges for Mediation (GEMME).

Abbreviations

AAA	American Arbitration Association
ABA	American Bar Association
ABGB	Allgemeines Bürgerliches Gesetzbuch
AC	Appeal Cases
ACAS	Advisory, Conciliation and Arbitration Services
ACR	Association of Conflict Resolution
ADR	Alternative Dispute Resolution
ADR Act	Act on Promotion of Use of Alternative Dispute Resolution
afl	Aflevering
AG	Amtsgericht
ALI	American Law Institute
All ER (Comm)	All England Law Reports (Commercial Cases)
AME	Association Nationale des Médiateurs
AMF	Autorité des marchés financiers
AMG	Advocate Medical Group
APMF	Association pour la Médiation Familiale
App Div	Appellate Devision
ARGE Baurecht	Arbeitsgemeinschaft für privates Bau- und Architektenrecht im Deutschen Anwalt Verein
ARM	Automatic Referral to Mediation
Art/Arts	article/articles
ÄrzteG	Ärztegesetz
AS	Aksjeselskap
ASA	Association Suisse de l'Arbitrage
Atty	Attorney
AußStrG	Außerstreitgesetz
AVMF	Association vaudoise pour la médiation familiale
Avtl	Avtaleloven
B2B	business to business
B2C	business to consumer
BAG	Berufsausbildungsgesetz
BEinstG	Behinderteneinstellungsgesetz
BFJR	Byggebransjens Faglig Juridiske Råd
BGB	Bürgerliches Gesetzbuch
BGBl	Bundesgesetzblatt
BGE	Bundesgerichtsentscheidung
BGH	Bundesgerichtshof
BGStG	Bundes-Behindertengleichstellungsgesetz
BIS-Justiz	Betriebliches Informationssystem der Justiz
BlgNR	Beilagen zu den stenographischen Protokollen des Nationalrates

BORA	Berufsordnung der Rechtsanwälte
BT-Drucks	Bundestagsdrucksachen
BVerfG	Bundesverfassungsgericht
B-VG	Bundes-Verfassungsgesetz
BW	Burgerlijk Wetboek
c	circa
C trav	Code du travail
C civil	Code civil
C cons	Code de la consommation
C2C	consumer to consumer
CA	Cour d'appel
CAF	Caisse d'Assurances Familiales
Cal Civ Proc Code	California Code of Civil Procedure
Cal Evidence Code	California Evidence Code
CAM	Camera Arbitrale Milano
CAMS	Court of Appeal Mediation Scheme
Cass Civ I	Cour de cassasion (1ère Chambre civile)
Cass Civ II	Cour de cassasion (2ème Chambre civile)
Cass com	Cour de cassation (Chambre commerciale)
Cass Soc	Cour de cassation (Chambre sociale)
CC	Civil Code
CCBE	Council of Bars and Law Societies in Europe
CCFLR	Centre for Child and Family Law Reform
CCP	Code of Civil Procedure
CDU	Christlich Demokratische Union
CEDR	Center for Effective Dispute Resolution
CEPANI	Belgian Centre for Mediation and Arbitration
CEPEJ	European Commission for the Efficiency of Justice
Cf	confer
CGB	Commissie Gelijke Behandeling
Ch	chapter
Ch	Chancery Division
CHF	Swiss franc
CIArb	Chartered Institute of Arbitrators
Cir	Circuit
Civ	Civil Division
CIV	Civil
CJEU	Court of Justice of the European Union
Cm	Command
CMC	Civil Mediation Council
CNDS	Commission nationale de déontologie de la sécurité
Co	Company
CO	Code of Obligations
CoA	Court of Appeal
COJ	Code de l'organisation judiciaire
con	consideration

CORECOM	Comitato Regionale per le Comunicazioni
Corp	Corporation
CP	Consultation Paper
CPC	Code de procédure civile
CPD	Continuing Professional Development
CPIL	Code on Private International Law
CPR	Civil Procedure Rules
CPR	Center for Public Resources
CPR	International Institute for Conflict Prevention and Resolution
Ct of App	Court of Appeals
DC	District of Columbia
DGCCRF	Direction Générale de la Concurrence, de la Consommation et de la Répression des Fraudes
Difi	Direktoratet for forvaltning og IKT
DIS	Deutsche Institution für Schiedsgerichtsbarkeit eV
Diss	Dissertation
DIS-SchGO	DIS-Schiedsgutachtensordnung
Dl	Domstolloven
Doc	Document
EHRR	European Human Rights Reports
eV	eingetragener Verein
EC	European Commission
ECCM	European Code of Conduct for Mediators
ECC-Net	European Consumer Centres Network
ECHR	European Convention on Human Rights
ECJ	European Court of Justice
ed/eds	editor/editors
EDF	Électricité de France
edn	edition
EEA	European Economic Area
eg	for example
EG ZPO	Einführungsgesetz zur Zivilprozessordnung
EGZPO	Gesetz betreffend die Einführung der Zivilprozessordnung
EO	Exekutionsordnung
ErläutRV	Erläuternde Bemerkungen zur Regierungsvorlage
et al	and others
etc	et cetera
EU	European Union
EWCA	Court of Appeal of England and Wales
EWHC	High Court of Justice of England and Wales
F	Federal
f/ff	and following
FAFML	Federal Act on the Freedom of Movement for Lawyers

FamFG	Gesetz über das Verfahren in Familiensachen und in den Angelegenheiten der freiwilligen Gerichtsbarkeit
FamPra.ch	Die Praxis des Familienrechts
Fed R Civ Proc	Federal Rules of Civil Procedure
FENAMEF	Fédération Nationale pour la Médiation Familiale
FH	Mediationsforum Schweiz
FINMA	Financial Market Supervisory Authority
FINMAC	Financial Instruments Mediation Assistance Centre
FIN-NET	Financial Dispute Resolution Network
Fla Stat Ann	Florida Statutes Annotated
FLBA	Family Law Bar Association
FMA	Family Mediators Association
FMC	Family Mediation Council
FMG	Fernmeldegesetz
fn/fns	footnote/footnotes (reference to a footnote outside the chapter)
FOR	Forskrift
FOS	Financial Ombudsman Service
FT	Folketingstidende
FTU	Forbrukertvistutvalget
Gemme	European Association of Judges for Mediation
GP	Gesetzgebungsperiode
GPM	Groupement pro Médiation
GRDR	Guide for Regulating Dispute Resolution
HALDE	Haute autorité de lutte contre les discriminations
HR	Hoge Raad
ibid	in the same place
IBR	Immobilien & Baurecht
IC	Insolvency Code
ICC	International Chamber of Commerce
ICSID	International Centre for Settlement of Investment Disputes
IDR	Internal Dispute Resolution
ie	that is
IEF	Institut für systemische Entwicklung und Fortbildung
IFLA	Institute of Family Law Arbitrators
IFM	Institut für Mediation
IKT	Informasjons- og kommunikasjonsteknologi
Innst O	Innstillinger til Odelsting
IOB	Insurance Ombudsman Bureau
IPRG	Internationales Privatrechtsgesetz
IT	Information Technology
JAB	Bericht des Justizausschusses
JAMS	Judicial Arbitration and Mediation Service
JC	Judicial Code

JCP G	La Semaine juridique—Edition générale
JO	Journal Officiel
JPY	Japanese Yen
KassGer ZH	Kassationsgericht des Kantons Zürich
KindNamRÄG	Kindschafts- und Namensrechts-Änderungsgesetz 2013
KMS	Koordination Mediation Schweiz
KO	Konsumentombudsmannen
KOV	Konsumentverket
LBM	Landelijk bureau Mediation
LG	Landgericht
LGBl	Landesgesetzblatt
lit	Letter
LJ	Lord Justice
LJN	Landelijk Jurisprudentie Nummer
Ltd	Limited
MRPC	Model Rules of Professional Conduct
mv	med videre
MARC	modes alternatifs de règlement des conflits
MARD	modes amiables de résolution des différends
Md	Maryland
MEDEF	Mouvement des entreprises de France
MIAM	Mediation Information and Assessment Meeting
Minn	Minnesota
MoJ	Ministry of Justice
MRG	Mietrechtsgesetz
ND	Northern District
n/nn	footnote (reference within the chapter)
NAI	Nederlands Arbitrage Instituut
NB	Nota Bene
NCCUSL	National Conference on Commissioners for Uniform State Laws
NCPC	Nouveau Code de procédure civile
Nds	Niedersachsen
NF	Norsk fabrikasjonskontrakt
NFM	National Family Mediation
NJ	Nederlandse Jurisprudentie
NJW	Neue Juristische Wochenschrift
NMI	Nederlands Mediation Instituut
no	number
No	Number (of an Act, Report)
NOK	Norwegian Krone
nos	numbers
NOU	Norges offentlige utredninger
nr	number

Nr	Nummer
NS	Norsk Standard
NTK	Norsk Totalkontrakt
Núm	Numero
Nw	Nieuw
NY	New York
NYU	New York University
OFCOM	Federal Office of Communications
OG ZH	Obergericht Zürich
OGH	Oberster Gerichtshof
OJ	Official Journal
Otprp	Odelstingsproposisjoner
OTS	Ordinance on Telecommunications Services
OUA	Organismo Unitario Avvocatura
p/pp	page/pages
para/paras	paragraph/paragraphs
PCC	Professional Practice Consultant
PL	Product Liability
plc	Public Limited Company
PRIME	Project integrated mediation
QBD	Queen's Bench Division
r/rr	rule/rules
RabelsZ	Rabels Zeitschrift für ausländisches und internationales Privatrecht
RAND Corp	Research and Development Corporation
RATP	Régie autonome des transports Parisiens
RCC	Reclame Code Commissie
reg	regulation
rev	revised
Rev arb	Revue de l'arbitrage
RIS-Justiz	Rechtsinformationssystem-Justiz
RJC	Restorative Justice Council
RME	Réseau des Médiateurs en Entreprise
RTDCiv	Revue trimestrielle de droit civil
RTDCom	Revue trimestrielle de droit commercial et de droit économique
RTR-GmbH	Rundfunk und Telekom Regulierungs-GmbH
Rv	Burgerlijke Rechtsvordering
s/ss	section/sections
SAV	Schweizerischer Anwaltsverband
SchiedsVZ	Zeitschrift für Schiedsverfahren
SchKG	Bundesgesetz über Schuldbetreibung und Konkurs
SDM	Schweizerischer Dachverband für Mediation

SGOA	Stichting Geschillenoplossing Automatisering
SI	Statutory Instrument
SINTEF	Stiftelsen for industriell og teknisk forskning
SKWM	Schweizerische Kammer für Wirtschaftsmediation
SNCF	Société nationale des chemins de fer français
SOBau	Schlichtungs- und Schiedsordnung für Baustreitigkeiten
SPD	Sozialdemokratische Partei Deutschlands
SSR	Studiecentrum Rechtspleging
SSW	Südschleswigscher Wählerverband
St	Saint
Sup Ct	Supreme Court
SVM	Schweizerischer Verein für Mediation
SZ	Entscheidungen des österreichischen Obersten Gerichtshofes in Zivilsachen
TAR	Regional Administrative Tribunal of Lazio
TCA	Telecommunications Act
TCC	Technology and Construction Court
TFEU	Treaty on the Functioning of the European Union
TGI	Tribunal de grande instance
TI	Tribunal d'instance
TK	Tweede Kamer
Tvl	Lov om mekling og rettergang i sivile tvister/Tvisteloven
USC	United States Code
UCLA	University of California, Los Angeles
UDAF	Union Départementale des Associations Familiales
UK	United Kingdom
UN	United Nations
UNCITRAL	United Nations Commission on International Trade Law
UNIDROIT	International Institute for the Unification of Private Law
UPIM	Union Professionnelle Indépendante des Médiateurs
US	United States
USIP Press	United States Institute of Peace Press
v	versus
VAT	Value Added Tax
VerG	Vereinsgesetz 2002
Vogl	Lov om voldgift/Voldgiftloven
vol/vols	volume/volumes
VSC	Victoria Supreme Court
VwVG	Federal Act of 20 December 1968 on Administrative Procedure
WD Oklahoma	Western District of Oklahoma
WLR	Weekly Law Reports
WL	Westlaw
WODC	Wetenschappelijk Onderzoek- en Documentatiecentrum

ZAK	Zentrum für Agogik
ZivMediatG	Zivilrechts-Mediations-Gesetz
ZivRÄG	Zivilrechts-Änderungsgesetz 2004
ZPO	Zivilprozessordnung
ZR	Blätter für Zürcherische Rechtsprechung
ZZPInt	Zeitschrift für Zivilprozess International

Part 1

Fundamental Issues

1

Guide for Regulating Dispute Resolution (GRDR): Principles[1]

FELIX STEFFEK AND HANNES UNBERATH (COORDINATORS), LIN ADRIAN, ALDO DE MATTEIS, GIUSEPPE DE PALO, FRÉDÉRIQUE FERRAND, REINHARD GREGER, JANA HÄRTLING, ULRIKE JANZEN,[2] SHUSUKE KAKIUCHI, LARS KIRCHHOFF, PETER G MAYR, ISAAK MEIER, KRISTIN NEMETH, MACHTELD PEL, ANNEKEN K SPERR AND IVAN VEROUGSTRAETE

THIS DOCUMENT RECOMMENDS structures and principles for the regulation of dispute resolution in civil and commercial matters. The recommendations are a first attempt to provide guidelines for a value-based and coherent regulation of dispute resolution. The principles refer to court proceedings as well as to alternative dispute resolution (ADR). Since this is a Herculean task, the principles suggested are only a first starting point to inspire further development. They are not comprehensive and, instead, aim to encourage further discussion. The structures and principles are recommendations for the regulation of dispute resolution, not for the practice of dispute resolution. As a consequence, issues that are important in practice, for example methods of dispute resolution, but that should not be regulated are not mentioned. This is both in the interest of clarity and the avoidance of over-regulation.

The recommendations are formulated against a comparative and international background. They have an open structure in order to allow for regional and local adjustments and to allow further developments of dispute resolution practice. They may serve to inform the formulation of model rules, regional directives or specific legislative acts. The recommendations start with more general issues and proceed to more specific topics.

[1] For an explanation of the principles see chapter 2, which contains the principles and comments.

[2] The views expressed are only the author's own opinions and may not in any circumstances be regarded as stating an official position of the German Federal Ministry of Justice.

I. DISPUTE RESOLUTION MECHANISMS

A. Choice of Procedure

The regulation of dispute resolution should start with and focus on the parties. Generally, the parties and not the state should choose the dispute resolution mechanism (principle of self-determination or party choice of process). While consensual dispute resolution is preferable over resolution forced on (one of) the parties, there is no preference of one sort of dispute resolution mechanism over another. Regulation may reflect, however, that certain dispute resolution mechanisms may be particularly well suited for specific types of disputes.

B. Regulating Dispute Resolution

The regulation of dispute resolution mechanisms both within a single jurisdiction and internationally should follow principles that permit rational choices to be made by the parties and include clear criteria informing that choice.

C. Functional and Modular Approach

A modular approach referring to the characteristics of dispute resolution procedures facilitates principled regulation. The following characteristics can be used to classify dispute resolution mechanisms; they generally refer to the control of or choice by the parties:

- *Initiation control: whether the parties' consent is needed to initiate the procedure;*
- *Procedure control: whether the parties determine the procedure;*
- *Result-content control: whether the parties determine the content of the result (ie whether the procedure is non-evaluative);*
- *Result-effect control: whether the parties' consent is needed for the result to be binding;*
- *Neutral choice control: whether the parties choose the neutral;*
- *Information control: whether the procedure and the information obtained during the procedure is private;*
- *Interest-based: whether the procedure is interest- or rights-based;*
- *Intermediary: whether the procedure includes intermediation by a third person.*

D. Policy Choice

Regulation of dispute resolution should be based on the following fundamentals: normative individualism (as expressed in human and constitutional rights), party choice, just dispute resolution for the parties and efficiency. Individuals have a right to effective and fair dispute resolution.

E. Principles

Currently, only general principles for the regulation of dispute resolution are desirable.

II. INFRASTRUCTURE AND FRAMEWORK

Citizens have a right of access to effective and fair dispute resolution. The state is responsible for organising and financing an adequate court and enforcement system. Additionally, the state has to provide citizens with a reliable legal framework for alternative dispute resolution and should, within the means available, support such alternative forms of dispute resolution.

III. COSTS

A. General

Generally the parties should carry the costs of resolving their dispute by the use of ADR procedures, while the cost of court proceedings may be partially borne by the general public. In procedures where the parties do not have initiation control, the costs of the procedure and reasonable party expenses should be borne according to the procedures for cost assessment appropriate in the legal system. In procedures with initiation control the parties should by default share the costs of the procedures and pay their own expenses. Mandatory extrajudicial dispute resolution may not impose costs to a degree that hinders access to the courts.

B. Cost Subsidies

Access to courts must not be impeded by prohibitive costs. Subsidies for alternative dispute resolution mechanisms may be justified if information and decision deficits exist, if certain procedures have intrinsic advantages or more generally on grounds of efficiency. Cost subsidies should avoid setting incentives favouring one kind of resolution mechanism merely for cost reasons.

C. Legal Aid

Legal aid for court proceedings should be provided to parties in financial need if they can demonstrate a more likely than not probability of being successful. Alternatively, legal aid could be provided based on the sole criteria of demonstrated financial need. Legal aid should not set incentives for parties to opt for court proceedings instead of alternative dispute resolution for cost reasons only. A necessary reaction may be the introduction of legal aid for alternative dispute resolution mechanisms.

IV. DISPUTE RESOLUTION CLAUSES

A. General

Dispute resolution clauses should be binding and enforceable in the same manner as other contracts are binding and enforced. Interim or conservation measures should generally remain possible as a dispositive default rule.

B. Specifics

The invalidation or later modification of dispute resolution clauses should follow general legal principles. The more control the parties have as regards (1) the procedure, (2) the choice of the neutral, (3) the content and (4) the effect of the result, the less there is a need for restricting and policing the validity of dispute resolution clauses.

V. CHOICE OF DISPUTE RESOLUTION PROCEDURE

A. General

Regulation should ensure an early, informed and undistorted choice of a dispute resolution procedure with the lowest possible transaction costs. Regulation should ensure that the parties are in a position to choose by matching their interests with the intrinsic characteristics of the resolution procedures. The state may provide options and alternatives for situations where the parties do not prefer the same dispute resolution mechanism.

B. Centralised or Decentralised Approach

Centralised and decentralised approaches to facilitate an early, informed, undistorted and less expensive choice of a dispute resolution mechanism are both reasonable. Counsel and the neutral should be under a duty to monitor the adequacy of the choice and point out if the choice needs to be modified. In case of information and decision deficits as regards choice, primarily incentives and subsidiarily mandatory rules may be necessary.

C. Sanctions

Cost, damage and procedural sanctions for parties who hinder or prolong dispute resolution without a good and proportionate reason can be justified. Before turning to cost sanctions, however, alternative and less intrusive means to correct decision deficits should be considered.

D. Transfer to Other Dispute Resolution Mechanisms

The above principles apply equally to a transfer between dispute resolution mechanisms.

E. Good Practice

Comparative analysis and empirical research reveal good practice models for regulating the choice of dispute resolution procedures. Research and assessment are essential for continued monitoring of what are the best ways to ensure early and good choices of dispute resolution procedures.

VI. CONFIDENTIALITY

A. General

Dispute resolution procedures, where the parties have information control, should be facilitated by enabling confidentiality rules.

B. Regulatory Tools and Approaches

Confidentiality of dispute resolution procedures, where the parties have information control, needs to be ensured in both substantive and procedural law. Confidentiality rules should cover all relevant persons and different types of information carriers. The subject matter to which the rules on confidentiality apply should be delineated. However, limits to confidentiality may be necessary. In particular, abuse of the confidentiality rules needs to be addressed, as well as the protection of third parties and the prevention and detection of crime.

VII. LIMITATION AND PRESCRIPTION PERIODS

Limitation and prescription periods should be suspended from the start until the end of any dispute resolution procedure. For all procedures the details of regulation should refer to the characteristics of initiation control and result effect control.

VIII. NEUTRAL

A. General

The more control the parties have as regards initiation control, neutral choice control, result-content control and result-effect control, the less intensive the regulation of the intermediary's neutrality and qualification needs to be.

B. Neutrality

The legislature has to ensure that the parties' choice of the neutral does not suffer from information asymmetry or decision deficits. If the parties have neutral choice control and result-effect control, the intensity of regulation may be lower.

C. Qualification

The less the parties control the choice of the neutral, the initiation, the result-content and the result-effect of a dispute resolution mechanism, the more the state needs to ensure the qualification of the neutral. Generally, however, it is recommended to opt for as little intrusive regulation as necessary.

If the parties control the choice of the neutral and the initiation or the effect of the procedure, a market approach or an incentive approach may be advisable.

If the parties have neutral choice control, but do not have control over the initiation of the procedure, either the incentive approach or the authorisation approach is recommended.

If the parties neither control the choice of the neutral nor the initiation, an authorisation approach is recommended.

If the parties have no control over initiation, neutral choice and result-effect, the state needs to opt for an authorisation approach.

IX. PROCEDURE

If the parties have neither initiation control nor both result-content and effect control, procedural safeguards are necessary. If the parties have initiation control but no result-content or effect control, a weaker form of state-ensured procedural safeguards is advisable.

X. COUNSEL

Generally, parties should have the right to be accompanied and advised by counsel. Full representation in procedural acts should also generally be allowed. Where the procedure specifically depends on personal participation of the parties, regulation may require the parties to appear in person.

XI. STATE (JUDICIAL) REVIEW OF RESULTS

If the parties have control over the result-content and effect of the procedure, a state (judicial) review of the result beyond that applying to contracts in general is not recommended. If the parties do not control the result-content and effect, there should be the possibility for a state review of the results. The degree of the state review should distinguish whether the party bound to the result had control over the initiation of the procedure or not.

XII. ENFORCEABILITY

Enforceability should require the participation of the state or a representative charged with state functions. Results controlled by the parties should not ex post be submitted to a court-like result review. The availability and the path to enforceability should generally not be designed in a way that it indirectly influences the choice of a dispute resolution mechanism.

XIII. TRANSPARENCY

Transparency can be used to indirectly control the quality of procedures. Care needs to be taken not to infringe the justified confidentiality interests of the parties.

XIV. CONSUMERS

Specific rules for consumer dispute resolution are required concerning, in particular, initiation control through dispute resolution clauses and the governance structures of industry-financed resolution systems.

XV. RULE-MAKER

Further research as regards the identification and assessment of rule-makers is desirable. Dispute resolution mechanisms with procedure control by the parties should generally not be influenced unnecessarily by mandatory state law. Rules with an enabling and protection function should generally be made by actors with high-level regulatory authority and wide geographical reach.

XVI. TYPE OF RULES

A. General

As regards conduct rules, in cases of doubt, dispositive rules over mandatory rules or even no regulation should be preferred. As regards enabling rules, state regulation is always needed to create the necessary tools and rights. To remedy information and decision deficits, regulations setting incentives or even imposing mandatory rules may be (temporarily) advisable.

B. Good Practice

Rules should be principled, clear and accessible. The development of dispute resolution practice should not be hampered by overly rigid regulation.

XVII. PROCEDURE DESIGN

It is essential to incentivise lawyers, judges, accountants, notaries, tax advisers, insurance companies and other gatekeepers to act in the parties' dispute resolution interest. Further measures can be information campaigns, institutionalised information boards and mandatory dispute resolution training within the university and education sector. The characteristics and effects of dispute resolution mechanisms need to be understandable. Online dispute resolution requires particular thought and may require specific regulation.

2

Guide for Regulating Dispute Resolution (GRDR): Principles and Comments

FELIX STEFFEK AND HANNES UNBERATH (COORDINATORS), LIN ADRIAN, ALDO DE MATTEIS, GIUSEPPE DE PALO, FRÉDÉRIQUE FERRAND, REINHARD GREGER, JANA HÄRTLING, ULRIKE JANZEN,[1] SHUSUKE KAKIUCHI, LARS KIRCHHOFF, PETER G MAYR, ISAAK MEIER, KRISTIN NEMETH, MACHTELD PEL, ANNEKEN K SPERR AND IVAN VEROUGSTRAETE

THIS DOCUMENT RECOMMENDS structures and principles for the regulation of dispute resolution in civil and commercial matters. The recommendations are a first attempt to provide guidelines for a value-based and coherent regulation of dispute resolution. The principles refer to court proceedings as well as to alternative dispute resolution (ADR). Since this is a Herculean task, the principles suggested are only a first starting point to inspire further development. They are not comprehensive and, instead, aim to encourage further discussion. The structures and principles are recommendations for the regulation of dispute resolution, not for the practice of dispute resolution. As a consequence, issues that are important in practice, for example methods of dispute resolution, but that should not be regulated are not mentioned. This is both in the interest of clarity and the avoidance of over-regulation.

The recommendations are formulated against a comparative and international background. They have an open structure in order to allow for regional and local adjustments and to allow further developments of dispute resolution practice. They may serve to inform the formulation of model rules, regional directives or specific legislative acts. The recommendations start with more general issues and proceed to more specific topics. Each recommendation is first introduced by a short explanation. The structures and principles proposed follow the explanation in italics.

[1] The views expressed are only the author's own opinions and may not in any circumstances be regarded as stating an official position of the German Federal Ministry of Justice.

I. DISPUTE RESOLUTION MECHANISMS

A. Choice of Procedure

At the centre of dispute resolution are the individuals who are party to and affected by the dispute. These individuals know the dispute and their interests best; hence, they should be the starting point and focus of designing dispute resolution mechanisms. It follows that—as a starting point—the parties and not the state should choose the resolution mechanism. Thus, there is no general preference of one dispute resolution mechanism over another. While peaceful and consensual dispute resolution is to be preferred over resolution forced on (one of) the parties, consensual dispute resolution requires the consent of all involved. If one of the parties to the dispute does not cooperate, state dispute resolution, ultimately in the form of a court decision, may be necessary and appropriate. Hence, court proceedings are not better or worse than alternative dispute resolution procedures; they are simply more suited for some disputes and less suited for others. While, in principle, there is no preference for a certain type of dispute resolution mechanism, certain dispute resolution mechanisms may be particularly well suited for specific types of disputes.

The regulation of dispute resolution should start with and focus on the parties. Generally, the parties and not the state should choose the dispute resolution mechanism (principle of self-determination or party choice of process). While consensual dispute resolution is preferable over resolution forced on (one of) the parties, there is no preference of one sort of dispute resolution mechanism over another. Regulation may reflect, however, that certain dispute resolution mechanisms may be particularly well suited for specific types of disputes.

B. Regulating Dispute Resolution

The advancement and institutionalisation of dispute resolution mechanisms displays a remarkably creative development and diversity. Common forms are negotiation, mediation, conciliation, ombudsman procedures, arbitration and court procedures. However, additional forms and variants of these procedures have been developed. Additional forms are, for example, neutral evaluation, fact-finding procedures, mini-trials, judgment proposals and adapted as well as hybrid court procedures. Variants include devices such as mandatory negotiation, mandatory mediation and combinations such as mediation-arbitration and conciliation-court proceedings. The regulatory approaches to be found are diverse both within legal systems, if one compares various mechanisms in any given jurisdiction, and across legal systems, when comparing internationally the approaches of different countries as regards any single form of dispute resolution.

Against this background, principled regulation of dispute resolution is desirable. This avoids distortions in the choice of dispute resolution mechanisms locally and internationally. The promise is better choices for the individuals as well as just and more efficient results for society. The great diversity in the practice and regulation of dispute resolution mechanisms should not lead to the conclusion that principled regulation of dispute resolution is unattainable. It is possible if a functional and modular approach is taken which openly communicates the underlying policy choice.

The regulation of dispute resolution mechanisms both within a single jurisdiction and internationally should follow principles that permit rational choices to be made by the parties and include clear criteria informing that choice.

C. Functional and Modular Approach

The variety of dispute resolution mechanisms can be characterised by referencing the following central functional features, which all relate to the control of the individuals: initiation control, procedure control, result-content control, result-effect control, neutral choice control and information control (privacy). Additional characteristics, such as whether the mechanism is interest-based (or rights-based) or whether an intermediary is involved, can be added. This approach is modular in two respects: further types of dispute resolution mechanisms and characteristics can be added depending on analytical and regulatory need. Regulatory questions can then be discussed referring to the control characteristics named above. For example, mediation and arbitration share the characteristics that their use is voluntary by the parties (initiation control), that the parties choose the neutral (neutral choice control) and that the procedure is private (information control), and as a consequence these characteristics pose similar regulatory questions. However, in mediation the parties have control over the content of the result (result-content control, ie non-evaluative), they have control over the effect of the result (result-effect control) and the procedure is interest-based; by contrast, in arbitration there is neither result-content nor result-effect control, and arbitration is usually rights-based. These different characteristics can be used to develop diverging regulatory principles.

The functional and modular approach suggested allows the formulation of regulatory principles that capture the essence of the procedures yet, at the same time, avoid getting lost in the jungle of intranational and international diversity. Also, the modular approach is able to capture changes in practice and law over time. It is a dynamic concept that allows adding procedures and characteristics, and by formulating the characteristics from the perspective of the individual it ensures that the individual's role as regulatory anchor is not forgotten. Hence, the characteristic 'initiation control' is used instead of 'mandatory'. For further explanation of this modular approach see Chapter 3.

A modular approach referring to the characteristics of dispute resolution procedures facilitates principled regulation. The following characteristics can be used to classify dispute resolution mechanisms; they generally refer to the control of or choice by the parties:

- *Initiation control: whether the parties' consent is needed to initiate the procedure;*
- *Procedure control: whether the parties determine the procedure;*
- *Result-content control: whether the parties determine the content of the result (ie whether the procedure is non-evaluative);*

- *Result-effect control: whether the parties' consent is needed for the result to be binding;*
- *Neutral choice control: whether the parties choose the neutral;*
- *Information control: whether the procedure and the information obtained during the procedure is private;*
- *Interest-based: whether the procedure is interest- or rights-based;*
- *Intermediary: whether the procedure includes intermediation by a third person.*

D. Policy Choice

The principles suggested here are based on the following fundamentals: normative individualism as well as just and efficient dispute resolution. The ethical concept of normative individualism puts the individual at the centre of regulatory questions and requires the state to justify the limitation of individual freedom. Normative individualism is the foundation of human and constitutional rights which govern local and regional procedural laws. It follows from normative individualism that the self-determined individual is primarily responsible for dealing with his or her conflicts. The self-determination of individuals is an open concept. The individuals take their decisions separately for themselves and collectively as a group. The expression 'party choice' may refer to both situations—decisions by separate individuals and decisions by groups of individuals. As a group the individuals have public interests and may decide to foster further-reaching values such as the interest of future generations in the environment. The individual interests inform the public interests. Conflicts between individual interests and between individual and group interests may, but need not always, require legislative solutions.

Efficient dispute resolution is necessary to allow the state to offer and maintain a sustainable system of dispute resolution. As the public means available for financing dispute resolution are not unlimited, the available means should be put to efficient use. In the interests of the individuals, process choices should be economically accessible and cost-efficient for the parties wherever possible. Individual interests and efficiency in the interest of society need to be balanced. This cannot be achieved by way of a mathematical algorithm, but is rather an exercise of educated judgement.

Regulation of dispute resolution should be based on the following fundamentals: normative individualism (as expressed in human and constitutional rights), party choice, just dispute resolution for the parties and efficiency. Individuals have a right to effective and fair dispute resolution.

E. Principles

The recommendations formulated here are general principles. With a view to the diversity of dispute resolution practice and law, and in order not to restrict the dynamic and creative development of dispute resolution, currently only general principles for ADR are desirable. They are, nonetheless, necessary to develop coherent and principled systems of dispute resolution. They can be used in two ways in particular. First, they can be referred to in formulating recommendations and model rules for the regulation of specific types of dispute resolution mechanisms, such as mediation, ombudsman procedure and arbitration. Second, they can be directly used as a basis to draft concrete laws, regulations and codes at a local or regional level.

Currently, only general principles for the regulation of dispute resolution are desirable.

II. INFRASTRUCTURE AND FRAMEWORK

The self-determination of the parties places the responsibility for solving disputes primarily in the hands of the parties. The state is called on to provide the parties with the necessary enabling and—as necessary—conduct rules, ie an adequate normative framework for dispute resolution. In this sense, the citizens have a right of access to effective and fair dispute resolution. It also follows that the state is not responsible for organising and financing a comprehensive institutional *infrastructure* for dispute resolution that comprises all ADR mechanisms. The state merely has to provide a reliable legal *framework* for alternative dispute resolution mechanisms and should, within the means available, support alternative forms of dispute resolution.

Due to the state monopoly on the enforcement of rights, the situation is altogether different regarding court procedures. In this respect, the state is responsible not only for providing a normative framework but also for setting up—ie organising and financing—an adequate and comprehensive court and enforcement system. It is especially needed for those cases when a consensual dispute resolution is not possible. This system needs to be adequately accessible as regards its cost and time framework for the enforcement of rights. In this sense, citizens have a right of access to justice. ADR mechanisms should not be used by the state as a substitute for the adequate organisation and financing of court and enforcement procedures.

Citizens have a right of access to effective and fair dispute resolution. The state is responsible for organising and financing an adequate court and enforcement system. Additionally, the state has to provide citizens with a reliable legal framework for alternative dispute resolution and should, within the means available, support such alternative forms of dispute resolution.

III. COSTS

A. General

Generally, the parties to a dispute should carry the costs of resolving their dispute. However, since ensuring access to justice is required by the rule of law, the cost of court proceedings may be partially borne by the general public. The costs of the procedure (neutral, experts, clerks, etc) and reasonable party expenses in procedures without initiation control can be allocated with reference to the outcome (for example according to the degree of losing) or according to other principles. Previously established cost rules for court procedures can serve as a point of orientation to develop the rules for alternative dispute resolution mechanisms where the parties do not control the initiation.

In procedures with initiation control of the parties a dispositive default rule should provide for the sharing of the costs of the procedure between the parties and the payment of party expenses by the relevant individual party. In alternative dispute resolution mechanisms where the parties do not have initiation control (mandatory ADR), the right of access to justice requires that the costs of alternative dispute resolution are not prohibitive so that as a consequence the parties would be hindered in their access to the courts.

Generally the parties should carry the costs of resolving their dispute by the use of ADR procedures, while the cost of court proceedings may be partially borne by the general public. In procedures where the parties do not have initiation control, the costs of the procedure and reasonable party expenses should be borne according to the procedures for cost assessment appropriate in the legal system. In procedures with initiation control the parties should by default share the costs of the procedures and pay their own expenses. Mandatory extrajudicial dispute resolution may not impose costs to a degree that hinders access to the courts.

B. Cost Subsidies

States have to offer a court system that is accessible as regards costs. This finds its justification in the state's monopoly on power. Whether the state subsidises dispute resolution mechanisms other than the court system should depend on the following three aspects: (1) Do information and decision deficits exist as regards certain mechanisms? (2) Do certain mechanisms intrinsically offer more advantageous conditions for the resolution of specific disputes? (3) Do the subsidies create cost savings or even positive cost income effects for the state?

Cost subsidies should never reach a degree such that the parties to a dispute lose the self-interest to find a solution themselves or such that an incentive is created to prefer one kind of dispute resolution mechanism over another merely for cost reasons.

Access to courts must not be impeded by prohibitive costs. Subsidies for alternative dispute resolution mechanisms may be justified if information and decision deficits exist, if certain procedures have intrinsic advantages or more generally on grounds of efficiency. Cost subsidies should avoid setting incentives favouring one kind of resolution mechanism merely for cost reasons.

C. Legal Aid

Legal aid for court proceedings should be given to parties who for financial reasons would otherwise not be in a position to bring or defend a claim in instances where they can show a strong claim, ie a more likely than not probability of being successful. Beyond this, the state may opt to provide legal aid based only on economic need without regard to the strength of the claim. The specific requirement for legal aid for court proceedings is justified due to the specific function of the court procedure as a counterweight to the state's monopoly on power.

With respect to legal aid for court proceedings, care needs to be taken, however, that no incentives are set so that parties in financial need opt for court proceedings instead of alternative disputes resolution for monetary reasons only. This would breach the principle that generally the party should be in a position to choose the dispute resolution mechanism according to the suitability of its intrinsic characteristics in relation to the specific dispute. Depending on the level of legal aid for court proceedings, legal aid for alternative dispute resolution mechanisms should be provided. The focus of legal aid for alternative dispute resolution should not be on whether a party has a more likely than not chance to win in court, but rather on whether the dispute is well suited for the characteristics of the dispute mechanism envisaged.

Legal aid for court proceedings should be provided to parties in financial need if they can demonstrate a more likely than not probability of being successful. Alternatively, legal aid could be provided based on the sole criteria of demonstrated financial need. Legal aid should not set incentives for parties to opt for court proceedings instead of alternative dispute resolution for cost reasons only. A necessary reaction may be the introduction of legal aid for alternative dispute resolution mechanisms.

IV. DISPUTE RESOLUTION CLAUSES

A. General

Dispute resolution clauses should be binding and enforceable. Such clauses are based on the voluntary decision of the parties. Their consent carries the presumption of efficiency and justice. The obligations undertaken under an individual clause should be central to its effect. Legislatures should enable parties to use clauses with effect in procedural law, such as the (temporary or permanent) unavailability of court and other dispute resolution procedures. Generally, however, interim or conservation measures should be possible in spite of a dispute resolution clause. Consideration should be given to allow parties to exclude such measures contractually within certain limits.

Dispute resolution clauses should be binding and enforceable in the same manner as other contracts are binding and enforced. Interim or conservation measures should generally remain possible as a dispositive default rule.

B. Specifics

Parties can waive their right to insist on a dispute resolution clause as long as it is based on the autonomous decision of the parties. The waiver of rights based on dispute resolution clauses operates against the background of constitutional law, contract law and the law in other areas. The protection of the right of access to justice requires that dispute resolution clauses can be challenged before the state courts. The more control the parties have as regards (1) the procedure, (2) the choice of the neutral, (3) the content and (4) the effect of the result, the less there is a need for policing dispute resolution clauses. Particular relevance needs to be given to the result-effect control of the parties in this regard. Hence, for example, arbitration clauses need to be subject to a higher degree of scrutiny than mediation clauses because mediation results require the consent of the parties; arbitration results do not. There may be complex issues of consent and enforcement if all parties are not in agreement.

The invalidation or later modification of dispute resolution clauses should follow general legal principles. The more control the parties have as regards (1) the procedure, (2) the choice of the neutral, (3) the content and (4) the effect of the result, the less there is a need for restricting and policing the validity of dispute resolution clauses.

V. CHOICE OF DISPUTE RESOLUTION PROCEDURE

A. General

An early, informed and undistorted choice of the adequate dispute resolution procedure by the parties is essential. Additionally, transaction costs, for example the cost for acquiring the necessary information and understanding the resolution mechanisms available, should be as low as possible. Legal rules should ensure that the parties take these decisions based on the adequacy of the intrinsic characteristics of the resolution procedure for the resolution of the conflict. Legal systems should to the extent possible avoid that external factors not connected to the dispute and the intrinsic characteristics of the resolution mechanism distort this choice.

If information and decision deficits relating to the choice of dispute resolution mechanisms exist, rule-makers should, first of all, put the parties themselves in a position to make the best choice. It is the dispute and the interests of the parties which are concerned; hence the party's decision-making process should be at the centre of possible regulatory intervention. Conflict diagnosis and dispute resolution choice should be an important and integral part of procedural and substantial law. When the parties' preferred choices do not coincide, the state may provide options and alternatives.

Regulation should ensure an early, informed and undistorted choice of a dispute resolution procedure with the lowest possible transaction costs. Regulation should ensure that the parties are in a position to choose by matching their interests with the intrinsic characteristics of the resolution procedures. The state may provide options and alternatives for situations where the parties do not prefer the same dispute resolution mechanism.

B. Centralised or Decentralised Approach

The choice of the appropriate dispute resolution procedure can be facilitated either by more centralised or more decentralised approaches. More centralised approaches establish means such as dispute boards, early dispute conferences, settlement conferences with judicial personnel and multi-door fora that foster the early and informed decision-making process of the parties by establishing a rather centralised dispute distribution mechanism. More decentralised approaches employ obligations of the parties to inform themselves as well as each other and duties of their counsel to inform and advise. Currently, either of these approaches seems reasonable. Both approaches can be combined.

In any case, counsel and the neutral overseeing the various dispute resolution procedures should be under a duty to constantly monitor the adequacy of the choice taken and point out to the parties if their choice turns out to be questionable. Depending on the degree of information and decision deficits experienced, the setting of cost incentives to modify the choice should be considered. In appropriate cases, the parties may choose to modify or change their initial choice of process. Only if this does not cure information and decision deficits should mandatory referrals be considered. Mandatory prescription of certain procedures may in particular be considered in the interest of third parties that are affected by the dispute, for example children in custody disputes. Mandatory ADR needs to be regulated in such a way that access to court justice is not overly restricted in terms of time and costs. Some legal systems have prohibited mandatory ADR procedures for certain classes of cases, eg constitutional challenges to laws.

Centralised and decentralised approaches to facilitate an early, informed, undistorted and less expensive choice of a dispute resolution mechanism are both reasonable. Counsel and the neutral should be under a duty to monitor the adequacy of the choice and point out if the choice needs to be modified. In case of information and decision deficits as regards choice, primarily incentives and subsidiarily mandatory rules may be necessary.

C. Sanctions

The dispute between two or more persons creates a monopoly for dispute resolution. The individual needs the cooperation of the other party to solve the dispute consensually. This can justify cost and damage sanctions for those parties who hinder or prolong dispute resolution without a good and proportionate reason. One consequence is the loser-pays principle in court proceedings (in legal systems that use a loser-pays rule); another consequence may be cost, damage or procedural sanctions if one party proposes a suitable dispute resolution mechanism that the other party rejects without a good and proportionate cause. However, cost sanctions should be a means of last resort. Before establishing such sanctions, other less intrusive legislative approaches, such as information improvement and positive incentives, should be considered.

Cost, damage and procedural sanctions for parties who hinder or prolong dispute resolution without a good and proportionate reason can be justified. Before turning to cost sanctions, however, alternative and less intrusive means to correct decision deficits should be considered.

D. Transfer to Other Dispute Resolution Mechanisms

Ideally, the parties should be in a position to transfer from one dispute resolution mechanism to another if the initial choice turns out to be inappropriate. Here, the above-mentioned principles should equally apply, which means the transfer should happen without delay, on an informed basis, without decision distortions and at low transaction costs. These principles should be implemented in substantive and in procedural law. The above principles as regards incentives for transfer or mandating transfer also apply.

In order to set incentives for a correct initial choice of the dispute resolution mechanism, the costs for dispute resolution may rise for the parties due to the transfer. The increase in costs should not, however, be prohibitive to transfer.

The above principles apply equally to a transfer between dispute resolution mechanisms.

E. Good Practice

The following tools may facilitate the early and correct choice of dispute resolution procedures:

- In centralised as well as decentralised approaches, easily accessible, understandable information about possible resolution options is important. Low-barrier steps for starting resolution procedures are also key. Here, information and connection providers can help.
- Self-tests, check lists, questionnaires and counselling for the parties that help the individuals to understand the characteristics of the dispute and match these characteristics with the appropriate dispute resolution mechanism. Such self-tests can be distributed in paper form or be offered online.
- Rules to deal with information and decision deficits need to be concrete and designed in a way that compliance is ensured. Example: instead of a general duty of lawyers to advise clients on dispute resolution possibilities, it is better to have a concrete duty which not only specifies what information is to be acquired and the point(s) in time at which advice needs to be provided to the client, but also requires documentation (eg in a form to be submitted to court).
- Double summons by courts, which means that the court sets two dates—the first for the start of an ADR mechanism and the second for the resumption of court proceedings.

Comparative analysis and empirical research reveal good practice models for regulating the choice of dispute resolution procedures. Research and assessment are essential for continued monitoring of what are the best ways to ensure early and good choices of dispute resolution procedures.

VI. CONFIDENTIALITY

A. General

Dispute resolution procedures, where the parties have information control, should be facilitated by enabling rules that allow the parties to keep the information pertaining to the dispute confidential, unless prohibited by appropriate law.

Dispute resolution procedures, where the parties have information control, should be facilitated by enabling confidentiality rules.

B. Regulatory Tools and Approaches

The legal basis for confidentiality can be state and contract law, but it needs to be ensured in both substantive and procedural law. Confidentiality needs to be guaranteed in all subsequent dispute resolution procedures. Rules on confidentiality need to cover all relevant persons: the parties, the neutral(s), counsel, translators, experts, other third parties and the assistants of all such persons. The substantive law needs to allow the parties to contract for discretion and other confidentiality duties; here dispositive law is generally well suited. Procedural law needs to equip parties with a right to refuse to testify as well as with restrictions on the later submission of facts and evidence insofar as they have been obtained in the alternative dispute resolution procedure. As regards the scope of the confidentiality rules, they need to cover different types of information carriers and transmission. However, the abusive use of a certain dispute resolution procedure with the sole intent to exclude information from another procedure needs to be addressed, as well as the protection of third parties and the prevention and detection of crime. In this regard, the right to submit evidence needs to be respected. Hence, the confidentiality rules should, in particular, be limited to the matter of the dispute submitted to a certain procedure. Information the other party had access to before the initiation of the procedure should not fall under the confidentiality rules.

Confidentiality of dispute resolution procedures, where the parties have information control, needs to be ensured in both substantive and procedural law. Confidentiality rules should cover all relevant persons and different types of information carriers. The subject matter to which the rules on confidentiality apply should be delineated. However, limits to confidentiality may be necessary. In particular, abuse of the confidentiality rules needs to be addressed, as well as the protection of third parties and the prevention and detection of crime.

VII. LIMITATION AND PRESCRIPTION PERIODS

Limitation and prescription periods should be suspended from the start until the end of any dispute resolution procedure. The suspension should refer to legal claims as well as other rights (particularly substantive and procedural limitation and prescription periods). The suspension should only have legal effect for the parties to the procedure and not have legal effects on third parties. The scope of affected claims and rights is determined by the matter submitted to the dispute resolution procedure.

The suspension should start with the agreement of the parties to start a specific procedure where they have initiation control and with the unilateral action of one party where the parties do not have initiation control. Where the parties have agreed to use one or certain procedures in a dispute resolution clause, the suspension should generally start with the initiation of the specified procedure(s) by one of the parties. Where the parties have result-effect control, the suspension should end with the statement of one party, both parties or (if possible) the neutral that the procedure has ended or when an agreement is reached. Where the parties do not have result-effect control, the suspension should end when the result becomes finally binding. To allow for a determination of the start and the end of a procedure where the parties have result-effect control, presumptions and documentation obligations can be used.

Limitation and prescription periods should be suspended from the start until the end of any dispute resolution procedure. For all procedures the details of regulation should refer to the characteristics of initiation control and result-effect control.

VIII. NEUTRAL

A. General

The appropriate regulatory intensity for ensuring the neutrality and qualification of the intermediary depends on four characteristics of the dispute resolution mechanism, namely whether the parties have (1) initiation control, (2) neutral choice control, (3) result-content control and (4) result-effect control. The more control the parties have as regards these four issues, the less intensive the regulation needs to be of the intermediary's neutrality and qualification. Among these characteristics, neutral choice control and result-effect control have the greatest importance.

The more control the parties have as regards initiation control, neutral choice control, result-content control and result-effect control, the less intensive the regulation of the intermediary's neutrality and qualification needs to be.

B. Neutrality

Where the parties have common neutral choice control, the legislature has to ensure that the parties' choice does not suffer from information asymmetry or decision deficits. This requires ex ante information and ex post updating if necessary. Particular attention as regards neutrality needs to be given to industry-financed dispute resolution schemes. If the parties have neutral choice control and result-effect control, there is a presumption for relaxing the intensity of regulation.

The legislature has to ensure that the parties' choice of the neutral does not suffer from information asymmetry or decision deficits. If the parties have neutral choice control and result-effect control, the intensity of regulation may be lower.

C. Qualification

The less control the parties have as regards the choice of the neutral, the initiation, the result-content and the result-effect of a procedure, the more the state needs to ensure the qualification of the neutral. For conflict resolution procedures where the parties have common control over the choice of the neutral and the initiation or the effect of the procedure, two types of regulatory approaches can be recommended: the market approach and the incentive approach. When choosing the market approach, the state does not regulate the corresponding education and admission to the activity of serving as a neutral in the particular ADR procedure. Instead, the neutrals, their organisations, the parties and academia develop practice standards and guidelines for their implementation. When choosing the incentive approach, the state does not require authorisation as a precondition for acting as a neutral, but sets incentives in order to fulfil certain qualification criteria. This can be done by awarding a qualification seal to those who fulfil certain qualification criteria or by creating advantageous legal consequences for those who fulfil such criteria, for example as regards confidentiality standards and professional duties. If the market of those offering neutral services and those requesting them consistently fails to develop stable quality and information systems, the legislature should consider trying the incentive approach. The authorisation approach, under which the state sets up a state-administered (ministry, courts, etc) admission procedure to the activity of serving as a neutral, may not be advisable for the procedures defined above. It should generally be respected that party self-determination entails the right to choose the neutral. Hence, it is generally recommended to opt for as little intrusive regulation as possible. Dispute resolution procedures that are based not on rights but on interests should not be restricted to professionals with a legal education.

For conflict resolution procedures where the parties have neutral choice control but do not have control over the initiation of the procedure, the use of one of two regulatory approaches is recommended, namely the incentive model or the authorisation model. If the parties do not have control over the choice of the neutral and no initiation control, the authorisation approach is recommended. If the parties do not control the initiation, neutral choice and result-effect of a procedure, then the state needs to opt for an authorisation approach. If the procedure is rights-based, the admission requirements need to ensure legal qualification.

The less the parties control the choice of the neutral, the initiation, the result-content and the result-effect of a dispute resolution mechanism, the more the state needs to ensure the qualification of the neutral. Generally, however, it is recommended to opt for as little intrusive regulation as necessary.

If the parties control the choice of the neutral and the initiation or the effect of the procedure, a market approach or an incentive approach may be advisable.

If the parties have neutral choice control, but do not have control over the initiation of the procedure, either the incentive approach or the authorisation approach is recommended.

If the parties neither control the choice of the neutral nor the initiation, an authorisation approach is recommended.

If the parties have no control over initiation, neutral choice and result-effect, the state needs to opt for an authorisation approach.

IX. PROCEDURE

The individual's private autonomy encompasses not only the right to contract over substance but also the right to to contract over procedure. Hence, it is only where the individual has neither initiation control nor both result-content and effect control that procedural safeguards aiming for a correct and just result become necessary. If the parties have initiation control but no result-content or effect control, a weaker form of state-ensured procedural safeguards is advisable. Legal justice and fairness as regards the procedure need to be adapted to the various characteristics of the dispute resolution procedures (procedural integrity). In particular, in case of evaluative procedures, ie procedures where the parties do not have result-content control, the neutral needs to explain to the parties the evaluation standards applied, and the neutral has to hear the parties as regards the evaluation.

If the parties have neither initiation control nor both result-content and effect control, procedural safeguards are necessary. If the parties have initiation control but no result-content or effect control, a weaker form of state-ensured procedural safeguards is advisable.

X. COUNSEL

As regards the role of counsel, it needs to be distinguished whether counsel accompanies the party or whether counsel represents the party (ie the party need not be present). Generally, parties should have the right to be accompanied and advised by counsel in all procedures.

Full representation in procedural acts should also generally be allowed. However, where the procedure specifically depends on the personal participation of the parties to the dispute, the state may require the parties to appear and act personally.

Generally, parties should have the right to be accompanied and advised by counsel. Full representation in procedural acts should also generally be allowed. Where the procedure specifically depends on personal participation of the parties, regulation may require the parties to appear in person.

XI. STATE (JUDICIAL) REVIEW OF RESULTS

If the parties have control over the result-content and effect of the procedure, there should not be a state (judicial) review of the result beyond that applying to contracts in general. If the parties do not have control over the result-content and effect, there should be the possibility for a state review of the results, particularly in the form of judicial review. The degree of the state review needs, however, to distinguish whether the individual bound to the result has control over the initiation of the procedure or not. If the parties have control over the initiation of the procedure, then a lower degree of state review is recommended while a high degree of review should be offered by the state if the parties do not have initiation control. The state review should also distinguish whether the underlying procedure is rights-based or interest-based. The result of an interest-based procedure should only be submitted to a weak rights-based review that checks for public policy infringements.

If the parties have control over the result-content and effect of the procedure, a state (judicial) review of the result beyond that applying to contracts in general is not recommended. If the parties do not control the result-content and effect, there should be the possibility for a state review of the results. The degree of the state review should distinguish whether the party bound to the result had control over the initiation of the procedure or not.

XII. ENFORCEABILITY

Formal state enforcement of the results of a conflict resolution procedure may not always be necessary and desired. Where desired by the parties, enforceability should be possible. The enforceability of the result of a dispute resolution procedure should generally require the participation of the state. This is based on the state's monopoly on power and the necessary protection afforded by this principle to the debtor. The participation of the state can take the form of representative participation, for example in the form of public notaries charged with equivalent protective functions. The degree of state monitoring to which the content of the to-be-enforced result is subjected should not have the effect that results controlled by the parties are submitted ex post to a court-like result review of the subject matter.

For procedures with result-effect control, the parties should be offered as many paths to enforceability as are necessary to allow them to choose the dispute resolution mechanism initially without being influenced by the availability of enforceability. In particular, the parties to a dispute should not indirectly be forced to turn to lawyers or public notaries for enforceability by requiring their participation in the procedure as precondition for enforcement. One solution would be the possibility of submitting the result of a dispute resolution procedure to a court which declares its enforceability and only checks for the validity of the agreement and—possibly—breach of public policy rules. In addition, enforceability might be denied if the agreement affects third parties (eg children).

Enforceability should require the participation of the state or a representative charged with state functions. Results controlled by the parties should not ex post be submitted to a court-like result review. The availability and the path to enforceability should generally not be designed in a way that it indirectly influences the choice of a dispute resolution mechanism.

XIII. TRANSPARENCY

Transparency can be used to regulate the behaviour of neutrals and their organisations indirectly. If the state requires neutrals and their organisations to publish information on their structures and practice, care needs to be taken not to infringe the confidentiality interests of the parties.

Transparency can be used to indirectly control the quality of procedures. Care needs to be taken not to infringe the justified confidentiality interests of the parties.

XIV. CONSUMERS

A. General

Information and decision deficits as well as rational ignorance can affect consumers as regards the choice and conduct of dispute resolution. Hence, specific rules for consumer dispute resolution are required. Consumers are, in particular, natural persons acting for purposes outside their trade or profession with professional counterparts, ie persons acting for commercial or professional purposes. Often rules pertaining to dispute resolution concerning consumers can take the form of complementary rules, so that it is not necessary to establish a separate dispute resolution system for consumers. Instead, the existing systems can be modified if necessary.

B. Specifics

A specific issue for consumer protection is initiation control. Here, for procedures where the parties have initiation control, the regulatory solution can be mandatory rules as regards unfair contract terms (in particular as regards dispute resolution clauses). Particular attention is merited by procedures where the parties do not have control over the effect of the result. If consumers are still directed by asymmetric information and decision structures towards a certain type of dispute resolution mechanism, then this mechanism can be reclassified from initiation-control to no-initiation-control with the consequence of the higher regulatory safeguards described here.

Close regulatory supervision of governance structures is needed for consumer dispute resolution mechanisms such as ombudsman procedures that are financed by the relevant industry. Also, state monitoring and possibly action may be necessary in cases where such or other institutions work together with repeat players on the industry side while the consumers are not repeat players. This becomes relevant in particular if the repeat industry players generate a substantial proportion of the mechanism's fee income. A possible solution to governance issues of privately funded consumer dispute resolution bodies can be the requirement of (at least) equal representation of consumer representatives on the governing boards.

Specific rules for consumer dispute resolution are required concerning, in particular, initiation control through dispute resolution clauses and the governance structures of industry-financed resolution systems.

XV. RULE-MAKER

A. General

Possible state rule-makers are, inter alia, the parliament, the executive branch and the courts. Possible private rule-makers are, inter alia, chartered associations, private dispute resolution providers, independent institutions, the parties and the neutral in a particular case.

B. Choice

The research and assessment regarding the identification and assessment of rule-makers as regards dispute resolution has just begun. While such knowledge is desirable in the interest of informed rule-making, at this stage it is difficult to develop a coherent set of principles. A first starting point could be that those dispute resolution mechanisms with procedure control by the parties should generally not be influenced unnecessarily by mandatory state law. Instead, the development of rules and practice might be left to the parties, the neutral and the professional organisations, unless otherwise mentioned here (see, for example, the principles above regarding confidentiality and neutrals). Rules with an enabling and protection function should generally be made by actors with high-level regulatory authority as well as accountability and wide geographical reach.

Further research as regards the identification and assessment of rule-makers is desirable. Dispute resolution mechanisms with procedure control by the parties should generally not be influenced unnecessarily by mandatory state law. Rules with an enabling and protection function should generally be made by actors with high-level regulatory authority and wide geographical reach.

XVI. TYPE OF RULES

A. General

The following types of rules can be distinguished at a first level: (1) enabling rules that empower the individuals to shape their relationships; and (2) conduct rules that set boundaries on individual behaviour and prescribe, forbid or allow a specific form of conduct directly. Conduct rules that require or prohibit certain conduct are in general accompanied by sanctions in case of their breach. At a second level, the following types can be distinguished: mandatory, semi-mandatory and dispositive statutory law, regulations, codes, model agreements, contracts, etc.

In general, it cannot be said whether a comprehensive and detailed regulatory approach is better than a restricted approach. As regards the regulation of ADR through conduct rules, in cases of doubt, a softer approach (for example dispositive rules rather than mandatory rules) or even no regulation should be preferred. As regards regulation of ADR through enabling rules, state regulation is sometimes needed to create the necessary tools and rights for the individuals. Examples include the above recommendations as regards confidentiality and enforcement. Finally, to remedy information and decision deficits, regulations setting incentives or even imposing mandatory rules may be (temporarily) advisable. The enabling and guiding rules necessary should integrate ADR institutionally in substantive and procedural law.

As regards conduct rules, in cases of doubt, dispositive rules over mandatory rules or even no regulation should be preferred. As regards enabling rules, state regulation is always needed to create the necessary tools and rights. To remedy information and decision deficits, regulations setting incentives or even imposing mandatory rules may be (temporarily) advisable.

B. Good Practice

Rules should be clear and accessible. Regulation should also follow a principled and systematic approach in order to be understood and embraced by parties to a dispute and professionals. When regulating, care should be taken not to give preference to one dispute resolution mechanism through the wording of the rules. To avoid this, in drafting general rules ADR could be defined as comprising mediation, conciliation, ombudsman procedure, arbitration, etc, as well as combinations of these procedures, and then the term ADR could be used subsequently. If, however, preference is to be given to one procedure for reasons of particular positive characteristics or in response to information and decision deficits, emphasis on this particular procedure is (temporarily) in order.

There is a considerable amount of new developments in practice and research. It is important to publicise and study 'best practices' in respect of assessment, research and evaluation. This is additional and supplementary to any regulation, and can lead to changes in regulatory schemes. Dispute resolution is a flexible field and its development should not be hampered by overly rigid regulation.

Rules should be principled, clear and accessible. The development of dispute resolution practice should not be hampered by overly rigid regulation.

XVII. PROCEDURE DESIGN

Comparative empirical evidence shows that it is essential to incentivise lawyers, judges, accountants, notaries, tax advisers, insurance companies and other gatekeepers to act in the parties' dispute resolution interest. Principal-agent problems arise all too easily, ie situations in which the gatekeepers influence the course of dispute resolution in their own interests instead of the parties' interest. Countermeasures can be taken on the side of the parties as well as on the side of the gatekeepers. The parties can be equipped with information and decision rights to influence the choice and course of dispute resolution. The gatekeepers can be positively incentivised by aligning their financial and temporal interests with the parties' interests, or their actions can be guided through procedural rules and substantive duties.

Further measures can be directed to the public in the form of information campaigns, institutionalised information boards and mandatory dispute resolution training within the university and education sector. Also, giving ADR programmes a physical presence in court buildings should be considered in order to allow for easy access and information. When institutionalising methods for conflict diagnosis, internet-based platforms should be considered. Moreover, within its own organisational realm, the state can take a leading role in interest- and efficiency-based dispute resolution.

The characteristics and effects of dispute resolution need to be understandable, which very often is not the case. At times, locally diverse and confusing dispute resolution structures should be simplified and unified at a higher geographical level. Where unification is not needed, the rule-making can be left to the parties, the neutrals and their organisations.

Communication by electronic means should be an integral part of dispute resolution and its regulation. Online dispute resolution requires particular thought and may require specific regulation.

It is essential to incentivise lawyers, judges, accountants, notaries, tax advisers, insurance companies and other gatekeepers to act in the parties' dispute resolution interest. Further measures can be information campaigns, institutionalised information boards and mandatory dispute resolution training within the university and education sector. The characteristics and effects of dispute resolution mechanisms need to be understandable. Online dispute resolution requires particular thought and may require specific regulation.

3

Principled Regulation of Dispute Resolution: Taxonomy, Policy, Topics

FELIX STEFFEK

I. PRINCIPLED REGULATION

A. Introduction

SHOULD REGULATION OF dispute resolution be based on principles? Is it possible to develop such principles on a sound methodical basis? Can such principles contribute meaningfully to law-making and standard-setting in the field of dispute resolution? This chapter argues that these three questions can be answered in the affirmative. First, the desirability, challenge and approach as regards principled regulation of dispute resolution are set out. Then a taxonomy of dispute resolution mechanisms is developed. This is followed by a discussion of policy decisions to be made and the identification of regulatory topics to be dealt with. Finally, it is shown how the taxonomy, policy and topics can be developed into principles of regulation. The chapter concludes with a summary and identifies further possible areas of research. The focus of this paper is on disputes in the realm of civil and commercial law.

B. Desirability

Principled regulation means a coherent, intelligible, systematic and reasoned approach to law-making and standard-setting.[1] This calls for an analytical, comprehensive and fact-based understanding of the relevant realities that may or may not be in need of regulation. It also demands a transparent discussion of underlying values and policy decisions, ideally leading to acceptance by those affected. Finally, it requires an informed identification of topics in regulatory need and a sound and consistent method to translate values and policy into laws and standards.[2] Consequently, principled regulation promises *justice* across the various types of dispute resolution mechanisms. Coherent and intelligible rules and standards improve choice and implementation at the level of both the individual and the institutions of the state.

By contributing to just dispute resolution, principled regulation also fosters *freedom, equality* and *efficiency*. An intelligible and just system of dispute resolution increases the freedom and private autonomy of the citizens by providing them with a predictable framework that connects behaviour with responsibility. The coherent and systematic translation of policy into rules and standards guarantees equality within mechanisms of dispute resolution, across different means of resolving conflicts and in cross-border conflicts. Finally, a reasoned and educated approach to the design of the rules and institutions of dispute resolution helps to prevent information and decision deficits.

[1] *Cf* R Cotterrell, 'Law's Community: Legal Theory and the Image of Legality' (1992) 19 *Journal of Law and Society* 405, 407ff, 415ff.

[2] On improving the quality of regulation see R Baldwin, 'Better Regulation: The Search and the Struggle' in R Baldwin, M Cave and M Lodge (eds), *The Oxford Handbook of Regulation* (Oxford, Oxford University Press, 2010) 259ff; for examples see Better Regulation Task Force, *Principles of Good Regulation* (London, 2003); Australian Law Reform Commission, *Principled Regulation* (2002) 131ff; D Mandelkern (ed), *Report on Better Regulation—Final Report* (Brussels, 2001).

Better information and decision frameworks enable the individuals and the state to make better use of scarce goods, thereby contributing to efficient dispute resolution.[3]

C. Challenge

The desired goal of transnational principles for the regulation of dispute resolution faces serious challenges. First, there are *complexity* and *diversity* as regards dispute resolution laws and practice. The rise of alternative dispute resolution has led to a multitude of different dispute resolution procedures in many jurisdictions, some regulated, some unregulated, often through incoherent and unsystematic piecemeal legislation, which is further varied in practice.[4] Second, there is no comprehensive convergence of the rules and practices of conflict resolution in the jurisdictions of the EU or the wider world. Instead, the multitude of differing laws and practices is multiplied by a myriad of varying rules and dispute resolution methods applied in different countries.[5] Third, there is diversity in regulatory policies and dispute resolution cultures. Some legislatures and citizens tacitly or openly disagree as to what dispute resolution is about,[6] and societies do not always share the same social mechanisms for conflict resolution.[7]

D. Approach

In the approach suggested here, the complexity and diversity of dispute resolution laws, practices, policies and cultures are respected on two levels: (1) in the process of *designing* principles for regulating dispute resolution and (2) at the stage of *implementing* these principles through regulation. In the first stage, the complexity and diversity of existing dispute resolution laws, practices and cultures are captured through a modular method referring to functional characteristics of dispute resolution mechanisms and regulatory topics.[8] This functional, as opposed to technical, understanding of laws, practices and cultures allows a reduction of complexity, but still captures the essence of dispute resolution mechanisms. The functional approach reflects reality, facilitates transnational arguments and draws on the vast experience of the functional method of comparative law.[9] The modular structure provides an adaptive

[3] *Cf* C Veljanovski, 'Economic Approaches to Regulation' in R Baldwin, M Cave and M Lodge, *The Oxford Handbook of Regulation* (Oxford, Oxford University Press, 2010) 17ff.

[4] *Cf* the description of conflict resolution rules and practice in the country chapters of this book.

[5] As regards mediation, see the comparison of more than 20 jurisdictions in KJ Hopt and F Steffek (eds), *Mediation: Principles and Regulation in Comparative Perspective* (Oxford, Oxford University Press, 2013); as regards different approaches to consumer dispute resolution in the EU see CJS Hodges, I Benöhr and N Creutzfeld-Banda, *Consumer ADR in Europe* (Oxford, Hart Publishing, 2012).

[6] See, eg the analysis of ADR policy in England and Wales in Chapter 7.

[7] *Cf* K Avruch, *Culture and Conflict Resolution* (Washington, DC, United States Institute of Peace Press, 1998).

[8] For more details on a functional taxonomy of dispute resolution mechanisms see below II; for a functional identification of regulatory topics see below IV.

[9] R Michaels, 'The Functional Method of Comparative Law' in R Zimmermann and M Reimann (eds), *The Oxford Handbook of Comparative Law* (Oxford, Oxford University Press, 2008) 339–82; K Zweigert and H Kötz, *Introduction to Comparative Law*, 3rd edn (Oxford, Clarendon Press, 1998) in particular pp 32ff.

framework and allows issues to be addressed with—as appropriate—an enhanced or lessened degree of intricacy. In order to respect the diversity encountered in existing regulatory policies and strategies, the regulatory proposals made are accompanied by an express and transparent disclosure of their normative foundations. This comprises a scientific approach based on available empirical research and open reasoning, thus facilitating a rational discussion.

Complexity and diversity of laws, practices, policies and cultures can in addition be respected at the *implementation stage* of the principles for regulating dispute resolution. The high level and modular types of principles presented in the Guide for Regulating Dispute Resolution (GRDR)[10] allow taking into account differing and complex local, as well as regional, laws, practices, policies and cultures. The general and modular formulation of the principles allows for adaptation and choice when designing model laws or concrete legislation. Such adaptation is—in particular, but not solely[11]—facilitated by referring to local concepts of law and by providing alternatives on the input and the output side of the principles. Principle structures such as 'A should be governed by the general law of consumer contracts' or 'if B then W or X, if C then Y or Z' provide flexibility as regards the complex and differing environments in which new regulation is implemented while maintaining a coherent, systematic and reasoned approach.

II. TAXONOMY

A. Matrix

Principled regulation of dispute resolution requires a taxonomy of dispute resolution mechanisms. The taxonomy anchors regulation through a better understanding of the regulatory environment and facilitates coherent, intelligible, systematic and reasoned law-making and standard-setting. Here a taxonomy based on a matrix of dispute resolution mechanisms is proposed.[12] The matrix has four essential characteristics, which are explained in the following text: (1) The matrix is constructed from the *perspective of the parties* to a dispute; (2) the matrix uses *intrinsic characteristics* of dispute resolution mechanisms; (3) the dispute resolution mechanisms are described using a *functional and comparative method*; and (4) the matrix has a *modular structure*.

[10] See Chapters 1 (Principles only) and 2 (Principles and Comments).

[11] For a more detailed discussion on dealing with diversity see below V.C.

[12] For taxonomies from other perspectives, see eg SB Goldberg, FEA Sander, NH Rogers and SR Cole, *Dispute Resolution*, 6th edn (New York, Wolters Kluwer, 2012) 1ff; CJ Menkel-Meadow, LP Love, AK Schneider and JR Sternlight, *Dispute Resolution*, 2nd edn (New York, Aspen Publishers, 2011) 22; S Blake, J Browne and S Sime, *A Practical Approach to Alternative Dispute Resolution* (Oxford, Oxford University Press, 2011) 23f; PWC (PriceWaterhouseCoopers) and Europa University Viadrina Frankfurt (Oder), *Commercial Dispute Resolution* (Frankfurt am Main and Frankfurt an der Oder, 2005) 15ff; S Smith and J Martinez, 'An Analytical Framework for Dispute Systems Design' (2009) 14 *Harvard Negotiation Law Review* 123, 129ff; FEA Sander and L Rozdeiczer, 'Matching Cases and Dispute Resolution Procedures' (2006) 11 *Harvard Negotiation Law Review* 1, 12ff.

A first version of the matrix, representing essential dispute resolution mechanisms and their core features, might look like Table 1.

Table 1

	Parties Together Have…					
	Initiation Control	Procedure Control	Result-Content Control	Result-Effect Control	Neutral Choice Control	Information Control
Negotiation	Yes	Yes	Yes	Yes	N/A	Yes
Mediation	Yes	Yes	Yes	Yes	Yes	Yes
Conciliation	Yes	Yes	No	Yes	Yes	Yes
Arbitration	Yes	Yes	No	No	Yes	Yes
Adjudication	No	No	No	No	No	No

B. Design

i. Perspective of the Parties

The matrix reduces the complexity of laws and practices by describing dispute resolution mechanisms through their essential features. These features are determined from the perspective of the parties, since they are the normative starting point and focus of regulation.[13] The features facilitate the distinction of whether or not the parties together[14] control a certain aspect of the dispute resolution. Hence, the matrix uses the following features to describe dispute resolution mechanisms, all to be understood from the viewpoint of the parties:

- *Initiation control*: whether each party's consent is needed to initiate the dispute resolution mechanism;
- *Procedure control*: whether the parties determine the procedure;
- *Result-content control*: whether the parties determine the content of the result of the dispute resolution—this corresponds to whether the mechanism is evaluative;
- *Result-effect control*: whether the parties' consent is needed for the result-content to be binding;
- *Neutral choice control*: whether the parties choose the neutral;
- *Information control*: whether the parties control the disclosure of information, ie whether the procedure is private.

ii. Intrinsic Characteristics

The matrix uses characteristics that are as intrinsic as possible to capture the diversity of dispute resolution mechanisms, both within and across jurisdictions. In other

[13] This normative foundation is substantiated in more detail under III.

[14] Later it is explained how an extended version of the matrix allows differentiating whether one party (as opposed to the parties together) controls a certain aspect of the dispute resolution mechanism.

words, the matrix tries to identify core properties of dispute resolution mechanisms that are (as far as possible) independent of their variations in different regulatory or cultural contexts.[15] By referring to the essential characteristics of the different dispute resolution mechanisms, the matrix tries to facilitate a clear analysis and to allow for transjurisdictional comparability. Since dispute resolution mechanisms are—sometimes more, sometimes less—shaped by law, this can result in an abstraction only to a certain degree from local laws and practices. Still, the (relative) intrinsic characteristics allow for a clearer understanding of the core features and for better transnational communication. This taxonomy approach also corresponds well with regulatory questions. It facilitates the distinction between regulatory questions and essential characteristics. Hence, the matrix does not contain regulatory topics. Instead, regulatory topics are introduced later as a separate category[16] and then considered in connection with the characteristics of dispute resolution mechanisms.

The approach of using (relatively) intrinsic descriptions explains why there are no characteristics used such as 'duration' or 'costs'. Empirical cross-country comparisons show that the duration and costs are less an essential character of certain dispute resolution mechanisms and more a consequence of legal and organisational circumstances, both in general and in the specific case. Take, for example, the duration of litigious court proceedings in first instance courts which was determined by the Council of Europe for the year 2010 in the countries covered in this book (as far as data is available):[17] Austria, 129 days; Switzerland, 132 days; Norway, 158 days; Germany, 184 days; Denmark, 186 days; France, 279 days; and Italy, 493 days. The consideration that litigious court proceedings at first instance in Italy take more than three times longer than in Austria reveals the difficulty of assigning an intrinsic duration characteristic to court proceedings.[18] A similar argument could be made for the costs of court proceedings[19] and for comparisons across different dispute resolution mechanisms.[20] However, if empirical research were to identify intrinsic patterns as regards duration or cost in relation to specific dispute resolution mechanisms, these patterns could be used as characteristics in the matrix proposed.

[15] On the distinction of intrinsic properties from extrinsic properties, each of which can have the quality of being more or less prevalent, see *D Lewis*, 'Extrinsic Properties' (1983) 44 *Philosophical Studies* 197; for an overview of the debate on intrinsicness see R Cameron, 'Intrinsic and Extrinsic Properties' in R Le Poidevin, P Simons, A McGonigal and R Cameron (eds), *The Routledge Companion to Metaphysics* (London and New York, Routledge, 2009) 265ff. Here we are less concerned with the philosophical debate on intrinsicness than with identifying core properties of dispute resolution mechanisms as independently as possible from regulatory and practical variations.

[16] See IV.

[17] Council of Europe (The European Commission for the Efficiency of Justice), *European Judicial Systems—Edition 2012 (Data 2010)* (Strasbourg, 2012) 184.

[18] For an empirical attempt to explain cross-country differences in the duration and costs of court proceedings, see S Djankov, R La Porta, F Lopez-de-Silanes and A Shleifer, 'Courts' [2003] *Quarterly Journal of Economics* 453ff.

[19] *Cf* the estimated costs of court proceedings in a standard business case in the Member States of the EU in ADR Center (Rome), *The Cost of Non ADR—Surveying and Showing the Actual Costs of Intra-Community Commercial Litigation: Survey Data Report* (Rome, 2010) 47.

[20] *Cf* the statistical comparison of court adjudication and mediation in KJ Hopt and F Steffek, 'Mediation: Comparison of Laws, Regulatory Models, Fundamental Issues' in KJ Hopt and F Steffek (eds), *Mediation: Principles and Regulation in Comparative Perspective* (Oxford University Press, 2013) 3, 99ff.

iii. Functional and Comparative Characteristics

The identification of intrinsic characteristics is closely linked with a functional and comparative method. The matrix is not designed with a view towards one particular legal system. The categories used in the matrix are not the result of using the technical terminology for dispute resolution mechanisms and describing the technical legal rules applied in one certain jurisdiction. Instead, the descriptions try to capture the function of dispute resolution mechanisms from a transnational perspective. They are less concerned with rules and more with their effects, less with doctrinal structures and more with events.[21] Real life matters, as does the function of law both for the individuals themselves and for their relationship to society. This requires law-external yardsticks from other academic disciplines, such as—but not limited to—ethics, economics, sociology and psychology. Comparing the function of certain dispute resolution mechanisms and their regulation in different jurisdictions helps to reveal their core characteristics. Legal comparison helps to identify which rules and legal elements are the results of particular legal and cultural contexts and which characteristics are essential to a certain dispute resolution mechanism.

The functional and comparative method has consequences for both types of category used in the matrix, for the characteristics employed and for the terminology adopted for dispute resolution mechanisms. The characteristics refer to function and not to law. Hence, the question whether each party's consent is needed to start a procedure is referred to as 'initiation control' and not as 'right to bring an action' or the like. Similarly, the dispute resolution mechanisms are termed according to their functional characteristics and not according to a literal translation of legal terminology from a particular jurisdiction. Hence, 'mediation' describes a dispute resolution mechanism where the parties control the initiation, procedure, content and effect of the result, the choice of the neutral and whether information becomes public. If a mechanism with such characteristics in a particular legal system is termed 'conciliation' instead of 'mediation', it would still be classified as 'mediation' here.[22] Where the mechanism at issue has all these same characteristics with the exception of the neutral now being responsible for proposing a non-binding result, the matrix value for 'result-content control' accordingly changes with the effect that such a procedure would be dealt with under 'conciliation'. The matrix contains classifications according to their respective functions in the legal systems analysed, not according to the terminology used there.

iv. Modular Structure

The matrix has no fixed number of dispute resolution mechanisms (lines) or characteristics (columns). The matrix above can be *reduced or extended*. An extension can satisfy the interest in further dispute resolution mechanisms or the relevancy of characteristics that are not represented in the version of the matrix above. A reduction of the matrix can help to focus on particular issues or reduce complexity in order to make regulation manageable.

[21] R Michaels, 'The Functional Method of Comparative Law' in R Zimmermann and M Reimann (eds), *The Oxford Handbook of Comparative Law* (Oxford, Oxford University Press, 2008) 339, 342.

[22] As to terminology confusions concerning 'mediation' and 'conciliation' see Hopt and Steffek, 'Mediation: Comparison of Laws, Regulatory Models, Fundamental Issues' 16, 107.

In addition to adaptability, the modular structure provides two important features for analysis and regulation. First, the modular structure facilitates the *identification of common characteristics and differences* between dispute resolution mechanisms. Considering the above matrix, it is easy to see that mediation and arbitration share the parties' common control of initiation, procedure, choice of the neutral and information. The main differences are that in mediation the parties together also control the content and the (binding) effect of the result, while in arbitration that is not the case.

Second, the characteristics can be used as *regulatory anchors*.[23] Employing the matrix above, one could, for example, anchor the regulation of professional education with reference to the following characteristics:[24] Can a party be forced into a procedure (initiation control)? Can the parties choose the neutral (neutral choice control)? Do the parties control the content of the procedure (result-content control)? Is the result binding on them (result-effect control)? Regulation can be anchored in the characteristics either indirectly at the level of procedure design or directly at the level of translating the characteristics into the wording of rules and standards. A characteristics-oriented view of dispute resolution mechanisms might be a little unfamiliar at first, but it comes with the advantage of avoiding unjust and inefficient regulation due to a limited piecemeal view. In order to provide the full picture of dispute resolution, the matrix above contains the two extreme poles of resolution mechanisms, namely negotiation and court adjudication.

C. Extending the Matrix

The extended matrix in Table 2 illustrates its modular structure and affords the opportunity to discuss further aspects of the taxonomy suggested here.

D. Modules and Differentiation

i. Modular Flexibility and Complexity

The extended matrix in Table 2 reflects the modular flexibility of the taxonomy suggested here. Dispute resolution mechanisms and characteristics have been added to the basic version of the matrix,[25] drawing from the descriptions and analyses of the country chapters in this book and beyond. Hence, for example, expert opinion,[26] mini-trial,[27] ombudsman[28] and mandatory arbitration[29] procedures have been added. The modular structure reveals that the current development of various types of dispute resolution procedures can be understood as modular variations of a common core of

[23] For further details and examples see below V.

[24] For an example see principle 8 in Chapters 1 and 2.

[25] See II.A.

[26] See, eg Chapter 9 (Germany), III.D.

[27] See, eg Chapter 15 (USA), IV.

[28] See, eg Chapter 14 (Switzerland), I.F.

[29] See, eg Chapter 15 (USA), V; for rules on mandatory non-binding arbitration see ch 718 s 1255 of the 2012 Florida Statutes, available at <www.flsenate.gov/Laws/Statutes/2012>.

Table 2

	Initiation Control	Procedure Control	Result-Content Control	Result-Effect Control	Neutral Choice Control	Information Control	Interest-Based	Intermediation
Negotiation	Yes	Yes	Yes	Yes	N/A	Yes	Yes	No
Mandatory Negotiation	No	Yes	Yes	Yes	N/A	Yes	Yes	No
Mediation	Yes	Yes	Yes	Yes	Yes	Yes	Yes	Yes
Mandatory Mediation	No	Yes	Yes	Yes	Yes	Yes	Yes	Yes
Conciliation	Yes	Yes	No	Yes	Yes	Yes	Yes	Yes
Mandatory Conciliation	No	Yes	No	Yes	Yes	Yes	Yes	Yes
Court Conciliation	No	No	No	Yes	No	Yes	No	Yes
Settlement Conference	No	No	No	Yes	No	Yes	No	Yes
Neutral Evaluation	Yes	Yes	No	Yes	Yes	Yes	No	Yes
Expert Opinion	Yes	Yes	No	Yes	Yes	Yes	No	Yes
Binding Expert Opinion	Yes	Yes	No	No	Yes	Yes	No	Yes
Mini-trial	Yes	Yes	No	Yes	Yes	Yes	No	Yes
Ombudsman	Yes	No	No	No	No	Yes	No	Yes
Mandatory Ombudsman	No	No	No	No	No	Yes	No	Yes
Arbitration	Yes	Yes	No	No	Yes	Yes	No	Yes
Mandatory Non-binding Arbitration	No	Yes	No	Yes	No	Yes	No	Yes
Mandatory Arbitration	No	Yes	No	No	Yes	Yes	No	Yes
Collection Procedure	No	No	No	Yes	No	Yes	No	Yes
Judgment Proposal	No	No	No	Yes	No	No	No	Yes
Adjudication	No	No	No	No	No	No	No	Yes

characteristics. The emergence of almost all possible variations of the characteristics employed demonstrates the desire for differentiated and tailored dispute resolution.

While the extended matrix mirrors the variety of dispute resolution mechanisms and their characteristics, its modular structure helps to handle the complex reality of dispute resolution. Compare, for example, the characteristics of court conciliation and settlement conferences. The matrix above reveals that the essential characteristics are the same. This indicates that the regulatory challenges and principles are similar for both types of procedures. The same applies to neutral evaluation, expert opinion and mini-trial as well as to binding expert opinion and arbitration. The analytical aspect of the modular structure helps to reduce the complexity of laws and practices while still capturing the essence of dispute resolution mechanisms. From a law-making perspective, the ability to determine the similarities and differences in features creates a clear and manageable basis of regulation.

ii. Differentiation

The additional dispute resolution mechanisms and characteristics demonstrate that the matrix can be used to steer through complexity while at the same time providing the necessary differentiation. Take, for example, the characteristics of dispute resolution procedures set out in the columns of the extended table. These characteristics are still designed from the perspective of the parties and try to capture the functional and intrinsic features of the various dispute resolution mechanisms.[30] The extended table contains two new characteristics:

- *Interest-based*: whether the procedure is interest- or rights-based;
- *Intermediation*: whether there is an intermediation in the procedure, ie whether a third person contributes to the conflict resolution.

Further differentiating characteristics could be introduced. This shall be illustrated using the just-provided example concerning neutral evaluation and expert opinion.[31] Even though the matrix has been extended, neutral evaluation and expert opinion share the same characteristic values. What is the difference? A possible differentiating aspect could be whether the mechanism covers the whole dispute or only a part of it. Generally, neutral evaluation is understood to do the former and expert opinion the latter. If this difference was thought to be a relevant regulatory anchor, the characteristic 'whole dispute covered' could be introduced into the matrix and referred to when designing regulation.

The matrix still comprehends the characteristics as representing all parties involved, ie the parties together. For example, if a dispute resolution mechanism like the ombudsman procedure is binding only on one party and not the other, the 'result-effect control' characteristic is displayed as 'No'. This approach is taken since it will more clearly signal regulatory anchors such as the protection of parties who are bound by a mechanism, here the ombudsman procedure. An alternative to this approach would be to introduce characteristics such as 'result-effect control only for one party/

[30] For more details see above II.B.
[31] See II.D.i.

for consumer'. Then the asymmetric characteristic of the dispute resolution mechanism would be signalled even more strongly.

The matrix structure presented here is open for other terminologies and features. Other properties than the ones chosen here can be used. The matrix is sealed in neither its basic nor its extended version. Both are mere examples of how the taxonomy suggested here could be used. Rather, it is expected that further variations and future developments in the field of dispute resolution mechanisms and in their characteristics will require adaptions of the matrix. Its modular structure based on the perspective of the parties and a functional understanding of dispute resolution mechanisms will be able to accommodate such changes.

III. POLICY

A. Normative Individualism

The question of which legal rules are just is answered by the discipline of legal ethics. In legal ethics normative individualism is the generally accepted position. It provides the essential starting point for normative arguments on regulating dispute resolution: just law requires justification in relation to the individual concerned. This fundamental principle is shared by many legal and political philosophers from the common law and the civil law traditions, such as Thomas Hobbes,[32] John Locke,[33] Robert Nozick,[34] Ronald Dworkin,[35] John Rawls,[36] Immanuel Kant,[37] Jean-Jacques Rousseau,[38] Norbert Hoerster[39] and Dietmar von der Pfordten.[40] While these authors differ in many of the essential requirements for justice, they agree on one fundamental thesis: whether a legal rule is just or not is to be determined in relation to all those individuals who are affected by that rule. This is referred to here as normative individualism. Often other terminology is used to express the idea of normative individualism, such as humanism, subjectivism, self-determination, private autonomy, human rights and democracy.[41] Ultimately terminology does not matter too much in this regard; rather, the individual is the source and focus of just law. This is founded in the fact that individuals require a justification in instances where they are affected by regulation.

Normative individualism excludes the possibility of justifying legal rules by reference to arguments that are not ultimately grounded in the interests of individuals. Hence, arguments based on state, society, economy, order, environment, etc are only a possible source of justification if they can ultimately be traced back to individuals.

[32] T Hobbes, *Leviathan* (London, Andrew Crooke, 1651).
[33] J Locke, *Two Treatises of Government* (London, Awnsham Churchill, 1690).
[34] R Nozick, *Anarchy, State, and Utopia* (New York, Basic Books, 1974).
[35] R Dworkin, *Taking Rights Seriously* (Cambridge, MA, Harvard University Press, 1977).
[36] J Rawls, *A Theory of Justice*, rev edn (Cambridge, MA, Belknap Press, 1999).
[37] I Kant, *Die Metaphysik der Sitten, Erster Theil: Metaphysische Anfangsgründe der Rechtslehre*, 2nd edn (Königsberg, Friedrich Nicolovius, 1798).
[38] J Rousseau, *Du Contrat Social, ou Principes du Droit Politiques* (Amsterdam, M Rey, 1762).
[39] N Hoerster, *Ethik und Interesse* (Stuttgart, Reclam, 2003).
[40] D von der Pfordten, *Rechtsethik*, 2nd edn (München, CH Beck, 2011).
[41] D von der Pfordten, 'Normativer Individualismus und das Recht' *JuristenZeitung* 2005, 1069.

The economy or the state as such, abstracted from their relevance for individuals, cannot justify laws that impact individuals. In other words, the economy and the state do not have a purpose in themselves; instead, they serve the individuals that take part in markets and constitute the state. Hence, normative individualism deals with groups, societies and states, but it does so from the perspective of the individual and not of the collective. Normative individualism, however, does not equal or promote egoism. The individuals themselves determine their interests, and amongst them may be interests in solidarity and society. Normative individualism is an open concept insofar as the interests of individuals are not imposed by a third party. Instead, the individual person determines his or her interests.[42]

The interests of the individuals are the basis on which the justness of a legal rule is determined. This requires weighing and balancing interests. One approach can be to consider the degree to which interests are related to the individual or to society. This requires assessing whether the implementation of an interest has effects on others and requires the cooperation of others. The more others are affected and needed, the more the individual has to accept that the interests of other individuals might justify interference.[43] It is not necessarily a deficit that the method of weighing and balancing interests can only be superficially indicated here.[44] Rather, the evaluation and appreciation of interests is part of the implementation of the principles for regulating dispute resolution. Interests and their relative value differ from jurisdiction to jurisdiction. The principles developed here aim to provide a framework that allows for such differences. In this regard, the various suggestions made by legal ethics and political philosophy can be understood as suggestions how to weigh and balance the interests of individuals.

While it is helpful to develop the regulation of dispute resolution from the perspective of legal ethics and normative individualism, it is not necessary to resort to ethical arguments every step of the way. Normative individualism is the foundation of human and constitutional rights. This is true, for example, for the United Nations' Universal Declaration of Human Rights,[45] the International Covenant on Civil and Political Rights,[46] the International Covenant on Economic, Social and Cultural Rights,[47] the European Convention on Human Rights,[48] the Charter of Fundamental Rights of the EU[49] and the constitutions of the countries represented in this book. Hence, these human rights, in particular as they concern dispute resolution, are oriented towards the individual. The conventions and constitutions mentioned concretise the requirements of normative individualism through the human and constitutional rights they enshrine. These conventions and constitutions are thus a good working basis for regulating dispute resolution.

[42] For one possible approach to determine interests see Hoerster, *Ethik und Interesse* 37ff.

[43] See, eg von der Pfordten, *Rechtsethik* ch 8.

[44] See further, eg III.D.

[45] General Assembly Resolution 217 A (III) of 10 December 1948, UN Doc A/810, 71.

[46] General Assembly Resolution 2200 A (XXI) of 16 December 1966, UN, *Treaty Series*, vol 999, p 171.

[47] General Assembly Resolution 2200 A (XXI) of 16 December 1966, UN, *Treaty Series*, vol 993, p 3.

[48] Council of Europe, *European Treaty Series*, No 5, Rome, 4 November 1950.

[49] Proclamation 2000/C of 7 December 2000, Official Journal of the European Communities C 364/1 of 18 December 2000.

B. Consequences of Normative Individualism

Normative individualism has consequences for the regulation of dispute resolution. It places the individual and the conflict perceived by the individual at the centre of regulation. Dispute resolution mechanisms should be designed from the perspective of the individuals concerned.[50] They should not be regulated by referring to abstract notions like state, public interest or economy without those notions indirectly expressing the interests of individuals. As a consequence, the taxonomy developed above uses characteristics from the perspective of the individuals to describe dispute resolution mechanisms. The interests of the individuals at the centre of regulatory thought are determined by the individuals themselves, not by a third person. Thus, the individual determines his or her interests in resolving the conflict and determines which mechanism serves these interests best. It follows from this self-determination that—as a starting point—there should not be a state-set preference of one dispute resolution mechanism over another. The self-determination of the individual as regards the resolution of his or her conflicts places the responsibility for conflict resolution with the individual in the first place.

If, first of all, the individual is responsible for resolving his or her conflicts, the state must provide a framework which allows the individual to resolve conflicts in a self-determined and effective way. Since different disputes require different resolution methods,[51] the state needs to offer rules that facilitate adequate private dispute resolution. Individuals have a right of access to a framework that allows for just private dispute resolution (*access to private dispute resolution*).[52] Private dispute resolution mechanisms should be designed in a coherent, intelligible and accessible way. The individuals should—as a starting point—be put in a position to choose between the mechanisms according to their interests and conflict needs. Generally, enabling rules should be given priority, followed by incentivising rules, with mandatory law being the last resort.[53] Normative individualism starts with the freedom and self-determination of the individual, but it may still justify regulation. Law may be needed to implement interests (eg enabling rules that allow keeping information confidential in court proceedings) or to protect interests against unjustified third-party harm. Normative individualism and the principle of self-determination in conflict resolution require the state to justify limiting legislation. If there is doubt as to whether regulation is justified or not, regulation that limits self-determination should be avoided.

Within the array of dispute resolution mechanisms, state court procedures and enforcement systems take on a special role. They are the necessary counterweights to the state's monopoly on power. The exclusive nature of the state's monopoly on power imposes organisational and financial duties on the state to provide access to justice in the form of an accessible and effective court and enforcement system (*access to*

[50] Similarly the legislative objectives in Japan (Chapter 11, II): the 'appropriate realisation of the rights and interests of the people'; consequently, empirical research by the Dutch Ministry of Security and Justice has taken the perspective of the citizens affected, see Chapter 12 (Netherlands), I.A.

[51] *Cf* Chapter 15 (USA), I: 'one size of legal process does not fit all'.

[52] *Cf* Chapter 14 (Switzerland), IV.C: 'right of access to a fair dispute resolution'.

[53] *Cf* for mediation Hopt and Steffek, 'Mediation: Comparison of Laws, Regulatory Models, Fundamental Issues' 121.

state justice).[54] Due to the primary responsibility of the individuals as regards private dispute resolution mechanisms, the state is not under a similar organisational and financial duty as regards dispute resolution mechanisms alternative to the court and enforcement procedures. Here, organisational and financial duties may, however, arise from further circumstances.

C. Freedom, Equality, Efficiency

Three principles of particular relevance for just regulation from the perspective of normative individualism are freedom, equality and efficiency. *Freedom* as the basis of self-determination is fundamentally built into legal ethics rooted in normative individualism as every limitation of the interests of an individual through law needs to be justified. Similarly, *equality* is an indispensable principle of such an approach to legal ethics as a limitation of the interests of an individual cannot be justified if the limitation does not apply to other individuals equally.[55] Equality here is understood as treating essentially similar situations the same and essentially dissimilar situations differently.[56] Freedom and equality are paramount and, again, may conflict so that policy decisions have to be made based on the interests affected. In the following text the third principle, efficiency, is dealt with more in detail. The reason is not that this principle takes higher priority than freedom and equality. Rather, it seems that currently questions of efficiency in the practice of regulating dispute resolution are particularly and widely discussed.

Efficiency is an element of justice because individuals expect that their affiliation to a certain society increases the realisation of their interests.[57] Otherwise there would not be any reason to be part of that society. A fundamental way in which a society can enhance the realisation of the interests of its members is to use resources more efficiently than the members could on their own. If scarce resources are used more efficiently in a society, then the individuals who are part of this society can realise more of their interests.[58] Put simply, the efficient use of goods increases freedom, since the individuals can then do more. It should be stressed that the aim of efficiency is to increase the range of realisable interests the individuals have. The content of these interests is determined by the individuals. Some interests may be related to material welfare, others may be related to immaterial goals. As a result, efficiency in this context is ultimately not oriented towards monetary profit. Practically, however, due

[54] *Cf* Art 14(1) International Covenant on Civil and Political Rights; Art 6(1) European Convention on Human Rights; Art 47 Charter of Fundamental Rights of the European Union; German Constitutional Court (Bundesverfassungsgericht), *Neue Juristische Wochenschrift* 2003, 1924ff.

[55] *Cf* for an early source on legal equality Aristotle, *Politics* (*Πολιτικά*), translated by B Howett (Kitchener, Ontario, Batoche Books, 1999) Book 4, p 87 (1291b 30); on equality in dispute resolution and justice R Dworkin, *A Matter of Principle* (Cambridge, MA, Harvard University Press, 1985) 65ff, 205ff; on legal equality from the perspective of the civil law tradition Radbruch, *Rechtsphilosophie* 127f.

[56] *Cf* HLA Hart, *The Concept of Law*, 2nd edn (Clarendon Press, Oxford, 1994) 155ff; Rawls, *A Theory of Justice* ch 38; German Constitutional Court (Bundesverfassungsgericht), *Neue Juristische Wochenschrift* 1951, 877, 878f.

[57] *Cf* von der Pfordten, *Rechtsethik* 505f.

[58] Generally on the economic concept of efficiency R Cooter and T Ulen, *Law & Economics*, 6th edn (Boston, Pearson Education, 2012) 13f; E Mackaay, *Law and Economics for Civil Law Systems* (Cheltenham, Edward Elgar, 2013) 14ff.

to the exchange function of money,[59] gains and costs expressed in monetary values play a significant role as a yardstick for efficiency.[60] Since it is the interests of the individuals that count in the end, efficiency serves the satisfaction of the interest of the individuals, both material and immaterial. In other words, efficiency maximises the realisation of interests; in this context in particular, this corresponds to the interests that concern dispute resolution.[61] Monetary gain is a significant—but not exclusive—yardstick to measure efficiency in this sense.

Which particular role does efficiency play for the regulation of conflict resolution? The resources employed by the individuals and the state[62] to resolve conflicts should be used as efficiently as possible. Public means available for the organisation of conflict resolution institutions and the finance of conflict resolution mechanisms are limited. The efficient use of available resources increases the realisation of the individuals' interest in conflict resolution. Hence, dispute resolution mechanisms should be designed with an eye on the cost–benefit relationship. As a consequence, regulation may reflect that certain dispute resolution mechanisms are particularly well suited for specific types of disputes. Information and decision deficits may justify regulation in order to prevent inefficient decisions. Such deficits are reported in research from most—if not all—countries represented in this book.[63] The market does not always seem to work.[64] Here, a possible field of regulation concerns specific rules for consumers.[65]

In line with the justice requirements based on normative individualism presented above, the efficiency principle also argues that individuals should be responsible for resolving their conflicts in the first place. State-set incentives carrying the result that persons would lose their interest in self-responsible dispute resolution would lead to externalities[66] and conflict transfers from the individuals to the state. Hence, a residual interest in the resolution of disputes in terms of cost, time or personal involvement should be maintained. The state should not offer dispute resolution that does not require a financial or temporal commitment from either party.

As the principle of self-determination of process, the efficiency principle cautions against, but does not exclude, mandatory referral to a specific kind of conflict resolution mechanism. Mandatory referral is easily blind to the characteristics and the

[59] The exchange function of money in the realm of justice is already dealt with by Aristotle, *Nicomachean Ethics*, translated by WD Ross (Kitchener, Ontario, Batoche Books, 1999) Book 5, 79ff (1133a and 1133b).

[60] On the exchange function of money AA Alchian, 'Why Money?' (1977) 9 *Journal of Money, Credit and Banking* 133; K Brunner and AH Meltzer, 'The Uses of Money: Money in the Theory of an Exchange Economy' (1971) 61 *The American Economic Review* 784.

[61] On the concept of maximisation Cooter and Ulen, *Law & Economics* 13, 44f.

[62] State resources are ultimately provided by the citizens; hence the reduction of state costs is supported by normative individualism.

[63] *Cf* for Austria Chapter 4, I.B; for Belgium Chapter 5, I.B; for Denmark Chapter 6, II.A; for England Chapter 7, II.Bff; for France Chapter 8, I.C; for Germany Chapter 9, I.C; for Italy Chapter 10, I.C; for Japan Chapter 11, I.F; for the Netherlands Chapter 12, I.C; for Norway Chapter 13, I.C; for Switzerland Chapter 14, IV (passim); and for the USA Chapter 15, VI.

[64] See, eg the empirical research by PWC and Europa University Viadrina Frankfurt (Oder), *Commercial Dispute Resolution* 15ff.

[65] *Cf* Hodges, Benöhr and Creutzfeld-Banda, *Consumer ADR in Europe*; as an example see the recent Directive 2013/11/EU of the European Parliament and of the Council of 21 May 2013 on alternative dispute resolution for consumer disputes and amending Regulation (EC) No 2006/2004 and Directive 2009/22/EC (Directive on consumer ADR) [2013] OJ L165, 3ff.

[66] Generally on externalities Cooter and Ulen, *Law & Economics* 39f, 105, 166ff; Mackaay, *Law and Economics for Civil Law Systems* 104ff, 205f.

efficiency of dispute resolution. There is a danger of automatic wrong choice. Mandatory referral should only be used as a last solution to information and decision deficits.[67] If information and decision deficits persist, the first option should be incentive setting; mandatory rules and referral should be the last option.[68]

D. Balance and Dynamic

Normative individualism, as it is understood here, is based on the individuals and their interests. Freedom and equality are deeply rooted within normative individualism. In the realm of regulating dispute resolution, this translates into self-determination of dispute resolution and equal access to and treatment in dispute resolution mechanisms. As the interests of individuals may differ, so may freedom and equality conflict. From the perspective of legal ethics, this first requires an assessment of the interests involved and, second, a decision on the just balance of these interests. As indicated, a possible approach would be to consider the orientation of the interests affected by possible legislation, ie whether an interest is more oriented towards the individual concerned or more towards the community of others that the individual is part of.[69] Accordingly, the more others are affected and needed, the more the individual has to accept that the interests of other individuals might justify interference with his or her own interests.

This concept, which can only be sketched briefly here, is dynamic in multiple aspects. The *interests of individuals differ* between the individuals as well as between communities and societies, and they differ over time.[70] This is particularly so since the interests are not imposed by a third person, but are those of the individuals. In addition, the factual circumstances within which the individuals develop their interests are subject to change.[71] This dynamism explains why the content of justice may differ between societies and evolve over time. However, the fact that an interference with an interest of an individual becomes more difficult to justify the less this interest requires the cooperation of other individuals, and the less this interest interferes with other individuals, guarantees a stable core of self-determination. As a consequence, interests such as life, thoughts and beliefs cannot be interfered with since—per se—they do not require the cooperation of or interfere with others.[72] Interests in the realm of dispute resolution, however, often require the *cooperation* of others or *impact* on the interests of others. Theories on legal ethics and political justice can be understood as providing models on how such conflicts of interests should be decided. Since the interests of individuals in different communities and jurisdiction differ, it is not possible to formulate universal and at the same time very detailed principles for just regulation of

[67] *Cf* G De Palo and MB Trevor (eds), *EU Mediation—Law and Practice* (Oxford, Oxford University Press, 2012) 7f; N Alexander, *International and Comparative Mediation—Legal Perspectives* (AH Alphen aan den Rijn, Kluwer Law International, 2009) 148ff on court referral.

[68] Similarly H Unberath, 'Auf dem Weg zu einer differenzierten Streitkultur—Neue gesetzliche Rahmenbedingungen für die alternative Konfliktlösung' *JuristenZeitung* 2010, 975, 979f.

[69] *Cf* von der Pfordten, *Rechtsethik* ch 8.

[70] Hoerster, *Ethik und Interesse* 37ff.

[71] Consider, for example, developments and changes in science, the environment and the general welfare level.

[72] These interests—per se—are to be distinguished by the translation of life, thoughts or beliefs into actions.

dispute resolution. Rather, more general and flexible principles of the sort presented in the GRDR[73] may reflect the differing interests.

To give just one example of the different requirements of justice in regulating dispute resolution, one might consider the requirement of financial aid for dispute resolution.[74] Assuming that individuals have an interest in both access to courts and alternative dispute resolution, they will have an interest in financial aid if they cannot afford access to the courts and ADR. Further interests involved are those of the other persons involved in the conflict. If financial aid were financed through taxes, all individuals who would have to contribute to the funding of the financial aid scheme would be concerned as well. Here the difference between the state court and enforcement system and alternative dispute resolution mechanisms becomes tangible. The state's monopoly on power forbids the individual from privately enforcing rights, and instead the state has to offer the state court and enforcement system. Since an individual that cannot afford to use this system would be completely excluded from the implementation of his or her rights where the other party is not inclined to concede these rights, justice requires the provision of legal aid for court proceedings. By contrast, there is no state monopoly on alternative dispute resolution. Hence, the case for interfering with the interests of others by forcing them to finance legal aid for ADR is less compelling. An essential argument as to whether justice requires such financing turns on the general welfare level of the society in question. The higher the welfare level, the more justified are taxes to finance the interest in ADR of individuals in financial need.

The efficient regulation of dispute resolution has two elements of justice that can be distinguished. First, there are regulatory interventions that increase efficiency without negatively impacting any interests. Take, for example, dispositive contract law enabling the parties to agree on the result of consensual dispute resolution.[75] Such rules that maximise the realm of realisable interests without limiting interests are always desirable from the perspective of legal ethics. Second, there are rules that increase efficiency by limiting the interests of one or more individuals involved. Regulation in the interest of efficiency can have negative impacts both on freedom and on equality. Freedom is limited if laws establish incentives or even prescribe a certain behaviour. Equality is concerned if laws allow differences in participation and results in order to increase efficiency. In this second type of cases the interests maximised by laws fostering efficiency have to be weighed against the interests limited. Again, the interest in resolving disputes where consensual solutions are not possible has high importance. Hence, access to the state court and enforcement system cannot be limited due to efficiency reasons in states with adequate welfare levels.[76] In other cases, eg when considering mandatorily prescribing specific procedural steps or specific dispute resolution mechanisms in certain situations, the interests concerned have to be assessed and balanced. Issues to consider can be the number and kind of interests, their being oriented

[73] See Chapters 1 and 2.

[74] In more detail see F Steffek, 'Mediation und Justiz' in C Fischer and H Unberath (eds), *Das neue Mediationsgesetz—Rechtliche Rahmenbedingungen der Mediation* (Munich, CH Beck, 2013) 29, 41ff.

[75] Leaving aside here possible issues of 'sticky default rules' and information and decision asymmetries; on sticky default rules see I Ayres, 'Regulating Opt-Out: An Economic Theory of Altering Rules' (2012) 121 *Yale Law Journal* 2032, 2084ff.

[76] Such welfare levels are reached, for example, in the states represented in this book.

towards society or the individual, etc.[77] On the basis of normative individualism as it is being argued here, it is important to note that justice and efficiency are not opposite goals. Instead, justice is the leading aim of law, and what is just is determined on the basis of the interests the individuals within a jurisdiction have. Efficiency as well as other principles can contribute in fulfilling these interests.

IV. TOPICS

A. Identification

In addition to a taxonomy of dispute resolution mechanisms and a reasoned approach to policy decisions, principled regulation requires the identification of possible regulatory topics. A systematic and coherent approach is, again, facilitated by using a modular approach to regulatory topics. This requires distinguishing between the identification of topics that may be in need of regulation and the decision whether—and what kind of—regulation is actually necessary. There should not be an automatic assumption that the identification of a regulatory topic always leads to regulation.

There are many ways to identify possible topics of regulation: individuals in a society may call for certain rules in order to foster their interests. Indirectly, individuals may reveal regulatory needs in standard and individual contracts, especially if standard clauses are developed and consistently used that are not reflected in state made law.[78] A comparison of laws can reveal regulatory issues that have been addressed in other jurisdictions.[79] In addition, a comparison of the regulation of different dispute resolution mechanisms within one jurisdiction may reveal possible topics. One might, for example, compare the rules on mediation, conciliation and ombudsman procedure within one jurisdiction and the issues that regulation addresses or does not address in these procedures. Also, other disciplines of law may be used as sources of inspiration. For example, one might draw from the regulatory discussion as regards corporate governance[80] or from the solution of principal-agent problems in companies,[81] and consider the governance of dispute resolution institutions and principal-agent problems in dispute resolution.

[77] *Cf* Chapter 12 (Netherlands), II.A.ii.

[78] Cf the contract clauses in M McIlwrath and J Savage, *International Arbitration and Mediation—A Practical Guide* (AH Alphen aan den Rijn, Kluwer Law International, 2010) 413ff; KP Berger, *Private Dispute Resolution in International Business—Negotiation, Mediation, Arbitration, vol II: Handbook*, 2nd edn (AH Alphen aan den Rijn, Kluwer Law International, 2009).

[79] *Cf* the differences in topics regulated in the country chapters in this book; for further examples of comparative analysis see A Ingen-Housz (ed), *ADR in Business—Practice and Issues Across Countries and Cultures*, vol II (AH Alphen aan den Rijn, Kluwer Law International, 2011); N Alexander, *Global Trends in Mediation*, 2nd edn (AH Alphen aan den Rijn, Kluwer Law International, 2006).

[80] See, eg AM Fleckner and KJ Hopt (eds), *Comparative Corporate Governance—A Functional and International Analysis* (Cambridge, UK, Cambridge University Press, 2013).

[81] Generally on principal-agent problems J Armour, H Hansmann and R Kraakman, 'Agency Problems and Legal Strategies' in R Kraakman, J Armour, P Davies, L Enriques, H Hansmann, G Hertig, KJ Hopt, H Kanda and E Rock (eds), *The Anatomy of Corporate Law—A Comparative and Functional Approach*, 2nd edn (Oxford, Oxford University Press, 2009) ch 2.

B. Essential Topics

Using the described approaches and a modular structure, the following possible regulatory topics for dispute resolution can be identified (descriptive examples in brackets):[82] infrastructure and framework (organisation and finance of dispute resolution institutions); costs of dispute resolution (division between the parties and between the parties and the state, cost subsidies, legal aid); dispute resolution clauses (validity, enforceability); choice of dispute resolution procedures (timing, adequacy, centralised or decentralised infrastructure, transfer to other dispute resolution mechanisms, incentives and sanctions); confidentiality (substance, affected persons, procedure, limits); limitation and prescription periods (range, timing, proof); intermediaries (neutrality, qualification, duties, choice); procedure (safeguards, standards); counsel (role, representation, duties); state (judicial) review of results (applicability, intensity); enforceability (state participation, degree of result control, alternative paths); transparency (supervision); consumers (choice of mechanisms, contract clauses, governance of dispute resolution institutions); rule-maker (parliament, executive branch, courts, associations, parties, intermediaries); type of rules (enabling rules, conduct rules, mandatory or dispositive rules, kind of regulation, comprehensive or restricted approach); procedure design (incentives of those involved, information, online dispute resolution). Again, it should be emphasised that naming a topic does not imply that regulation is necessary; it only means that consideration should be given to whether and, if so, how regulation may be advisable.

V PRINCIPLES

A. From Taxonomy, Policy and Topics to Principles

Finally, using (1) the topics of regulation,[83] (2) the guidelines of legal ethics for just regulation[84] and (3) the taxonomy of dispute resolution mechanisms[85] as ingredients, principles for regulating dispute resolution can be developed. The *topics of regulation* serve as a starting point and determine possible areas of regulatory intervention. As already indicated, the identification of a regulatory topic should not automatically lead to the conclusion that regulation is desirable.

The *policy guidelines* developed from the background of legal ethics help to determine whether regulation is necessary and, if so, how the legal rules should be designed. On a transnational level, only more generally formulated principles such as the ones presented in this book can be determined. Differences in local environments, cultures and interests of the individuals constituting societies do not allow principles that are both universal and highly detailed. However, the principled approach to regulation suggested here can also be used to develop more detailed regulation on a local level, concerning one jurisdiction, or on a regional level, concerning similar jurisdictions

[82] These topics correspond with the topics covered by the GRDR in Chapters 1 and 2.
[83] See IV.
[84] See III.
[85] See II.

(like the Member States of the EU). In these instances, the principles suggested here can be used as a starting point and then be combined with local or regional interests and requirements of justice to develop specific regulation.

The *taxonomy of dispute resolution mechanisms* proposed in this chapter can be used as a regulatory anchor. Principles for regulating dispute resolution can refer to the categories of dispute resolution mechanisms and their characteristics. The functional and modular logic of the taxonomy facilitates systematic and coherent regulation that can manage complexity and diversity. When using the principled approach to regulation to develop concrete laws, the taxonomy can be used in two ways. First, the dispute resolution mechanisms and their characteristics can be used to formulate the wording of legislation. Then legislation can, for example, refer to whether the parties have initiation control, procedure control, result-content control, result-effect control, neutral choice control or information control. Second, the taxonomy can be used as a theoretical background without directly using the characteristics in the wording of the law. To illustrate the principled approach to regulating dispute resolution, two principles and their development will be explained in the following text. The two examples are taken from Chapters 1 and 2; hence they are examples of transnational principles of dispute resolution.

B. Examples

i. Costs

The first example of the development of regulatory principles from topics, policy guidelines and taxonomy is taken from the field of financing dispute resolution.[86] In terms of a regulatory *topic*, the question is who should generally bear the costs of dispute resolution. Due to the state's monopoly on power, a differentiation is made between the costs for court proceedings and those for alternative dispute resolution.[87] This example concentrates on the costs of alternative dispute resolution only and who should generally bear those costs as a regulatory starting point. Hence, regulatory questions concerning the costs of mandatory ADR, state subsidies and legal aid are not dealt with in this example.[88]

Using the *policy* guidelines developed above, three principles are relevant: self-determination in dispute resolution, equality in dispute resolution and efficiency. For the regulatory question at issue, these three principles all point in the same direction: the parties should share the costs of the procedure of alternative dispute resolution, and should bear additional costs individually. One obvious equality argument for sharing the procedure costs is the equal distribution of contributions. A second equality argument is based on the idea that the parties can expect equal treatment in the procedure if they fund the procedure equally. The sharing of procedure costs is supported by efficiency arguments. The parties will each have an interest in organising a procedure that maximises support in resolving their dispute while minimising

[86] *Cf* principle III (Costs) in Chapters 1 and 2.
[87] *Cf* above III.B and D.
[88] On those issues see Chapter 2, Principle III.

the resources used. A similar efficiency argument can be made for holding each party accountable for additional costs incurred on an individual basis. It would create undesired incentives if a party had to carry costs for services that benefit only the other party. Self-determination of dispute resolution, however, argues in favour of allowing each party to determine whether and which costs should be incurred individually in the interest of conflict resolution. Also, self-determination of dispute resolution is an argument against imposing a mandatory cost rule on parties to alternative dispute resolution and for imposing instead only a dispositive default rule.

Finally, the *taxonomy* of dispute resolution mechanisms helps in the formulation of the relevant regulatory principle. The regulatory approach has been developed with a view to alternative dispute resolution mechanisms into which the parties cannot be forced. These are mechanisms like mediation, conciliation, expert opinion, mini-trial and arbitration, which all require the consent of both parties to commence.[89] In the taxonomy developed above, this feature is described as 'initiation control' of the parties. Now, upon integrating regulatory topic, policy decisions and taxonomy into a regulatory principle, one could formulate: *In procedures with initiation control the parties should by default share the costs of the procedures and pay their own expenses.*

ii. Qualification

The second example of the development of principles for regulating dispute resolution concerns the qualification of third-party intermediaries, eg the qualification of mediators, conciliators, experts, ombudsmen, arbitrators and judges. A comparison of laws reveals considerable uncertainties and inconsistencies regarding the question whether and, if so, which degree of qualification the state should prescribe for different kinds of intermediaries. A prime example of such inconsistencies is the qualification requirements for mediators and arbitrators. The laws of some jurisdictions impose stricter qualification requirements for mediators than for arbitrators even in cases where the commencement of both procedures requires the parties' consent.[90] This seems inconsistent, since the arbitrator decides on the content of the dispute resolution and this decision is binding, while the mediator does not impose a decision and the parties can decide whether they want to be bound or not. One would rather expect higher qualification requirements for the intermediary who has more influence on the result.

Considering the *policy guidelines* developed above, the principles of self-determination, equality and efficiency are relevant. Self-determination and efficiency argue that the starting point should be the free choice of intermediaries and their qualifications. Together, the parties have an interest in choosing an intermediary who has the qualifications to fulfil their interests in dispute resolution, but they do not have an interest

[89] Consent is also given where a party, while not suffering from any information or decision deficits, has previously agreed to a dispute resolution clause but no longer agrees when, at some later point, the procedure is in fact set to commence. Nevertheless, it bears emphasis that the commencement of the procedure in spite of such opposition is a function of the earlier consent. Private autonomy entails the right to bind oneself for a later point in time knowing that at this later point one might prefer not to be bound anymore.

[90] *Cf* the qualification requirements for mediators in ss 5 and 6 German Mediation Law (Mediationsgesetz), which do not find an equivalent in ss 1025ff German Code of Civil Procedure (Zivilprozessordnung) applying to arbitrators.

in 'overpaying' for qualifications that are not needed in their specific case. Self-determination and efficiency are of course also relevant for the intermediaries, who—as a starting point—should be free to decide on the level of qualification they prefer to acquire. The parties, however, can only take self-determined and efficient decisions on the qualifications of the intermediary they choose if they do not suffer from information or decision deficits. This also concerns equality in cases where the qualifications of the intermediary are sufficient for the interests of one party but not for the interests of the other party. Hence, regulation should prevent information asymmetry and decision deficits. Compared to mandatory qualification rules, this results in less interference with the interests of those affected—another policy guideline developed above.

There is a second aspect to consider, namely the influence the intermediary has on the resolution of the dispute. The greater the influence of the intermediary, the stronger the case for state regulation of qualification requirements. Again, this is supported by self-determination, equality and efficiency considerations. Where the influence of the intermediary on the procedure and the result of the dispute resolution mechanism increases, the parties' interest in laying their fate in the hands of a person who is sufficiently qualified to take just decisions increases correspondingly. Here normative individualism provides a good guideline: the qualification should ensure that the intermediary's decisions impacting the parties' interests are just. Also, from the efficiency viewpoint, increasing legal qualification requirements make sense in situations in which the parties would generally expect certain qualification standards. Thus contracting costs can be avoided by requiring such qualification as a matter of law. A further relevant issue is whether or not the parties can be forced into a procedure against their will, ie whether the parties have initiation control. If the parties do not have such control, as in mandatory mediation, mandatory arbitration and court proceedings, the state has a particular responsibility to provide qualification standards that guarantee a justified influence of the intermediary in the procedure. This is especially true if the state additionally has a monopoly on a certain procedure, as is the case for court and enforcement proceedings.

The formulation of a principle of regulation has to deal with two particular issues. First, the discussion on the required level of qualification is far from being settled.[91] Thus, the principle needs to be worded openly in order to allow the factoring in of further insights. Second, the principle needs to find a simple but clear expression for 'influence of the intermediary on the procedure and result of the conflict resolution' that is still able to capture the essence of the many procedures concerned. Here the characteristics of the *taxonomy* developed above can be used. The influence of the intermediary can be described using the characteristics of whether or not the parties have initiation control, result-content control, result-effect control and, of course, the degree to which they choose the intermediary. Integrating these thoughts into a principle, one could state:[92] *The less the parties control the choice of the neutral, the initiation, the result-content and the result-effect of a dispute resolution mechanism,*

[91] *Cf* by way of example, the unsettled discussion on mediator qualification analysed from a comparative law perspective in Hopt and Steffek, 'Mediation: Comparison of Laws, Regulatory Models, Fundamental Issues' 79ff.

[92] These two sentences are the first sentences of principle VIII.C. See Chapters 1 and 2 for more details.

the more the state needs to ensure the qualification of the neutral. Generally, however, it is recommended to opt for as little intrusive regulation as necessary.

In addition to these general principles, further specifications can be made depending on the characteristics of dispute resolution mechanisms. For these specifications, the reader is referred to Chapter 2, principle VIII.C. At this point, just one of these concretisations shall be introduced. To frame further concretisations, three regulatory approaches to the qualification of intermediaries can be distinguished: the market approach, the incentive approach and the authorisation approach.[93] In the *market approach* the state refrains from the regulation of education and admission to the activity of serving as an intermediary. Instead, the intermediaries, their associations, the parties and academia develop practice standards. In the *incentive approach* the state abstains from authorisation as a precondition for acting as an intermediary, but sets incentives to fulfil certain qualification criteria. One option is to award a qualification seal to those who fulfil certain qualification conditions. Another option is to create advantageous legal consequences for those who meet such conditions, for example concerning confidentiality and professional duties. Under the *authorisation approach* the state sets up a state-administered (ministry, courts, etc) admission procedure for access to acting as an intermediary. Where the parties choose the intermediary and control the commencement or the result effect of a dispute resolution mechanism, self-determination and efficiency support the market or the incentive approach. The relevant principle could then read:[94] *If the parties control the choice of the neutral and the initiation or the effect of the procedure, a market approach or an incentive approach may be advisable.*

C. Diversity

The GRDR aims to respect local and regional diversity.[95] Very detailed and rigid rules would not be appropriate at this stage. Many dispute resolution mechanisms are under development and in flux. Inflexible in-depth principles would hinder development. There needs to be room for variation. This is especially true for transnational principles for regulating dispute resolution. Different states should be able to experiment with different approaches and this will bring insights into what works best. Due to differing environments, cultures and interests, there are also substantial reasons arguing against comprehensive transnational convergence. Hence, for transnational principles for regulating dispute resolution only more abstract, high-level principles are advisable. The modular method as regards regulatory topics and taxonomy employed in the design of the principles allows menu choice. As regards the fundamental policy choices, the approach used here not only aims to be transparent but also uses the generally accepted position of normative individualism, and is open as regards the appreciation and balancing of interests. In this way, local and regional normative differences can be respected in the implementation of the principles.

[93] For further details on these regulatory models see Hopt and Steffek, 'Mediation: Comparison of Laws, Regulatory Models, Fundamental Issues' 80ff.

[94] This is the third sentence of principle VIII.C (see Chapter 2).

[95] See above I.D.

The last example given above[96] illustrates a further method to deal with diversity and still maintain a principled approach to regulation. This sample principle reads: *If the parties control the choice of the neutral and the initiation or the effect of the procedure, a market approach or an incentive approach may be advisable.* It illustrates how diversity can be respected on the input and the output side. On the input side, the principle is flexible as to whether the parties control the initiation *or* the effect of the dispute resolution mechanism, as long as they can choose the neutral. On the output side, the principle leaves room to decide between a market and an incentive approach. Needless to say, there are many different variants in the implementation of each of these approaches. A further technique used to deal with diversity is the dynamic reference to local and regional concepts. For example, principle XIV suggests consumer protection as regards dispute resolution contract clauses, but refers to the differing local consumer protection levels by considering solely consumer protection. The principle reads in this regard: *Specific rules for consumer dispute resolution are required concerning, in particular, initiation control through dispute resolution clauses.*

VI. CONCLUSION

A. Summary

Principled regulation of dispute resolution at the local, regional and transnational levels is desirable. A coherent, intelligible, systematic and reasoned approach to regulation promises just dispute resolution. It fosters freedom, equality and efficiency, and, above all, it respects the interests of those affected by conflicts. It also improves decisions and the implementation of dispute resolution at the level of the individuals and the institutions of the state. However, principled regulation faces the challenge of diversity and complexity in regulation, practice, culture and policy. It is suggested that these challenges can be dealt with by a modular and flexible approach to the development of principles for regulating dispute resolution. This approach rests on three pillars: (1) a functional and modular taxonomy of dispute resolution mechanisms; (2) a transparent normative framework, which is based on normative individualism and is open for further development; and (3) a modular identification of regulatory topics.

The *taxonomy* suggested here describes dispute resolution mechanisms from the perspective of the individuals who are affected by a conflict. The taxonomy aims to describe all dispute resolution mechanisms and their variants, including negotiation, mediation, conciliation, expert opinion, ombudsman procedure, mini-trial, arbitration and court adjudication. The characteristics are embedded in a flexible modular structure and try to capture the intrinsic qualities of the different dispute resolution mechanisms. To discover these characteristics, a functional and comparative method is applied. In particular, the following characteristics of dispute resolution mechanisms are identified, all to be understood from the perspective of the parties:

- *Initiation control*: whether each party's consent is needed to initiate the dispute resolution mechanism;

[96] At the end of V.B.ii.

- *Procedure control*: whether the parties determine the procedure;
- *Result-content control*: whether the parties determine the content of the result of the dispute resolution—this corresponds to whether the mechanism is evaluative;
- *Result-effect control*: whether the parties' consent is needed for the result-content to be binding;
- *Neutral choice control*: whether the parties choose the neutral;
- *Information control*: whether the parties control the disclosure of information, ie whether the procedure is private;
- *Interest-based*: whether the procedure is interest- or rights-based;
- *Intermediary*: whether there is an intermediation in the procedure, ie whether a third person contributes to the conflict resolution.

Defining the characteristics from the perspective of the parties corresponds with the normative basis of this paper: *normative individualism*. This normative approach is the generally accepted foundation in legal ethics and political philosophy, as well as the basis of human rights in international conventions and national constitutions. According to normative individualism, a legal rule is just if it can be justified in relation to each individual affected. In the context of regulating dispute resolution, normative individualism demands that one consider in particular the interests of the individuals affected by a conflict. Normative individualism does not, however, promote egoism, and is well able to take account of societies and the state. From this perspective, societies and the state are constituted by the individuals and their interests. These interests are not imposed by an outsider but are determined by the individuals themselves. Such interests can be material or immaterial, they can be self-concerned or be oriented towards others, and they can be egoistic or in solidarity with others. Of course, the decision which legal rule is just requires an evaluation and balancing of the interests involved. One possible approach is to consider the degree to which interests are related to the individual or to society. This requires assessing whether the implementation of an interest has effects on others and requires the cooperation of others. The more others are affected and needed, the more the individual has to accept interference based on the interests of other individuals. Guiding principles are freedom, equality and efficiency, which may conflict at times but which are all rooted in normative individualism. Efficiency is an element of justice, since individuals usually expect that their affiliation to a society increases the realisation of their interests.

Normative individualism has consequences for the regulation of dispute resolution: dispute resolution mechanisms should be designed from the perspective of the individuals involved. The individuals have a right of access to a legal framework that facilitates just private dispute resolution. Further than that, the state's monopoly on power sits alongside the organisational and financial duties of the state to provide an accessible and effective court and enforcement system. The starting point is self-determination and equality in dispute resolution. However, information asymmetries and decision deficits may justify regulation. The first option should be enabling rules, followed by incentive-setting rules; mandatory rules and referral should be the last option. The normative foundation suggested and introduced only very briefly here is an open concept. Interests of individuals differ within jurisdictions and between jurisdictions, and they evolve over time. Consequently, while there is a stable core of justice requirements underlying law, the content of justice may differ between jurisdictions and over time. The wider framework proposed in this chapter may accommodate locally and regionally differing interests. As a consequence, only relatively abstract and high-level principles for regulating dispute resolution are suggested. When they are implemented, local and regional notions of justice can be added.

The *topics* of regulation are identified, once again, using a modular approach. To identify a topic of regulation does not suggest that state regulation is the best answer. It just means that thought should be given to whether and, if so, how regulation is advisable. Topics can be identified, for example, through an analysis of standard contracts, comparison of regulation between different dispute resolution mechanisms, comparison of laws and cross-fertilisation from other fields of regulation. The principles of regulation suggested here employ topics like costs, dispute resolution clauses, choice of procedure, confidentiality, counsel, enforceability, transparency and consumers. Starting with the topics of regulation, the normative policy guidelines answer the question whether and, if so, which regulation is necessary. The principles of regulation can then be formulated using the characteristics of dispute resolution mechanisms developed in the taxonomy as regulatory anchors.

The GRDR suggested in this book can be used on three levels. First, it can be used to develop principles[97] or model laws[98] for specific dispute resolution mechanisms or regional framework rules, such as directives[99] and recommendations[100] in the EU. These model laws, directives and recommendations are the basis on which concrete local laws are developed in a subsequent step. Second, the principles suggested can be used to draft local laws, such as state law, or regional laws, such as regulations in the EU. In this case, the principles directly inform applicable laws. Third, the principles can be used by practitioner associations and other bodies as a background when drafting professional standards.[101]

B. Further Research

The discussion of transnational principles of regulating dispute resolution has just begun. Further research is necessary on all aspects of regulation, including the taxonomy of dispute resolution mechanisms, normative foundations and the topics of regulation. It is suggested that there is a close link between these three elements of regulation. Amongst these elements the normative foundations have a leading role. More than determining solely policy choices, whether to regulate and how to regulate, the normative basis also shapes the understanding of dispute resolution mechanisms.

[97] *Cf* ALI/UNIDROIT Principles of Transnational Civil Procedure [2004] *Uniform Law Review* 758–808; for background information on these Principles see M Andenas, N Andrews and R Nazzini (eds), *The Future of Transnational Civil Litigation* (London, British Institute of International and Comparative Law, 2004); R Stürner, 'The Principles of Transnational Civil Procedure' (2005) 69 *RabelsZ* 201–54.

[98] *Cf* UNCITRAL Model Law on International Commercial Conciliation, A/RES/57/18 (2002); UNCITRAL Model Law on International Commercial Arbitration A/RES/61/33 (2006); National Conference of Commissioners on Uniform State Laws, Uniform Mediation Act (approval 2001, revision 2003).

[99] *Cf* Directive 2008/52/EC of the European Parliament and of the Council of 21 May 2008 on certain aspects of mediation in civil and commercial matters, Official Journal L 136, 24 May 2008, 3ff.

[100] *Cf* Commission Recommendation 2001/310 of 4 April 2001 on the principles for out-of-court bodies involved in the consensual resolution of consumer disputes, Official Journal L 109, 19 April 2001, 56ff.

[101] *Cf* European Code of Conduct for Mediators, available at <http://ec.europa.eu/civiljustice/adr/adr_ec_code_conduct_en.pdf>.

Here the individuals affected by a conflict are the source and focus of justice. Consequently, the characteristics of those mechanisms are defined from the perspectives of those individuals. As the normative perceptions change, so will the understanding of dispute resolution mechanisms.

The three elements of regulation used here are not abstract, instead resting on concrete individuals and their interests. They also depend on the social, economic and environmental circumstances of these individuals and societies. Here further empirical research on the interests of individuals in dispute resolution can contribute to better regulation. It is suggested that such empirical and theoretical further research is worthwhile in the interest of justice and, above all, in the interest of the individuals affected by conflict.

BIBLIOGRAPHY

ADR Center (Rome), *The Cost of Non ADR—Surveying and Showing the Actual Costs of Intra-Community Commercial Litigation: Survey Data Report* (Rome, 2010)

Alchian, AA, 'Why Money?' (1977) 9 *Journal of Money, Credit and Banking* 133–40

Alexander, N, *Global Trends in Mediation*, 2nd edn (AH Alphen aan den Rijn, Kluwer Law International, 2006)

Alexander, N, *International and Comparative Mediation—Legal Perspectives* (AH Alphen aan den Rijn, Kluwer Law International, 2009)

ALI/UNIDROIT, 'Principles of Transnational Civil Procedure' [2004] *Uniform Law Review* 758–808

Andenas, M, Andrews, N and Nazzini, R (eds), *The Future of Transnational Civil Litigation* (London, British Institute of International and Comparative Law, 2004)

Aristotle, *Nicomachean Ethics* (ἠθικὰ Νικομάχεια), translated by WD Ross (Kitchener, Ontario, Batoche Books, 1999)

Aristotle, *Politics* (Πολιτικά), translated by B Howett (Kitchener, Ontario, Batoche Books, 1999)

Armour, J, Hansmann, H and Kraakman, R, 'Agency Problems and Legal Strategies' in R Kraakman, J Armour, P Davies, L Enriques, H Hansmann, G Hertig, KJ Hopt, H Kanda and E Rock (eds), *The Anatomy of Corporate Law—A Comparative and Functional Approach*, 2nd edn (Oxford, Oxford University Press, 2009) 35–53

Australian Law Reform Commission, *Principled Regulation—Federal Civil & Administrative Penalties in Australia*, Report 95, December 2002

Avruch, K, *Culture and Conflict Resolution* (Washington, DC, United States Institute of Peace Press, 1998)

Ayres, I, 'Regulating Opt-Out: An Economic Theory of Altering Rules' (2012) 121 *Yale Law Journal* 2032–116

Baldwin, R, 'Better Regulation: The Search and the Struggle' in R Baldwin, M Cave and M Lodge (eds), *The Oxford Handbook of Regulation* (Oxford, Oxford University Press, 2010) 259–78

Berger, KP, *Private Dispute Resolution in International Business—Negotiation, Mediation, Arbitration, vol II: Handbook*, 2nd edn (AH Alphen aan den Rijn, Kluwer Law International, 2009)

Better Regulation Task Force, *Principles of Good Regulation* (London, 2003)

Blake, S, Browne, J and Sime, S, *A Practical Approach to Alternative Dispute Resolution* (Oxford, Oxford University Press, 2011)

Brunner, K and Meltzer, AH, 'The Uses of Money: Money in the Theory of an Exchange Economy' (1971) 61 *The American Economic Review* 784–805

Cameron, R, 'Intrinsic and Extrinsic Properties' in R Le Poidevin, P Simons, A McGonigal and R Cameron (eds), *The Routledge Companion to Metaphysics* (London and New York, Routledge, 2009) 265–75

Cooter, R and Ulen, T, *Law & Economics*, 6th edn (Boston, Pearson Education, 2012)

Cotterrell, R, 'Law's Community: Legal Theory and the Image of Legality' (1992) 19 *Journal of Law and Society* 405–22

Council of Europe (The European Commission for the Efficiency of Justice), *European Judicial Systems—Edition 2012 (Data 2010)* (Strasbourg, 2012)

De Palo, G and Trevor, MB (eds), *EU Mediation—Law and Practice* (Oxford, Oxford University Press, 2012)

Djankov, S, La Porta, R, Lopez-de-Silanes, F and Shleifer, A, 'Courts' [2003] *Quarterly Journal of Economics* 453–517

Dworkin, R, *A Matter of Principle* (Cambridge, MA, Harvard University Press, 1985)

Dworkin, R, *Taking Rights Seriously* (Cambridge, MA, Harvard University Press, 1977)

Fleckner, AM and Hopt, KJ (eds), *Comparative Corporate Governance—A Functional and International Analysis* (Cambridge, Cambridge University Press, 2013)

Goldberg, SB, Sander, FEA, Rogers, NH and Cole, SR, *Dispute Resolution—Negotiation, Mediation, Arbitration, and Other Processes*, 6th edn (New York, Wolters Kluwer, 2012)

Hart, HLA, *The Concept of Law*, 2nd edn (Oxford, Clarendon Press, 1994)

Hobbes, T, *Leviathan—Or the Matter, Forme, & Power of a Common-wealth Ecclesiasticall and Civill* (London, Andrew Crooke, 1651)

Hodges, CJS, Benöhr, I and Creutzfeld-Banda, N, *Consumer ADR in Europe* (Oxford, Hart Publishing, 2012)

Hoerster, N, *Ethik und Interesse* (Stuttgart, Reclam, 2003)

Hopt, KJ and Steffek, F (eds), *Mediation: Principles and Regulation in Comparative Perspective* (Oxford, Oxford University Press, 2013)

Hopt, KJ and Steffek, F, 'Mediation: Comparison of Laws, Regulatory Models, Fundamental Issues' in KJ Hopt and F Steffek (eds), *Mediation: Principles and Regulation in Comparative Perspective* (Oxford, Oxford University Press, 2013) 3–130

Ingen-Housz, A (ed), *ADR in Business—Practice and Issues Across Countries and Cultures*, vol II (AH Alphen aan den Rijn, Kluwer Law International, 2011)

Kant, I, *Die Metaphysik der Sitten, Erster Theil: Metaphysische Anfangsgründe der Rechtslehre*, 2nd edn (Königsberg, Friedrich Nicolovius, 1798)

Lewis, D, 'Extrinsic Properties' (1983) 44 *Philosophical Studies* 197–200

Locke, J, *Two Treatises of Government—In the Former, the False Principles and Foundation of Sir Robert Filmer, and His Followers, are Detected and Overthrown—The Latter is an Essay Concerning the True Original, Extent, and End of Civil-Government* (London, Awnsham Churchill, 1690)

Mackaay, E, *Law and Economics for Civil Law Systems* (Cheltenham, Edward Elgar, 2013)

Mandelkern, D (ed), *Report on Better Regulation—Final Report* (Brussels, 2001)

McIlwrath, M and J Savage, J, *International Arbitration and Mediation—A Practical Guide* (AH Alphen aan den Rijn, Kluwer Law International, 2010)

Menkel-Meadow, CJ, Love, LP, Schneider, AK and Sternlight, JR, *Dispute Resolution—Beyond the Adversarial Model*, 2nd edn (New York, Aspen Publishers, 2011)

Michaels, R, 'The Functional Method of Comparative Law' in R Zimmermann and M Reimann (eds), *The Oxford Handbook of Comparative Law* (Oxford, Oxford University Press, 2008) 339–82

Nozick, R, *Anarchy, State, and Utopia* (New York, Basic Books, 1974)

PWC (PriceWaterhouseCoopers) and Europa University Viadrina Frankfurt (Oder), *Commercial Dispute Resolution—Konfliktbearbeitungsverfahren im Vergleich* (Frankfurt am Main and Frankfurt an der Oder, 2005)

Radbruch, G, *Rechtsphilosophie*, 3rd edn (Leipzig, Quelle & Meyer, 1932)
Rawls, J, *A Theory of Justice*, rev edn (Cambridge, MA, Belknap Press, 1999)
Rousseau, J, *Au Contrat Social, ou Principes du Droit Politique* (Amsterdam, M Rey, 1762)
Sander, FEA and Rozdeiczer, L, 'Matching Cases and Dispute Resolution Procedures: Detailed Analysis Leading to a Mediation-Centered Approach' (2006) 11 *Harvard Negotiation Law Review* 1–41
Smith, S and Martinez, J, 'An Analytical Framework for Dispute Systems Design' (2009) 14 *Harvard Negotiation Law Review* 123–69
Steffek, F, 'Mediation und Justiz' in C Fischer and H Unberath (eds), *Das neue Mediationsgesetz—Rechtliche Rahmenbedingungen der Mediation* (Munich, CH Beck, 2013) 29–45
Stürner, R, 'The Principles of Transnational Civil Procedure' (2005) 69 *RabelsZ* 201–54
Unberath, H, 'Auf dem Weg zu einer differenzierten Streitkultur—Neue gesetzliche Rahmenbedingungen für die alternative Konfliktlösung' *JuristenZeitung* 2010, 975–81
Veljanovski, C, 'Economic Approaches to Regulation' in R Baldwin, M Cave and M Lodge (eds), *The Oxford Handbook of Regulation* (Oxford, Oxford University Press, 2010) 17–38
von der Pfordten, D, 'Normativer Individualismus und das Recht' *JuristenZeitung* 2005, 1069–80
von der Pfordten, D, *Rechtsethik*, 2nd edn (Munich, CH Beck, 2011)
Zweigert, K and Kötz, H, *Introduction to Comparative Law*, 3rd edn (Oxford, Clarendon Press, 1998)

Part 2

Regulation of Dispute Resolution

4

Regulation of Dispute Resolution in Austria: A Traditional Litigation Culture Slowly Embraces ADR

PETER G MAYR AND KRISTIN NEMETH

I. CHARACTERISTICS OF ADR

A. Current Situation in Austria

AS A GENERAL observation, it has to be said that the predominant form of dispute resolution in Austria is litigation before the domestic state courts. Civil procedure in this sense comprises not only traditional litigation as regulated in the Civil Procedure Act (Zivilprozessordnung, ZPO), but also a less formal procedure known as *Außerstreitverfahren* (non-contested procedure) regulated in a separate act, the Außerstreitgesetz (AußStrG). It has to be pointed out in this context that the AußStrG is reserved for conflict resolution in areas such as family matters, inheritance matters and condominium disputes, and therefore deals with issues which have always been viewed as ADR-appropriate.

In 2011 the Austrian courts had to deal with 615,913 traditional civil disputes and 376,849 less formal (AußStrG) matters.[1] For other forms of dispute resolution statistical data hardly exist; sometimes private collections of data are available. Recently various regulatory authorities which also serve as conciliation bodies for consumer disputes—eg authorities dealing with broadcast and telecommunications (Rundfunk und Telekom Regulierungs-GmbH, RTR-GmbH), energy (E-Control) and the railway (Schienen-Control-GmbH)—have started to publish annual reports regarding their conciliation activities. The biggest of these regulatory authorities, namely the RTR-GmbH, deals with approximately 5,000 cases per year in the field of telecommunication law,[2] a very small number compared to the number of cases resolved in court.

Austrian scholars and practitioners agree that the current preference for court proceedings is best explained in the historical context: Austria has a long tradition of this form of dispute resolution, which in the view of the legislature is one of the most important pillars of the social legal order.

This is supported by a—compared to other jurisdictions—very well functioning judiciary. Indeed, despite a few drawbacks in recent history, the Austrian judiciary still enjoys great public confidence. The latest report of the European Commission for the Efficiency of Justice revealed that Austria is well under the European average when it comes to length of procedure: the usual duration of a case in Austria is 129 days, compared to the European average of 287 days.[3] It must also be mentioned that approximately 30 per cent of the litigated cases are resolved without entry of judgment because the parties reach an agreement and settle in court.

The current situation thus leaves little room for alternative forms of dispute resolution.

B. Appropriateness of Dispute Resolution Form

If a party wants a quick, effective and cheap way to deal with an (undisputed) money claim, which can be enforced against the opponent, he would choose a summary procedure (*[obligatorisches] Mahnverfahren*) whereby the court decides in favour of the claimant without conducting a trial, issuing a payment order (*Zahlungsbefehl*). In 2011 approximately 86 per cent of the civil disputes before the regional courts (Bezirks-

[1] These numbers are published on the website of the Austrian Ministry of Justice: <www.justiz.gv.at>; see P Mayr, 'Neue Rechtstatsachen aus der Zivilgerichtsbarkeit' [2009] *Österreichisches Anwaltsblatt* 54ff.

[2] 4,258 applications for conciliation were brought in 2009, 4,403 were brought in 2010 and 5,470 in 2011; see the Activity Report of the Conciliation Body: <www.rtr.at/de/komp/alleBerichte>.

[3] See the report *Efficiency and Quality of Justice* (2010 edn) of the European Commission for the Efficiency of Justice (CEPEJ), distributed by the Austrian Ministry of Justice under the heading *Bericht der CEPEJ: Die österreichische Justiz arbeitet rasch und günstig*; see also G Stawa, 'Effizienz der Justiz im europäischen Vergleich' [2011] *Österreichisches Anwaltsblatt* 510.

gerichte) were solved that way. In only 9.3 per cent of these cases was the payment order formally challenged (by submitting an *Einspruch*, with which full proceedings are demanded).[4] In all other cases the payment order became enforceable.

On the other hand, there is wide consensus in Austria that for many cases litigation is not the best dispute resolution approach. However, practice is lagging behind: despite various attempts of the legislator to make ADR more popular, the courts are called upon far too often, even in cases which do not seem to require state interference or where state interference is not suitable, such as in family law.

The various forms of ADR have advantages and disadvantages. Although this report cannot discuss these features in detail, in general it can be said that:

- Mediation is most suitable for disputes between parties who have a special relationship which they want or have to continue after termination of the dispute;
- Conciliation procedures are suitable for small consumer claims;
- Expert opinions are suitable for cases in which the determination of certain facts proves to be the main problem; and
- Arbitration is most suitable for complex international commercial disputes.

II. THE LEGISLATOR'S APPROACH

A. The Regulation of ADR in General

In Austria, ADR is not comprehensively regulated. This report can only focus on ADR mechanisms which are subject to legislation. The fate of the many other, non-regulated ADR schemes in Austria is hard to predict, as there is not even a register of any kind. The only 'official' list (which is, however, neither comprehensive nor up to date) is available at the ECC-Net homepage, which names 15 'notified' ADR institutions in Austria,[5] nine of them based on legislation (Schienen-Control, E-Control, RTR-GmbH, and several patient conciliation bodies), the other six not being regulated. Among the latter, the Internet Ombudsman is probably the most important institution, handling approximately 5,000 complaints per year.[6] An example of a very important institution that is not part of this list is the (unregulated) Common Conciliation Body of the Austrian Credit Sector (Gemeinsame Schlichtungsstelle der Österreichischen Kreditwirtschaft), which conducted 112 conciliation proceedings in 2011.[7] This conciliation body is, however, a member of the financial dispute resolution network FIN-NET.[8]

[4] Of 509,623 civil proceedings at the regional courts (Bezirksgerichte), 433,972 were summary filings in nature; in 40,279 cases full proceedings (*Einspruch*) were demanded; for the numbers see the general information system of the Austrian Judiciary (*Betriebliches Informationssystem der Justiz (BIS-Justiz) 2011* 32). See also Mayr, 'Neue Rechtstatsachen aus der Zivilgerichtsbarkeit' 60f.

[5] See <www.europakonsument.at> and n 49.

[6] See <www.ombudsmann.at>: this was the number of cases reported in the Annual Report 2011. The report also explains that the number of complaints rose significantly between 2005 and 2010, from 5,000 to 10,000 cases per year, allegedly because of the existence of many products and services offered 'free of charge' on the internet. The majority of these offers have in the meantime disappeared from the web, which explains the decrease in the number of complaints reported in 2011.

[7] See <www.bankenschlichtung.at/docs/Jahresbericht.pdf>: after 268 written complaints and enquiries.

[8] See <ec.europa.eu/internal_market/fin-net/members_de.htm>.

i. The Effect of Regulation on the Use of ADR

The regulation of an ADR mechanism definitely has an encouraging effect in the sense that regulation leads to publicity and guarantees that the respective instrument 'survives' for a certain amount of time. Moreover, if an ADR mechanism is regulated, there is a higher chance that fundamental procedural principles are observed. On the other hand, recent regulatory incentives have shown that regulation itself is not sufficiently encouraging for conflicting parties to rely on ADR in practice. In other words: as long as the public does not recognise the respective ADR mechanism as a useful tool, legislation is only of limited effect.

ii. The Reasons to Regulate

The predominant reason given by the legislature in favour of regulation of ADR is the attempt to reduce the workload of the courts and therefore minimise costs, regardless of whether this reason is stated expressly or not. Quality and appropriateness of dispute resolution only play secondary roles. Recently, the need to implement EU law has become an important third reason.

The prevailing reason presented in academia[9] is the need to optimise and differentiate the means of dispute resolution. However, publications analysing this approach in detail are rather rare.

B. Incentives to Use Certain Types of ADR

Austrian procedural law contains no rules that deal with ADR in the early conflict resolution phase in general, which means there is no legal provision that would help the parties to a dispute to choose the best conflict resolution method for their individual problem. The limited possibilities for trial judges to point out alternatives means—albeit without any legal consequences—will be discussed below in II.F.

In the latter stages of a conflict there is also no real legislative support for ADR. For the time being, parties cannot be forced to use alternative means of dispute resolution; needless to say, there are no sanctions if they do not use ADR.

The only rule that comes close to a legislative incentive can be found in family law, where parties can apply for financial support from the state if they decide to use

[9] E Bajons, 'Außergerichtliche Güteverfahren als Mittel der Prozessvermeidung und Konfliktlösung' (1984) *Österreichische Juristen-Zeitung* 368; P Mayr and A Schmidt, 'Gesetzlich geregelte Alternativen innerhalb und außerhalb des Zivilprozesses in Österreich' [1987] *Zeitschrift für Vergleichende Rechtswissenschaft* 227; H Krejci, 'Recht ohne Gerichte' in P Doralt and C Nowotny (eds), *Kontinuität und Wandel: Beiträge zum Unternehmensrecht. Festschrift für Walther Kastner zum 90. Geburtstag* (Orac, 1992) 251; N Michalek, 'Streitbeilegung ohne Gerichte' in Österreichische Juristenkommission (ed), *Kritik und Fortschritt im Rechtsstaat* (Verlag Österreich, 1994) 13; P Mayr, 'Neuigkeiten bei der außergerichtlichen Streitbeilegung in Österreich' in M Ganner (ed), *Die soziale Funktion des Privatrecht. Festschrift für Heinz Barta zum 65. Geburtstag* (Linde, 2009) 245; P Mayr, 'Aktuelle Entwicklungen und Probleme bei den Rechtsschutzalternativen' in R Geimer, R Schütze and T Garber (eds), *Europäische und Internationale Dimensionen des Rechts. Festschrift für Daphne-Ariane Simotta* (LexisNexis, 2012) 375; P Mayr, 'Alternative Dispute Resolution (ADR) in Austrian and European Law' in V Rijavec and T Ivanc (eds), *Cross-border Civil Proceedings in the EU (Conference Papers)* (Pravna fakulteta, 2012) 1.

mediation.[10] This rule is, however, unique in the Austrian legal order, and there are no other comparable provisions.

If the use of ADR is compulsory in the pre-trial stage, as is the case in the law regarding liberal professions, private associations as well as housing and neighbour relations, no special incentives are needed.[11]

C. The Role of Legal Culture

Legal culture definitely plays an important role when it comes to the choice of the appropriate dispute resolution form. The Austrian legislature has long favoured a classical court procedure, which in the legislature's view is one of the predominant tasks of the social legal order. Alternatives have only been considered in the last decade. This is shown, for example, by the increasing legislation in the field of out-of-court settlement. Also the recent amendments in arbitration law are much more in favour of using arbitration as an alternative than before (see the Schiedsrechts-Änderungsgesetz 2006).[12]

D. Advisory Duties of Lawyers

Austrian law contains no general obligation of lawyers to advise clients about alternatives and their advantages and disadvantages before going to court, apart from the few fields where the use of ADR is compulsory.

The Guidelines for Practising Lawyers (Richtlinien zur Ausübung des Rechtsanwaltsberufes),[13] however, contain a special Article XII (sections 63–65) dealing with the relationship between the legal profession and mediation.

Moreover, in 2004 a compulsory course on mediation and out-of-court settlement was introduced into the training provisions for future lawyers, though the course was cancelled in 2010.[14]

E. Restriction of Access to Court with a View to Alternative Dispute Resolution

A few fields of law require compulsory ADR proceedings before the parties can refer

[10] Section 39c of the Law Regarding the Financial Support of Families (Familienlastenausgleichsgesetz, FLAG) BGBl 1967/376, last amended by BGBl I 1999/136; see J Stadlmaier, 'Familienmediation: Einladung zum konstruktiven Miteinander' [2011] *iFamZ—Interdisziplinäre Zeitschrift für Familienrecht* 54.

[11] See below II.E.

[12] BGBl (Official Gazette of the Republic of Austria) I 2006/7; see also below III.E.

[13] See the Guidelines regarding the exercise and supervision of the legal profession (Richtlinien für die Ausübung des Rechtsanwaltsberufes und für die Überwachung der Pflichten des Rechtsanwaltes und des Rechtsanwaltsanwärters, RL-BA 1977) published on the website of the Austrian Bar Association <http://www.rechtsanwaelte.at/downloads/rl_ba10052011.pdf> or E Feil and F Wennig, *Anwaltsrecht* (7th edn, Linde, 2012) 641ff.

[14] See the critical remarks by B Knötzl, 'Außergerichtliche Streitbeilegung. Konfliktlehre in der anwaltlichen Praxis—Ein "Alien"?' [2010] *Österreichisches Anwaltsblatt* 584; and in response J Weixelbaum, 'Auch überbordender Eifer kann schaden! Eine Replik des ÖRAK zum Beitrag von Mag Bettina Knötzl' [2010] *Österreichisches Anwaltsblatt* 591.

their conflict to court.[15] It must be stressed, however, that these cases only amount to a small percentage of the overall disputes in Austria. They are outlined in the following subsections.

i. Liberal Professions

Numerous laws regulating liberal professions (practising lawyers, notaries, public accountants and tax advisers, the medical profession, civil engineers, etc) contain a rule stipulating that disputes between members of the respective professions require compulsory conciliation proceedings before a claim can be referred to the state courts.[16]

The Law Regarding Doctors (Ärztegesetz 1998)[17] shall serve as an example: according to section 94(1) ÄrzteG the members of the Medical Chamber are obliged to call the Conciliation Committee of the Medical Chamber regarding disputes arising between doctors in relation to the exercise of their profession or in relation to their activities as members of the professional group before initiating litigation or private prosecution. As long as the conciliation proceedings run, prescription periods and other time limits are suspended for up to three months. A civil action or private prosecution may only be brought after termination of the three-month period, or at an earlier date if the conciliation process is terminated at that earlier date (section 94(3) and (4) ÄrzteG). Details shall be regulated in specific rules of procedure issued by the Austrian Chamber of Doctors.[18]

ii. Private Associations

According to section 3(1) no 10 of the Law Regarding Private Associations (Vereinsgesetz 2002, VerG),[19] the articles of association have to include rules regarding the resolution of disputes resulting from the special legal relationship between the association and its members as well as between members. Section 8 VerG further stipulates that, according to section 8(1) VerG, disputes resulting from the above-mentioned relationship have to be referred to a conciliation body. If the proceedings before that body do not end earlier, parties can only file a claim with the court in charge after six months have elapsed from the referral for conciliation, ie the admissibility of the claim is only suspended. The possibility of bringing proceedings to the courts can, however, be excluded completely if an arbitral tribunal is set up according to sections 577ff ZPO. Section 8(2) VerG also sets forth that, to a certain extent, the articles of association have to regulate procedural questions, ie rules on the composition of the conciliation

[15] See Mayr, 'Neuigkeiten bei der außergerichtlichen Streitbeilegung in Österreich' 250ff and Mayr, 'Aktuelle Entwicklungen und Probleme bei den Rechtsschutzalternativen' 382ff.

[16] For more details see P Mayr, 'Die Schlichtungstätigkeit der Kammern der freien Berufe' (1995) *Wirtschaftsrechtliche Blätter* 269.

[17] BGBl I 1998/169. See also s 54 of the Law Regarding the Chamber of Dentists (Zahnärztekammergesetz) BGBl I 2005/154.

[18] According to s 118(4) of the Law Regarding Doctors (ÄrzteG 1988) these rules of procedure have to contain specific provisions regarding conciliation, the competence of the conciliation committee, its members and their appointment, the period they sit and the regional distribution of cases taking into consideration the high reputation of the medical profession.

[19] BGBl I 2002/66; see P Mayr, 'Vereinsstreitigkeiten zwischen Schlichtungseinrichtung, Gericht und Schiedsgericht' [2009] *Österreichische Juristen-Zeitung* 39.

body as well as guidelines on the election or appointment of its members, particularly with regard to their impartiality. There is also a rule stipulating that both parties of a dispute must be heard.

iii. Housing

Under the heading 'decision of the municipality', section 39 of the Austrian Tenancy Act (Mietrechtsgesetz, MRG)[20] lays down that certain disputes arising from leases in certain municipalities[21] can only be subject to civil proceedings if the case is initially referred to the municipality. Otherwise a civil claim is inadmissible.[22] The municipality has to undertake all necessary investigations and first of all attempt to achieve an amicable agreement. If no agreement is reached, the municipality will start proceedings which are partly governed by the Außerstreitgesetz, and therefore civil procedural law, and partly by rules of administrative procedure, ie the General Administrative Procedure Rules (Allgemeines Verwaltungsverfahrensgesetz, AVG).[23] The decision of the municipality is enforceable, and there is no legal remedy against it. It is, however, automatically and immediately void when a complaint is filed within four weeks of the decision being served on the parties (section 40(1) MRG). The civil courts can also be called upon if the proceedings are not brought to an end within three months (section 40(2) MRG). The described rules (sections 39, 40 MRG) are also applicable to certain proceedings under the Condominium Act (Wohnungseigentumsgesetz, WEG 2002, section 52(3)), under the Law Regarding Heating Costs (Heizkostenabrechungsgesetz, HeizKG, section 25(2)) and under the Limited Profit Housing Act (Wohnungsgemeinnützigkeitgesetz, WGG, section 22(4)).

In all these cases, dispute resolution is therefore shifted—temporarily—from the state courts to an administrative authority. This so-called successive competence is considered acceptable under the Austrian constitutional principle of separation of powers.[24] Despite this competence to actually decide a dispute, the municipality is still referred to as a 'conciliation body'. This is due to section 39(3) MRG, which outlines the attempt to find a peaceful solution.

iv. Neighbour Disputes

Article III of the Civil Law Amendment 2004 (Zivilrechtsänderungsgesetz, ZivRÄG 2004)[25] introduced a compulsory ADR mechanism for certain disputes between neigh-

[20] BGBl 1981/520 as amended.

[21] These are the cities of Graz, Innsbruck, Klagenfurt, Leoben, Linz, Mürzzuschlag, Neunkirchen, Salzburg, St. Pölten, Stockerau and Vienna.

[22] For the history of these provisions see P Mayr, 'Die Entwicklung der wohnrechtlichen Schlichtungsstellen' [2003] *Wohnrechtliche Blätter* 349; for important constitutional issues see P Mayr and I Rath-Kathrein, 'Verfassungsrechtliche Fragen der wohnrechtlichen Schlichtungsstellen' [2013] *Wohnrechtliche Blätter* 67ff.

[23] See in particular P Heindl and F Lenk, *Das Verfahren vor der Schlichtungsstelle* (Verlag Österreich, 2003).

[24] See eg L Adamovich, B Funk and G Holzinger, *Österreichisches Staatsrecht* vol 2 (Springer, 1998) 106 (no 27.019); H Mayer, *Das österreichische Bundes-Verfassungsrecht* (4th edn, Manz, 2007) 331; R Walter, H Mayer and G Kucsko-Stadlmayer, *Grundriss des österreichischen Bundesverfassungsrechts* (10th edn, Manz, 2007) no 558, the latter two with further references.

[25] BGBl I 2003/91 (in force 1 July 2004).

bours.[26] If a neighbour contends that he is deprived of natural light or air by trees or other plants, he has to choose one of three possible alternatives before he may initiate civil proceedings: he can refer the dispute to a conciliation body for an amicable solution (section 364(3) of the Austrian General Civil Code, Allgemeines Bürgerliches Gesetzbuch, ABGB); he can submit an application for a pre-trial court settlement according to section 433(1) ZPO; or—if the owner of the plant or tree agrees[27]—he can lay the dispute in the hands of a mediator. It is only if no amicable agreement is reached within three months from the application or the beginning of the conciliation or mediation proceedings that the neighbour can file a claim with the competent regional court (Article III no 1). A respective confirmation of the conciliation body, court or mediator that a peaceful solution could not be found must be submitted together with the claim (Article III no 4). Otherwise, a complaint is inadmissible;[28] it has to be dismissed *ex officio* at any stage of the proceedings.

When the ZivRÄG refers to a 'conciliation body' it does not mean every institution that offers conciliation, but only those which are established by the Notaries' Chamber, the Bar Association or a legal person under public law. Furthermore, only a mediator who fulfils the requirements of the Civil Mediation Act (Zivilrechts-Mediations-Gesetz, ZivMediatG)[29] can act as a mediator in neighbour disputes (Article III no 2).

If the parties do not agree on an alternative mode, the costs of the conciliation, judicial settlement proceedings or mediation are first borne by the neighbour who seeks the remedy. If no agreement is reached, the costs are treated as pre-trial costs in the court proceedings (Article III no 3).

According to the legislative materials,[30] it was the express goal of the new regulation to primarily handle disputes arising in relation to the 'right to light' out of court. One reason for the new rule was to avoid an even greater workload for the courts; another was the attempt to achieve better solutions by profiting from the means of alternative dispute resolution, as they have the advantage of not only focusing on the legal issues but also trying to investigate and identify the underlying (non-legal) reasons of the dispute. This constitutes a real advantage in comparison to court proceedings, where the judge can, of course, also try to achieve a peaceful solution, but is ultimately always restricted to deal with the arguments brought by the parties. Frequently, judges also do not have the time or means to investigate the non-legal aspects of a dispute.

[26] A similar rule is contained in s 79m of the Law Regarding Genetic Engineering (Gentechnikgesetz), BGBl 1994/510 as amended by BGBl I 2004/126.

[27] According to the prevailing opinion this agreement guarantees the principle of voluntary mediation (see below III.B).

[28] See the explanatory remarks of the government bill (ErläutRV 173 BlgNR 22. GP 7f) which explicitly mention the inadmissibility of the claim if the parties do not fulfil these requirements; see also OGH 4 September 2007, 4 Ob 146/07k [2007] *SZ—Entscheidungen des österreichischen Obersten Gerichtshofes in Zivilsachen* no 140 = [2008] *Juristische Blätter* 51; OGH 11 December 2007, 4 Ob 196/07p [2007] *SZ—Entscheidungen des österreichischen Obersten Gerichtshofes in Zivilsachen* no 192 = [2008] *Juristische Blätter* 315.

[29] See below III.B and, in particular, P Glavac, 'Mediation im Nachbarschaftsrecht' [2006] *immolex—Neues Miet- und Wohnrecht* 177; I Auer, 'Mediation—die Lösung von Nachbarkonflikten' [2012] *immolex—Neues Miet- und Wohnrecht* 274; see also A Illedits and K Illedits-Lohr, *Handbuch zum Nachbarrecht*, 2nd edn (LexisNexis, 2007) no 739ff and *Nachbarrecht kompakt*, 2nd edn (LexisNexis, 2008) no 207ff.

[30] See the legislative materials (173 BlgNR 22. GP 1, 6f and 24f) and G Kathrein,'Mehr Licht!' [2003] *ecolex—Fachzeitschrift für Wirtschaftsrecht* 894, 898 as well as 'Das neue Nachbarrecht', in Österreichische Notariatskammer (ed), *Festschrift für Nikolaus Michalek zum 65. Geburtstag* (Manz, 2005) 175, 189.

v. The Disabled

According to section 10(2) of the Act Regarding the Equal Treatment of Disabled Persons (Bundes-Behindertengleichstellungsgesetz, BGStG),[31] court proceedings can only be brought after first submitting the case to the Federal Social Welfare Office (Bundessozialamt) for conciliation. The claim is only admissible if the conciliation procedure does not lead to a settlement within three months from its beginning.[32] The referral for conciliation suspends the time limit for initiating court proceedings; as soon as the Federal Social Welfare Office serves upon the parties the confirmation that the conciliation was not successful, the suspension ceases (section 10(4) BGStG).[33] Within three months of delivery, each party can file a claim with the courts (section 10(5) BGStG). More details regarding the procedure are regulated in sections 14ff BGStG.

Also section 7k(1) of the Disabled Persons Employment Act (Behinderteneinstellungsgesetz, BEinstG)[34] states that certain rights under this law can be enforced in court only if the case is first referred to conciliation according to sections 14 ff BGStG. Again, a claim is only admissible after the expiry of a three-month period, running from the beginning of the conciliation, in which a settlement could not be reached. In cases of termination of employment or dismissal, the period is reduced to one month. If a case is referred to conciliation, the time limits for initiating court proceedings are suspended (section 7k(4) and (5) BEinstG).

vi. Apprentices

According to section 15 of the Act Regarding Apprentice Training (Berufsausbildungsgesetz, BAG),[35] an apprenticeship can be terminated by either the employer or the apprentice at any time during the first three months of the training ('probationary period'). Afterwards the apprenticeship can be terminated only by mutual agreement or unilaterally by either the employer or the apprentice if one of the 'important reasons' listed in section 15(3) and (4) BAG is given. Moreover, a new section 15a BAG—introduced by an amendment of 2008[36]—now provides for an additional possibility of unilateral termination at the end of the first or second year of the training. This new form of termination does not require the existence of certain important

[31] BGBl I 2005/82 as amended by BGBl I 2008/67; lately M Risak, 'Die Mediation im Arbeitsrecht' [2012] *Österreichische Juristen-Zeitung* 392f.

[32] It is therefore a temporary inadmissibility of the claim. The legislative materials state that the rules follow the example of conciliation in disputes between neighbours.

[33] The legislative materials (ErläutRV 836 BlgNR 22. GP 11) state in this regard: 'If conciliation seems unpromising from the beginning, because the parties do not want to refer the dispute to this form of conflict resolution, the Federal Social Welfare Office has to confirm that fact, even if the three months have not yet expired'.

[34] BGBl 1970/22 as amended by BGBl I 2005/82 and BGBl I 2008/67. The legislative materials (ErläutRV 836 BlgNR 22. GP 15f) state that the pre-trial conciliation procedure was also introduced to remove some workload from the courts and that it is expected that most cases of discrimination would ultimately not be dealt with in court but be solved earlier.

[35] BGBl 1969/142. An identical rule can be found in s 135 Landarbeitsgesetz 1984 (dealing with the special employment relationship of people working in agricultural and forestry services) as amended by BGBl I 2008/82.

[36] BGBl I 2008/82.

reasons, but follows a rather complex set of prerequisites,[37] eg the compulsory conduct of mediation proceedings according to the Civil Mediation Act.[38]

F. Referral to ADR

The possibility of arriving at a court settlement instead of a judgment has already been pointed out above in I.A. At any stage of the proceedings, a judge may support the parties in reaching such a solution (section 204(1) first sentence ZPO and section 258(1) no 4 ZPO). On the other hand, Austrian law establishes no general duty of judges to either carry out alternative procedures or refer a dispute to ADR. The only provisions which point slightly in that direction are the following: when negotiating a court settlement, the judge—among others—can also name certain dispute resolution centres if it 'seems appropriate' (section 204(1) second sentence ZPO). Furthermore, parties can be called before a member of the panel or another judge outside the panel in order to negotiate a court settlement, if they agree (section 204(2) ZPO).

In non-contested proceedings the court can even suspend the proceedings for a period of up to six months, if an amicable agreement between the parties seems achievable (section 29 AußStrG). The provision explicitly mentions ADR mechanisms in this respect, which could encourage such an agreement, but also points out that an alternative method must not endanger any interests of one or both parties or the public if the protection of such interests would be guaranteed in the court proceedings. From 1 February 2013 a third provision has contributed to this new concept: in child custody cases, section 107(3) no 2 AußStrG allows the judge to refer parties to a compulsory initial meeting in order to consider the use of mediation or conciliation.[39]

G. The Regulation of ADR and Constitutional/Human Rights Law

According to Article 6 ECHR and Article 47 of the Charter of Fundamental Rights, every person is entitled to a fair and public hearing within a reasonable time by an independent and impartial tribunal established by law. According to the prevailing opinion,[40] however, this does not preclude a compulsory pre-trial ADR procedure (or procedure before an administrative authority) unless it prevents the court proceedings as such or delays them for an unreasonable time. This view was recently confirmed by the CJEU.[41]

[37] For more details see P Mayr, 'Die Zwangsmediation im Berufsausbildungsrecht' in H Barta et al (eds), *Analyse und Fortentwicklung im Arbeits-, Sozial- und Zivilrecht. Festschrift Martin Binder* (Linde, 2010) 295ff; F Burger, '10 Stolpersteine auf dem Weg zum Ausbildungsübertritt' [2010] *Zeitschrift für Arbeits- und Sozialrecht* 162ff and M Risak, 'Die Mediation im Arbeitsrecht' 393ff.

[38] See below III.B.

[39] KindNamRÄG 2013 BGBl I 2013/15; see R Thunhart, 'Können Eltern gegen ihren Willen zur Zusammenarbeit mit außergerichtlichen Institutionen gezwungen werden?' [2011] *iFamZ—Interdisziplinäre Zeitschrift für Familienrecht* 139 and P Mayr, 'Case Note' [2012] *Österreichische Notariatszeitung* 347.

[40] See eg C Grabenwarter, *Europäische Menschrechtskonvention* (5th edn, Beck, 2012) s 24 comment 58 or H Fink, *Die sukzessive Zuständigkeit im Verfahren in Sozialrechtssachen* (Springer, 1995) 75f.

[41] Case C-317/08 *Alassini/Telecom Italia* [2010] *Zeitschrift für Konfliktmanagement* 92 (with a commentary by G Wagner) = [2010] *Europäische Zeitschrift für Wirtschaftsrecht* 550.

Even in cases of compulsory pre-trial ADR proceedings, the parties are free to directly refer their dispute to the court if it is clear from the start that the ADR mechanism does not grant the level of protection the ECHR requires.[42]

H. ADR and International (Soft) Law

The UNCITRAL Model Law on International Commercial Conciliation (2002) has not yet had any influence on Austrian law.[43]

There is also no obvious influence of the two Commission Recommendations of 1998 and 2001 concerning principles for out-of-court bodies resolving consumer disputes.[44] It can be assumed, however, that the Austrian conciliation bodies especially designed and reserved for consumer disputes, eg in the fields of telecommunication law,[45] postal law,[46] energy law[47] and travel law,[48] follow these Recommendations, although it should be noted once more that the list of notified conciliation bodies in Austria published online is neither comprehensive nor up to date.[49]

III. APPROACH TOWARDS SPECIFIC ADR INSTRUMENTS

A. Negotiation

In Austria, 'negotiation' in the context of this study is not subject to regulation at all. Academia and practice are only slowly starting to show an interest in this area.[50] There is no relevant case law. Therefore the latest publication dealing with the use of ADR

[42] See eg OGH 17 March 2005, 2 Ob 41/04z [2005] *Juristische Blätter* 801 = [2005] *ecolex—Fachzeitschrift für Wirtschaftsrecht* 915 = [2005] *Österreichisches Recht der Wirtschaft* 549 and <www.ris.bka.gv.at> (RIS-Justiz): RS0094154; P Mayr, 'Vereinsstreitigkeiten zwischen Schlichtungseinrichtung, Gericht und Schiedsgericht' 542f.

[43] (Briefly) addressed by S Perner and C Völkl, 'Conciliation, Mediation, ADR' [2003] *Österreichische Juristen-Zeitung* 495, 498ff.

[44] Commission Recommendation of 4 April 2001 on the principles for out-of-court bodies involved in the consensual resolution of consumer disputes [2001] OJ L109/56 and Commission Recommendation of 30 March 1998 on the principles applicable to the bodies responsible for out-of-court settlement of consumer disputes [1998] OJ L115/31; see P Mayr and M Weber, 'Europäische Initiativen zur Förderung der alternativen Streitbeilegung' [2007] *Zeitschrift für Rechtsvergleichung* 165ff.

[45] See s 122 Telecommunication Act 2003 (Telekommunikationsgesetz, TKG) BGBl I 2003/70.

[46] See s 53 Postal Law (Postmarktgesetz, PMG) BGBl I 2009/123.

[47] See s 26 Energy Control Act (Energie-Control-Gesetz, E-ControlG) BGBl I 2010/110.

[48] See s 78a Railroad Act (Eisenbahngesetz 1957) BGBl 1957/60 as amended by BGBl I 2006/125 and s 139a Aviation Act (Luftfahrtgesetz) BGBl 1957/253 as amended by BGBl I 2006/88.

[49] This list contains 15 institutions which fulfil the requirements of recommendation 98/257/EC. See <www.europakonsument.at> and above n 5.

[50] See B Birnbaum and M Allmayer-Beck, 'Konfliktlösung ohne gerichtliche Entscheidung durch Verhandeln und Mediation' [1997] *Österreichisches Anwaltsblatt* 612; I Greiter, *Kreativität bei Verhandlungen und im Alltag* (Manz, 2001); 'Kommunikation und Rhetorik für den Anwalt in der täglichen Praxis' [2010] *Österreichisches Anwaltsblatt* 361 and 474; G Kreuzbauer, 'Ausbildung in juristischer Argumentation und Rhetorik' in E Schweighofer et al (eds), *Informationstechnik in der juristischen Realität* (Verlag Österreich, 2004) 57; E Schäfer, 'Schiedsgerichtsbarkeit und Mediation' in H Torggler (ed), *Praxishandbuch Schiedsgerichtsbarkeit* (Nomos, 2007) 9ff; see also C Bouhafa, R Fucik, S Kleindienst-Passweg and R Rath, *Verhandeln vor Gericht* (Verlag Österreich, 2011).

in Austria rightly pointed out that—except in the field of mediation—ADR is hardly existent in Austria.[51]

Generally it can be said that the rules applying to mediation and conciliation also seem appropriate for the area of negotiation; therefore an analogous application of the respective rules seems possible.

Austrian substantive law knows a form of liability in the pre-contractual stage (*culpa in contrahendo*) if certain duties of disclosure or duties of care are infringed during negotiation or contract preparation. This area of law is mainly defined by case law. One possibility leading to pre-contractual liability is the case that one of the parties abstains from concluding a contract despite having left no doubt that the contract would be concluded. This concept could possibly also be invoked in regard to negotiations in the meaning of the current study where negotiations are broken off contrary to good faith.

There are no specific rules in regard to conflict of laws and jurisdiction.

B. Mediation

Mediation is the most comprehensively regulated form of alternative dispute resolution in Austria. The Austrian legislator tackled this field of law rather early, even before European activities were noticeable. Also, in practice, mediation is relied upon most often.

i. The Scope of Application of the Austrian Mediation Laws

In 2003, the Austrian Parliament enacted a Civil Mediation Act (Zivilrechts-Mediationsgesetz, ZivMediatG),[52] which entered into force on 1 May 2004 and has not been changed since.[53]

According to the legislative materials, the primary goal of the new law was to create a legal framework for mediation safeguarding the interests of both clients and qualified mediators.[54]

The law, therefore, does not attempt to comprehensively regulate mediation and its procedure but, rather, aims to provide for a high-quality standard. After a few

[51] M Allmayer-Beck, 'Außergerichtliche Streitbeilegung—ADR, das unbekannte Wesen' [2011] *Österreichisches Anwaltsblatt* 421.

[52] BGBl I 2003/29; see S Ferz and E Filler, *Mediation* (Wiener Universitätsverlag, 2003) and G Falk and G Koren, *Zivilrechts-Mediationsgesetz* (Verlag Österreich, 2005); see also G Hopf, 'Das Zivilrechts-Mediations-Gesetz' [2004] *Österreichische Juristen-Zeitung* 41; P Oberhammer and T Domej, 'Ein rechtlicher Rahmen für die Mediation in Österreich' [2003] *Zeitschrift für Konfliktmanagement* 144; M Roth and K Markowetz, 'Bundesgesetz über Mediation in Zivilrechtsachen—Ein erster Überblick über die neuen Bestimmungen' [2004] *Juristische Blätter* 296; Markus Roth and D Gherdane, 'Österreich' in K Hopt and F Steffek (eds), *Mediation* (Mohr Siebeck, 2008) 105; B Laukemann, 'Das österreichische Mediationsgesetz: Eine Standortbestimmung im Lichte seiner Regelungsstruktur und praktischen Bewährung' [2007] *Internationale Zeitschrift für Zivilprozess* 91, all with further references.

[53] The Principality of Liechtenstein has enacted a Civil Mediation Act which is identical with the Austrian regulation; LGBl (Official Journal of the Principality of Liechtenstein) 2005/31; in force 1 May 2005; see P Mayr, 'Die Mediationsgesetze von Österreich und Liechtenstein' [2008] *Liechtensteinische Juristen-Zeitung* 90.

[54] See the legislative materials (ErläutRV 24 BlgNR 22. GP 1).

general provisions (sections 1–3), it deals with the establishment of an advisory board for mediation (sections 4–7); the prerequisites for registration as a mediator and the procedure leading to registration, as well as the administration of the list of mediators (sections 8–14); the prerequisites and the procedure leading to the registration of vocational institutions and vocational preparation courses for mediation in civil matters, as well as the administration of the relevant list (sections 23–28); the rights and duties of the registered mediators (sections 15–21); and finally the effects of mediation on prescription periods and other time limits (section 22).

Most of the provisions thus refer to registration and the rights and duties of registered mediators, not to the procedure itself. The majority of the rules of the Civil Mediation Act are mandatory; in particular, the rules regarding the duties of the mediator (section 16) cannot be amended by party agreement.

Mediation was introduced by law in the following fields: neighbour disputes (Article III Civil Law Amendment, ZivRÄG 2004),[55] the law of the disabled (section 15 of the Law Regarding the Equal Treatment of the Disabled)[56] and apprentice training (section 15 of the Law Regarding Apprentice Training).[57]

In practice, the most important field of activity concerns family matters. Furthermore, mediation is deployed in employment cases, education, building, housing, economy, environmental matters, etc,[58] ie also in fields to which the existing rules do not directly apply, as the Civil Mediation Act limits its scope to mediation in civil matters (section 1(1)). Of course, the rules are also followed in other mediation cases in practice. A general competence to introduce mediation in areas other than civil matters has so far been rejected by the Austrian federal legislature, as several cases fall within the legislative competence of the *Länder*.[59] The existing rules, however, seem appropriate to serve as an example for the regulation of mediation in other areas in the future.

In 2011 Austria enacted the EU Mediation Act in order to implement the Mediation Directive (which came into force on 1 May 2011).[60] In order to maintain the high

[55] See II.E.iv.

[56] See II.E.v.

[57] See II.E.vi.

[58] See eg s 16(2) Umweltverträglichkeitsprüfungsgesetz 2000 (Law Regarding Environmental Risk Assessments; BGBl 1993/697 as amended); S Ferz and J Pichler (eds), *Mediation im öffentlichen Bereich* (Verlag Österreich, 2003); A Jungbauer-Komarek and A Gobiet, *Konfliktlösung im Bauwesen und Projektmediation* (Neuer Wissenschaftlicher Verlag, 2005); S Ferz, 'Der Beitrag der Mediation zur Optimierung von Behördenverfahren im Anlagerecht' in F Merli and S Greimel (eds), *Optimierungspotenziale bei Behördenverfahren* (Linde, 2009) 99; M Allmayer-Beck, 'ADR im Wohnungseigentum—Gedanken eines österreichischen Rechtsanwalt-Mediators' [2003] *Zeitschrift für Konfliktmanagement* 260 and 'ADR im Wohnungseigentum' [2006], *immolex—Neues Miet- und Wohnrecht* 173; J Stabentheiner, 'Überlegungen zum Einsatz von Mediation im Wohnrecht' [2004] *Wohnrechtliche Blätter* 291; 'Mediation im Mietrecht?' in Österreichische Notariatskammer (ed), *Festschrift für Nikolaus Michalek zum 65. Geburtstag* (Manz, 2005) 373; C Kothbauer, 'Mediation im Mietrecht—Chancen und Grenzen' [2006] *immolex—Neues Miet- und Wohnrecht* 169 and many others, including recently B Gratz, 'Mediation im öffentlichen Bereich' [2012] *RFG—Recht & Finanzen für Gemeinden* 86.

[59] See G Hopf, 'Erfahrungen mit dem österreichischen Mediationsgesetz' [2010] *Rabels Zeitschrift für ausländisches und internationales Privatrecht* 759, 761f.

[60] BGBl I 2011/21; see B Kloiber, 'Die Mediations-Richtlinie und ihre Umsetzung in Österreich' [2011] *Zeitschrift für Rechtsvergleichung* 119; U Scheuer, 'Regelungen zur Mediation in Österreich nach Umsetzung der Mediations-Richtlinie' in R Fucik et al (eds), *Jahrbuch Zivilverfahrensrecht 2011* (Neuer Wissenschaftlicher Verlag, 2011) 197; 'Zum Stand der Mediation in Österreich' [2012] *Zeitschrift für Konfliktmanagement* 21; R Fucik, 'EU-MediatG und ZivMediatG—ein Überblick' [2011] *Österreichische Juristen-Zeitung* 941.

Austrian standard, it was only implemented to the extent required by the Directive.[61] Consequently, the new law only applies to cross-border disputes in civil and commercial matters (see Article 2 Mediation Directive). A tiny extension of the scope can be found in section 2(1) 1 no 5 EU Mediation Act, as the Austrian Law also includes Denmark.

The rest of the EU Mediation Act is rather restricted and more or less identical to the Directive: besides the scope of application (section 1) and definitions (section 2), it contains rules regarding the confidentiality of mediation (section 3) and the effects of mediation on prescription periods (section 4). In order to implement Article 6 Mediation Directive, the Austrian Civil Procedure Rules were amended, introducing a new section 433a ZPO: the result of mediation in civil matters can be the basis for a court settlement, which is then immediately enforceable.[62] As this rule is applicable not only to mediation in cross-border cases but to all kinds of mediation, it can actually be seen as an important step towards a greater emphasis of mediation in general.

According to the prevailing opinion, a valid mediation agreement (as well as a conciliation agreement) does not lead to a dismissal of a claim for formal reasons but on account of (momentary) unenforceability. However, in such cases the court does not act *ex officio* but only upon an application of the defendant.[63]

ii. The Duties of Mediators

The Austrian Civil Mediation Act regulates the duties of a mediator in great detail. Due to the scope of application of the Act, these duties only apply to mediators who are registered in the list of mediators of the Ministry of Justice. Registration is not reserved to certain professional groups; the rules of the Civil Mediation Act apply notwithstanding the profession of a mediator, and therefore apply to lawyers and non-lawyers in the same way; a certain quality standard is guaranteed by the registration process.

The most important rules are the following:

- Prohibition of remuneration for arranging mediation or recommending mediators (section 15(2)).
- Specification of relationships and conditions that endanger the neutrality of the mediator (section 16(1)).
- The mediator may act only upon agreement of the parties. He has the duty to inform the parties about the characteristics and legal consequences of mediation in

[61] See the legislative materials (ErläutRV 1055 BlgNR 24. GP 3 and JAB 1125 BlgNR 24.GP 1).

[62] See U Frauenberger-Pfeiler, 'Zur "Vollstreckbarmachung" von Mediationsvereinbarungen' in R Fucik et al (eds), *Jahrbuch Zivilverfahrensrecht 2010* (Neuer Wissenschaftlicher Verlag, 2011) 237; U Scheuer, 'Vollstreckbarer Mediationsvergleich und neue Regelungen für grenzüberschreitende Mediationsverfahren' [2011] *Zivilrecht aktuell* 147; U Frauenberger-Pfeiler and M Risak, 'Der prätorische Mediationsvergleich' [2012] *Österreichische Juristen-Zeitung* 798.

[63] C Hausmaninger in H Fasching and A Konecny (eds), *Kommentar zu den Zivilprozessgesetzen* vol IV/2, 2nd edn (Manz, 2007) s 581 ZPO comment 175ff and the relevant Austrian case law: OGH 23 May 2006, 4 Ob 54/06d (2006) *SZ—Entscheidungen des österreichischen Obersten Gerichtshofes in Zivilsachen* no 78; 2 September 2008, 8 ObA 28/08p [2009] *Österreichisches Recht der Wirtschaft* 99 with a commentary by P Gatternig and K Gatternig, 'Zulässigkeit und Wirkung von Schlichtungsvereinbarungen in Arbeitsverträgen' [2009] *Österreichisches Recht der Wirtschaft* 282; <www.ris.bka.gv.at> (RIS-Justiz): RS0033687 and RS0045298.

civil matters as well as the duty to personally, directly and impartially conduct the mediation according to good faith (section 16(3)).
- The mediator must inform the parties about the need to consult further experts, especially regarding legal questions, or on the question of how to formulate the mediation outcome in order to achieve the intended result (section 16(3)).
- The mediator has duties of documentation regarding the beginning, the conduct and the termination of mediation (section 17(1)).
- Upon the parties' request, the mediator must set out the mediation results, including the steps required to realise these results, in writing (section 17(2)).
- The mediator has a strict duty of confidentiality regarding all information gained during mediation (section 18).
- It is compulsory for the mediator to possess personal liability insurance (section 19).
- The mediator has to attend continuing education (section 20).

In case of a breach of these duties, the penal provisions (sections 31 and 32) apply. In certain cases it is also possible to have mediators removed from the list of mediators (section 14).

Sections 9 and 10 the Civil Mediation Act state a few general prerequisites the mediator has to fulfil, such as having obtained a certain age, trustworthiness and carrying compulsory insurance. Section 10 addresses qualifications which have to be safeguarded by attending a certain number of courses during the training of future mediators.

The EU Mediation Act, on the other hand, only contains a duty of confidentiality (section 3), but this applies to both non-registered and registered mediators. The latter also have to act in conformity with the Civil Mediation Act (section 5(1) EU Mediation Act). Non-registered mediators who conduct mediation in cross-border disputes have to inform the parties of the fact that they are not subject to the national rules (section 5(2) EU Mediation Act).

Mediators are liable according to the general rules of civil law. They are experts in the meaning of section 1299 of the Austrian General Civil Code and bear an increased duty of care.[64]

iii. The Duties of the Parties

The Austrian laws on mediation do not contain duties of the parties. Even if otherwise agreed, each party can withdraw from the mediation at any time. This derives from section 16(2) Civil Mediation Act, according to which the mediator can act only upon agreement of the parties, and from section 17(1) Civil Mediation Act, according to which mediation terminates if one of the parties declares so.

Remuneration is not regulated, but is left to party agreement. It will normally be dealt with in the contract of services concluded with the mediator.

[64] See C Völkl and S Perner, 'Die Haftung von Schiedsrichtern und Mediatoren' [2006] *Österreichische Notariatszeitung* 129, 134f.

iv. Enforceability of Meditation Agreements

Generally, a mediation agreement constitutes an out-of-court settlement (section 1380 ABGB), which is not immediately enforceable. The state courts do not automatically supervise such an agreement.

With the introduction of the new section 433a ZPO (in force since 1 May 2011), it is now possible to conclude a court settlement with every regional court (Bezirksgericht) regarding the contents of a written mediation agreement without having to file a claim first. In this respect, the court bears the same rights and duties as with an ordinary court settlement.[65]

Like any other court settlement, a mediation settlement is immediately enforceable (section 1 no 5 Enforcement Act, Exekutionsordnung, EO).

v. Court-based Mediation Programmes

Austria has not so far introduced any court-based mediation programmes. The Austrian Civil Mediation Act does not touch upon the relationship between mediation and court procedure, and therefore does not distinguish at all between court mediation, out-of-court mediation and mediation initiated by the court.[66]

Two provisions are relevant in this respect, although it should be pointed out that they do not constitute real duties to transfer a case to ADR: according to section 204(1) second sentence ZPO, the court must point out the possibility of mediation and other conciliation bodies when trying to achieve a court settlement. Moreover, section 29 AußStrG regulates the possibility of interrupting the proceedings if an amicable agreement of the parties achieved by an ADR institution can be expected. A further step towards a real referral, however, is the new section 107(3) no 2 AußStrG, which gives the judge the opportunity to at least order an initial meeting to discuss ADR.[67]

vi. Cross-border Conflicts and Mediation

It has already been mentioned that the Civil Mediation Act (also) applies to cross-border mediation exercised by registered mediators (section 5(1) EU Mediation Act). It is only in regard to cross-border disputes according to Article 2 Mediation Directive and section 2(1) no 3 EU Mediation Act that the rules of the EU Mediation Act also apply. The registered mediator has a duty to inform the parties in this respect.

[65] See n 62 and B Kloiber, 'Mediations-Richtlinie und ihre Umsetzung in Österreich' 126f, as well as G Kodek in H Fasching and A Konecny (eds), *Kommentar zu den Zivilprozessgesetzen* vol III, 2nd edn (Manz, 2004) s 433 ZPO comment 19.

[66] See G Hopf, 'Erfahrungen mit dem österreichischen Mediationsgesetz' 762ff, 764.

[67] KindNamRÄG 2013 BGBl I 2013/15; see II.F and E Gitschthaler (ed), *Kindschafts- und Namensrechts-Änderungsgesetz 2013* (Manz, 2013); P Barth, A Deixler-Hübner and G Jelinek (eds), *Handbuch des neuen Kindschaftsrechts- und Namensrechts* (Linde, 2013).

C. Conciliation

i. General

There are not many legal norms regarding conciliation in Austria. Only the Law Regarding Private Associations (VerG) contains a rather precise provision as already mentioned above in II.E.ii: according to section 8(1), the articles of association have to provide for a conciliation procedure. Moreover, the articles have to contain rules on the composition of the conciliation body and the appointment of its members, as well as their impartiality. The articles of association also have to address the right of both parties of a dispute to be heard (section 8(2) VerG).

In other fields of law, conciliation is only partly regulated: sometimes the rules just deal with the suspension of prescription periods (eg medical malpractice law), sometimes the delay of the maturity date is subjected to regulation (eg in energy law). The competences of the conciliation bodies are similarly different: sometimes the conciliation body only tries to encourage the parties to come to an amicable solution or reports its opinion to the parties. Very often the respective laws contain an obligation of the affected enterprise to co-operate and to disclose information (eg in telecommunication and postal law).

The Act Regarding Energy Control (Energie-Control-Gesetz) limits the maximum duration of a conciliation procedure to six weeks, within which an amicable solution is to be found. In consumer cases, the Austrian Federal Chamber of Labour (Bundesarbeitskammer) participates in the proceedings. The Law Regarding E-Control also expressly regulates the participation of experts in the conciliation proceedings.

The respective conciliation bodies enact individual rules of procedure that are more or less identical. It is important to state that, as a general rule, conciliation never constitutes an obstacle to proceedings before the state courts. If an amicable solution is not found earlier, the conciliation procedure normally ends with the proposal of a solution by the respective conciliation body. The acceptance of such a proposal constitutes an out-of-court settlement. Otherwise the parties are free to initiate court proceedings. In order to speed up the conciliation proceedings, time limits are kept rather short.

All conciliation mechanisms mentioned are free of cost; however, parties have to bear their own costs. Representation (eg by a lawyer or a consumer organisation) is possible.

ii. The Duties of the Conciliator

Besides the general duty to try to achieve an amicable solution or to propose such a solution to the parties, Austrian law has not established special duties for the members of a conciliation body. Some obligations might, of course, derive from the general principles of private law.

iii. Scopes of Application, International Law and Cross-border Situations

Conciliation is mandatory in housing law and neighbour relations, as well as regarding disputes within private associations, and therefore plays a significant role in these areas.[68] It is also common in respect of conflicts between doctors and patients.[69] Consumer disputes in the fields of telecommunication, energy and transport of persons are additional important areas of conciliation, the respective rules being almost identical.[70]

As pointed out above (II.H), there is no noticeable influence of the UNCITRAL Model Law on International Commercial Conciliation;[71] nor have the Commission Recommendations been followed. Questions regarding the applicable law and questions of jurisdiction are similarly not subject to specific regulation in Austria.

D. Expert Opinions

i. General

Expert opinions are deployed in different areas of the law, mainly in insurance contract law, company law, plant engineering projects (*Anlagebauprojekte*) and the international sale of goods.[72] They appear in different forms, depending on whether their scope is to (1) amend an existing contract or the law (*vertragsergänzende, vertrags- oder rechtsabändernde Schiedsgutachtenverträge*) or (2) whether they are designed to determine certain facts (*feststellende Schiedsgutachtenverträge*). The legal nature of expert opinions has been discussed extensively for a long time. They cannot be classified clearly, instead existing at the interface between substantive and procedural law. There is common consensus in Austria that the first group is substantive in nature.[73] Regarding the other group, there is disagreement among scholars. Further, the classification as either substantive or procedural has consequences with regard to their substantive validity and their treatment in a subsequent civil or arbitral process, as well as regarding the application of principles of procedural law.[74] The Austrian Supreme Court (Oberster Gerichtshof, OGH), on the other hand, classifies all expert opinions as substantive and consequently rejects the application of the Austrian rules of procedure.[75]

[68] See above II.E.iii and iv.

[69] See A Leischner, *Streitbeilegung in medizinischen Haftungsfällen* (Manz, 2007); B Jahn, *Außergerichtliche Konfliktlösung im Gesundheitswesen* (Manz, 2009); P Mayr, 'Aktuelle Entwicklungen und Probleme bei den Rechtsschutzalternativen' 392f.

[70] Dazu etwa P Mayr, 'Aktuelle Entwicklungen und Probleme bei den Rechtsschutzalternativen' 396ff.

[71] See <www.uncitral.org/pdf/english/texts/arbitration/ml-conc/03-90953_Ebook.pdf>.

[72] C Koller in C Liebscher, P Oberhammer and W Rechberger (eds), *Schiedsverfahrensrecht* I (Springer, 2012) no 3/8.

[73] This is the prevailing opinion in Austria; see B Garger, *Das Schiedsgutachtenrecht* (Manz, 1996) 61f, 135; C Hausmaninger in H Fasching and A Konecny (eds), *Kommentar zu den Zivilprozessgesetzen* vol IV/2, 2nd edn (Manz, 2007) s 581 ZPO comment 140f; see also H Fasching, *Lehrbuch des österreichischen Zivilprozessrechts*, 2nd edn (Manz, 1990) no 2168.

[74] The most convincing opinion being probably expressed by B Garger, who stated that such expert opinions constitute a special type of contract, partly procedural partly substantive in nature: B Garger, *Schiedsgutachtenrecht* 185ff and B Garger, *Das Sachverständigenverfahren im Versicherungsvertragsrecht* (Springer, 2002) 87f. C Hausmaninger in H Fasching and A Konecny (eds), *Kommentar zu den Zivilprozessgesetzen* vol IV/2, 2nd edn (Manz, 2007) s 581 ZPO comment 141 states that such expert opinions are procedural agreements.

[75] OGH 21 April 1966, 1 Ob 71/66 SZ—*Entscheidungen des österreichischen Obersten Gerichtshofes in Zivilsachen* vol 39 no 75; 12 October 1978, 7 Ob 657/78 SZ—*Entscheidungen des österreichischen Obersten*

It is sometimes difficult to distinguish agreements to rely on expert opinions from arbitration agreements. Whereas the latter aim at deciding a dispute, the former only provide the basis for a decision.[76] The interpretation as one or the other largely depends on the interpretation of the parties' intentions.[77]

ii. Duties of the Expert and their Enforcement, Special Procedural Rules (Fair Procedure)

The duties (and rights) of the expert are determined in the contract concluded between the expert and the parties (*Schiedsgutachtervertrag*). This is normally a contract of service, as the expert owes a certain outcome.[78] In case of a breach of such a contract, the general rules of civil law apply. This mainly regards the rules on late performance (sections 918ff ABGB), bad performance (sections 922ff ABGB) and contractual damages (sections 1293ff ABGB). According to section 1299 ABGB, the expert bears an increased duty of care.

The outcome of an expert opinion generally binds the parties and the court. Anything else would contradict the underlying aim of avoiding long and costly court proceedings. The discussion of the nature of the binding effect is colourful and reflects the different viewpoints of the legal nature of the expert opinion itself. In the view of the Austrian Supreme Court, the expert opinion binds the parties like a contractual agreement.[79] The parties can make this effect dependent on certain prerequisites; they can also agree that there is no binding effect at all.[80] If there is no such agreement, the expert opinion cannot be challenged like an ordinary contract,[81] but only in especially severe cases. If an amending expert opinion constitutes an infringement of the law or contradicts the principles of good faith (in the meaning of section 879 ABGB), or if it is obviously unfair (*offenbar unbillig*), it can be challenged before the civil courts.[82] An expert opinion determining certain facts can be challenged if it is obviously incorrect; it is not, however, automatically void if it is wrong solely because of the use of wrong methods, wrong materials or because of calculation errors.[83] If the expert opinion is

Gerichtshofes in Zivilsachen vol 51 no 139; 26 July 1996, 1 Ob 501/96 *SZ—Entscheidungen des österreichischen Obersten Gerichtshofes in Zivilsachen* vol 69 no 168; 2 September 2009, 7 Ob 75/09v, *Versicherungsrechtliche Entscheidungen* no 2305.

[76] C Koller in C Liebscher, P Oberhammer and W Rechberger (eds), *Schiedsverfahrensrecht* vol I no 3/12.

[77] C Koller in C Liebscher, P Oberhammer and W Rechberger (eds), *Schiedsverfahrensrecht* vol I no 3/15, who provides a lot of examples.

[78] See B Garger, *Sachverständigenverfahren* 122ff.

[79] OGH 26 July 1996, 1 Ob 501/96 *SZ—Entscheidungen des österreichischen Obersten Gerichtshofes in Zivilsachen* vol 69 no 168; 17 December 2007, 2 Ob 236/07f [2008] *Österreichisches Recht der Wirtschaft* 462.

[80] C Koller in C Liebscher, P Oberhammer and W Rechberger (eds), *Schiedsverfahrensrecht* vol I no 3/21.

[81] See eg OGH 26 July 1996, 1 Ob 501/96, *SZ—Entscheidungen des österreichischen Obersten Gerichtshofes in Zivilsachen* vol 69 no 168 and <www.ris.bka.gv.at> (RIS-Justiz): RS0106359; C Hausmaninger in H Fasching and A Konecny (eds), *Kommentar zu den Zivilprozessgesetzen* vol IV/2, 2nd edn (Manz, 2007) s 581 ZPO comments 153 and 157.

[82] C Koller in C Liebscher, P Oberhammer and W Rechberger (eds), *Schiedsverfahrensrecht* vol I no 3/22.

[83] See recently OGH 27 April 2011, 9 Ob 42/10g [2011] *Österreichisches Recht der Wirtschaft* 526; earlier OGH 26 July 1996, 1 Ob 501/96 *SZ—Entscheidungen des österreichischen Obersten Gerichtshofes in Zivilsachen* vol 69 no 168; see also <www.ris.bka.gv.at> (RIS-Justiz): RS0016769, RS0106360, RS0081234; s 64(2) of the Insurance Contract Act (VersVG, Versicherungsvertragsgesetz).

void and the parties have not agreed on a different mode, the determination of facts falls into the responsibility of the court.[84]

According to the Austrian Supreme Court, the rules of arbitration are not applicable to expert opinions, unless the parties agree otherwise.[85] There is also no successive competence of the civil courts.[86] Many authors argue, however, that some procedural principles should also apply to expert opinions, among them the principle of the impartiality of the expert, the parties' right to be heard and the parties' right to participate in the collection of evidence as well as to comment on the evidence. They consequently argue for the possibility of challenging the expert opinion in case of a breach of these fundamental principles.[87]

iii. Scope of Application, Cross-border Situations

It has already been described under subsection (i) that expert opinions are deployed in several areas of the law in Austria.[88] They are most important, as a practical matter, in the insurance sector.[89] Three provisions of the Austrian Insurance Contract Act (Versicherungsvertragsgesetz, VersVG 1958)[90] contain explicit rules—namely section 64, regarding insurance other than life assurance; section 158l, regarding insurance for legal expenses; and section 184, regarding accident insurance—mainly regulating the scope of the expert opinion and repeating the general principles mentioned above. The Austrian insurance sector knows numerous sets of general terms and conditions[91] for the various sectors of non-life insurance[92] which are not binding but serve as a model for the individual contracts. Many of them contain rules on expert opinions. These rules, however, only apply if they become part of the agreement. The various general terms and conditions mainly regulate the following: the requirement that the agreement be in writing, the subsidiary application of the procedural rules of arbitration, and the scope and limits of expert opinions. Sometimes they also contain confidentiality duties; sometimes the experts have to be chosen from among a certain professional group; sometimes there are model rules relating to cost-bearing.

When determining the applicable law, the legal nature of expert opinions has to be taken into consideration. As far as clearly substantive content is concerned, an expert opinion is governed by the law of the state with the closest connection (see section 36 IPRG and Article 4 Rome I Regulation). In cases with a close connection to an existing

[84] This is the prevailing opinion, although Austrian law lacks a provision like the German Civil Code s 319(1).

[85] Which is common in the insurance industry other than life assurance, see the standard terms and conditions (Art 9(2) ABS): 'If not regulated differently, the rules of the ZPO regarding arbitration apply'.

[86] C Hausmaninger in H Fasching and A Konecny (eds), *Kommentar zu den Zivilprozessgesetzen* vol IV/2, 2nd edn (Manz, 2007) s 581 ZPO comment 155.

[87] C Hausmaninger in H Fasching and A Konecny (eds), *Kommentar zu den Zivilprozessgesetzen* vol IV/2, 2nd edn (Manz, 2007) s 581 ZPO comment 156; H Fasching, *Lehrbuch des österreichischen Zivilprozessrechts*, 2nd edn (Manz, 1990) no 2169. See also OGH 24 September 1981, 7 Ob 623/81 (1982) *Österreichische Juristenzeitung* EvBl no 77; <www.ris.bka.gv.at> (RIS-Justiz): RS0045277.

[88] See B Garger, *Schiedsgutachtenrecht* 12ff; C Hausmaninger in H Fasching and A Konecny (eds), *Kommentar zu den Zivilprozessgesetzen* vol IV/2, 2nd edn (Manz, 2007) s 581 ZPO comment 150.

[89] For a detailed discussion see B Garger, *Sachverständigenverfahren*.

[90] BGBl 1959/2.

[91] See <www.vvo.at/musterbedingungen/index.php>.

[92] There are also standardised terms regarding life assurance with a slightly different concept, which shall not be described here.

contractual relationship between the parties, the outcome can therefore also be that the expert opinion is governed by the law that is applicable to this contract. For its procedural content, the governing law can only be the *lex fori*.

E. Arbitration

i. General

In 2006, the Austrian legislator enacted the Schiedsrechts-Änderungsgesetz 2006,[93] which completely restructured the rules applying to arbitration (sections 577–618 ZPO).[94] The reform aimed at creating a modern arbitration law according to the example of the UNCITRAL Model Law on International Commercial Arbitration. The legislature, however, wanted to provide not only for a legal framework for international commercial arbitration, but also for other arbitral procedures.[95] The UNCITRAL Model Law was followed to a great extent.

ii. Arbitration Procedure

In general, the mode of the arbitration procedure is subject to party agreement. If there is no agreement, the arbitral tribunal acts according to sections 594ff ZPO and on its own discretion (section 594(1) 1 ZPO).

There are, however, also a few mandatory provisions which the parties cannot deviate from: according to section 594(2) ZPO, the parties have to be treated in a fair way and every party has the right to be heard (see Article 6 ECHR). Furthermore, the right of the parties to be represented or to seek consultation by third parties must neither be excluded nor restricted (section 594(2) ZPO).

If the existing procedural law or the agreement regarding the mode of procedure is infringed, the parties have an obligation to report the infringement. If an infringement is not immediately reported, it cannot be challenged later in the proceedings (section 570 ZPO). Infringements of mandatory provisions need not be reported; they can still lead to an action for annulment later.

In certain cases of breach of fundamental procedural rights (section 611(2) ZPO), the decision of the arbitral tribunal has to be annulled by the state courts;[96] this occurs normally upon application of a party (action for annulment according to section 611

[93] BGBl I 2006/7; for a detailed discussion see C Hausmaninger in H Fasching and A Konecny (eds), *Kommentar zu den Zivilprozessgesetzen* vol IV/2, 2nd edn (Manz, 2007) and recently C Liebscher, P Oberhammer and W Rechberger (eds), *Schiedsverfahrensrecht* vol I (Springer, 2012), as well as a list of literature in G Kodek and P Mayr, *Zivilprozessrecht* (facultas, 2011) before no 1106.

[94] The Principality of Liechtenstein soon took the Austrian reform as an example to enact almost identical rules in Liechtenstein. See P Mayr, 'Das neue Schiedsverfahrensrecht in Liechtenstein' [2010] *Jus & News* 297 and [2011] *Jus & News* 17; H Schumacher, 'Das neue Schiedsverfahren' [2011] *Liechtensteinische Juristen-Zeitung* 105.

[95] See the legislative materials: ErläutRV 1158 BlgNR 22. GP 1 and JAB 1236 BlgNR 22.GP 1.

[96] Reasons for annulment regard questions of competence, whether the subject matter can be dealt with by way of arbitration (s 611(2) no 1 and 3 ZPO), the deprivation of parties' procedural rights (s 611(2) no 2 ZPO), the composition of the arbitral tribunal (s 611(2) no 4 ZPO) or *ordre public* reasons (s 611(2) no 5 and 8 ZPO), as well as any reason which would enable the reopening of civil proceedings according to s 530 ZPO (s 611(2) no 6 ZPO).

ZPO), but in two cases—if the matter cannot be subject to arbitration by law or if the decision constitutes an infringement of the Austrian *ordre public*—can also occur *ex officio* (section 613 ZPO).

iii. Enforcement

An arbitral award has the same force as a non-appealable decision of the court (section 607 ZPO). According to the Austrian Enforcement Act, an Austrian arbitral award is immediately enforceable (section 1 no 16 EO). Recognition and enforcement of foreign arbitral awards are governed by section 614 ZPO and sections 79 ff EO, unless there are special conventions or special rules of EU law. The New York Convention on the Recognition and Enforcement of Foreign Arbitral Awards of 10 June 1958 is also important in this respect.[97]

iv. Cross-border Situations

The Austrian rules regarding arbitration apply to national as well as cross-border cases. The scope of application of section 577 ZPO is generally[98] determined by the principle of territoriality: if the parties have agreed on an arbitral tribunal situated in Austria, this tribunal has to apply the Austrian arbitration rules. Regarding the applicable substantive law, section 603 ZPO provides for the primary application of the rules the parties have agreed upon, which is generally seen as an agreement to apply the rules of law in force other than the rules of private international law. In the absence of a choice, the arbitral tribunal has to apply the rules it thinks are appropriate (section 603(2) ZPO).

IV. POLICY QUESTIONS

The question whether ADR should be regulated at all or left unregulated has to be seen against the background that ADR is, after all, meant to be the *alternative* to traditional, state-regulated dispute resolution. Therefore one might consider that ADR should not be subject to legislation at all but, rather, be left to the self-regulation of the market. The last few decades have shown, however, that ADR has become increasingly popular and has gained more and more importance—not so much in Austria, but definitely on an international level. Therefore a certain amount of regulation (such as the Austrian example of mediation) seems advisable in order to avoid undesirable developments and malpractice.

In our view and from what is possible at the moment in Austria, regulation should be limited to providing a general framework. This general legal framework should also, however, provide for certain principles of procedure in the field of ADR.

In our view, the state—besides creating the said framework—ought to stay with

[97] Ratified by Austria in 1961: BGBl 1961/200; see D Czernich, *New Yorker Schiedsübereinkommen* (LexisNexis, 2008).

[98] Some (Austrian) rules referred to in s 577(2) ZPO are applicable even if the seat of the arbitral tribunal is not in Austria or has not been determined yet.

its traditional core task in the form of a vertical approach, ie the responsibility to provide for and encourage a well-functioning form of traditional civil litigation as a last resort for conflict resolution. This main task, however, should not be an obstacle to the setting up of a framework regulation for ADR. The state should also provide for a regulation of the interrelation between state court proceedings and ADR, as well as for the supervision of the quality of ADR services.[99]

An important policy argument regards the costs of ADR in civil law: in our view, the costs should generally be borne by the parties according to their individual agreement, which can of course also state that one party bears all the costs. In cases of compulsory pre-trial, ADR the state should provide for a form of legal aid, which is already the case in neighbour disputes.[100] Also, in certain other cases of optional ADR a certain form of financial support would seem favourable, especially in regard to the fact that referring a case to ADR always contributes to a reduction of the workload of the courts.[101]

As far as procedural guarantees are concerned, we think that the state should provide for a framework and a kind of minimum guarantee that the use of ADR does not deprive the parties of their otherwise guaranteed rights and does not constitute procedural disadvantages. Because of the Austrian constitutional principle of legality (Article 18 of the Austrian Constitution, Bundes-Verfassungsgesetz, B-VG), this framework regulation and also all further state enhancement generally need a basis in law (enacted by the Austrian Parliament or the European legislature), especially as general principles of procedure are concerned. Rarely, the rules are not based on a specific law but triggered by model projects of the Ministry of Justice. Austrian Mediation is, for instance, based on a model project of the 1990s.

Partly, the state rules have to be mandatory (eg as far as the principle of fair trial is regarded). They can, however, also be designed as optional measures that the parties and/or the court can choose as an alternative, such as with arbitration. Regarding cross-border disputes, a model law seems desirable.

When it comes to effectively supporting parties in deciding whether and in which stage of the proceedings to use ADR, we find it difficult to establish and determine general criteria. Maybe the personal relationships of the parties could help to distinguish the suitableness of the respective form of dispute resolution ('personal' or 'non-personal' conflicts). Because of the described difficulties, the Austrian legislature has up to now chosen a rather flexible approach in section 204(1) second sentence ZPO: the court has to point out relevant ADR schemes if that step 'seems appropriate'. In non-contested proceedings the court can also interrupt the proceedings in cases in which an 'amicable solution using a form of ADR can be expected' (section 29(1) AußStrG; rules on non-contested procedures). The new section 107(3) AußStrG will go even slightly further, as it can lead to a mandatory first consideration of ADR. It is a general tendency in Austria to place conflicts between parties who will continue to have a relationship after the conflict resolution into the forum of non-contested

[99] See eg H Unberath, 'Auf dem Weg zu einer differenzierten Streitkultur—Neue gesetzliche Rahmenbedingungen für die alternative Konfliktlösung' [2010] *Juristenzeitung* 975, 978.

[100] See ss 64b and 433 ZPO.

[101] Such as in s 39c of the Law Regarding the Financial Support of Families (Familienlastenausgleichsgesetz, FLAG; see n 10), which sets forth that mediation can be financially supported by the state.

proceedings, which are characterised by a special focus on amicable conflict solution.[102] It must not be forgotten, however, that they are still court proceedings and must not be mistaken as a form of ADR.

On the other hand, Austria is still reluctant to introduce compulsory ADR in the pre-trial stage. Respective rules can be found in neighbour relations and housing law, as well as the law of liberal professions (see II.C). It seems realistic to perhaps expand these rules to the fields of marriage and family law. The introduction of a general duty to use ADR in the pre-trial stage, however, is not advisable in our view. History has shown that such a measure bears the danger that the usage of ADR will turn into a mere time- and cost-consuming formality, which would thus hurt the image of ADR. Instead, we favour the voluntary use of ADR rather than a system of state intervention in the form of sanctions in general.

In this respect, the main task of the state is to ensure that parties relying on ADR do not suffer disadvantages. The state has to guarantee the impartiality of the ADR institutions and the right to fair trial (in the meaning of Article 6 ECHR) as two core principles. It is also necessary to provide for a regulation of the effects of ADR on prescription periods and other time limits. They should be interrupted or suspended in the same way as if court proceedings were initiated.

The ideal case would be that the parties can refer their dispute voluntarily to the relevant ADR institution if a better solution can be expected. A necessary prerequisite in that respect is appropriate and objective information on how ADR works in general as well as on the particular ADR institution at issue. The duty to provide such general information should in our view lie with the state, and should be made available online and in leaflets (all free of cost). It should also include a list of all ADR institutions that meet a certain standard. Moreover, the state should introduce a form of financial support for such institutions so that conflict resolution can ideally be offered free of cost.

One problem is that it is certainly difficult to ascertain whether the parties have been properly informed about the existence of ADR alternatives, especially if the parties have voluntarily chosen to refer their conflict to the court and not—despite its appropriateness—to the relevant ADR institution. A possible solution in this respect could be to introduce a duty of the representing lawyers to document in their pleadings that an attempt to find an amicable solution has taken place and failed and/or why such an attempt has not been made. This duty would have to be accompanied by certain sanctions in case of breach (eg regarding the restitution of costs) in order to prevent lawyers from simply including a standardised phrase. In our view, however, it is not justified to introduce a general cost sanction for parties who actively decide against using ADR measures after having been properly informed: generally, the immediate referral of a conflict to a court must not be sanctioned. A better way to sanction the non-usage of ADR can possibly be found in the field of legal aid. When assessing whether a party shall be granted legal aid in court proceedings, the court could take into consideration whether the party has referred the conflict to the appropriate ADR institution first and/or whether the party has rejected the involvement of such an institution without proper reasons.

[102] See eg P Mayr and R Fucik, *Das neue Verfahren außer Streitsachen* (3rd edn, facultas, 2006) nos 16f and 114.

A genuine duty to refer a dispute to ADR before being able to initiate court proceedings should, however, be introduced only in special circumstances.

BIBLIOGRAPHY

Adamovich, LK, Funk, B-C and Holzinger, G, *Österreichisches Staatsrecht* vol 2 (Springer, 1998)

Allmayer-Beck, M, 'ADR im Wohnungseigentum—Gedanken eines österreichischen Rechtsanwalt-Mediators' [2003] *Zeitschrift für Konfliktmanagement* 260ff

Allmayer-Beck, M, 'ADR im Wohnungseigentum' [2006] *immolex—Neues Miet- und Wohnrecht* 173ff

Allmayer-Beck, M, 'Außergerichtliche Streitbeilegung—ADR, das unbekannte Wesen' [2011] *Österreichisches Anwaltsblatt* 421ff

Auer, I, 'Mediation—die Lösung von Nachbarkonflikten' [2012] *immolex—Neues Miet- und Wohnrecht* 274ff

Bajons, E-M, 'Außergerichtliche Güteverfahren als Mittel der Prozessvermeidung und Konfliktlösung' [1984] *Österreichische Juristen-Zeitung* 368ff

Barth, P, Deixler-Hübner, A and Jelinek, G (eds), *Handbuch des neuen Kindschaftsrechts- und Namensrechts* (Linde, 2013)

Birnbaum, B and Allmayer-Beck, M, 'Konfliktlösung ohne gerichtliche Entscheidung durch Verhandeln und Mediation' [1997] *Österreichisches Anwaltsblatt* 612ff

Bouhafa, C, Fucik, R, Kleindienst-Passweg, S and Rath, R-M, *Verhandeln vor Gericht* (Verlag Österreich, 2011)

Burger, F, '10 Stolpersteine auf dem Weg zum Ausbildungsübertritt' [2010] *Zeitschrift für Arbeits- und Sozialrecht* 162ff

Czernich, D, *New Yorker Schiedsübereinkommen* (LexisNexis, 2008)

Falk, G and Koren, G, *Zivilrechts-Mediationsgesetz* (Verlag Österreich, 2005)

Fasching, HW, *Lehrbuch des österreichischen Zivilprozessrechts* (2nd edn, Manz, 1990)

Fasching, HW and Konecny, A (eds), *Kommentar zu den Zivilprozessgesetzen* vol III (2nd edn, Manz, 2004)

Fasching, HW and Konecny, A (eds), *Kommentar zu den Zivilprozessgesetzen* vol IV/2 (2nd edn, Manz, 2007)

Feil, E and Wennig, F, *Anwaltsrecht* (7th edn, Linde, 2012)

Ferz, S, 'Der Beitrag der Mediation zur Optimierung von Behördenverfahren im Anlagerecht' in F Merli and S Greimel (eds), *Optimierungspotenziale bei Behördenverfahren* (Linde, 2009) 99ff

Ferz, S and Filler, E, *Mediation* (Wiener Universitätsverlag, 2003)

Ferz, S and Pichler, J (eds), *Mediation im öffentlichen Bereich* (Verlag Österreich, 2003)

Fink, H, *Die sukzessive Zuständigkeit im Verfahren in Sozialrechtssachen* (Springer, 1995)

Frauenberger-Pfeiler, U, 'Zur "Vollstreckbarmachung" von Mediationsvereinbarungen' in R Fucik et al (eds), *Jahrbuch Zivilverfahrensrecht 2010* (Neuer Wissenschaftlicher Verlag, 2010) 237ff

Frauenberger-Pfeiler, U and Risak, M, 'Der prätorische Mediationsvergleich' [2012] *Österreichische Juristen-Zeitung* 798ff

Fucik, R, 'EU-MediatG und ZivMediatG—ein Überblick' [2011] *Österreichische Juristen-Zeitung* 941ff

Garger, B, *Das Schiedsgutachtenrecht* (Manz, 1996)

Garger, B, *Das Sachverständigenverfahren im Versicherungsvertragsrecht* (Springer, 2002)

Gatternig, P and Gatternig, K, 'Zulässigkeit und Wirkung von Schlichtungsvereinbarungen in Arbeitsverträgen' [2009] *Österreichisches Recht der Wirtschaft* 282ff

Gitschthaler, E (ed), *Kindschafts- und Namensrechts-Änderungsgesetz 2013* (Manz, 2013)

Glavac, P, 'Mediation im Nachbarschaftsrecht' [2006] *immolex—Neues Miet- und Wohnrecht* 177ff

Grabenwarter, C, *Europäische Menschrechtskonvention* (5th edn, Beck, 2012)

Gratz, B, 'Mediation im öffentlichen Bereich' [2012] *RFG—Recht & Finanzen für Gemeinden* 86ff

Greiter, I, *Kreativität bei Verhandlungen und im Alltag* (Manz, 2001)

Greiter, I, 'Kommunikation und Rhetorik für den Anwalt in der täglichen Praxis' [2010] *Österreichisches Anwaltsblatt* 361ff and 474ff

Heindl, P and Lenk, F, *Das Verfahren vor der Schlichtungsstelle* (Verlag Österreich, 2003)

Hopf, G, 'Das Zivilrechts-Mediations-Gesetz' [2004] *Österreichische Juristen-Zeitung* 41ff

Hopf, G, 'Erfahrungen mit dem österreichischen Mediationsgesetz' [2010] *Rabels Zeitschrift für ausländisches und internationales Privatrecht* 759ff

Illedits, A and Illedits-Lohr, K, *Handbuch zum Nachbarrecht* (2nd edn, LexisNexis, 2007)

Illedits, A and Illedits-Lohr, K, *Nachbarrecht kompakt* (2nd edn, LexisNexis, 2008)

Jahn, B, *Außergerichtliche Konfliktlösung im Gesundheitswesen* (Manz, 2009)

Jungbauer-Komarek, A and Gobiet, A, *Konfliktlösung im Bauwesen und Projektmediation* (Neuer Wissenschaftlicher Verlag, 2005)

Kathrein, G, 'Mehr Licht!' [2003] *ecolex—Fachzeitschrift für Wirtschaftsrecht* 894ff

Kathrein, G, 'Das neue Nachbarrecht' in Österreichische Notariatskammer (ed), *Festschrift für Nikolaus Michalek zum 65. Geburtstag* (Manz, 2005) 175ff

Kloiber, B, 'Die Mediations-Richtlinie und ihre Umsetzung in Österreich' [2011] *Zeitschrift für Rechtsvergleichung* 119ff

Knötzl, B, 'Außergerichtliche Streitbeilegung. Konfliktlehre in der anwaltlichen Praxis—Ein "Alien"?' [2010] *Österreichisches Anwaltsblatt* 584ff

Kodek, GE and Mayr, PG, *Zivilprozessrecht* (facultas, 2011)

Kothbauer, C, 'Mediation im Mietrecht—Chancen und Grenzen' [2006] *immolex—Neues Miet- und Wohnrecht* 169ff

Krejci, H, 'Recht ohne Gerichte' in P Doralt and C Nowotny (eds), *Kontinuität und Wandel: Beiträge zum Unternehmensrecht. Festschrift für Walther Kastner zum 90. Geburtstag* (Orac, 1992) 251ff

Kreuzbauer, G, 'Ausbildung in juristischer Argumentation und Rhetorik' in E Schweighofer et al (eds), *Informationstechnik in der juristischen Realität* (Verlag Österreich, 2004) 57ff

Laukemann, B, 'Das österreichische Mediationsgesetz: Eine Standortbestimmung im Lichte seiner Regelungsstruktur und praktischen Bewährung' [2007] *Zeitschrift für Zivilprozess International* 91ff

Leischner, A, *Streitbeilegung in medizinischen Haftungsfällen* (Manz, 2007)

Liebscher, C, Oberhammer, P and Rechberger, WH (eds), *Schiedsverfahrensrecht* vol I (Springer, 2012)

Mayer, H, *Das österreichische Bundes-Verfassungsrecht* (4th edn, Manz, 2007)

Mayr, PG, 'Die Schlichtungstätigkeit der Kammern der freien Berufe' (1995) *Wirtschaftsrechtliche Blätter* 269 ff

Mayr, PG, 'Die Entwicklung der wohnrechtlichen Schlichtungsstellen' [2003] *Wohnrechtliche Blätter* 349ff

Mayr, PG, 'Die Mediationsgesetze von Österreich und Liechtenstein' [2008] *Liechtensteinische Juristen-Zeitung* 90ff

Mayr, PG, 'Neue Rechtstatsachen aus der Zivilgerichtsbarkeit' [2009] *Österreichisches Anwaltsblatt* 54 ff

Mayr, PG, 'Neuigkeiten bei der außergerichtlichen Streitbeilegung in Österreich' in M Ganner (ed), *Die soziale Funktion des Privatrecht. Festschrift für Heinz Barta zum 65. Geburtstag* (Linde, 2009) 245ff

Mayr, PG, 'Vereinsstreitigkeiten zwischen Schlichtungseinrichtung, Gericht und Schiedsgericht' [2009] *Österreichische Juristen-Zeitung* 39ff

Mayr, PG, 'Das neue Schiedsverfahrensrecht in Liechtenstein' [2010] *Jus & News* 297ff and [2011] 17ff

Mayr, PG, 'Die Zwangsmediation im Berufsausbildungsrecht' in H Barta et al (eds), *Analyse und Fortentwicklung im Arbeits-, Sozial- und Zivilrecht. Festschrift Martin Binder* (Linde, 2010) 295ff

Mayr, PG, 'Aktuelle Entwicklungen und Probleme bei den Rechtsschutzalternativen' in R Geimer, RA Schütze and T Garber (eds), *Europäische und Internationale Dimensionen des Rechts. Festschrift für Daphne-Ariane Simotta* (LexisNexis, 2012) 375ff

Mayr, PG, 'Alternative Dispute Resolution (ADR) in Austrian and European Law' in V Rijavec and T Ivanc (eds), *Cross-border Civil Proceedings in the EU (Conference Papers)* (Pravna fakulteta, 2012) 1ff

Mayr, PG, 'Case Note' [2012] *Österreichische Notariatszeitung* 347ff

Mayr, PG and Fucik, R, *Das neue Verfahren außer Streitsachen* (3rd edn, facultas, 2006)

Mayr, PG and Rath-Kathrein, I, 'Verfassungsrechtliche Fragen der wohnrechtlichen Schlichtungsstellen' [2013] *Wohnrechtliche Blätter* 67ff

Mayr, PG and Schmidt, A, 'Gesetzlich geregelte Alternativen innerhalb und außerhalb des Zivilprozesses in Österreich' [1987] *Zeitschrift für Vergleichende Rechtswissenschaft* 227ff

Mayr, PG and Weber, M, 'Europäische Initiativen zur Förderung der alternativen Streitbeilegung' [2007] *Zeitschrift für Rechtsvergleichung* 165ff

Michalek, N, 'Streitbeilegung ohne Gerichte' in Österreichische Juristenkommission (ed), *Kritik und Fortschritt im Rechtsstaat* (Verlag Österreich, 1994) 13ff

Oberhammer, P and Domej, T, 'Ein rechtlicher Rahmen für die Mediation in Österreich' [2003] *Zeitschrift für Konfliktmanagement* 144ff

Perner, S and Völkl, C, 'Conciliation, Mediation, ADR' [2003] *Österreichische Juristen-Zeitung* 495ff

Risak, M, 'Die Mediation im Arbeitsrecht' [2012] *Österreichische Juristen-Zeitung* 392f

Roth, M and Markowetz, K, 'Bundesgesetz über Mediation in Zivilrechtsachen—Ein erster Überblick über die neuen Bestimmungen' [2004] *Juristische Blätter* 296ff

Roth, M and Gherdane, D, 'Österreich' in KJ Hopt and F Steffek (eds), *Mediation* (Mohr Siebeck, 2008) 105ff

Schäfer, E, 'Schiedsgerichtsbarkeit und Mediation' in H Torggler (ed), *Praxishandbuch Schiedsgerichtsbarkeit* (Nomos, 2007) 9ff

Scheuer, U, 'Regelungen zur Mediation in Österreich nach Umsetzung der Mediations-Richtlinie' in R Fucik et al (eds), *Jahrbuch Zivilverfahrensrecht 2011* (Neuer Wissenschaftlicher Verlag, 2011) 197ff

Scheuer, U, 'Vollstreckbarer Mediationsvergleich und neue Regelungen für grenzüberschreitende Mediationsverfahren' [2011] *Zivilrecht aktuell* 147ff

Scheuer, U, 'Zum Stand der Mediation in Österreich' [2012] *Zeitschrift für Konfliktmanagement* 21ff

Schumacher, H, 'Das neue Schiedsverfahren' [2011] *Liechtensteinische Juristen-Zeitung* 105ff

Stabentheiner, J, 'Überlegungen zum Einsatz von Mediation im Wohnrecht' [2004] *Wohnrechtliche Blätter* 291ff

Stabentheiner, J, 'Mediation im Mietrecht?' in Österreichische Notariatskammer (ed), *Festschrift für Nikolaus Michalek zum 65. Geburtstag* (Manz, 2005) 373ff

Stadlmaier, J, 'Familienmediation: Einladung zum konstruktiven Miteinander' [2011] *iFamZ—Interdisziplinäre Zeitschrift für Familienrecht* 54ff

Stawa, G, 'Effizienz der Justiz im europäischen Vergleich' [2011] *Österreichisches Anwaltsblatt* 510ff

Thunhart, R, 'Können Eltern gegen ihren Willen zur Zusammenarbeit mit außergerichtlichen Institutionen gezwungen werden?' [2011] *iFamZ—Interdisziplinäre Zeitschrift für Familienrecht* 139

5

Regulation of Dispute Resolution in Belgium: Workable Solutions?

IVAN VEROUGSTRAETE

I. CHARACTERISTICS OF ADR

A. Commonly Deployed Dispute Resolution Procedures

THE NORMAL DISPUTE resolution procedure is resolution by court decision. Every year, the Belgian court system produces more than 900,000 judicial decisions (civil and criminal) for a population of about 11 million. There are many reasons for this high figure: the court system is not very expensive; there are no meaningful restrictions on the right of appeal; there are numerous courts; judicial delay is not significant (with a few exceptions); and the judiciary is, generally speaking, honest and reasonably competent.

The alternatives to adjudication are not very attractive. For example, arbitration tends to be very expensive, slow and formal. Hence, the number of arbitrations in Belgium is low, though no reliable figures are available. Arbitration has become increasingly institutionalised (as in most other countries bound by the same international treaties). It is no longer considered as an alternative dispute resolution mechanism, except when it is combined with mediation.

According to the rules of civil procedure—to a large extent contained in the 1967 Code judiciaire (hereinafter Judicial Code)—conciliating parties is not part of a judge's mandate. There is no general principle of law holding that judges should attempt to conciliate parties.[1] The business of the judge is still, as it was in the nineteenth century, to render a legal decision according to the legal rules laid down by the Parliament. Creating precedents and providing a shrewd interpretation of thousands of statutes is still the judge's main and most visible duty. It is therefore not surprising that referrals to mediation by the courts are rare (no official figures have been released). Referrals are, however, frequent in family law cases, either at the appeal level or at the first instance level, as it would appear that parties like the idea of staying empowered concerning issues that are quite personal.

The weaknesses of referrals to mediation are the following: the judges simply do not have the time to organise such referrals. Particularly in simple, straightforward cases (invoices, seizures) or cases for which ADR mechanisms would be clearly inappropriate (test cases, insolvency cases), adjudication is advisable.

Conventional mediation is more common. It is rare that courts are asked to formally ratify a conventional mediation agreement, and no reliable statistics are available. A recent attempt has, however, been made by the Brussels mediation centre to quantify the number of conventional mediations in Belgium (see Table 1).

Table 1: The Number of Conventional Mediations in Belgium

	Civil and commercial	Family	Social	Others
2010	3,117	1,166	477	192
2011	3,228	1,328	494	199
2012 (first 6 months)	2,171	812	332	134

There are probably many more mediations, but these figures show an increase in the number of classical mediations.

Mediation in criminal matters has experienced a revival, but no statistics are available. Mediations in criminal matters are quite time consuming and the desire for short-term efficiency has made it less popular. Additionally, public prosecutors are allowed to enter into formal settlements without much ado, and this also has made criminal mediation less attractive. Med-arbitration and various other forms of ADR are also rather exceptional. Settlements in courts, ie settlements inspired by the sitting judge, are frequent particularly at the level of the *juge de paix*. No statistics are available. Experience shows that a legal prerequisite for an attempt at conciliation to be made by the parties prior to a hearing in court, and organised by the courts, is totally ineffective. Parties go through the motions in labour law cases or in landlord and tenant cases, but this is simply a waste of time and money.

[1] Unwritten general principles of the law are rules created (or recognised) by the Cour de cassation which have almost as much binding effect as a regular statute.

Some legal provisions have created ADR-like organisations for particular disputes concerning public services or entities:

- Office of the Ombudsman for the Postal Sector (Law of 21 March 1991 on the reform of certain economic public companies);
- Ombudsman for the NMBS Group (Law of 21 March 1991 on the reform of certain public enterprise companies(for railway issues));
- Ombudsman Service for Telecommunications (Law of 21 March 1991 on the reform of certain public enterprise companies);
- Ombudsman Service for Energy (Royal Decree of 28 January 2008 *relatif au service de médiation pour l'énergie*; Law of 29 April 1999 *relative à l'organisation du marché de l'électricité*; Law of 12 April 1965 *relative au transport de produits gazeux et autres par canalisations*);
- Federal mediation service 'Patient Rights';
- Mediation in some insolvency cases (statute of 30 January 2009 on the reorganisation of enterprises);
- The *médiateur des dettes* in cases of personal insolvency.

These official (and mostly free of charge) systems are not ADR systems as such but have earned a good reputation for their ability to settle cases.

Concerning *consumer issues or consumer-related issues*, many commissions have been created at the initiative of the business community. These commissions give (mostly binding) advice to business entities. Many of these commissions or ombudsmen are operational, but their activity is not transparent and academia is quite critical of these operations. In banking and insurance disputes, for instance, the business ombudsman is financed by the banking or insurance sector and is not fully independent, or at least does not have the appearance of an independent body. This is particularly true for banking disputes.

Some examples of such private organisations providing a conciliation procedure (organised by the profession itself) are:

- Real Estate Conciliation, Arbitration and Mediation Board;
- Arbitration Commission for Consumers and Textile Carers;
- Furniture Disputes Commission;
- Travel Disputes Commission;
- Second-hand Vehicle Reconciliation Commission;
- Construction Reconciliation Commission;
- Mediation Service Banks—Credits—Investments;
- Insurance Ombudsman.

Each has its own characteristics, weaknesses and strong points.

A centralised official system (Belmed) provides access to a multitude of bodies which provide some form of mediation or settlement (<www.belmed.fgov.be>). The system run by the Ministry of Economic Affairs screens the questions and forwards the case to the most appropriate organisation. When consulting Belmed or filing a petition, the parties may attach any documents they want (in pdf form).The platform gives access to all possible kinds of conciliation systems, even to those that are not very transparent or impartial. The fine distinctions made between the impartial and transparent organisations promoted by the state and those promoted by the business entities are not taken account of by the system.

Mediation is also present in a variety of areas, such as relating to schools, neighbourhoods and workplaces, sometimes with non-professional and non-trained mediators who work free of charge. They are indeed an alternative to adjudication because even in these contexts a tendency to go to court for relatively insignificant reasons has been observed in the last 30 years.

The number and variety of types of mediation make it very hard to maintain a general view over the efficiency and weaknesses of the ADR system. Legal scholars have a rather critical view on this multitude of ADR schemes, and the web of ADR mechanisms makes ADR less than transparent and confusing for citizens.

B. Does the Market Work?

The market works in the sense that the court system has provided most of the answers needed, because it is a rather simple way to approach and solve the disputes. The market has made arbitration irrelevant except in a few complex cases; it has made mediation even less attractive. It is only in recent months that the displeasure with the official court system has become strong enough to enhance the chances of mediation or other ADR proceedings. The citizens or companies involved in a dispute will normally attempt a negotiation, and if this does not work they will go straight to the courts. The usefulness of a neutral is slowly gaining in recognition.

It is, however, hard to pretend that the market works in the sense that the most efficient system of dispute resolution will prevail in the end. The litigants do not always have efficiency as their main purpose: they may feel more at ease in a system in which a public authority decides on the issues. A decision made by a judge will also have a punishing effect on the losing party, which may be what the winning party always wanted. Irrational behaviour on the part of the parties should never be excluded—even in a free market. Pointing out that mediation is cheaper is not the ultimate argument in favour of mediation.

II. GENERAL APPROACH OF THE LEGISLATOR AS REGARDS THE REGULATION OF ADR AND ADJUDICATION

A. Existing Regulations

The Belgian legislator has regulated the various forms of dispute resolution in some detail. A clear distinction has been made (in civil and commercial litigation) between adjudication, judicial mediation (ie referrals to mediation), conventional mediation, settlements in court and arbitration. These various forms of dispute resolution are included in the Belgian Judicial Code (as separate chapters), which gives the rather misleading impression of a multi-door, coherent court system.

The official view has been that, by regulating and promoting mediation (and arbitration and settlements in court), the legislator has enhanced the image and efficiency of justice in general and made sure that justice would be done and would be seen to be done. A modest intervention in legal aid for mediation has also been provided (less generous than for adjudication).[2] The practical organisation of mediation has not been taken care of (this has been done only for conciliation). The details of institutionalised ADR will be seen later on. It cannot be denied that, by giving a name and a framework to ADR, the legislator has fostered it, though the general result has been less than overwhelming.

B. Incentives to Use Certain Types of ADR

The legislator has ratified the various international conventions on *arbitration* with the idea that it should be an acceptable way to settle disputes. This legislation has not been very successful: the high cost of arbitration has as a consequence that very few disputes (except in international commercial transactions) are submitted to the process. In fact, even when an arbitration clause is included in private contracts, the claimant will very often ignore the arbitration path in favour of summary proceedings. Whatever the contracts may provide, they cannot exclude that a party has recourse to summary proceedings. A clause excluding the possibility of summary proceedings would be considered a violation of public policy.

The very detailed way in which *mediation* has been regulated in the Judicial Code should normally favour this form of dispute resolution before that point when a conflict becomes totally entrenched. If an agreement to mediate has been included in the contract between the parties, the party who would go straight to the judge would have to face an exception by the defendant, and the judge would suspend the proceedings in order to allow the parties to attempt a mediation (see below II.B). Initiating a mediation at an early stage suspends prescription and also has the value of serving as a formal notice (which is important for the calculation of interest on monetary amounts). In family law cases, the judge has to inform the parties of the possibility of mediation before he even starts with the hearings.

The elaboration of mediation in the Judicial Code has worked to a limited extent. In most cases there are still lawyers to be paid in any event, and the general public is not (yet) convinced that mediation is much cheaper than judicial proceedings, even when it knows what mediation is about.[3]

Culture plays an important role, albeit a less important role than monetary issues. There is a long tradition of going to court to claim compensation for all kinds of prejudice. Negotiation or settlements reached out of court do happen, of course, and are frequent, but at the slightest displeasure Belgian citizens go to court. Lawyers also traditionally prefer court adjudication. The legislator added mediation and arbitration to the Code of Judicial Procedure, and also provided legal aid for ADR, but these devices are considered foreign to normal proceedings.

Lawyers are not required to advise their clients on the possibilities of ADR. The judge might do so—and in fact is bound to do so in family litigation—but the lawyers

[2] Young lawyers who have to provide their services for a fixed amount of money (paid by the federal state) receive less public credit for assistance in a successful mediation than even for an unsuccessful procedure in court.

[3] Research made by Giuseppe di Palo concerning the cost of adjudication in Italy and Belgium has shown that mediation could in fact be much cheaper: Workshop before the European Parliament, 21 May 2011.

are not obliged to fully inform their clients as to the advantages of alternative dispute resolution systems. Deontologically they are required to give a rough estimate of the cost and risks of judicial proceedings, but they are not required to tell the clients about all the possible alternatives. To the extent that mediation will become a true alternative at some future time, the duty to inform the client is becoming more pressing.

C. Restriction of Access to Courts as an Incentive

Access to Belgian courts is almost unrestricted. In fact, the right to have a day in court is almost without limits. Even the right to appeal is very rarely limited, and access to the Cour de cassation is only partially restricted (the most important restriction being the compulsory assistance of specialised lawyers in most civil and commercial law cases).

Exploring the possibility of a settlement out of court before going to court is not mandatory as a rule. This is true for all kinds of alternatives. It is even more true for mediation. The legislator views mediation as a totally optional operation and—according to the actual provisions of the law—estimates that it would be against the fundamental principles of mediation to force the parties to enter into a mediation.

The law does provide for some rare exceptions: in labour disputes the parties have to attempt a conciliation (ie a settlement submitted to the court, which is not a mediation) before the case can be heard on the merits. Such exceptions aside, it is fair to say that ADR procedures as a rule are not a pre-condition for starting proceedings, except when the contract between the parties contains a clause to that effect (see below III).

The judge may, however, decide on his own motion or at the request of one or both parties that a case should be referred to an alternative dispute resolution mechanism, particularly to mediation. This can be done at any moment of the proceedings by a summary written ruling, or even by an oral decision that is mentioned in the minutes of the hearing. The judge is not supposed to refer the dispute to another court official, but if he opts for mediation, he has to choose (as a rule) a mediator from among the officially accredited mediators. The proceedings will be suspended during the mediation. The mediator will have to report to the judge if the mediation fails or lasts more than the time span provided.

The judge can also appoint a court expert with the task of attempting to conciliate the parties and, if this fails, giving an expert opinion on matters described by the judge. This is routinely done in many cases. In construction cases, patent cases and personal injury cases, the appointment of an expert who is supposed to attempt to reconcile the parties happens every day in most courts.

The possibility given to the judge to refer a case to mediation does not limit the rights of the parties to have their day in court. In all instances the mediator acts in this context under a kind of supervision of the judge, and the parties are allowed to stop a mediation any time they wish. The agreements have to be ratified by a court decision which will examine whether the agreement is compatible with the public policy of the land.

No objections have been raised concerning the so-called privatisation of justice. This is not surprising, as the mediation proceedings stay in the judicial ambit.

The Belgian Court de cassation has not yet decided whether a refusal—without good reason—to enter a mediation could allow the judge to impose the costs of the proceedings to the reluctant party—even if the reluctant party has prevailed on the merits. The Judicial Code does not provide a straight answer to that question. It is likely that a judgment in tort based on abuse of the right to refuse any ADR proceedings would be upheld (the damages would be the costs of the court proceedings). This should be done with prudence, as no one can be compelled to enter into an agreement.

No violation of the constitution or of the human rights conventions derived from this judicial policy have been mentioned in legal literature. In this regard, the European Directive 2008/52/EC does not infringe on the European Convention on Human Rights (ECHR) or on Article 47 of the Treaty on the Functioning of the European Union.

The legislator has been very reluctant to restrict access to the courts in general, even long before ADR schemes became popular or even before the European Court of Human Rights stressed the importance of free access to an impartial judge. Fostering ADR by restricting access to the judge—for instance. by making pre-adjudication mediation or conciliation mandatory, or by imposing a financial penalty on those who would unreasonably refuse a mediation or attempt at settlement—is simply not done. The judges might allocate costs of the proceedings in an astute way when a party clearly abuses its rights, but the abuse must be obvious and serious.

III. APPROACH TOWARDS SPECIFIC ADR INSTRUMENTS

A. Negotiation[4]

Pre-contractual negotiations are subject to precise rules mostly based on case law of the Cour de cassation. The Civil Code does not provide specific legislation on this subject.

However, if a statute tends to protect one of the parties involved and is of the nature of a *droit impératif* (*ius cogens*), the protected party cannot waive its rights and retains the possibility of seeking the annulment of such agreement. This is, of course, also the case with regards to public policy: the parties cannot bargain around the principle. The negotiations in labour law cases, consumer cases, and landlord and tenant cases will never be completely subject to party autonomy.

If a negotiation is attempted in the post conflict stage, the parties will have to take into account that an adjudication might be unavoidable when the dispute concerns matters governed by *ius cogens* or public policy.

Breaking off negotiations in the post-conflict stage could eventually entail the liability of the party which breaks off the negotiations in bad faith or with negligence.[5] However, an action to force another party to negotiate would be rejected on the basis of the principle *nemo potest cogi ad factum,* even if there was a prior agreement to negotiate in case of conflict.

[4] 'Negotiation' in the context of this study primarily refers to negotiations in the post-conflict stage taking place without the assistance of a third-party neutral. The concept includes negotiations assisted by partisan lawyers.

[5] B De Coninck and C Delforge, 'La rupture des négociations et le retrait intempestif de l'offre. Régime général et sanctions' in M Vanwijck-Alexandre and P Wery (eds), *Le processus de formation du contrat* (Brussels, Larcier, 2004) 73ff.

The parties can indeed make binding agreements on the way they will negotiate. Contracts can be the result of progressively more binding agreements (in the way of letters of intent, options, granting of certain preferences, etc).[6] These agreements may also concern eventual negotiations at a post-conflict stage.

Refusing to enter into further negotiations would imply that an action in tort could be successful. In summary proceedings, the judges could go one step further if maintaining a provisional situation would be the only way to avoid further damages.

The applicable law as to the duties concerning the negotiations in the conflict stage would be determined according to the provisions of Regulation (EC) No 864/2007—Rome II not only in the EU but also in external relations outside of the EU (Article 98 of the Code de droit international privé).

B. Mediation

i. The Basic Regulation

Mediation is regulated in detail in the Judicial Code. The provisions are deemed to concern the judicial proceedings and therefore are binding on the parties irrespective of the contract they may have entered into. Mediation is considered as a matter of procedure and not as a contractual matter.

Mediation should be clearly distinguished from conciliation.[7] Conciliation in this narrow sense is quite successful (particularly by the juges de paix—Amtsgerichte). These conciliations will be briefly discussed later in below III.C. The rules on conciliation are also part of the Judicial Code (Articles 731ff).

The first chapter of the title of the Judicial Code concerning mediations contains general principles. They are applicable to all types of mediation. The second chapter concerns voluntary mediation, and the third concerns judicial mediation. The text of these provisions is an unofficial translation made by the Belgian Centre for Mediation and Arbitration (CEPINA).

CHAPTER 1—GENERAL PRINCIPLES

Article 1724
Any dispute which can be the subject matter of a settlement agreement may be submitted to mediation. This is also the case for:

1° disputes related to the matters referred to in Chapters V and VI of the Fifth Title, in Chapter IV of the Sixth Title and in the Ninth Title of the First Book of the Civil Code;
2° disputes related to matters referred to in Title Vbis of the Third Book of the Civil Code;

[6] W Van Gerven and S Covemaeker, *Verbintenissenrecht* (Leuven, Acco, 2006) 160f.

[7] The term conciliation is used here as the attempt by a judge in the course of judicial proceedings to settle the conflict. It is expressly regulated in the Judicial Code and has nothing in common with mediation or any other type of free conciliation. In other jurisdictions this could be quite different. For example, conciliation (in German: *Schlichtung*) can be used in legal writings in Germany or Italy for all procedures that result in a non-binding recommendation of the conflict manager regarding the dispute as a whole. Thus, the term may, for instance, cover the instruments of early neutral evaluation or mini-trial. Some jurisdictions (as also the UNCITRAL Model Law) do not differentiate between mediation and conciliation.

3° disputes introduced in accordance with sections I to IV of Chapter XI of the Fourth Book of the Fourth Part of the Judicial Code;
4° disputes arising from *de facto* cohabitation.

Public legal entities may take part in a mediation in the cases provided for by the law or by a Royal Decree decided by the Council of Ministers.

Article 1725
§ 1. Any contract may contain a mediation clause, by which the parties agree to have recourse to mediation with respect to any dispute relating to the validity, the conclusion, the interpretation, the performance or the breach of the contract before having recourse to any other dispute resolution method.
§ 2. The Court or the Arbitral Tribunal to which a dispute is submitted which is the subject of a mediation clause shall suspend the examination of the case if requested by any party, unless, with regard to the dispute in question, the mediation clause is invalid or has ceased to exist. The plea must be raised before any other plea or defense. The examination of the case may be continued once the parties, or any one of them, has notified the registry and the other parties that the mediation has ended.
§ 3. The mediation clause does not prevent requests for provisional or conservatory measures. The filing of such requests does not imply any waiver of the mediation.

Article 1726
§ 1. The Commission mentioned in Article 1727 may accredit mediators who satisfy at least the following conditions:

1° possess, by present or past activity, the qualification required by the nature of the dispute;
2° can demonstrate, as the case may be, training or experience appropriate for the practice of mediation;
3° present the guarantees of independence and of impartiality necessary to practice mediation;
4° have not been convicted to a condemnation registered in a criminal record and held to be incompatible with the function of an accredited mediator;
5° have not incurred a disciplinary or administrative sanction held to be incompatible with the function of an accredited mediator; nor to have had the accreditation withdrawn.

§ 2. The accredited mediators follow a permanent education programme recognised by the Commission mentioned in Article 1727.
§ 3. This article applies equally when a panel of mediators is called upon.

Article 1727
§ 1. A Federal Mediation Commission is created, composed of a General Commission and a Special Commissions.
§ 2. The General Commission is composed of six members specialized in mediation, being two notaries, two lawyers and two representatives of mediators who do not practice as lawyers or notaries.

In the composition of the General Commission care shall be taken to have all fields of practice represented in a balanced manner.

The General Commission is composed of an equal number of Dutch-speaking and French-speaking members.

For every effective member an alternate member is appointed.

The rules for the publication of vacancies, the filing of applications and the presentation of the members are set forth in a ministerial decree.

The effective and alternate members are appointed by the Minister of Justice, on the basis of a reasoned presentation:

- from the Association of Flemish Bars (*Orde van Vlaamse Balies*) for any lawyer belonging to the said Association;
- from the Association of French and German speaking Bars (*l'Ordre des barreaux francophones et germanophones)* for any lawyer belonging to the said Assocation;
- from the Royal Federation of Notaries, for any notary;
- from the representative organisations of those mediators who do not practice as a lawyer or as a notary.

The term of office as an effective member lasts for four years and is renewable.

§ 3. The General Commission appoints from within its own members and for a period of two years, its chairman and vice-chairman, the vice-chairman replacing the chairman as needed, as well as a secretary, these functions being assigned alternately to a Dutch-speaking and a French-speaking person. In addition, the chairmanship and vice-chairmanship are held alternately by notaries, lawyers and by mediators who do not practise as a lawyer or as a notary.

The General Commission establishes its internal regulations.

In order to deliberate and decide validly, the majority of the members of the Commission must be present. If an effective member is absent or excused, his alternate replaces him. The decisions are taken by simple majority of votes. If the votes are even, the chairman or the vice-chairman who replaces him has the casting vote.

§ 4. Three Special Commissions are created in order to give advice to the General Commission:

- a Special Commission for Family Matters;
- a Special Commission for Civil and Commercial Matters;
- a Special Commission for Social Matters;

These Special Commissions are composed of specialists and practitioners of each of the said types of mediation, namely:

Two notaries, two lawyers and two representatives of those mediators who do not practice as a lawyer or as a notary.

The Special Commissions are composed of as many Dutch-speaking members as French-speaking members.

For each effective member, an alternate member is appointed.

The rules for the publications of vacancies, the filing of applications and the presentation of members are set forth in a Ministerial Decree.

The effective and alternate members are appointed by the Minister of Justice, on the basis of a reasoned presentation:

- from the Association of Flemish Bars (*Orde van Vlaamse Balies*) for any lawyer belonging to the said Association;
- from the Association of French speaking and German speaking Bars (*l'Ordre des barreaux francophones et germanophone)* for any lawyer belonging to the said Association;
- from the Royal Federation of Notaries, for any notary;
- from the representative organisation of those mediators who do not practice as a lawyer or as a notary.

The term of office as effective member lasts for four years and is renewable.

§ 5. Each Special Commission appoints from within its own members and for a period of two years, its chairman and vice-chairman, the vice-chairman replacing the chairman as needed, as well as a secretary, the said functions being assigned alternately to a Dutch-speaking and a French-speaking person.

The Special Commission establishes its internal regulations.

In order to deliberate and decide validly, the majority of the members of the Special

Commission must be present. If an effective member is absent or excused, his alternate replaces him. The decisions are taken by simple majority of votes. If the votes are even, the chairman or the vice-chairman who replaces him has the casting vote.
§ 6. The General Commission has the following tasks:

1° to accredit providers of mediation training and the training they provide;
2° to determine the criteria for the accreditation of mediators by type of mediation;
3° to accredit mediators;
4° to withdraw, either temporarily or definitely, the accreditation of mediators who no longer satisfy the conditions set forth in article 1726;
5° to determine the procedure for accrediting and for withdrawing, temporarily or definitely, the title of mediator;
6° to establish the list of mediators and to distribute same to the Courts;
7° to establish a Code of Conduct and to determine the sanctions deriving therefrom.

The decisions of the Commission are reasoned.
§ 7. The Minister of Justice puts at the disposal of the Federal Mediation Commission the personnel and means necessary to operate.

The King determines what allowance may be granted to the members of the Federal Mediation Commission.

Article 1728
§ 1. All documents and communications made during and for the purpose of a mediation process are confidential. They may not be used during any judicial, administrative or arbitral procedure or in any other dispute resolution procedure and they are not admissible as evidence, not even as an out-of-court confession. The duty of confidentiality can only be lifted with the consent of the parties with a view to allowing *inter alia* a Court to homologate settlement agreements.

If this duty of confidentiality is violated by one of the parties, the Court or Arbitral Tribunal decides whether any damages may be granted. Any confidential documents that are nevertheless communicated or which are relied upon by a party in violation of the duty of confidentiality are *ex officio* excluded from the proceedings.

Without prejudice to the requirements of the law, the mediator may not disclose the facts with which he becomes acquainted as a result of his function. He may not be called upon by the parties as a witness in civil or administrative proceedings relating to the facts with which he has become acquainted in the course of the mediation. Article 458 of the Criminal Code is applicable to the mediator.
§ 2. During and for the purpose of his office, the mediator, with the consent of the parties, may examine third parties who consent thereto or, if required due to the complexity of the case, may call upon an expert specializing in the subject matter. The latter are bound by the duty of confidentiality set forth in § 1 (1°). § 1 (3°) is applicable to the expert.

Article 1729
Each party may terminate at any moment the mediation proceedings on a without prejudice basis.

CHAPTER II—VOLUNTARY MEDIATION

Article 1730
§ 1. Any party may propose to the other parties, regardless of any other judicial or arbitral proceedings, before, during or after the conduct of judicial proceedings, to have recourse to a mediation procedure. The parties appoint the mediator by mutual consent or call upon a third party to make the appointment.

§ 2. If the proposal is sent by registered mail and if it contains a claim to a right, it shall be assimilated to the formal notice referred to in Article 1153 of the Civil Code.
§ 3. Under the same conditions, the proposal shall suspend the limitation period of the claim related to the said right during one month.

Article 1731
§ 1. The parties decide by mutual agreement, with the assistance of the mediator, upon the rules for the conduct of the mediation as well as its duration. This agreement is confirmed in writing in a mediation protocol signed by the parties and by the mediator. The mediation costs and fees are payable in equal shares by the parties, unless agreed otherwise by the parties.
§ 2. The mediation protocol contains:

1° the name and domicile of the parties and their counsel;
2° the name, description and address of the mediator, and, as the case may be, the indication that the mediator is accredited by the Commission mentioned in Article 1727;
3° the restatement of the voluntary character of mediation;
4° a brief summary of the dispute;
5° the restatement of the principle of the confidentiality of all communications exchanged during the mediation;
6° the method by which the fees of the mediator are fixed, the fee rate as well as the terms of payment;
7° the date;
8° the signature of the parties and of the mediator.

§ 3. The signature of the protocol suspends the limitation period for the duration of the mediation.
§ 4. Unless expressly agreed by the parties, the suspension of the limitation period ends one month after one of the parties or the mediator inform the other party or parties of its wish to terminate the mediation. This notification is done by registered mail.

Article 1732
If the parties reach a settlement, it is set out in a document dated and signed by the parties and by the mediator. If the mediator is accredited, this is mentioned.

This written document sets out the precise commitments of each party.

Article 1733
When a settlement agreement is reached, and if the mediator who has conducted the mediation is accredited by the Commission mentioned in Article 1727, the parties or one of the parties may submit for homologation by the competent Court the settlement agreement reached in accordance with Articles 1731 and 1732. This is done in accordance with Articles 1025 to 1034. The request can however be signed by the parties themselves, if it emanates from all the parties to the mediation. The mediation protocol is attached to the request.

The Court may only refuse the homologation of the settlement agreement if it is contrary to public policy or, in the case of a mediation in family matters, if the agreement is against the interests of under age children.

The homologation has the same effect as a judgment in the sense of Article 1043.

CHAPTER III—COURT-INSTIGATED MEDIATION

Article 1734
§ 1. At every stage of the proceedings, even in summary proceedings, but not in proceedings before the Supreme Court (*Hof van Cassatie/Cour de cassation*) or before the Case Allocation Court (*arrondisssementsrechtbank/tribunal d'arrondissement*), at the joint request

of the parties or on its own initiative but with the consent of the parties, a Court in pending proceedings may order a mediation, as long as the case has not been closed for the purposes of rendering a judgment. The parties agree on the name of the mediator, who must be accredited by the Commission mentioned in Article 1727.

By way of derogation to the above paragraph, the parties, jointly and on a reasoned basis, may ask the Court to appoint a non-accredited mediator. Unless the mediator proposed by the parties obviously does not satisfy the conditions set forth in Article 1726, the Court shall accede to this request if the parties demonstrate that no accredited mediator with the required skills is available to conduct the mediation.

§ 2. Any decision that orders mediation shall expressly mention the agreement of the parties, the name, the description and the address of the mediator and shall determine the initial duration of his term of office, which may not exceed three months, and shall also indicate the date to which the case is postponed, which is the first useful date after the expiration of said time limit.

§ 3. At the latest at the hearing mentioned in § 2, the parties shall inform the Court of the result of the mediation. If they have not reached a settlement agreement, they may request a new time limit or ask that the proceedings be continued.

§ 4. The parties may request a mediation, either in the writ initiating the proceedings, or at the hearing, or by simple written request filed with, or sent to, the Court clerk. In the latter case, the case is scheduled within fifteen days following the said request.

The Court clerk convokes the parties by judicial notification, and, as the case may be, their counsel by ordinary mail. If it is a joint request of the parties, they and, as the case may be, their counsel are convoked by ordinary mail.

§ 5. When the parties jointly request that a mediation be ordered, the time limits in relation to the proceedings are suspended as from the date on which they formulate their request.

As the case may be, the parties or any one of them may request new time limits so as to have the case ready for the hearing mentioned in § 2 or in Article 1735, § 5.

Article 1735

§ 1. Within eight days after the rendering of the decision, the Court clerk sends to the mediator by judicial notification a certified copy of the judgment. Within eight days, the mediator informs by ordinary mail the Court and the parties of the place, date and time for the beginning of his office.

§ 2. The mediation may concern a part or the entirety of the dispute.

§ 3. During the mediation the dispute continues to be laid before the Court, which, at any time, may take such measures as it deems necessary. At the request of the mediator or any of one of the parties, the Court may put an end to the mediation even before expiry of the time limit which has been set.

§ 4. At any time during the proceedings, the appointed mediator, with the agreement of the parties, may be replaced by another accredited mediator. This agreement is signed by the parties and is included in the file.

§ 5. The case may be brought back before the Court prior to the date initially set by means of a simple written declaration filed with, or sent to, the registry by the parties or by anyone of them. A Court hearing is scheduled within fifteen days following the said request.

The Court clerk convokes the parties by judicial notification and, as the case may be, their counsel by ordinary mail. In case of a joint request of the parties, they are convoked, and, as the case may be, their counsel by ordinary mail.

Article 1736

The mediation is conducted in accordance with the provisions of Articles 1731 and 1732.

When his term of office has expired, the mediator informs the Court in writing whether or not the parties have reached a settlement agreement.

If the mediation leads to a settlement agreement, even if the agreement is only partial, the parties or any one of them, in accordance with Article 1043, may ask the Court to homologate the said agreement.

The Court may refuse the homologation of the settlement agreement only if it is contrary to public policy or, in the case of a mediation in family matters, if the agreement is against the interests of under age children.

If the mediation has not led to a full settlement agreement, the Court proceedings are resumed at the date set, but the Court has the right, if it deems it so appropriate and with the consent of all the parties, to extend the term of office of the mediator for such time limit as it determines.

Article 1737
It is not possible to appeal against any Court decision ordering the mediation, extending its duration or putting an end to the mediation.

ii. The Transposition of the EU-Directive—Some Assets of the National Legislation

The basic legislation on mediation has not been amended following Directive 2008/52/EC. The Belgian government considered that it would be pointless to further implement the directive as the domestic legislation essentially covers all of the issues addressed by the directive. It officially notified the Commission that no further implementation was required.

There has been only one significant change after the directive was enacted. A statute of 5 April 2011 concerning divorce proceedings obliges the judge to inform the parties on the possibility of mediation and allows the judge on his own initiative to stay the proceedings to allow the parties to consider mediation (new Articles 1254, § 4/1, 1255, § 6 and 1280 of the Judicial Code). In all other regards, the existing procedure of Articles 1724–37 of the Judicial Code remains in force (the basic general statute on mediation, introduced in the Judicial Code on 21 February 2005). No distinction is made between domestic proceedings and transnational proceedings.

Provisions of the law which differ from the requirements of Directive 2008/52/EC or could be specific for Belgian law without infringing on the Directive are the following:

- Mediation involving public entities is only possible if a statute or a royal decree has allowed the public entities to enter into a mediation; this is disappointing indeed, although the reason for including this provision was mainly of a technical nature (the supremacy of the state vis-à-vis the citizen);
- An accreditation system is provided, with the accreditation given to mediators and to training centres by a Federal Commission on Arbitration. Various provisions of the law reserve some positive effects of the mediation protocols and agreements to agreements made under the supervision of an accredited mediator. There is no provision concerning the recognition of mediators trained abroad or recognised elsewhere in the EU.
- If an agreement to mediate in cases of conflict was included into a contract and one of the parties immediately sues the other party, the judge can stay the proceedings if one of the parties raises this exception (Article 1725 Judicial Code)(ie it cannot be raised *ex officio*).
- The confidentiality requirements are very strict. They concern not only the mediator

but also the parties, even if they do not provide this by a specific agreement; even an expert who could be appointed during the mediation by the parties with the assent of the mediator would be bound by the obligation of secrecy. This provision makes a Belgian mediation rather attractive compared to the Dutch and UK types of mediation which take a less favourable view on confidentiality (particularly in the UK, the judges do not fully respect the requirements of confidentiality).

- Legal assistance for mediation is provided; the amounts covered are very limited.
- Entering a conventional mediation has legally defined effects: it has the effects of a formal notice (important for the interest due) and suspends the statute of limitations for one month (Article 1730 Judicial Code); signing the mediation protocol suspends prescription as long as the mediation proceedings last.
- The minimum content of the mediation agreement is more precise than in the Directive.
- The agreement made under the supervision of an accredited mediator can be ratified by the court upon request of even one of the parties and has the value of a judgment when it is ratified; the judge can only reject the demand of ratification on the grounds of public policy or if in family matters it is contrary to the interests of the children.
- Referral by a judge to mediation can be made at all stages of proceedings (with the exception of proceedings before the Cour de cassation or a special court that handles jurisdiction issues).
- Noteworthy: it is generally admitted that active professional judges cannot be mediators (almost none of them are accredited in any event); retired judges can be mediators but need, of course, a state accreditation like any other mediator.
- Various provisions regulate the way that judicial mediation and ordinary proceedings are linked.
- The mediation agreement concluded after a referral can be ratified by the judge; the application made by one of the parties can only be rejected on narrow grounds.
- Mediation remains a fundamentally voluntary process: mandatory mediation is miles apart from the mediation concept embodied in the Judicial Code. This is partly due to the fact that there are few historic instances of mandatory conciliation (labour; some landlord and tenant cases), and these did not prove successful. However, it is not excluded that a party—even a winning one—would have to pay part of the costs of the proceedings if the party had unreasonably refused to at least attempt a mediation (this might be considered as an abuse of rights, but the abuse must be obvious and significant).

iii. Mediation Clauses and Some Other Elements Favouring Mediation

A mediation clause does not prevent an action before a state court. However, the provisions of Article 1725 Judicial Code further the mediation process:

> § 2. The Court or the Arbitral Tribunal to which a dispute is submitted which is the subject of a mediation clause shall suspend the examination of the case if requested by any party, unless, with regard to the dispute in question, the mediation clause is invalid or has ceased to exist. The plea must be raised before any other plea or defense. The examination of the case may be continued once the parties, or any one of them, has notified the registry and the other parties that the mediation has ended.

> § 3. The mediation clause does not prevent requests for provisional or conservatory measures. The filing of such requests does not imply any waiver of the mediation.

The mediation process can also be aided within certain limits by the existence of an official accreditation system of the mediators active in Belgium, with the fortunate consequence that the accredited mediators have their liability insured and are bound by deontological rules. The mediation process is also furthered by the suspension of the statute of limitations, even if the mediation is just a conventional one.

There is no formal way to contest the impartiality of the mediator. Regulating this possibility would have been useless—according to Belgian law—as any party may stop the mediation at any time. It is fortunate that the legislator did not engage in that type of regulation.

iv. Duties of the Mediator—Liability

The mediators are bound to respect the applicable codes of conduct. The European code of conduct will most often be the code to which the mediators will refer themselves. All mediation centres include the respect of some deontological code in their internal rules, which the affiliated mediators have to accept before being recognised. The codes are routinely referred to in all mediation agreements.

The code of conduct contains provisions on:

- Competence
- Advertising
- Independence and neutrality
- Impartiality
- Procedure
- Fairness of the process
- End of the process
- Fees
- Confidentiality

The liability of the mediator for malpractice or some other reason will create a contractual liability towards the parties (even if the mediation was instigated by the court). This implies that the liability will take into account the conduct which could be expected by the parties from the particular mediator. The parties can expect that he will act as any prudent and competent mediator would act.

If the mediator is a lawyer, he will incur some specific liability if he allows or supervises the drafting of an agreement which would run counter to the public policy of the jurisdiction in which the agreement has to be enforced. Liability is also incurred if he terminates the mediation without providing for a formal implementation of the agreement when this is usual or to be expected in the circumstances of the case. If he is only acting on an advisory level and not purely legal level in family matters, this would, of course, be different. The formal implementation will be left to the parties and their lawyers.

Another, more complex, aspect concerns the obligations of the mediator to secure full fairness of the proceedings, particularly if one of the parties is not assisted by a (competent) lawyer and the other party is assisted by a skilled lawyer. There is an ongoing discussion, related to the fundamental task of the mediator, as to whether the mediator should inform the weaker party about his rights. The approach might be different, though not necessarily, when the mediation is held in a multi-party context. Much depends on the approach to mediation (evaluative or not). The courts in Belgium have not yet made a decision on this kind of issue.

Liability in tort could be theoretically possible if the mediator encourages a settlement which is fraudulent towards absent parties or towards the state (eg by organising some tax avoidance).

There seem to be rather few disputes involving the liability of the mediator. The accreditation allows a screening of the mediators. A clear manifestation of the small number of liability situations is the low level of the insurance for civil liability: around €120 a year (for 2013).

v. Duties of the Parties

It has already been mentioned that each party may terminate the mediation at any time on a without prejudice basis (Article 1729 Judicial Code). This is a basic principle: mediation is supposed to be a completely free commitment. Nevertheless, a party could abuse this right to terminate the mediation and could be liable in tort for a significant, clear and obvious abuse of a right. This is true for conventional and for court-connected mediation.

The fees of the mediator are to be borne by both parties on an equal basis (unless the parties decide otherwise). There is no regulation concerning the fee, but legal aid provides only limited relief. The courts would decide in court-instigated mediation whether the fee of the mediator is reasonable.

vi. Enforcement

Agreements resulting from mediation are not enforceable as such, unless they are included in an authentic act of a notary public. Normally they should be homologated by a court before being enforceable (see Article 1733 Judicial Code).

There have been very few demands to ratify mediation agreements. There are no known refusals to homologate mediation agreements. The reasons not to enforce an agreement should be exceptional. There is a clear tendency in legal literature and in the case law of the Cour de cassation to limit the effect of the public policy requirement as much as possible (in all fields of law).

vii. Court Programmes

A few courts have organised systematic court referrals in commercial law and in family law. These programmes are moderately successful and have been praised (Court of Appeal Ghent; Brussels Court of First Instance; Commercial Court Namur and Commercial Court Liège). Referrals remain exceptional, mostly on account of a lack of time of the judges involved. Judges who have carefully prepared a court hearing are reluctant to let a third party decide on the matter. The limited experience of judges who do make such referrals has also been that the mediators did not bother to inform the judges on the issue of the dispute.

viii. Cross-border

The same rules apply in cross-border and domestic situations. Mediations held in Belgium would be run according to the national procedural rules. It is not a matter of choice of law. Having a mediation organised in Belgium—even if it has transnational aspects—according to non-Belgian procedural rules (among others concerning the confidentiality requirements) would run counter to the idea of the Judicial Code.

C. Conciliation

Conciliation is understood in this chapter to be a method of settlement in court. The obligations of fairness applicable to all court proceedings would be similarly applicable. It would be unlawful, for instance, to have a caucus with one of the parties as this would violate Article 6 of the ECHR.

The conciliator would necessarily be the judge himself. Increasingly, the legal literature considers that the judge who attempts to conciliate the parties and fails in this attempt should withdraw from the case and not adjudicate the matter himself, at least if he made a formal attempt to conciliate the parties. Just asking questions of the parties and nudging them gently to an agreement should not be considered as a formal attempt to reach a settlement. This type of conciliation is very informal and very successful.

All other forms of conciliation are left to the discretion of the parties, conciliation being understood as any form of negotiation involving a third party as a more or less neutral participant. The parties are free to negotiate whatever agreement they want and to ask the help of third parties in their settlement as long as they do not violate any *ius cogens* or do not infringe on public policy.

The schemes mentioned above run by the business organisations are examples of conciliation schemes run by professional conflict managers appointed and paid by the sector involved. Provided advice is not binding and could not be because it is widely felt that the conflict manager is not independent (or is even not impartial). This practice leans more towards negotiation than towards a true conciliation by a neutral.

The cross-border element can be important. When the schemes are purely conventional, and there is no reference to an existing system of ADR, the parties are not bound to the procedural rules of the land. The parties are free to choose whatever law they prefer, but of course will not have the possibility of obtaining an easy homologation of their agreement.

D. Expert Opinion[8]

The role of the expert will be fundamentally different, depending on whether he has been appointed by a judge or appointed by one or more parties.

[8] Expert Opinion. Reference here is to expert opinions that are used in the context of a dispute resolution as opposed to expert opinions or evaluations occurring in regular negotiations. A dispute is a social conflict between at least two subjects. The difference between conciliation and expert opinions is that conciliation concerns the dispute as a whole whereas expert opinions cover only certain aspects of the dispute.

The rules applicable to the expert opinions of an expert appointed by a judge—even if he has been appointed during a mediation procedure (as an incident to a mediation)—will be those of the Judicial Code. These rules are extremely detailed. The judge-appointed expert has a quasi-judicial role, although he is legally barred from giving his own legal views on the subject matter in dispute (he may only advise on facts in the broadest sense of the word). He has to comply with procedural standards (right of defence among others) and has to report to the court which appointed him. His fee is also determined by the court.

The courts appoint experts in all kinds of cases, and there seems to be no limit to the domains in which they are active: building law, intellectual property, family law, insolvency liquidation, taxation, etc. The law has further made a distinction between ordinary experts and some specific categories of experts in the fields of intellectual property (IP) and taxation, with specific authority being accorded by law to their findings (*saisie-description* in respect of IP, and binding decision authority for taxation and expropriation matters).

Parties may also appoint an expert. If both parties agree to give a task to an expert, they may also decide that his opinion will be binding on the parties. The contract appointing the expert will determine how the expert has to act and according to which rules. Contesting a binding opinion of such an expert will only be possible on the basis of the contract.

Experts are allowed to work on an international basis. This, indeed, is one of the major reasons to appoint an expert. As the judge is only allowed to operate in his own country, he will be relieved to have the opportunity to appoint an expert who can act abroad. The expert acting abroad can fulfil his task without compelling the foreign residents to act or to refrain from acting. He will not infringe on the sovereignty of a foreign state, which allows the judge to give a mission to the expert which will be fulfilled abroad.

E. Arbitration

Arbitration is in fact not an alternative to court litigation. It is truly a marginal phenomenon, except in respect of international commercial transactions. Arbitration has never worked well in Belgium. Belgian law closely follows the obligations of the international conventions, and adapts its legislation from time to time to remain competitive with foreign arbitration centres. The arbitration procedure mimics the normal adjudication procedure—excessively so, sometimes.[9]

The arbitration convention or the parties can decide which law will be applied in the arbitration (according to Regulation (EC) No 593/2008—Rome I) and within the limits of that regulation. This implies that even *ius cogens* can be avoided. The validity of the choice of law allowing a principal to choose another law than the Belgian law to determine the validity of the termination of an agency agreement made with a Belgian agent has been successfully challenged.

[9] See 'Le nouveau règlement d'arbitrage du Centre belge d'arbitrage et de médiation (CEPANI)' *Revue de Droit International et de Droit Comparé (RDIDC)* 1/2013, 99.

The parties will decide which rules on arbitration are applicable: this choice is theirs.

The enforcement and recognition of arbitration awards follow the internationally recognised usual rules on recognition and enforcement of arbitral awards. Belgium has adhered to all major arbitration treaties.

IV. POLICY RECOMMENDATIONS

- ADR deserves a minimum regulation. This is, in any event, not an optional question, as a Directive exists. However, it is surprising that the enactment of the Directive has prompted regulatory reactions or legislative work which have proved to be controversial and awakened sleeping dogs (competence of the *Länder*; confidentiality).
- Providing a general framework would be sufficient (for mediation and settlements in court). The aforementioned ADR should be better integrated into the general rules on civil procedure.
- An integrated system is preferable: the courts are already implicated (ratifying, appointing experts, screening mediators). Mediation should be part of the judicial civil system. This would enhance the prospects of mediation and would be a cornerstone of a multi-door system.
- As mediation would be part of the court system, it seems appropriate that the system should carry part of the costs (at least in the case of court-instigated mediation). The parties who attempted a mediation should at a minimum be rewarded by a refund of the normal court costs.
- Fundamental choices should be made by the legislator, but the legislator should refrain from giving overly detailed regulations. The courts could be called upon to establish additional, further detailed regulations which could be easily changed or modified. The general approach tends to leave to the parties the possibility of organising themselves as they wish.
- In the early stages of a conflict the parties should enter into negotiations rather than involve a neutral. This is particularly true in the business world.
- Less invasive methods are to be preferred over mandatory ADR. Pre-trial compulsory methods have not worked out very well in systems in which the courts work reasonably well. The parties do not see the point of avoiding the court system at all costs.
- Cost penalties are mostly unfair and, moreover, might violate the right to a day in court. Incentives to mediate coupled with selective pressure exercised by the judge to enter into a mediation and potentially reach a settlement in court seem more promising. Providing a better substantive organisation of the mediators to whom the judges make referrals would be an excellent step forward.[10]

[10] Some premises should be made available for the meetings in a limited number of courts in the country; the courts should have a list at hand of 'good' mediators; a judge in each province could be appointed to supervise the use of ADR.

BIBLIOGRAPHY

De Coninck, B and Delforge, C, 'La rupture des négociations et le retrait intempestif de l'offre. Régime général et sanctions' in M Vanwijck-Alexandre and P Wery (eds), *Le processus de formation du contrat* (Brussels, Larcier, 2004) 73–132

Van Gerven, W and Covemaeker, S, *Verbintenissenrecht* (Leuven, Acco, 2006)

'Le nouveau règlement d'arbitrage du Centre belge d'arbitrage et de médiation (CEPANI)' *Revue de Droit International et de Droit Comparé (RDIDC)* 1/2013, 99

6

Regulation of Dispute Resolution in Denmark: Mediation, Arbitration, Boards and Tribunals

LIN ADRIAN

I. INTRODUCTION

RESOLVING DISPUTES WITHOUT going to court has been part of Danish legal culture for centuries.[1] Today's landscape of alternative dispute resolution[2] consists of an established practice of arbitration, a long-lived tradition of specialised complaint boards and tribunals, and the emergence of mediation over the past two decades.[3] Arbitration, boards and tribunals have over time become increasingly institutionalised and a well-established form of ADR. They are adjudicative in nature and so legally embedded that, although they technically constitute ADR mechanisms, today in many ways they are more traditional than alternative.

Denmark does not have a comprehensive, national regulation of ADR. Each area

[1] For an extensive history of, for example, legal mediation in Denmark see V Vindeløv, 'Mediation in Danish Law: In Retrospect and Perspective' in N Alexander (ed), *Global Trends in Mediation* (Köln, Centrale für Mediation, 2003).

[2] In this chapter the term ADR will be used for processes that are alternatives to court proceedings, see DH Yarn (ed), *Dictionary of Conflict Resolution* (San Francisco, Jossey-Bass Publishers, 1999) 17ff.

[3] Other forms of ADR, such as conciliation, early neutral evaluation and summary jury trials, are not found in Denmark. Expert opinion and conciliation are built into adjudication of civil cases and exist as independent ADR mechanisms on such a limited basis that they will not be covered by this chapter.

of practice is governed by a host of autonomous initiatives that are not coordinated or necessarily interconnected. Arbitration and certain areas of mediation have been regulated by legislation, as this chapter will show, but there is no overriding legislation setting forth rules of ADR on a broader scale. Likewise, there is no national initiative on promoting ADR in general—whether publicly or privately—and there is no national certification system in place either.

Approximately 63,000 civil cases were resolved by litigation in 2012.[4] Data on ADR is sparse, but from the accessible data combined with anecdotal evidence, it seems safe to assume that about 20,000–25,000 cases are resolved by ADR mechanisms annually—the majority by boards and tribunals.[5] This suggests that, even though a significant number of conflicts are resolved in ADR, litigation is still the most commonly applied method of third party intervention in legal disputes.

Mediation is practiced in many areas in Denmark—legal as well as non-legal. This chapter concentrates on ADR involving non-criminal legal disputes, but mediation in criminal cases will be discussed briefly.[6] The different areas of ADR are best dealt with separately. Primary attention will be paid to mediation, which will be discussed first. Arbitration and tribunals and boards will then be covered briefly, and incentives to ADR described. In the final section, policy-related issues regarding regulation will be discussed.

II. MEDIATION

In the following sub-sections, mediation in various legal areas of practice will be described in turn. However, before addressing the specifics, it makes sense to turn attention to four prominent features of mediation in Denmark on a more general level. These are that mediation is based on a set of explicit values, that it is dominated by a facilitative ideology, that current law is not the centre of attention and that mediation is practised by trained mediators. These features are reflected in legislation, in ethical guidelines from professional organisations and in mediation practice.

First, mediation is based on and intrinsically intertwined with a set of *values*. The one overriding value is the dual notion that the parties know best what the conflict is about and how it should be resolved. In other words, the parties are considered the experts of their own lives, and this is realised through the general mediation principle of self-determination. Other values include considering dialogue desirable in conflict and considering individuality and relationship as being intertwoven.[7] The importance

[4] Available at: <www.domstol.dk/om/talogfakta/statistik/Pages/civilesager.aspx>. This is a total number for municipal courts, appeals courts and the Supreme Court. The majority of cases, about 66,000, are heard on the municipal court level.

[5] A number of providers were surveyed in 2011 and their input is combined with public statistics and my own estimates based on working in the field of ADR for many years. Hence, this figure should be read with a corresponding degree of caution.

[6] The labour market in Denmark is based on a widespread use of various dispute resolution mechanisms. However, this is a wholly separate and extensive area, which is too excessive to be included in this chapter. Further information can be found in eg J Kristiansen, 'Conciliation, Mediation and Arbitration in Denmark' in F Valdés Dal-Ré (ed), *Labour Conciliation, Mediation and Arbitration in European Union Countries* (Ministerio De Trabajo Y Asuntos Sociales, Colección Y Estudios, Núm. 53, 2003) 103–20.

[7] For these and other values see V Vindeløv, *Mediation* (Copenhagen, Djøf Publishing, 2007) 23ff.

of the values lies in their ability to guide practice and differentiate between mediation on the one side and authoritative mechanisms of conflict resolution, such as litigation, on the other side, both in terms of the role of the third party, the role of the parties and the role of law.[8]

Secondly, mediation in Denmark is dominated by a *facilitative* ideology, ie the role of the mediator is to guide the process and generally not to make recommendations or evaluations with regard to the substance of the dispute.[9] This is the foundation of the majority of training, and is reflected in the legislation and ethical guidelines. As pointed out by, for instance, Dorothy Della Noce, James A Wall and Suzanne Chan-Serafin, mediation is not always practised in accordance with the way it is presented in theory.[10] However, an empirical study of court-connected mediation in Denmark suggests that mediators are in fact predominantly facilitative, supporting anecdotal evidence on this point.[11]

Thirdly, the resolution of disputes in mediation is generally based on *current law* only to the extent that parties choose to involve the law in their considerations. Mediators do not have an obligation to involve the rule of law on the matter at hand. Rather, they are obligated to let the parties decide what rules and norms *they* want to apply as long as the agreement does not involve criminal action (and for court-connected mediators does not conflict with mandatory legislation).

Fourthly, mediation is generally practised by *trained* mediators. Although, there are no certification or national minimum training requirements, most mediation is practised after some level of basic training. Basic training varies in length from as little as four to seven days, spread over potentially a number of months to as much as a two-year part-time university-level programme.[12] It deserves mention, too, that mediation is an academic field in its own right in Denmark and an elective part of the curriculum at the major law schools.[13] This contributes to the development of mediation in theory as well as in practice.

In the following sections, the main areas of mediation (court-connected mediation, public-sector mediation in family matters, mediation by lawyers and arbitration institutions, and victim–offender mediation) and the regulation of each area will be discussed in turn. Due to Denmark's exemption from EU regulation in the judicial area, Denmark is not bound by Directive 2008/52/EC of the European Parliament and

[8] This differentiation is illustrated by seeing mediation and adjudication as belonging to different paradigms for conflict resolution, see Vindeløv, *Mediation* 27ff. Mediation belongs to the so-called 'new paradigm' where, inter alia, both parties are taken into consideration and parties must participate actively, as opposed to the so-called 'old paradigm' (to which adjudication belongs), where a third party settles a conflict typically with one party winning and the other losing.

[9] For facilitative and evaluative mediation see LL Riskin, 'Understanding Mediators' Orientations, Strategies, and Techniques: A Grid for the Perplexed' (1996) 1 *Harvard Negotiation Law Review* 7 and LL Riskin, 'Decisionmaking in Mediation: The New Old Grid and the New New Grid System' (2003–04) 79 *Notre Dame Law Review* 1.

[10] See, eg DD Noce, 'Evaluative Mediation: In Search of Practice Competencies' (2009) 27 *Conflict Resolution Quarterly* 195, and JA Wall and S Chan-Serafin, 'Do Mediators Walk Their Talk in Civil Cases' (2010) 28 *Conflict Resolution Quarterly* 3, 11ff.

[11] See L Adrian, *Mellem retssag og rundbordssamtale—retsmægling i teori og praksis* (Copenhagen, Jurist- og Økonomforbundets Forlag, 2012).

[12] For the two-year master programme at the Law Faculty at the University of Copenhagen see <jura.ku.dk/uddannelser/efterogvidereuddannelse/master/>.

[13] At the Law Faculty of the University of Copenhagen there is also a full professorship in mediation, as well as an executive master programme.

of the Council of 21 May 2008 on certain aspects of mediation in civil and commercial matters, and the Directive has not been transposed into national legislation on a voluntary basis.[14]

A. Court-connected Mediation of Civil Cases

Mediation and civil court cases have historical roots. From 1795 to 1952, Denmark had a system of mediation boards operating *outside* the court system. As a general rule, parties who wished to file a civil suit were required to attempt to mediate the case as a prerequisite to initiating court proceedings. In 1952, mediation moved *inside* the courts and became judicial in nature. Mediation was integrated into the adjudication process and judges were required to try to settle the case as part of their judicial activities. Judicial mediation remains an integral part of civil proceedings, but has very little in common with modern day mediation, and in 2003 a pilot project regarding mediation of civil cases as an *alternative* to adjudication was initiated in four municipal courts and one appeals court. The pilot project was evaluated in 2005.[15] In accordance with studies on party satisfaction in other arenas and in other countries, the majority of the parties were somewhat or completely satisfied with their mediation and would recommend court-connected mediation to others. Furthermore, the evaluation showed that the parties entered agreements in 64 per cent of the cases and that only approximately 5 per cent of civil cases relevant for mediation were in fact mediated, leaving plenty of room for expansion.

Encouraged by the positive reviews of users, court-connected mediation of civil cases was made a permanent feature of the Danish judicial system in all courts except the Supreme Court by an addition to the Danish Administration of Justice Act (Chapter 27) in 2008. The legislation was accepted by a unanimous and unusually supportive Parliament.[16] The purpose of implementing a system of court-connected mediation was to provide citizens with a manner of resolving their disputes which is *qualitatively* different from adjudication and judicial mediation in the course of adjudication which is based on current law. The government hoped that by providing a dispute resolution process where the parties' interests, needs and future could be addressed and where the parties could influence the proceedings, they would reach solutions to their conflict that they considered more satisfactory than court rulings. Furthermore, mediation of civil cases would further the overall goal of providing the public with more flexible forms of dispute resolution. During the legislative debate in Parliament, various parties supported the general goal of providing a different process, and to some a secondary motivation was the hope that mediation might lead to less adjudication and thus indirectly provide a more efficient justice system.[17]

[14] The directive is listed alongside mediation initiatives in a description of other countries and a recommendation from the Council of Europe in the preparatory work leading to regulation of court-connected mediation, but there is nothing to suggest that the content of the directive has influenced the legislation in any way.

[15] J Roepstorff and B Kyvsgaard, *Forsøg med retsmægling—en evalueringsrapport* (Copenhagen, Justitsministeriets Forskningsenhed, 2005).

[16] See discussions in Parliament, 13 December 2007, FT 2007–08.

[17] See discussions in Parliament, 13 December 2007, FT 2007–08.

All courts except the Supreme Court are obliged to provide mediation services in civil actions, and judges and attorneys with special training in mediation can serve as mediators.[18] Mediators are administratively appointed to each case from the court's panel of mediators.[19] According to preliminary, unofficial statistical information, 422 cases were mediated successfully in 2011.[20] Mediation is offered to parties after filing of the case and payment of the filing fee. Participation is voluntary and the parties can withdraw from the process at any time—no 'punishment' is imposed either for declining mediation or for not reaching a solution in mediation. The process is confidential for all involved, and mediators are exempt from the general duty to give evidence if the case proceeds in court. Mediation is offered free of charge and can take place at any point in time during the adjudicative process, but in most instances mediation takes place soon after the case is filed. When mediation is accepted by the parties, the legal proceedings are brought to a halt. Court-connected mediation is carried out in accordance with a structured mediation model, which emphasises facilitative mediation.[21] As a general rule, mediator action such as providing suggestions for solutions or evaluating the merit of the case occurs on a very limited basis, this being possible only when the parties ask for such input and the mediator finds it appropriate. Attorneys may attend mediations, but the parties and not the lawyer play the principal role in the process. For example, the parties always participate, they present the matter at hand themselves and they do more of the talking than their lawyers.[22] Should the case not be resolved in mediation, the mediator cannot participate as judge or attorney in the case, and information about what has transpired in mediation cannot become part of the subsequent litigation unless the parties agree to it.

If the case is resolved in court-connected mediation, the parties can choose to make it enforceable by requesting that the agreement be added to the court records. If they do so, the legal effect of the mediated agreement is equated with the legal effect of settlements made in the course of adjudication and can be accordingly enforced (see Administration of Justice Act sections 270 and 478). Otherwise, the parties' agreement is binding in the same manner as any private agreement made in Denmark, but in most instances the parties have to obtain a judgment before it can be enforced. Unless the parties decide otherwise, they each carry their own expenses occurring from mediation. With regard to potential liability, mediators are liable like other professionals, and are subject to the general rules of damages in Danish law.

In terms of how court-connected mediation is practised, an empirical study suggests that mediators primarily practise a facilitative mediation style, as mentioned earlier, and the parties and not the attorneys play the principal role in the course of the medi-

[18] At any point in time during litigation, parties can choose to mediate a case privately, in which case the regulation of court-connected mediation does not apply.

[19] Approximately 40% of the cases are mediated by mediators with an attorney background and 60% by mediators with a judicial background, according to available data in a mailing from the national court administration dated 12 August 2011. There is considerable interaction between the two groups of mediators and, among other aspects, they are offered joint supplementary training by the court administration and have cooperated in establishing ethical guidelines for court-connected mediation.

[20] According to a mailing from the national court administration dated 20 September 2012. More recent statistical information is unfortunately unavailable. There is reason to believe that this is an underestimation due to inaccuracies in the data collection.

[21] For details on this model, the reflexive model, see Vindeløv, *Mediation*.

[22] For court-connected mediation in practice see Adrian, *Mellem retssag og rundbordssamtale—retsmægling i teori og praksis*.

ation meeting and in deciding the outcome.[23] Furthermore, the parties in about 50 per cent of the cases that are successfully resolved in mediation reach agreements that include other elements than would be possible in a judgment. At the same time, the study suggests that court-connected mediation unintendedly seems to import features from the adjudicative system, such as focusing on issues that are relevant from a judicial perspective and using primarily legal jargon in the phrasing of the agreement.

The legislation on court-connected mediation is characterised by the minimal framework provided by a few sections found in Chapter 27 of the Administration of Justice Act (Retsplejeloven); this legislation notably omits issues such as a definition of mediation, the role of the parties and the mediator, participation in mediation and the model of mediation. Those issues are addressed only in the preparatory work carried out by a governmental committee.[24] Preparatory work plays an independent role as a source of law in Denmark, but it does not carry the same weight as legislation proper. In addition to regulation by legislation and preparatory work, court-connected mediation is regulated in a set of ethical guidelines for practice issued by the national court administration. This eclectic form of regulation has the advantage of being flexible, leaving room for designing and conducting mediations in a manner suitable to each specific case with the possibility of maximum influence by the parties. The disadvantage is that matters important from a mediation perspective—such as the emphasis on facilitative mediation—are regulated in sources of law that carry less weight than legislation. Hence, they are easier to ignore and may lose power over time. A more detailed legislative regulation of the most important aspects of mediation from a *mediation* perspective rather than a *legal* perspective would be more effective in emphasising the importance of mediation features and simultaneously be more effective in protecting mediation as a distinct dispute resolution feature.

B. Public Sector Mediation in Family Matters

Regional state administrations[25] are the entry points for resolving disputes regarding custody, visitation, residence and other disagreements between parents who no longer live together. In a one-year period from 1 February 2010 to 31 January 2011, the regional state administrations handled a total of about 20,000 cases regarding these matters.[26] Regional state administrations make administrative decisions about visitation rights if no agreement is reached by the parents, whereas custody and residence

[23] Adrian, *Mellem retssag og rundbordssamtale—retsmægling i teori og praksis*.

[24] See Administration of Justice Act, Chapter 27, and Betænkning nr 1481, *Reform af den civile retspleje V—Retsmægling* (Copenhagen, Justitsministeriet, 2006).

[25] Called '*statsforvaltninger*'. A total of five *statsforvaltninger* cover five different geographical regions. At the time of the writing (March 2013), a merger of the five *statsforvaltninger* is proposed by the government.

[26] See *Statistik om forældreansvarslovens effekt i de sager, der behandles i statsforvaltningerne*, (Copenhagen, Family Law Department, 2011). About 8,000 of the cases regarded custody and residence. Some of these were undisputed, since the regional state administration handles disputes as well as sanctions agreements regarding custody. However, since parents came to an agreement in approximately 2,300 or 26% of these cases, the remainder were definitely disputed cases. This leaves the number of disputed cases regarding custody and residency at somewhere between 5,700 and 8,000, and the total number of disputes handled between 17,700 and 20,000.

matters are referred to court if the parents are unable to arrive at an agreement at the regional state administration level (see sections 14, 17 and 21 of the Parental Responsibility Act (lov om forældreansvar)). The primary tool for resolving these matters are administrative meetings with parents conducted by a lawyer alone or a lawyer working in tandem with either a psychologist or social worker with expertise in children. If these meetings do not result in agreement, the parents are offered mediation or counselling by an expert on children.

Mediation in family matters was introduced nationwide in 2001 as a pilot project and it was evaluated in September 2004.[27] Overall, 71 per cent of the parents found the mediation altogether successful. In 84 per cent of the cases the parents arrived at an agreement or partial agreement; in 52 per cent of the cases the agreement was more or less upheld after six months, in another 23 per cent less so and in 19 per cent not at all. Based on the positive evaluation of the pilot project, the service continued and was incorporated in the Parental Responsibility Act in 2007. The legislation is rather brief, stating that the regional state administration offers parents and children mediation if they disagree on custody, residence or visitation, as well as in other situations where there is a need for mediation (see section 32). The Parental Responsibility Act authorises the responsible ministry to provide more detailed regulation of mediation if deemed necessary (section 42(5)), which is done in a statutory Decree on Custody, Residence and Visitation (sections 16–19) and in two sets of guidelines.[28] In addition, a set of ethical guidelines regulates mediation in this area.

According to the ministerial Guideline on Visitation, mediation is defined as an alternative to third-party decisions which aims to assist parents in negotiating an acceptable solution.[29] The guideline goes on to describe the mediator as neutral and as working in a facilitative rather than evaluative manner; consequently, the mediator cannot make any ruling in the case if the parties do not reach an agreement.

Mediation is confidential as far as the mediators are concerned. They are covered by the general rule of confidentiality covering civil servants. Moreover, an additional rule of confidentiality is imposed on the mediators as they are not allowed to pass on information from the mediation to colleagues working on the legal case, and likewise their colleagues are barred from requesting information from the mediators unless the parties agree to it (see section 19 of the statutory Decree on Custody, Residence and Visitation). There is no confidentiality rule governing the parties, but parties often make a good faith agreement whereby confidentiality is a part of the mediation.

Mediation is offered free of charge and is voluntary. It is up to the parties to enter mediation and they can terminate their participation at any point in time. The parents must participate in the mediation personally and may bring a lawyer or someone else, but commonly choose not to. If the parties reach an agreement concerning custody and visitation, the parties can choose to make the agreement enforceable. According to the ministerial Guideline on Custody, mediations are carried out in a couple of

[27] CS Henriksen, M Malmgren and MM Juul, *Konfliktmægling i statsamterne* (Copenhagen, CASA, 2004).

[28] For the different types of regulation in Denmark (statute, statutory decree, guidelines etc) see P Blume, *Legal Method in Danish Law* (Copenhagen, Djøf Publishing, 2011).

[29] Vejledning nr 70 from 27/09/2012 om samvær, 3.6.3.2.

three- to four-hour meetings.[30] Even though mediation—according to the Parental Responsibility Act—includes mediations with children, this is not yet being practised.[31]

The principal idea of the Danish legislation regarding disputes over children in the event of divorce is that parents maintain joint responsibility regarding the children by caring for them and by cooperating and making joint decisions regarding the major matters concerning the children. The legislation is aimed at the rights of children rather than the rights of parents, and parental cooperation and the decisions made by the parents themselves are considered to be in the best interests of the children. This ideology has become more manifest over the last decade and is mirrored in the legislation. The inclusion of mediation in the Parental Responsibility Act both emphasises this ideology and makes mediation services mandatory. By stating that the regional state administration has to offer mediation, it is not possible to administratively cease this service.

So far, attention has been given to disputes over children. However, separation and divorce are also dealt with by the regional state administrations. Separation and divorce can be granted by administrative licence if the spouses agree to the central terms of the separation or divorce. If they are unable to come to an agreement by themselves or with the assistance of a case officer, they may be offered mediation (see section 41 of the Marriage and Matrimonial Causes Act (lovbekendtgørelse nr 38 af 15/01/2007 om ægteskabs indgåelse og opløsning)). Mediation in these matters is provided by the regional state administration in exactly the same manner as described above in disputes concerning children, and sometimes both matters are combined in the mediation. If the parties still cannot agree regarding the conditions of the divorce, the case is turned over to the courts for decision.

A total of 613 mediations were carried out in the regional state administrations in 2010 and 243 in the first six months of 2011.[32] Unfortunately these numbers are not broken down into disputes regarding divorce and those regarding children, but historically most mediations have concerned disputes about children.[33] In the first couple of years after the introduction of mediation, the number of cases mediated was lower than later experienced, which can be expected in a period of implementation. Since then, however, the number has remained relatively stable. This might indicate that the number of mediated cases has reached an ideal level. Another explanation is that the regional administrative administrations have curbed the increase in mediations by encouraging other (and cheaper) forms of dispute handling. In any event, the regional state administrations are obliged to continue offering mediation services, which can serve as an illustration of an advantage of legislative regulation seen from a mediation perspective: even in financially difficult times a relatively expensive service (as seen from a short-term perspective at least) cannot be eliminated.

[30] See Vejledning nr 70 from 27/09/2012 om samvær. Due to financial limitations, the option of holding two meetings is rarely used.

[31] See Vejledning nr 70 from 27/09/2012 om samvær.

[32] According to the most recent statistical information from the Family Law Department under the Ministry of Justice.

[33] This assessment being based on years of personal experience with consultation regarding mediation at the regional state administrations.

C. Mediation in Other Areas

Other than state-supported initiatives, mediation is implemented in a variety of areas, such as in schools, workplaces, doctor–patient relations and landlord–tenant disputes. In these areas, mediation is not primarily an alternative to adjudication, but mediations may lead to cases being resolved without going to court. For the purpose of this chapter, only a few mediation initiatives in the legal arena will be briefly addressed.

i. Mediation by Lawyers

In 2003, a group of lawyers formed an organisation called 'Danske Mediatoradvokater' (Danish Mediator Lawyers),[34] affiliated with the Danish Bar Association.[35] Today, 170 lawyers with mediation training promote and provide mediation. Although the bulk of their cases concern legal disputes, they offer mediation in other areas as well. The organisation appoints mediators upon request, which is once a month on average. Information on how many mediations are conducted by this group of mediators is unavailable, but anecdotal evidence suggests that the number is rather limited.

The overall framework for mediations conducted by mediator-lawyers is outlined in a standard contract that all parties sign prior to entering mediation, as well as in a set of ethical guidelines covering the conduct of mediators.[36] Accordingly, mediation is voluntary and confidential for all involved. The role of the mediator-lawyer is to assist the parties in resolving the dispute themselves. The parties may bring their lawyers to the mediation, but they are required to attend personally. If one party in the dispute is a legal entity, a person with authority to enter an agreement must participate. The mediator must be neutral and impartial, and cannot act as advisor to the parties or make any decisions regarding the conflict. The Danish Mediator Lawyers have adapted a rule that also governs court-connected mediation, stating that mediators are not obliged to evaluate the strengths and weaknesses of the legal aspects of the case or to intervene if the parties arrive at a solution that is different from the likely outcome of adjudication or arbitration (paragraph 4.9 in the standard contract).

The fee for the mediation has to be reasonable, and the general rule is that each party covers his or her own expenses and pays half of the fee for the mediation. In accordance with the general rules for attorney fees in Denmark, contingency fees in mediation are not permitted (ethical guidelines paragraphs 4.3 and 4.4).

ii. Mediation by Arbitration Institutions

The two primary arbitration institutions offer mediation as well, but apparently their

[34] See <www.mediatoradvokater.dk/>.

[35] In addition to this organisation, the Danish Bar Association supported the setting up of another mediation agency, The Danish Mediation Institute, in 2007; see <www.mediationsinstituttet.com/#/344234/> for further information. The Mediation Institute has never managed to establish itself as a significant actor on the mediation scene, and at the time of writing (March 2013) a merger with Danish Mediator Lawyers is under way.

[36] The standard contract as well as the ethical guidelines are available in Danish from their website <www.mediatoradvokater.dk>.

mediation services are seldom used.[37] Each of these organisations has issued rules for mediation that resemble those of the Danish Mediator Lawyers.[38] However, they differ in one important aspect, as the role of the mediator operating under the arbitration organisations' guidelines includes making suggestions for settlement. This is probably a spillover from the main activity of the institution, providing decisions in the form of arbitration awards. Furthermore, a mediator is prohibited from meeting with the parties privately according to one of the organisation's guidelines.[39] Here also, this may very well be attributable to the procedures governing the main activity of the institution, arbitration, which may in turn be inspired by the procedural rules governing litigation.

iii. Victim–Offender Mediation

The first government initiative on mediation dates back to 1994 and was in the area of victim–offender mediation.[40] Since mediation in this area is offered as a supplement and not an alternative to criminal proceedings, unlike as in Norway, for instance, it is not ADR per se. However, since the method employed is mediation and since the area is subject to national legislation and generally subject to international interest, it is worth closing this section on mediation initiatives in Denmark by making a few brief comments on this system and its regulation.

After years of being a pilot project in a few police districts, victim–offender mediation was made available nationwide effective from January 2010 and was regulated by legislation in the Mediation in Criminal Matters Act (lov nr 467 af 12/06/2009 om konfliktråd i anledning af en strafbar handling). In the proposal for the legislation and in the discussions in Parliament, out of consideration for the victim, the offender and society at large,[41] the reasons for implementing mediation in this area were in line with general restorative justice ideas.[42] For victims, the purpose is to provide an opportunity of coming to terms with the incident, hopefully restoring a feeling of safety. For offenders, the purpose is to provide an opportunity of assuming responsibility for the incident, leading to more responsible behaviour in the future, which might lead to less criminal behaviour to the benefit of society at large.

Mediation services are offered by the police and most often made available prior to trial. Such a service is offered free of charge on a voluntary basis in cases where the offender has largely admitted to the crime. Lay persons are used as mediators and they receive training in mediation. A confidentiality rule is in place for mediators, who are

[37] According to statistical information from the Danish Institute of Arbitration, only a few cases are mediated each year; see <www.voldgiftsinstituttet.dk/dk/Menu/Statistik>. The same situation seems to be true for the Arbitration Tribunal for Construction, but, as it has not been possible to obtain statistical information from this tribunal, this information cannot be verified.

[38] See <www.voldgiftsinstituttet.dk/dk/Service/English> for the rules governing mediation in the Danish Institute for Arbitration and <www.voldgift.dk/> for the rules governing the Arbitration Tribunal for Construction.

[39] See s 8 in the rules governing mediation by the Arbitration Tribunal for Construction.

[40] For a description of victim–offender mediation during the pilot project period, see V Vindeløv, *Konfliktmægling—en refleksiv model*, 2nd edn (Copenhagen, Jurist- og Økonomforbundets Forlag, 2008) 359ff.

[41] See Betænkning nr 1501 om Konfliktråd (Copenhagen, Justitsministeriet, 2008) and discussions in Parliament, 26 and 27 January 2009, FT 2008–09.

[42] For restorative justice see H Zehr, *Changing Lenses* (Scottdale, PA, Herald Press, 1990) and G Johnstone and DW Van Ness (eds), *The Handbook of Restorative Justice* (Cullompton, Willan Publishing, 2007).

also privileged from giving testimony. There is no similar rule for parties, but they can agree on good-will confidentiality between themselves. Even though mediation is not an alternative to criminal proceedings, participation may lead to a reduced sentence at the discretion of the judge of the case; in some—but far from all—cases it has just such an effect.

Through the implementation of the legislation from 2010 to 2012, a total of 1,905 mediations were conducted.[43] All types of crimes can be mediated. However, assault is by far the most common type, followed by robbery and burglary. According to an evaluation of victim–offender mediation from 2012, more than 80 per cent of participants found the mediation to be successful and in about half of the cases the parties entered a written agreement.[44]

Like the regulation of mediation of family matters, the legislation governing victim–offender mediation is somewhat brief, empowering the National Commission of the Danish Police to issue more detailed regulations. This authorisation had been used to issue only limited further regulations, and the authorisation to regulate, for instance, the way mediators work and how the mediation session is conducted has not been used.[45] In addition to the legislation proper, victim–offender mediation is regulated in detail in the preparatory work and, since the legislation and additional regulation is rather limited, the preparatory work by default plays an important role in regulating both the work of the mediators as well as organisational matters.[46] Victim–offender mediation shares this feature with court-connected mediation of civil cases (for a discussion of the consequences of this type of regulation, see section II.A above).

The legislation on victim–offender mediation does not have incentives for participation other than making the services easily available and offering mediation free of charge. However, the possibility of a reduced sentence, which is not a right by legislation but a discretionary option granted to judges, may serve as an incentive for offender participation—though very few offenders cited this as a reason for choosing mediation.[47]

III. ARBITRATION

A single rule from 1683 served as the only regulation of arbitration for almost 300 years.[48] According to this rule, courts were excluded from trying cases when the parties had entered an agreement to arbitrate, and arbitration rulings were binding and could not be tried by courts. After more than a decade of debate in the 1960s and 1970s on whether more extensive legislation was necessary and what should be included,

[43] See <www.konfliktraad.dk/konfliktraad-i-tal>.

[44] FK Hansen, *Evaluering af konfliktråd—den landsdækkende ordning* (Copenhagen, CASA, 2012) 90ff.

[45] See bekendtgørelse nr 1081 af 15/09/2010 om konfliktråd i anledning af en strafbar handling (ministerial Decree on Mediation in Criminal Matters).

[46] No ethical guidelines have been issued as to this type of mediation.

[47] For the offender, the primary reasons given for participation were to apologise and show consideration to the victims. Only very few offenders chose mediation hoping to have their sentence reduced. For the victims, the primary reasons for choosing mediation were meeting the offender and being provided an explanation for the offending behaviour. See Hansen, *Evaluering af konfliktråd—den landsdækkende ordning* 84ff.

[48] Danske Lov (Danish Law) s 1-6-1.

the first Arbitration Act was passed in 1974. The Act mirrored the ambivalence of its origin by being rather brief and non-inclusive, eg by leaving decisions as to how the case should be prepared and conducted to the arbitrator(s) in each case. The Act was in part inspired by international trends in arbitration and permitted the implementation of the New York Convention from 1958 (the Convention on the Recognition and Enforcement of Foreign Arbitral Awards). In the years to come, the Act turned out to be insufficient and unable to match international legislative developments, including those of other Scandinavian countries, which have inspired Denmark in many legislative matters.

Heavily influenced by the UNCITRAL Model Law on International Commercial Arbitration from 1989 and by legislation enacted primarily in Sweden and Norway, which is also based on the Model Law, a revised and much more comprehensive Arbitration Act was implemented in 2005. Because of the very brief and superficial nature of the 1974 Act, it is fair to say that national regulation of arbitration only came into place with this new Act.

The Arbitration Act (Voldgiftsloven) covers arbitration by agreement. Arbitration agreements can be made with respect to future as well as to existing conflicts and are legally binding. Hence, a court will reject hearing a case with an arbitration stipulation. With a few notable exceptions, most of the regulations in the Act are non-mandatory. The parties cannot decide on the applicability of the Act, the matters that can be decided by arbitration, the relationship between arbitration and adjudication or the enforceability of the award, but, other than that, the parties to the dispute are free to make their own decisions as to most other aspects of the arbitration. They can decide on the composition and authority of the tribunal, the requirements of the award, cost and security, etc.

In terms of the conduct of the proceedings, the Arbitration Act has adopted Articles 18 and 19 from the UNCITRAL Model Law. Hence, this is another area where the parties are free to agree on their own terms, with two exceptions: namely, the parties must be treated equally and each party must be provided the opportunity to present their own case (see sections 18 and 19 of the Arbitration Act). If the parties have not agreed on procedure, the tribunal carries out the proceedings in the manner it deems appropriate (see section 19). The bulk of arbitration in Denmark is conducted by two private arbitration institutions: the Danish Institute of Arbitration (Voldgiftsinstituttet)—a non-profit organisation founded in 1981—and the Arbitration Tribunal for Construction (Voldgiftsnævnet for bygge- og anlægsvirksomhed). Both of these institutions are bound by the Arbitration Act, including its procedural rules. Using the parties' right to design the conduct of the proceedings, each has implemented quite detailed rules of procedure that the parties must agree to follow when using those institutions' arbitration services.[49] The total number of arbitrations has generally been on the rise for at least the past 15 years.[50] The Arbitration Tribunal for Construction has the highest number of cases, the last available statistical information showing that 541 cases were handled in 2006–07. In the Danish Institute of Arbitra-

[49] The procedural rules for the Danish Institute of Arbitration can be found in English at <www.voldgiftsinstituttet.dk/en/Menu/Arbitration> and the Arbitration Tribunal for Constructions procedural rules can be found in Danish at <www.voldgift.dk>.

[50] See J Juul and PF Thommesen, *Voldgiftsloven*, 2nd edn (Copenhagen, Forlaget Thomson, 2008) 24 for statistical information for 1995–2007.

tion, 89 cases were handled in that same period, whereas a total of 87 cases were filed in 2011.[51]

The UNCITRAL Model Law's Article 28 has been incorporated into section 28 of the Arbitration Act. Hence, the tribunal makes the award on the basis of the rules of law chosen by the parties. If the parties fail to make such a choice, the tribunal will choose. The tribunal is only allowed to base its award on equity (*ex aequo et bono* and *amiables compositeurs*) if the parties have expressly authorised it to do so. Prior to the 2005 Arbitration Act, it was generally assumed that a Danish tribunal could do so without express authorisation. However, since arbitration is not a dispute resolution mechanism chosen in order to let a tribunal make decisions based on rules other than those applied by a court of justice but, rather, is chosen in order to achieve efficiency, competence and to some extent confidentiality,[52] this understanding was changed by the revision of the Arbitration Act and the approach brought in accordance with the UNCITRAL Model Law, thereby being adjusted to the rules governing arbitration in other countries.

In principle, a court of justice cannot review an arbitration award and setting aside an arbitral award is, in general, possible only in a very limited number of situations (see Arbitration Act, section 37). These are similar to those of the Model Act, Article 34, and include situations where the parties have to provide proof that, for example, the agreement is not valid under the law to which the parties have subjected it or the agreement includes decisions on matters beyond the scope of the submission to arbitration. If a court finds that the subject matter of the dispute cannot be subject to arbitration or if the award is in conflict with the public policy of the state, the award can similarly be set aside.

Arbitration is not excluded if the subject matter of the case concerns mandatory law in part or in full.[53] However, the arbitration tribunal is bound by mandatory rules, and it is assumed—contrary to the general principle that a court of justice cannot review the content of an award—that the court can to some extent review and set aside arbitration awards that are in conflict with the public policy of the state in those instances where mandatory rules have been ignored or wrongly applied by an arbitration tribunal to an unacceptable degree.[54] To date, however, no court decision has been issued in respect this matter. Hence, there is legal uncertainty on this point.

The Arbitration Act has adopted the New York Convention, Article V (as has the UNCITRAL Model Law in Article 36), in ruling that international arbitration awards are recognised and can be enforced in Denmark by equating international and national awards (see section 38). Recognition and enforcement can be refused only under the same circumstances as listed in the New York Convention, Article 36 (see the Arbitration Act, section 39). These include, for example, situations where a party to an arbitration agreement was to some extent incapacitated, the party against whom the award is invoked was not given proper notice of the appointment of an arbitrator, or the recognition or enforcement would be contrary to the public policy of the state.

As is apparent, regulation of arbitration in Denmark has been heavily influenced by

[51] The most recent available statistics are available at <www.voldgiftsinstituttet.dk/dk/Menu/Statistik>.
[52] Juul and Thommesen, *Voldgiftsloven* 267.
[53] Juul and Thommesen, *Voldgiftsloven* 54.
[54] Juul and Thommesen, *Voldgiftsloven* 60ff.

international rules and practice. It is an example of the potentially substantial impact of an international model law, and this impact is probably in part caused by business considerations and the international nature of arbitration.

IV. BOARDS AND TRIBUNALS

Many conflicts are resolved before going to court by bringing the dispute before one of the countless boards and tribunals.[55] These treat disputes concerning a variety of subject matters, ranging from the smaller complaint boards, which deal with complaints concerning undertakers, driving instruction schools, electrical installations or holiday homes, on to more widely used boards of broader interest, which address consumer complaints concerning merchandise, insurance, medical malpractice and banking. Some boards and tribunals are set up by the government, for example the Consumer Complaints Board (Forbrugerklagenævnet) and the Rent Control Board (Huslejenævn) that each municipality must have. Others are private and typically organised by trade organisations, sometimes in collaboration with the governmental Danish Consumer Agency. One such example is the Insurance Complaints Board (Ankenævnet for Forsikring). If the private consumer board meets certain criteria, they can receive governmental approval. Consequently, they are covered by the general regulation concerning consumer complaints in the Consumer Complaints Act, and this serves as a quality stamp.

Even though boards and tribunals differ tremendously in set-up, size, caseload, type of case, procedure, etc, many of them share some central features. First of all, they provide simple access to justice. It is generally easy and inexpensive to file a complaint, as many boards and tribunals provide complaint forms, together with readily understood information about how to register a complaint, on a website.[56] Hence, a complaint can be filed without the assistance of a lawyer. Fees vary, but are usually very low. In the three largest boards (the Rent Control Boards, the Consumer Complaints Board and the Insurance Complaints Board), the fees (for 2012) are €18, €21 and €27 respectively. Many boards are chaired by professionals with a legal background. Governmentally recognised boards and tribunals are all chaired by judges from the court system, giving them a fair amount of legitimacy.

Complaints in most boards and tribunals are handled and decided upon in writing, and decisions are based on the application of current law. Their rulings can usually be challenged in court. Rulings in governmentally approved consumer boards can be enforced if the business does not object to the ruling within 30 days of service according to the Consumer Complaints Act, section 4.

As is apparent, tribunals generally employ summary legal processes with third parties making rulings based on law. They serve as an alternative dispute resolution mechanism by resolving many disputes short of going to court, but they share critical

[55] It is not possible to secure a complete account of the number of cases resolved by these bodies each year. In addition, it has not been possible to locate all boards and tribunals for this contribution. Test samples from the most well known and likely most-used boards and tribunals suggest that at least 18,000 cases were heard in this manner in 2011.

[56] For an example of such a website (in Danish) see <www.ankeforsikring.dk>; for the complaint form see <www.ankeforsikring.dk/Hvordan_man_klager.aspx>.

aspects of litigation by being adjudicative and by being based on the logic of law in both procedures used and the type of ruling.

V. INCENTIVES TO USE ADR

The primary incentive for the use of alternative dispute resolution in Denmark lies in the ADR mechanism itself, it being quicker, cheaper, private, less formal and sometimes providing better solutions to the disputes at hand. There is no national strategy for creating incentives to use ADR and there is no punishment for not pursuing ADR, such as incurring the other party's legal costs in a future litigation as a consequence of merely declining ADR. Incentives are provided more indirectly—for example, by providing some ADR services for free or at a very low cost, as mentioned above, or through the filing fee system of the Danish courts. In court cases, only about half the fee is paid upon the filing of the case, the other half being paid when the case is scheduled for trial. This encourages settlements before trial, including the use of ADR to achieve this.

Incorporating an option of referral to mediation in legislation is another example of an indirect incentive, and is found in the Danish Rent Acts. Rent Control Boards and Tenant Boards resolve a variety of conflicts and can encourage—but not order—the parties to seek mediation (see, for example, section 105 of the Rent Act for Social Housing (lov om leje af almen boliger)).[57] Including a mediation option in legislation adds legitimacy to the process and increases awareness of this form of dispute resolution, which may in turn lead to increased use.

According to the Danish Bar Association's ethical guidelines from 2011, Article 16.9, lawyers are not required to advise clients on alternative dispute resolution mechanisms, but at a suitable point in time they ought to advise their client to settle the case or refer the case to mediation or the like.[58] The wording of this rule is new. A similar rule used to state that a lawyer must aim to provide the most inexpensive solution to the client's problem and, when appropriate, advise the client of the advantages of settling the case and/or the possibility of alternative dispute resolution. Among other changes, the wording 'alternative dispute resolution' has been amended to 'mediation or the like'. This does not exclude ADR mechanisms other than mediation, but it certainly highlights mediation over others, indicating that mediation is the preferred means of ADR. The reason may be that lawyers are very active in promoting and offering mediation (as described above in II.C.i) in collaboration with the Danish Bar Association, which issues the ethical guidelines. Another change is from 'must' to 'ought', making it less of an obligation to advise about ADR than it was before.

[57] An example of including ADR in developing legislation is found in the new Police Complaint Act, which came into effect on 1 January 2012. In the preparatory work, the new police complaint agency is authorised to launch a mediation pilot project in police misconduct cases. See Betænkning nr 1507, *Behandling om behandling af klager over politiet* (Copenhagen, Justitsministeriet, 2009) 162ff.

[58] *De advokatetiske regler*, Advokatrådet, 1 October 2011.

VI. REGULATION OF MEDIATION AND POLICY MATTERS

The discussion of regulation and policy matters in this final section will focus on mediation. Arbitration has already been subjected to regulation and to the development of an international model law. Tribunals and boards are usually embedded in very national contexts and, even though it is possible to be inspired by activities in other countries, it is an area that traditionally has strong ties to national regulation and legislation. Mediation, however, is an international and transnational activity that is being advanced in many countries and in many areas at the moment. Therefore, the issue of regulation on a national as well as on an international level is particularly relevant. Even so, it makes sense to continuously push for international definitions of all forms of ADR in order to ensure that each maintains its characteristics and in order to make the distinction between them clear to the consumers of dispute resolution services.

Opponents of the regulation of mediation often argue that the intrinsic values of informality and flexibility will be quelled if the field is regulated, and that regulation will lead to precisely the formal and legalised form of dispute resolution to which mediation is supposed to be an alternative. Even though this may be true if the regulation is too far-reaching and disrespectful of the nature of mediation, a careful and well-prepared regulation will probably rather lead to the *protection* of the values of mediation—it could, for example, be a way of securing specific mediation practices and avoiding others. In addition, some level of regulation could provide legitimacy, quality assurance and transparency in the field.

Many other forms of ADR are summary *rights-based* legal processes that have emerged from a need to provide dispute resolution mechanisms that are cheaper, faster and more straightforward than going to court. Even though mediation meets some of the same needs, it is fundamentally different. Mediation is an *interest and needs-based* dispute resolution method with heavy emphasis on the self-determination of the parties; law, by contrast, plays only a secondary role.[59] Ensuring these aspects of mediation ought to be the principal tenet of any regulation of the field.

Based on the Danish experience, where regulation of mediation has served as an impetus for mediation, it makes sense to develop an international model law which could inspire legislation at the national level, as has been the case in the area of arbitration with the UNCITRAL Model Law. Had a model law of mediation been in place prior to current Danish legislation, it might very well have influenced the development of that legislation. In mediation, a model law ought to be a general legal framework and include areas of principal importance from a mediation perspective, as well as from a legal perspective. If necessary, more detailed regulation ought to be pursued at the national level, so that rules can be tailored to the specific needs in the specific setting. However, even at the national level, regulation of mediation through legislation generally ought to be kept at a very general level, leaving more detailed regulation to other relevant bodies, such as providers of mediation services and professional mediator organisations.

From a perspective which takes a combined account of both mediation and legal

[59] See Adrian, *Mellem retssag og rundbordssamtale—retsmægling i teori og praksis* and L Adrian, 'Om standpunkter, interesser og behov' (2008) 68(4) *Kart og Plan* for more on needs and interests in mediation.

aspects, a number of areas ought to be included in a model law. A definition of mediation,[60] party self-determination, the facilitative role of the mediator and the voluntary participation by parties naturally belong in a regulation. Mediation is conducted without the procedural safeguards of legal processes, such as publicity, decision-making based on current law and a right of appeal. Hence, the protection of the parties lies in being able to enter and leave the process freely. This includes not having to risk incurring financial burdens or other types of 'punishment' for not participating in mediation or for not entering into a particular agreement. Protection of the parties also lies in the principle of self-determination combined with the mediator assuming a facilitative rather than an evaluative role. This ensures that mediators do not make decisions for the parties or make legal evaluations on a basis that is incomplete compared to adjudication, where judgment is passed only after the case is fully exposed, witnesses are heard, etc. In addition to protecting the parties, ensuring the principles central to mediation—voluntary participation and self-determination—through regulation safeguards the process from being colonised by legal features which might lead to mutation and result in mediation becoming more like early neutral evaluation or arbitration, which some observers see as a real threat.[61] Mediation belongs to one paradigm of conflict resolution and adjudicative processes to another, and regulation can act to support this differentiation.[62]

A model law ought to address the issue of confidentiality for mediators and the involved parties, including mediators being privileged from giving testimony in future court proceedings. Furthermore, the question of enforceability ought to be addressed. It seems fair to encourage enforceability as an option but not as an obligation. Making mediation agreements enforceable per se may influence the mediation process negatively by making enforceable aspects of the conflict the primary issue of mediation, by focusing primarily on enforceable solutions (and not, for example, on providing opportunity for an apology) and by making parties more hesitant to enter into agreements altogether.

Finally, the quality in practice ought to be addressed in a model law. This includes making adequate training of mediators a mandatory prerequisite for practicing mediation as well as making adherence to a set of ethical guidelines mandatory.

The Danish experience with regulation of mediation seems to indicate that regulation adds to the legitimacy of mediation. When mediation gets political attention and is subject to discussions on a government level, it automatically exudes a sense of being part of mainstream dispute resolution rather than a niche activity. This helps pave the way for mediation in areas where more adjudicatory forms of dispute resolution have traditionally reigned. Regulation also commits a variety of agencies to either provide mediation or other ADR services, or to consider implementing ADR activities as part of their dispute resolution options.

[60] An example of a definition worth imitating is found in Art 3 of the Directive 2008/52/EC of the European Parliament and of the Council of 21 May 2008 on certain aspects of mediation in civil and commercial matters: 'Mediation' means a structured process, however named or referred to, whereby two or more parties to a dispute attempt by themselves, on a voluntary basis, to reach an agreement on the settlement of their dispute with the assistance of a mediator.

[61] See Vindeløv, *Mediation* 255ff, and K Kovach and LP Love, 'Mapping Mediation: The Risk of Riskin's Grid' (1998) 3 *Harvard Negotiation Law Review* 71.

[62] For the different paradigms see Vindeløv, *Mediation* 27ff.

The Danish experience with the regulation of mediation also shows that governmental regulation tends to address the primarily legal aspects of mediation and leave out principal aspects of mediation seen from a mediation point of view. This leaves mediation open to taking on many forms and may potentially blur the characteristics of mediation. A regulation—whether national or international—should include legal aspects as well as mediation aspects, and should further include protection of proper mediation practice. Otherwise, mediation risks losing its central features and with that its justification and legitimacy. Consequently, mediation could turn out to be a short-lived attempt at providing a real alternative to adjudication.

BIBLIOGRAPHY

Adrian, L, *Mellem retssag og rundbordssamtale—retsmægling i teori og praksis* (Copenhagen, Jurist- og Økonomforbundets Forlag, 2012)
Adrian, L, 'Om standpunkter, interesser og behov' (2008) *Kart og Plan* 68(4)
Blume, P, *Legal Method in Danish Law* (Copenhagen, Djøf Publishing, 2011)
Hansen, FK, *Evaluering af konfliktråd—den landsdækkende ordning* (Copenhagen, CASA, 2012)
Henriksen, CS, Malmgren, M and Juul, MM, *Konfliktmægling i statsamterne* (Copenhagen, CASA 2004)
Johnstone, G and Ness, DW Van (eds), *The Handbook of Restorative Justice* (Cullompton, Willan Publishing, 2007)
Juul, J and Thommesen, PF, *Voldgiftsloven*, 2nd edn (Copenhagen, Forlaget Thomson, 2008)
Kristiansen, J, 'Conciliation, Mediation and Arbitration in Denmark' in F Valdés Dal-Ré (ed), *Labour Conciliation, Mediation and Arbitration in European Union Countries* (Ministerio De Trabajo Y Asuntos Sociales, Colección Y Estudios, Núm 53, 2003) 103–20
Kovach, K and Love, LP, 'Mapping Mediation: The Risk of Riskin's Grid' (1998) 3 *Harvard Negotiation Law Review* 71
Noce, DD, 'Evaluative Mediation: In Search of Practice Competencies' (2009) 27 *Conflict Resolution Quarterly* 193
Riskin, LL, 'Understanding Mediators' Orientations, Strategies, and Techniques: A Grid for the Perplexed' (1996) 1 *Harvard Negotiation Law Review* 7
Riskin, LL, 'Decisionmaking in Mediation: The New Old Grid and the New New Grid System' (2003–04) 79 *Notre Dame Law Review* 1
Roepstorff, J and Kyvsgaard, B, *Forsøg med retsmægling—en evalueringsrapport* (Copenhagen, Justitsministeriets Forskningsenhed, 2005)
Vindeløv, V, 'Mediation in Danish Law: In Retrospect and Perspective' in N Alexander (ed), *Global Trends in Mediation* (Köln, Centrale für Mediation, 2003) 121–35
Vindeløv, V, *Mediation* (Copenhagen, Djøf Publishing, 2007)
Vindeløv, V, *Konfliktmægling—en refleksiv model*, 2nd edn (Copenhagen, Jurist- og Økonomforbundets Forlag, 2008)
Wall, JA and Chan-Serafin, S, 'Do Mediators Walk Their Talk in Civil Cases' (2010) 28 *Conflict Resolution Quarterly* 3
Yarn, DH (ed), *Dictionary of Conflict Resolution* (San Francisco, Jossey-Bass Publishers, 1999)
Zehr, H, *Changing Lenses* (Scottdale, PA, Herald Press, 1990)

Reports from Parliamentary Commissions

Betænkning nr 1481 *Reform af den civile retspleje V—Retsmægling* (Copenhagen, Justitsministeriet, 2006)

Betænkning nr 1501 om Konfliktråd (Copenhagen, Justitsministeriet, 2008)

Betænkning nr 1507 *Behandling om behandling af klager over politiet* (Copenhagen, Justitsministeriet, 2009)

7

Regulation of Dispute Resolution in England and Wales: A Sceptical Analysis of Government and Judicial Promotion of Private Mediation

HAZEL GENN, SHIVA RIAHI AND KATHERINE PLEMING

I. INTRODUCTION

THIS CHAPTER REVIEWS contemporary ADR development in England and Wales. It is not intended to provide a comprehensive guide or analysis, since the last 15 years or so has seen a proliferation of private dispute resolution services, processes and schemes directed at different areas of civil, family, commercial and administrative law disputes, as well as community based initiatives. There is now a market in private dispute resolution services and, while there are no official data about the volume of mediations, arbitrations or other ADR processes taking place, provider organisations all talk of increases in caseloads.[1] The focus of the chapter is principally on mediation, since it is the development of this ADR process that has figured most significantly in justice system policy debates and is where the growth and visibility of private providers has been most noticeable. Section II of the chapter offers an overview of government and judicial policy on mediation since the mid-1990s. Section III provides a more factual description of the scope of mediation and arbitration services in the English dispute resolution landscape, together with a discussion of regulation and standards

II. OVERVIEW OF MODERN ADR POLICY AND DEVELOPMENT

A. Definitions

Alternative dispute resolution is an umbrella term which is generally applied to a range of techniques for resolving disputes other than by means of traditional court adjudication—for example, mediation, early neutral evaluation, arbitration, neutral expert

[1] For a recent discussion of the privatisation of civil justice see H Genn, *Why the Privatisation of Civil Justice is a Rule of Law Issue*, 36th FA Mann Annual Lecture, November 2012, available at <www.ucl.ac.uk/laws/academics/profiles/docs/Hazel/36th%20F%20A%20Mann%20Lecture%20Website.pdf>. The annual reports of the ICC show a gradual upward trend in arbitrations; CEDR the largest commercial mediation provider published statistics for 2004 showing an upward trend and a significant increase following the case of *Dunnett v Railtrack* in 2002.

fact-finding, MedArb (a mixture of mediation and arbitration) and mini-trials.[2] With the exception of arbitration and mini-trials, most forms of ADR are species of facilitated settlement. A critical feature of all forms of ADR is that they are dispute resolution processes conducted in private. Both the process and outcome of the procedures are generally confidential to the parties. Like other types of out-of-court settlement, the terms of mediated agreements are not publicly known.

Despite the range of processes included under the ADR umbrella or within the ADR tent, the focus of current ADR policy in England and the rest of the UK is on mediation rather than other forms of private dispute resolution. The basic definition of mediation is that of a voluntary process in which a neutral third party assists disputing parties to reach a consensual solution to their dispute. This characteristic distinguishes mediation from partisan negotiations carried out between lawyers on behalf of their clients. In classic 'facilitative' mediation, the mediator has no authority to impose a solution on the parties and the aim of the mediation is to achieve a settlement, or at least a clarification of the issues in dispute. Mediation can be undertaken at any point in a dispute, including after court proceedings have commenced or even during a trial. The outcome of successful mediation is an agreement enforceable in contract. Private mediation in the UK is conducted on a 'without prejudice' basis, meaning that, as a general rule, nothing revealed or discussed at the mediation may be disclosed to the court should the mediation fail and proceedings continue.

The use of the word 'alternative' in ADR/mediation discourse tends to be interpreted as alternative to judicial processes and adjudication. Mediation is said to be better than litigation for the resolution of family and non-family civil disputes because it is cheaper and quicker than trial; because it is a flexible procedure that can achieve settlement in a wide range of disputes; because it is capable of achieving creative solutions that would not be available in court adjudication; because it focuses on the commercial realities of disputes rather than legal technicalities; because it can repair damaged relationships; because it can reduce conflict; and because it is less stressful for parties than court procedures.

Although a wide range of dispute resolution processes are currently in use in the UK—including negotiation, mediation, arbitration, conciliation and ombudsmen schemes—it is private mediation that has grabbed the attention of policy-makers and the judiciary, and it is the emerging and growing profession of mediators that is ensuring that mediation stays high on the justice system agenda. Compared with the complexity of federal systems, justice policy in the UK is relatively straightforward, even after devolution. While Scotland and Northern Ireland have devolved responsibilities for justice policy, in each of the jurisdictions of the UK the administration is in a position to determine and enforce a unitary policy. As a result, it is possible to talk about a single broad policy agenda relating to ADR in the UK which has led to similar developments in England and Wales, Scotland and Northern Ireland. While this chapter concentrates on the policy in England and Wales, reference is also made, where relevant, to other parts of the UK.[3]

[2] For a comprehensive survey of the field see H Brown and A Marriott, *ADR Principles and Practice*, 3rd edn (London, Sweet & Maxwell, 2011). See also K Mackie, D Miles, W Marsh and T Allen, *The ADR Practice guide: Commercial Dispute Resolution*, 3rd revised edn (West Sussex, Tottel Publishing, 2007), ch 3.

[3] In Northern Ireland a relatively cautious approach is being taken in policy terms as discussed in Northern Ireland Department of Justice, *Access to Justice Review Northern Ireland*, August 2011,

B. Mediation Policy Development

Although arbitration and conciliation have been used in England as alternative techniques for the resolution of civil and commercial disputes at least since the 1950s,[4] the contemporary history of ADR, and in particular mediation, dates back little further than the early 1990s. However, the mediation movement in Britain over the last 15–20 years has been enormously successful in establishing a firm place in policy debates on the administration of civil and family justice.[5] In many ways it has taken the lead and framed the content of justice policy debate outside of the criminal sphere. The mediation movement has challenged the purpose of the civil and family justice systems, the value of public courts, the relevance of judicial determination to modern disputes and the legal profession's commitment to representative advocacy. We have witnessed a revolution in dispute resolution discourse. At the beginning of the twenty-first century in England and Wales at least, political arguments, judicial speeches and policy pronouncements about how civil and family justice should be working now focus on how to encourage or force more people to mediate, on worrying about why more people are not mediating, and on promoting the value of mediation to the justice system and society as a whole.[6] This is a remarkable success story, and the root of the movement's rhetorical achievement can be found in its ability to communicate simple (if empirically unverified) messages to policy-makers struggling to manage justice system costs.

As the British government's crime control policies of the past decade have increased expenditure on criminal legal aid, criminal courts and prisons, the Ministry of Justice has looked with an increasingly critical eye at its expenditure on civil and family disputes and even judicial review cases, encouraged by the voices of mediation leaders, who argue that not only is the expenditure unnecessary—serving only the interests of

60–69, available at <www.dojni.gov.uk/index/publications/publication-categories/pubs-criminal-justice/access-to-justice-review-final-report.pdf>. In Scotland the approach is also somewhat more cautious than in England and Wales: see Consumer Focus, *Ensuring Effective Access To Appropriate and Affordable Dispute Resolution, The final report of the Civil Justice Advisory Group*, January 2011, available at <www.consumerfocus.org.uk/scotland/files/2011/01/Civil-Justice-Advisory-Group-Full-Report.pdf>. The Law Reform Commission of Ireland, however, has recommended the introduction of a statutory framework for mediation and conciliation. See *Alternative Dispute Resolution: Mediation and Conciliation,* November 2010, available at <www.lawreform.ie/_fileupload/consultation%20papers/cpADR.pdf>.

[4] For a comprehensive survey of the field see Brown and Marriott, *ADR Principles and Practice*.

[5] For an extended account and critique see H Genn, *Judging Civil Justice, The 2008 Hamlyn Lectures* (Cambridge, Cambridge University Press, 2009) ch 3.

[6] Numerous speeches by leading judicial figures and government ministers over the past decade demonstrate the interest in promoting mediation. See, eg Lord Phillips of Worth Matravers, Lord Chief Justice of England and Wales, *Alternative Dispute Resolution: An English Viewpoint*, speech, India, 29 March 2008, available at <www.judiciary.gov.uk/Resources/JCO/Documents/Speeches/lcj_adr_india_290308.pdf>; Sir A Clarke, Master of the Rolls, *The future of civil mediation*, speech to Annual Mediation Council Conference, Birmingham, 8 May 2008, available at <www.judiciary.gov.uk/Resources/JCO/Documents/Speeches/mr_mediation_conference_may08.pdf>. See also the Legal Services Consultation Document, *A New Focus For Civil Legal Aid: Encouraging Early Resolution; Discouraging Unnecessary Litigation* (London, Department for Constitutional Affairs, 2004) and the government response, Department for Constitutional Affairs, *A New Focus for Civil Legal Aid: Encouraging Early Resolution; Discouraging Unnecessary Litigation*, Response to Consultation 22/07/04, available at <www.dca.gov.uk/response-litigation.pdf>, which focused on family cases and 'discouraging unnecessary publicly-funded litigation'. On judicial review see also V Bondy, M Doyle and V Reid, 'Mediation and Judicial Review—Mind the Research Gap' (2005) 10 *Judicial Review* 220, <http://www.publiclawproject.org.uk/downloads/MindResGap.pdf>.

lawyers—but that court processes and adjudication are potentially damaging to the interests of parties and to the wider society.

The focus on the asserted potential of mediation to save justice system expenditure is evident around the world. Indeed, much of the interest in mediation has grown out of the perceived failure of civil courts to meet the demand for efficient and affordable justice. In some parts of the world, both the criminal and civil courts are overloaded, with cases taking years to be processed and concluded. Legal costs are often high and disproportionate, and enforcement can be difficult. Some legal systems are corrupt. In many places there is little or no legal aid funding, so few means for low income groups to obtain quality legal representation. It is therefore unsurprising that the campaign for mediation, with its confident promise of diversion, healing and cost-saving, has been welcomed in many jurisdictions. Certainly, the adoption of pro-mediation policies by governments is an easier and cheaper option than attempting to fix or invest in dysfunctional systems of adjudication. But government interest in promoting and, more importantly, mandating mediation for civil, commercial and family cases in England has not been a panic response to overloaded courts. The driver is far more about cost-saving—to ease the pressure on the legal aid bill and to reduce the demand for court and judge time. As the minister responsible for legal aid pointed out quite candidly in July 2009, in the government's view mediation of family disputes provides quick outcomes and

> can also deliver big savings to the tax-payer, with disputes resolved through mediation costing half as much as those in the courts. A significant saving at a time when we're actively trying to sustain the best legal aid system in the world.[7]

In policy debates the benefits of mediation are generally expressed in opposition to adjudication, despite the fact that most civil and family cases are settled out of court, rather than by means of judicial determination. Around 90 per cent of civil disputes formally commenced in the courts conclude on the basis of an out-of-court settlement, and this has been the modal pattern in English civil litigation throughout the twentieth century. In the past 20 years the decline in full blown trials has been quite dramatic. and we have witnessed the phenomenon in civil justice of what has been termed 'the Vanishing Trial'.[8] Research on English trials shows that, although the number of criminal trials is increasing, trial rates in the civil courts have stabilised at a level that is well below previous decades. Figure 1 shows the issue of proceedings in the Queen's Bench Division of the High Court (excluding the Administrative Court) and reflects the basic run of private law disputes. During the period shown from the early 1960s to the mid-1990s there was a steep increase in the number of cases being commenced in the Queen's Bench Division—a trend that had been in place since the mid-1930s. However, in common with other jurisdictions around the world, since the mid-1990s England has witnessed a reduction in the number of cases being issued in

[7] Lord Bach, Legal Aid Minister in the Ministry of Justice, speech in Birmingham, 9 July 2009, launching the family mediation pilot scheme.

[8] M Galanter, 'A World Without Trials' (2006) 7 *Journal of Dispute Resolution* 7; HM Kritzer, 'Disappearing Trials? A Comparative Perspective' (2004) 1 *Journal of Empirical Legal Studies* 735, 752.

Figure 1. Proceedings issued in the Queen's Bench Division of the High Court, 1962–2011. Based on data derived from Ministry of Justice, *Judicial and Court Statistics 2011* (2012), <www.justice.gov.uk/downloads/statistics/courts-and-sentencing/jcs-2011/judicial-court-stats-2011.pdf>.

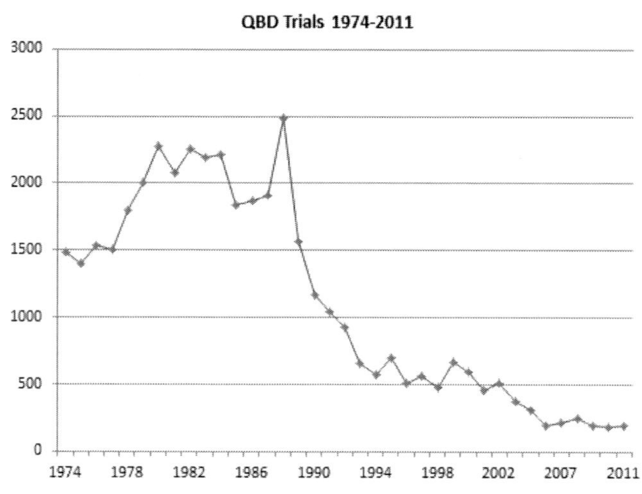

Figure 2. Trials in the Queen's Bench Division of the High Court, 1974–2011.

court and in the absolute number of cases coming to trial for authoritative adjudication, as shown in Figure 2.[9]

The cases that go to trial—even those involving the issue of formal legal proceed-

[9] There has been a significant downturn in trials dating back to 1955. See further Genn, *Why the Privatisation of Civil Justice is a Rule of Law Issue*; Kritzer, 'Disappearing Trials?'; Genn, *Judging Civil Justice*, ch 2; R Dingwall and E Cloatre, 'Vanishing Trials? An English Perspective' (2006) 1 *Journal of Dispute Resolution* 51.

ings—are the tiny tip of a large dispute pyramid or iceberg.[10] By definition, they are the cases that are the most contentious, where the parties and their representatives have not been able to achieve a resolution through pre-issue negotiation. But, despite this pattern of declining trials in England and Wales, the government and some sections of the senior judiciary have been determined since the mid-1990s to divert those disputes that are commenced in court away from public judicial determination and into private dispute resolution. The remainder of this part of the chapter traces the policy and supporting arguments.

C. Judicial Promotion of Mediation in Civil Justice Reform

An important starting point in the development of mediation policy in the English courts was Lord Woolf's fundamental review of the civil justice system of England and Wales and his *Access to Justice* reports of 1995[11] and 1996,[12] which signalled a minor revolution in court procedures for civil disputes. Lord Woolf devoted a chapter in his Interim Report to the subject of 'Alternative Approaches to dispensing Justice', in which he stated that ADR had the 'obvious' advantage of saving scarce judicial resources as well as a variety of benefits for litigants. He did not, however, propose that ADR should be compulsory either as an alternative or as a preliminary to litigation. He said,

> I do not think it would be right in principle to erode the citizen's existing entitlement to seek a remedy from the civil courts, in relation either to private rights or to the breach by a public body of its duties to the public as a whole.[13]

A fundamental premise of the Access to Justice Final Report was that court proceedings should be issued as a last resort, that all cases should be settled as soon as possible, and that ADR should be tried before and after the issue of court proceedings in order to achieve early settlement. While the 1995 *Interim Report* provided encouragement for litigants to consider using ADR, the tone was more directive in the 1996 *Final Report,* which warns that:

> [T]he court will encourage the use of ADR at case management conferences and pre-trial reviews, and will take into account whether the parties have unreasonably refused to try ADR or behaved unreasonably in the course of ADR.[14]

So convinced was Lord Woolf of the benefits of mediation that his 1996 Final Report placed a responsibility on the courts to encourage its use and provided them with power to punish parties deemed to have unreasonably refused an offer of mediation.[15]

[10] For estimates of the proportion of civil disputes that involve the issue of legal proceedings and trial see H Genn, *Paths to Justice: What People Do and Think About Going to Law* (Oxford, Hart Publishing, 1999); P Pleasence et al, *Causes of Action* (Norwich, The Stationery Office, 2004).

[11] Lord Woolf, *Access to Justice: Interim Report to the Lord Chancellor on the Civil Justice System in England and Wales* (London, Her Majesty's Stationary Office, 1995).

[12] Lord Woolf, *Access to Justice: Final Report to the Lord Chancellor on the Civil Justice System in England and Wales* (London, Her Majesty's Stationery Office, 1996).

[13] Lord Woolf, *Interim Report* 6.

[14] Lord Woolf, *Final Report* 5.

[15] CPR r 1.4 (2) and CPR r 26.4: stay of proceedings for settlement at the court's instigation.

Although it was not proposed that litigants in civil disputes should be compelled to mediate before or after the issue of proceedings, the inclusion in the Civil Procedure Rules (CPR) of a judicial power to direct the parties to attempt ADR, coupled with the court's discretion to impose a costs penalty on those who behave unreasonably during the course of litigation,[16] created a situation in which parties would understandably feel that they had no choice if it was suggested by a judge or by their opponent.

When the new procedure rules were implemented in 1999, all judges serving in civil courts were given training to raise awareness of ADR generally and, specifically, to alert them to the potential benefits of mediation in the resolution of civil disputes.

D. Pre-action Protocols

An essential element in the reforms was the introduction of codes of conduct which regulated how disputing parties should behave prior to the commencement of legal proceedings. The CPR enable the court to take into account the extent of the parties' compliance with relevant pre-action protocols when making orders about who should pay costs.[17] The court can ask the parties to explain what steps were taken to comply prior to the start of the claim. Where there has been a failure of compliance by a party, the court may ask that party to provide an explanation.

There are now 12 of these protocols in force covering different dispute types, including clinical negligence, construction and engineering, housing possession, actions for judicial review, professional negligence and low-value road accident claims. There have been various versions of these protocols and all now contain a paragraph on ADR. For example, the current version of the general protocol provides as follows:

> Starting proceedings should usually be a step of last resort, and proceedings should not normally be started when a settlement is still actively being explored. Although ADR is not compulsory, the parties should consider whether some form of ADR procedure might enable them to settle the matter without starting proceedings. The court may require evidence that the parties considered some form of ADR.[18]

The pre-action protocol for professional negligence contains a similar provision:

> The parties should consider whether some form of alternative dispute resolution procedure would be more suitable than litigation, and if so, endeavour to agree which form to adopt. Both the Claimant and professional may be required by the Court to provide evidence that alternative means of resolving their dispute were considered. The Courts take the view that litigation should be a last resort, and that claims should not be issued prematurely when a settlement is still actively being explored. Parties are warned that if the protocol is not followed (including this paragraph) then the Court must have regard to such conduct when determining costs.

[16] CPR 26.4 and Part 44 costs discretion. 'The court will encourage the use of ADR at case management conferences and pre-trial reviews, and will take into account whether the parties have unreasonably refused to try ADR.' Factors to be taken into account when deciding costs issues include 'the efforts made, if any before and during the proceedings in order to try and resolve the dispute'.

[17] See CPR r 44.3(5)(a).

[18] Civil Procedure Rules, Rules and Directions. Practice Direction—Pre-Action Conduct, para 8, available at <www.justice.gov.uk/courts/procedure-rules/civil/rules/pd_pre-action_conduct#IDANRA2>. These rules apply to civil litigation and not to family proceedings.

E. Court-attached Mediation Schemes

Following the lead provided by Lord Woolf in his civil justice reforms in the late 1990s and early 2000s, enthusiastic judges in courts around England collaborated with mediation providers to set up court-attached mediation schemes offering no- or low-cost, time-limited mediation, held on court premises for litigants who had already commenced court proceedings. The first and largest of these court-based mediation schemes was established in a county court trial centre in central London (Central London County Court) in 1996. Although the courts administered the schemes, the mediations themselves were undertaken initially on a pro bono basis by trained mediators keen to try out their newly acquired skills. Several of these schemes continued until around 2007, and evaluation research commissioned by the government is referred to later in the chapter.

F. Judicial Development of Mediation Law

Perhaps the most important development relating to mediation of civil and commercial disputes and England and Wales has been the strategy of the senior judiciary in seeking to create pressure to mediate through high-profile common law decisions. Despite the enthusiasm for mediation shown by some sections of the judiciary in the late 1990s and early 2000s, the voluntary uptake of mediation and use of these court-attached mediation schemes between 1996 and 2001 remained low. Starting in 2002, it seems that there was orchestrated action resulting in a number of landmark cases in which the senior judiciary sought to clarify the approach of the courts to the role of ADR in civil disputes.

In the case of *Cowl*[19] in 2002, Lord Woolf held that, as a matter of law, parties are required to consider ADR before starting legal proceedings, particularly where public money was involved. This was followed more significantly by *Dunnett v Railtrack*,[20] in which Lord Justice Brooke in the Court of Appeal held that Railtrack's refusal to contemplate mediation prior to the appeal (after it had been suggested by the Court) was sufficient to deny them their legal costs. The message of *Dunnett v Railtrack* was reinforced in the later case of *Hurst v Leeming*,[21] in which Mr Justice Lightman held that it is for the judge to decide whether a refusal to mediate was justified. While judges will accept valid reasons for not wanting to proceed with ADR, such reasons must be fully justifiable if the party wishes to avoid being penalised by the court. A further case in 2003 confirmed the risks for parties if they unreasonably refused to try ADR or withdrew unreasonably from an ADR process.[22] However, the high-water mark in the line of cases came in May 2003, when the High Court made another significant decision in relation to the use of ADR. The case of *Royal Bank of Canada Trust Corporation Ltd v Secretary of State for Defence*[23] centred on a point of law

[19] *Cowl and Others v Plymouth City Council* [2001] EWCA (Civ) 1935.

[20] *Dunnett v Railtrack plc* [2002] EWCA (Civ) 2003.

[21] [2001] EWHC 1051 (Ch), but judgment given on 9 May 2002 after the *Dunnett* decision.

[22] *Leicester Circuits Ltd v Coates Brothers plc* [2003] EWCA (Civ) 290—withdrawal from mediation is contrary to the spirit of the Civil Procedure Rules (March 2003).

[23] [2003] EWHC 1479 (Ch).

relating to a lease. The claimant was willing to try to resolve the dispute by ADR, but the Ministry of Defence rejected the suggestion on the ground that the dispute involved a point of law that required a 'black and white' answer. In the High Court, the department was successful on the point of law, but the judge refused to award the department its legal costs as a result of its refusal to mediate. The judge stated that the reason given for refusing mediation (ie that the case involved a point of law) did not make the case unsuitable.[24]

In 2004, the tide appeared to turn somewhat in the Court of Appeal case of *Halsey v Milton Keynes General NHS Trust*,[25] in which Lord Justice Dyson said that there should be no presumption in favour of mediation and that, where there was a question of denying a winning party their legal costs, the burden was on the losing party to show that there would have been a real prospect of a mediation succeeding. This case was initially greeted with considerable concern by mediation providers, being viewed as something of a retreat on mediation by the senior judiciary. However, since 2004 there has been a campaign by senior judicial figures to undermine its authority and to re-establish the importance of parties involved in litigation attempting to mediate their claims. In a later case, in 2005, guidance given by Lord Justices Rix and Ward reinforced the danger of not responding positively to an offer to mediate. They determined that, even where an offer to mediate was made before the institution of court proceedings, a refusal may be regarded as unreasonable in the subsequent award of costs. The clear message of the ruling is that ADR must be considered pre-action and that cost consequences may flow from an unreasonable refusal to engage in ADR even at the pre-action stage.[26] In a robust and very recent High Court decision in 2012[27] from the Technology and Construction Court, it was held that, where one party fails to accept another party's offer to mediate, and where the court generally believes that such a mediation would have had a reasonable prospect of success, such conduct by an obdurate party must be taken into account by the court when it comes to exercise its discretion in relation to costs. Any costs sanctions will be imposed from the time a party refuses to mediate, not from when a proposed mediation may have taken place. In this context, the unreasonable refusal was simply based on a failure to respond to an offer to mediate.

G. Government Policy

Government policy on mediation in relation to civil disputes initially rather lagged behind judicial enthusiasm and activism. However, towards the end of the twentieth

[24] CEDR, the leading commercial mediation provider organisation, commenting on the decision, said that it 'follows in a direct line from *Dunnett v Railtrack*, *Hurst v Leeming* and *Leicester Circuits v Coates Industries*, providing further examples of failed arguments to avoid mediation. More specifically, the case makes it clear that it is dangerous for a government party to ignore its own public undertaking to use ADR.' CEDR 'Public Sector—A Culture Change?' (2003) 32 *Resolutions* 6, available at <www.cedr.co.uk/news/resolutions/resolutions32.pdf>.

[25] [2004] EWCA (Civ) 576.

[26] *Burchell v Bullard and others* [2005] EWCA (Civ) 358.

[27] *PGF II SA v OMFS Company and another* [2012] EWHC 83 (TCC); see also the comment by CEDR pointing out that it is dangerous to fail to respond to an offer to mediate. Silence can be interpreted by the courts as an unreasonable refusal to mediate, T Allen, 'Don't Ignore a Request to Mediate. *Halsey* Applied! A Note on *PGF II SA v OMFS Company* [2012] EWHC 83 (TCC)', available at <www.cedr.com/articles/?301>.

century, as pressure on justice budgets became more severe and legal aid expenditure continued to rise, ministers became more interested in the promise of mediation. In 1998 the government signalled its interest in shifting dispute resolution attention away from the courts. In its landmark white paper, *Modernising Justice*, published in 1998,[28] the government made clear that it was seeking to improve the range of options available for dispute resolution. Despite the high settlement rate of civil cases, from 2001 onwards it has been explicit government policy to reduce the proportion of disputes resolved by resort to the civil courts. The 2004–09 government justice strategy included a target to reduce civil court hearings by 5 per cent by March 2008, despite the fact that trial rates in the High Court and county courts (other than small claims) had already plunged. The key instrument for achieving this target was the encouragement, both in and outside the court structure, of the use of ADR.

The government's determination to promote mediation was manifested in the Access to Justice Act 1999, which included the cost of mediation within the legal aid system and signalled that parties should first try ADR options before seeking legal aid for legal representation. This emphasis on mediation has been reinforced in subsequent documents and through the Commission's Funding Code, the 2005 version of which indicates that 'an application for funding may be refused if there are complaint systems, ombudsman schemes or forms of alternative dispute resolution which should be tried before litigation is pursued'.[29] Interestingly, the ADR section of the Code's Decision-Making Guidance states that 'all forms of ADR are accepted to have *at least equal validity* [emphasis added] to court proceedings', and goes on to point out that decisions about legal aid may be contingent on willingness to enter mediation.[30] Moreover, the Guidance contains a clear preference for mandatory mediation as a means of overcoming the preference of parties to litigate—or at least to initiate court proceedings:

> Most solicitors or clients who are considering or are engaged in litigation seem to prefer to continue litigating rather than attempting mediation. The Commission believes that it is in the interests of clients for more non-family cases to attempt mediation and that some solicitors or clients will not properly consider mediation unless required to do so.[31]

By 2005 the orthodoxy concerning mediation had become enshrined in the legal aid rules. The Legal Aid Funding Code for that year opines as a matter of uncontested fact that ADR is about 'solving problems rather than imposing solutions through an adjudicative process. In many cases it can yield creative and far-reaching solutions to issues that are not able to be addressed within the court process.' Among the reasons given in the Funding Code for choosing ADR as a dispute resolution method is apparently the fact that 'it works quickly . . . because it is not about establishing blame, parties find it easier to discuss matters openly and to entertain creative solutions'.

[28] Lord High Chancellor, *Modernising Justice* (London, Lord Chancellor's Department, 1998), available at <webarchive.nationalarchives.gov.uk/+/http://www.dca.gov.uk/consult/access/mjuspap.pdf>.

[29] Legal Services Commission, 2005 Funding Code Criterion 5.4.3.

[30] Funding Code Guidance Amendments: 'A New Focus for Civil Legal Aid'. Non-Family Guidance, Part 7, Alternative Dispute Resolution (Legal Services Commission, 2005).

[31] Ibid, s 7.6(6).

Finally, ADR is 'generally better for participants and their future relationship with one another than the confrontation of adjudication'.[32]

H. Mandatory Mediation in Civil Disputes

Although Lord Woolf's enthusiasm for ADR led to critical changes in civil procedure and the development of common law rules promoting mediation, he had not been in favour of compulsory mediation. However, commercial providers and other mediation enthusiasts have not shared his concerns. Frustration at the low voluntary uptake of mediation in civil disputes and some unease about the number of trained mediators without work led mediation providers in the early 2000s to press the government to take a more radical approach. It was argued by a coalition of mediation practitioners and judges that a pilot compulsory mediation scheme should be set up. The justification for such a step was that, even if disputing parties were forced against their will to undergo a mediation experience, the attractions of the process would overcome resistance and the parties would be likely to settle. Moreover, compulsion would rapidly expose a large number of people to the positive experience of mediation, thus leading to the kind of 'take-off' that had to date been elusive. Positive experience in Canada of a large mandatory mediation programme for civil disputes gave some credence to this argument,[33] and in March 2004 a one-year mandatory pilot scheme was set up in Central London County Court, where the voluntary scheme had been running for some years. Cases were automatically referred to mediation (ARM) and, while it was possible for parties to object to the referral, any unreasonable refusal to mediate would lead to costs sanctions. Unfortunately, the launch of the scheme coincided precisely with a ruling by the Court of Appeal in the case of *Halsey*[34] that the court had no power to compel parties to enter a mediation process. It is difficult to assess precisely what impact the Halsey judgment had on the behaviour of those who were automatically referred to mediation during the course of the pilot, but there can be little doubt that the judgment did not help. The result of the pilot was almost exactly the opposite of what happened in Canada. While the Canadians experienced only a handful of cases in which the parties opted out of the mandatory mediation scheme, in the ARM pilot about 80 per cent of those referred to mediation objected to the referral and, following the Halsey judgment, the court seemed to be uneasy about forcing people to mediate against their will.[35] Indeed, it was a classic example of policies colliding and of the danger of extrapolating from one culture to another. The applicability across jurisdictions of procedural innovations depends, among other things, on the culture of litigation, the formal court structures for dispute resolution, the characteristics of disputes and the costs rules.

A decision that the pilot had been largely unsuccessful was effectively taken after the experience of the first six months, although the scheme was allowed to run its

[32] Legal Services Commission, The Funding Code: Decision Making Guidance p 126.

[33] RG Hann and C Baar, *Evaluation of the Ontario Mandatory Mediation Program (Rule 24.1): Final Report—The First 23 Months* (Ontario, Ministry of the Attorney General, 2001).

[34] *Halsey v Milton Keynes General NHS Trust* [2004] EWCA (Civ) 576.

[35] H Genn et al, *Twisting Arms: Court Referred and Court Linked Mediation under Judicial Pressure*, (London, Ministry of Justice, 2007).

course for a full year before being abandoned. What is instructive, however, in the current context is the fact that, despite the failure of the ARM pilot, the appetite for mandatory mediation for civil disputes continues among mediators, the judiciary and the Ministry of Justice, and is now being revived for family disputes.

I. Learning from Court-attached Mediation Schemes

As part of its programme of promoting mediation, the government invested quite heavily in evaluating a number of court-based mediation schemes and we have therefore learned quite a lot about mediation of civil disputes.[36] We know, for example, that, despite the promotion of mediation and the pressure exerted by the judiciary, there has been a relatively weak 'bottom-up' demand even for very-low-cost court-linked mediation schemes. This is particularly so for cases involving personal injury, where historically the vast majority of cases have settled without adjudication. Although the value of mediation is generally compared with trial and adjudication, the challenge for mediation policy since the mid-1990s has been that it is seeking to encourage facilitated settlement in a system in which settlement is in any case the norm. Since most cases settle, mediation is principally offering the possibility of accelerated settlement, but in the early stages of a dispute at least, many litigants may not be ready to compromise, which is what mediation largely demands.

Interviews with mediating parties and observations of mediations have also revealed that the principal motivation for agreeing to mediate was to avoid the anticipated cost, delay and uncertainties of trial, and, more recently, to avoid the risk of adverse cost penalties being imposed under the Civil Procedure Rules. To that extent, the interest of mediating parties was primarily in outcome, not in the mediation process.

As far as party satisfaction is concerned, evaluations of court-annexed mediation schemes show high levels of satisfaction among those who have volunteered to enter the process. On the question of speed and cost, analysis of large-scale data from court-based mediation schemes compared with control data provides no evidence to suggest any difference in case length durations between mediated and non-mediated cases.[37] The same analysis does, however, show that time limited mediation can avoid trials in cases not involving personal injury, either through immediate settlement or by bringing the parties closer to settlement so that they can settle before trial.[38]

The perceptions of mediators, parties and their lawyers is that successful mediation can save cost, but it is difficult to estimate how much, since, although the touchstone is always trial, the overwhelming majority of cases would not proceed to trial and

[36] H Genn, *Central London Pilot Mediation Scheme, Evaluation Report* (London, Department for Constitutional Affairs, 1998); L Webley, P Abrams and S Bacquet, *Evaluation of Birmingham Fast and Multi Track Mediation Scheme* (London, Department for Constitutional Affairs, 2006); S Prince and S Belcher, *An Evaluation of the Effectiveness of Court-based Mediation Processes in Non-Family Civil Proceedings at Exeter and Guildford County Courts* (London, Department for Constitutional Affairs, 2006); Genn et al, *Twisting Arms*; M Doyle, *Manchester Small Claims Mediation Scheme Evaluation* (London, Department for Constitutional Affairs, 2006); J Enterken and M Sefton, *Evaluation of Reading Small Claims Mediation Scheme* (London, Department for Constitutional Affairs, 2006); S Prince, *Evaluation of Exeter Small Claims Mediation Scheme* (London, Department for Constitutional Affairs, 2006).

[37] Genn et al, *Twisting Arms* 71.

[38] Ibid, 73.

would not therefore incur the costs of trial.[39] On the other hand, it is also clear that unsuccessful mediation may increase the costs for parties (estimated at between £1,500 and £2,000),[40] and this fact raises serious questions for policies that seek to pressure parties to enter mediation unwillingly.[41]

The other important lesson from mediation programmes for civil and commercial disputes is that most settlements involve simply a transfer of money. Only a small minority of settlements are in any way creative or provide something different from what would be available in court. It also seems clear that claimants significantly discount their claims in reaching mediated settlements.[42]

Not all mediated cases result in settlement. Settlement rates in court-based mediation schemes have varied,[43] and statistical analysis of a large number of mediated cases in civil disputes shows that it is difficult to predict which factors lead to settlement. It seems to be a function of unobservable factors, such as personalities, depth of grievance, degree of conflict, willingness to negotiate and compromise. Indeed, analyses of the outcome of mediation in these court-based schemes show that the readiness of parties to mediate is an important factor in settlement.[44] Put simply, cases are more likely to settle at mediation if the parties enter the process voluntarily rather than being pressured into the process, and increased pressure to mediate depresses settlement rates. Thus, one broad conclusion of evaluation research has been that facilitation and encouragement, together with selective and appropriate pressure, are likely to be more effective and possibly efficient in producing settlements than blanket coercion to mediate. These findings chime with learning from court-based mediation programmes in the Netherlands.[45]

J. The Future of Mediation Policy

Despite the evidence that willingness to mediate is critical to achieving a settlement at the end of the mediation process, that there are financial and other costs to unsuccessful mediation, and that it is important to tailor dispute resolution processes to the dispute, the enthusiasm of policy-makers in the UK, and particular England and Wales, for mediation remains largely undimmed. In some jurisdictions it is becoming more pronounced, with a growing interest in compulsory mediation for civil and

[39] Ibid, 107.

[40] Ibid, 110 and 183.

[41] See also results of a recent evaluation of judicial mediation in employment discrimination disputes which found no saving in cost or time: P Urwin et al, *Evaluating the Use of Judicial Mediation in Employment Tribunals* (London, Ministry of Justice, 2010), available at <www.justice.gov.uk/downloads/publications/research-and-analysis/moj-research/evaluating-judicial-mediation-march10.pdf>. The study found that judicial mediation was an expensive process to administer and was not offset by the estimated benefits (both direct and indirect) of the process.

[42] Genn, *Central London Evaluation* 71; Webley, Abrams and Bacquet, *Birmingham Evaluation* 70–71.

[43] See the studies referred to in n 36.

[44] This emerges from the findings of the ARM pilot and analyses of the voluntary mediation scheme at Central London County Court, where the settlement rate declined from a high of 62% in 1998 to below 40% in 2000 and 2003. This interpretation for the falling settlement rate is supported by the views of mediators interviewed for that study, Genn et al, *Twisting Arms* ch 6.

[45] M Pel, *Referral to Mediation: A Practical Guide for an Effective Mediation Proposal* (The Hague, SDU Uitgevers, 2008) ch 1.

family disputes.[46] Although the case for private mediation has traditionally been framed around process—quicker, cheaper, less stressful than trial—it is increasingly being presented not merely as a useful alternative or supplement to public courts, but as an equal or, indeed, preferable method of handling disputes. Moreover, despite the private nature of ADR, government is now arguing that diverting legal disputes away from the courts and into mediation is a strategy that will increase access to justice—a claim that requires some scrutiny. It is arguable, although fiercely contested by mediation enthusiasts, that mediation has little to do with access to justice. It is neither about access to the courts nor about just outcomes. A successful mediation outcome is a settlement that the parties 'can live with'. The outcome of mediation is not about *just* settlement, it is *just about settlement*—and private settlement at that. A critical feature of ADR is its privacy. Both the process and outcome of the procedures are private and generally confidential to the parties, who pay themselves for the process.

Following the election of a coalition government in 2010, the first clear policy statement on the justice system was the Ministry of Justice's Transforming Justice agenda. Set in the context of the global financial crisis and the need to save £2billion from the justice budget by 2014–15, the government outlined its intention to reform legal aid, to simplify court processes, rationalise the court estate by closing courts, merge the administration of courts and tribunals, and focus policy on alternatives to court. These proposals were accompanied by a new civil justice rhetoric which presented court proceedings as an unnecessary drain on public resources, and public funding for civil and family disputes through legal aid as an incitement to litigate rather than a means of facilitating access to justice.[47] It was argued that the fiscal climate required a tightening of belts and that what was needed was more mediation, although this was accompanied by an assurance that mediation 'is not just about cost-cutting and pushing people away from the justice system'. Interestingly, this view seems to be reserved only for individual citizens, since the Ministry has recently developed a concurrent policy of promoting the British justice system and legal services to international commercial enterprises for the resolution of business disputes.

In March 2011 the Ministry of Justice published another set of proposals aimed at procedure in the civil courts.[48] The title of the paper, 'Solving Disputes', communicates the current philosophy and approach, which is to represent the cases that come to court for determination on the merits as problems in search of resolution—the message and language of mediation. The paper refers back explicitly to the Woolf Review Reports and reminds us that the fundamental premise of the Woolf Reforms was that court

[46] This is true in Australia. See, eg Australian Government, Attorney General's Department, *A Strategic Framework for Access to Justice in the Federal Civil Justice System*, September 2009, available at <www.ag.gov.au/LegalSystem/Documents/A%20Strategic%20Framework%20for%20Access%20to%20Justice%20in%20the%20Federal%20Civil%20Justice%20System.pdf> 95–96; see also the Australian Attorney General's proposals to amend the Family Law Act 1975 to permit mediators to be able to give an arbitral ruling in mediation if agreement cannot be reached.

[47] '[Legal aid] has encouraged people to bring their problems before the courts too readily, even sometimes when the courts are not well placed to provide the best solutions. This has led to the availability of taxpayer funding for unnecessary litigation.' Ministry of Justice, *Proposals for Reform of Legal Aid in England and Wales*, November 2010, available at <www.justice.gov.uk/downloads/consultations/legal-aid-reform-consultation.pdf/>.

[48] Ministry of Justice, *Solving Disputes in the County Courts: Creating a Simpler, Quicker and More Proportionate System. A Consultation on Reforming Civil Justice in England and Wales*, Consultation Paper CP6/2011, March 2011, (London, Ministry of Justice, 2011), available at <www.official-documents.gov.uk/document/cm80/8045/8045.pdf>.

proceedings are not the best or most appropriate route for civil disputes. The paper argues that cases which settle between issue and trial are a waste of court resources and judicial time. This suggestion conveniently fails to acknowledge that it is only the threat of coercion that brings defendants to the negotiating table.[49]

Perhaps the most worrying aspect of the tone of the paper was its rejection of the language of justice. We are told that the court system needs to 'focus more on dispute resolution . . . for the majority of its users, rather than the *loftier ideals of "justice"* [emphasis added], that cause many to pursue their cases beyond the point that it is economic for them to do so'. The vision for the new system is one 'where many more avail themselves of the opportunities provided by less costly dispute resolution methods, such as mediation—to collaborate rather than litigate'—so not a 'justice' system at all, or at least not one that is concerned with substantive justice. A mandatory mediation system will be imposed so that most cases will be required to go through mediation before being considered for judicial determination.

The terms of reference of the fundamental review of family justice launched by the British government in 2010 stated explicitly that mediation is the preferred approach to dealing with disputes following relationship breakdown.[50] The Final Report of the Family Justice Review published in 2011 recommended that all family disputes in English courts go through a mandatory MIAM (mediation information and assessment meeting) unless there is evidence of domestic abuse.[51] The government published their response to the recommendations in June 2012, stating that they would introduce legislation to ensure that, in every case, evidence of attendance at a meeting with a mediator will be required before a case can proceed to court. Exemptions would apply for cases involving domestic violence.[52]

K. Mediation and the Withdrawal of Legal Aid

In November 2010 the Justice Minister announced his proposals for changes to the provision of legal aid. The document suggested no significant changes to the scope of criminal legal aid, but a dramatic cutting-down of the scope of civil and family legal aid, losing support for advice and representation for, among other things, employment, immigration, welfare benefits and housing cases. In presenting these proposals, it was argued that the measures were needed to 'stop the encroachment of unnecessary litigation into society'. What is particularly troubling is the way that arguments about mediation are woven seamlessly into the justificatory fabric. In a disingenuous line of argument, the government seeks to present the removal of civil legal aid as a social

[49] We know that judicial determination is not necessary to settle every case, and we know from research and judicial statistics that the vast majority of civil cases in which formal proceedings are issued eventually settle without a judicial determination. However, without that threat, without the potential to institute proceedings, claimants would not be in a position to settle their disputes. They would be left without a remedy. For discussion of settlement rates in county court litigation see Genn et al, *Twisting Arms*, especially 57–61.

[50] See *Fundamental Review of Family Justice, Final Report, 2011, Terms of Reference, Annex 2*, available at <www.education.gov.uk/publications/eOrderingDownload/FJR-2011.pdf>.

[51] *Family Justice Review, Final Report*, November 2011, available at <www.justice.gov.uk/downloads/publications/moj/2011/family-justice-review-final-report.pdf>.

[52] Ministry of Justice and Department of Education, *Government Response to Family Justice Review*, June 2012, available at <www.education.gov.uk/publications/eOrderingDownload/CM-8273.pdf>.

benefit rather than what it is—a removal of an important access to justice vehicle for the most disadvantaged groups in society. The approach adopted by the government is to suggest that legal aid is an 'incitement to litigate' and a barrier to dispute resolution, whereas private mediation promotes harmony and settlement. The Minister tells us that, 'the courts should not be used as arenas of conflict, argument and debate when a more mature and considered discussion of the issues at hand between parties could see a better outcome for them'.

Despite a valiant fight by politicians, the legal profession, the advice sector and even some senior members of the judiciary, the legal aid proposals became law in May 2012[53] and the removal of most civil cases from the legal aid system has been accomplished—wreaking potentially irrevocable changes to our legal aid system and to access to civil and family justice.

In June 2011 the campaigning organisation Justice issued an intentionally powerful press release warning that the combined effect of changes to legal aid together with compulsory mediation will be the 'economic cleansing' of the civil courts. The statement argued that in the future 'courts and lawyers will be only for the rich. The poor will make do as best they can with no legal aid and cheap, privatised mediation. There will be no equal justice for all—only [for] those with money.'[54]

L. Judiciary and Government—a Parting of the Ways?

What we are now seeing is a slight bifurcation between the views of the senior judiciary and policy-makers. The judiciary are beginning to display some nervousness about the emphasis on private dispute resolution. More than a decade after the reforms of civil justice, with resources for civil justice severely strained and a change in the leadership of the judiciary, we are hearing a more nuanced analysis of the issues. For example, in an address to the Civil Mediation Council's Annual conference shortly after his appointment in 2009, the Lord Chief Justice emphasised the need for an effective civil justice system and hinted at some concerns about the prospect of compulsory mediation. Lord Judge said:

> If I were to enter into the debate on whether the court process could or should have the power to compel mediation, in effect as part of its own process, I should have to speak for a very long time . . . on this I have to confess to an underlying concern not so much directed at the mediation issue, which is about too many people telling too many other people what they must do and thus compel an additional step in the process of litigation.[55]

At the corresponding conference a year later, Lord Neuberger, the Master of the Rolls and Head of Civil Justice, gave rather more cautious support for the mediation 'project' than that expressed by his two immediate predecessors:

> [L]et us not get carried away by zeal. Zeal for justice, zeal for one's client are fine, but zeal for a form of dispute resolution or any other idea, theory, or practice is not so healthy. It

[53] Legal Aid, Sentencing and Punishment of Offenders Act 2012.

[54] See <www.justice.org.uk/data/files/resources/282/press210611.pdf>.

[55] The Right Honourable the Lord Judge, Lord Chief Justice of England and Wales, speech to the Third Civil Mediation Council National Conference, 14 May 2009, available at <www.judiciary.gov.uk/Resources/JCO/Documents/Speeches/lcj-mediation-council-conf-140509.pdf>.

> smacks of fanaticism, and it drives out one of the three most important qualities a lawyer should have—scepticism or, if you prefer, objectivity. (The others being honesty and ability.) Overstating the virtues of mediation will rebound in the long term, even in the medium term, to the disadvantage of mediation.[56]

In his recent comprehensive review of costs in civil litigation, Lord Justice Jackson considered the role of mediation in the resolution of civil disputes. He rejected the submission by mediation providers that procedural judges should impose sanctions on parties who had not mediated prior to the issue of proceedings without a good reason. He also rejected the suggestion that 'compulsion may even be needed' to ensure that procedural judges implement such a policy. Lord Justice Jackson favoured an approach that would support education and facilitation of ADR rather than coercion.

Most recently, Lord Neuberger has sought to emphasise the public purpose of courts and to reject the notion that judicial determination represents a failure of the justice system rather than being fundamental to its purpose. There seems to be some deeper thinking going on about what it means to deliver justice in the realm of civil disputes. He argued that neither arbitration nor ADR can provide a framework for securing the enforcement of rights and the rule of law, and that without the framework provided by formal adjudication 'they would be mere epiphenomena'.[57] In November 2010 Lord Neuberger gave a speech that he provocatively entitled 'Has Mediation Had its Day?'[58] He argued that the increasing emphasis on mediation and ADR may well be 'antipathetic to our commitment to equal access to justice, to our commitment to a government of law'. He went on to say that:

> Citizens are bearers of rights; they are not simply consumers of services. The civil justice system exists to enable them to secure those rights. It does not exist to merely supply a service, which like a bar of chocolate may be consumed.

The judiciary have articulated their concern about mandatory mediation more recently in their response to the government's proposal to introduce mandatory mediation for a wide range of civil claims. In his response to the government, Lord Justice Jackson argued that, while he felt that mediation should be encouraged, he did not support compulsory mediation, not least because of his concerns that it can increase cost and delay. For high-value civil disputes, Jackson LJ urges caution about judges recommending mediation too soon and that whether it is appropriate depends on the nature of the case. He is opposed to the EU Mediation Directive (Directive 2008/52/EC on Certain Aspects of Mediation in Civil and Commercial Matters) being extended to apply to domestic cases, suggesting that this would add a raft of unwelcome rules 'to no useful purpose'.

In a collective response to proposals for mandatory mediation of civil claims, the judiciary have stated that, while recognising the benefits of ADR, they feel that it is not

[56] Lord Neuberger of Abbotsbury, Master of the Rolls, *Educating Future Mediators*, speech to the Fourth Civil Mediation Council National Conference, London, 11 May 2010, available at <www.judiciary.gov.uk/Resources/JCO/Documents/Speeches/mor-cmc-conference-speech-11052010.pdf>.

[57] Lord Neuberger of Abbotsbury, Master of the Rolls, *Equity, ADR, Arbitration and The Law: Different Dimensions of Justice*, The Fourth Keating Lecture, Lincoln's Inn, 19 May 2010, available at <www.judiciary.gov.uk/Resources/JCO/Documents/Speeches/mr-keating-lecture-19052010.pdf>.

[58] Lord Neuberger of Abbotsbury, Master of the Rolls, *Has Mediation Had Its Day?*, The Gordon Slynn Memorial Lecture 2010, 10 November 2010, available at <www.judiciary.gov.uk/Resources/JCO/Documents/Speeches/moj-speech-mediation-lectureA.pdf>.

suitable for resolving all civil disputes. They highlight the need for courts to remain in control of the progress of proceedings. The judiciary do not support a system of compulsory mediation involving private mediators and consider that, in general, it is essential to have a proper, rigorous accreditation system for mediators.

III. THE ADR LANDSCAPE

A. Processes

In the UK, ADR is generally understood to describe all dispute resolution methods other than court proceedings, including negotiation, mediation, conciliation, arbitration, adjudication, and early neutral evaluation and ombudsmen schemes.[59] There is a broad range of ADR processes in the UK, including both adjudicative and non-adjudicative processes. The most commonly deployed ADR mechanisms differ in the UK according to the type of dispute and the category under which the dispute falls. The most frequently used ADR processes are mediation, conciliation, arbitration, adjudication and ombudsmen schemes. There are two hybrid processes which are closely linked to mediation: mediation–arbitration (MedArb) and arbitration–mediation (ArbMed). Neither is widely used, but each may occasionally be appropriate for use in a particular dispute.

B. Providers

The largest providers of commercial mediation are CEDR (Centre for Effective Dispute Resolution) and ADR Group. CEDR provides mediation services, as well as training and consultancy services. CEDR has both in-house mediators and a panel of mediators from a variety of professional backgrounds, including practising accountants, architects, bankers, barristers, company directors, engineers, insurers, loss adjusters, solicitors and surveyors, numbering over 150 in total.[60] ADR Group also specialises in commercial mediation, as well as being known for their family mediation work. They also offer training, consultancy and dispute resolution services by mediators from both law and non-law backgrounds. ADR Group manages over 500 commercial mediation appointments each year.[61] Other commercial mediation organisations include the Academy of Experts, the Chartered Institute of Arbitrators, ADR Chambers and the Royal Institute of Chartered Surveyors. In addition to these organisations, many law firms and barristers' chambers provide mediation services.

In family mediation, ADR Group is again a large provider, with approximately 100 accredited specialist family mediators. Additional family mediation providers include the College of Mediators, the Family Mediators Association (FMA) and National Family Mediation (NFM). The College of Mediators provides mediators who have

[59] For a comprehensive analysis of the main ADR categories, see J Crook, 'What is Alternative Dispute Resolution (ADR)?' in JC Betancourt (ed), *What is Alternative Dispute Resolution (ADR)?* (London, Chartered Institute of Arbitrators, 2010) 1.

[60] Centre for Effective Dispute Resolution 2012, available at <www.cedr.com/>.

[61] ADR Group 2012, available at <www.adrgroup.co.uk/index.php>.

backgrounds in law, counselling, social work, health, employment and business. The FMA is a registered charity which specialises in promoting the use of mediation nationally, as well as assisting people to find registered mediators. NFM is a voluntary sector provider of mediation and counselling services. NFM undertakes 65 per cent of all publically funded family mediation.[62] All four organisations are members of the Family Mediation Council, the quasi-regulatory body for family mediation, and offer training as well as mediation services.

The largest provider of employment dispute services is the Advisory, Conciliation and Arbitration Services (ACAS). ACAS functions as an advisory body to promote better employment relations. As part of this, they offer arbitration and mediation services. Hearings are dealt with by an independent arbitrator, who is appointed on a case-by-case basis and not employed directly by ACAS. ACAS also provides independent mediators, as well as mediation training to assist employers in developing their own workplace mediation schemes. Mediation at Work is another provider offering independent mediation services and workplace conflict resolution training.

C. The Funding of ADR

The main source of funding for civil and commercial ADR cases is private, though that funding may come in different forms. One such way is for disputants to engage with an arbitrator or mediator through an ADR organisation. The organisation collects the cost from the parties and is then responsible for paying the arbitrator/mediator. Other organisations will function simply as referral bodies and will put a party in touch with a mediator from their panel. Parties who wish to engage a mediator or arbitrator directly may do so, though they or the practitioner assume the administrative burdens. The cost of mediation can become a topic of the mediation itself, with the parties choosing to include costs as part of the settlement agreement. Following the case of *Wilkinson* in 1998,[63] legal aid was made available to contribute to the cost of mediation in eligible civil cases, although there is currently little legal aid available to support either mediation or legal advice for civil disputes. Some government support exists for telephone mediation of small claims, as discussed later.

D. Arbitration

Arbitration goes back a long way in English legal history. It has been argued that arbitration was an integral part of the informal machinery of dispute settlement that existed alongside the courts of law in fifteenth-century England, settling feuds, making peace and restoring harmonious social relations between disputing neighbours.[64]

Modern commercial arbitration is national and international big business. While generally categorised as one of the main ADR processes, it is distinctive from most

[62] National Family Mediation 2012, available at <www.nfm.org.uk/about/nfm>.

[63] (1998) 26 EHRR CD131.

[64] E Powell, 'Settlement of Disputes by Arbitration in Fifteenth-Century England' (1984) 2 *Law and History Review* 21.

other methods, which largely constitute different types of facilitated settlement.[65] Arbitration is essentially private, specialist adjudication on the merits. While rarely any cheaper or quicker than judicial determination in court, it offers something valuable and different for business disputes. Arbitration procedures and outcomes are regulated by the Arbitration Act 1996. Commercial arbitration is binding and arbitral decisions have very limited opportunities for review by courts. Arbitral decisions are given by specialist decision-makers chosen by the parties. Procedures are subject to the rules of natural justice, but the proceedings and the determinations are private and remain confidential to the parties. So what arbitration offers, which is different from public courts, is specialist decision-makers and, crucially, confidentiality. This means that commercially sensitive information is not in the public domain and determinations do not create precedents. English commercial arbitration law is seen as attractive not only to domestic parties but internationally, and English commercial providers offer their services worldwide.

The central feature of the arbitration process is the arbitration agreement. If an individual is not party to an arbitration agreement, that person can neither initiate nor be subjected to arbitration. In the case of a valid arbitration agreement, the courts have limited jurisdiction to grant some forms of interim relief, support the arbitral process if it breaks down, offer a supervisory function to ensure the standards of justice, and enforce the award.[66]

The main rules regarding the costs of arbitration are set out in the English Arbitration Act in sections 59–65, based primarily on the idea that costs should be recoverable by the successful party. However, given that the determination of 'success' can sometimes be a difficult one, the issues of awarding costs can become less straightforward.

E. Current Regulation of Arbitration

The regulatory framework for arbitration in the UK is provided by statute, with the current primary regulation being the Arbitration Act 1996. The 1996 Act sets out as its main objective 'the fair resolution of disputes by an impartial tribunal'.[67] In addition to statutory regulation, much of the arbitration process itself is regulated by the rules of various arbitral bodies who distinguish formal and ad hoc arbitration. Many of these institutions will each have their own regulatory mechanisms and codes of conduct. However, the 1996 Act sets out several notable provisions.

Under the 1996 Act, the court has powers to remove an arbitrator should there be justifiable doubts as to his impartiality, qualifications, or capacity (section 24), enforce peremptory orders of a tribunal (section 42), secure the attendance of witnesses (section 43), determine preliminary points of law (section 45) and provide for appeal on point of law, unless otherwise agreed by the parties (section 69).

The mandatory provisions of the 1996 Arbitration Act require some minimum procedure. Arbitration cannot take place without an arbitration agreement, and there can be no arbitration initiated by, or conducted against, a person who is not a party to

[65] For a comprehensive survey of the field see Brown and Marriott, *ADR Principles and Practice*.
[66] Brown and Marriott, *ADR Principles and Practice* 117–18.
[67] Arbitration Act 1996, s 1.

the arbitration agreement.[68] There is a degree of flexibility in arbitration proceedings in England and Wales, with the 1996 Act stipulating that the parties may organise the proceedings as they so wish. The Act recognises 'party autonomy' by permitting the parties and the arbitrators' freedom in the organisational processes.[69] The Act does give extensive procedural control to arbitrators (section 34), while also maintaining that such control must be exercised in a way compatible with the yardsticks of economy, expedition and fairness (section 33).

The Act also makes several provisions regarding the enforcement of awards. Under section 66, the court's permission is required in order to enforce an arbitral award in the UK. Awards made in England and Wales can, by leave of the court, be enforced in the same manner as a judgment or order of the court to the same effect.[70] It should be noted that the court cannot cure a deficiency within the award in its enforcement order.[71] An application for permission to enforce an award may be made without notice in an arbitration claim form, although the court may nevertheless require that the application be served on the other party.[72] However, section 63(3) provides for an exception to this if the person against whom the award is sought can show that the tribunal lacks the jurisdiction to make such an award. Awards themselves can also be challenged on the grounds of substantive jurisdiction of the tribunal (section 67). They can also be challenged on the grounds of serious irregularities, such as a failure by the tribunal to comply with its general duties, failure to conduct the proceedings in accordance with the procedure agreed by the parties, or any uncertainty or ambiguity as to the effect of the award. Should the court find a serious irregularity, the court can decide whether to submit the award for reconsideration or to set aside the award entirely (section 68). The provisions for awards made outside of England and Wales are found in part 3 of the Act. Sections 100–03 provide for enforcement of arbitral awards under the New York Convention. Given that section 103 reflects the provisions of Article 5 of the New York Convention, the ability to challenge the enforcement of these awards is much more difficult. Section 99 provides for enforcement of arbitral awards made in certain countries under the Geneva Convention 1927. In general, the court will interfere with the enforcement of awards only when a specific provision of the Act has entitled it to do so.

F. Mediation

Mediation is a private, confidential, consensual process in which a third-party neutral assists disputing parties to reach a settlement. Mediators and the mediation process are unregulated and unsupervised. Settlements are enforceable in contract but are confidential to the parties, and information obtained during an unsuccessful mediation cannot be referred to in any subsequent legal proceedings. The principal claims

[68] Brown and Marriott, *ADR Principles and Practice* 117.

[69] This freedom to organise the procedure is restricted by basic principles of fairness, for example natural justice.

[70] Arbitration Act 1996, s 66(1).

[71] *Walker v Rowe* [1999] 2 All ER (Comm) 961.

[72] Civil Procedure Rule 62.18(1) and (2).

for mediation are generally made by contrasting it with trial. Thus it is presented as cheaper, quicker, less risky, more creative and more harmonious than legal proceedings.

Mediators do not give a decision on legal cases but adopt a problem-solving approach which helps disputing parties to reach a settlement that they can live with. It is seen as offering win–win outcomes in which there are no losers. The cost of mediation is paid by the parties.

G. Civil/Commercial Disputes

The vast majority of civil/commercial disputes end on the basis of an out-of-court settlement negotiated between solicitors. Between 85 and 95 per cent of disputes conclude in this way, even after the issue of court proceedings.[73]

Other than arbitration, which is governed by statute, ADR is unregulated in the UK and this lack of regulation has resulted in limited statistical data. However, CEDR conducts biennial 'mediation audits' based on internet surveys of commercial mediators. Data from the fifth mediation audit in 2012 suggest that the market for commercial mediation in the UK is growing, with approximately 8,000 mainstream commercial and civil cases mediated per year. The commercial mediation market is dominated by a select few mediators. A group of just over 100 individuals are involved in around 85 per cent of all non-scheme commercial cases (in 2010, 90 individuals held 85 per cent); and within this group, some 60 individuals are involved in 70 per cent of all cases (in 2010, 50 individuals held 70 per cent).[74] Mediation is clearly seeing a significant growth in the commercial sector.[75]

H. Court-based Mediation Schemes

Court-based mediation schemes are those in which the court incorporates mediation in a number of ways. The most common approach in England is where the judge advises or directs parties to attempt mediation or where mediators use the court premises. A number of schemes have run in county courts across England and Wales with differing degrees of success (as discussed above). The Leeds Combined Court Centre pilot had high rates of satisfaction from participants, though an overall low take-up. The Central London County Court mediation scheme was a primarily voluntary scheme except for the Automatic Referral to Mediation Scheme, which gave participants in the scheme an opt-out of mediation, though only where considered justifiable. The scheme was evaluated most recently in 2007, when concern was expressed at the pressure by

[73] Genn et al, *Twisting Arms* ch 2.

[74] CEDR, *The Fifth Mediation Audit*, Annual Review 2012, available at <www.cedr.com/docslib/The-MediatorAudit2012.pdf>.

[75] See the recent article by J Swift, 'Ex-Halliwells Partners Prepare for Mediation with Liquidators over £20m Windfall', *The Lawyer*, 12 April 2012. This will be a real test for the still-burgeoning form of alternative dispute resolution. The fact that the parties could agree on a mediator at all is, if nothing else, a good start. Anything else they can agree on after that will be a shining endorsement for this particular brand of dispute resolution, see <www.thelawyer.com/ex-halliwells-partners-prepare-for-mediation-with-liquidators-over-%C2%A320m-windfall/1012150.article>.

courts to mediate.[76] Another notable scheme was the Exeter small claims scheme, where voluntary solicitors acted as mediators to provide short mediation meetings to individuals referred by the court. Judges were available to immediately make orders upon a decision being reached. The report found that 70 per cent of cases settled before trial.[77] From 2007 all county court mediation in England and Wales is organised through the Civil Mediation Directory,[78] not through individual courts.

I. Commercial Court ADR Orders

The Commercial Court is a court within the Queen's Bench Division of the High Court with specialist jurisdiction over commercial matters. Judges of the Court have specialist knowledge and experience of commercial affairs. Since 1993 commercial court judges have been actively encouraging the use of ADR. In 1996 the Court issued a practice statement providing that at a preliminary stage of the case the judge would consider whether the action was particularly appropriate for ADR and, if so, he could invite the parties to take positive steps to set in motion ADR procedures. The judge has the power to adjourn the case to enable the parties to use ADR and, if he deems it appropriate, he may make an ADR order. Such an order requires the parties to exchange lists of neutrals; endeavour in good faith to agree on a neutral to conduct ADR; and 'take serious steps to resolve their dispute by ADR'; and, if the case is not finally settled, the parties are to inform the court by letter what steps towards ADR have been taken and why those steps have failed.

Research evaluating the Court's practice and its effect, commissioned by the government and published in 2002, concluded that ADR orders were generally thought to have a positive or neutral impact on settlement. Although only a minority of orders led to ADR taking place, experience of successful ADR after an order was overwhelmingly positive. ADR orders were said to have had a significant impact on commercial practice and the advice given by the legal profession to clients about commercial dispute resolution. The broad conclusion was that an individualised approach to the direction of cases toward ADR is more appropriate and likely to be more effective than general pressure by courts in all cases to attempt mediation at an early stage in the litigation process.[79]

J. The Court of Appeal Mediation Scheme (CAMS)

The Court of Appeal has been administering a mediation scheme since 1996, and in 2003 this was put on a more formal footing in collaboration with CEDR. Single judges can, when considering permission to appeal, recommend the scheme is used when granting the permission, or the scheme is open to both sides if they decide that they wish to use it. The current fee is £850 plus VAT per party, which will buy four

[76] Genn et al, *Twisting Arms*.

[77] Prince and Belcher, *Exeter Evaluation*.

[78] See <www.civilmediation.justice.gov.uk/>.

[79] H Genn, *Court-based ADR Initiatives for Non-family Civil Disputes: The Commercial Court and the Court of Appeal* (London, Lord Chancellor's Department, 2002).

hours' preparation time and five hours' mediation time of a mediator belonging to the court-supervised panel. If the case is not settled through the mediation, the court is simply informed that the appeal is to proceed. A settlement rate of about 50 per cent is achieved. The object of CAMS is to offer a good settlement process early in the life of any appeal where mediation is felt worthwhile and to settle it if possible, but, if not, to let the appeal run its course with the Court.

Recently Court of Appeal judges together with CEDR have decided to initiate a pilot scheme within the CAMS operating on the assumption that any contractual, personal injury or clinical negligence claim in which no more than £100,000 as claimed (excluding costs) is at stake should be referred to the CAMS for mediation unless there are good reasons why not.[80] Unless a judge exceptionally directs otherwise, the parties in such cases will be informed that case papers are automatically recommended for mediation to CEDR. If the parties agree to mediate, a panel of accredited CAMS mediators will be nominated by CEDR. The selected mediator will bring the parties together to try to reach a settlement. If there is a settlement, the case will not go back to the Court of Appeal. Lord Justice Rix commented on the advantages that this scheme would provide:

> Judges regularly see cases in the Court of Appeal which could easily have been resolved at an earlier stage through the use of mediation. Parties may not be poles apart, but litigation can have a corrosive effect for which mediation can provide a balm.[81]

Parties will have a maximum of 10 weeks to set a mediation date in compliance with the single judge's recommendation before CEDR reports back to the Civil Appeals Office that mediation has not been agreed. The appeal will then continue, but the parties may be exposed to costs sanctions if the Court later considers that ignoring the single judge's recommendation to mediate was unreasonable when dealing with costs.

CAMS will remain available for any other appeal where parties want to use it or where the single judge recommends its use, regardless of the issues or value at stake. No one will be compelled to settle, nor will the court be told why a case did not settle at mediation, unless all parties agree to waive the privilege attached to the mediation process at the appeal hearing.

K. Low-value Civil Disputes

A small claims mediation service has been established to deal with disputes of less than £5,000 which provides a mediation officer based in every court area in England and Wales. Where proceedings have been issued and the parties agree, the mediator can conduct mediations by telephone, or in some cases in a room at court. A recent study comparing litigants' experience of small claims mediation with small claims hearings found that overall satisfaction with the mediation process was high—though no higher, it seems, than with small claims hearings; levels of satisfaction with specific

[80] See the recent article by K Dowell, 'CoA Pilots Mediation Scheme in Bid to Cut Litigation Costs', *The Lawyer*, 4 April 2012, available at <www.thelawyer.com/1012099.article>.

[81] Judiciary of England and Wales, *New Pilot to Show Mediation Can Work for the Court of Appeal* (March 2012), see <http://www.judiciary.gov.uk/media/media-releases/2012/news-release- mediation-pilot-court-of-appeal>.

aspects of the mediation process were more varied (and with regard to convenience of arrangements, were low); most respondents for whom mediation produced a settlement reported that the outcome was fair, but strong belief in the fairness of mediated outcomes appeared lower than for outcomes of small claims hearings.[82]

L. Construction Disputes

In some areas, such as construction disputes, a norm exists for a particular form of ADR to be used within the industry—such as 'adjudication'.[83] Adjudication as a means of dispute resolution is compulsory in any contract for construction works to be carried out in England, Scotland or Wales. It only applies to contracts in writing, and it does not apply to contracts with a house owner for domestic works. It covers agreements for architectural, surveying or design work, for provision of labour for construction operations, and advice on building, landscaping, engineering, and interior and exterior decoration. The adjudicator is the decision maker in the process, who will have experience in dispute resolution and will usually be a professional, such as a surveyor, architect or engineer.

M. Expert Determination

Expert determination is generally a binding dispute resolution procedure that is well recognised in almost all areas of commercial life. Expert determination is normally used to resolve disputes and issues of a technical or specialist nature. Its origins rest in valuation and it is regarded as a more informal type of ADR. It is not commonly used in matters which are likely to give rise to extensive factual disputes requiring the review of extensive documentary and factual witness evidence. This type of ADR is less suited to purely legal disputes since, typically, expert determination clauses do not envisage the appointment of legally qualified individuals. Expert determination clauses arise perhaps most commonly in two contexts: where some form of valuation is required, and where an expert scientific or professional opinion is needed to resolve the disputes which have arisen.

Unlike the more established procedural areas of arbitration and mediation, the case law on expert determination is a lot less developed. An expert's remit is entirely dependent on contractual provisions, and there are generally no back-up rules of procedure and process.[84] The procedure adopted by the expert is likely to be overseen by the governing contractual terms. There are numerous appointing authorities[85] in England and Wales that may be used in appointing a relevant expert.

[82] L Bello, *Small Claims, Big Claims, Consumers' Perceptions of the Small Claims Process*, Consumer Focus, October 2010, see <www.consumerfocus.org.uk/files/2010/10/Small-claims-WEB-FILE.pdf>.

[83] S Blake, J Browne, and S Sine, *A Practical Approach to Alternative Dispute Resolution* (Oxford, Oxford University Press, 2011) 22.

[84] P Heneghan and L Orr, *Practice note on Expert Determination*, Practical Law Company online database (2011), see <uk.practicallaw.com/>.

[85] Examples include The Chartered Institute of Arbitrators; The Expert Witness Institute; The Institute of Actuaries; The Centre for Effective Dispute Resolution; The International Chamber of Commerce; The Law Society of England and Wales; London court of International Arbitration; The General Council of the

The primary duties of the expert are to remain both impartial and independent. The expert must be stringent in adhering to the task assigned by the parties and a material departure from instructions could result in a challenge made to the determination of the expert.[86] The court has the power to instruct the expert to provide reasons for his conclusions and failure to do so could also result in the determination being deemed void.[87]

Experts' decisions cannot generally be enforced without further court action or arbitration proceedings on the decision—whether internationally or domestically. If there is a specific clause in the governing contract related to expert determination and its binding power, then breach of this would ultimately be breach of contract and remedies for this would be applicable.

There is no specific or general requirement for the rules of due process or natural justice to be followed in order for an expert determination to be binding and valid between the parties.[88] Since expert determinations comprise decisions made in private contractual relations, they are not susceptible to judicial review on such grounds as failing to observe due process.

N. Workplace Mediation

Under employment legislation, employment disputes are required to go through a compulsory conciliation process using the services of the government agency ACAS, even though it serves as an independent and impartial body.[89] Conciliation is very similar to mediation involving a third-party neutral who seeks to achieve a settlement between the parties. Conciliation tends to be more directive than classic mediation, and is often conducted simply by a series of telephone conversations with the parties. Conciliation can take the form of both individual and collective rights, with individual conciliation focusing on disputes such as unfair dismissal or the infringement of an individual right. The conciliator's role is not to offer advice as to the likely outcome, but instead to explain the relevant law or suggest options to encourage resolution. Should an agreement fail to be reached, any negotiations or discussions cannot be used as evidence in a tribunal hearing as they remain confidential. Collective conciliation is used when disputes focus more on working conditions, pay, job losses, redundancy or pensions. In collective conciliation the role of the conciliator is to liaise with both sides to promote the best procedure, carrying the proposals between the parties, and in general promoting trust and resolution between the parties. Pre-claims concili-

Bar of England and Wales; The Chartered Institute of Management Accountants; Royal Institute of British Architects etc.

[86] *Jones v Sherwood Computer Services plc* [1992] 1 WLR 277 (a case decided in 1989).

[87] See the case of *Halifax Life Limited v The Equitable Life Assurance Society* [2007] EWHC 503 (Comm), where a declaration that an expert determination was not final and binding was sought on the ground that the expert had materially departed from the agreed terms of reference by failing to provide any adequate reasons for his decision.

[88] See *Bernhard Schulte GmbH & Company KG v Nile Holdings Limited* [2004] EWHC 977 (Comm) and *Barclays Bank PLC v Nylon Capital LLP* [2011] EWCA (Civ) 826 per Thomas LJ, para 37.

[89] See <www.acas.org.uk/index.aspx?articleid=356>.

ation is offered by ACAS to be used in situations where a dispute is likely to lead to a tribunal in order to attempt to resolve the dispute in a more proactive way.

In addition to offering conciliation and mediation services, ACAS also offers arbitration for industrial disputes. It is offered as an alternative to employment tribunals and will only hear cases of unfair dismissal or cases involving flexible working legislation. The choice to arbitrate under this scheme means that parties relinquish their right to have the case heard in front of an employment tribunal.

O. Family Disputes

The principal method of family dispute resolution, other than court processes, is bipartisan solicitor negotiation and/or mediation. Family mediation is generally conducted by trained family mediators—generally not legally qualified—without parties' legal advisers being present. Mediation covers division of property and arrangements for children. Government policy is to compel divorcing couples to attempt mediation before having access to court proceedings. Recent government statements make clear that policy is to try and get separating couples into mediation before seeking legal advice:

> Our experience is that too many people still approach a solicitor for a court resolution in the first instance when a dispute arises and mediation is a secondary consideration for them. We need a culture change to shift parental attitudes so that meeting the needs of children is put centre stage, not whether the parent can win or lose at court.[90]

As a result, anyone applying to court for a divorce is now required to attend a MIAM to discuss with a mediator whether mediation would be suitable for them.

A recent development in the field of family law ADR is an increased use of arbitration to settle family disputes. The Institute of Family Law Arbitrators (IFLA) recently proposed a scheme, which is the result of collaboration between Resolution (a national organisation of family lawyers committed to non-confrontational divorce, separation and other family problems), the Family Law Bar Association, the Chartered Institute of Arbitrators and the Centre for Child and Family Law Reform, aimed at enabling family disputes to be resolved by arbitration. The arbitration is conducted under the Family Arbitration Rules, which were developed by IFLA specifically for the scheme.[91] The emphasis on promoting the use of mediation in family law has been reinforced by judges and lawyers calling for no-fault divorce processes.[92]

The procedure for family mediation is rather different from that in civil/commercial mediations. Lawyers are generally not present in family mediations. Instead, parties

[90] Minister JS Djangoly, speech, 16 April 2012, to Law Society Family Mediation Conference, available at <www.justice.gov.uk/downloads/about/moj/our-ministers-board/speeches/djanogly-law-society-event.doc>.

[91] See <ifla.org.uk> for details on IFLA scheme.

[92] See the recent article by A Melton, 'Divorce—The Blame Game', *The Lawyer*, 9 April 2012, for commentary on Sir Nicholas Wall's (President of the High Court Family Division) statement that in his opinion the time had come for 'no-fault' divorce, available at <www.thelawyer.com/divorce-the-blame-game/1012117.article>. See also the article by J Hyde, 'Jackson Calls for Mediation Education', *Law Society Gazette*, 15 March 2012, 4(1), and also P Randolph's article on why litigation is so preferred to mediation, where he argues that there is an urgent social need to dissuade people from unnecessarily entering into prolonged litigation disputes, 'Compulsory Mediation?' (2010) 160 *New Law Journal* 499.

have the opportunity to check any proposed settlements with their lawyers before anything becomes binding. In some models, however, lawyers are completely discouraged from being involved. Mediators are expected not to advise parties on their rights or what the potential outcomes might be should the case go to court. Lawyers who act as mediators are expected to make clear that they are acting as a mediator and not as a lawyer, and are expected to take a non-directive and non-advisory role.

Unlike civil/commercial mediators, family mediators are required to have a consultant/supervisor to assist in dealing with the sensitive nature of family mediation's subject matter. Thus the role of professional practice consultant (PCC) was created in order to support a family mediator in their practice. A PCC is required for all family mediators, regardless of experience or seniority.

In general in the UK, it is rare for children to be directly involved in the mediation process. However, mediators who do involve children are expected to have specialised training and to give special regard as to how to best communicate with children effectively. When mediating with children, mediators are responsible for obtaining agreement from the parents as to the objectives of the meeting and ensuring everyone is properly prepared. The goal is to discuss the wishes and feelings of the children, without undermining parental authority.

P. Mediation in Judicial Review Cases

Despite the special nature of citizen–state judicial review cases, in which citizens challenge decisions of public bodies, there has been increasing interest on the part of some sections of the judiciary and government in encouraging ADR. The current Judicial Review Pre-Action Protocol provides that parties should consider whether some form of alternative dispute resolution procedure would be more suitable than litigation and, if so, endeavour to agree which form to adopt. Moreover, both the claimant and defendant may be required by the court to provide evidence that alternative means of resolving their dispute were considered. Parties are warned that if the protocol is not followed then the court must have regard to such conduct when determining costs.[93]

Independently funded research published in 2009[94] assessed the value and limits of mediation as an alternative to, or used alongside, judicial review. The research was devised to consider, in the specific context of judicial review, government and mediator claims that mediation can lead to savings in costs as well as in court time, and provide remedies and solutions to disputes that cannot be offered by the court. The researchers were concerned to explore the use of mediation in the context of judicial review, which they argue not only has an important constitutional function, but, compared to other forms of civil litigation, already offers flexibility, low costs and speed. The researchers also felt that claims as to the value of mediation needed to be examined in light of the realities of judicial review litigation. For example, a large proportion of judicial review claims end in settlements negotiated between the parties, with little input from

[93] Pre-Action protocol for Judicial Review, Civil Procedure Rules, May 2012, available at <www.justice.gov.uk/courts/procedure-rules/civil/protocol/prot_jrv>.

[94] V Bondy and L Mulcahy, with M Doyle and V Reid, *Mediation and Judicial Review: An Empirical Research Study*, Public Law Project, 2009, available at <www.publiclawproject.org.uk/documents/MediationandJudicialReview.pdf>.

the court. Therefore, any aspects of added value that mediation may offer need be considered in relation to bilaterally negotiated settlements as well as in relation to judicial determinations. The researchers were also interested in principled concerns, such as the importance of a transparent supervisory role for the court, the need to create precedents and the retreating role of adjudication in public law.

The research concluded that litigation, or the threat of it, brings public bodies to the negotiating table. An offer of mediation is unlikely to be accepted by the defendant until judicial review is a potential course of action. And once a judicial review claim has been threatened or issued, cases that can settle do so, usually as a result of discussions between the parties' lawyers. Mediation can offer added value in the sense of better outcomes in some cases, but it will be difficult to justify the additional cost of mediation when a bilateral negotiation can settle the claim. On the question of cost savings, the researchers concluded that there was no empirical basis for the assertion that mediation in judicial review cases would save costs. Their interviews with lawyers and mediators did not support the claim that mediation is cheaper than litigation and have highlighted how difficult it is to generalise.

> It is clear that in some situations a successful mediation will be cheaper than a lengthy and complex court hearing, but more expensive in other situations . . . In the absence of empirical data to support the assertion that mediation is cheaper than litigation in the context of judicial review, how does this claim arise and why is it repeatedly rehearsed? . . . Mediation providers have a financial and ideological interest in promoting mediation and they have formed a powerful and persuasive lobby. What better way to recruit support from the establishment than the promise of savings on costs, both in terms of public funding and of judges' time? It is not suggested that claims about costs savings are made in bad faith, but it is suggested that, certainly in the context of judicial review, where there is no evidence to support them, uncritical adherence to them could have significant implications for both policy and practice. For example, the assumption that mediation is cheaper is at the core of the rationale for costs sanctions against a party who 'unreasonably' refuses to mediate.[95]

Q. Community/Neighbourhood Mediation

Community/neighbourhood mediation is a type of mediation which focuses on interpersonal and social disagreements within a community, attempting to keep such disputes out of the legal system. Mediators in this type of mediation are generally volunteers from within the community. The most common types of dispute covered involve neighbours and relate to noise problems, verbal abuse, mischievous behaviour of children, disagreements over pets, boundary disputes, environmental issues, parking disputes, or inter-group disputes. The second significant category of community mediation is that in schools and among peers. Peer mediation allows for students to resolve disputes amongst themselves by offering them training and support to do so. In the UK a number of mediation schemes have been introduced training both students and teachers to deal with handling conflicts and disputes. Other types of mediation include mediation among the elderly, gang mediation and victim–offender mediation, which will be addressed in greater depth in the following section. Given

[95] Ibid, 69–70.

the non-commercial nature of community/neighbourhood mediation, funding depends heavily on the community itself or on charities funding such activities. Alternatively, a managing agency may engage volunteer mediators to carry out the tasks. Because of the emotional nature of many disputes dealt with via community mediation, the mediations are generally conducted by two individuals acting as co-mediators.

R. Mediation in the Criminal Justice System

The use of victim–offender mediation (restorative justice) is intended to achieve a number of objectives, including 'repairing (as far as possible) or making up for the damage and hurt caused by the crime' by the offender to the victim (or victim's family).[96] In theory, criminal mediation provides an opportunity for healing and possible restitution for the victim in a way that the formal criminal justice system does not. While the use of criminal justice mediation varies from scheme to scheme, most schemes exclude the most serious violent and sexual offences. On the other hand, some mediation processes have been used in manslaughter and murder cases between the offender and the victim's family. Generally, criminal mediation most commonly deals with vandalism, assault, antisocial behaviour orders and road traffic offences.

The most common form of criminal mediation is in the form of victim and offender mediation. These schemes were established to allow victims of a crime to engage an offender directly to discuss his actions and agree how he should make amends. The redress can take the form of restitution, whether it is in the form of financial restitution or through community service, or even just an apology. The schemes are also meant to have a rehabilitative impact on offenders. Since the 1980s, several victim–offender mediation schemes have been launched, including the National Association of Victim's Support Scheme as well at the four experimental schemes carried out across England by the Home Office. Restorative justice mediation also takes place at the community level with police forces taking a key role in referring cases to community justice panels and community mediation services. Police also take a role in resolving conflict informally, a practice which has become known as 'street restorative justice'. The Restorative Justice Council provides accreditation, consultancy and quality assurance for the field of restorative justice mediation.

S. UK Regulation of Mediation

There is no Mediation Act controlling mediation practice and procedure. There is no current state control in the UK of the training, appointment or performance of mediators.[97] As discussed above in II, there are numerous references to ADR in the CPR, and many judicial and government initiatives to promote mediation and to exert pressure on disputing parties to enter into mediation processes before having access to court proceedings and judicial determination. However, common law developments

[96] M Wright, *Justice for Victims and Offenders: A Restorative Response to Crime* (Berkshire, Open University Press, 1991) 41.

[97] A Boon, R Earle and A Whyte, 'Regulating Mediators?' (2007) 10 *Legal Ethics* 26.

and government policy do not regulate the process itself.[98] Court-attached mediation schemes operate using private mediators, as do the schemes in which the courts direct or recommend ADR (for example, Commercial Court ADR orders and the Court of Appeal Mediation Scheme).

The pre-action protocols provide encouragement for parties to consider mediation at the earliest possible stage. The Practice Direction on Pre-action Conduct[99] states that parties should consider whether some form of ADR procedure would be more suitable than litigation and, if so, attempt to agree which form to adopt. The Practice Direction states that starting proceedings should usually be a stage of last resort, and proceedings should not normally be started when a settlement is still actively being explored. Although ADR is not compulsory, the guidance on pre-action conduct stresses that both parties should consider whether some form of ADR procedure might enable them to settle the matter without commencing proceedings. If proceedings do take place, both parties may be required to provide evidence that alternative means of resolving the dispute were considered.[100] Parties are warned that if this provision is not followed then the court must have regard to such conduct when determining costs. English case law (discussed earlier) makes clear that there is a requirement under the common law for parties to attempt to resolve civil disputes by ADR at the earliest opportunity and that unreasonable refusal to agree to engage in ADR when suggested by an opponent may lead to the party being penalised by the court through the award of costs.

As discussed earlier, the government intends to compel ADR as a preliminary first stage in small claims, but again this service is likely to be provided by private mediators and there is no quality control regime that will monitor and guarantee standards. In family cases the Family Procedure Rules 2010, which came into force on 6 April 2011, oblige the court to consider the use of alternative dispute resolution at every stage.

Thus the current regulatory position in relation to mediation is that there is significant common law and practice 'regulation' of the conduct of disputes aimed at encouraging, if not pushing, disputing parties into mediation, but there is no supervision or regulation of standards of performance or practice of mediators themselves.

T. EU Regulation of Mediation

The initial success of mediation in Europe and the enthusiasm of numerous proponents of alternative dispute resolution led to the harmonisation of mediation legislation in EU Member States by the Directive on Certain Aspects of Mediation in Civil and Commercial Matters (2008/52/EC), which was adopted on 23 April 2008 and came into force on 13 June 2008.[101] The Directive was enacted with the objective of facilitating access to alternative dispute resolution. It required Member States (with the exception of Denmark) to bring into force the laws, regulations and administra-

[98] Blake, Browne and Sime, *A Practical Approach to Alternative Dispute Resolution*.

[99] Para 8.1, Practice Direction on Pre-Action Conduct.

[100] Ibid. See also para 4.4(3).

[101] See <www.wbginvestmentclimate.org/advisory-services/regulatory-simplification/alternative-dispute-resolution/upload/Directive-202008-52-EC_en.pdf>.

tive provisions necessary to comply with this Directive before 21 May 2011. Though intended to deal with cross-border disputes, the Directive expressly says that 'Nothing should prevent Member States from applying such provisions also to internal mediation processes'. About two-thirds of EU Member States have incorporated the Directive into national legislation. While some have chosen to incorporate domestic disputes into the changes in national laws, others, like the UK, have not. In addition to the 2008 Directive, the EU Parliament has recently passed a resolution in October 2011 calling for, among many other things, an increase in public awareness of ADR mechanisms as well as calling on the Commission to explore setting out minimum standards of ADR across sectors as well as encouraging Member States to develop their existing ADR schemes. To encourage the coordinated development and implementation of mediation, a European Association of Judges for Mediation also exists, known as Gemme.

Directive 2008/52/EC of the European Parliament relating to mediation has been given effect in England and Wales by amendment to the Civil Procedure Rules, specifically rules 78.23–78.28 (the Civil Procedure (Amendment) Rules 2011 (SI 2011/88)). This new section in part 78 made provisions relating to confidentiality of proceedings as well as the suspension of the limitation period during mediation. More specifically, rules 78.24 and 78.25 relate to Article 6 of the Directive (Enforceability of agreements resulting from mediation) by allowing for parties to apply for mediation settlement orders, and rules 78.26–78.28 relate to Article 7 (Confidentiality of mediation) requiring an application to be made under particular procedural requirements before any mediation evidence can be disclosed. Consequential amendments are made to rules in other CPR Parts, most significantly to rules 5.4C (Supply of documents to a non-party from court records) and 31.3 (Right of inspection of a disclosed document). In CPR Update 55, published in March 2011, Practice Direction 78 was amended by the addition of provisions supplementing rule 78.24 (Making a mediation settlement enforceable). In addition to the changes made in the CPR, the UK has also implemented the Directive through the Cross-Border Mediation (EU Directive) Regulations 2011, which came into force on 20 May 2011. This legislation made provisions to amend primary and secondary legislation, for example, amendments to legislation such as new section 207A of the Employment Rights Act 1998, which extends time limits in certain cross-border disputes. It also makes provisions regarding mediation evidence providing that

> a mediator or mediation administrator has the right to withhold mediation evidence in civil and commercial judicial proceedings and arbitration (reg 9) as well as allowing the court to make orders to disclose evidence upon agreement by the parties or where considerations of public policy or enforcement of the settlement require the court to do so (reg 10).

As mentioned previously, within the UK, these changes to national legislation apply only in situations of cross-border disputes rather than any domestic disputes.

A mediation clause does not prevent an action before the courts in the UK. Although many commercial contracts have dispute resolution clauses that require the parties to attempt mediation before resorting to arbitration or litigation, eventual access to the courts is not prevented. This is not surprising, as the mediator does not resolve disputes but merely acts as facilitator to help the parties achieve an agreed settlement, and no settlement can take place unless both disputing parties agree to it. Historically, the courts in England and Wales have been reluctant to enforce mediation clauses on the basis that they are too uncertain—an express agreement to negotiate is not a contract 'because it is too uncertain to have any binding force'.[102] However, the strong public policy in favour of mediation and ADR, and the development of specific procedures for mediation, have led the courts to lend their support to 'mediation-first' clauses where they are sufficiently certain, where there is no need for an agreement at any stage before matters can proceed, where the administrative processes for selecting a party to resolve the dispute and to pay that person are defined, and where the process or at least a model of the process is set out in the contract. The courts cannot make a party agree, but they can order a party to comply with specific contractual clauses, such as to send representatives with the requisite authority to take part in a formal mediation procedure under the auspices of a named institute. On that basis, alternative dispute resolution clauses are enforced.[103] But the contractual requirement to mediate must require mediation, rather than merely offer the parties the option.[104] Mediation is also encouraged and supported by court procedure rules and practice guides.

U. What Are the Duties of Mediators?

The state does not regulate mediation in England and Wales, nor does any one professional body have overall control over accreditation. It thus follows that there is no single code of conduct. As there is no national legislative standard for mediators, duties will be imposed by the parties or by a mediation organisation if the mediator belongs to one. Guidance for mediators will come primarily from the code of practice or code of conduct of the organisation to which that mediator belongs. The code covers issues such as qualifications, impartiality, confidentiality, conflicts of interest, ethical requirements and conduct, as well as providing the baseline for good quality practice. One duty that is imposed by case law is that of confidentiality for statements made in the course of conciliation or, by logical extension, mediation. It would appear that there is growing support for a statutory regime for mediation and this is discussed further in the final section below.

The Civil Mediation Council's (CMC) Code of Good Practice for Mediation Organizations was developed to supplement the CMC Registered Mediation Organization Scheme, which sets out the administrative details of becoming a mediation organisation registered with the CMC. The CMC Code of Practice is quite brief, setting out a few rules each under the headings of Mediators, Mediations, Administration, Complaints and Standards, Insurance and Ethics & Equality.

In practice, it is common for most standard-form mediation agreements to include a mediator immunity clause. This clause attempts to exclude the mediator's liability for negligence, breach of contract and other civil wrongs as a means of protecting their position. However, such clauses cannot absolve mediators where wrongs such as fraud have been committed. It is also common for mediators to carry professional indemnity

[102] HG Beale (general ed), *Chitty on Contracts*, 30th edn, vol 1 (London, Sweet & Maxwell, Thomson Reuters, 2008) paras 2–136, citing, among other cases, *Walford v Miles* [1992] 2 AC 128 and *Willis Management (Isle of Man) Ltd v Cable and Wireless plc* [2005] EWCA (Civ) 806, [24], [26].

[103] *Cable & Wireless plc v IBM United Kingdom Ltd* [2002] 2 All ER (Comm) 1041 and KMJ Lewison, *The Interpretation of Contracts*, 5th edn (London, Sweet & Maxwell, 2011) para 18.08.

[104] *Balfour Beatty Construction Northern v Modus Corvest* (Blackpool) [2008] EWHC 3029.

insurance. Where mediators are signatories to the mediation agreement, breach of this will be breach of contract. There is also an implied term in the agreement that the mediator will carry out his role exercising reasonable care and skill. There are two further sources of liability that a mediator may be subjected to: breach of fiduciary duty and negligence claims.

A point of contention remains with these claims of how it is possible to determine if a mediator has breached his duty of care. Academics still question whether and if an all-embracing standard of care will ever be formulated due to the individualistic, flexible nature of mediation and the varying levels that mediators work at.[105] There are no decided cases under English law where a claim has been made against a mediator for breach of contract, misrepresentation, negligence or breach of fiduciary duty.[106]

There are several quality control mechanisms in place (predominantly private), including the Ministry of Justice's restricted permission to only allow mediations handled by the National Mediation Helpline to be provided by organisations accredited by the CMC.[107] The CMC is not a regulatory body; however, it does provide accreditation schemes for mediation providers which require the providers to demonstrate that their schemes meet the requirements regarding adequate training and insurance, supervision and mentoring, efficient administration and allocation of mediators, and the adoption of a code of conduct. Thus the CMC takes on a quasi-regulatory role.

Mediation is generally a non-binding process. If the parties fail to agree on an outcome, the mediation will be deemed to have 'failed' and the dispute may proceed to litigation. However, if the parties reach a settlement, then any agreed terms set out in the settlement agreement (a document in which both parties have formally recorded their agreement and signed it) will be contractually enforceable. A decision cannot be imposed on the parties in a mediation and, though mediators may encourage a settlement, they cannot coerce the parties into one. Coercive behaviour undermines the self-determining nature of mediation and might also violate the mediator's code of conduct.

V. Should There Be More Regulation of ADR?

It has been argued in the English context that unregulated, mass dispute resolution provision is 'aberrant'.[108] Developed legal systems assure quality through judicial selection and training, and through procedural rules and a system of appeals. Arbitration is governed by statute, which provides protection for parties in relation to arbitrators and offers limited opportunity for review of arbitral awards. However, no similar protections exist for parties entering mediation.

Effective mediators and conciliators require a complex set of skills that depend on

[105] D Spencer and M Brogan, *Mediation Law and Practice* (Cambridge, Cambridge University Press, 2006).

[106] P Rowe, *Atkin's Court Forms—Alternative Dispute Resolution*, vol 6(2) (London, LexisNexis, 2008). See *Tapoohi v Lewenberg* [2003] VSC 410 for a Commonwealth case where there was no written mediation agreement but one party alleged that the mediator had put pressure on the parties to sign a settlement agreement.

[107] P Rowe, *Atkins Court Forms—Alternative Dispute Resolution*, vol 6(2).

[108] Boon, Earle and Whyte, 'Regulating Mediators?' 33.

personal attributes and good quality training. Concerns about quality control flow from variable training and standards of performance in the context of a private dispute resolution process that has the capacity to magnify rather than minimise power imbalances between parties. The role of mediators is currently unregulated and they are unaccountable. The nature and extent of their responsibilities is not clearly articulated and ethical codes, where they exist, vary. These matters are particularly important when parties attend mediation sessions without their legal advisers and when it is clear that mediators have considerable opportunity for the exercise of covert power during the course of mediations and in the design of settlement agreements. The development of common agreed standards of training and performance would promote confidence in those offering mediation services. However, if a growing proportion of cases are likely to be forcibly diverted from normal litigation procedures into ADR processes, it might be argued that the government has some responsibility in assuring the standards of those providing such services. In common with many professions, mediation providers seem keen to self-regulate rather than have a regulatory regime imposed.

Some commentators believe that pressure for some kind of regulation of mediator standards and practice is growing.[109] It is suggested that the public expect mediators to be properly skilled and qualified, although there is no concrete evidence to support this suggestion. On the other hand, the increased emphasis on mandatory mediation, and especially that being applied by government and through court rules, suggests that the public ought to be able to rely on the fact that mediators are appropriately qualified and perform to a good professional standard. While all mediation organisations have criteria for practice, there is no consistency between them and, indeed, there is a substantial degree of competition between commercial mediation providers. There is, apparently, no cross-recognition of accreditation of members. A number of mediation organisations that previously performed a quasi-regulatory function have now ceased to exist, leaving something of a vacuum. The CMC was established in 2003 and has become an accepted umbrella body for civil, commercial and workplace mediation. However, although it encourages good practice, it has no regulatory function. Practitioners may choose to join a mediation organisation in order to be supported and obtain clients, but membership is voluntary and mediation organisations are only able to regulate those who join and remain members.

Areas that are currently unregulated include:

- *Selection of people for training as mediators*: There are currently no consistent basic qualifications for selection to be trained as a mediator but, given the very wide range of people training to become mediators and the diversity of subject areas, it is difficult to envisage a successful regulatory regime.
- *Training, accreditation and continuing professional development*: The competence of mediators in the UK is generally assessed by their trainers during training. There is no common system for competence testing and no national standards for competence testing in England. Competence assessment is different from accreditation which requires more than mere observation. Accreditation may require adherence to codes of practice, a period between training and accreditation during which skills

[109] Ibid. Marriott and Brown also make a strong case for some form of regulation, Brown and Marriott, *ADR Principles and Practice* 613–15.

are developed, commitment to continuing professional development, and so on. However, in the UK, mediation organisations have different standards and criteria for accreditation, and they do not collaborate to produce common standards.

- *Accountability and supervision*: Because of the confidential nature of mediation there is no accountability and no right of appeal. While family mediation has incorporated the concept of supervision into practice, this is not generally the case for civil/commercial mediation.

W. Quasi-regulatory/Supervisory Bodies

The CMC has a quasi-regulatory function in that it accredits civil, commercial and workplace mediation providers, not individual mediators. Under its constitution, the CMC's objective is to 'create a culture of good practice by encouraging research, continuing education and quality standards in the field; by issuing codes of good practice; and by conducting accreditation of mediation providers and through them individual mediators'.[110]

The Family Mediation Council is also not a regulatory body, but an umbrella organisation covering the main providers of family mediation in England and Wales. It publishes a code of practice, provides initial training and continuing professional development.[111]

The Restorative Justice Council has a national register of practitioners and publishes codes of practice. Registered practitioners are required to adhere to the code and there are standards for training, supervision and continuing professional development.[112]

In the absence of formal regulation of mediation in the UK, anyone without training or qualifications is able to offer mediation services to the public. While there has been little enthusiasm for moving towards a statutory regime in the past, it has been suggested that the balance is now shifting towards creating a regulatory regime and that this is gaining impetus since the introduction of EU initiatives discussed earlier.[113] On the other hand, the European Parliament has made clear that they would not want legislative action setting out minimum standards if that would constrain diversity of ADR practices and developments.[114]

BIBLIOGRAPHY

Allen, T, 'Don't Ignore a Request to Mediate. *Halsey* Applied! A Note on *PGF II SA v OMFS Company* [2012] EWHC 83 (TCC)', <www.cedr.com/articles/?301>

Australian Government, Attorney General's Department, *A Strategic Framework for Access to Justice in the Federal Civil Justice System*, September 2009, <www.ag.gov.au/LegalSystem/

110 See <www.civilmediation.org/about-cmc>.

111 See <www.familymediationcouncil.org.uk/>.

112 See <www.restorativejustice.org.uk/trainers/>.

113 Marriott and Brown, *ADR Principles and Practice* 627–27.

114 European Parliament, Resolution of 25 October 2011 on alternative dispute resolution in civil, commercial and family matters (2011/2117(INI), Horizontal Approach to ADR, no 4.

Documents/A%20Strategic%20Framework%20for%20Access%20to%20Justice%20in%20the%20Federal%20Civil%20Justice%20System.pdf>

Beale, HG (general ed), *Chitty on Contracts*, 30th edn, vol 1 (London, Sweet & Maxwell, Thomson Reuters, 2008)

Bello, L, *Small Claims, Big Claims, Consumers' Perceptions of the Small Claims Process*, Consumer Focus, October 2010, <www.consumerfocus.org.uk/files/2010/10/Small-claims-WEB-FILE.pdf>

Blake, S, Browne, J and Sine, S, *A Practical Approach to Alternative Dispute Resolution* (Oxford, Oxford University Press, 2011)

Bondy, V, Doyle, M and Reid, V, 'Mediation and Judicial Review—Mind the Research Gap' (2005) 10 *Judicial Review* 220

Bondy, V and Mulcahy, L, with Doyle, M and Reid, V, *Mediation and Judicial Review: An Empirical Research Study*, Public Law Project, 2009, <www.publiclawproject.org.uk/documents/MediationandJudicialReview.pdf>

Boon, A, Earle, R and Whyte, A, 'Regulating Mediators?' (2007) 10 *Legal Ethics* 26

Brown, H and Marriott, A, *ADR Principles and Practice*, 3rd edn (London, Sweet & Maxwell, 2011)

CEDR, 'Public Sector—A Culture Change?' (2003) 32 *Resolutions* 6, <www.cedr.co.uk/news/resolutions/resolutions32.pdf>

CEDR, *The Fifth Mediation Audit*, Annual Review 2012, <www.cedr.com/docslib/TheMediatorAudit2012.pdf>

Clarke, Sir A, Master of the Rolls, *The Future of Civil Mediation*, speech to Annual Mediation Council Conference, Birmingham, 8 May 2008, <www.judiciary.gov.uk/Resources/JCO/Documents/Speeches/mr_mediation_conference_may08.pdf>

Consumer Focus, *Ensuring Effective Access to Appropriate and Affordable Dispute Resolution, The Final Report of the Civil Justice Advisory Group*, January 2011, <www.consumerfocus.org.uk/scotland/files/2011/01/Civil-Justice-Advisory-Group-Full-Report.pdf>

Crook, J, 'What is Alternative Dispute Resolution (ADR)?' in Betancourt, JC (ed), *What is Alternative Dispute Resolution (ADR)?* (London, Chartered Institute of Arbitrators, 2010) 1–43

Department for Constitutional Affairs, *A New Focus for Civil Legal Aid: Encouraging Early Resolution; Discouraging Unnecessary Litigation*, Response to Consultation 22/07/04, <www.dca.gov.uk/response-litigation.pdf>

Dingwall, R and Cloatre, E, 'Vanishing Trials?: An English Perspective' (2006) 7 *Journal of Dispute Resolution* 51

Djangoly, JS, Minister, speech, 16 April 2012, to Law Society Family Mediation Conference, <www.justice.gov.uk/downloads/about/moj/our-ministers-board/speeches/djanogly-law-society-event.doc>

Dowell, K, 'CoA Pilots Mediation Scheme in Bid to Cut Litigation Costs', *The Lawyer*, 4 April 2012, <www.thelawyer.com/1012099.article>

Doyle, M, *Manchester Small Claims Mediation Scheme Evaluation* (London, Department for Constitutional Affairs, 2006)

Enterken, J and Sefton, M, *Evaluation of Reading Small Claims Mediation Scheme* (London, Department for Constitutional Affairs, 2006)

Family Justice Review, Final Report, November 2011, <www.justice.gov.uk/downloads/publications/moj/2011/family-justice-review-final-report.pdf>

Galanter, M, 'A World without Trials' (2006) 7 *Journal of Dispute Resolution* 7

Genn, H, *Central London Pilot Mediation Scheme, Evaluation Report* (London, Department for Constitutional Affairs, 1998)

Genn, H, *Paths to Justice: What People Think and Do about Going to Law* (Oxford, Hart Publishing, 1999)

Genn, H, *Court-based ADR Initiatives for Non-family Civil Disputes: The Commercial Court and the Court of Appeal* (London, Lord Chancellor's Department, 2002)

Genn, H et al, *Twisting Arms: Court Referred and Court Linked Mediation under Judicial Pressure* (London, Ministry of Justice, 2007)

Genn, H, *Judging Civil Justice, The 2008 Hamlyn Lectures* (Cambridge, Cambridge University Press, 2009)

Genn, H, *Why the Privatisation of Civil Justice is a Rule of Law Issue*, 36th FA Mann Annual Lecture, November 2012, <www.ucl.ac.uk/laws/academics/profiles/docs/Hazel/36th%20F%20A%20Mann%20Lecture%20Website.pdf>

Hann, RG and Baar, C, *Evaluation of the Ontario Mandatory Mediation Program (Rule 24.1): Final Report—The First 23 Months* (Ontario, Ministry of the Attorney General, 2001)

Heneghan, P and Orr, L, *Practice Note on Expert Determination*, Practical Law Company online database (2011), <uk.practicallaw.com/>

Hyde, J, 'Jackson Calls for Mediation Education', *Law Society Gazette*, 15 March 2012, 4(1)

Judge, The Right Honourable the Lord, Lord Chief Justice of England and Wales, speech to Third Civil Mediation Council National Conference, 14 May 2009, <www.judiciary.gov.uk/Resources/JCO/Documents/Speeches/lcj-mediation-council-conf-140509.pdf>

Justice, Press Release, 21 June 2011, <http://www.justice.org.uk/data/files/resources/282/press210611.pdf>

Kritzer, HM, 'Disappearing Trials? A Comparative Perspective' (2004) 1 *Journal of Empirical Legal Studies* 735

Law Reform Commission of Ireland, *Alternative Dispute Resolution: Mediation and Conciliation*, November 2010, <www.lawreform.ie/_fileupload/consultation%20papers/cpADR.pdf>

Legal Services Consultation Document, *A New Focus for Civil Legal Aid: Encouraging Early Resolution; Discouraging Unnecessary Litigation* (London, Department for Constitutional Affairs, 2004)

Lewison, KMJ, *The Interpretation of Contracts*, 5th edn (London, Sweet & Maxwell, 2011)

Lord High Chancellor, *Modernising Justice* (London, Lord Chancellor's Department, 1998), <http://webarchive.nationalarchives.gov.uk/+/http://www.dca.gov.uk/consult/access/mjuspap.pdf>

Mackie, K, Miles, D, Marsh, W and Allen, T, *The ADR Practice Guide: Commercial Dispute Resolution*, 3rd revised edn (West Sussex, Tottel Publishing, 2007)

Melton, A, 'Divorce—The Blame Game', *The Lawyer*, 9 April 2012, <www.thelawyer.com/divorce-the-blame-game/1012117.article>

Ministry of Justice, *Proposals for the Reform of Legal Aid in England and Wales*, Cm7967 November 2010, <www.justice.gov.uk/downloads/consultations/legal-aid-reform-consultation.pdf/>

Ministry of Justice, *Solving Disputes in the County Courts: Creating a Simpler, Quicker and More Proportionate System, A Consultation on Reforming Civil Justice in England and Wales*, Consultation Paper CP6/2011, March 2011 (London, Ministry of Justice, 2011), <www.official-documents.gov.uk/document/cm80/8045/8045.pdf>

Ministry of Justice and Department of Education, *Government Response to Family Justice Review*, June 2012, <www.education.gov.uk/publications/eOrderingDownload/CM-8273.pdf>

Neuberger of Abbotsbury, Lord, Master of the Rolls, speech to the Fourth Civil Mediation Council National Conference, Educating Future Mediators, London, 11 May 2010, <www.judiciary.gov.uk/Resources/JCO/Documents/Speeches/mor-cmc-conference-speech-11052010.pdf>

Neuberger of Abbotsbury, Lord, Master of the Rolls, *Equity, ADR, Arbitration and the Law: Different Dimensions of Justice*, The Fourth Keating Lecture, Lincoln's Inn, 19 May 2010,

<www.judiciary.gov.uk/Resources/JCO/Documents/Speeches/mr-keating-lecture-19052010.pdf>

Neuberger of Abbotsbury, Lord, Master of the Rolls, *Has Mediation Had it's Day?*, The Gordon Slynn Memorial Lecture 2010, 10 November 2010, <www.judiciary.gov.uk/Resources/JCO/Documents/Speeches/moj-speech-mediation-lectureA.pdf>

Northern Ireland Department of Justice, *Access to Justice Review Northern Ireland*, August 2011, <www.dojni.gov.uk/index/publications/publication-categories/pubs-criminal-justice/access-to-justice-review-final-report.pdf>

Pel, M, *Referral to Mediation: A Practical Guide for an Effective Mediation Proposal* (The Hague, SDU Uitgevers, 2008)

Phillips of Worth Matravers, Lord, Lord Chief Justice of England and Wales, *Alternative Dispute Resolution: An English Viewpoint*, speech, India, 29 March 2008, <http://www.judiciary.gov.uk/Resources/JCO/Documents/Speeches/lcj_adr_india_290308.pdf>

Pleasence, P et al, *Causes of Action* (Norwich, The Stationery Office, 2004)

Prince, S, *Evaluation of Exeter Small Claims Mediation Scheme* (London, Department for Constitutional Affairs, 2006)

Prince, S and Belcher, S, *An Evaluation of the Effectiveness of Court based Mediation Processes in Non-Family Civil Proceedings at Exeter and Guildford County Courts* (London, Department for Constitutional Affairs, 2006)

Powell, E, 'Settlement of Disputes by Arbitration in Fifteenth-Century England' (1984) 2 *Law and History Review* 21

Randolph, P, 'Compulsory Mediation?' (2010) 160 *New Law Journal* 499

Rowe, P, *Atkin's Court Forms—Alternative Dispute Resolution*, vol 6(2) (London, LexisNexis, 2008).

Spencer, D and Brogan, M, *Mediation Law and Practice* (Cambridge, Cambridge University Press, 2006)

Swift, J, 'Ex-Halliwells Partners Prepare for Mediation with Liquidators over £20m Windfall', *The Lawyer*, 12 April 2012, <www.thelawyer.com/ex-halliwells-partners-prepare-for-mediation-with-liquidators-over-%C2%A320m-windfall/1012150.article>

Urwin, P, et al, *Evaluating the Use of Judicial Mediation in Employment Tribunals* (London, Ministry of Justice, 2010), <www.justice.gov.uk/downloads/publications/research-and-analysis/moj-research/evaluating-judicial-mediation-march10.pdf>

Webley, L, Abrams, P and Bacquet, S, *Evaluation of Birmingham Fast and Multi Track Mediation Scheme* (London, Department for Constitutional Affairs, 2006)

Woolf, HK, *Access to Justice: Interim Report to the Lord Chancellor on the Civil Justice System in England and Wales* (London, Her Majesty's Stationery Office, 1995)

Woolf, HK, *Access to Justice: Final Report to the Lord Chancellor on the Civil Justice System in England and Wales* (London, Her Majesty's Stationary Office, 1996)

Wright, M, *Justice for Victims and Offenders: A Restorative Response to Crime* (Berkshire, Open University Press, 1991)

8

Regulation of Dispute Resolution in France: Evolutions and Challenges

FRÉDÉRIQUE FERRAND

I. CHARACTERISTICS OF ADR

A. Dispute Resolution Procedures Most Commonly Deployed in France

IN FRANCE THERE is no very recent general official statistical data available with regard to mediation or arbitration. The number of cases referred to mediation is not mentioned in either the brochure *Les chiffres clés de la Justice 2011* or in the *Annuaire Statistique de la Justice 2011–2012*.[1] The *Rapport Guinchard 2008*,[2] however, mentions that a mediator is appointed by the court in 1.5 per cent of the cases before appellate courts and 1.1 per cent before first instance courts. Mediation seems to be used essentially in family matters.[3] It is likely that the use of mediation has increased in the 10 last years;[4] however, no precise statistics confirm this perception. Statistical data are available in respect of the cases brought before court and before conciliators (*conciliateurs*).

Before civil courts of first instance,[5] 2010 saw 952,412 new cases brought before the tribunaux de grande instance (TGI),[6] 706,979 before the tribunaux d'instance (TI),[7] 102,908 before the juridictions de proximité[8] and 217,661 before the conseils de prud'hommes.[9] During the same year, 930,999 cases were concluded before the TGI (18,856 by conciliation, settlement *(transaction)* or admission *(acquiescement)*), 662,411 before the TI (5,662 by a conciliation of the parties), 99,291 before the juridictions de proximité and 205,653 before the conseils de prud'hommes (12,258 by a conciliation). It appears that since 2004 the percentage of cases settled during proceedings has not been increasing but has remained more or less constant, except before labour courts (*conseils de prud'hommes*), where it has been regularly decreasing.

[1] Only mediations in criminal matters have been subject to statistics: in 2010, 21,598 *médiations pénales* took place (11,953 with success, 9,645 failed), see *Annuaire statistique de la Justice 2011–2012* (Paris, Documentation française, 2012) 113, report also available on the website of the French Ministry of Justice at <www.justice.gouv.fr/art_pix/stat_annuaire_2011-2012.pdf>.

[2] *Rapport Guinchard, L'ambition raisonnée d'une justice apaisée* (Paris, Documentation française, 2008) 161. The same figures for 2001 can also be found in E Serverin, 'Le médiateur civil et le service public de la justice' [2003] *Revue trimestrielle de droit civile (RTDCiv)* 243 and are based on a study called *La médiation judiciaire en chiffres, Situation au 31 octobre 2001* by C Moreau, B Munoz-Perez and E Serverin (Paris, Ministère de la Justice, Cellule Études et Recherches, 2002). This study only deals with mediation ordered by court (ie *médiations judiciaires*).

[3] In 2006: 5,095 non-judicial family mediation processes and 3,710 by court order; those figures are very low in comparison with the 360,000 cases brought before the family judge the same year, see *Rapport Guinchard, L'ambition raisonnée d'une justice apaisée*, ibid.

[4] Especially due to some new legal provisions allowing the judge to enjoin the parties to take part in a mediation information session.

[5] Before the appellate courts (cours d'appel) 243,967 new cases were brought in 2010; 233,577 were terminated, under which 903 were concluded by a settlement between the parties (*conciliation*), which is less than the previous years (1,448 settlements in 2008, 1,128 in 2009): see *Annuaire statistique de la Justice 2011–2012* 29.

[6] *Annuaire statistique de la Justice 2011–2012* 31. TGI have jurisdiction in civil matters when the value of the claim exceeds €10,000 and in some special matters.

[7] *Annuaire statistique de la Justice 2011–2012* 35. TI have jurisdiction in civil matters where the value of the claim is between €4,000 and €10,000, as well as in some special matters.

[8] *Annuaire statistique de la Justice 2011–2012* 37. Juridictions de proximité have jurisdiction for small claims that do not exceed €4,000. These courts will soon be eliminated (1 January 2015) in order to make the jurisdiction rules in the first instance courts clearer and simpler.

[9] *Annuaire statistique de la Justice 2011–2012* 41. The conseils de prud'homme decide on cases regarding labour law (employment contracts, dismissal, redundancy, etc).

Table 1: Statistics on the Activity of the Conciliateurs de Justice, 2005–10

	2005	2006	2007	2008	2009	2010
Number of conciliateurs de justice	1,808	1,809	1,794	1,799	1,777	1,810
Number of cases brought before them	123,174	121,909	127,389	122,787	124,792	130,715
Number of cases settled	70,875	68,543	70,399	73,261	72,024	75,919
Settlement rate (in %)	57.5	56.2	55.3	59.7	57.7	58.1

Source: *Annuaire statistique de la justice 2011–2012.*

Before the *conciliateurs de justice*[10] (conciliators), 130,715 disputes were brought in 2010, of which 75,919 were settled, which means a 58.1 per cent settlement rate (see Table 1).[11]

B. Strength and Weaknesses of These Dispute Resolution Mechanisms

Mediation (*médiation*) is an appreciated dispute resolution mechanism, and most parties who use it are satisfied. However, it is not yet well known and needs further incentives. It is especially suited for family conflicts,[12] for example, for issues regarding parental responsibilities. It is also praised in labour law and sometimes in commercial law.

Conciliation (*conciliation*) can take place either before court proceedings (between the parties in an informal way or before the conciliateur) or during proceedings before the court in charge of the case since 'to conciliate parties is part of the mandate of the judge' (Article 21 CPC, Code de procédure civile),[13] so that conciliation by the judge belongs in France to the *principes directeurs de la procédure*. However, the French judge seldom takes time to try to suggest a settlement.[14] The conciliation process before the conciliateur de justice leads to good results; it is, however, restricted to rights that are at the free disposal of the parties. In practice, most disputes brought before the conciliateur de justice are modest with regard to the value of the claim, and concern housing (unpaid rents, inventory of fixtures, etc), neighbourhood disputes, sales between private persons, false information, etc.

[10] In 2010 there were 1,810 *conciliateurs de justice* in France (1,807 in 2004, 1,808 in 2005, 1,809 in 2006, 1,794 in 2007, 1799 in 2008 and 1,777 in 2009), see *Annuaire statistique de la Justice 2011–2012* 307.

[11] Ibid. The number of disputes brought before the *conciliateurs de justice* for settlement did not seem to increase: 122,713 in 2004, 123,174 in 2005, 121,909 in 2006, 127,389 in 2007 and 122,787 in 2008 and the success rate remained the same (between 55.3 and 57.5%), see *Annuaire statistique de la Justice 2011–2012* 307. However, since 2009, more cases have been brought before them (124,792 in 2009 and 130,715 in 2010) so that a '*regain de la conciliation*' can be asserted.

[12] See *Rapport Guinchard, L'ambition raisonnée d'une justice apaisée* 163.

[13] Parties can also conciliate during the expertise proceeding, see Art 281 CPC: 'If the parties have reached a settlement, the expert will observe that his mission has become without purpose; he will so report to the judge. The parties may request from the judge to deliver an enforceable certificate to the document containing their agreement.'

[14] The practice differs from one judge to another.

Arbitration is praised for its discretion, confidentiality and the parties' power to define the scope and nature of the arbitrator's mission. However, it can be very expensive and is not always a rapid way of obtaining a solution to the dispute.

C. Practical Use and Theoretical Appropriateness

Since the statistics are incomplete, it is difficult to compare practical use and theoretical appropriateness. With regard to the conciliation before conciliateurs de justice, although its appropriateness with regard to small claims over rights at the parties' free disposal has been underlined and although the quality of the conciliateurs' work has often been stressed,[15] the statistics show that the number of disputes brought before them was slightly decreasing until 2008. However, subsequent to the majority of the statistics from 2008, Act No 2010-1165 of 1 October 2010 'relatif à la conciliation et à la procédure orale en matière civile, commerciale et sociale' has modified the CPC in order to extend the possibility of a conciliation by the conciliateur de justice, so that the future statistics could show a new increase in the number of conciliations. This tendency can already be noticed in the statistical data available for 2009 and 2010.[16]

II. GENERAL APPROACH OF THE LEGISLATOR AS REGARDS THE REGULATION OF ADR AND ADJUDICATION

A. Regulation of ADR

With regard to ADR[17] mechanisms, French law makes a distinction between arbitration, mediation and conciliation. Arbitration is regulated in the fourth book of the CPC (Articles 1442–527). It has been reformed recently by Decree No 2011-48 of 13 January 2011 in order to reflect case law, and to promote both arbitration and France as a location for arbitration.

Conciliation is regulated in several ways and was already regulated in the Code of Civil Procedure 1806:

- First, as a general task of the judge in Articles 21, 127 and 128[18] CPC, who may, however, delegate this task to a conciliateur de justice (Articles 129-1 to 129-5 CPC) where legal provisions allow such a delegation (ie before tribunaux d'instance, juridictions de proximité, tribunal de commerce and tribunal paritaire des baux ruraux);

[15] See eg *Rapport Guinchard, L'ambition raisonnée d'une justice apaisée* 156ff: this kind of conciliation allows a 'rapid, free and effective treatment of the disputes' (157).

[16] See n 11.

[17] ADR mechanisms were called in French *Modes alternatifs de règlement des conflits* (MARC). Since the new *décret* No°2012-66 of 20 January 2012, the new terminology is *Modes amiables de résolution des différends* (MARD).

[18] Art 127 CPC: 'Parties may reconcile, on their initiative or upon that of the judge, throughout the proceeding'; Art 128 CPC: 'The conciliation must be attempted, unless otherwise provided, at the place and the time that the judge deems favourable. The judge who has the duty to try to conciliate the parties may enjoin them to meet a conciliateur de justice who shall inform them about the matter and the procedure of conciliation.'

- Second, as a sometimes mandatory preliminary phase of the proceedings (see eg Articles L 1411-1(2) and R 1454-10ff Code du Travail (C trav) for labour courts[19]) or as a proceeding stage that is not mandatory but is, however, suggested and regulated, as before the tribunal d'instance or the juridiction de proximité (Article 845f CPC);
- Third, as a non-judicial process before the conciliateur de justice (regulated in Decree No 78-381 of 20 March 1978 and the CPC amended by Decree No 2012-66 of 20 January 2012), whose task is to facilitate outside a judicial proceeding the *règlement amiable* of disputes regarding rights that are at the parties' free disposal; and
- Fourth, in specific provisions applying to special kinds of disputes, such as those involving the lease of a dwelling (Article 20 of Law Act No 89-462 of 6 June 1989 and Decree No 2001-653 of 19 July 2001), over-indebtedness (*surendettement*) of natural persons not subject to a professional insolvency proceeding (Article L 331-6 Code de la consommation, C cons), or medical accident or hospital-acquired infection (Articles L 1142–4ff Code de la santé publique creating *commissions de conciliation et d'indemnisation*).

Mediation has been regulated in the CPC since Law Act No 95-125 of 8 February 1995 and Decree No 96-652 of 22 July 1996 (see Articles 131-1 to 131-15 CPC). However, only judicial mediation (*médiation judiciaire*, meaning mediation ordered by court with the parties' consent) was dealt with in the CPC, not *médiation extrajudiciaire* (before and/or outside judicial proceedings). Ordonnance No 2011-1540 of 16 November 2011 and Decree No 2012-66 of 20 January 2012 introduced regulations on *médiation extrajudiciaire* in the Code of Civil Procedure, which now has a specific Book V dedicated to the '*résolution amiable des différends*' (amicable settlement of disputes, Articles 1528–68 CPC), with a first title dealing with conventional mediation and conciliation (Articles 1530 and 1531 CPC). See also the specific provisions for divorce proceedings (Article 255 C civil) or parental responsibilities (Article 373-2-10 C civil).

There are also more specific provisions for some areas, such as those related to the *médiateur du cinéma* (Decree No 83-86 of 9 February 1983), the *médiateur bancaire* (Article 315-1 Code monétaire et financier), the *médiateur de l'énergie* (Law Act No 2006-1537 of 7 December 2006) or even the *médiateur du net*.[20] Moreover, some regulations deal more specifically with the family mediator (*médiateur familial*).[21]

France has now (after some delay) implemented the European Directive of 21 May 2008[22] by two separate bills: an Ordonnance[23] No 2011-1540 of 16 November 2011 '*portant transposition de la directive 2008/52/CE*' and a Décret No 2012-66 of

[19] Labour courts have a special *bureau de conciliation*, which tries to settle the dispute between the parties. If no settlement can be reached, the *bureau de jugement* gives a judgment.

[20] Forum des droits de l'internet, see <www.mediateurdunet.fr>. However, the forum ceased its mediation activity in December 2010 because it did not receive any further subsidies from the state.

[21] Decree No 2003-1166 of 2 December 2003 creating a state diploma for family mediators.

[22] See F Ferrand, 'La transposition en droit français et en droit allemande de la directive 2008/52/CE du 21 mai 2008 relative à certains aspects de la médiation en matière civile—Confrontation des conceptions nationales en matière de règlement amiable des différends' (2011) 16 *Zeitschrift für Zivilprozess International (ZZPInt)* 29.

[23] An *ordonnance* is a bill enacted by the government with the authorisation of the Parliament in matters normally allocated to the Parliament.

20 January *'relatif à la résolution amiable des différends'*. The ordonnance modifies Law Act No 95-125 of 8 February 1995 (chapter 1 has been titled *La médiation* and includes a new section 1 containing general provisions regarding the definition of mediation (Article 21), the principle of confidentiality with the exceptions stated in the European Directive (Article 21-3) and the possibility for the parties to request the approval of the settlement reached during the mediation process in order to make it enforceable, *homologation* (Article 21-5).

Decree No 2012-66 of 20 January 2012 modifies Book V of the CPC, which is now dedicated to the *'résolution amiable des différends'* (Articles 1528ff) and consists of three titles: (1) mediation and conciliation outside judicial proceedings, so-called *conciliation conventionnelle* and *médiation conventionnelle en dehors d'une procédure judiciaire*;[24] (2) *procédure participative* (a kind of collaborative law; see below II.B.v);[25] and (3) common provisions.

Since the enactment of Law Act No 2010-1609 of 22 December 2010, Article 2238 of the French Civil Code has contained a general rule on prescription (time limits): prescription is suspended from the day when the parties to a dispute decide to use mediation or conciliation or, where there is no written mediation or conciliation agreement, from the day of the first mediation or conciliation meeting. The same applies in case of a *convention de procédure participative*.[26] If one of the parties, both of the parties or the mediator or conciliator declares that the mediation or conciliation procedure is terminated, the statute of limitation begins to run again for a period of at least six months.

i. No Clear Encouraging Effect of Legal Regulation on the Use of ADR

It cannot be stated that legal regulation has already had an encouraging effect on the use of ADR. Most litigants are not aware of the possibility of making use of such ADR mechanisms. Therefore, most of the proposals made by commissions working on ADR insist upon the necessity of informing[27] not only potential litigants,[28] but also the attorneys and the judges themselves (eg through in-service training). Also, in the professional schools for future judges or lawyers, special attention should be paid to ADR mechanisms. The aim is to modify the judicial culture and to promote the 'culture of mediation'[29] and conciliation.

Informing the litigants of the possibility of mediation can also be provided for by an order of the judge requiring the parties to attend an information session on mediation (see Article 255 C civil for divorce and Article 373-2-10 C civil for parental responsibilities proceedings).

[24] This first title is divided in two chapters: Chapter 1: *La médiation conventionnelle*; Chapter 2: *La conciliation menée par un conciliateur de justice*.

[25] Chapter 1: *La procédure conventionnelle*; Chapter 2: *La procédure aux fins de jugement*.

[26] See II.A.v.

[27] See *Rapport Guinchard, L'ambition raisonnée d'une justice apaisée* 161ff; *Rapport Magendie, Célérité et qualité de la justice. La médiation: une autre voie* (Paris, Documentation française, 2008) 78f.

[28] By way of an information sheet sent to the litigants by the secretary of the tribunal and by the presence of mediators inside the court at the hearing (as audience).

[29] See *Rapport Guinchard, L'ambition raisonnée d'une justice apaisée* 161.

ii. Reasons to Encourage and Regulate ADR Procedures

The principal reasons given by the legislator for encouraging ADR procedures are the following:

- To reduce the number of cases brought before court for adjudication and to better allocate the modest resources of civil justice;
- To achieve better access to (informal) justice for small claims, especially where consumers hesitate to seise a court because of the low value at stake;
- To realise a quick way to reach a solution of the dispute; and
- To obtain a better quality of justice and acceptance in disputes regarding personal matters like divorce, parental responsibilities and all the fields in which the parties have to keep in contact in the interest of common children or where business relations should be maintained. The parties to the dispute are made responsible for the solution of their conflict and are to themselves find the way out of the conflict.

The view in academia is mostly that ADR should be promoted but should not replace access to state courts: it is an alternative and not a substitute way (*voie alternative et non substitutive*).[30] ADR should be seen as a supplementary offer and not as a mandatory pre-trial condition. Not all disputes are suited to be solved by ADR mechanisms that should guarantee diversity and security.[31] The judge should also more often make use of his/her general power to conciliate the parties. ADR can contribute to the reconstruction of social links and the promotion of a more participative justice.

B. Incentives to Use Certain Types of ADR

i. Regulation in the Early Conflict Resolution Phase

In France, there is no specific regulation in this phase. It is only when the claimant (or both parties by joint petition, *requête conjointe*) seises the court that the practice of *double convocation* may apply:[32] the secretary of the tribunal (*greffe*) simultaneously summons the parties, first, to a session before the conciliator and, secondly, in case the parties do not reach a settlement, to appear before the court that will then give judgment. In practice, it happens increasingly frequently that a conciliator is present at the hearing of the court and that the parties are invited to meet him/her in order to try to reach a settlement of their dispute.

However, for repeated disputes over the exercise of parental responsibilities or over maintenance towards children, in which the court has already given judgment, Law Act No 2011-1862 of 13 December 2011 *relative à la repartition des contentieux*

[30] See eg L Cadiet, 'Des modes alternatifs de règlement des conflits en général et de la médiation en particulier' in Société de la legislation comparé (ed), *La médiation* (Paris, Dalloz, 2009) 13, 25f.

[31] Ibid.

[32] Before the tribunal d'instance and the jurisdiction de proximité, see Art 845 CPC as modified by Decree No 2010-1165 of 1 October 2010: 'Le juge s'efforce de concilier les parties. Le juge peut également, à tout moment de la procédure, inviter les parties à rencontrer un conciliateur de justice aux lieu, jour et heure qu'il détermine. Les parties en sont avisées, selon le cas, dans l'acte de convocation à l'audience ou par une lettre simple. L'avis indique la date de l'audience à laquelle l'affaire sera examinée afin que le juge constate la conciliation ou tranche le litige. L'invitation peut également être faite par le juge à l'audience.'

et à l'allègement de certaines procédures juridictionnelles has, for an experimental period of three years, created before some tribunaux de grande instance a duty for the parent(s) to first make an attempt at a family mediation before again seising the court. If this is not done, the claim will not be admissible. This is the first provision on mandatory mediation in French civil law. Some exceptions to this obligation are stated: joint petition of both parents aiming at the approval of their agreement in order to make it enforceable (*homologation*); legitimate ground not to make use of mediation; risk for the parties that their right to have access to the court within a reasonable time will be violated.

At present, a few legal provisions allow the judge to order the parties to meet with a mediator. For example, with regard to disputes relating to the exercise of parental responsibilities (*exercice de l'autorité parentale*), Article 373-2-10 C civil provides for a specific procedure. First, the judge must try to conciliate the parties. Consistent with this effort, and in order to facilitate a consensual exercise of parental responsibilities, he can also suggest a mediation. If the parties consent, he can then appoint a family mediator. He can also, without the parties' consent, enjoin them to meet a family mediator, who will inform them about the object and conduct of such a measure. Decree No 2010-1395 of 12 November 2010 has added some details; specifically, the parties are informed of the court's order either by letter or during a hearing before court, and are provided with the following details: the name of the family mediator or the appointed association, as well as the place, the date of the meeting with the mediator and the date of the next court hearing. The same Decree creates a magistrate *coordonnateur de l'activité en matière de droit de la famille et des personnes* (a judge in charge of coordinating the court activity in family matters)[33] before the tribunal de grande instance and the appellate court.

ii. Incentives

French law has not opted for financial incentives. Therefore, the court is not allowed to adjust its award of costs to reflect a party's failure to cooperate in an ADR mechanism. No special benefit can be expected, except the possibility for the parties who settle their case to have their *transaction*[34] (settlement contract) approved by the court, which makes it enforceable (*exécutoire*).[35]

iii. Comparison with the Incentives to go to Court

It cannot be said that the French regulations contain incentives to use ADR (nor do they contain incentives to go to court). Until now, litigants have been better informed about court proceedings than about available ADR mechanisms. However, this is slowly changing.

[33] See Arts R 213-9-1 and R 312-13-2 Code de l'organisation judiciaire.

[34] Under French law a *transaction* is a contract by which the parties terminate a dispute which has arisen; it must be made in writing, see Art 2044 C civil.

[35] It is not only the court that can make a settlement (*transaction*) enforceable. The Cour de cassation (the highest French Court for civil and criminal matters) has recently ruled that such a *transaction* may also be received by a public notary, who may make it enforceable (Cass Civ II, 21 October 2010, No 09-12378, *Recueil Dalloz* 2011, 493 with comment from S Chassagnard-Pinet).

iv. The Role of Legal Culture in the Choice of a Dispute Resolution Mechanism—Promotion of Specific ADR Mechanisms

The French legislator first regulated conciliation by the court itself and then by the conciliateur de justice, the latter being created in 1978. The idea of conciliation has its roots in French legal culture with the justices of peace (*juges de paix*). France was more familiar with the mechanism of judicial or non-judicial conciliation than with mediation.

Rules on mediation came later (1995); in the Law Act of 8 February 1995 and the Decree of 22 July 1996, mediation is designed as judicial mediation, ie as a mediation ordered by the judge with the parties' consent. Judicial mediation is seen in this context as an alternative to court.[36] Purely contractual mediation without the court being seised (*médiation extrajudiciaire*) was not covered by those initial legal provisions. *Médiation extrajudiciaire* is now regulated in the CPC due to the implementation of the European Directive of 21 May 2008 (see the new Book V of the CPC).[37]

Currently, the legislator should attempt to promote both types of ADR without clarifying the differences between the processes of conciliation and of mediation. However, at this stage, the judge is always entitled to try to conciliate parties (Article 21 CPC), whereas he may not act as a mediator.

v. Information Duties of Lawyers towards Their Clients

In France, lawyers are not required to advise clients as to ADR procedure before seising the court. They should advise their clients and inform them about the possible outcome of the court proceedings.

The recent Law Act No 2010-1609 of 22 December 2010 has created a new ADR mechanism in which lawyers play an important role: the *convention de procédure participative*, designed in a way somewhat similar to the collaborative law approach encountered in North America (Articles 2062–68 C civil).[38] Parties to a dispute may—before seising the court or the arbitrator(s)—agree in a contract (the *convention de procédure participative*) to try to reach together in good faith a settlement of their dispute if it is related to rights that are at their free disposal.[39] The agreement is entered into in writing for a limited period of time (Article 2062 C civil) and mentions the object of the dispute, as well as the documents and information that should be disclosed between the parties (Article 2063 C civil). As long as the *convention de procédure participative* is applicable, the parties may not bring a claim into court, except where a party does not abide by the *convention* (Article 2065 C civil). If the parties manage to reach a settlement (in full or in part), they can submit it to the court for approval (*homologation*), which will make the agreement enforceable (*exécutoire*, Article 2066 C civil). If they do not settle their dispute, they may submit this outcome

[36] For a very critical view of this reform, see B Gorchs, 'La médiation dans le procès civil: sens et contresens' [2003] *Revue trimestrielle de droit civil (RTDCiv)* 409.

[37] For more see II.A.

[38] See F Rongeat-Oudin, 'Les avocats à la conquête du règlement amiable des différends' *La Semaine juridique—Edition générale (JCP G)* 2011, no 1097.

[39] But exceptionally such an agreement may also be entered into in cases of divorce or legal separation (Art 2067 CPC). By contrast, it is prohibited in labour disputes (Art 2064(2) C civil).

to the court and do not have to make an attempt at conciliation or mediation if such an attempt would otherwise be required by law (Article 2066(2) C civil). Decree No 2012-66 of 20 January 2012 regulates in detail the *procédure participative* that has been integrated in the CPC (Articles 1542–64 CPC). The CPC now dedicates two chapters to this specific mechanism. Chapter 1 deals with the *procédure conventionnelle* (Articles 1544–55 CPC) that takes place between the parties and their lawyers. Chapter 2 regulates the *procédure aux fins de jugement*: here, either the parties can reach a settlement and one or all of them can then request the judge to approve the settlement in order to make it enforceable (Article 1557 CPC), or the parties cannot agree[40] or can only partially agree.[41] In the latter instance, the case is then called to trial to be decided (Article 1558 CPC); there is in general no further preparation of the case (*mise en état*), and the case is decided by the court panel to which it had originally been assigned.

The role of the lawyers is important in this context since they can take the initiative to suggest the use of such an agreement before seising a court. Apparently, some French lawyers have already done so in family disputes, especially in divorce cases.

C. Restriction of Access to Courts with a View to Alternative Dispute Resolution

i. ADR Procedures Are Not a Precondition for Starting Proceedings before a State Court

In principle, ADR procedures are not a precondition for starting proceedings before a state court. However, before some civil courts or in some matters a first phase, called *tentative de conciliation* (conciliation attempts), has to take place. This normally takes place before the judge. The judge may also delegate the conciliation attempt to a conciliateur de justice. Decree No 2010-1165 of 1 October 2010 has enlarged the range of cases in which the judge may do so: now, not only the tribunal d'instance or the juridiction de proximité may delegate the conciliation attempt to the conciliateur de justice, but also the commercial court[42] and the tribunal paritaire des baux ruraux (a court specialised in disputes regarding rural leases).

As already mentioned,[43] for recurring disputes about the exercise of parental responsibilities or about maintenance towards children—as to which the court has already rendered judgment—Law Act No 2011-1862 of 13 December 2011 has created, on an experimental basis before some tribunaux de grande instance, a duty for the parent(s) to first make an attempt at family mediation before again seising the court. Otherwise the renewed claim would not be admissible.

ii. Mechanisms in Place that Allow a Court to Refer a Dispute to an Alternative Dispute Resolution Mechanism

The court may refer a dispute to an ADR mechanism, but only with the parties'

[40] See Arts 1562–64 CPC.
[41] See Art 1560 CPC.
[42] Arts 831ff and 860–2 CPC.
[43] See II.B.i.

consent. There is no special regulation before the claim is brought before court. Therefore, the parties are generally not obliged to make use of ADR as a pre-trial step.

a. Conciliation. The role of conciliation and especially of so-called *conciliation déléguée* was clarified and extended by Decree No 2010-1165 of 1 October 2010.[44] There are two kinds of conciliation: *conciliation conventionnelle*, which takes place before civil proceedings, and *conciliation déléguée*, when a claim has already been brought before court.

When the court is seised, in certain cases or before certain courts (labour court, some civil courts such as the tribunal d'instance, juridiction de proximité) a mandatory conciliation attempt shall take place (*tentative préalable de conciliation*). This attempt can take place before the judge, who is always entitled to conciliate the parties (at any stage of the proceedings) since it is part of his/her mandate (Article 21 CPC).[45] Before the civil courts already mentioned, the commercial court (tribunal de commerce) and the tribunal des baux ruraux, the judge may also decide to delegate this task to a *conciliateur de justice*[46] except in two cases: (i) if the claimant or the defendant refuses such a delegation; and (ii) in divorce or legal separation proceedings. If the parties settle their case, a document is signed by them and the conciliator (*constat de conciliation, constat d'accord*). The parties can request the approval (*homologation*) of the settlement by the court in order to make it enforceable.

Before the tribunal d'instance and the juridiction de proximité, the parties can receive a double summons (*double convocation*) to a conciliation and, in case of the failure to reach a settlement, to a later trial (Article 845 CPC since Decree No 2010-1165 of 1 October 2010).

In other cases, the conciliation attempt is not mandatory; however, the judge may try to conciliate the parties at any stage of the proceedings. If special provisions allow him to delegate his conciliation task, he may also delegate it to a *conciliateur de justice* (Article 129-1 CPC). He may also appoint, with the parties' consent, a mediator who shall 'hear the parties and confront their points of view in order to facilitate the finding of a solution to their conflict' (Article 131-1 CPC). The mediation can relate to the whole dispute or only to part of it (Article 131-2 CPC), and can be entrusted to a natural person or to an association (Article 131-4 CPC). If the parties settle, they can request from the court the approval (*homologation*) of their settlement (Article 131-12 CPC), which then becomes enforceable.

Conciliateurs de justice are appointed by decision of the Premier Président of the appellate court (cour d'appel) on proposal of the first instance civil judge called the juge d'instance. The public prosecutor has to give his opinion on the application. The conciliateur is initially appointed for one year; a subsequent appointment is possible for two years, with further possible reappointments every two years thereafter. The conciliator must have had at least three years of experience in legal matters. See Articles 2 and 3 of Decree No 78-381 of 20 March 1978 '*relatif aux conciliateurs de justice*'.

[44] See Arts 129-1ff CPC.

[45] See also Arts 834f CPC for the tribunal d'instance.

[46] See Arts 831ff CPC. This kind of conciliation is called *conciliation déléguée* in contrast to *conciliation extrajudiciaire* which is agreed upon by the parties without any judicial intervention.

b. Mediation and Mediators. Mediation is never mandatory (with the exception of the specific provisions contained in Law Act No 2011-1862 of 13 December 2011,[47] relating to some family matters). When it takes place, it is never carried out by court officials; the dispute is referred to external service providers that can be private individuals or associations.

At present, there is no genuine possibility for quality control by the judge who appoints a mediator. This is one of the reasons why the French civil judges still seldom make use of the mediation option.[48] However, Decree No 2003-1166 of 2 December 2003 has created a state diploma for médiateurs familiaux.[49] Most of those mediators work within structures connected with the state, such as associations receiving subsidies from the state, the Caisse d'Assurances Familiales or the Union Départementale des Associations Familiales. The state diploma 'médiateur familial' follows a transdisciplinary approach and consists of 560 hours[50] (490 hours of theory and 70 hours of practice) in a maximum period of three years. In family mediation, statistics from 2001 show that associations are mostly appointed as mediators,[51] whereas individuals rather than associations are commonly appointed in general civil cases.

D. Impact of Human Rights Law on the Regulation of ADR

The main limitation resulting from human rights law relates to the right of access to justice (Article 6(1) ECHR). In a decision of 23 September 1994 (*Hokkanen v Finland*),[52] the European Court of Human Rights ruled that 'conciliation should not be ordered if former attempts show that it would fail or, in case of a court order relating to custody, if the order should be enforced immediately in the child's interest and for serious reasons'.

E. No Influence of the UNCITRAL Model Law on International Commercial Conciliation

French law did not follow the UNCITRAL Model Law on Conciliation 2002 since conciliation has existed in France since the early activities of *juges de paix*. More recently, it was again asserted as an important task of the court in the New Code of Civil Procedure enacted in 1975. The *conciliateurs de justice* were then created in 1978. However, most of the principles contained in the UNCITRAL Model Law on International Commercial Conciliation also apply under French law of mediation and conciliation, especially those relating to communication between the conciliator and parties, disclosure of information, confidentiality, admission of evidence in other proceedings and the possibility of making the settlement agreement enforceable (although

[47] Mentioned in II.B.

[48] See E Serverin, 'Le médiateur civil et le service public de la justice' 235f.

[49] See also *Arrêté* of 12 February 2004 and *Circulaire* of 30 July 2004.

[50] Law: 63 hours; psychology: 63 hours; sociology: 35 hours.

[51] See Moreau, Munoz Perez and Serverin, *La médiation judiciaire civile en chiffres, Situation au 31 octobre 2001* 10ff. In 2001, family judges had appointed a family mediator in only 0.8% of the cases.

[52] No 50/1993/445/524.

the judge retains this power to make the agreement enforceable in a non-contentious proceeding—*procédure gracieuse*).

F. Special Rules for Consumers

Consumer protection is one of the areas in which an effective access to justice is sought, irrespective of the often low value of the claim. Therefore, several ADR mechanisms have been created in order to protect consumers without requiring them to bring a claim into court.

In its answer to the public consultation on the use of ADR in disputes related to commercial transactions in the EU, France describes 35 ADR schemes concerning such disputes which have found application. Some are public (like the former *Médiateur de la République*,[53] who has recently been replaced (in 2011) by the *Défenseur des droits*,[54] or the commissions de règlement des litiges de consummation, aimed at solving consumer disputes), others are private (eg the mediator of the Fédération française des sociétés d'assurances for insurance disputes, or the *médiation bancaire*, bank mediation and other mediators inside companies like GDF-SUEZ). Some provide a regional coverage (commission on resolution of consumer disputes), others a national coverage (eg the *médiateur du net* for disputes arising from internet transactions,[55] who existed until 31 December 2010,[56] or the *médiateur de l'Autorité des marchés financiers*, AMF,[57] who participates in the FIN-NET network of the European mediators in the area of financial services[58]). Eighty per cent of the cases are resolved within 30–90 days.

The MEDEF (employers' association) has collected information from several sectors

[53] The *médiateur de la République* received 56,971 cases in 2004, 59,974 in 2005, 62,822 in 2006, 65,077 in 2007, 65,530 in 2008, 76,286 in 2009 and 79,046 in 2010. Where mediation took place, the success rate was 94% in 2010, see *Annuaire statistique de la Justice 2011–2012* 283. The *médiateur de la République* was in charge of seeking out-of-court settlements of disputes between citizens and public services (such as state and regional administrative entities). His interventions were free for citizens.

[54] The new *Défenseur des droits* created in 2011 is an independent constitutional authority in charge of ensuring that rights and freedoms are respected by any public or private person or body in the framework of public services, see *loi organique* No 2011-333 and *loi ordinaire* No 2011-334 of 29 March 2011. He also has to defend and promote the child's best interest and rights, to fight against prohibited discriminations and to promote equality. The *Défenseur des droits* has, as of 1 May 2011, replaced the *médiateur de la République*, the *Défenseur des enfants*, the *Haute autorité de lutte contre les discriminations* (HALDE) and the *Commission nationale de déontologie de la sécurité* (CNDS). For example, any person having a dispute with an administrative or public service body may seise him (*Mission médiation avec les services publics*).

[55] The Forum du droit de l'internet proposed online mediations with regard to disputes connected to the law of the internet, see <www.foruminternet.org>.

[56] The subsidies from the Ministry of Industry ceased in December 2010 so that the Forum stopped and could not accept any new mediation cases. During the preceding seven years (2004–10), 13,000 national disputes were brought before the Forum with a success rate of 87%.

[57] See the report presented in May 2011 by this mediator for the stock exchange activities, *Recueil Dalloz* 2011, 1481. The report suggests promoting out-of-court settlement, especially mediation, by the AMF Ombudsman, for example in the case of many similar disputes. In 2010, 396 mediation requests were received (in 2009 there were 735 mediation requests); the decrease can partly be explained by the extension of the powers of Bank ombudsmen in 2008. In 2010, 520 mediation procedures took place; 40% led to a settlement; 74% were closed within six months.

[58] The AMF Ombudsman's activity covers the following institutions: investment providers, most investment intermediaries, most securities intermediaries, some pension providers; the financial products covered are most investments, most securities and some pensions.

(RATP (bus and metro in Paris), SNCF (French railways), GDF-SUEZ, La Poste, EDF, insurance companies, BNP Paribas (French bank) and from the mediator for electronic communication) which show that the number of mediation cases is increasing: from 10,620 in 2007 to 13,420 in 2008 and to 18,880 in 2009, which corresponds to an increase of more than 20 per cent per year.

Some mediation schemes are instituted by law according to one of two possible features: as a public body (as in the energy sector, Law Act of 7 December 2006) or as a result of an obligation placed on companies to appoint a mediator (eg Law Act of 11 December 2011 imposing on the banks the duty to create a *médiation bancaire*).

France has created[59] the Commission for Consumer Mediation (*Commission de la médiation de la consommation*), whose tasks include having to elaborate a charter of best practices, suggesting appropriate measures to promote non-judicial mediation and publishing a report each year.

However, it seems that some sectors, like tourism and transport, do not have enough consumer redress mechanisms. In order to inform consumers, the French Direction Générale de la Concurrence, de la Consommation et de la Répression des Fraudes[60] now has an information portal on mediation on its website and has published a brochure on mediation for consumers.

The French position is that ADR should remain as voluntary processes which should not be systematically subject to specific law provisions. However, in certain sectors where the consumers' interests are especially important, law is called upon to provide an ADR scheme or oblige the relevant professionals to create such a scheme. This is the case in France, for instance, in the energy sector[61] and for banking activities. The French government stated the aim of generalising mediation as a consumer dispute resolution model by July 2012.

Whether the Commission Recommendation of 4 April 2001 on the principles for out-of-court bodies involved in the consensual resolution of consumer disputes, C(2001) 1016, has been followed is not easily answered in a general way. Some mediators are genuinely independent (eg *médiateur de l'énergie*[62]); others are financed by the companies themselves (insurance companies, telephone and internet companies, etc).[63] The degree of independence therefore varies from one mediator to another. Transparency is aimed at, but the information provided to consumers can still be improved. Effectiveness seems to have been achieved since the necessary period for solving the dispute is in most cases rather short, and the procedure is most of the time free of charge for the consumer, who is never obliged to use a legal representative.

[59] Law Act No 2010-737 of 1 July 2010 and Decree No 2010-1221 of 18 October 2010. See also Art L 534-7 and Art L 331-6 Code de la consommation.

[60] General Direction for Competition, Consumption and Sanction of Frauds.

[61] In 2009 the recommendations of the médiateur de l'énergie were followed by 88% of the professionals and by 70% of the retailers. In 2010 the success rate of the médiateur des communications électroniques reached 87%, see *Réponse des autorités françaises sur le recours au règlement extrajudiciaire des litiges pour régler des litiges relatifs aux transactions et aux pratiques commerciales dans l'Union européenne*, March 2011, available at <www.sgae.gouv.fr/gcp/webdav/site/sgae-internet-sgae/shared/04_Consultations_publiques/201104/20110323_ReponseFR_Reglement_extrajudiciaire_des_litiges.pdf>.

[62] His budget is financed by ~ 0.2% of the taxes for the public service of electricity.

[63] However, Recommendation C (2001) 1016 does not apply to customer complaint mechanisms operated by a business and concluded directly with the consumer or to such mechanisms carrying out such services by or on behalf of a business (I.2).

III. APPROACH TOWARDS SPECIFIC ADR INSTRUMENTS

A. Negotiation

i. Nature of the Rules Applicable to the Pre-contractual Stage of Negotiation

There is no specific rule with regard to negotiations between parties in conflict. However, a recent act (Loi No 2010-1609 of 22 December 2010) has created a new procedure called '*procédure participative assistée par avocat*'. When parties to a dispute agree to follow this scheme, they sign a *convention de procédure participative*, which will allow them to negotiate—with their lawyers' assistance—a settlement (Article 1544 CPC) in cases where the rights in dispute are at their free disposal.[64] The agreement is entered into in writing for a limited period of time (Article 2062 C civil), and states the object of the dispute as well as the documents and information that should be disclosed between the parties (Article 2063 C civil). As long as the *convention de procédure participative* is applicable, the parties may not bring a claim into court, except where a party does not abide by the agreement to negotiate in good faith and to disclose the agreed documents (Article 2065 C civil). The statute of limitation (*prescription*) does not run but is suspended during the negotiation phase and for six months following its cessation. At the end of the negotiation within the framework of a *procédure participative*, there are two possibilities:

- The parties have reached an agreement that can be made enforceable by the court in a quick and simple non-contentious proceeding (*procédure gracieuse*);[65] or
- The parties could not reach a settlement[66] (or reached only a partial one)[67] and any of them may then seise the court in an expeditious and uncomplicated manner. If a legal provision requires a preliminary conciliation or attempt at mediation, the parties are exempted from this effort (Article 1558 CPC). The court proceedings will also be quicker since the *mise en état de l'affaire* (preparation of the case) will already have taken place (Article 1559 CPC).

The parties who fulfil the specified legal conditions may apply for judicial aid (*aide juridique*) for the negotiation phase within a *convention de procédure participative*. A Decree (No 2012-66 of 20 January 2012) regulating in detail the *procédure participative* has been enacted and integrated into the CPC.

More generally, French contract law never obliges parties to contract. Nevertheless, they should negotiate in good faith. If one of them suddenly breaks off the negotiations without any legitimate reason, he/she can be made liable and may have to pay damages to the other party. Duties to negotiate are not enforceable.

[64] Such an agreement may also exceptionally be entered into in cases of divorce or legal separation (Art 2067 CPC), but it will be subject to the family judge's scrutiny. By contrast, it is prohibited in labour disputes (Art 2064(2) C civil). For more details see II.B.v.

[65] See Art 1557 CPC: one of the parties or all the parties may make a request to the judge to make the settlement enforceable. A copy of the *convention de procedure participative* shall be added to a request which is otherwise not admissible.

[66] See Art 1562 CPC.

[67] See Arts 1560 and 1561 CPC.

ii. Liability for Breaking Off Negotiations in Bad Faith

In general, French contract law is based on the parties' freedom to contract or not. However, if one of the parties in negotiation does not negotiate in good faith and breaks off the negotiation phase in a sudden way without giving legitimate reasons for this, this party can be made liable (torts: *responsabilité délictuelle*).

B. Mediation

i. Sources of Regulation on Mediation—Areas in Which Mediation is Deployed—Implementation of the European Directive No 2008/52 of 21 May 2008

The general trend in France is to promote mediation not only in civil and commercial disputes, but also in minor criminal cases and in administrative law.[68] As already explained, there are nowadays special provisions in several sectors of activity;[69] there are also more general provisions in the Code of Civil Procedure. The provisions are mostly contained in Law Acts and Decrees or *Arrêtés* made by the government. Conciliation and mediation clauses are also increasingly frequent in contracts; they are generally valid, except if they reduce or make ineffective the right of access to justice. However, case law seems to restrict the extent of clauses imposing on the parties a preliminary conciliation attempt before seising the court.[70]

French law distinguishes between judicial mediation (*médiation judiciaire*) and non-judicial mediation (*médiation extrajudiciaire*).[71] Until the implementation in France of European Directive 2008/52/EC of 21 May 2008, only judicial mediation (and conciliation) was regulated in the Code of Civil Procedure. However, since the implementation

[68] See Circulaire of 7 September 2009 relative au recours à la transaction pour la prévention et le règlement des litiges portant sur l'exécution des contrats de la commande publique, NOR: ECEM0917498C, Journal Officiel (JO) 18 September 2009, 15,230 and even more recently Circulaire of 6 April 2011 relative au développement des recours à la transaction pour régler amiablement les conflits, NOR: PRMX1109903C, JO 8 April 2011, 5,248. These two documents drafted by the offices of the prime minister aim at encouraging settlements (transactions) by the administration in order to spare public money and to facilitate a quick compensation for the parties.

[69] For the bank sector see, eg Art L 315-1 Code monétaire et financier, and for financial services related to stock exchange, Art L 621-19 du code monétaire et financier (L'Autorité des marchés financiers est habilitée à recevoir de tout intéressé les réclamations qui entrent par leur objet dans sa compétence et à leur donner la suite qu'elles appellent. Elle propose, lorsque les conditions sont réunies, la résolution amiable des différends portés à sa connaissance par voie de conciliation ou de médiation. La saisine de l'Autorité des marchés financiers, dans le cadre du règlement extrajudiciaire des différends, suspend la prescription de l'action civile et administrative. Celle-ci court à nouveau lorsque l'Autorité des marchés financiers déclare la médiation terminée. L'Autorité des marchés financiers coopère avec ses homologues étrangers en vue du règlement extrajudiciaire des litiges.)

[70] See Cass Soc, 7 March 2007, No 05-45157; S Amrani-Mekki, 'La clause de conciliation' (2009) 14 *Zeitschrift für Zivilprozess International (ZZPInt)* 83, especially 90, fn 16.

[71] See the definitions provided by Ch Jarrosson in *Rapport Magendie, Célérité et Qualité de la Justice, La médiation, une autre voie* 16: médiation judiciaire: 'médiation engagée sur proposition du juge, à l'occasion d'une action en justice pendante devant lui'. Médiation conventionnelle or non judiciaire: 'médiation qui se déroule sur le fondement du seul accord des parties, que celui-ci soit intervenu avant ou après la naissance du litige'.

through Ordonnance No 2011-1540 of 16 November 2011[72] and Decree No 2012-66 of 20 January 2012,[73] the CPC also contains provisions on non-judicial conciliation and mediation (*médiation et conciliation conventionnelles*). The new Article 1530 CPC gives a definition of such conciliation and mediation.[74] The new Article 1531 states the principle of confidentiality with the two exceptions contained in the European Directive. Articles 1532–35 CPC regulate non-judicial mediation: the mediator must be a natural or a legal person (Article 1532) who has to fulfil certain legal conditions (no criminal convictions, no serious administrative or disciplinary sanctions, possessing the required qualifications with regard to the nature of the dispute, having appropriate training or experience with regard to the practice of mediation, Article 1533 CPC). The court that would have had jurisdiction over the dispute makes the out-of-court settlement enforceable on request of all parties, or of one of them with the consent of the others, under Articles 1534 and 1565 CPC.[75]

Mediation is especially developed in family matters[76] and in commercial disputes,[77] and sometimes also in labour disputes.[78] There are specific provisions with regard to family matters (eg Article 255 C civil for divorce proceedings and Article 373-2-10 C civil for disputes related to the exercise of parental responsibilities).[79]

Even though the implementation of Directive 2008/52/EC into French law only occurred after some delay, most of the requirements contained in the Directive were already met in France before the implementation (eg suspension of prescription in Article 8 of the Directive, enforceability of agreements resulting from mediation in Article 6, confidentiality of mediation in Article 7). The main issue that needed

[72] See B Gorchs-Gelzer, 'Regard critique sur l'ordonnance n°2011-1540 transposant la directive médiation' *Droit et Procédures* 2012, 2; N Nevejans, 'L'ordonnance du 16 novembre 2011, Un encouragement au développement de la médiation' *La Semaine juridique—Edition générale (JCP G)* 2012, no 148.

[73] See F Rongeat-Oudin, 'Le règlement amiable des différends est en bonne marche!', *La Semaine juridique—Edition générale (JCP G)* 2012, no 157; B Gorchs-Gelzer, 'Le décret du 20 janvier 2012 relatif à la résolution amiable des différends, Une cote mal taillée entre changement des mentalités et continuité des pratiques', *Droit et Procédures* 2012, 117.

[74] 'Tout processus structuré, par lequel deux ou plusieurs parties tentent de parvenir à un accord, en dehors de toute procédure judiciaire en vue de la résolution amiable de leur différend' with the help of an impartial and competent third party chosen by the parties.

[75] See also Art 1535 CPC: 'An agreement reached by parties during a mediation process and made enforceable by the competent authority of another Member State of the EU is recognised and made enforceable in France under the conditions of Arts 509 2ff CPC' (ie same proceeding as for declaration of enforceability in the EC Regulation Brussels I).

[76] See *Rapport Magendie, Célérité et Qualité de la Justice, La médiation, une autre voie,* 27: before the tribunal de grande instance Paris, between 2005 and 2007, the number of mediations increased enormously (47 in 2005, 282 in 2007) but remains low. See also C Chabault-Marx, 'A propos de la médiation familiale: vers une judiciarisation du dialogue?' *Recueil Dalloz* 2012, 43; D Calderon-Bruneau, 'La médiation familiale' *Droit Famille 2011*, Fiche pratique no 1.

[77] See, eg the statistics provided by the CMAP (Centre de Médiation et d'Arbitrage de Paris), which was created in 1995 (<www.cmap.fr>) and in 2010 dealt with 300 mediation cases (70% of them led to a settlement). In 2010, 50% the mediators of the CMAP were lawyers and former judges, 38% were company managers and 12% were free professionals, such as architects or doctors. In 2007, the Paris commercial court ordered 25 mediations (16 were successful), see *Rapport Magendie, Célérité et Qualité de la Justice, La médiation, une autre voie* 34.

[78] See *Rapport Magendie, Célérité et Qualité de la Justice, La médiation, une autre voie* 40ff, the description by B Brenneur of the mediation practice before the social chamber of the appellate court Grenoble (in five years, more than 1,000 mediations with a success rate of 70%).

[79] A specific decree also regulates the conditions for becoming a family mediator (Decree No 2003-1166 of 2 December 2003), see II.C.ii. There are also special provisions and mediation procedures in different sectors of activity, see II.F.

regulation as a result of the Directive was the *médiation conventionnelle* (mediation outside the court and not ordered by the judge). Such regulation can now be found in the Code of Civil Procedure (Articles 1530ff CPC) and in Law Act No 95-125 of 8 February 1995.

ii. Legal Effects of a Mediation Clause

Already in 2003,[80] the French Cour de cassation had ruled that a conciliation clause makes the claim inadmissible (*irrecevable*): the claimant must first take part in a conciliation attempt and only in case of a failure to reach a settlement may he/she bring a claim into court.

The same applies in case of a mediation clause, as ruled by the Cour de cassation on 8 April 2009.[81] The claim's admissibility may even be raised for the first time during the appellate proceedings.[82]

However, Decree No 2009-302 of 18 March 2009, on unfair clauses (*clauses abusives*) in contracts concluded with consumers, established a 'grey list' of clauses that are (rebuttably) presumed to be unfair and therefore void. This list contains clauses which have as their aim, or result, the suppression or hindrance of the consumer's exercise of claims or means of recourse before state courts, eg by obliging the consumer to seise an arbitration court or to use only an out-of-court settlement mechanism.

The appointment of the mediator is the judges' task in the case of a judicial mediation. For non-judicial mediation, the parties may freely choose their own mediator. There is no special procedure in order to challenge the mediator's impartiality, but if the mediation is not judicial, any party may stop the mediation process at any time. If the mediation has been ordered by the court with the parties' consent, the judge may at any time stop the mediation procedure at a party's or the mediator's request (Article 131-10(1) CPC), or even *ex officio* if the '*bon déroulement de la médiation paraît compromis*' (the progress of mediation seems to be jeopardised).

iii. Duties of Mediators

It does not make any difference whether or not the mediator is a lawyer. French legal provisions do not require that the mediator be a lawyer. Decree No 2012-6 of 20 January 2012, which implemented the European Directive of 21 May 2008 and

[80] Cour de cassation, chambre mixte, 14 February 2003, Nos 00-19.423 and 00-19.424: 'Mais attendu qu'il résulte des Arts 122 et 124 du nouveau Code de procédure civile que les fins de non-recevoir ne sont pas limitativement énumérées; que, licite, la clause d'un contrat instituant une procédure de conciliation obligatoire et préalable à la saisine du juge, dont la mise en oeuvre suspend jusqu'à son issue le cours de la prescription, constitue une fin de non-recevoir qui s'impose au juge si les parties l'invoquent; qu'ayant retenu que l'acte de cession d'actifs prévoyait le recours à une procédure de conciliation préalable à toute instance judiciaire pour les contestations relatives à l'exécution de la convention, la cour d'appel en a exactement déduit l'irrecevabilité du cédant à agir sur le fondement du contrat avant que la procédure de conciliation ait été mise en oeuvre.' The same solution was reached in a decision of 28 April 2011, No 10-30721, where a party claimed for subrogation against an architect (the conciliation clause contained in the contract concluded with the architect applies to the claimant even if he had no personal knowledge of the clause).

[81] Cass Civ I, 8 April 2009, No 08-10866, *Recueil Dalloz* 2009, 1284.

[82] Cass Com, 22 February 2005, No 02-11519, *La Semaine juridique—Edition générale (JCP G)* 2005, I, 183, no 3, comment Th Clay.

regulates not only cross-border but also domestic ADR (MARD, *modes amiables de résolution des différends*), only requires (Article 1533 CPC) that the mediator:

(a) Has the required qualification (with regard to his/her present or past activity) with regard to the nature of the dispute; or
(b) Has had appropriate training or experience with regard to the practice of mediation.

The mediator should also meet the requirements of good moral character (he should not have been sentenced on the grounds of a criminal offence, see Articles 131-5 and 1533, 1° CPC).

It was only for family mediators that Decree No 2003-1166 of 2 December 2003 created a state diploma.[83]

There is no express rule on the information that the mediator is required to provide to the parties. However, it is self-evident that he/she shall inform the parties about the mediation process itself (see eg Article 255 C civil).

With regard to the fairness of mediation proceedings, at present, Article 131-5, 5° CPC only requires that the mediator shall '*présenter les garanties nécessaires à l'exercice de la médiation*' (present all necessary guarantees to exercise mediation).

If the mediator who has been appointed by the court were to not fulfil his duties, the court could decide, on the request of a party or *ex officio*, to stop the mediation. In the case of a non-judicial mediation (*médiation conventionnelle* out of court), all or one of the parties could decide to terminate the mediation process. The mediator is liable for malpractice based on the general legal provisions relating to torts (Articles 1382ff Code civil). However, such a compensation claim does not seem to have ever been brought before a court.

The main French professional mediation structures[84] drafted the Code de déontologie du médiateur et de la mediation, stating the values and common practices that should be promoted and respected. The main principles are freedom, independence, neutrality, impartiality, confidentiality, responsibility and fairness. All mediators belonging to those mediation structures shall commit themselves to following the Code. With regard to the mediator's liability, the Code de déontologie (Code of Ethics and Compliance) states that the mediator guarantees the peaceful and dispassionate course of the mediation process; if he has doubts with regard to a proposed agreement's feasibility, compatibility with the public order or fairness, he shall invite the parties to consult a lawyer before accepting a binding settlement of the dispute. The mediator who violates the rules stated in the Code de déontologie can be removed from the list of mediators of the association whose membership he claims (see Part 3 of the Code).

France has not established any special mechanism with a view to establishing the quality of the service before selecting the mediator or after the mediation has taken place. This is one of the reasons why judges seldom suggest mediation to the parties.

[83] 560 hours of training over three years (law: 63 hours; psychology: 63 hours; sociology: 35 hours); see also II.C.ii.

[84] Académie de la Médiation, Association Nationale des Médiateurs Européens, Association Nationale des Médiateurs, Association pour la Médiation Familiale, Fédération Nationale pour la Médiation familiale, Fédération Nationale des Centres de Médiation, Médiation-Net, Réseau des Médiateurs en Entreprise, Union Professionnelle Indépendante des Médiateurs.

Another reason is that mediation can slow down the course of civil proceedings. The judges see mediation not as a substitute to civil justice but as an alternative which is appropriate in some, but not all, disputes.

iv. Duties of the Parties

The parties are free to choose whether or not to consent to mediation (except in the very exceptional and limited case of mandatory mediation in respect of some family issues, as introduced into French law by Law Act No 2011-1862 of 13 December 2011[85]). They are also free to withdraw from the mediation at any time and without any special justification.

Concerning remuneration of mediators: in the case of a mediation ordered by court, the parties (or one of them)[86] shall pay a deposit (*provision, consignation*) to the court's secretary (*greffe*) for the mediator's remuneration.[87] At the end of the mediation process, Article 131-13 CPC applies and the court determines what that remuneration will be. Factors affecting the amount set by the judge include the complexity of the dispute and the quality of the mediation.

When the mediation is conventional (ie has not been ordered by court), the mediator and the parties agree on the remuneration that will be paid to the mediator. In most cases, the different associations have fixed rates (approximately €250 per hour of mediation for a legal person, €150 per hour for a natural person); some propose a fixed price for a total of six hours. A price list is provided by the CMAP (Centre de Médiation et d'Arbitrage de Paris) for business disputes.[88]

The costs of family mediation depend on the parties' income, so that one hour costs between €3 (for a person living from state aid as a welfare recipient) and €131 for the highest incomes. The Code de déontologie requires that the financial situation of the family should be taken into account when determining the family mediator's remuneration. Moreover, the first information meeting on mediation shall be free of charge. Family mediation functions at subsidised costs, since the state funds (at least in part) the associations offering such mediation schemes.[89]

[85] See II.B.a.

[86] See Art 131-6(2) CPC.

[87] If the parties do not pay the consignation in court, the mediation order lapses and the court proceedings continue (Art 131-6(3) CPC).

[88] The mediation costs depend on the value at stake, on the nature of the disputants (two legal entities, or a company and a natural person) and on the national or international nature of the dispute, see <www.cmap.fr/Reglements-et-baremes/Baremes-de-frais-et-honoraires-35-fr.html>. One hour of mediation costs between €300 and €500; in the case of a mediation ordered by court, €300. The CMAP statistics for 2010 show that in 24% of the mediation cases the costs were less than €2,000, in 36% between €2,000 and €5,000, in 29% between €5,000 and €10,000, and in 11% greater than €10,000. The average duration of a business mediation is 10–30 hours (in 58% of the cases dealt with by the CMAP; it was less than 10 hours in 34% and more than 30 hours in 18%). In 2010 the mediation cases before the CMAP were related to non-fulfilment of contractual obligations (42%), disputes in company law or between shareholders (25%), intellectual property (20%), labour disputes (1%) and other fields (12%).

[89] The Ministry of Justice grants subsidies for mediation to each appellate court. These courts then sharing the funds between the different locally active family law associations.

v. Enforceability of Agreements Resulting From Mediation

Mediation agreements are not enforceable as such, but on the parties' request the court can approve (*homologation*) the agreement, which makes it enforceable (Article 131-12 CPC). Decree No 2012-66 of 20 January 2012 *relatif à la resolution amiable des différends* contains several provisions dealing with the enforceability of agreements resulting from mediation (see Articles 1534 and 1535 CPC, which are specific to mediation *conventionnelle*, and Articles 1565 to 1568 CPC, which apply to agreements resulting from mediation, conciliation or *procédure participative* assisted by lawyers and even to agreements reached without any such procedure). For *médiation conventionnelle*, the request (*demande en homologation de l'accord issu de la mediation*) is made by all the parties or by one of them with the express consent of the others (Article 1534 CPC). The court that approves the agreement and makes it enforceable is the one that would have had jurisdiction if the case had been brought to a state court (Article 1565 CPC). The judge may not change the wording of the agreement (Article 1565(2) CPC). In most cases, the court will decide on the approval (*homologation*) request without any hearing, unless the judge thinks a hearing of the parties is necessary (Article 1566(1) CPC). If the request is rejected, appeal is available (Article 1566(3) CPC).

The judge is not legally required to approve and make enforceable the mediation agreement: especially in labour disputes, the Cour de cassation has ruled that the judge shall scrutinise the agreement and verify whether the rights of each party are preserved.[90] In most other cases, the judge does not engage in a rigorous scrutiny but only a limited one (scrutiny being had with regard to the matters in dispute—are they at the parties' free disposal—and to the French *ordre public*).

Where the rights in dispute are not at the parties' free disposal (family law, parental responsibilities, etc), the court verifies whether the mediation agreement is consistent with the best interests of the child. Mostly, the court accepts agreements reached between parents.

vi. Court-based Mediation Programmes[91]

Some cases which are taken to the courts could be resolved through mediation. The French government policy encourages court users to think about mediation before making an application to court, and courts have the power to suggest mediation as a way of resolving suitable disputes. However, when the judge suggests mediation and the parties give their consent, that mediation does not usually take place in the courtroom.[92] The court appoints the mediator for a limited period of time and informs

[90] Cass Soc, 18 July 2001, *Bulletin des arrêts de la Cour de cassation* V, no 279.

[91] See also above II.A.

[92] However, in some courts, the mediator can be present at the first hearing: the judge asks the parties whether they would consider mediation, and if they consent they can immediately have a first meeting with the mediator. For family matters see, eg *Rapport Magendie, Célérité et Qualité de la Justice, La médiation, une autre voie* 43ff: family mediation associations organise a kind of 'mediation permanence' that facilitates the use of mediation by the family judge and allows the judge to enjoin the parties to attend an information meeting on mediation. Before the Paris tribunal de grande instance, the order is followed in 80% of the cases by the parties' agreement to attempt mediation.

the parties about the date at which the case will be heard again before court;[93] the mediator shall let the court know as soon as possible whether he/she accepts the mediation case (Article 131-7(2) CPC). The mediator convenes the parties as soon as he/she has been informed by the court that the consignation has been paid by the parties (Article 131-7(3) CPC). At the end of the mediation procedure, the court determines the mediator's remuneration.

In France, the judge may try to conciliate the parties at any stage of the proceedings (Article 21 CPC). He acts then as a *conciliateur*. He never acts as a mediator, in contrast to the German *richterliche Mediation*.

C. Conciliation

i. Nature of the Rules Applicable to Conciliation—Procedure to Be Followed by the Conciliator

The rules applicable to conciliation are mostly of a procedural nature. However, the result of a conciliation attempt can be a *transaction* (settlement, compromise), which is defined and regulated in the Civil Code (Articles 2044–58).[94]

a. Conciliation judiciaire (Judicial Conciliation). As a general principle, the judge may at any stage of the proceedings try to conciliate the parties (Article 21 CPC). This is one of his/her general tasks. He may also, under some conditions,[95] delegate this task to a *conciliateur de justice* (Articles 129-1 to 129-5 CPC). Sometimes, the French CPC requires a conciliation attempt as a mandatory preliminary phase of the court proceedings (see eg Articles L 1411-1(2) and R 1454-10ff Code du travail (C trav) for labour courts[96]), or suggests it and regulates this proceedings stage (Articles 845–46 CPC for claims brought before the tribunal d'instance or the juridiction de proximité). Where the judge delegates the conciliation attempt to the conciliateur de justice, the conciliation process generally takes place in the courthouse

b. Conciliation extrajudiciaire (Non-judicial Conciliation). Conciliation can also take place as a non-judicial process before the *conciliateur de justice* (regulated in Decree No 78-381 of 20 March 1978 and in the CPC, Articles 1536–41), whose task is to facilitate outside a judicial proceeding the *règlement amiable* of disputes regarding rights that are at the parties' free disposal.

The *conciliateurs de justice* number about 1,810 in France.[97] In 2010 (the most

[93] Art 131-6(1) CPC.

[94] See Art 2044 C civil: 'A compromise is a contract by which the parties settle an arisen controversy, or prevent a controversy from arising. That contract must be made in writing.' Art 2052: 'Compromises have, between the parties, the authority of *res judicata* of a final judgment. They may not be attacked on account of an error of law, nor on account of loss.'

[95] Such a delegation (*conciliation déléguée*) is possible before tribunaux d'instance, juridictions de proximité, tribunaux de commerce and tribunaux paritaires des baux ruraux.

[96] Labour courts have a special *bureau de conciliation* which tries to settle the dispute between the parties. If no settlement can be reached, the *bureau de jugement* gives a judgment.

[97] 1,807 in 2004, 1,808 in 2005, 1,809 in 2007, 1,794 in 2008 and 1,777 in 2009, see *Annuaire statistique de la Justice 2011–2012* 307. There are roughly three *conciliateurs de justice* per 100,000 inhabitants, see *L'activité des conciliateurs de justice en 2003* (Infostat Justice no 78, November 2004).

recent statistics) they had to deal with 130,715 disputes[98] and were able to settle 75,919 (= 58.1 per cent),[99] which is a satisfying result. They work for free (*bénévolement*) so that the parties do not have to bear any costs when requesting the conciliator to make a conciliation attempt.

The *conciliateur* can be seised either directly by a party or, where a preliminary conciliation attempt is required by law, by delegation of the court. In most cases (93 per cent), until the recent reform effected by Decree No 2010-1165 of 1 October 2010 enlarging the possibilities for the court to delegate conciliation to a *conciliateur de justice*,[100] the *conciliateur* was directly contacted by the parties.[101]

To be appointed as a *conciliateur de justice* requires at least three years of experience in legal matters.[102] The President of the appellate court appoints *conciliateurs* by court order for one initial year, after a proposal by the *juge d'instance* (first instance single judge). After this first year, a two-year renewal is possible several times (Article 3 Decree No 78-381 of 20 March 1978). Most *conciliateurs* (86 per cent in 2003) are male and relatively old (80 per cent are over 60 years old, 30 per cent even older than 70).[103] In 2003, 86 per cent were retired; many of them were former judges, lawyers, civil servants or managers.

They can easily be seised *sans forme* (without any form requirement) by natural persons or legal entities (Art1536 CPC). They hold regular office hours two or three times a month at either city hall or some other location in one of the town's districts, and any person may have access to them during this 'legal permanence'; they can also be present at the civil court or in a *maison de justice et du droit*.

The *conciliateur de justice* has powers and duties: he hears the parties; with the parties' consent, he can be assisted by a second conciliateur; he can visit the places related to the dispute; and he can hear any person that knows about the issue at stake (Articles 129-3 and 1538 CPC). He has a duty of confidentiality, so may not disclose information obtained or findings made during the conciliation procedure (Article 129-3(2) CPC).[104]

Where the parties can at least partly resolve the dispute by means of conciliation, a *constat d'accord* (written agreement) may be drafted and signed by the parties

[98] 122,713 in 2004, 123,174 in 2005, 121,909 in 2006, 127,389 in 2007, 122,787 in 2008 and 124,792 in 2009, see *Annuaire statistique de la Justice 2011–2012* 307.

[99] 69,475 in 2004 (56.6%), 70,875 in 2005 (57.5%), 68,543 in 2006 (56.2%), 70,399 in 2007 (55.3%), 73,261 (59.7%) in 2008 and 72,024 (57.7%) in 2009, see *Annuaire statistique de la Justice 2009-2010* (Paris, Documentation française, 2010) 307.

[100] But not in divorce or legal separation proceedings. See also II.C.b.

[101] See *L'activité des conciliateurs de justice en 2003* 2. In 2007, in 91% of the cases; in 9% of the cases the civil court of first instance (tribunal d'instance) delegated the conciliation attempt to the *conciliateur*, see JC Magendie and JF Thony (eds), *Célérité et qualité de la justice: Les conciliateurs de justice 2010*, available at <www.ca-paris.justice.fr/art_pix/rapport_Les_conciliateur_justice_Cour_d_appel_de_Paris_Avril_2010.pdf>, 4.

[102] See Art 2(2) Decree No 78-381 of 20 March 1978: 'personnes justifiant d'une expérience en matière juridique d'au moins trois ans, que leur compétence et leur activité qualifient particulièrement pour l'exercice de la fonction'.

[103] See *L'activité des conciliateurs de justice en 2003* 4.

[104] When he/she is first appointed, the conciliateur shall swear an oath ('je jure de loyalement remplir mes fonctions avec exactitude et probité et d'observer en tout les devoirs qu'elles m'imposent', see Art 8(2) Decree No 78-381 of 20 March 1978). See also Art 129-3(2) CPC: the conciliateur's findings and the declarations made by the parties or third parties during the conciliation procedure may not be used in the subsequent proceeding before court without the parties' consent. They may never been used in other proceedings.

and the *conciliateur* (Article 1540 CPC).[105] Each party receives a copy of the settlement agreement and the conciliator promptly sends a copy to the civil court of first instance (tribunal d'instance). Any party may then request the civil court to approve (*homologuer*) the agreement in order to make it enforceable,[106] except if one party opposed judicial approval and enforceability (*homologation*) in the settlement agreement (Article 1541(1) CPC[107]).

Each year, the *conciliateur de justice* shall draft a report and submit it to the President of the appellate court and to the civil court of first instance (tribunal d'instance).

A national report was drafted in 2010 on the activity and role of the French *conciliateurs de justice*.[108] Their intervention is well appreciated, and the report formulates 11 proposals:

- to strengthen the relations between *conciliateurs de justice* and the courts;
- to improve the recruitment of *conciliateurs de justice;*
- to develop the training of the *conciliateurs de justice;*
- to achieve greater transparency in their ethics and compliance rules;[109]
- to organise and utilise specialised *conciliateurs* for the commercial courts;
- to improve the manner in which a *conciliateur de justice* is seised;
- to improve conciliation by preselecting the cases;
- to regulate the consequences of conciliation on time limitations;
- to secure the results of conciliation;
- to draft models for the *conciliateurs* in order to harmonise their practices; and
- to develop more statistical material on conciliation by the *conciliateurs de justice.*

With regard to conciliation, there are also specific provisions applying to particular kinds of disputes, such as the lease of a dwelling (Article 20 of Law Act No 89-462 of 6 June 1989 and Decree No 2001-653 of 19 July 2001) or over-indebtedness (*surendettement*) of natural persons not subject to professional insolvency proceedings (Article L 331-6 C cons). In these cases, the party who would like to bring a claim to court shall first seise the conciliation commission. Only if no settlement can be reached between the parties may one or both of them together seise the state court.

ii. Duties of the Conciliator and Enforcement of these Duties

The conciliator shall be independent, impartial, neutral, competent in legal matters and able to communicate with the parties. He shall act promptly and respect confidentiality.[110]

[105] The drafting of such a written agreement is required where a party waives a right, Art 1540(2) CPC.

[106] The state court may refuse to make the settlement agreement enforceable if it is contrary to public policy. In such a case, the agreement remains valid between the parties; however, the use of legal measures or coercion as based on an enforcement order is not allowed.

[107] In the case of a cross-border dispute, the request shall be made by all the parties or by one but with the express consent of the others, see Art 1542(2) CPC. This consent may be contained in the agreement.

[108] Magendie and Thony (eds), *Célérité et qualité de la justice, Les conciliateurs de justice.*

[109] An ethics and compliance guide should be drafted and be given to the conciliator when he swears the oath. The guide should also explain the role of a *conciliateur* (to suggest or induce a possible solution) and stress his necessary skills (efficiency, competence, impartiality, neutrality), see Magendie and Thony (eds), *Célérité et qualité de la justice, Les conciliateurs de justice* 16.

[110] Magendie and Thony (eds), *Célérité et qualité de la justice, Les conciliateurs de justice* 108.

If the civil court has delegated the conciliation attempt to the *conciliateur de justice*, the *conciliateur* shall inform the judge about any difficulties encountered during the conciliation process. The civil judge may stop the conciliation procedure at any time (at a party's request or even on his own motion), especially if the progress of conciliation appears to be endangered (Article 129-4 CPC).

If the *conciliateur de justice* infringes the rules related to his duties and his status, the President of the appellate court, after receiving the opinions of the public prosecutor and the first instance civil judge (*juge d'instance*) and after hearing the conciliator himself, can dismiss the *conciliateur* from his post (Article 3(2) Decree No 78-381 of 20 March 1978). The dismissal order shall contain reasons. Such an action constitutes a disciplinary hearing.

The *conciliateur de justice* can also be subject to criminal or civil liability in the event of a breach of law related to his functions. He should therefore take out an insurance policy against civil liability. The state is not liable for the faults of a *conciliateur de justice*.

iii. Areas in Which Conciliation is Deployed

A conciliation attempt is mandatory in labour disputes and in certain civil disputes (especially in family law for divorce, legal separation, etc). These conciliation attempts take place before the civil judge. However, in some civil and commercial cases, the civil judge may delegate the conciliation to a *conciliateur de justice*.

Non-judicial conciliation (*conciliation extrajudiciaire*) occurs directly by seising the conciliateur and relates to disputes resorting to the jurisdiction of tribunal d'instance or juridiction de proximité, eg disputes between an individual and a company, or between individuals, concerning neighbourhood conflicts, lease, consumer contracts, unpaid debts,[111] or bank and insurance contracts.

iv. Influence of the UNCITRAL Model Law or the Commission Recommendation 2001

Conciliation has existed in France for a considerable time. Therefore, the UNCITRAL Model Law 2002 and the Commission Recommendation 2001 have not had a significant influence on the French regulations.

D. Expert Opinion

i. Nature of the Rules Applicable to Expert Opinions

In France, expert opinion is very seldom used as an ADR technique.

The French CPC contains provisions on experts, but in the framework of civil proceedings, where the court holds it necessary to appoint an expert to obtain information on technical issues (the expert may never give a legal opinion to the court, Article 238(3) CPC). The courts appoint an expert in disputes having a complicated technical

[111] See *L'activité des conciliateurs de justice en 2003* 2.

nature (construction, medical malpractice, sometimes intellectual property). The same procedural rules[112] apply independent of the area. The parties can conciliate while the expert is in the process of researching and formulating an opinion; see Article 281 CPC, which states that

> [I]f the parties have reached a settlement, the expert will notice that his mission has become without purpose; he will so report to the judge. The parties may request the judge to deliver an enforceable certificate to the document containing their agreement.

The parties could also agree on the appointment of an expert *non judiciaire* (which means outside court proceedings) on technical issues in dispute. They may then settle their case and agree on a compromise (*transaction*) that they can request the court to make enforceable (*homologation*). The role of the *expert non judiciaire* is not regulated by law.

ii. Duties of the Expert and Enforcement of these Duties

The CPC only regulates the duties of the judicial expert (*expert judiciaire*) appointed by the court (Articles 273ff CPC). He/she shall comply with procedural fundamental principles such as *principe contradictoire* (ie he has to hear all the parties and give them an opportunity to express their views), independence and impartiality.

E. Arbitration

i. Influence of the UNCITRAL Model Law on International Commercial Arbitration

French legal provisions on arbitration are contained in the CPC. Two major reforms have taken place. The first was in 1980 (Decree No 80-354 of 14 May 1980) and 1981 (Decree No 81-500 of 12 May 1981), when the provisions on arbitration were integrated in the New Code of Civil Procedure. The second one was occasioned by Decree No 2011-48 of 13 January 2011 *portant réforme de l'arbitrage*, which came into force on 1 May 2011 and is aimed at modernising the French law of domestic and international arbitration. Rules regarding arbitration agreements, enforcement and notice of arbitration awards have become more flexible. The powers of the arbitration court have been strengthened especially with regard to interim measures. Also, the legal provisions on means of recourse against the arbitration award have been clarified and the permissible avenues of challenge have been restricted. The 2011 reform aims at making France even more attractive as a potential place for arbitration

Many of the principles contained in the UNCITRAL Model Law on International Commercial Arbitration have been followed by French national regulations. This holds true especially since 2011 (eg Article 17 of the Model Law on the power of the arbitral tribunal to order interim measures; and similarities between the new French provisions in Article 1518 CPC and Article 34 of the UNCITRAL Model Law whereby an application for setting aside is admitted as the exclusive recourse against an arbitral award),

[112] Arts 232–48 and 263–84-1 CPC; see also Law Act No 71-498 of 29 June 1971 *relative aux experts judiciaires*.

but this assessment is also accurate to a certain extent in respect of rules applicable prior to 2011 (eg French case law on the competence of an arbitral tribunal to rule on its jurisdiction—called *principe compétence-compétence*—in line with Article 16 of the UNCITRAL Model Law; similarities between the French provisions on enforcement of arbitration awards and Articles 35 and 36 of the UNCITRAL Model Law; freedom of the parties to determine the applicable rules of procedure; equal treatment of the parties). When reading the 2011 version of the French legal provisions on arbitration, it appears that many of the solutions recommended in the UNCITRAL Model Law 1985 as amended in 2006 have been followed.

ii. Minimum Procedural Standards to be Followed

Procedural standards in arbitration have been stated by the CPC and in case law. Arbitrators are neither mediators nor conciliators; they have the power to decide on the dispute. Therefore, they are required to follow some fundamental principles of procedure, such as the ones stated in Articles 4–10, 11(1) and 13–21 CPC (the principle of party initiative; *principe dispositif*;[113] no *infra* or *ultra petita*; parties shall invoke the facts on which their claims or defences are based; rules on burden of proof; necessity of summoning the parties before deciding the case (due notice); *principe contradictoire*— namely, the right to be heard and to be informed about contentions of fact or law and evidence presented by the other party; the right to be afforded the opportunity to respond to legal arguments that the court is considering to follow *ex officio*; and, more generally, defence rights). Article 6(1) ECHR (right to a fair trial) also applies before French arbitration courts.[114]

Decree No 2011-48 of 13 January 2011 reforming arbitration also requires that parties and arbitrator(s) shall act and conduct the arbitration proceeding 'avec célérité et loyauté' (promptly and in a fair way, Article 1464(3) CPC).

Case law does not allow the arbitration court to base its award on factual or legal evidence without giving the parties an opportunity to express their views.

iii. Restricted Possibility to Abrogate Mandatory Law in Arbitration

In principle, the arbitrator or arbitration court shall decide the dispute in accordance with the rules of law (Article 1478 CPC for domestic arbitration and Article 1511 CPC for international arbitration[115]). The French Cour de cassation has ruled that, where the dispute may be subject to arbitration, the arbitral tribunal shall apply the mandatory legal provisions under the possible scrutiny of the state court (which can set aside an arbitration award that violates mandatory law).[116]

However, the arbitral tribunal shall decide as *amiable compositeur* (*ex aequo et*

[113] The scope of the proceeding is determined by the claims and defences of the parties in the pleadings, including amendments, see Art 4 CPC.

[114] See S Guinchard, C Chainais and F Ferrand, *Procédure civile, Droit interne et droit de l'Union européenne,* 31st edn (Paris, Dalloz, 2012) no 2299.

[115] In international arbitration, in accordance with such rules of law as are chosen by the parties as applicable to the substance of the dispute, see Art 1511 CPC (same contents as Art 28 UNCITRAL Model Law on international commercial arbitration).

[116] Cass Com, 9 April 2002, *Bulletin des arrêts de la Cour de cassation* IV, no 69.

bono) if the parties have expressly authorised it to do so (Articles 1478 and 1512 CPC).

In the latter situation, the question arises whether mandatory law can be abrogated in arbitration. The Cour de cassation held that *amiable composition* means a clearly expressed will of the parties to exempt the arbitral tribunal from applying the rules of law[117] so that the parties accept in advance that the arbitrators will deviate from legal provisions.[118] However, in several decisions, the French highest court requires from the *amiables compositeurs* that they shall apply substantive rules based on fundamental public policy, such as the regulations on prices,[119] customs rules[120] and legal provisions on commercial leases.[121] This means that, even where mandatory law based on public policy (*lois de police*) is applicable to the dispute, arbitration is not excluded;[122] however, the arbitral tribunal must apply the mandatory law.

iv. Rules of Enforcement

An arbitration award is not enforceable per se; it needs an *exequatur* by the state court (tribunal de grande instance). The winning party requests from the civil court the *exequatur* (non-contentious proceeding, *procédure gracieuse*).

For domestic arbitration, see Articles 1487 and 1488 CPC. An arbitration award is subject to enforcement only based upon an *exequatur* order (*ordonnance d'exequatur*) made by the civil court called the tribunal de grande instance. The *exequatur* proceeding is not *contradictoire*, which means that the party against whom enforcement is sought is not informed and is not entitled to make any submissions on the application at this stage of the proceedings. The court shall not grant *exequatur* if the arbitration award is manifestly contrary to the public policy; if the court does not grant *exequatur*, its order shall state the reasons (Article 1488 CPC).

The order on declaration of enforceability (*ordonnance d'exequatur)* is not subject to any means of recourse (Article 1499 CPC), except where enforceability has been rejected by the court (in this latter case an appeal may be brought before the appellate court, Article 1500 CPC).

For international arbitration, see Articles 1514–17 CPC. An international arbitration award is also made enforceable by an *exequatur* order of the civil court (tribunal de grande instance) if the award is not contrary to the international public order (Articles 1514 and 1516 CPC). In the first stage of the enforcement proceeding, the party against whom enforcement is sought is not informed and is not entitled to make any submissions on the application at this stage of the proceedings. A court order denying enforceability shall state the reasons (Article 1517 CPC).

With regard to the admissibility of a means of recourse against the enforcement order (*ordonnance d'exequatur*), a distinction has to be made between the interna-

[117] Cass Civ II, 13 May 1991, *Bulletin des arrêts de la Cour de cassation* II, no 145.

[118] CA Paris, 14 January 2003, *Revue trimestrielle de droit commercial et de droit économique (RTDCom)* 2003, 478.

[119] Cass Civ II, 20 December 1965, *Revue de l'arbitrage (Rev arb)* 1966, 16.

[120] Cass Com, 4 March 1980, *Revue de l'arbitrage (Rev arb)* 1981, 35 with comment by Ph Fouchard.

[121] Cass Civ, 13 December 1978, *Revue de l'arbitrage (Rev arb)* 1979, 359.

[122] See Cass Civ I, 8 July 2010, No 09-67013: even if a party invokes a French *loi de police* (here a provision of the French Commercial Code, Art L 442-6-I-5), the arbitration clause contained in the contract and giving jurisdiction to a foreign arbitral tribunal is valid and shall apply.

tional arbitration awards given in France and those given abroad. With regard to the first category, the court order denying enforceability can be challenged by an appeal (Article 1523 CPC), whereas no appeal is admissible against a positive enforcement order, except for a *recours en annulation* (application for setting aside) made upon one of the five grounds listed in Article 1520 CPC.[123]

For the latter category, in all cases the court order on the enforceability of the arbitration award is subject to appeal (Article 1525 CPC).

IV. POLICY RECOMMENDATIONS

A. Necessity to Regulate ADR with Regard to its Connection with Civil Justice

ADR should be regulated with regard to its connection with civil justice. Where an ADR mechanism is used after a claim has been brought into court, it should be integrated in the course of the proceedings, and the court should be given powers to fix a hearing after a lapse of time and either make enforceable an agreement reached by the parties or decide on the case. Also, the main principles to be followed by conciliators or mediators should be clearly stated in some relevant regulation (independence, impartiality, duty to hear all the parties, etc). Furthermore, the effect of a mediation or conciliation procedure on prescription (time limits) should be precisely regulated.

The regulation should nevertheless not be overly detailed; it should be limited to providing a general legal framework for particular ADR procedures, except with regard to ADR integrated in or connected to the civil court system.

B. Nature of State Intervention in Supporting ADR

The state should:

- actively support ADR as an alternative to civil justice, especially by financing in part family mediation associations and by creating a procedure to establish the enforceability of the settlement reached by the parties after use of an ADR mechanism; and
- offer procedures of conciliation and/or mediation within the civil justice system with coordination undertaken by the court itself.

C. Costs of Conflict Resolution

ADR can only become popular if there are financial incentives for using it.

[123] (1) The arbitration court has wrongly decided it had jurisdiction or it did not have jurisdiction; (2) the arbitration court was not validly constituted/convened in the case at hand; (3) the arbitration court has ruled without respecting the terms of the submission to arbitration or on matters beyond the scope of the submission to arbitration; (4) the *principe de la contradiction* has been violated; (5) the enforcement of the arbitration award is contrary to international public policy.

First, parties who would receive judicial aid if they sued before court should also receive judicial aid for ADR procedures.

Secondly, family law conflicts are often appropriate for mediation, but the spouses or parents hesitate because they are deterred by the possible cost of mediation. Mediation may at the same time avoid repeated claims; therefore, the state should (at least partly) subsidise the associations that perform family mediation.

In other disputes, eg in business conflicts, there is no reason why the state should totally or partly carry the costs of the conflict resolution procedure.

D. Promotion of ADR Mechanisms by the State

In France, when mediation is criticised, it is often because of the vagueness of the mechanism, its being only minimally regulated, and because a judge who orders mediation with the parties' consent has in fact no real possibility to investigate the quality of the mediation/mediator.

Therefore, a certain general regulation by the Parliament (or, in France, by government decree, since civil procedure numbers among those areas in which the government has the power to enact decrees)[124] is necessary with regard to the duties of a mediator or conciliator, the general principles to be followed and the consequences of an agreement reached by the parties (in respect of matters such as enforceability).

Charters of mediation or codes of ethics for mediators are also useful, and should be drafted by the main mediation structures (eg associations) acting together. The violation by a mediator of the rules stated in such a charter or code would lead to sanctions (eg the mediator would be struck off the list of mediators of the association to which he belongs).

Finally, as has sometimes been attempted in France, an agreement between a court and the local bar association[125] can be very helpful since the lawyer (*avocat*) often plays a filtering role with regard to ADR. It could even be configured as a close collaboration between judge and lawyer in order to determine which cases might be appropriate for mediation. This is being considered by some civil courts in France.

E. Effective Approaches for the Parties/Decision-makers to Understand at an Early Stage What the Conflict is About and to Which Forum it Should Go

Many judges in France have had the experience that it is not necessarily the cases which they would recommend for ADR (mediation, conciliation) that ultimately prove amenable to an out-of-court settlement.

[124] See Arts 34 and 37 of the French Constitution of 1958.

[125] See eg *Protocole relatif à la médiation civile* signed between the Cour d'appel of Paris and the local bar (Ordre des avocats du Barreau de Paris) in *Rapport Magendie, Célérité et Qualité de la Justice, La médiation, une autre voie* 90f.

The practice followed by some French courts to sign an agreement with the local bar association in order to organise the selection of the cases that could be appropriate for mediation or conciliation is probably to be recommended. Also a list of criteria or indicators prepared jointly by the court and other professionals could be useful.

F. ADR Should Not Be a Compulsory Pre-trial Procedure

Several models designing ADR as a compulsory pre-trial procedure (see the German model based on section 15a EGZPO) have failed. ADR should not be seen as an always necessary pre-trial step or as suitable for each kind of conflict. It should probably be distinguished in respect of the nature of the dispute. Convincing the parties of the advantages of ADR is probably more promising than imposing on them the duty to take part in a compulsory pre-trial procedure which will not be suited to all kinds of dispute.

However, the state court should be given the power (and even the duty) to first try to conciliate the parties. Only where such a conciliation attempt fails should the case be resolved by a court judgment following a contested proceeding. This would be a first step towards 'appropriate' dispute resolution.

The most promising interventions in order to promote ADR are probably:

i. To supply information (brochures sent by the court secretary; national mediation day; the important role of mediation associations to promote this kind of ADR; accessibility of information at, for instance, city halls; etc).
ii. To organise the presence of mediators or mediation associations inside the court so that at the first hearing of a case the judge can suggest to the parties (if it seems appropriate to do so) that they immediately attend an information meeting on mediation with a mediator being present at the hearing or at least present in the court building.
iii. To coordinate inside the civil court system the use of ADR mechanisms, eg by appointing a coordinating judge who can provide an overview of the practices and their possible improvement.
iv. To use the system of 'double summons'. The court simultaneously summons parties to a mediation or conciliation meeting with a private mediator or conciliator (outside the court or in the court's facilities), while at the same time giving a second, later date for a court hearing; if the parties do not appear before the mediator or do not reach a settlement, they will be heard by the court at the later date.
v. To better facilitate the enforcement of agreements reached after a mediation or a conciliation process.

Conversely, I am not convinced that cost penalties should be used as an incentive. They lead to a pressure on the parties, who could feel 'obliged' to reach a settlement. In such a case, the settlement is not 'free', but forced, such that a party may wish to refrain from fulfilling his/her obligations. Moreover, it is not always easy for the court to decide that a party has unreasonably failed to cooperate or has cooperated in bad faith in settlement endeavours.[126] In France, cost penalties would be seen as a serious restriction of the right of effective access to court.

BIBLIOGRAPHY

Annuaire statistique de la Justice 2009–2010 (Paris, Documentation française, 2010)
Annuaire statistique de la Justice 2011–2012 (Paris, Documentation française, 2012)
L'activité des conciliateurs de justice en 2003, Infostat Justice November 2004 (Paris, Ministère de la Justice, 2003)
Amrani-Mekki, S, 'La clause de conciliation' (2009) 14 *Zeitschrift für Zivilprozess International (ZZPInt)* 83
Cadiet, L, 'Des modes alternatifs de règlement des conflits en général et de la médiation en particulier' in Société de la législation comparée (ed), *La médiation* (Paris, Dalloz, 2009), 13–28
Calderon-Bruneau, D, 'La médiation familiale' *Droit Famille 2011*, Fiche pratique no 1
Chabault-Marx, C 'A propos de la médiation familiale: vers une judiciarisation du dialogue?' *Recueil Dalloz* 2012, 43
Ferrand, F, 'La transposition en droit français et en droit allemande de la directive 2008/52/CE du 21 mai 2008 relative à certains aspects de la médiation en matière civile—Confrontation des conceptions nationales en matière de règlement amiable des différends' (2011) 16 *Zeitschrift für Zivilprozess International (ZZPInt)* 29
Gorchs, B, 'La médiation dans le procès civil: sens et contresens' [2003] *Revue trimestrielle de droit civil (RTDCiv)* 409
Gorchs-Gelzer, B, 'Le décret du 20 janvier 2012 relatif à la résolution amiable des différends, Une cote mal taillée entre changement des mentalités et continuité des pratiques' *Droit et Procédures* 2012, 117
Gorchs-Gelzer, B, 'Regard critique sur l'ordonnance n°2011–1540 transposant la directive médiation' *Droit et Procédures* 2012, 2
Guinchard, S, Chainais, C and Ferrand, F, *Procédure civile, Droit interne et droit de l'Union européenne*, 31st edn (Paris, Dalloz, 2012)
Magendie, JC and Thony, JF (eds), *Célérité et qualité de la justice: Les conciliateurs de justice* April 2010, available at <www.ca-paris.justice.fr/art_pix/rapport_Les_conciliateur_justice_Cour_d_appel_de_Paris_Avril_2010.pdf>
Moreau, C, Munoz-Perez, B and Serverin, E, *La médiation judiciaire en chiffres, Situation au 31 octobre 2001* (Paris, Ministère de la Justice, Cellule Études et Recherches, 2002)
Nevejans, N, 'L'ordonnance du 16 novembre 2011, Un encouragement au développement de la médiation' *La Semaine juridique—Edition générale (JCP G)* 2012, no 148
Peulvé, C, 'La dimension processuelle de la procédure participative' *Les Petites Affiches (LPA)* 16 April 2012, no 76, 6
Rapport Guinchard, L'ambition raisonnée d'une justice apaisée (Paris, Documentation française 2008)

[126] *Cf* Principle 24.1 ALI/Unidroit Principles of Transnational Civil Procedure:

24.1 The court, while respecting the parties' opportunity to pursue litigation, should encourage settlement between the parties when reasonably possible.
24.2 The court should facilitate parties' participation in alternative-dispute-resolution processes at any stage of the proceeding.
24.3 The parties, both before and after commencement of litigation, should cooperate in reasonable settlement endeavours. The court may adjust its award of costs to reflect unreasonable failure to cooperate or bad-faith participation in settlement endeavours.

Rapport Magendie, Célérité et Qualité de la Justice, La médiation, une autre voie (Paris, Documentation Française, 2008)

Rongeat-Oudin, F, 'Le règlement amiable des différends est en bonne marche!' *La Semaine juridique—Edition générale (JCP G)* 2012, no 157

Rongeat-Oudin, F, 'Les avocats à la conquête du règlement amiable des différends' *La Semaine juridique—Edition générale (JCP G)* 2011 no 1097

Serverin, E, 'Le médiateur civil et le service public de la justice' (2003) *Revue trimestrielle de droit civile (RTDCiv)* 229

9

Regulation of Dispute Resolution in Germany: Cautious Steps towards the Construction of an ADR System

BURKHARD HESS AND NILS PELZER

I. CHARACTERISTICS OF ADR

A. Overview—Statistical Data

THERE IS NO reliable statistical data concerning the use of the different ADR practices. However, it may be said that apart from negotiation, which cannot be reasonably documented in statistics, litigation before state courts is the most commonly used dispute resolution procedure.

The official statistics presented by the Federal Office of Justice (*Bundesamt für Justiz*) mainly contain data on dispute resolution by the German state courts. According to these statistics, roughly 1.6 million civil lawsuits are filed in German courts every year, and the trend is decreasing.[1] In contrast, state-approved conciliation bodies (*Gütestellen*, *Schiedsstellen*) recorded 12,252 actions in civil matters in 2011, comprising data of 12 of the 16 federal states (*Länder*).[2] Of these proceedings, 53.1 per cent were settled amicably. The amount of cases has slightly decreased since the peak of 13,196 cases was reached in 2002.[3] The statistics show that, in those federal states with compulsory conciliation mechanisms,[4] these compulsory proceedings were predominant.[5]

With regard to terminology, it should be noted that 'mediation' and 'conciliation' (*Schlichtung*) have often been used interchangeably in legal practice.[6] Both expressions designate the amicable settlement of a dispute by the parties with the help of a neutral person. While 'conciliation' was the original expression used for the amicable settlement of disputes, the term 'mediation' has become more popular during the last decade. Therefore, mediation techniques may be used even if a dispute resolution mechanism is labelled as 'conciliation'. Yet mediation is now defined in section 1(1) of the newly enacted Mediation Law (Mediationsgesetz) as being a confidential and structured procedure in which the parties voluntarily and on their own initiative try to reach an amicable resolution of their dispute with the support of one or more mediators.

It is generally assumed that private mediation is not yet widely used: only

[1] In 2011, 1,199,758 new lawsuits were filed at the local courts (Amtsgericht, AG) and 372,605 lawsuits were filed at the regional courts (Landgericht, LG). In 1995, the numbers had been 1,751,448 and 418,807, respectively. See Bundesamt für Justiz, 'Geschäftsentwicklung der Zivilsachen in der Eingangs- und Rechtsmittelinstanz' (25 September 2012), see <www.bundesjustizamt.de/nn_2103252/DE/Themen/Buergerdienste/Justizstatistik/Geschaeftsbelastungen/Geschaeftsentwicklung__Zivilsachen,templateId=raw,property=publicationFile.pdf/Geschaeftsentwicklung_Zivilsachen.pdf>.

[2] No statistical data was available for the states of Baden-Württemberg, Bavaria, Bremen and Hamburg.

[3] Bundesamt für Justiz, 'Übersicht über die Tätigkeit der Schiedspersonen' (5 October 2012), see <www.bundesjustizamt.de/cln_115/DE/Themen/Buergerdienste/Justizstatistik/Schiedspersonen/Schiedspersonen__Gesamtuebersicht,templateId=raw,property=publicationFile.pdf/Schiedspersonen_Gesamtuebersicht.pdf>.

[4] See below II.C.ii.

[5] For example, in the state of Sachsen-Anhalt, 459 of the reported 518 conciliation proceedings in 2010 were compulsory, see Bundesamt für Justiz, 'Übersicht über die Tätigkeit der Schiedspersonen und vergleichbarer Stellen im Jahr 2010' (13 October 2011), see <www.bundesjustizamt.de/cln_349/DE/Themen/Buergerdienste/Justizstatistik/Schiedspersonen/Schiedspersonen__2010,templateId=raw,property=publicationFile.pdf/Schiedspersonen_2010.pdf>.

[6] B Hess, 'Mediation und weitere Verfahren konsensualer Streitbeilegung—Regelungsbedarf im Verfahrens- und Berufsrecht?' in *Verhandlungen des 67. Deutschen Juristentages Erfurt 2008* (Munich, Beck, 2008) vol 1, F 30; *cf* the legislative materials to the first draft of the Mediation Law, BT-Drucks 17/5335, 14. But see C Stubbe, 'Schiedsgutachten als modernes ADR Instrument' [2006] *German Arbitration Journal (SchiedsVZ)* 150, 152, who claims that, contrary to Anglo-American legal systems, conciliation (as defined here) and mediation can be clearly distinguished in German law.

2,000–2,500 private mediations per year have been estimated.[7] However, court-based mediation seems to have been more successful. During the past 10 years, the use of mediation has increased considerably, especially in family matters.[8] According to the estimates of the authors, 10,000–15,000 judicial mediation proceedings take place in German courts each year; unfortunately, no reliable data is available for Germany as a whole. According to the Ministry of Justice of Lower Saxony, approximately 2,400 judicial mediations are launched at the courts of this state each year, with the settlement rate being approximately 80 per cent.[9] In the state of Schleswig-Holstein, 1,108 judicial mediations took place in 2010.[10]

As a result, it can be stated that a genuine market for private mediation in Germany has not yet been established, although an increasing number of lawyers and other professionals have attended courses on mediation. Most of the (relatively few) practising mediators earn money through mediation training rather than from mediation sessions.[11] Many private mediators, most of them lawyers, and the professional organisations of lawyers and mediators have claimed that this is due to an unfair intrusion of judicial mediation into an area of private dispute resolution because judicial mediation, as part of the court proceedings, was free of additional costs.

Consumer disputes are increasingly frequently dealt with under ombudsman schemes. In contrast to a mediator, an ombudsman decides a case on its merits, but the decision is binding only for the business party and not for the consumer.[12] The most prominent examples of ombudsman schemes are the ombudsmen for financial and insurance matters, established in 1992 and 2001 respectively. In 2011, the Ombudsman of the German private commercial banks dealt with 8,268 applications[13] and the Ombudsman of the German insurance companies received 17,733 applications.[14]

A 2005 study conducted by PricewaterhouseCoopers and the University of Frankfurt/Oder[15] revealed that companies mostly use negotiations to solve commercial

[7] S Kirchhoff, 'Ein kleiner Schritt für den Gesetzgeber, aber ein großer für die Mediation?—Entstehung und Hintergründe des Nds Mediations- und Gütestellengesetzes' [2007] *Zeitschrift für Konfliktmanagement* 138.

[8] In particular, *cf* s 135 of the Act on the Procedure in Family Matters and in Matters of Non-contentious Jurisdiction (Gesetz über das Verfahren in Familiensachen und in den Angelegenheiten der freiwilligen Gerichtsbarkeit—FamFG), see below II.A.ii.

[9] See Ministry of Justice of Lower Saxony, 'Mediation an niedersächsischen Gerichten', see <www.mj.niedersachsen.de/portal/live.php?navigation_id=3787&article_id=10690&_psmand=13>.

[10] See a joint request of five of the six political groups of the Landtag (the state parliament) of Schleswig Holstein: political groups of CDU, SPD, FDP, Bündnis 90/Die Grünen and SSW, 'Antrag der Fraktionen von CDU, SPD, FDP, Bündnis 90/Die Grünen und des SSW, Zukunft der gerichtsinternen Mediation sichern' Schleswig-Holsteinischer Landtag Drucks 17/2276.

[11] J Risse, 'Das Mediationsgesetz—eine Kommentierung' [2012] *German Arbitration Journal (SchiedsVZ)* 244, 251; M von Schubert, 'Die Mediationsklausel/Mediationsvereinbarung' in KJ Schiffer (ed), *Mandatspraxis, Schiedsverfahren und Mediation: Übersichten, Bewertungshilfen, Checklisten, Praxishinweise, Schiedsordnungen, Muster*, 2nd edn (Cologne, Heymann, 2005) para 884; P Tochtermann, 'Mediation in Germany' in KJ Hopt and F Steffek (eds), *Mediation: Principles and Regulation in Comparative Perspective* (Oxford, Oxford University Press, 2013) 528.

[12] Hess, 'Mediation' (2008) F 31; Tochtermann, 'Mediation' (2013) 524.

[13] Ombudsmann der privaten Banken, 'Tätigkeitsbericht 2011' (August 2012), see <www.bankenverband.de/publikationen/ods/ombudsmann-taetigkeitsbericht-2011/ombudsmann-taetigkeitsbericht-2011/download>, 107.

[14] Ombudsmann für Versicherungen, 'Jahresbericht 2011', see <www.versicherungsombudsmann.de/Ressourcen/PDF/Jahresbericht-2011.pdf>, 79.

[15] PricewaterhouseCoopers and University of Frankfurt/Oder, 'Commercial Dispute Resolution: Konfliktbearbeitungsverfahren im Vergleich' (April 2005), see <www.europa-uni.de/de/forschung/institut/institut_ikm/publikationen/Studie_Commcercial_Dispute_Resolution_2005.pdf>.

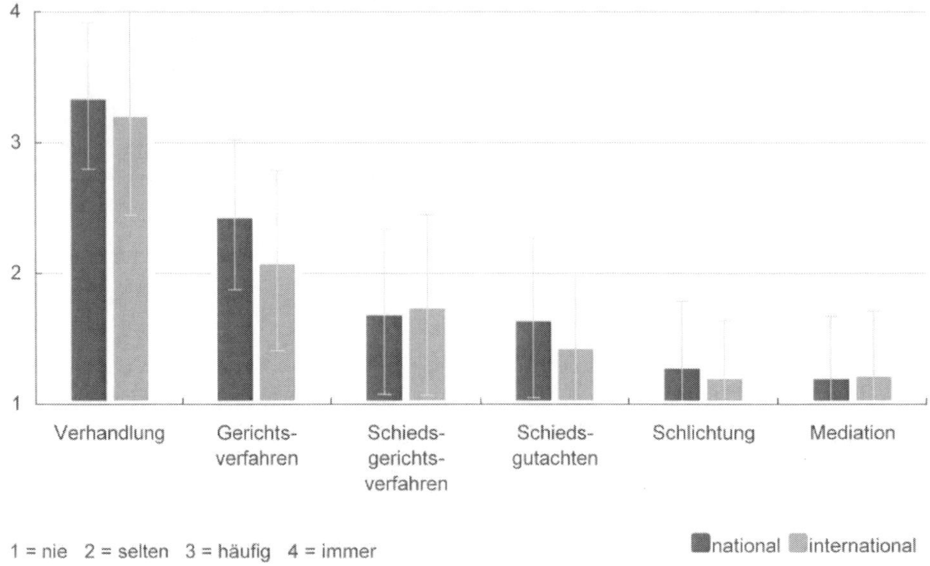

Figure 1. Use of conflict resolution mechanisms.

Source: PricewaterhouseCoopers and University of Frankfurt/Oder, 'Commercial Dispute Resolution' (2005) 7. The terms translate as follows (from left to right): Negotiation, Litigation, Arbitration, Expert opinions, Conciliation, Mediation. 1 = never, 2 = seldom, 3 = often, 4 = always.

conflicts; conventional court proceedings ranked second (see Figure 1). Arbitration and expert opinions were used to a considerably lesser extent, whereas conciliation and mediation were least used. However, 83 per cent of the companies interviewed had already had practical experience with ADR procedures.

Compared to the number of cases filed in state courts, ADR figures are still very low. The preference for state courts may be explained by the fact that resolving conflicts by means of litigation is a tradition deeply rooted in German legal culture. The judiciary is generally regarded as efficient, fair and impartial, and judges enjoy a good reputation and prestige in German society. Access to the courts is rather easy even for less well-off claimants. Legal aid is available and many citizens are covered by insurance for legal fees. Therefore, there has been little reason to consider alternatives.[16] Moreover, the cost structures of the German procedural laws provide for legal certainty and offer the winning party full compensation of all litigation costs according to the 'loser pays principle'.[17] On the other hand, it should be noted that, due to the increasing awareness of lawyers and businesses of ADR, mediation clauses are increasingly incorporated into commercial contracts.[18]

[16] See also R Greger, 'Die Reglementierung der Selbstregulierung: Zum Referentenentwurf eines Mediationsgesetzes' [2010] *Zeitschrift für Rechtspolitik* 209, 212.

[17] Hess, 'Mediation' (2008) F 116f.

[18] See also Tochtermann, 'Mediation' (2013) 529.

B. Strengths and Weaknesses of the Different Dispute Resolutions Mechanisms

The dispute resolution mechanism that best suits a situation can only be individually determined for each case by the parties concerned. This evaluation not only aptly describes the situation in Germany, but can be transferred to most other jurisdictions. Generally it can be stated that ADR has the advantages of being fast, confidential and flexible. Mediation or conciliation may be preferable if the parties wish or have to maintain their relationship (such as for businesses or neighbours). Compared to litigation and arbitration, these mechanisms may not only be cheaper but also less time-consuming. In particular, mediation techniques provide the potential to find solutions which are perceived by both parties as fair and satisfactory.[19] This can also be favourable in family matters: an amicable divorce is often reasonable when the couple has joint children or if maintenance has to be paid over a long period of time.

For small consumer claims, ombudsman proceedings may provide a convenient and risk-free way for consumers to assert their claims. Court-based mediation combines the authority and legal expertise of a judge with the opportunity to find an amicable solution and relatively low costs. Both arbitration and expert opinions feature the special professional and industry expertise of the arbitrator or expert. Arbitration is especially well suited for cross-border business contracts, not only because bias towards the home jurisdiction of one party may be avoided but also because an arbitral award may easily be enforced worldwide pursuant to the New York Convention.[20]

C. The Need for an ADR Market

ADR is a developing market, mostly in family disputes, but also in commercial matters. In family matters, the most prominent area relates to parental responsibility. In commercial matters, hybrid dispute resolution clauses providing for negotiation, mediation and arbitration have become increasingly popular (regrettably, no specific statistical data is available). However, the figures clearly indicate that most disputes that are not resolved by negotiation are brought before the courts. As demonstrated above, this is due to several factors that favour judicial dispute resolution in Germany. A fundamental change in this mentality does not appear to be imminent.

However, it would be premature to assert that the German market is well balanced. The study by PricewaterhouseCoopers and the University of Frankfurt/Oder revealed the positive attitude of businesses towards ADR.[21] Overall, negotiation was considered to be the most advantageous approach, followed by mediation, conciliation and binding expert opinions. State-court litigation ranked last and was assessed as inconvenient in many aspects. When asked about the requirements for successful dispute resolution, many companies expressed their wish to maintain business relations and to

[19] For an empirical study, see M Leiss, 'Empirische Erkenntnisse zur Mediation im Wirtschaftsrecht' [2007] *German Arbitration Journal (SchiedsVZ)* 139.

[20] The Convention on the Recognition and Enforcement of Foreign Arbitral Awards of 1958 has been acceded to by 147 states; *cf* UNCITRAL, 'Status 1958—Convention on the Recognition and Enforcement of Foreign Arbitral Awards' (2012), see <www.uncitral.org/uncitral/en/uncitral_texts/arbitration/NYConvention_status.html>.

[21] PricewaterhouseCoopers and University of Frankfurt/Oder, 'Commercial Dispute Resolution' (2005) 4.

actively frame both the process and the result of the resolution of disputes, which also points in the direction of ADR. As a result, it can be concluded that company preferences diverge to a great extent from their actual behaviour. This may be explained with the fact that court actions are conceived as inevitable;[22] another, perhaps more plausible, explanation is that companies are reluctant to take the risk to follow new paths of conflict resolution.[23] It can also be assumed that many lawyers still avoid mediation because they have no experience in this regard and, as a consequence, the parties lack information concerning ADR. Moreover, lawyers' fees are higher if a case is brought to a court.[24]

Another issue is the proper use of negotiation techniques. Many cases brought before state courts and arbitral tribunals—some say more than half of all arbitration proceedings[25]—are resolved by amicable settlement. It may be argued that mediation techniques could help the parties settle these disputes more efficiently, saving both time and costs.[26] There is thus still some potential regarding the use of mediation.

II. THE REGULATION OF ADR

A. General Regulation of ADR

German law does not provide for any comprehensive regulation on ADR. Before the new Mediation Act[27] was enacted in July 2012, sparse provisions were found at the federal level, at the state level and (mostly) in private regulations of professional and consumer organisations. In its Article 1, the Mediation Act contains the Mediation Law, which provides for a basic framework for mediation. The Mediation Law closely follows the pattern of the EU Mediation Directive,[28] but deals with domestic mediation. It addresses the basic aspects of mediation, such as the duties of the mediators and rules for the mediation session (section 2), conflict of interests of the mediator (section 3), confidentiality of the mediation process and training requirements (sections 4 and 5).[29]

Provisions concerning judicial mediation were basically non-existent until the Mediation Act was passed.[30] The Mediation Act finally introduced the concept of the *Güterichter* (conciliation judge) in the Code of Civil Procedure (Zivilprozessordnung, ZPO) and expressly mentions mediation as a possible conflict resolution technique of the conciliation judge in the wording of section 278(5) ZPO. Thus, judicial media-

[22] Ibid.

[23] J Risse and C Wagner, 'Mediation im Wirtschaftsrecht' in F Haft and K Gräfin von Schlieffen (eds), *Handbuch Mediation*, 2nd edn (Munich, Beck, 2009) ch 23 para 2.

[24] Tochtermann, 'Mediation' (2013) 538.

[25] German Maritime Arbitration Association, 'GMAA—Why?', see <www.gmaa.de/en/faqs/gmaa-why>; *cf* Risse and Wagner, 'Mediation im Wirtschaftsrecht' (2009) para 5, who mention a figure of more than 60%.

[26] Risse and Wagner, 'Mediation im Wirtschaftsrecht' (2009) para 5.

[27] Gesetz zur Förderung der Mediation und anderer Verfahren der außergerichtlichen Konfliktbeilegung of 21 July 2012, promulgated on 25 July 2012 in Bundesgesetzblatt 2012, Part I, No 35, 1577.

[28] Directive 2008/52/EC of the European Parliament and of the Council of 21 May 2008 on certain aspects of mediation in civil and commercial matters.

[29] M Ahrens, 'Mediation und Güterichter—Neue Regelungen der gerichtlichen und außergerichtlichen Mediation' [2012] *Neue Juristische Wochenschrift* 2465.

[30] However, since 2002, the civil courts have been able to stay the proceedings in order to permit the parties to attempt an out-of-court settlement (*außergerichtliche Streitschlichtung*), *cf* below II.C.ii.

tion has now found a place in the Code of Civil Procedure.[31] Similar provisions on judicial mediation are now found in other procedural codes (on family, labour, social and administrative matters) as amended by the Mediation Act.

With regard to other areas of ADR, regulation is still fragmented. Since the 1990s, several legislative initiatives have sought to encourage ADR techniques in the German judicial landscape. The most prominent (and unsuccessful) attempt was section 15a of the Introductory Act to the Code of Civil Procedure (Gesetz betreffend die Einführung der Zivilprozessordnung, EGZPO). This provision permits the federal states to establish compulsory conciliation procedures for small claims (up to €750) as well as certain libel, discrimination and neighbour disputes. The majority of the federal states have enacted special conciliation laws (*Schlichtungsgesetze*), which may contain provisions concerning both compulsory and voluntary conciliation.

There are no special regulations concerning negotiation as a dispute resolution mechanism, nor does German law explicitly provide for expert opinion proceedings. However, expert opinions with binding force are subject to the fragmentary contract law rules of sections 317–19 of the Civil Code (Bürgerliches Gesetzbuch, BGB), at least according to prevailing opinion.[32] These provisions do not directly address expert opinions, but rather concern the specification of performance by a third party. However, Germany's highest court in civil matters, the Bundesgerichtshof (Federal Court of Justice), has argued that they may be applied analogously.[33] Non-binding expert opinions have only rarely been discussed in legal literature so far.[34]

By contrast, arbitration is comprehensively regulated in book 10 of the Code of Civil Procedure (sections 1025–68 ZPO), modelled after the UNCITRAL model law on international commercial arbitration.

i. Stimulating Effects of Regulation

Putting ADR mechanisms on a legal basis is certainly likely to promote knowledge about the different mechanisms by communicating the mere existence of ADR to potentially interested parties.[35] Legal certainty is achieved. It has been said that enacting a mediation law has the psychological effect of a 'legislative accolade' because mediation will be intuitively considered to be officially recognised and endorsed.[36]

Cost incentives for the settlement of disputes are found in the legislation on the costs of civil proceedings. If the parties settle the case, they are not required to pay a fee for the judgment. Furthermore, settlement is encouraged by an augmentation of the statutory lawyers' fee. These provisions also apply to judicial mediation. The new law on mediation provides for further incentives as it gives the states the freedom to

[31] B Hess, 'Mediation Judges in Germany: Mutual Interference of EU Standards and National Developments' in CH van Rhee (ed), *Essays on the Role of Judges and Parties in China and Europe* (Dordrecht, Springer, forthcoming).

[32] *Cf* below IV.A.i.

[33] BGH *Neue Juristische Wochenschrift—Rechtsprechungs-Report Zivilrecht* 2000, 279, 281; M Würdinger in FJ Saecker and R Rixecker (eds), *Münchener Kommentar zum Bürgerlichen Gesetzbuch*, 6th edn (Munich, Beck, 2012) s 317, comment 38.

[34] See, eg Stubbe, 'Schiedsgutachten als modernes ADR Instrument' (2006) 150ff.

[35] Risse, 'Das Mediationsgesetz' (2012) 244f.

[36] G Wagner, 'Grundstrukturen eines deutschen Mediationsgesetzes' (2010) 74 *Rabel Journal of Comparative and International Private Law (RabelsZ)* 794, 797.

further reduce the statutory costs of litigation (regarding court costs) if the parties opt for mediation (within or outside of the court system).

In family matters, the courts may order the parties to take part in a free information session on mediation, *cf* sections 135(1) and 156(1)(3) of the Act on the Procedure in Family Matters and in Matters of Non-contentious Jurisdiction (Gesetz über das Verfahren in Familiensachen und in den Angelegenheiten der freiwilligen Gerichtsbarkeit, FamFG). According to section 156(2) FamFG, the judge may endorse a settlement on parental custody reached by family mediation (even without any intervention of a lawyer) in a court-approved settlement.[37] However, parties are not obliged to attempt mediation.

ii. Objectives of Regulating ADR

The objective of providing a legal basis for mediation under the new Mediation Law was to generally encourage ADR. The legislature expected that more cases would be taken out of the mainstream court system in order to reduce bottlenecks in court proceedings. For the conflicting parties, on the other hand, mediation may have the advantage of being less stressful, cheaper and faster.

However, judicial mediation turned out to be a very controversial issue during the lengthy legislative process of the Mediation Act. Federal states with programmes on judicial mediation argued that the early experiments were working efficiently, whereas lawyers' associations, the bar and some federal states (such as Baden-Württemberg) recommended that the new Act should only promote private mediation, claiming that judicial mediation entailed more work for the courts. The underlying fear was that cheap mediation by the courts was unwelcome competition for private mediation. As judicial mediation was eventually included in the new Act, it is expected that the controversy will now end.[38]

As far as arbitration is concerned, the aim of implementing the UNCITRAL Model Law was to establish Germany as a preferred venue for arbitration and to assist arbitration institutions. Although any assessment is difficult, it seems that these goals were met at least to a certain extent. Since the millennium, the arbitration activities of the German Institution of Arbitration (Deutsche Institution für Schiedsgerichtsbarkeit, DIS), one of the most prominent services for arbitration, have increased considerably.[39]

B. Incentives

i. Cost Incentives

In Germany, cost incentives for ADR have been discussed in the context of the draft of the Mediation Act. Incentives can be either positive or negative. On the one hand,

[37] Hess, 'Mediation' (2008) paras F 50ff.

[38] See below III.B.vi.

[39] In 2011, 178 new arbitration proceedings were commenced; see German Institution of Arbitration, 'DIS Statistics 2011', available at <www.dis-arb.de/en/39/content/statistik-id53>. In 2002, there had only been 77; see 'Deutsche Institution für Schiedsgerichtsbarkeit eV (DIS)' [2003] *German Arbitration Journal (SchiedsVZ)* 178.

there can be sanctions such as the dismissal of a legal aid application or higher legal costs at court if the parties have not attempted ADR before commencing court proceedings. On the other hand, legal aid could be granted for mediation, and court fees might be reduced if the parties have successfully conducted a court-annexed or court-based mediation.[40]

Pursuant to section 114 ZPO, an application for legal aid can be dismissed on the basis of frivolity if the applying party is not willing to take part in mediation. One may argue that ADR is not mandatory and that the right of access to justice prohibits this, but if the opposing party offers a fair and promising mediation, the applicant does not need to rely on public assistance.[41]

Cost sanctions if a party refuses to take part in ADR proceedings—as based on the English model—were discussed by legal scholars but were not adopted by the Mediation Act. This would have entailed many additional problems. However, discretionary cost provisions, such as section 91a ZPO, may be interpreted in an ADR-friendly way.[42]

An incentive for in-court mediation (now called *Güterichter* proceedings[43]) is the fact that, unlike private mediation, mediation by the courts is free of additional costs. Legal fees are considerably lower if a settlement is reached in this way.[44]

The Mediation Act did not directly introduce positive cost incentives into German law, but allows the federal states to reduce or abolish certain legal fees if a claim is withdrawn after a successful ADR procedure. Additionally, the claimant's statement of claim must include that ADR is intended or has been commenced or that the court had suggested an ADR procedure.[45] This gives the parties an incentive to reach a settlement during mediation so as to save litigation costs.[46] It remains to be seen if the federal states will make use of this authorisation at times when public exchequers are short of cash.

The grant of legal aid comprises the lawyer's fees for an out-of-court settlement attempt. However, the mediator's fees are not included and state agencies, such as those providing debt counselling or youth aid, must be used instead when available.[47] Therefore, a needy claimant is more likely to go to court than conduct mediation.

The Mediation Act has not widened the scope of legal aid for ADR. However, section 7 of the Mediation Law allows the federal government and the federal states to cooperate in order to conduct research projects to evaluate the consequences of financial assistance for mediation for the federal states. This gives an opportunity to introduce experimental projects concerning legal aid for mediation at some courts—under conditions similar to ordinary legal aid. This regulation was criticised as being too timid,[48] but one has to keep in mind that it is hard to estimate the budgetary burden a general regulation of 'mediation aid' would entail.[49]

[40] Hess, 'Mediation' (2008) F 113.
[41] Ibid, F 114.
[42] Ibid, F 117.
[43] See below III.B.vi.
[44] Ibid, F 132.
[45] Arts 7 and 7a Mediation Act.
[46] Risse, 'Das Mediationsgesetz' (2012) 253f.
[47] Hess, 'Mediation' (2008) F 114f.
[48] Greger, 'Reglementierung' (2010) 212f.
[49] See Hess, 'Mediation' (2008) F 115f.

ii. The Role of Legal Culture

For a long time, ADR was not regulated at all, and court adjudication was considered the best dispute resolution mechanism.[50] In particular, the provision of section 15a EGZPO (allowing the introduction of mandatory conciliation prior to small claims proceedings) gave the impression that it complicated access to the courts (and thus lessened the case load of the courts) instead of promoting ADR.[51] However, things have begun to change, especially since the Mediation Law came under discussion, and the legislature's attitude towards ADR has become increasingly positive.

iii. Advisory Duties of Lawyers

Section 1(3) of the Rules on the Professional Practice for Lawyers (Berufsordnung der Rechtsanwälte, BORA) requires lawyers to advise their clients to solve their legal problems in the most favourable way. A lawyer is therefore obliged to suggest solving a conflict by way of mediation if this is the dispute resolution method most appropriate for the respective case. This duty is reinforced by the fact that, pursuant to the revised section 253(3)(1) ZPO as of July 2012, the statement of claim must indicate whether mediation or another ADR method was unsuccessfully attempted and whether there are compelling reasons not to resort to alternative dispute resolution. Therefore, the lawyer drafting a statement of claim is indirectly obliged to consider whether mediation is useful in the respective case and must advise his clients accordingly. The provision, however, becomes meaningless if lawyers use standard phrases to state that an amicable settlement seems impossible or the like.[52] If a lawyer violates the obligation of section 1(3) BORA, he may be held liable for damages.[53] However, in practice, evidence of a correlation to actual damage is difficult to establish.[54]

C. Restriction of Access to Courts

i. Mandatory ADR Proceedings

The new Mediation Act does not provide for compulsory mediation prior to court proceedings. However, as mentioned before, section 15a EGZPO allows the federal states to establish compulsory conciliation procedures with regard to small claims not exceeding €750, defamation claims and neighbour disputes as well as certain claims resulting from a violation of the General Equal Treatment Law (Allgemeines Gleichbehandlungsgesetz). Eleven of the 16 federal states[55] have made use of this provision by enacting conciliation laws (*Schlichtungsgesetze*). As far as small claims are con-

[50] However, conciliation as an alternative to civil justice has been a topic of discussion since the late eighteenth century, see ibid F 9f.

[51] Ibid, F 32.

[52] Tochtermann, 'Mediation' (2013) 535; M Henssler and C Deckenbrock, 'Das neue Mediationsgesetz: Mediation ist und bleibt Anwaltssache!' [2012] *Der Betrieb* 159, 162.

[53] Ahrens, 'Mediation und Güterichter' (2012) 2469.

[54] Tochtermann, 'Mediation' (2013) 535.

[55] The states where there is no compulsory conciliation are Berlin, Bremen, Hamburg, Saxony and Thuringia.

cerned, however, conciliation can be easily circumvented. The conciliation laws contain exemption clauses for the case of court proceedings being initiated by filing a payment order according to sections 688ff ZPO (see section 15a(2)(5) EGZPO). In this case, the parties do not have to undergo a conciliation procedure before filing the claim at court. In the past, claimants opted for the payment order in most cases.

Consequently, as of 2012, seven states had once again abolished the requirement of prior conciliation for small claim proceedings.[56] Three states had never included it from the beginning.[57] Only Baden-Württemberg has kept this prerequisite so far, but its Secretary of Justice recently announced plans to abolish compulsory conciliation as a whole, since it prolongs court proceedings and increases the costs of litigation.[58]

ii. Court-annexed ADR and the Güterichter Model

According to the newly introduced section 278a ZPO, a court may suggest that the parties attempt mediation or any other ADR proceedings. If the parties agree, the court orders a stay of the litigation. Even before the Mediation Act came into force, the law had permitted the court to stay proceedings and to suggest an ADR procedure out of court.[59] However, this provision was seldom applied in practice; judges were reluctant to promote dispute resolution out of court (inter alia, for constitutional reasons) and the parties expected and preferred an attempt by the judge to settle the case. Finally, the additional costs of a mediation conducted out of court were regarded as an impediment.[60]

Pursuant to section 278(5) ZPO as amended by the Mediation Act, a judge may also refer a dispute to a conciliation judge (*Güterichter*) for judicial mediation.[61] According to the wording of the provision, a *Güterichter* procedure may even be imposed on the parties against their will,[62] but it remains to be seen whether this will take place in practice.[63] The Committee on Legal Affairs (*Rechtsausschuss*) of the Bundestag assumed in its draft that such a procedure requires the consent of the parties.[64]

Court-annexed mediation is regarded to be preferable to proceedings before a settlement judge—the settlement judge is deemed to be a last resort if court-annexed mediation is not available.[65] Concerning quality assurance of external neutrals, only the provisions of the Mediation Law and professional law are applicable.[66]

[56] Bavaria, Brandenburg, Hesse, North Rhine-Westphalia, Saarland, Saxony-Anhalt, Schleswig-Holstein.

[57] Mecklenburg-West Pomerania, Lower Saxony, Rhineland-Palatinate.

[58] Ministry of Justice of Baden-Württemberg, 'Justizminister strebt Abschaffung des Schlichtungsgesetzes an' (12 July 2012), see <www.jum.baden-wuerttemberg.de/servlet/PB/menu/1277899/index.html?ROOT=1153239>.

[59] The old s 278(5) ZPO read as follows (translation provided by Samson Übersetzungen GmbH, Dr. Carmen von Schöning, available at <www.gesetze-im-internet.de/englisch_zpo/index.html>): 'Where appropriate, the court may suggest to the parties that they pursue dispute resolution proceedings out of court. Should the parties to the dispute decide to do so, s 251 shall apply mutatis mutandis.'

[60] Tochtermann, 'Mediation' (2013) 571.

[61] See below III.B.vi.

[62] B Hess, 'Perspektiven der gerichtsinternen Mediation in Deutschland' (2011) 124 *Zeitschrift für Zivilprozess* 137, 159 fn 140.

[63] See H Walter, 'Der Güterichter nach dem Mediationsgesetz—echte Mediation oder richterliche Schlichtung?' (2012) 45 *Spektrum der Mediation* 60, 62, who approves of compulsory *Güterichter* proceedings.

[64] Legislative materials, BT-Drucks 17/8058, 21.

[65] Legislative materials, BT-Drucks 17/5335, 30.

[66] See below III.B.ii.

D. The Impact of Constitutional Law

As far as a mandatory conciliation hearing as a requirement for filing a claim at court is concerned, it was questionable whether this violates the procedural rights of the claimant. The Bundesverfassungsgericht (Federal Constitutional Court) has ruled that mandatory ADR does not violate Article 19(4) of the German constitution, the Basic Law (Grundgesetz, GG). This provision stipulates that if any person's rights are violated by a public authority, he or she may have recourse to the courts. The Constitutional Court convincingly held that the amicable solution of a conflict is usually preferable to a decision of a court.[67]

For a long time, there was a great deal of controversy as to whether the right to be heard (enshrined in Article 103 of the Basic Law) applies to judicial mediation. The question of whether in-court mediation forms part of the judicial system within in the meaning of Article 92 of the Basic Law is equally disputed.[68] Most scholars argued that the principles of fair trial only apply to adjudication.[69] However, the purpose of the right to be heard is to protect the parties and to prevent the parties from being reduced to mere objects.[70] But even if judicial mediation is subject to certain fundamental rights, caucuses might still be allowed with the consent of the parties if the other party is informed about results that may promote a settlement.[71] As a rule, caucuses should be used conservatively.

According to the new section 278 ZPO, judicial mediation is regarded as part of judicial activity and, consequently, the fundamental guarantees of a fair trial and the right to be heard are applicable.

E. The Impact of the UNCITRAL Model Law on International Commercial Conciliation (2002)

The UNCITRAL Model Law on International Commercial Conciliation did not influence the German legislation. According to the first draft of the Federal Ministry of Justice, in preparing the Mediation Act the legislative objectives were to regulate mediation (out-of-court mediation, court-annexed mediation and mediation by the courts themselves), to create a due legal basis for judicial mediation, and to transpose the Mediation Directive into German law.[72]

[67] BVerfG *Neue Juristische Wochenschrift—Rechtsprechungs-Report Zivilrecht* 2007, 1073, 1074 (1 BvR 1351/01).

[68] See R Wimmer and U Wimmer, 'Verfassungsrechtliche Aspekte richterlicher Mediation' [2007] *Neue Juristische Wochenschrift* 3243.

[69] H Eidenmüller, 'Vertrags- und verfahrensrechtliche Grundfragen der Mediation: Möglichkeiten und Grenzen privatautonomen Konfliktmanagements' in S Breidenbach (ed), *Konsensuale Streitbeilegung: Akademisches Symposion zu Ehren von Peter F Schlosser aus Anlass seines 65. Geburtstages* (Bielefeld, Gieseking, 2001) 76.

[70] B Hess, 'Rechtsgrundlagen der Mediation' in F Haft and K Gräfin von Schlieffen (eds), *Handbuch Mediation*, 2nd edn (Munich, Beck, 2009) ch 43 para 54.

[71] Ibid.

[72] Directive 2008/52/EC of the European Parliament and of the Council of 21 May 2008 on certain aspects of mediation in civil and commercial matters.

F. ADR and Consumer Protection

Mediation clauses are subject to judicial review according to sections 305ff BGB on the protection against surprising or unfair clauses. Furthermore, the case law of the European Court of Justice on dispute resolution clauses for consumers is equally applicable.

The Commission Recommendation of 4 April 2001 on the principles for out-of-court bodies involved in the consensual resolution of consumer disputes, C(2001) 1016 (Recommendation 2001/310/EC), has not been expressly taken into consideration.[73] However, dispute resolution schemes organised by businesses often refer either to Recommendation 2001/310/EC or to Commission Recommendation 98/257/EC on the principles applicable to the bodies responsible for out-of-court settlement of consumer disputes. The Ombudsman Scheme of the Private Commercial Banks and other ombudsman schemes in the banking sector are members of the Financial Dispute Resolution Network (FIN-NET) and have therefore committed themselves to comply with the principles of Commission Recommendation 98/257/EC.

III. SPECIFIC ADR INSTRUMENTS

A. Negotiation

Negotiation clauses as a dispute resolution mechanism have not been a focus of research among German legal scholars. A much better understood topic is the validity of amendment clauses, which oblige the parties to renegotiate a contract if the law (particularly section 313 BGB) would otherwise allow a party to cancel the contract or amend it with the help of a court.[74] Nevertheless, the legal and practical implications are comparable.

Multi-tiered dispute resolution clauses (*Eskalationsklauseln*), which frequently occur in international commercial contracts, usually contain a duty to negotiate as a first level of dispute resolution. The question which regularly arises in these cases is what happens if one party commences arbitration without having conducted negotiations.

As for all ADR clauses, a distinction can be drawn between 'soft' and 'hard' negotiation clauses.[75] While a soft negotiation clause (*Sprechklausel*, literally a 'speaking clause'[76]) merely gives the parties an option to negotiate before commencing an adjudication or arbitration proceeding, a hard negotiation clause is designed to make prior negotiation compulsory. The following remarks only refer to hard negotiation clauses.

The agreement to negotiate contains substantive (contract) law and procedural elements. If a party brings a claim to the court (or arbitral tribunal) without prior

[73] The enactment of this recommendation was questionable, see B Hess, *Europäisches Zivilprozessrecht* (Heidelberg, Müller, 2010), ch 10 paras 136ff.

[74] A Nelle, *Neuverhandlungspflichten: Neuverhandlungen zur Vertragsanpassung und Vertragsergänzung als Gegenstand von Pflichten und Obliegenheiten* (München, Beck, 1994) 2 and passim; T Finkenauer in *Münchener Kommentar zum Bürgerlichen Gesetzbuch* s 313, comments 122f.

[75] KP Berger, 'Rechtsprobleme von Eskalationsklauseln' in B Bachmann, S Breidenbach et al (eds), *Grenzüberschreitungen: Beiträge zum Internationalen Verfahrensrecht und zur Schiedsgerichtsbarkeit, Festschrift für Peter Schlosser zum 70. Geburtstag* (Bielefeld, Gieseking, 2001) 20.

[76] See von Schubert, 'Die Mediationsklausel/Mediationsvereinbarung' (2005) para 837.

negotiation, the action will be rejected as temporarily inadmissible. This is a generally accepted view in the legal literature and is in line with rulings of the Bundesgerichtshof regarding other ADR mechanisms. In this respect, the clause generates procedural effects. The *pactum de non petendo* contained in the negotiation clause does not have a material effect in most cases, since the parties do not want to suspend their substantive rights, but only legal action.[77]

Quite obviously, there is no obligation to reach an agreement.[78] However, one may ask whether an obligation to negotiate is enforceable as such. This is highly doubtful,[79] because it is the parties themselves who decide on how to fulfil their negotiation duty, not a judge. Therefore, a judgment would be vague, and any answer or suggestion of the other party would suffice.[80] Such a judgment would be worthless, and a complaint would therefore be dismissed for lack of need for legal relief. In addition, the enforcement of the judgment would be unreasonable. However, if a party does not comply with the obligation to negotiate, costs expended in vain by the other party and other potential damages may be successfully claimed on the basis of sections 241(2) and 280(1) BGB.[81] The negotiation agreement may contain a liquidated damages clause. On the other hand, no damages can be claimed for the loss of the opportunity to reach an agreement since an obligation to reach an agreement does not exist.[82] The same also applies if negotiations are cancelled in bad faith. According to section 241(2) BGB, an obligation may also require that each party takes into account the rights, legal interests and other interests of the other party. However, in practice it may be difficult to prove that actual damages have occurred.

Like other ADR clauses, negotiation clauses are therefore mainly indirectly enforced by the court by admitting a case only when prior negotiations have failed. To facilitate evidence in this regard, negotiation clauses may provide for the requirement of written notice in order to establish failure.

B. Mediation

i. The Mediation Law of 2012 and the Implementation of the Mediation Directive

According to its Article 12, Directive 2008/52/EC on certain aspects of mediation in civil and commercial matters (hereinafter referred to as the Directive) had to be implemented by 31 May 2011. Although the Directive only addresses cross-border situations, there was a consensus that this opportunity should be taken to broadly implement the Directive and to adopt a comprehensive set of rules to foster mediation in Germany. An ongoing political debate was launched in 2007. The Federal Ministry of

[77] Therefore, a negotiation clause does not contain a deferment of mutual claims; *cf* A Hacke, *Der ADR Vertrag: Vertragsrecht und vertragliche Gestaltung der Mediation und anderer alternativer Konfliktlösungsverfahren* (Heidelberg, Verlag Recht und Wirtschaft, 2010) 119.

[78] See von Schubert, 'Die Mediationsklausel/Mediationsvereinbarung' (2005) para 826.

[79] For the following arguments, see Nelle, *Neuverhandlungspflichten* (1994) 309f.

[80] *Cf* von Schubert, 'Die Mediationsklausel/Mediationsvereinbarung' (2005) para 827.

[81] Ibid, 322f.

[82] Ibid, 324.

Justice commissioned a comparative study,[83] and the German Jurists Forum (Deutscher Juristentag), the single most important political forum on law reform in Germany, put the subject on its agenda in autumn 2008.[84] In July 2012, a Mediation Act finally entered into force, more than a year after the expiry of the transposition deadline of the Directive. The most controversial issue of the legislative process had been judicial mediation.[85]

The new Mediation Law of 2012 only provides for a few binding rules. Most issues, such as rules of the mediation process, and duties of the mediator and the parties, are left to the codes of conduct of mediation organisations and mediation agreements. There are no rules which apply in default of agreement.

The definition of 'mediation' given in section 1 Mediation Law[86] is in line with Article 3(a) of the Directive. It was not regarded as necessary to emphasise that 'two or more parties' can take part in a mediation proceeding.[87] However, unlike the first draft and Article 3(a) of the Directive, the final version of the Mediation Law does not mention mediation conducted by a judge. Nevertheless, pursuant to section 41(8) ZPO, a judge is disqualified by law from exercising judicial office if he has been involved in former ADR proceedings concerning the matter in question. The provision therefore expresses the concept underlying Article 3(a) of the Directive.

The Mediation Law is neither restricted to cross-border cases within the scope of Article 2 of the Directive (see recital 8 of the Directive) nor expressly confined to civil and commercial matters as stated in Article 1(2) of the Directive.

As far as the quality of mediation is concerned (Article 4 of the Directive), the Mediation Law seeks to protect it by introducing the title of a *zertifizierter Mediator* (certified mediator), as described by sections 5 and 6. The first draft of the Mediation Law stated that there is a conflict between the interest of consumers in a transparent mediation market and the need for advancement of mediation not regulated by law.[88] At first, it was therefore considered sufficient to set up common minimum standards. However, the final version of the Law entitles the Federal Ministry of Justice to create rather detailed outlines of training requirements. It should be noted that this only refers to certified mediators. It is unclear what requirements apply to an uncertified mediator, who, according to section 5(1) of the Mediation Law, also has to prove that he has the necessary knowledge and experience to conduct mediation proceedings.[89] The reinforced training requirements are attributable to successful lobby work—mediation training is a profitable business.[90] It is unclear whether they may sustainably enhance the quality of mediation in practice.[91]

Section 278a ZPO incorporates the rule that a court may invite the parties to use

[83] K Hopt and F Steffek (eds), *Mediation: Rechtstatsachen, Rechtsvergleich, Regelungen* (Tübingen, Mohr Siebeck, 2008).

[84] Hess, 'Mediation' (2008).

[85] See below III.B.vi.

[86] See above I.A.

[87] Legislative materials, BT-Drucks 17/5335, 13.

[88] Ibid, 18.

[89] Henssler and Deckenbrock, 'Das neue Mediationsgesetz' (2012) 167.

[90] Risse, 'Das Mediationsgesetz' (2012) 251. The average costs for a mediation training amount to €5,000–8,000, *cf* J Risse, 'Mediator' in M Hies (ed), *Perspektiven für Juristen 2013* (Munich, e-fellows.net, 2012) 195.

[91] Hess, 'Mediation' (2008) F 127.

mediation in order to settle the dispute as stipulated in Article 5 of the Directive. As described above,[92] a mandatory information session on mediation may be ordered by the court in certain family matters according to sections 135 and 156 FamFG. This is in line with Article 5 of the Directive.

The enforceability of agreements resulting from mediation (Article 6 of the Directive) had been an issue during the drafting process of the Mediation Act. The solution that was eventually accepted determined that a settlement with the help of a mediator is not per se enforceable. However, there are manifold possibilities to obtain an enforceable title.[93]

The Committee on Legal Affairs of the Bundestag has correctly pointed out that this is in line with the Directive,[94] since Article 6(2) only requires that the content of the agreement may be made enforceable by a court or other competent authority.[95]

Section 4 of the Mediation Law implements Article 7(1) of the Directive, regulating the confidentiality of mediation. The exception of *ordre public* in section 4(2) of the Mediation Law has been formulated slightly more narrowly than Article 7(1)(a) of the Directive, speaking of *schwerwiegende Beeinträchtigung* (severe harm) to the physical or psychological integrity of a person. This is allowed by Article 7(2) of the Directive, under which Member States may enact stricter measures to protect the confidentiality of mediation. Furthermore, according to section 4(3) of the Mediation Law, the confidentiality obligation does not apply to facts which are obvious or so insignificant that they do not need to be kept secret.

Concerning the effect of mediation on limitation and prescription periods (Article 8 of the Directive), there was no need for a special provision[96] because section 203 BGB generally stipulates that limitation is suspended in the case of negotiations.

The Mediation Law does not distinguish between different subject matters such as family or business disputes. It is therefore relevant for all kinds of mediation regardless of the nature of the dispute, except for mediation conducted by 'conciliation judges'.[97] As to court-related and in-court mediation, the special codes of procedure, such as the Administrative Procedure Code (Verwaltungsgerichtsordnung, VwGO) or the Labour Courts Act (Arbeitsgerichtsgesetz, ArbGG), refer to the ZPO or paraphrase it (*cf* Articles 4–6 and 8 of the Mediation Act).

ii. Private Mediation and the Courts

Similar to negotiation clauses, a claim will be rejected by the court as temporarily inadmissible if a party raises an objection with reference to the mediation clause.[98]

[92] At II.A.ii.

[93] See below III.B.v.

[94] BT-Drucks 17/8058, 21.

[95] Hess, *Europäisches Zivilprozessrecht* (2010) ch 10 para 142.

[96] This view is generally accepted, *cf* Hess, 'Mediation' (2008) F 113; G Wagner, 'Das neue Verjährungsrecht—Ein Segen für die außergerichtliche Streitbeilegung' [2002] *Zeitschrift für Konfliktmanagement* 103.

[97] JP Francken, 'Erforderliche Nachbesserungen im Mediationsgesetz und im Arbeitsgerichtsgesetz' [2012] *Neue Zeitschrift für Arbeitsrecht* 249, 251f; Ahrens, 'Mediation und Güterichter' (2012) 2469f.; see also below III.B.vi.

[98] H Unberath, 'Mediationsklauseln in der Vertragsgestaltung—Prozessuale Wirkungen und Wirksamkeit' [2011] *Neue Juristische Wochenschrift* 1320, 1321f; but see LG Heilbronn, *Immobilien- & Baurecht* 2010, 666.

Procedures to contest the impartiality of a mediator or a provision allowing a state court to replace a mediator or the like do not yet exist. The parties may, however, take the necessary precautions in their mediation agreement. The rules of procedure of a mediation association, to which the parties may refer in their agreement, may stipulate that the association will appoint a mediator if the parties do not come to an agreement after a certain period of time.[99] The rules of procedure may also contain a provision that applies in case a party questions the impartiality of the mediator. Due to the voluntary nature of mediation, the proceedings may in any case be terminated unilaterally.

If the mediator or the mediator's firm has already advised or represented one of the parties in the same matter prior to the commencement of mediation, this violates sections 3(2) and 3(3) of the Mediation Law. In this case, the mediation agreement is void according to section 134 BGB,[100] with the consequence that court action may be commenced directly and other steps are not necessary.

iii. Duties of the Mediator

The duties of the mediator are laid down in the mediation contract between the parties and the mediator as well as in statutory law.

First, the duties stipulated in the Mediation Law apply equally for all mediators. Section 2 of the Mediation Law incorporates several elements of the European Code of Conduct for Mediators[101] and imposes several duties of care on the mediator. The provisions of this section are non-mandatory, and the parties may derogate from them in their mediation contract.[102]

According to section 2(2), mediators have to make sure that the parties have understood the principles and the process of the mediation, and that they participate on a voluntary basis. The impartiality of mediators is stipulated in section 2(3); they have to guarantee that all of the parties are integrated in the mediation process in an appropriate and fair manner. Mediators may hold a caucus with each side upon approval of the parties. If the parties reach a settlement, section 2(6) stipulates that the mediator has to ensure that the parties have full knowledge of the facts and understand the content of the settlement. Furthermore, a mediator shall expressly mention that a party that is not professionally advised may have the agreement reviewed by external advisors. A final agreement may be documented in written form with the consent of the parties.

According to section 3(1) of the Mediation Law, a mediator must disclose to the parties any circumstances which might impede his impartiality and neutrality. When there are such circumstances, he may only carry out the mediation if the parties explicitly state that they do not have any objections. Pursuant to section 3(5), upon

[99] See, eg s 10(2) of the rules of procedure of the Bundesverband Mediation in Wirtschaft und Arbeitswelt, available at <www.bmwa.de/downloads/00verfahrensordnung_08_07.pdf>, or, for a more sophisticated clause, s 4.5 of the DIS Mediation Rules, available at <www.dis-arb.de/en/16/rules/dis-mediation-rules-id31>.

[100] This has not been explicitly decided by German courts, but can be inferred from other judgments of the Federal Court of Justice, *cf* Henssler and Deckenbrock, 'Das neue Mediationsgesetz' (2012) 165.

[101] Legislative materials, BT-Drucks 17/5335, 14. The text of the Code can be found at <ec.europa.eu/civiljustice/adr/adr_ec_code_conduct_en.pdf>.

[102] Risse, 'Das Mediationsgesetz' (2012) 247.

request a mediator has to inform the parties about his professional background as well as his mediation training and experience.

Section 4 of the Mediation Law stipulates that the mediator is bound to confidentiality concerning any information that has become known to him in the course of his duties. The mediator is also required to inform the parties about the scope of his confidentiality obligation.

Secondly, there are duties of professional law, which only apply for members of the respective professional groups. Pursuant to section 18 BORA, a lawyer is still subject to professional rules when acting as an intermediary, conciliator or mediator. Those rules basically include the same duties as imposed on mediators by the Mediation Law and thus reinforce the latter; for example, sections 43a(2) and 2 BORA constitute an obligation of the lawyer to maintain confidentiality. Additionally, lawyers are obliged to prevent a clash of interests, which implies that a mediator may not advise either party after the mediation has taken place.

Notaries acting as mediators are subject to the same duties of confidentiality and impartiality: *cf* sections 14(1)(2) and 18 of the Federal Notary Law (Bundesnotarordnung, BNotO). Beyond these obligations, before the notarisation of a mediation settlement, a notary has to ascertain the will of the parties, clarify the facts and instruct the parties regarding the settlement's legal implications, as stipulated by section 17(1) of the Notarisation Act (Beurkundungsgesetz). Generally speaking, notaries have a greater responsibility to ensure the fairness of the outcome of the mediation (section 14 BNotO).

iv. Enforcement of Duties and Mediators' Liability

If a mediator violates an obligation arising from the mediation agreement, he may be held liable according to general contract law rules (sections 241(2) and 280ff BGB). Notaries acting as mediators are also subject to the liability provision under section 19(1) BNotO. However, in practice, it is generally very difficult for a party to enforce such a claim because a link between the violation of the duty of the mediator and concrete damages is very difficult to prove.

v. Mechanisms Ensuring the Quality of Mediation

One of the major weaknesses of the new Mediation Law is that there is no provision incorporating measures against misconduct of mediators or conditions which may lead to the withdrawal of the accreditation as a certified mediator. Mechanisms ensuring that mediation standards are met usually take effect before a conflict arises: the mediator's certificate may guarantee a certain standard and a 'brand' that parties can follow. In addition, section 5(3) of the Mediation Law requires certified mediators to undergo continuing training programmes to maintain their certificate. Lastly, for economic reasons, mediation organisations will try to ensure high standards in order to maintain their reputation. To sum up, quality is so far ensured by 'soft measures', and the legislature has relied on market forces.

vi. Duties of the Parties

The duties of the parties are not explicitly stipulated by statutory law, and the situation has not changed since the Mediation Law entered into force. The duties of the parties are regulated by the mediation agreement and the rules of procedure of mediation associations, which can be incorporated into the agreement. There is a general duty to cooperate with regard to the mediation process and to negotiate in good faith; this follows from section 242 BGB. According to the principle of *pacta sunt servanda*, both parties are obliged to appoint a mediator, at least to attend the first meeting (and, depending on the situation, a caucus) and to comment on the substance.[103] The parties also have to pay an advance of costs and, where applicable, the fees of a mediation association.[104]

Since mediation is based on the principle of voluntariness, the parties are free to withdraw from mediation at any time and without any justification once the mediation procedure has started.[105] This right has now been codified in section 2(5) of the Mediation Law. The mediation agreement or the rules of procedure may provide for conditions under which a termination of mediation is valid. For example, section 8.1(2) of the DIS Mediation Rules states that mediation may be terminated 'by declaration of one party, provided that at least one mediation meeting or no mediation meeting within two months after confirmation of the mediator took place. The written declaration is addressed to the other party and the mediator.'[106]

It is not quite clear from its wording that the confidentiality obligation of section 4 of the Mediation Law does not apply to the parties themselves. An agreement concerning confidentiality may, however, be included in the mediation agreement or the rules of procedure, as, for example, in section 10.1 DIS Mediation Rules.[107]

The remuneration of mediators is not regulated by law, but is usually agreed between the parties. According to section 34(1) of the Lawyers' Remuneration Law (Rechtsanwaltsvergütungsgesetz, RVG), lawyers acting as mediators shall work towards an agreement concerning fees. If no agreement is reached, civil law rules apply, which means that the usual remuneration is deemed to be agreed upon. In practice, fees amount to €200–600 per hour in commercial disputes and €50–250 per hour for family mediations.[108]

vii. Enforcement of Mediation Agreements

The first draft of the Mediation Act proposed to introduce a new section 796d ZPO, providing for a simple and cost-efficient way to obtain an enforceable mediation settlement.[109] It was intended that notaries and local courts should be able to accept the settlement and declare its enforceability. This provision was entirely deleted during the legislative process.

[103] Unberath,'Mediationsklauseln' (2011) 1322; Tochtermann, 'Mediation' (2013) 549.

[104] Tochtermann, 'Mediation' (2013) 551.

[105] Unberath, 'Mediationsklauseln' (2011) 1322.

[106] German Institution of Arbitration (DIS), 'DIS Mediation Rules (in force as from May 1, 2010)', see <www.dis-arb.de/en/16/rules/dis-mediation-rules-id31>.

[107] Ibid.

[108] Tochtermann, 'Mediation' (2013) 542.

[109] BT-Drucks 17/5335, 7 and 21.

Nevertheless, German law provides for several ways to transform an out-of-court settlement into an enforceable title under sections 794ff ZPO. On the one hand, the settlement may be registered or confirmed before a notary or court, or by a state or state-approved conciliation body. If the notary is involved in the mediation process, the notary may also issue a declaration of enforceability. Settlements reached by judicial mediation are enforceable titles according to section 794(1) ZPO.[110] On the other hand, if lawyers reach a mediation settlement on behalf of the parties, it may be declared enforceable by the civil courts according to section 796a and the following sections of the ZPO.[111] The deletion of the draft section 796d ZPO thus serves the interests of lawyers.[112] However, the German Federal Bar (Bundesrechtsanwaltskammer) has rightly pointed out that there is no obligation for non-lawyer mediators to take out professional liability insurance. Consumers would thus not be protected in the event of problems.[113] It is nonetheless regrettable that the legislature did not take up the proposals in legal literature to streamline and simplify the existing legal framework.[114]

viii. Court-based Mediation Programmes

With the revision of the ZPO, which entered into force in 2002,[115] one of the intents of the legislature was to improve settlements by judges. Section 278(2) ZPO as amended, which is modelled on section 54 ArbGG, provides for a 'mandatory conciliation hearing', stipulating that the courts have to attempt a settlement between the parties before the beginning of the hearing.[116] While the new provision was criticised

[110] S 794 ZPO reads as follows (translation provided by Samson Übersetzungen GmbH, Dr Carmen von Schöning, available at <www.gesetze-im-internet.de/englisch_zpo/index.html>): 'Compulsory enforcement may furthermore be pursued: 1. Based on settlements concluded by the parties, or between one of the parties and a third party, in order to resolve the legal dispute either in its full scope or as regards a part of the subject matter of the litigation, before a German court or before a dispute-resolution entity established or recognised by the Land department of justice (Landesjustizverwaltung), as well as based on settlements that have been recorded pursuant to s 118(1) third sentence or s 492(3) for the record of the judge; . . .'

[111] S 796a ZPO reads as follows (translation provided by Samson Übersetzungen GmbH, Dr Carmen von Schöning, available at <www.gesetze-im-internet.de/englisch_zpo/index.html>):

> (1) A settlement reached by attorneys on behalf of the parties they represent, upon having been correspondingly authorised, shall be declared enforceable, upon corresponding application being made by a party, if the debtor has subjected himself in such settlement to immediate compulsory enforcement and the settlement has been deposited, specifying the date on which it was reached, with a local court in the district of which one of the parties had its general venue at the time the settlement was reached.
> (2) Sub-s (1) shall not apply should the settlement be directed at the issuance of a declaration of intent or should it concern the existence of a tenancy relationship for residential premises.
> (3) The declaration of enforceability shall be refused to be issued if the settlement is invalid or if its recognition would violate public order.

[112] Ahrens, 'Mediation und Güterichter' (2012) 2468. However, it would be incorrect to say that a lawyer-mediator is in a far better position than a mediator with a non-legal background, eg a psychologist. According to its wording, s 796a ZPO requires both parties to be represented by an attorney. But see Henssler and Deckenbrock, 'Das neue Mediationsgesetz' (2012) 167.

[113] Bundesrechtsanwaltskammer, 'Stellungnahme der Bundesrechtsanwaltskammer zum Referentenentwurf eines Gesetzes zur Förderung der Mediation und anderer Verfahren der außergerichtlichen Konfliktbeilegung BRAK-Stellungnahme 27/2010' (October 2010), available at <www.brak.de/w/files/stellungnahmen/Stn27-2010.pdf>, 19f. For other disadvantages of the proposal, see Greger, 'Reglementierung' (2010) 210.

[114] Hess, 'Mediation' (2008) para 165.

[115] Gesetz zur Reform des Zivilprozesses as of 27 July 2001, Bundesgesetzblatt 2001, part I, p 1887.

[116] S 278(2) ZPO reads as follows (translation provided by Samson Übersetzungen GmbH, Dr Carmen von Schöning, available at <www.gesetze-im-internet.de/englisch_zpo/index.html>): 'For the purposes of

by legal scholars as being too formal, unnecessary and unsuited for civil litigation, judges at the regional court (Landgericht) of Göttingen (in Lower Saxony) developed a new approach to settlement.[117] Influenced by the ADR movement that had reached Germany in the mid-1990s, the judges studied and applied the techniques and tools of mediation at the conciliation hearings in their court.[118] For the implementation of mediation in the German civil process, they adapted the new statutory provisions to their needs,[119] the most important step being the introduction of a 'mediation judge'. With the parties' consent, a case could be transferred to another judge of the same court, who would immediately hold a hearing using mediation techniques. Once a settlement was reached, the judge originally competent to make the decision on the merits of the case registered the settlement in the protocol. If the mediation was not successful, the case was quickly decided on the merits by the competent judge. The new procedure proved to be very successful: about 30 per cent of all cases were sent to the mediation judges, the rate of amicable settlements in these cases being about 88.5 per cent. Accordingly, the number of amicable settlements at the regional court rose from one-third to one-half of all cases.[120]

In Bavaria, the Ministry of Justice initiated a similar project in 2005–07 at courts including the Regional Courts of Augsburg and Nuremberg. However, in order to avoid any conflict with the bar, the judges were not called mediation judges, but *Güterichter* (conciliation judges).[121] This model was not as successful as the model in Göttingen, but the settlement rates were equally improved. However, the judges involved disapproved of the term *Güterichter,*[122] preferring to call themselves *Richtermediatoren* (mediation judges) on their court websites.[123]

From 2003 to 2010, the mediation movement within the German judiciary gained considerable ground. The pilot projects were regarded as successful and several federal states (Hamburg, Schleswig-Holstein, Berlin, Mecklenburg-West Pomerania and Rhineland-Palatinate) adopted specific judicial mediation programmes. In 2008, there were almost 140 mediation judges at more than 30 regional courts and higher regional

arriving at an amicable resolution of the legal dispute, the hearing shall be preceded by a conciliation hearing unless efforts to come to an agreement have already been made before an out-of-court dispute-resolution entity, or unless the conciliation hearing obviously does not hold out any prospects of success. In the conciliation hearing, the court is to discuss with the parties the circumstances and facts as well as the status of the dispute thus far, assessing all circumstances without any restrictions and asking questions wherever required. The parties appearing are to be heard in person on these aspects.'

[117] It should be noted that the local bar fully supported the project, see G Spindler, 'Gerichtsinterne Mediation in Niedersachsen' [2007] *Zeitschrift für Konfliktmanagement* 79. In Lower Saxony and other federal states, particularly in Bavaria, pilot projects were also supported by the State Ministries of Justice (at least in the initial stage), see below.

[118] Due to lack of public resources and sufficient support from their ministries, many judges paid for professional mediation training themselves, Tochtermann, 'Mediation' (2013) 533.

[119] Accordingly, the legality of the pilot project was disputed in legal literature, see (for a critical assessment) H Prütting, 'Ein Plädoyer gegen Gerichtsmediation' (2011) 124 *Zeitschrift für Zivilprozess* 163; against Hess, 'Perspektiven' (2011) 137–62.

[120] Recent surveys report settlement rates of about 80%.

[121] This term was created in the face of severe criticism from the bar, which considered mediation a genuine part of private dispute resolution, outside of the court system. According to these critics, mediation is merely a task for lawyers and other experts operating in the private sector.

[122] The new—but inelegant—expression of the German language was created by the Bavarian Ministry of Justice for obviously political reasons in order to avoid any similarity with mediation.

[123] See, eg <www.justiz.bayern.de/imperia/md/content/stmj_internet/gerichte/amtsgerichte/wolfratshausen/familie/infoblatt_mediation.pdf> or <www.vgh.bayern.de/mediation.htm> for an administrative court.

courts in 8 of 16 federal states (25 per cent of all regional courts).[124] Many courts adopted similar proceedings—the expansion often took place without the involvement of the competent Ministries of Justice, but mainly on the initiative of the judges involved. A genuine 'mediation movement' grew within the judiciary: judges trained other judges in mediation techniques, and courts used the facilities of the internet to promote local mediation proceedings. As a result, 'local rules on mediation' were developed at the local and regional levels, sometimes promoted by the Ministries of Justice and sometimes regarded with much suspicion.[125]

As has been stated previously, judicial mediation had been a very controversial issue during the legislative process of the Mediation Act. Federal states with judicial mediation programmes proposed to include judicial mediation in the ZPO, while lawyers' associations, the bar and some federal states (like Baden-Württemberg) recommended that the new Act should strictly promote private mediation. Basically, court mediation was contested because of its success. Many private mediators, most of them lawyers, as well as the professional organisations of lawyers and mediators, claimed that judicial mediation was an unfair intrusion in an area of private dispute resolution because judicial mediation—as part of the court proceedings—was free of additional costs.

The first draft by the Federal Ministry of Justice tried to avoid this conflict by a provision authorising the federal states to provide for judicial mediation in their respective jurisdictions. The Committee on Legal Affairs of the Bundestag—a board almost completely dominated by lawyers—then proposed to amend the bill by legalising the Bavarian conciliation judge concept in an enhanced form.[126] In the proposal, dispute resolution by conciliation judges was considered a distinct procedure—although it was stated that mediation could be used as one tool amongst others. The proposal was adopted by the Bundestag in December 2011. However, the bill was stopped by the Bundesrat in January 2012. The Bundestag/Bundesrat mediation committee (*Vermittlungsausschuss*) finally agreed on a compromise by mediating the dispute over the Mediation Act: although the title of conciliation judge (*Güterichter*) was maintained, the amendment of the ZPO expressly states that such judges may use mediation as a technique.[127] This is a very positive outcome. Since mediation forms part of the ZPO, conciliation judges must respect mandatory procedural guarantees.[128] On the other hand, all federal states are obliged to provide for settlement judges in their courts—a comprehensive and uniform regime was set up in the area of judicial mediation. A judge is not precluded from carrying out a complete mediation procedure as he may independently choose the dispute resolution method.[129] Finally, it remains to be seen whether the judges will use the legal expression *Güterichter*.[130] It seems possible that

[124] Hess, 'Perspektiven' (2011) 141f.

[125] After a change of the government, the pilot project in Lower Saxony faced considerable problems as the new government regarded mediation as a matter for lawyers and not for judges.

[126] BT-Drucks 17/8058, 17.

[127] The new provision of s 278(5) ZPO reads as follows (translation by the authors): 'The court may refer the parties to the dispute to a designated judge who is not competent to make a decision (conciliation judge) for the conciliation hearing and additional conciliation attempts. The conciliation judge may use all methods of dispute resolution including mediation.'

[128] See also Ahrens, 'Mediation und Güterichter' (2012) 2469.

[129] Ibid; against E Carl, 'Vom richterlichen Mediator zum Güterichter' [2012] *Zeitschrift für Konfliktmanagement* 16, 19.

[130] But see s 9 of the Mediation Law, which allows judges to maintain the terminology of *gerichtlicher Mediator* (court mediator) only until 1 August 2013. It remains to be seen whether the courts will strictly apply this provision.

conciliation judges practicing mediation will continue to call themselves *Richtermediatoren* (mediator judges), just as was the case on Bavarian court websites.

C. Conciliation

German law does not strictly distinguish conciliation from mediation. In procedures according to section 15a EGZPO, the 'conciliator' may use mediation techniques as well. The same also applies, since the revision of section 278(5) ZPO, for the *Güterichter*, who, according to the revised wording, may use mediation as a dispute resolution method.

Concerning private mediation, there is some disagreement as to whether mediators can make their own proposals to solve disputes upon request by the parties.[131] These problems arise because the negotiation style is different if the parties have to convince the conciliator instead of the other party. Another problem occurs if the mediator has conducted caucuses with the parties and has gained special knowledge that one party does not have.

i. Legal Framework

A distinction must be made between the conciliation laws of the federal states and private conciliation agreements. The conciliation laws form part of procedural law. The procedural rules of the conciliation bodies established on the basis of these laws can also be qualified as procedural, as their legal basis is the respective conciliation law.

Concerning private conciliation, the legal situation is very similar to private mediation. It is generally accepted that the legal nature of a contractual agreement depends on its legal effects,[132] which might differ for every separate clause.[133] The currently prevailing opinion is that the main focus of a mediation or conciliation agreement is of a substantive nature and only those clauses concerning the relationship of ADR and state courts are of a procedural nature. The starting premise of these approaches is that procedural law only regulates the legal relations of the parties in proceedings before a state court (or another person with decision-making authority).[134] However, things can also be seen from a different perspective: the parties agree on a procedure designed for the reasonable conciliation of interests when a dispute arises. The mediation and conciliation rules which are often incorporated into ADR agreements provide for detailed procedural requirements. In addition, procedural law guarantees the parties' autonomy during the proceedings and helps to find the right solution on

[131] Risse and Wagner, 'Mediation im Wirtschaftsrecht' (2009) ch 23 para 93.

[132] See G Wagner, *Prozeßverträge: Privatautonomie im Verfahrensrecht* (Tübingen, Mohr Siebeck, 1998) 33ff.

[133] Ibid 39ff; Eidenmüller, 'Grundfragen der Mediation' (2001) 52ff.

[134] Wagner, *Prozeßverträge* (1998) 13; W Henckel, *Prozessrecht und materielles Recht* (Göttingen, Schwartz, 1970) 21, 24f.

the basis of sufficient but autonomously determined fact-finding.[135] Therefore, ADR contracts mainly contain procedural agreements.[136]

The applicability of procedural safeguards differs from case to case. Compared to mediation, conciliation is more similar to the three-pole dispute resolution model of state court adjudication. Procedural guarantees are thus more likely to be applicable in the case of conciliation. Moreover, the safeguard provisions of material law (eg concerning standard clauses) may also be applicable.[137]

Neither the UNCITRAL Model Law nor the Commission Recommendation has been formally transposed into German law.

ii. Duties of the Conciliator

Some conciliation laws impose duties of impartiality, independence and confidentiality on the parties, eg section 6 of the Conciliation Law (Schlichtungsgesetz) of Baden-Württemberg or section 8 of the Conciliation Law of Schleswig-Holstein. In addition, conciliation rules issued by the conciliation bodies on the basis of the conciliation laws may also provide for obligations of the conciliator.

If lawyers act as conciliators, their professional rules also apply.[138]

Lastly, conciliation contracts and incorporated conciliation rules of organisations such as the Chambers of Industry and Commerce (*Industrie- und Handelskammern*) often include duties of conciliators. A conciliator who violates any of these obligations may be held liable under contract law.

iii. Fields of Conciliation

Apart from labour law conflicts, where conciliation has a long-standing tradition, and subject matters covered by compulsory conciliation, conciliation can be applied in a variety of fields, such as commerce, construction, medical malpractice, legal advice, energy, transport and tourism. There are special conciliation bodies, mostly organised by professional bodies and the guilds of different crafts, which apply their own conciliation rules.[139] As described previously,[140] ombudsman schemes have increasingly been set up to deal with consumer complaints. As the outcome of these proceedings is binding for the non-consumer party, an ombudsman procedure does not fall within the concept of conciliation as defined in the glossary but, rather, is similar to arbitration.[141] The situation in Germany is highly diversified, especially in the field of consumer ADR, and this makes generalisations difficult.[142]

[135] G Hager, *Konflikt und Konsens: Überlegungen zu Sinn, Erscheinung und Ordnung der alternativen Streitschlichtung* (Tübingen, Mohr Siebeck, 2001) 84.

[136] Hess, 'Rechtsgrundlagen der Mediation' (2009) ch 43 paras 22–24; Hess, 'Mediation' (2008) F 26f.

[137] Hess, 'Rechtsgrundlagen der Mediation' (2009) ch 43 para 24.

[138] See above III.B.iii.

[139] See, eg the Arbitration and Conciliation Rules for Disputes in the Construction Industry: (Arbeitsgemeinschaft für privates Bau- und Architektenrecht im Deutschen Anwalt Verein—ARGE Baurecht), 'Schlichtungs- und Schiedsordnung für Baustreitigkeiten—SOBau)', available at <www.arge-bauschlichtung.de/sobau.doc>.

[140] Above I.A.

[141] Hess, 'Mediation' (2008) F 31; *cf* K Süß, *Streitbeilegungsmechanismen im Verbraucherrecht unter besonderer Berücksichtigung der australischen Rechtsordnung* (Frankfurt am Main, Lang, 2011) 196ff.

[142] I Benöhr, C Hodges and N Creutzfeldt-Banda, 'Germany' in I Benöhr, C Hodges and N Creutzfeldt-Banda, *Consumer ADR in Europe* (Oxford, Hart, 2012) 89.

D. Expert opinion

i. Legal Nature

The legal nature of (binding) expert opinions is highly controversial. While the Bundesgerichtshof has ruled that sections 317–19 BGB are applicable, some authors argue that provisions of procedural law, particularly those governing arbitration, are the only applicable provisions[143] and some argue that they may be applicable in addition.[144] The opinion of the Bundesgerichtshof implies that the nature of expert opinions is purely substantive.[145] However, from a theoretical perspective, non-binding and binding expert opinions cannot be precisely differentiated.[146] If the fact finding of the expert is to be legally binding, this outcome also has procedural effects (eg on the evaluation of evidence).[147] Consequently, both procedural safeguards and sections 1025ff ZPO should be applicable. However, some provisions on arbitration do not match with expert opinions, such as section 1031 ZPO concerning the form of an arbitration agreement.[148]

Non-binding expert opinions are not regulated and the parties are free to design ADR instruments as they wish. Therefore, non-binding expert opinions are permitted by German law.[149] Non-binding expert opinions can be reasonable as they still have a de facto binding effect.[150] It seems advisable not to treat non-binding expert opinions any differently than other ADR procedures. Procedural guarantees should therefore also be applicable.

ii. Duties of the Expert

The duty of the expert to render his opinion may be enforced if the expert has contractually agreed to do so. According to prevailing opinion, a court may render a decision instead of the expert upon request of a party if the parties have agreed that the expert may exercise equitable discretion and the expert does not render his decision in time, as is stipulated in section 319(1)(2) BGB. According to section 319(1)(1) BGB, the parties are not bound by a decision that is obviously unfair.

As has been said above, the expert is also bound by rules of procedural fairness. The application of section 1036 ZPO entails that the expert has to be independent

[143] See P Schlosser in Stein and Jonas, *Kommentar zur Zivilprozessordnung*, 22nd edn (Tübingen, Mohr Siebeck, 2002) preliminary notes to s 1025 comments 22ff, especially 32.

[144] See, eg Würdinger in *Münchener Kommentar zum Bürgerlichen Gesetzbuch* s 317 comment 41.

[145] V Rieble in Staudinger, *Kommentar zum Bürgerlichen Gesetzbuch, §§ 315–326, Leistungsstörungsrecht 2*, rev edn (Berlin, de Gruyter, 2009) s 317 comment 22.

[146] Schlosser in Stein and Jonas, *Kommentar zur Zivilprozessordnung* preliminary notes to 1025 comment 32.

[147] Würdinger in *Münchener Kommentar zum Bürgerlichen Gesetzbuch* s 317 comment 41.

[148] This provision cannot reasonably fulfil its warning function as far as expert opinions are concerned. See Schlosser in Stein and Jonas, *Kommentar zur Zivilprozessordnung* preliminary notes to s 1025 comment 33.

[149] Stubbe, 'Schiedsgutachten' (2006) 153.

[150] Ibid, 153f; R Greger and C Stubbe, *Schiedsgutachten: Außergerichtliche Streitbeilegung durch Drittentscheidungen* (Munich, Beck, 2007) 20ff.

and impartial.[151] The procedural rules of professional associations, such as the DIS, also stipulate obligations of equal treatment and respecting the right to be heard.[152]

iii. Fields of Expert Opinions

Expert opinions are most commonly used in the areas of engineering and construction. Recently, professional associations in this field have adopted specific rules on temporarily binding expert opinions (*Adjudikation*), which were largely inspired by the adjudication process in England.[153]

E. Arbitration

i. The Impact of the UNCITRAL Model Law on International Commercial Arbitration

Book 10 of the Code of Civil Procedure has been closely modelled on the UNCITRAL Model Law on International Commercial Arbitration.

ii. Procedural Standards

According to section 1042 ZPO, the parties have to be treated equally; each party has the right to be heard. The parties must be allowed representation by lawyers. The procedural rules may be determined by the parties themselves (they may refer to existing arbitration rules), subject to a few mandatory provisions stipulated in book 10 of the ZPO. If the rules have not been determined by the parties, they shall be determined by the arbitral tribunal at its discretion. As far as the taking of evidence is concerned, the arbitral tribunal is equally bound by fundamental rule-of-law principles.[154]

The claimant has to present his claim and the facts on which this claim is based, and the defendant has to state his position in this regard within the period determined by the parties or by the arbitral tribunal (section 1046(1) ZPO). Furthermore, according to section 1047(1) ZPO, the arbitral tribunal is free to decide if oral hearings shall be scheduled or if the proceedings are to be implemented on the basis of documents and other records, unless the parties have agreed otherwise.

iii. Mandatory Law

Mandatory procedural guarantees may not be abrogated. Pursuant to section 1059(2)

[151] Schlosser in Stein and Jonas, *Kommentar zur Zivilprozessordnung* preliminary notes to s 1025 comment 34.

[152] See, eg s 16 of the DIS Rules on Expert Determination: German Institution of Arbitration (DIS), 'DIS Rules on Expert Determination (in force as from May 1, 2010)', available at <www.dis-arb.de/de/16/regeln/dis-rules-on-expert-determination-id28>.

[153] C Stubbe, 'DIS-Schiedsgutachtensordnung (DIS-SchGO) und DIS-Gutachtensordnung (DIS-GO)' [2006] *German Arbitration Journal (SchiedsVZ)* 130. See further German Institution of Arbitration (DIS), 'DIS Adjudication Rules (in force as from July 1, 2010)', available at <www.dis-arb.de/de/16/regeln/dis-rules-on-adjudication-id30>.

[154] Schlosser in Stein and Jonas, *Kommentar zur Zivilprozessordnung* s 1042 comment 9.

(1)(d) ZPO, an arbitration award may be reversed if the arbitration proceedings violated a mandatory procedural provision and it is to be assumed that this has had an effect on the arbitration award.[155]

iv. Enforcement of Arbitral Awards

In order to be enforced, an arbitral award has to be declared enforceable before a court. The law distinguishes between domestic and foreign arbitral awards, depending on the venue of the arbitration proceedings (section 1043 ZPO). Domestic arbitral awards have to be declared enforceable if none of the grounds for reversal designated in section 1059(2) ZPO are given, while the enforceability of foreign arbitral awards depends on the requirements of Article V of the New York Convention. However, the differences are marginal, since section 1059(2) ZPO is largely modelled after Article V of the New York Convention. Pursuant to section 1062(1)(4) ZPO, the Higher Regional Court (Oberlandesgericht) has competence for the declaration of enforceability. Section 1063(1) ZPO stipulates that the opponent is to be heard prior to the decision. According to section 1065(1) ZPO, there is an appellate remedy for the decision of the court (complaint on points of law—*Rechtsbeschwerde*).

An arbitral tribunal is not authorised to take certain actions, such as taking evidence, that are reserved for judges. According to section 1050 ZPO, a court may provide support on request of the arbitral tribunal or, with the consent of the arbitral tribunal, upon request of a party. In this case, the procedural rules of the court apply, and the arbitral judges may attend the court hearing at which evidence is taken and may ask questions. For these measures, the local court (Amtsgericht) in the district of which the action is to be taken is the competent court (section 1062(4) ZPO).

According to section 1041(2) ZPO, a court may permit the enforcement of a measure of temporary relief that has been directed by the arbitral tribunal. It may reverse or modify the order later upon request of a party. The competent court for these measures is the Higher Regional Court (Oberlandesgericht), section 1062(1)(3) ZPO.

IV. POLICY RECOMMENDATIONS

As ADR is a very diverse and experimental area of dispute resolution, only minimum standards should be regulated. ADR must be considered a principally self-regulated area of law. Intervention by legislation should be limited to the interfaces with litigation (eg confidentiality) and enforcement. Intervention might also be necessary to protect weaker parties, and to monitor the quality and the self-regulation of the profession.

It is thus ambiguous whether regulation should be limited to providing a legal framework for particular ADR procedures. On the one hand, there is a need for

[155] There is a dilemma in international cases because Art V(1)(d) of the New York Convention stipulates that recognition and enforcement of an award may be refused if the arbitral procedure was not in accordance with the agreement of the parties, even if mandatory provisions were abrogated in this agreement. See Schlosser in Stein and Jonas, *Kommentar zur Zivilprozessordnung* s 1042 comment 3.

transparency, which may be achieved by a legal framework; on the other hand, private autonomy has to be respected. Legislators have to keep both sides of the coin in mind.

The state could intervene either by merely actively supporting ADR as an alternative or by offering such procedures as part of the state civil justice system; both approaches appear to have merit.

As far as mandatory ADR is concerned, experience has shown that this experiment was not successful in Germany,[156] especially concerning the undifferentiated approach towards small claims. Nevertheless, compulsory conciliation has been relatively successful in neighbour and libel disputes.[157] Here, greater regard has been paid to the 'mediability' of the subject matter. However, the best solution is still the targeted application of mediation on a case-to-case basis in court-annexed or in-court mediation.[158]

BIBLIOGRAPHY

Ahrens, M, 'Mediation und Güterichter—Neue Regelungen der gerichtlichen und außergerichtlichen Mediation' [2012] *Neue Juristische Wochenschrift* 2465

Benöhr, I, Hodges, C and Creutzfeldt-Banda, N, 'Germany' in I Benöhr, C Hodges and N Creutzfeldt-Banda, *Consumer ADR in Europe* (Oxford, Hart, 2012) 73–115

Berger, KP, 'Rechtsprobleme von Eskalationsklauseln' in B Bachmann, S Breidenbach et al (eds), *Grenzüberschreitungen: Beiträge zum Internationalen Verfahrensrecht und zur Schiedsgerichtsbarkeit, Festschrift für Peter Schlosser zum 70. Geburtstag* (Bielefeld, Gieseking 2001) 18–35

Carl, E, 'Vom richterlichen Mediator zum Güterichter' [2012] *Zeitschrift für Konfliktmanagement* 16

'Deutsche Institution für Schiedsgerichtsbarkeit eV (DIS)' [2003] *German Arbitration Journal (SchiedsVZ)* 178

Eidenmüller, H, 'Vertrags- und verfahrensrechtliche Grundfragen der Mediation: Möglichkeiten und Grenzen privatautonomen Konfliktmanagements' in S Breidenbach (ed), *Konsensuale Streitbeilegung: Akademisches Symposion zu Ehren von Peter F. Schlosser aus Anlass seines 65. Geburtstages* (Bielefeld, Gieseking, 2001) 45–100

Francken, JP, 'Erforderliche Nachbesserungen im Mediationsgesetz und im Arbeitsgerichtsgesetz' [2012] *Neue Zeitschrift für Arbeitsrecht* 249

Gottwald, W, 'Staatliche Maßnahmen zur Förderung der außergerichtlichen Mediation—empfiehlt sich eine "verordnete" Mediation?' [2007] *Aktuelle Juristische Praxis* 611

Greger, R, 'Die Reglementierung der Selbstregulierung: Zum Referentenentwurf eines Mediationsgesetzes' [2010] *Zeitschrift für Rechtspolitik* 209

Greger, R and Stubbe, C, *Schiedsgutachten: Außergerichtliche Streitbeilegung durch Drittentscheidungen* (Munich, Beck, 2007)

Hacke, A, *Der ADR Vertrag: Vertragsrecht und vertragliche Gestaltung der Mediation und anderer alternativer Konfliktlösungsverfahren* (Heidelberg, Verlag Recht und Wirtschaft, 2010)

Hager, G, *Konflikt und Konsens: Überlegungen zu Sinn, Erscheinung und Ordnung der alternativen Streitschlichtung* (Tübingen, Mohr Siebeck, 2001)

[156] See above II.C.i.

[157] Hess, 'Mediation' (2008) F 133f; W Gottwald, 'Staatliche Maßnahmen zur Förderung der außergerichtlichen Mediation—empfiehlt sich eine "verordnete" Mediation?' (2007) *Aktuelle Juristische Praxis* 611, 613.

[158] Hess, 'Mediation' (2008) F 134.

Henckel, W, *Prozessrecht und materielles Recht* (Göttingen, Schwartz, 1970)

Henssler, M and Deckenbrock, C, 'Das neue Mediationsgesetz: Mediation ist und bleibt Anwaltssache!' [2012] *Der Betrieb* 159

Hess, B, 'Mediation und weitere Verfahren konsensualer Streitbeilegung—Regelungsbedarf im Verfahrens- und Berufsrecht?' in *Verhandlungen des 67. Deutschen Juristentages Erfurt 2008* (Munich, Beck, 2008) vol 1 part F

Hess, B, 'Rechtsgrundlagen der Mediation' in F Haft and K Gräfin von Schlieffen (eds), *Handbuch Mediation*, 2nd edn (Munich, Beck, 2009) 1053–86

Hess, B, *Europäisches Zivilprozessrecht* (Heidelberg, Müller, 2010)

Hess, B, 'Perspektiven der gerichtsinternen Mediation in Deutschland' (2011) 124 *Zeitschrift für Zivilprozess* 137

Hess, B, 'Mediation Judges in Germany: Mutual Interference of EU Standards and National Developments' in CH van Rhee (ed), *Essays on the Role of Judges and Parties in China and Europe* (Dordrecht, Springer, forthcoming).

Hopt, K and Steffek, F (eds), *Mediation: Rechtstatsachen, Rechtsvergleich, Regelungen* (Tübingen, Mohr Siebeck, 2008)

Kirchhoff, S, 'Ein kleiner Schritt für den Gesetzgeber, aber ein großer für die Mediation?—Entstehung und Hintergründe des Nds. Mediations- und Gütestellengesetzes' (2007) *Zeitschrift für Konfliktmanagement* 138

Leiss, M, 'Empirische Erkenntnisse zur Mediation im Wirtschaftsrecht' (2007) *German Arbitration Journal (SchiedsVZ)* 139

Nelle, A, *Neuverhandlungspflichten: Neuverhandlungen zur Vertragsanpassung und Vertragsergänzung als Gegenstand von Pflichten und Obliegenheiten* (München, Beck, 1994)

Political groups of CDU, SPD, FDP, Bündnis 90/Die Grünen and SSW, 'Antrag der Fraktionen von CDU, SPD, FDP, Bündnis 90/Die Grünen und des SSW, Zukunft der gerichtsinternen Mediation sichern' Schleswig-Holsteinischer Landtag Drucks 17/2276

Prütting, H, 'Ein Plädoyer gegen Gerichtsmediation' (2011) 124 *Zeitschrift für Zivilprozess* 163

Risse, J, 'Das Mediationsgesetz—eine Kommentierung' [2012] *German Arbitration Journal (SchiedsVZ)* 244

Risse, J, 'Mediator' in M Hies (ed), *Perspektiven für Juristen 2013* (Munich), e-fellows.net, 2012)

Risse, J and Wagner, C, 'Mediation im Wirtschaftsrecht' in F Haft and K Gräfin von Schlieffen (eds), *Handbuch Mediation*, 2nd edn (Munich, Beck, 2009) 553–87

Saecker, FJ and Rixecker, R (eds), *Münchener Kommentar zum Bürgerlichen Gesetzbuch*, 6th edn (Munich, Beck, 2012)

von Schubert, M, 'Die Mediationsklausel/Mediationsvereinbarung' in KJ Schiffer (ed), *Mandatspraxis, Schiedsverfahren und Mediation: Übersichten, Bewertungshilfen, Checklisten, Praxishinweise, Schiedsordnungen, Muster*, 2nd edn (Cologne, Heymann, 2005) 269–73

Spindler, G, 'Gerichtsinterne Mediation in Niedersachsen' [2007] *Zeitschrift für Konfliktmanagement*, 79

Staudinger, *Kommentar zum Bürgerlichen Gesetzbuch, §§ 315–326, Leistungsstörungsrecht*, 2nd, rev edn (Berlin, de Gruyter, 2009)

Stein and Jonas, *Kommentar zur Zivilprozessordnung*, 22nd edn (Tübingen, Mohr Siebeck, 2002)

Stubbe, C, 'DIS-Schiedsgutachtensordnung (DIS-SchGO) und DIS-Gutachtensordnung (DIS-GO)' [2006] *German Arbitration Journal (SchiedsVZ)* 130

Stubbe, C, 'Schiedsgutachten als modernes ADR Instrument' [2006] *German Arbitration Journal (SchiedsVZ)* 150

Süß, K, *Streitbeilegungsmechanismen im Verbraucherrecht unter besonderer Berücksichtigung der australischen Rechtsordnung* (Frankfurt am Main, Lang, 2011)

Tochtermann, P, 'Mediation in Germany' in KJ Hopt and F Steffek (eds), *Mediation: Principles and Regulation in Comparative Perspective* (Oxford, Oxford University Press, 2013) 521–84

Unberath, H, 'Mediationsklauseln in der Vertragsgestaltung—Prozessuale Wirkungen und Wirksamkeit' [2011] *Neue Juristische Wochenschrift* 1320

Wagner, G, *Prozeßverträge: Privatautonomie im Verfahrensrecht* (Tübingen, Mohr Siebeck, 1998)

Wagner, G, 'Das neue Verjährungsrecht—Ein Segen für die außergerichtliche Streitbeilegung' [2002] *Zeitschrift für Konfliktmanagement* 103

Wagner, G, 'Grundstrukturen eines deutschen Mediationsgesetzes' (2010) 74 *Rabel Journal of Comparative and International Private Law (RabelsZ)* 794

Walter, H, 'Der Güterichter nach dem Mediationsgesetz—echte Mediation oder richterliche Schlichtung?' (2012) 45 *Spektrum der Mediation* 60

Wimmer, R and Wimmer, U, 'Verfassungsrechtliche Aspekte richterlicher Mediation' [2007] *Neue Juristische Wochenschrift* 3243

10

Regulation of Dispute Resolution in Italy: The Bumps in the Road to Successful ADR

GIUSEPPE DE PALO AND ASHLEY E OLESON

I. CHARACTERISTICS OF ADR[1]

A. Dispute Resolution Procedures Most Commonly Deployed in Italy

PRIOR TO 2011, the vast majority of cases in Italy were litigated in courts.[2] Starting in March 2011, in response to Italian Legislative Decree No 28 of March 2010 (Legislative Decree 28/2010), cases being resolved by alternative dispute resolution methods were on the rise. Legislative Decree 28/2010, specifically, enacted mandatory pre-trial mediation for many civil and commercial cases. However, in December 2012 the Italian Constitutional Court sent down a decision condemning Article 5(1) of Legislative Decree 28/2010, which described the provisions for mandatory mediation.[3] While much of Legislative Decree 28/2010 was left intact, the removal of Article 5(1) and various relative provisions throughout the decree has resulted in a sharp decline in the utilisation of mediation, which was quickly becoming the front runner of ADR options in Italy.

The Ministry of Justice (MoJ) found in its 2012 report that in 2010 there were 1,205,089 cases filed in the courts of first instance.[4] This reflects an average of 100,424 cases filed per month. In just the first month in which mandatory mediation was in effect (March 2011), a report from the Italian MoJ stated that 5,070 cases were submitted to mediation proceedings. Of those, 55 per cent were mandatory, 40 per cent were voluntary and 4 per cent were by judicial referral. In a MoJ study which analysed data for the period between the 1950s and 2011, it was shown that between 2010 and mid-2011 there were 102,179 fewer filings in the courts of first instance. Further-

[1] The authors graciously thank Atty Francesco Paolo Franza for his research assistance, as well Atty Chiara Massidda for her kind support in reviewing the chapter.

[2] On Friday, 9 August 2013, the Italian Parliament finally 'converted into law' the new mediation rules approved by the Government with the Law Decree 69 of 21 June 2013. After publication in the Italian Official Gazette, the parliamentary act containing the new mediation rules is expected to come into effect around mid-September 2013. Parliamentary approval of the mediation rules, including the controversial mandatory mediation requirement, resolves the constitutionality issue that led to the quashing of the mediation rules contained in Legislative Decree 28/2010 and, as a consequence, to the virtual cessation of mediation in Italy, as described in this chapter. The new rules essentially confirm the regulatory framework introduced with Legislative Decree 28/2010 with some significant changes, the most important of which are listed below. First, the mediation mandate is limited to a four-year trial period that ends September 2017. A mid-term review is to be conducted by the Minister of Justice by September 2015. Second, car accident disputes are exempted from mandatory mediation. Third, parties must be assisted by counsel in mediation. Last, judges are granted the power, at any stage in the dispute, to order the parties to mediation, not just to invite them. The 21 June 2013 version of the mediation rules did not include the four-year time limit, nor the need for mediating parties to be assisted by counsel. These changes were vigorously advocated by a sector of the Italian bar during the process of converting the Government decree into law, and the Parliament eventually accepted these changes. Based on the first official declarations, the Italian bar appears generally very satisfied with the new framework for mediation. In light of this, commentators predict that Italy is now set to witness an even bigger 'mediation explosion' than before, and this time a more stable one. As a related consequence, some predict that the Italian mediation model might inspire a number of other EU countries where, after many years of attempts to promote mediation, the process is used only occasionally. However, the regulatory history of mediation in Italy is far from finished. For instance, the legal requirement to be assisted by counsel in mediation runs contrary to Art 8(b) EU Directive on Consumer ADR (Directive 2013/11/EU of the European Parliament and of the Council of 21 May 2013 on alternative dispute resolution for consumer disputes and amending Regulation (EC) No 2006/2004 and Directive 2009/22/EC).

[3] Italian Constitutional Court, Judgment 272, 6 December 2012.

[4] Ministerio della Giustizia, 'Strumenti: Statische', see <www.giustizia.it/giustizia/it/mg_1_14_1.wp?facetNode_1=1_5_0&previsiousPage=mg_1_14&contentId=SST734820>.

more, between March 2011 and June 2012 there were 143,324 mediation filings.[5] All of this data indicates that the provisions contained in Legislative Decree 28/2010 were having positive effects, not just by increasing mediation filings, but by also reducing the burden on the court system.

A study presenting national data on arbitration found that both the number of arbitration cases and value of the cases settled have increased over the past few years.[6] The majority of these cases are conducted by the chambers of commerce based in Italian cities. However, statistics from the Camera Arbitrale Milano (CAM)—a large arbitration provider affiliated with the Chambers of Commerce in Milan—suggest that the use of arbitration has actually not increased significantly in recent years.[7] In 2011, the CAM reports that 130 requests for arbitrations were filed, a drop from 2009, which saw 158 applications. However, 129 proceedings were concluded in 2011 (equal to the number filed in 2010), while only 106 were concluded in 2009. Looking at the data over the last five years, the number of arbitrations performed at the CAM has increased slightly, but not by much.[8] Furthermore, in relation to the number of cases filed with the court system (figures denoted previously), 129 filings hardly makes a dent in the court backlog.

The inference to be drawn from the MoJ data is that mediation was becoming the most popular ADR method, documenting over 12,000 mediation requests filed in June 2012 alone. Of the cases filed with mediation organisations between 21 March 2011 and 30 March 2012, 77.2 per cent were mandatory and 19.7 per cent were voluntary, with about 0.5 per cent from a contractual mediation clause and 2.7 per cent of cases referred by a judge. It is interesting to note that the judicial referral percentage had risen from 1 per cent in September 2011. Though the increase is slight, this may indicate judges are realising more about the benefits of ADR. Regardless, thanks to the sharp decline in mediation filings resulting from the Constitutional Court judgment barring mandatory mediation,[9] arbitration might be the most utilised form of ADR currently. That is essentially to say that ADR in Italy is now virtually non-existent.

[5] Department of Judicial Organisation, Ministry of Justice Report, *Mediazione obbligatoria ex DL 28/2010: statistiche dal 21 marzo 2011 al 30 giugno 2012*.

[6] T Giovannini and V Renna, 'The Italian Experience of Arbitration and the Arbitration Rules of the Chamber of Arbitration of Milan: A Parallel View' (2010) 14 *Vindobona Journal of International Commercial Law and Arbitration* 297; citing the *Terzo rapporto annuale sulla diffusione della giustizia alternative in Italia*, see <www.camera-arbitrale.it/consulta.php?sez_id=26&Ing_id=7>. The study considered only institutional arbitration, including cases conducted by the chambers of arbitration set up by the chambers of commerce, or by Italian private institutions. It does not consider ad hoc arbitral proceedings, which are difficult to quantify.

[7] As stated on the website, 'The Chamber of Arbitration of Milan is a special branch of the Chamber of Commerce of Milan and specialises in commercial dispute resolution. The Chamber provides an array of services and tools known as ADR (Alternative Dispute Resolution), which allow for a resolution of disputes within time-limits and through methods that are different from—alternative to, thus—judicial proceedings. The resolution of disputes is one of the regulatory market functions attributed by law to the chambers of commerce (Italian Law No 580 of 1993).'

[8] In 2005, 99 requests were filed and 105 proceedings were conducted; in 2006, there were 102 filings and 99 performed; in 2007, there were 99 filings and 102 performed; in 2008, there were 118 filings and 86 performed. This, however, represents the data of only one of the many arbitration groups which are affiliated with the Italian chambers of commerce included in the study.

[9] Italian Constitutional Court, Judgment 272, 6 December 2012.

B. Strengths and Weaknesses of Certain Dispute Resolution Mechanisms

For disputants in Italy, litigation has the advantage of being a well-established and predictable process that is highly professionalised. Litigation is characterised by detailed procedural rules which provide disputants with some certainty and protection of individual rights throughout the process. The most prominent weakness in Italian litigation is the inefficiency of the process, as it is both time consuming and expensive (though it is not as costly as litigation in other comparative countries, eg the UK). Moreover, due to the procedural complexity, litigants can easily become lost in the process. Some argue that the attorneys and judiciary have little incentive to speed up the procedure, or to refer parties to forms of alternative dispute resolution, simply because they are comfortable with the status quo.[10]

As ADR processes, mediation and arbitration offer some similar benefits, but also differ in several respects. Like litigation, arbitration offers the benefit of being a formalised proceeding, though it is largely confined to specific areas of law, such as commercial contracts.[11] Arbitrators themselves are highly professionalised and have an extensive understanding of legal principles. Therefore, with arbitration the parties have the benefit of resolving their dispute in a forum which adheres closely to the law but is designed to be more efficient than courtroom litigation. However, because arbitration is largely tailored for use in specific industries, where parties habitually sign and enforce arbitration clauses, its drawback is that it is not a mechanism that is largely accessible to the general litigating public.

Voluntary mediation had been available to Italian litigants for almost two decades before Legislative Decree 28/2010 was enacted, yet it was never a popular choice. Mediation has been criticised as being an unstructured and expensive procedure. Furthermore, mediators have been disparaged for lacking the expertise required for fostering the just resolution of cases. Legislative Decree 28/2010 and accompanying Ministerial Decree 180 of 18 October 2010 (Ministerial Decree 180/2010), modified by Ministerial Decree 145 of 6 July 2011 (Ministerial Decree 145/2011), endeavoured to address these concerns. This framework has helped to further institutionalise the process by strengthening procedural rules and protections, standardising mediation costs and ensuring the quality of mediators.

The benefits of mediation are predicated upon vast reductions in cost and time, as well as the potential to forge agreements of superior quality. A recent European study looked specifically at the time and cost savings for cases resolved in mediation rather than litigation.[12] The study strove to discover the lowest possible percentage of media-

[10] G De Palo, *Cross-Border Commercial Mediation: How Legislation Affects Mediation Use*, see <www.europarl.europa.eu/comparl/juri/hearings/20071004/depalo5_en.pdf>.

[11] Code of Civil Procedure, Arts 806–40.

[12] ADR Center Study Report, 'Quantifying the Cost of Not Using Mediation: A Data Analysis', paper presented at the European Parliament, 23 May 2011. This study follows 'The Costs of Non ADR' study, funded by the European Commission as a part of the ADR Center project 'Lawyers in ADR'. 'The Costs of Non ADR' measured the costs of litigating and mediation in a country using the World Bank's Doing Business 2011 report, 'Enforcing Contracts' index. This index looked at the cost of litigating a sample case of contract enforcement in the capital city of each country, and represented the cost of litigation as a percentage of 200% of that country's gross national income. Using this standard indicator as a baseline allowed 'The Costs of Non ADR' to compare litigation and then mediation costs in each country and demonstrate the time and cost savings for the sample case.

tion success in which mediation would still result in savings of time and money when compared to litigation. This study predicted that Italy requires a success rate of only 28 per cent of mediated cases to reduce costs for litigants and courts, and of merely 4 per cent to reduce case processing time. The previously cited June 2012 Italian MoJ statistics found that, while only 35 per cent of mediation cases secured the participation of all parties, 48 per cent of these cases were successful. This data indicates that mediation had already been saving Italian disputants considerable amounts of time and money.

As mentioned, mediation and arbitration have some key differences. They are displayed throughout multiple jurisdictions and affect their suitability for certain types of disputes. Parties who select arbitration access a formalised procedure in which the arbitrator may issue a final decision. Further, because arbitration adheres to specific procedural and evidentiary principles, it is imperative that the neutral has an extensive technical knowledge of the law. Mediation, on the other hand, is procedurally informal. Still, while mediation is flexible in terms of evidence, process and formality, the mediator must be adept at the informal methods of engendering cooperation and compromise, while being able to visualise where all of the interests in a dispute convene.

C. Practical Use and Theoretical Appropriateness—The Market of ADR

In Italy, it would appear that theoretical appropriateness does not greatly affect the average party in their dispute resolution choice. Italian disputants have demonstrated, by their high rate of continued litigation use, that they prefer courtroom litigation—irrespective of whether their case is better suited for an ADR mechanism.

With reference to ADR mechanisms, practical use and theoretical appropriateness appear to be better aligned in the arbitration field than that of mediation. Arbitration procedures happen to be tailored conveniently for use in the commercial sector. Commercial arbitration cases tend to be of high value, with the Camera Arbitrale Milano reporting that the average arbitral dispute value in 2011 was €7,151,109,[13] so the formalised arbitration process is appealing to this industry.

On the other hand, the Italian mediation procedure is commonly the theoretically appropriate choice for the average disputant in civil and commercial cases, though practical use had always been lower than it should have been prior to Legislative Decree 28/2010.[14] Mediation in Italy that is only regulated by market principles, and legislation which supports it by only creating minimum standards, is not widely utilised. Prior to Legislative Decree 28/2010, the court backlog grew to 5.4 million pending cases, and the average time for resolution of a civil case had risen to eight years.[15] Suffice to say that the light-touch mediation legislation issued over the 20 years prior to Legislative

[13] *Cf* The Ministry of Justice reported that the average value of mediated cases from 21 March 2011 to 30 March 2012 was €118,299.00.

[14] According to the draft report on the adoption of Legislative Decree 28/2010, the disputes subject to mandatory mediation under Legislative Decree 28/2010 would have eventually constituted over 1 million of the cases currently pending before the Italian courts.

[15] G De Palo and L D'Urso, 'Explosion or Bust? Italy's New Mediation Model Targets Backlogs to 'Eliminate' One Million Disputes, Annually' (2010) 28(4) *CPR Alternatives* 93.

Decree 28/2010 was insufficient to motivate parties to use mediation services; it thus seems fairly evident that continuing the same agenda will not be successful in aligning theory with practice now.

The situation Italy found itself in during the period leading up to Legislative Decree 28/2010 highlighted a distinct paradox within the Italian litigation system. Throughout this era of mediation, the success rate was roughly 80 per cent of cases; however, the mere availability of competent mediation services was insufficient to persuade parties to choose mediation. In fact, mediation was voluntarily selected in only 0.1 per cent of cases.[16] With the regulatory framework of Legislative Decree 28/2010 and mandatory provisions in effect to augment the natural process of the market, practical use and theoretical appropriateness were converging. This union is reflected by the statistical information contained in the MoJ report cited above in part I.A.[17] Although some types of commercial cases are mediated under Legislative Decree 28/2010, the most frequently mediated subject areas were real estate (19 per cent) and landlord/tenant disputes (11 per cent).[18] However, mediation accessibility spans a wide area of subject matters, including finance and banking contracts, medical malpractice, inheritance, division of property and telecommunications law. It began to look as if the mandatory provision of Legislative Decree 28/2010 was finally going to drive mediation towards fulfilment of its true market potential; now, however, Parliament will determine whether mediation will rise again, and we must wait in anticipation.

II. REGULATORY APPROACH AS REGARDS ADR AND ADJUDICATION

A. Regulation of ADR

The dispute resolution procedures in Italy are highly regulated. Civil litigation is primarily regulated by the Code of Civil Procedure.

In terms of ADR, mediation is regulated by several recent statutes (as previously mentioned), namely Legislative Decree 28/2010 and Ministerial Decree 180/2010 (amended by Ministerial Decree 145/2011). This compilation of regulations endures even after the December 2012 Constitutional Court decision, though some of the components have been modified.

As to 'conciliation', it is important to note that the term is used in Italian law, in one sense, to refer to the technical settlement of the dispute at hand. However, forms of judicial conciliation exist as methods of resolution. These are generally found in specific subject areas, which are primarily codified in the Italian Code of Civil Procedure.

Italian arbitration is governed by the Code of Civil Procedure, Articles 806–40. In addition, Italy is a signatory to the 1958 New York Convention on the Recognition

[16] G De Palo, L D'Urso and R Gabellini, *Il Ruolo Dell'Avvocato Nella Mediazione* (Milan, Giuffrè, 2011). See also G De Palo, L D'Urso and D Golann, *Manuale del Mediatore Professionista*, 2nd edn (Milan, Giuffrè, 2010); De Palo, *Cross-Border Commercial Mediation*.

[17] Department of Judicial Organisation, Ministry of Justice Report, *Mediazione obbligatoria ex DL 28/2010: statistiche dal 21 marzo 2011 al 30 giugno 2012*.

[18] Ministry of Justice, Director of Statistics, *National Statistics Projection, 21 March 2011–30 September 2011*.

and Enforcement of Foreign Arbitral Awards, the 1961 Convention on International Commercial Arbitration and the 1965 ICSID (International Centre for Settlement of Investment Disputes) Convention.

i. Clear Encouraging Effect of Legal Regulation on the Use of ADR

The mere codification of ADR procedures does not seem to encourage use of these mechanisms.[19] Observing the data, we can see a drastic uptake in mediations after the implementation of Legislative Decree 28/2010, then a significant drop in filings once Constitutional Court judgment 272/2012 eliminated the mandatory provision. As the majority of Legislative Decree 28/2010 has been left intact, it is evident that the escalation in mediation filing was due not to the basic regulatory improvements to the process but, rather, to the obligation to attempt mediation in certain civil and commercial cases. It follows that cogent regulation of ADR mechanisms is necessary to bolster their utility.

ii. Reasons to Encourage and Regulate ADR Procedures

As mentioned, the Italian justice system is currently suffering from a significant case backlog and extremely long processing times for disputes litigated in the courts. Further, the Italian legal community seems only to respond to strongly regulated legal procedures; therefore, unregulated ADR mechanisms have traditionally been unsuccessful. Thus, to inspire litigants to utilise ADR, Italian legislators have input procedural regulations in an attempt to provide them with institutional support and the 'blessing' of the government.

Within various sections of these regulations, the Italian government and Parliament cite adherence to European Union standards. In the area of mediation, Parliamentary Law 69 of 18 June 2009 (Parliamentary Law 69/2009), Article 60—which delegated power to the government to enact a decree on mediation—supports the enactment of Legislative Decree 28/2010, citing that it was rendered in accordance with EU law (paragraphs 2 and 3). The decree further states that its enactment is pursuant to Directive 2008/52/EC of the European Parliament and of the Council on certain aspects of mediation in civil and commercial matters of 21 May 2008 (Directive 2008/52/EC).

In contrast, the regulatory reform for arbitration, brought on by the entry into force of Legislative Decree 40 of 2 February 2006 (Legislative Decree 40/2006), does not point to EU law as a motivating force. However, this decree substantially amended relative provisions of the Italian Code of Civil Procedure, and other national legislation on arbitration.

B. Incentives to Use Certain Types of ADR

i. Early Conflict Resolution Phase

With regard to the relevant statutes, all ADR procedures are available in the early

[19] See above I.C.

conflict resolution phase. They are usually initiated subsequent to election by the parties, or in compliance with mandatory procedures. Instances of judicial referral of cases to ADR procedures are possible, but do not occur often.

Parties who have prescribed arbitration or mediation as a condition within a contract must abide by those terms if a dispute arises. There are also statutory requirements in certain areas of judicial conciliation obliging parties to participate in this procedure before litigation.[20]

Italian law contains unique provisions which require that information on mediation be made available to the public—eg as explicitly outlined in Legislative Decree 28/2010, Article 21. These provisions have been implemented in order to assist disputants in making educated decisions about which dispute resolution mechanism is most appropriate for their case during the pre-conflict stage. Additionally, attorneys are required to provide their clients with information on all available types of resolution mechanisms.[21]

ii. Incentives

Every form of ADR that exists in Italy carries the key incentive of providing disputants with an alternative to engaging in the inefficient civil litigation process. Disputants in the mediation process are eligible for further financial incentives. These incentives, set out in Article 17 of Legislative Decree 28/2010, manifest as an exemption from the stamp tax when filing mediation documents, along with a tax exemption on the written final agreement itself (up to €51,646). Lastly, Article 20 outlines a tax credit applicable to the fee paid to the mediation organisation, reaching €500 if the mediation is successful and up to €250 if the mediation is unsuccessful.

Sanctions also exist to facilitate the effectiveness of the mediation process. Article 8(5) of Legislative Decree 28/2010 dictates technical sanctions that may be imposed upon parties who fail to participate in the mediation proceedings. Participants can be excused from proceedings without suffering sanctions if they show good cause. However, barring a good cause pardon, if a party fails to participate the issue could be raised during the subsequent court hearing.[22] As a result, the judge could make presumptions as to certain evidentiary issues during subsequent proceedings in accordance with the Code of Civil Procedure, Article 116(2).[23]

In cases of mandatory mediation, Article 13 of Legislative Decree 28/2010 endorsed monetary sanctions imposable by the court. These allowed the judge to oblige the winning party to compensate the losing party for their additional court costs if the amount awarded by the judge is the same as or similar to the settlement offer rejected during mediation. Further, the successful party would be required to replenish the state budget in the amount of the judicial procedural administration fees. Finally, in such a case, the victor would not be granted recompense for the court costs they had incurred. All of these sanctions, however, are presently barred by Constitutional Court judgment 272/2012.

[20] This is discussed in more detail in II.C.

[21] Legislative Decree 28, 4 March 2010, Art 4(3). This feature is discussed further in II.B.iv.

[22] Prior to Constitutional Court Judgment 272/2012, the judge could be apprised of this by a recorded mediator statement; however, now the issue must be raised by a party to the dispute if it is to be addressed.

[23] Legislative Decree 28, 4 March 2010, Art 8(5), Code of Civil Procedure, Art 116(2).

If analysed in the context of the Constitutional Court's reasoning, it could be argued that elimination of the specified punitive procedures may have been outside the scope of the Court's judgment as presented. The Court ruled that the provisions mandating mediation in some instances were unconstitutional as they violated constitutional Articles 76 and 77.[24] However, it is not necessary for such sanctions to be inextricably linked to mandatory mediation. These sanctions could also be quite valuable in aiding the reduction of the court system's case load if applied to voluntary cases. Moreover, there could be no question of injustice, as those disputants electing mediation would know that these sanctions are an associated risk and, as such, they could be a significant motivating factor to attempt negotiation.

There are no statutory financial incentives, or sanctions, for parties who arbitrate or engage in judicial conciliation or mediation.

iii. The Effect of Legal Culture on the Promotion and Selection of ADR Mechanisms

The Italian legal culture is pro-litigation and, as a result, utilisation of ADR remedies has remained low.[25] This is in spite of the fact that new legislative reforms have been introduced for both mediation and arbitration.[26] Compared to the volume of cases seen in the courts each year, today amicable dispute resolution mechanisms play a 'minimal role' in Italian civil case management.[27]

In consideration of the statistics cited above in part I, arbitration seems to have found its niche in pre-dispute contractual agreements. In this low-volume but high-value area, arbitration is growing more popular. However, it has not been a prevalent option for common civil cases. This is attributable to the predilection of the Italian legal community, the high costs of arbitration services and because the arbitral legal framework is largely tailored for commercial disputes.

In recent years, the Italian legislature has supported mediation as the preferred ADR mechanism to reduce the backlog of civil cases and case-processing time. In fact, prior to the implementation of Directive 2008/52/EC, Italy had enacted more legislation on mediation than any other European country.[28] However, despite these numerous regulatory instruments, mediation failed to take root in the Italian dispute resolution market, raising the concern that the legislative approach has been one inadvertently favouring quantity over quality.[29]

[24] The Constitutional Court found Art 5(1) to be in violation of Art 77 of the Italian Constitution, according to which 'The Government may not, without an enabling act of the Parliament issue a decree having force of law'. Regarding the latter assumed violation, it is claimed that the government (with Legislative Decree 28) went beyond the delegation received by the Parliament with Art 60, Law 69/2009. It is interesting to note that the Constitutional Court did not address the claimed violation of Art 24 of the Italian Constitution, protecting everyone's right to take judicial action to protect individual rights and legitimate interests, as well as, the right to a defence.

[25] G De Palo and L Cominelli 'Crisis of Courts and the Italian Mediation Debate' in N Alexander (ed), *Global Trends in Mediation* (Köln, Otto Schmidt, 2003) 213f.

[26] See Giovannini and Renna, 'The Italian Experience of Arbitration'; De Palo and Cominelli, 'Crisis of Courts and the Italian Mediation Debate', 213f.

[27] Giovannini and Renna, 'The Italian Experience of Arbitration'.

[28] De Palo, *Cross-Border Commercial Mediation.*

[29] Ibid. De Palo reports that, from January 1991 to 31 March 2005, the ADR Center managed 327 disputes through mediation, of which 277 had been initiated by one of the parties, 45 because of a contractual provision, 3 by law (telecommunications) and 2 by judicial referral. These results, and others, were published in *Top Legal* (June 2005).

Several theories have been put forth in an attempt to describe this phenomenon. However, the prevailing argument is that, in the broader legal and social context the Italian legal culture is hesitant to venture away from the courts and thus disrupt the status quo.[30] This attitude comes both from the bottom up and the top down. This means that, first of all, litigants are mistrustful of the new legislation, as well as of the mediators' abilities. In addition, attorneys are not advocating mediation (they are only held to an obligation to inform); and judges are not referring cases to mediation with any sort of frequency or vigour. This historical lack of popularity suggests that the issue is more cultural than political, as it has been exhibited across political party lines, by Italian citizens, attorneys and the judiciary.[31] This has, once again, been demonstrated by the brevity of the success of Legislative Decree 28/2010 and its failure to motivate the masses towards mediation without compulsion. The conclusion to be drawn is that the non-utilisation of mediation does not stem from a lack of dispute resolution options; rather, disputants have demonstrated that they prefer to resolve disputes in court regardless of expediency.[32]

This reality is predicated on a number of factors.[33] For example, there is a deeply rooted suspicion of lay judges (those who are not selected and trained as magistrates).[34] Another possible cause is the 'self-preservation' instinct of certain professionals who are in some way linked to the mediation process. Attorneys, notaries, accountants, tax experts, etc may fear that they will lose business or become redundant should mediation—which in Italy does not require parties to have legal representation—become the default dispute resolution choice. Most recently, with specific reference to the mandatory provision of the regulatory framework, opponents claimed that mediation under the law does not increase access to justice, but rather limits it because the mandatory requirement forces parties to undergo a procedure that is too expensive and conducted by mediators whose quality is not sufficiently regulated.

Hence, the question now raised by theorists is how to promote the use of mediation in the legal culture without compulsion.[35] In Italy, the government faces a society that is so pro-litigation that it needs to not only provide mediation services, but also to create a shift in the 'choice architecture'[36] under which, currently, disputants view litigation as the default option and ADR procedures with scepticism. Therefore, navigating the legal culture away from litigation—to lead participants to view mediation, if not as the default option, as a viable option—is a key factor in implementing Italian mediation legislation.[37]

[30] Ibid.

[31] De Palo and Cominelli, 'Crisis of Courts and the Italian Mediation Debate'.

[32] Ibid.

[33] Ibid.

[34] Ibid. De Palo and Cominelli compare the mediation case with the initial resistance to the justices of the peace, introduced in 1991. However, 15 years later, the data demonstrates the effectiveness of this 'new' dispute resolution process as only 10% of the decisions from that court are appealed.

[35] L Cominelli, 'Bringing Mediation to the Masses: The EU Regulatory Approach and the Italian Case', paper presented at the meeting 'Current Socio-legal Perspectives on Dispute Resolution' in Onati, Spain, 9 July 2010, see <air.unimi.it/bitstream/2434/149004/2/Onati_WS_Jul10_Cominelli.pdf>.

[36] D Watkins, 'A Nudge to Mediate: How Adjustments in Choice Architecture Can Lead to Better Dispute Resolution Decisions' (2010) 4 *The American Journal of Mediation* 1.

[37] See IV.C for proposed solutions.

iv. Duty of Lawyers to Inform their Clients

Obviously, when parties have contractually agreed to mediate or arbitrate, or when they must engage in judicial conciliation or mediation by statute, attorneys must advise their clients of this. Regardless of contractual or statutory obligations, though, lawyers should inform their clients when it is advisable to utilise an alternative dispute resolution procedure, out of adherence to general professional responsibility. Nevertheless, attorneys are presently obliged to inform their clients of the possibility of mediation under Legislative Decree 28/2010, Article 4(3) in all applicable cases.

The decree states that, when retained, an attorney must inform his client of the possibility of using mediation, as well as supply information about the financial incentives available. This information must be provided clearly in writing, signed by the client and filed with other court documents. If the lawyer fails to so inform, the client will be entitled to voidance of the entire attorney–client contract. The information provided, however, does not need to detail the risks or pitfalls of engaging in litigation. Its sole purpose is to ensure that parties are informed of the mediation process and availability. There are no specific advisory requirements for attorneys with respect to arbitration.

C. Restriction of Access to Courts with a View to Alternative Dispute Resolution

i. ADR Procedures as a Precondition for Court Proceedings

ADR procedures are required before commencing proceedings in court if parties have agreed to engage in mediation or arbitration by contract, or if the dispute falls under one of the statutory categories which require conciliation. Attempts at amicable settlement must precede trial in certain disputes arising in family law, labour law, agrarian law and telecommunications law. Legislative Decree 28/2010, Article 5(1) had required mediation attempts for other specific types of civil and commercial actions; however, as discussed, this has been nullified by the ruling of the Constitutional Court.[38]

ii. Court Referral to Alternative Dispute Resolution

Under Italian law, judges do not have the power to order a case to alternative dispute resolution. However, in cases where voluntary election of ADR is an option, the judge may invite the parties to mediate if upon review of the merits they believe the dispute to be a good candidate for ADR.[39]

In mediation, if parties to a dispute arising from a contract which contains an obligation to attempt arbitration or mediation proceed directly to court, the case will be suspended pending the required ADR process attempt. This action may occur upon the motion of a party or by the judge's initiative.[40] Such an order does not force parties to arbitrate or mediate, as there will be no sanctions if the parties do not go through

[38] Italian Constitutional Court, Judgment 272, 6 December 2012.

[39] Legislative Decree 28/2010, Art 5(2).

[40] Legislative Decree 28/2010, Art 5(5).

the ADR process. Rather, it clarifies that the court procedures are not available to the parties until arbitration or mediation has been attempted.

D. Constraints of ADR Regarding Constitutional and Human Rights Law

In Italy, domestic constitutional challenges arise when an alternative dispute resolution method interferes with access to justice. This right is recognised by Article 24 of the Italian Constitution, and is inviolable and non-disposable. The 2012 challenge of the mediation regulatory scheme by the leading Italian attorney group Organismo Unitario Avvocatura (OUA) in the Regional Administrative Tribunal of Lazio (TAR) submitted violation of access to justice as one of its central charges. The OUA also argued that, under Ministerial Decree 180/2010, mandatory pre-trial mediation is too expensive, and there are not sufficient quality guarantees of the mediation services. As a preliminary measure, however, the OUA argued that Legislative Decree 28/2010 exceeded the delegation of power from Parliamentary Law 69/2009.

The judge of the TAR found these challenges 'not manifestly baseless' and referred them to the Constitutional Court for review.[41] In the December 2012 decision, the Constitutional Court found that Article 5(1) of Legislative Decree 28/2010 exceeded the power delegated by Parliamentary Law 69/2009. It is important to note, however, that in a 57-page decision the Court did not once say that mandatory mediation, in and of itself, interferes with access to justice.[42]

Academics are currently debating the legality and appropriateness of mandatory pre-trial mediation under the Italian law. The contention surrounding this is rooted in the perception that mandatory mediation takes away the parties' right to choose. Some argue that, by simply removing the parties' voluntary act of choosing mediation, the benefit of mediation as a true facilitative procedure is invalidated. Therefore, mediation can only make a positive contribution to combating the dire civil litigation situation in Italy if it is voluntary.[43]

Others argue that exposure to the mediation process through voluntary and compulsory mediation, which complement one another and offer different benefits, may enable Italian disputants to achieve results that are superior to those attained using judicial resolution alone.[44] The interplay between these two arguments has continued in different forms, but the core remains the same: party-driven resolution cannot function at its best when parties are forced to participate; yet, the benefits of ensuring that parties are exposed to mediation are now undeniable.

[41] Regional Administrative Tribunal of Lazio, decision no 03202/2011 REG.PROV.COLL., referring cases nos 10937/2010 and 11235/2010 to the Italian Constitutional Court.

[42] Italian Constitutional Court, Judgment 272, 6 December 2012.

[43] P Giuggioli, 'La mediazione per la conciliazione: strumento utile se scelto liberamente dalle parti' in *Quarto rapporto sulla diffusione della giustizia alternativa in Italia* (Milan, ISDACI, 2010) 147–55.

[44] G Deodato, 'Il quarto rapporto: Conoscere per determinare i processi evolutivi della giustizia alternativa' in *Quarto rapporto sulla diffusione della giustizia alternativa in Italia* Milan, ISDACI, 2011) 5–10.

E. Special Rules for Consumers and the UNCITRAL Model Law on International Commercial Conciliation

Italian consumer rules address some of the principles contained in the Commission Recommendation of 4 April 2001 on the Principles for Out-of-Court Bodies involved in the Consensual Resolution of Consumer Disputes, C(2001) 1016. However, the Recommendation was not actually referenced during the ADR legislation drafting process. Considerations of impartiality and fairness are reflected, and standards designed to facilitate these aims have been imposed. Furthermore, Italy continues to make varied attempts to promote the dissemination of procedural information in an effort to divert appropriate cases to ADR mechanisms. Ultimately, the essence of ADR mechanisms is optimal effectiveness as the purpose of utilising these mechanisms is to avoid protracted and expensive litigation procedures.

Italy did not rely on the UNCITRAL Model Law in drafting its mediation legislation.[45]

III. APPROACH TOWARDS SPECIFIC ADR INSTRUMENTS

A. Negotiation

i. Nature of the Rules Applicable to the Pre-Contractual Stage of Negotiation

Article 1322 of the Italian Civil Code states that parties have the right and freedom to negotiate the content of a contract. However, during pre-contractual negotiations and the formation of the contract, parties are obliged to conduct themselves with good faith under Article 1337. There is no specific legislation on cross-border negotiation, nor, in practice, is there any distinction between national and cross-border rules.

ii. Enforceability of Duties to Negotiate

As mentioned in the previous section, Article 1322 of the Italian Civil Code asserts that parties have the privilege and independence to regulate the content of a contract. Accordingly, parties may create a contractual provision which pronounces that, should a dispute arise, the parties will first attempt to negotiate before pursuing formalised dispute resolution procedures. The duty of good faith required in the drafting phase of the contract is carried into the interpretation of the contract under Article 1366 of the Civil Code. However, as a contractual arrangement, an agreement to negotiate is binding but cannot effectively be enforced by either party beyond a request for damages.

iii. Liability for Breaking off Negotiations in Bad Faith

In 1942, Italy was the first European state to require that parties act in good faith

[45] See <www.uncitral.org/uncitral/en/uncitral_texts/arbitration/2002Model_conciliation_status.html>.

during pre-contractual negotiations.[46] 'Good faith' is not explicitly defined under Italian law, but it is generally considered to include disclosure of vital information, honesty, loyalty, fair dealing and a lack of fraud, malice or intent to deceive. Further, Italy is one of the countries in which '[g]ood faith is also the basis for many obligations which complete those expressly contained in the contract: obligations of information, of confidentiality, to act fairly, of cooperation and security'.[47]

Article 1460 of the Civil Code states that contractual liability is applicable if parties violate the terms of the contract or fail to act in good faith. Thus, refusal to negotiate a dispute when one is contractually obligated, or breaking off negotiations in bad faith, will be considered a breach and may carry liability for the breaching party. In this situation, rules of contractual liability under Articles 1218f of the Civil Code require the defaulting party to prove that the failure to perform was not their fault nor the result of a bad faith act.

B. Mediation

i. Sources of Regulation on Mediation

As established in previous parts, mediation in Italy is very closely regulated by legislation. The detailed rules that we see today are the result of a multistep process and multilevel efforts of the Italian government and legislature. The earliest forms of mediation regulation can be seen in the Codice Codacci Pisanelli of 1865, though the first of the more modern regulating instruments was enacted in 1931. This is when mediation was acknowledged as a dispute resolution option in public safety provisions. Mediation was codified in 1940 within the Code of Civil Procedure, and was designated as an internal court procedure conducted by judges. In the 1960s, Italy began using mediation in labour disputes. On 29 December 1993, Law 580 was passed, giving the chambers of commerce the ability to establish mediation and arbitration commissions for the resolution of disputes among companies, or between companies and their clients. Mediation then became available in the corporate, financial and intermediation areas following the enactment of Legislative Decree 5/2003.

Recently, the enactment of Directive 2008/52/EC signalled a new era in Italian mediation. Shortly thereafter, the Italian Parliament issued Law No 69/2009, in which Article 60 acknowledges mediation as a viable option in all civil and commercial disputes. Article 60 further delegated power to the Italian government to issue a decree on mediation for the implementation of Directive 2008/52/EC. As discussed previously, the result was Legislative Decree 28/2010, enacted on 4 March 2010. Shortly thereafter, Ministerial Decree 180/2010 provided the specific guidelines necessary to effectuate the provisions of Legislative Decree 28/2010, which governed mediation organisations, mediators, mediator training, and mediation costs. Subsequently, on 6 July 2011, Ministerial Decree 145/2011 amended Ministerial Decree 180/2010 by raising

[46] Association Henri Capitant, Société de législation comparée (eds), *European Contract Law. Materials for the Common Frame of Reference: Terminology, Guiding Principles, Model Rules* (Munich, Sellier, 2008).

[47] Ibid.

the requirements for mediator qualification and diminishing the costs of mandatory mediation procedures.

ii. Fields of Mediation and Conciliation

Mediation appears in many forms in different areas of Italian law. In Italy, the line between conciliation and mediation is somewhat ambiguous, as conciliation can refer to the simple resolution of a dispute, as well as a procedure aimed at resolving a dispute.[48] Therefore, the mediation and conciliation provisions are discussed jointly here.

a. Voluntary Mediation in Civil and Commercial Cases

As mentioned, Article 60 of the Parliamentary Law 69/2009 officially recognised mediation as a feasible option in all civil and commercial cases. While Article 5(1) of Legislative Decree 28/2010 had mandated mediation in certain types of civil and commercial cases (eg land rights, partition of property, hereditary succession, *successìon ereditarie, patti di famiglia, locazione, comodato* leases, loans, rental companies, medical malpractice, *diffamazione con il mezzo della stampa o con altro mezzo di*, defamation by the press or other means of advertising, contracts, insurance, or banking and finance), Constitutional Court judgment 272/2012 declared this mandate to have been enacted unconstitutionally. The cases falling into these categories can still be resolved through mediation, but it must be voluntarily elected by the parties. If mediation is selected, the financial incentives in Legislative Decree 28/2010[49] still apply.

b. Judicial Mediation

Italy does not have judicial mediation as envisioned by Directive 2008/52/EC, in which acting judges may conduct mediations themselves. Further, Italy does not use processes in which one judge may refer a case to another judge to conduct mediation.

c. Small Claims Mediation

Italian small claims cases are heard by a justice of the peace, who has the power to invite parties to mediate.[50] Alternatively, parties in the jurisdiction of this court may request mediation and employ a justice of the peace as the mediator.[51]

d. Consumer Law

Mediation or conciliation in consumer law first appeared in Parliamentary Law 580/1993, which allowed chambers of commerce to conduct conciliation proceedings at the behest of the parties. Section 140 of the Consumer Code states that parties may opt to initiate conciliation, pursuant to Law 580/1993, to resolve disputes arising between businesses and consumers.[52] This form of conciliation now works in conjunc-

[48] Though Legislative Decree 28/2010 is arguably the first statute which makes a clear distinction between the two.

[49] As described in II.B.ii.

[50] Code of Civil Procedure, Art 320.

[51] Code of Civil Procedure, Art 322.

[52] English translation of Italian Consumer Code, Art 140(1) states that parties may commence conciliation for cases arising under (a) prohibition order against actions damaging the interests of consumers and users; (b) suitable measures to remedy or eliminate the damaging effect of any breaches; or (c) orders to

tion with Legislative Decree 28/2010, in which Article 16 transposes these consumer conciliation procedures into the mediation arena. In Article 16 it is also indicated that inter-industry mediation groups can be created and maintained, so long as they are members of the official mediation registry.[53] Further, Article 15 provides for conciliation in class actions arising under Article 140-bis of the Consumer Code. Despite these opportunities, a lack of data on industrial movement towards mediation suggests that mediation is not widely employed in the area of consumer law at this time.

e. Telecommunication Law

In the telecommunication industry, mediation must be attempted to resolve disputes between consumers and companies as a precursor to a court hearing, via CORECOM (Comitato Regionale per le Comunicazioni)[54] Resolution 173/2007. Mediations are hosted by the chambers of commerce or regional CORECOM facilities (formed under the auspices of the Italian Authority of Communications, hereinafter called the Authority). Mediations that are unsuccessful, even in part, may be appealed to the Authority, or within the court system. As recently as 2012, the Authority, together with the Union of the Chambers of Commerce, drafted a memorandum which expounded upon the conditions of mediation in the telecommunications sector, with the goal of promoting its utilisation. In summary, the protocol states that: mediation settlements are enforceable; the mediator may not offer their own proposal;[55] and the disputants are only required to pay the tariff specific to the mediation proceedings.[56]

f. Family Law

During the first hearing of judicial separation proceedings, the judge has the authority to meet with the husband and wife, both separately and jointly, in order to attempt to reconcile the couple before advancing the proceedings.[57]

g. Labour Law

As mentioned above, labour law was one of the first sectors to utilise mediation in the resolution of legal disputes. Currently, for most labour cases, the parties may choose whether to attempt conciliation or mediation.[58] However, until 2010, mediation was mandatory for all forms of labour disputes. If the proceedings are successful, an agreement is drafted and signed by the parties and the members of the panel. If unsuccessful, the dispute continues in the courts.

A more recent development in labour law implemented mandatory mediation measures applicable specifically to the employee dismissal process. Law 92 of 28 June 2012 provides specific procedures that must be adhered to in circumstances of dis-

publish measures in one or more national or local daily newspapers where publicising measures may help to correct or eliminate the effects of any breaches.

[53] The registry is managed by the Ministry of Justice and the Ministry of Economic Development.

[54] Translation: Regional Committee for Communications.

[55] Formerly, the mediator could issue a settlement proposal when it seemed attainability of an agreement was unlikely; however, Constitutional Court judgment 272/2012 has eliminated this provision in all mediations now.

[56] In mediations there can also be a standard initiation fee, or a supplemental fee if a case is resolved successfully.

[57] Code of Civil Procedure, Art 708.

[58] Code of Civil Procedure, Arts 409–10.

missal based on financial reasons, eg a meeting between the employer and employee attempting mediation before the board.[59] The idea behind mandating this process is to ensure that the employer has given proper consideration to the action of dismissal, and has exhausted all other alternatives. In addition to mandatory mediation, Law 92/2012 provides for access to mediation or arbitration by voluntary election during a dismissal appeal.

h. Criminal Law

Legislative Decree 274 of 28 August 2000, Article 29(4) permits mediation in areas of criminal law which fall under the jurisdiction of the justice of the peace. In Italy, there are certain crimes that must be prosecuted by the state's attorney; however, in cases where this is not required, mediation can be attempted. It follows, then, that the injured party is obliged to initiate the proceedings.

iii. Transposition of Directive 2008/52/EC

As mentioned previously, Directive 2008/52/EC served as a major impetus for change in the Italian mediation sphere. Due to the case backlog in the courts and the extended processing time for disputes, and given the paradox already mentioned with respect to lack of participation in voluntary mediation procedures, Italy was ready for implementation of sweeping changes. The issuance of Directive 2008/52/EC provided Italian legislators with the occasion to make these changes and to ultimately enact the strong mediation regulations that Italy needed under the aegis of the Directive.

With respect to the core requirements of Directive 2008/52/EC, Legislative Decree 28/2010 provides specifically for procedures ensuring mediation as a form of redress,[60] enforcement of mediation agreements,[61] confidentiality of the proceedings,[62] tolling the statute of limitations[63] and providing information to the general public.[64] Additionally, Ministerial Decree 180/2010 provides the quality assurance provisions that Directive 2008/52/EC, Article 4 called for, by regulating the registration of mediation organisations, mediator qualifications, and training and certification requirements.

As noted earlier, Italian legislation goes beyond the Directive's mandate in certain respects. Legislative Decree 28/2010 provides financial incentives for parties who participate in mediation,[65] and also creates a requirement that attorneys inform clients of the option to mediate.[66] Most notably, Article 5(1) of Legislative Decree 28/2010 enacted mandatory mediation for select commercial and civil disputes. Though this provision has been barred by the Constitutional Court, these bold steps had previously drawn praise from the European Parliament and policymakers in other European countries.

In its 13 September 2011 Resolution on the Implementation of the Directive on

[59] This is specific to cases where the dismissal is a result of situations like job externalisation, organisational restructuring, and elimination of a position.

[60] Directive 2008/52/EC, Art 5; Legislative Decree 28/2010, Art 2.

[61] Directive 2008/52/EC, Art 6; Legislative Decree 28/2010, Art 12.

[62] Directive 2008/52/EC, Art 7; Legislative Decree 28/2010, Arts 9–10.

[63] Directive 2008/52/EC, Art 8; Legislative Decree 28/2010, Art 6.

[64] Directive 2008/52/EC, Art 9; Legislative Decree 28/2010, Art 21.

[65] Arts 17 and 20.

[66] This is discussed in II.B.iv.

Mediation in the Member States (the Resolution), the European Parliament highlighted the success seen in Italy, and other jurisdictions, that exceeded the minimum requirements of Directive 2008/52/EC.[67] The Resolution commended Italy, particularly, for taking bold steps to enact a mandatory mediation procedure, and pointed out how Italy was reaping the benefits of more effective dispute resolution despite the fact it was also experiencing political backlash from these provisions.[68] The Resolution also declared that when Italy rises above the internal dissent and begins to see the positive effects of mandatory mediation, mediation will be acknowledged as a viable, lower-cost and quicker alternative to the courts—not as just another required hurdle of the civil justice system.[69] The underlying message seems to be that the European Parliament's desire is for mediation to become an integral to the mainstream judicial resolution service structure both in Italy and beyond.

iv. Legal Effects of a Mediation Clause

Contract clauses which predetermine the mediation process and/or a mediation organisation are valid, with the available recourse to transfer the case to the courts if the mediation fails. As previously discussed, a mediation clause will be enforced by the judge if the parties bring a dispute directly to the court in an attempt to forego mediation. Upon the motion of a party, or of their own initiative, the judge will order a suspension of the proceedings whilst the parties participate in mediation.[70]

For Italian disputants, there are apparent and unique benefits to taking advantage of a mediation clause. Namely, the party who first files a mediation request receives preference in selecting the mediation organisation and location of the mediation.[71] This right grants the filing party the ability to select an organisation whose internal regulations are perceived to be most advantageous to them, or merely has rules and mediators the party feels most comfortable with.[72] The benefits of selecting the location and, possibly, the mediation organisation can be significant for any case. Thus, it is often in the parties' best interests to secure an advantage by predetermining the details of the eventual mediation, and establishing them in a written contract.

v. Procedures Available that Aid the Mediation Process

A myriad of procedural rules and protections support the mediation process in Italy. The beginning of the process is grounded in Legislative Decree 28/2010, which states that mediation is initiated when one party files a request for mediation with a registered mediation organisation,[73] or when parties are invited to mediate by a judge.[74] The mediation organisation must then appoint a mediator and set a meeting date

[67] European Parliament, Resolution of on the Implementation of the Directive on Mediation in the Member States: its impact on mediation and its take-up by the courts 2011/2026(INI), 13 September 2011.

[68] Ibid, points 4, 8 and 9.

[69] Ibid, point 10.

[70] Legislative Decree 28/2010, Art 5.

[71] Legislative Decree 28/2010, Art 4(1) and (2).

[72] Legislative Decree 28/2010, Art 3(1).

[73] Legislative Decree 28/2010, Art 4(1).

[74] Legislative Decree 28/2010, Art 5(2).

within 15 days of the filing, and immediately communicate this information to the opposing party so that everyone may be present at the initial meeting.[75]

A mediation organisation maintains a roster of mediators who are dually qualified by the Italian standards and the internal standards of the organisation. Larger mediation organisations may also offer mediators specialised in managing particular types of disputes. Naturally, the procedure for selection of a mediator for a specific case will vary among mediation organisations. The customary practice is to appoint a mediator whose qualifications are most suitable for the case.

vi. Mediators

a. Qualification. There are no restrictions as to the profession of the mediator, though many mediators tend to be attorneys or retired judges. However, mediators must hold a minimum of a three-year university degree or be enrolled in a professional society. Subsequently, mediators must complete mediator training and be recertified every two years. Newly trained mediators must assist another mediator with at least 20 mediation hours during their first two years of certification.

b. Mediator Duties. Concerning procedural guidelines and qualifications, mediators must adhere to the rules set forth in the legislation, particularly Legislative Decree 28/2010 and Ministerial Decree 180/2010, as amended by Ministerial Decree 145/2011. The mediator must respect all technical aspects of the proceedings, including the duty to be fair and impartial at all times. However, as no general code of conduct for mediators exists in Italy, mediators must adhere to the code of conduct adopted by their mediation organisation. Many of the Italian organisations have also adopted the European Code of Conduct for Mediators (ECCM); hence, it is used as a reference here.

Under the ECCM duties of care, mediators must be competent and knowledgeable in mediation procedures. This includes a requirement that they receive proper training, continuing education and certification.[76]

The duty of communication requires that Italian mediators maintain open communication with parties regarding the details of the mediation procedure, including describing each person's role in the process[77] and selecting appropriate dates for the mediation procedure.[78] In Italy, this process is often assisted by case managers within the mediation organisations. In order to ensure effective communication with the parties on the particulars of a case, the mediator is responsible for confirming that they have the requisite experience and, if applicable, expertise in a specific subject to properly manage the mediation at hand. Finally, the mediation organisation must also provide exact representations of the fees required for the mediation services.

Italian Legislative Decree 28/2010 describes the duty of loyalty in Article 14(2), stating that the mediator must sign a declaration of impartiality for each mediation they preside over. If there are possible grounds for bias, the mediator must immediately inform the parties and the organisation. Article 14(1) states that the mediator is forbidden from entering into any relationship with one of the parties that would

[75] Legislative Decree 28/2010, Art 8(1).
[76] ECCM, s 1.1.
[77] ECCM, s 3.1.
[78] ECCM, s 1.2.

create a conflict of interest. If a conflict arises, the mediator must disclose it immediately. Upon disclosure, even if the parties accept the relationship and still wish to proceed, the mediator may continue only if they are certain that their judgement will not be affected. The duty of impartiality mandates that no favour be assigned to either party, and the mediator must maintain an outward appearance of neutrality for the duration of the mediation. To further assure objectivity, Article 14(1) of Legislative Decree 28/2010 also prescribes that the mediator is not permitted to receive direct compensation from the parties.

The commencement of a mediation is signalled by the signing of a mediation agreement, which also serves to educate the participants about the mediation process and other procedural matters. The formalities of the mediation session are open to determination by the mediation organisations. Generally, there are no rules of evidence or fixed procedures for presenting facts or positions. In practice, under most ADR organisations' rules of procedure the parties and the mediator will agree upon the rules to be followed, and this agreement is treated as a binding contract. The flexibility of this process allows for open discussion of the issues and facilitates the free exchange of ideas. Thus, it becomes easier to determine the interests of the parties and to design a solution that satisfies those interests.

c. Enforcement of Duties. Enforcement of duties is the responsibility of the mediation organisation that employs the mediator. According to Article 6(4) of Ministerial Decree 180/2010 violations of the mediator's obligations and standards constitute a disciplinary offence punishable under existing rules of professional conduct.

This power is assigned to the mediation organisations, particularly due to the fact that if the mediator is found to be in violation of their professional obligations, the *organisation* may be liable for malpractice. According to Article 4(2)(b) of Ministerial Decree 180/2010 the mediation organisations are accountable for the mediator's conduct, and therefore must hold liability insurance of €500,000.00 to cover potential losses arising from misconduct. However, the mediation organisation may require its mediators to maintain their own insurance coverage.

There have been no reported cases, thus far, where clients have launched legal actions against mediation organisations or mediators.

d. Quality Assurance. The quality of mediation services in Italy is monitored by both state regulation and market principles. The state regulates mediation organisations, mediators and mediator training very closely. Under Article 16(1) of Legislative Decree 28/2010 mediation is to be administered exclusively by mediation providers registered by the Ministry of Justice under Ministerial Decree 180/2010. These organisations are responsible for conducting the mediation procedure, supervising mediators, mediator training and impartiality, and the overall quality of the proceedings. Furthermore, mediation providers must abide by certain regulations, set forth by ministerial decree, with respect to registering with the Minister of Justice and maintaining their eligibility.[79]

As previously discussed, the profession of the mediator is also carefully regulated, and Article 4(3) of Ministerial Decree 180/2010[80] places the responsibility of verifying

[79] Legislative Decree 28/2010, Art 3(2).

[80] As modified by Ministerial Decree 145/2011.

the qualification of mediators with the mediation organisation. The organisation, in its application to the Registrar, must attest that all of its mediators meet the requirements outlined above.[81] Additionally, the mediator must also maintain obligatory technical qualifications, including sufficient abilities in each language listed on their curriculum vitae. Further, if the mediator has asserted expertise in a certain area, they must be able to present adequate documentation of this proficiency. An individual who satisfies all of these requirements is eligible to apply for employment with a mediation organisation. Different mediation organisations have varied mediator qualification standards, owing to the fact that they may set internal requirements that are more demanding than the statute prescribes.

Upon receipt of a mediator's qualifications, the mediation organisation must principally review and certify that the mediator has all of the proper materials before referring them for inclusion in the state registry. As stated in Article 6 of Ministerial Decree 180/2010, when submitting the mediator's requirements to be included in the registry, the mediation organisation must furnish the state with: a declaration of availability signed by the mediator; the mediator's curriculum vitae; an attestation that the mediator meets all of the requirements listed above; and the appropriate documentation outlined in Article 4(3) (requirements of certification and criminal history). This information is maintained by the Director General of Civil Justice within the Office of the Attorney General. The current criminal history requirement holds that a prospective mediator must not have been: (i) convicted of a criminal offense (nor hold a non-suspended prison sentence); (ii) disqualified (permanently or temporarily) from public office; or (iii) subjected to restrictive measures resulting from criminal activities; and (iv) must not have received disciplinary sanctions aside from a simple warning.

Mediation quality is also implicitly regulated by rules governing mediator training. To this end, Article 17 of Ministerial Decree 180/2010 calls for the creation of a list of mediation organisations authorised to provide training to mediators. Training can be offered by public or private entities, so long as they are on the authorised list. Information on qualified training providers and training course requirements is maintained, once again, by the Director General of Civil Justice. Article 18 of Ministerial Decree 180/2010 provides details as to how an entity can become qualified to train mediators. To be entered onto the list, the organisation must submit a training curriculum consisting of no less than 50 hours, divided into theoretical and practical modules, which will accommodate a maximum of thirty participants. The courses are required to integrate simulations, and must be concluded with a final examination (lasting a minimum of four hours) on theory and practice.

e. Remuneration. While mediation fees have been set according to Ministerial Decree 145/2011, the mediator's fee has not been specifically prescribed. Ministerial Decree 145/2011 has set maximum cost limits on the full mediation process, to which mediation organisations must adhere, relative to the value of the case.[82] The mediator negotiates his fees with the mediation organisation. Normally, his fee would be a percentage of the

[81] In III.B.vi.

[82] See IV.A for the fee table.

preset figure. As previously mentioned, the mediator never receives payment directly from the parties; rather, all payment is arranged with the mediation organisation.[83]

vii. Duties of the Parties

Under the current regulatory framework, parties to a mediation may withdraw from the proceedings at any time, without providing any justification. Even in cases where mediation attempts have been inscribed in a contractual agreement, if a party decides not to acknowledge this obligation, there is no consequence or mode of enforcement that can keep them at the table. Further, under the current law, if a participant physically appears at a mediation proceeding but makes absolutely no effort to resolve the case, that still constitutes an official 'attempt' at mediation.

viii. Enforceability of Agreements resulting from Mediation

Article 12 of Legislative Decree 28/2010 provides that all mediation settlement agreements can be made enforceable when they are presented to, and approved by, the court. Comparable to other court orders, the agreement is entered as an official record by the mediator and subsequently becomes a writ of execution, permitting the placement of a judicial lien on the parties' assets.[84] Additionally, the agreement can be included in the judicial registrar of mortgages and claims.[85] However, the agreement cannot be made enforceable by this procedure if it contradicts public policy or mandatory regulations.[86] With respect to cross-border disputes, Article 12(1) states that the President of the Court in the jurisdictional area of enforcement is required to approve the written agreement, ensuring compliance with Directive 2008/52/EC.

ix. Court-based Mediation Programs

There are no court-based mediation programs in Italy. However, Legislative Decree 28/2010 sanctions the creation of mediation organisations by local bar associations, which can be situated in court-run facilities. The mediation organisation would not be in any way linked to the courts, but the bar association may carry out their mediation activities in a space provided by the court system, free of charge.

x. Cross-border Mediation

Legislative Decree 28/2010 does not distinguish between national and cross-border rules. The procedural regulations of court conciliation programs are not based on legislation, and in practice there is no distinction between national and cross-border rules.

[83] G De Palo and L Keller, 'Mediation in Italy, Alternative Dispute Resolution for All' in KJ Hopt and F Steffek (eds), *Mediation: Principles and Regulation in Comparative Perspective* (Oxford, Oxford University Press, 2013) 2.

[84] De Palo and D'Urso, 'Explosion or Bust?' 94.

[85] Ibid.

[86] Legislative Decree 28/2010, Art 12.

C. Conciliation

See the mediation and conciliation provisions discussed jointly above in part III.B.

D. Expert Opinion

i. Nature of the Rules Applicable to Expert Opinions

Experts are allowed to participate in ADR procedures when their expertise is appropriate and solicited by the mediation participants. Article 8(1) of Legislative Decree 28/2010 states that, with regard to mediation, the mediation organisation may appoint an expert in disputes which require specific technical skills. Section 4 dictates that the mediator may only select experts registered with the local court, and their services are to be compensated in accordance with the policies of the mediation organisation. The sections of the Italian Code of Civil Procedure relevant to arbitration do not outline special provisions for the use and role of experts.

In general, as regards expert opinions, there is no distinction between national and cross-border rules.

ii. Duties of the Expert and Enforcement of These Duties

In general, experts who participate in ADR proceedings must espouse professional standards equal to those required when they participate in court proceedings. This includes basic principles like impartiality and full consideration of information provided by both parties.

iii. Cases Where Experts Are Used

While no statistical data is available, in general, the use of experts in ADR proceedings ensues under the same circumstances that would necessitate their presence in court hearings.

E. Arbitration

i. Influence of the UNCITRAL Model Law on International Commercial Arbitration

Although one may find traces of the Model Law in the Italian arbitration legislation, especially in the area of international arbitration, following the 2006 reform of arbitration regulations and the inclusion of arbitration in the Code of Civil Procedure, Italian law is generally not considered to be marked by the Model Law.

ii. Minimum Procedural Standards to be followed

As noted above, Italian arbitration is codified in the Code of Civil Procedure, Articles 806–40. Italy is also a signatory to the 1958 New York Convention on the Recognition and Enforcement of Foreign Arbitral Awards, the 1961 Convention on International Commercial Arbitration and the 1965 ICSID Convention. While the rules on arbitration are formalised, they are generally not as strict as the procedural rules governing courtroom litigation.

Parties to an arbitral dispute can freely determine the procedural rules that apply. Normally, the parties do not lay down all of the procedural rules in the arbitration agreement, but rather select a set of arbitration rules designed by one of the arbitration organisations. Absent the parties' agreement, arbitrators can follow the procedural rules they deem to be most fitting. In practice, arbitrators comply with the procedures set out by the Code of Civil Procedure for court proceedings, together with a few specific rules concerning arbitral proceedings.

iii. Mandatory Law in Arbitration and Rules of Enforcement

Italian arbitration is largely a feature of contract. Therefore, the terms of the arbitration can be determined by the parties, so long as they adhere to the minimum procedural standards.

Judgments obtained in arbitration are final and enforceable.

iv. Rules applied to Cross-border Situations

With specific reference to the New York Convention, disputes between treaty members that are resolved and awarded within Italy are done so in accordance with the convention rules, and are enforceable under the same.[87]

IV. POLICY QUESTIONS

In general, ADR regulation in Italy reflects the principle that legislators should not be afraid to enact strong ADR requirements in order to create a true balance between alternative and judicial dispute resolution. In Italy, due to the inaccessibility of arbitration to the majority of disputants, mediation seems to be the ADR mechanism best suited to help unburden the court system and provide citizens with swifter access to dispute resolution. The following addresses a few policy points that have not been so explicitly stated previously, and discusses how ADR in Italy should look in the future, particularly the potential of mediation.

A. Costs of ADR

At the moment, the disputants carry all of the costs of mediation proceedings, though conditional legal aid funds are available. In response to exorbitant cost accusations, Ministerial Decree 145/2010 standardised the costs of mediation to increase affordability. Table 1 represents the maximum allowable limit of mediation fees.

Arbitration maintains a similar standardised cost approach. However, there are

[87] For further information see III.E.ii.

Table 1: The Maximum Allowable Limit of Mediation Fees in italy

Value of the claim (€)	Cost for each of the parties (excluding 21% VAT)
Up to €1,000	€65
From €1,001 up to €5,000	€130
From €5,001 up to €10,000	€240
From €10,001 up to €25,000	€360
From €25,001 up to €50,000	€600
From €50,001 up to €250,000	€1,000
From €250,001 up to €500,000	€2,000
From €500,001 up to €2,500,000	€3,800
From €2,500,001 up to €5,000,000	€5,200
Above €5,000,000	€9,200

no pre-set limitations by a legal authority. Therefore, there can be a wide range of variance among arbitration organisations. Parties to an arbitration are also required to pay all of the procedural costs, in addition to attorney fees. Table 2 is an example of the standard costs of arbitration from the leading arbitration provider in Italy, Camera Arbitrale Milano.[88]

Table 2: The Standard Costs of Arbitration by Camera Arbitrale Milano

Value of dispute(€)	Fees		
	Chamber of Arbitration	Sole arbitrator (min–max)	Arbitral panel (min–max)
Up to €25,000	€400	€600–1,500	€1,600–3,800
€25,001–50,000	€800	€1,500–2,500	€3,800–6,000
€50,001–100,000	€1,500	€2,500–4,500	€6,000 12,000
€100,001–250,000	€3,000	€4,500–10,000	€12,000–25,000
€250,001–500,000	€5,000	€10,000–20,000	€25,000–50,000
€500,001–1,000,000	€8,000	€20,000–30,000	€50,000–75,000
€1,000,001–2,500,000	€12,000	€30,000–50,000	€75,000 120,000
€2,000,001–5,000,000	€18,000	€50,000–80,000	€120,000–180,000
€5,000,001–10,000,000	€25,000	€80,000–100,000	€180,000–250,000
€10,000,001–50,000,000	€35,000	€100,000–130,000	€250,000–320,000
€25,000,001–50,000,000	€48,000	€130,000–180,000	€320,000–420,000
€50,000,001–100,000,000	€70,000	€180,000–230,000	€420,000–550,000
Above €100,000,000	€70,000 + 0.1% of the amount exceeding €100,000,000 to a maximum amount of €120,000	€230,000 + 0.05% of the amount exceeding €100,000,000	€550,000 + 0.12% of the amount exceeding €100,000,000

[88] Camera Arbitrale Milano, "Fees", see <www.camera-arbitrale.it/risolvi.php?sez_id=88&lng_id=14>.

B. Promotion of ADR Mechanisms by the State

The state should provide active support to enhance ADR mechanisms, and these activities should be managed by the appropriate regulatory authority. In Italy, the Italian Parliament maintains the ultimate authority to enact laws on ADR, though it may delegate this power to the government. However, because ADR procedures—particularly mediation—by their nature require the parties to retain a level of autonomy, regulation must permit the incorporation of primary stakeholders in formation of the process.

Arbitration is governed by international agreements and the Code of Civil Procedure. As a feature of a contract, the parties may affix additional regulatory features within these parameters.[89]

C. Election of the Appropriate Conflict Forum

In cases where parties have elected to participate in arbitration or mediation by contract, the parties are necessarily cognisant of the dispute resolution process in the pre-conflict phase. Therefore, they are already more inclined to follow through with the ADR mechanism prescribed in the contract by virtue of their predisposition to the idea. Apart from contractual cases, the residual informational and promotional approaches present in Italy have not been effective in motivating utilisation of diversified dispute resolution mechanisms.[90]

D. The Future of Mandatory Mediation Legislation

Though attorneys initially attacked mandatory mediation,[91] they have come to realise it was not just the Italian court system and the mediation community that prospered from increased use of mediation—they too were reaping benefits. Often, attorneys supplemented their business by taking on the role of mediator. Furthermore, though it is not required, more than 80 per cent of mediation participants were represented by counsel. Thus, contrary to the fears of the lawyers who challenged the mandatory mediation clause in Legislative Decree 28/2010, the condition actually helped them rather than hurt them.

The benefits for disputants have been discussed already at length but, to reiterate, parties who participate in mediation procedures as an alternative to directly filing with the court will be able to resolve their cases more expediently, in terms of both time and money. Moreover, they will have a better chance at crafting a mutually satisfactory and durable solution.

In the future, legislators could essentially enact a mandatory mediation statute identical to that which was drafted by the government. We know that this was effective in increasing mediation usage and relieving the court system—it even received

[89] Discussed in III.E.ii.

[90] See the previous sections.

[91] See II.D for more information on the challenge.

accolades from the European Commission and various national and international institutions. However, to do this would be to ignore the concerns of vital stakeholders in the mediation process, once again. That is to say, when enacting the most recent policy framework on mediation, the government failed to be mediation savvy. Then, when provided with the opportunity to remedy the resultant conflict with mediative tools, the government still failed to do so. This resulted in the ADR system Italy finds itself with today, or lack thereof.

Accordingly, it would be more prudent for Parliament to enact a new version of the law, utilising mediative competencies in doing so. In other words, the government, mediation and legal communities should use consensual resolution methods to draft a new law on mediation. Fortunately, it seems that this is just what they are doing, as negotiations have already begun to take place.

Multiple ideas have been proffered, but the popular suggestion in all circles considers the implementation of a trial period for mandatory mediation. For a three-year period, certain civil and commercial cases would require parties to attend a preliminary informational meeting to explore the resolution options that might be most appropriate for the case. If the parties and the mediator agree that the case is suitable for mediation, the proceedings can continue immediately at that conference. If, however, the parties determine the mediation forum is not equipped to handle their case, they may opt out and take their case to the courts, incurring only a minimal fee.

Observation of the data at the beginning of this chapter highlights the importance of an extended trial period. In particular, the data shows that when mediation was mandatory, there was an uptake in both mandatory and *voluntary* mediations,[92] leading us to deduce that mandatory exposure to mediation instigates a fortuitous 'tag-along' effect. Nevertheless, we have witnessed that the brief heyday of mandatory mediation was not sufficient to sustain systematic voluntary election of mediation as a dispute resolution mechanism. Theoretically, the idea of mediation need only resonate for a while longer, in order to offer assurance of its beneficent qualities. On the other hand, if disputants remain unconvinced of the advantages of mediation at the end of the three-year period, it will go away and they can resume resolving disputes via direct initiation with the courts.

The potential to opt out should alleviate some of the concerns of disputants who are required to mediate under the mandatory law. This option should also quell the allegation made by OUA condemning mandatory mediation as a violation of access to justice. Moreover, the 'opt-out' system also addresses the quality concerns raised in the OUA challenge. Due to the freedom of the parties to withdraw from the process, both the mediation organisation and the mediator will maintain competitive standards in order to convince disputants that they are best suited to handle their case. As a positive consequence, they will simultaneously be promoting mediation as a resolution method in general.

Some EU countries have implemented an 'opt-in' system, so to speak. Romania, for example, has attempted such a system whereby parties can choose whether to pursue mediation at the initial informational meeting, but failure to appear at this meeting

[92] Department of Judicial Organisation, Ministry of Justice Report, *Mediazione obbligatoria ex DL 28/2010: Statistiche dal 21 marzo 2011 al 30 giugno 2012.*

incurs a fine.[93] This route has been contemplated in Italy, but the opt-out system is still favoured. One primary reason for this is that, with a lack of 'good faith' requirement in Italy, a disputant may simply walk through the mediation door and walk back out again without giving mediation its due consideration, and not even suffer a minimal consequence. Secondly, the opt-in system usually requires an additional step to initiate the mediation process, whereas the proposed Italian model allows the mediation proceedings to begin at the initial information session.

If Italy truly wants to fix its broken justice system, it must start by recognising that mediation must be mandatory, at least for now. Furthermore, lawmakers and the mediation and legal communities need to be 'mediation savvy' in establishing new legislation, so that the advantages of mediation can be accessed and appreciated by all. Now that it is understood that all of the stakeholders' interests are actually aligned, revival of the mediation system should be readily attainable. Optimistically, the result would be for Italy to regain its place as a leading example of the maximum positive potential of ADR in Europe.

BIBLIOGRAPHY

ADR Center, 'Quantifying the Cost of Not Using Mediation: A Data Analysis', presented at the European Parliament, 23 May 2011

Association Henri Capitant, Société de législation comparée (eds), *European Contract Law. Materials for the Common Frame of Reference: Terminology, Guiding Principles, Model Rules* (Munich, Sellier, 2008)

Camera Arbitrale Milano. 'Fees', <www.camera-arbitrale.it/risolvi.php?sez_id=88&lng_id=14>

Ciuca, AE and Constantin-Adi, G, 'Romania' in G De Palo and M Trevor (eds), *EU Mediation Law and Practice* (Oxford, Oxford University Press, 2012)

Cominelli, L, 'Bringing Mediation to the Masses: The EU Regulatory Approach and the Italian Case', paper presented at the meeting 'Current Socio-legal Perspectives on Dispute Resolution' in Onati, Spain, July 9, 2010, <air.unimi.it/bitstream/2434/149004/2/Onati_WS_Jul10_Cominelli.pdf>

De Palo, G, 'Cross-Border Commercial Mediation: How Legislation Affects Mediation Use', <www.europarl.europa.eu/comparl/juri/hearings/20071004/depalo5_en.pdf> (2007)

De Palo, G and Cominelli, L, 'Crisis of Courts and the Italian Mediation Debate' in N Alexander (ed), *Global Trends in Mediation* (Köln, Otto Schmidt, 2003), 213–31

De Palo, G and D'Urso, L, 'Explosion or Bust? Italy's New Mediation Model Targets Backlogs to "Eliminate" One Million Disputes, Annually' (2010) 28(4) *CPR Alternatives* 93

De Palo, G, D'Urso, L and Gabellini, R, *Il Ruolo Dell'Avvocato Nella Mediazione* (Milan, Giuffrè, 2011)

De Palo, G, D'Urso, L and Golann, D, *Manuale del Mediatore Professionista*, 2nd edn (Milan, Giuffrè, 2010)

De Palo, G and Keller, L, 'Mediation in Italy, Alternative Dispute Resolution for All' in KJ Hopt and F Steffek (eds), *Mediation: Principles and Regulation in Comparative Perspective* (Oxford, Oxford University Press, 2013)

Deodato, G, 'Il quarto rapporto: Conoscere per determinare i processi evolutivi della giustizia

[93] AE Ciuca and G Constantin-Adi, 'Romania' in G De Palo and M Trevor (eds), *EU Mediation Law and Practice* (Oxford, Oxford University Press, 2012) 296.

alternativa' in *Quarto rapporto sulla diffusione della giustizia alternativa in Italia* (Milan, ISDACI, 2011) 5–10

Department of Judicial Organisation, Ministry of Justice Report, *Mediazione obbligatoria ex DL 28/2010: Statistiche dal 21 marzo 2011 al 30 giugno 2012*

European Commission, Commission Recommendation of 4 April 2001 on the Principles for Out-of-Court Bodies involved in the Consensual Resolution of Consumer Disputes, 1016

European Commission, European Code of Conduct for Mediators, 2 July 2004

European Parliament, Resolution of on the Implementation of the Directive on Mediation in the Member States: its impact on mediation and its take-up by the courts, 2011/2026(INI), 13 September 2011

Giovannini, T and Renna, V, 'The Italian Experience of Arbitration and the Arbitration Rules of the Chamber of Arbitration of Milan: A Parallel View' (2010) 14 *Vindobona Journal of International Commercial Law and Arbitration* 297

Giuggioli, P, 'La mediazione per la conciliazione: strumento utile se scelto liberamente dalle parti' in *Quarto rapporto sulla diffusione della giustizia alternativa in Italia* (Milan, ISDACI, 2010) 147–55

Ministerio della Giustizia. 'Strumenti: Statiche', <www.giustizia.it/giustizia/it/mg_1_14_1.wp?facetNode_1=1_5_0&previsiousPage=mg_1_14&contentId=SST734820>

Regional Administrative Tribunal of Lazio, decision no 03202/2011 REG.PROV.COLL

Watkins, D, 'A nudge to mediate: How adjustments in choice architecture can lead to better dispute resolution decisions' (2010) 4 *The American Journal of Mediation* 1.

LEGAL SOURCES

Directive 2008/52/EC of the European Parliament and of the Council on certain aspects of mediation in civil and commercial matters. 21 May 2008

Italian Constitutional Court, Judgment 272, 6 December 2012

Italian Government, Legislative Decree 28, 4 March 2010

Italian Government, Legislative Decree 40, 2 February 2006

Italian Government, 'Consumer Code', Legislative Decree 206, 6 September 2005

Italian Government, Legislative Decree 274, 28 August 2000

Italian Parliament, Code of Civil Procedure 1942 (Amended 1950)

Italian Parliament, Constituzione della Repubblica Italiana, 27 December 1947

Italian Parliament, Law 69, 18 June 2010

Italian Parliament, Law 92, 28 June 2012

Ministry of Justice, Ministerial Decree 145, 6 July 2011

Ministry of Justice, Ministerial Decree 180, 18 October 2010

UNCITRAL, 'Model Law on International Commercial Conciliation', 2002

11

Regulation of Dispute Resolution in Japan: Alternative Dispute Resolution and its Background

SHUSUKE KAKIUCHI

I. OVERVIEW OF THE DISPUTE RESOLUTION MECHANISMS IN JAPAN

IN JAPAN, THERE are five major types of dispute resolution mechanisms: (i) litigation; (ii) court-annexed mediation procedures (what we should rather call 'conciliation'); (iii) arbitration/mediation procedures provided by administrative organs; (iv) arbitration/mediation procedures provided by private associations; and (v) other, non-institutionalised, mechanisms, like negotiation and conciliation on a purely ad hoc basis. However, as the latter are invisible from our view because of the lack of statistics, although they certainly play a role, the first four categories will be focused on in this chapter.

Among these dispute resolution mechanisms, some procedures cover all kinds of civil disputes while others specialise in a specific type. Lawsuits, court-annexed mediation and dispute resolution services provided by bar associations belong to the first group, whereas many others fall in the latter.

A. Litigation

It is often said that the litigation rate in Japan is considerably lower than in other developed countries.[1] However, this does not mean that litigation plays only a marginal role in the landscape of dispute resolution in Japan. On the contrary, according to the statistical data, litigation is the most commonly used procedure to resolve civil disputes. As Table 1 shows, in 2010, 234,651 cases were brought to district courts, which are the courts of general jurisdiction at first instance, and 585,710 cases were

Table 1: Civil Cases per Population

Total population (× 1000)		Civil cases docketed for formal trial proceedings in courts of first instance			Cases per 1000 persons
		District courts[a]	Summary courts[b]	Total[c]	
1950	83,200	61,599	5,147	66,746	0.80
1955	89,276	60,300	82,675	142,975	1.60
1960	93,419	65,024	81,831	146,855	1.57
1965	98,275	91,966	66,389	158,355	1.61
1970	103,720	104,371	69,642	174,013	1.68
1975	111,940	92,414	56,506	148,920	1.33
1980	117,060	127,072	77,729	204,801	1.75
1985	121,049	128,547	232,418	360,965	2.98
1990	123,611	111,630	97,319	208,949	1.69
1995	125,570	152,016	245,749	397,765	3.17
2000	126,926	162,589	298,053	460,642	3.63
2005	127,767	145,395	355,714	501,109	3.92
2010	126,382	234,651	585,710	820,361	6.49

Source: Annual Report of Judicial Statistics.
[a] Including cases concerning personal status (eg divorce), over which family courts have had jurisdiction since 2004. District courts are the courts of general jurisdiction in civil matters.
[b] Summary courts have jurisdiction over cases with a claim value up to JPY 1,400,000 (about $1,600).
[c] The total of civil cases peaked in 2009 when it reached 905,588 per year.

[1] See eg Ch Wollschläger, 'Historical Trends of Civil Litigation in Japan, Arizona, Sweden and Germany: Japanese Legal Culture in the Light of Judicial Statistics' in H Baum (ed), *Japan: Economic Success and Legal System* (New York, Walter de Gruyter, 1997) 89.

brought to summary courts, which deal with disputes of lower value. These numbers are obviously higher than the number of cases brought to judicial mediation proceedings (see below Table 4).

There are two possible explanations for this paradox. First, there may be some other procedures, like negotiation or ad hoc mediation, which successfully manage a large amount of disputes but are invisible from our view because they do not appear in statistical data.[2] Another hypothesis is that there are no such successful dispute resolution procedures, and most of the latent disputes are left unattended or unrecognised. It is likely that many disputes are settled through negotiation between parties,[3] but the truth seems to lie somewhere between the two extremes. Whatever the case, it is worth noting that organised arbitration or mediation procedures provided by private organisations still remain to be developed in Japan (see below I.F).

B. Court-annexed Mediation (Conciliation)

Concerning court-annexed mediation, there are two kinds of procedures: attempts to compromise by the judge and court-annexed mediation procedures independent of lawsuits.

i. Attempts to Compromise by the Judge

First, there is the attempt to compromise by a judge. As Table 1 shows, about 820,000 new cases in total were brought to the courts in 2010. Judges, who are authorised to advise parties to compromise at any stage of the lawsuit (Article 89 Code of Civil Procedure[4]), make active use of this possibility, and a considerable number of cases have been terminated by settlements thus recommended by judges (see Tables 2 and 3).

ii. Court-annexed Mediation Procedures Independent of Lawsuits

The second type of court-annexed mediation procedures[5] are independent of lawsuits and are conducted by a mediation committee composed of one professional judge and two or more laypersons, who are selected from one of the following three categories: (i) individuals qualified as attorneys at law, (ii) experts with knowledge contributing to resolution of disputes in civil or family matters;[6] and (iii) other lay persons with sufficient experience in social life in general.

[2] The traditional explanation finds its basis in the so-called non-litigious character or mentality of the Japanese people: 'Commentators, both within and without Japan, are almost unanimous in attributing to the Japanese an unusual and deeply rooted cultural preference for informal, mediated settlement of private disputes and a corollary aversion to the formal mechanisms of judicial adjudication'. JO Haley, 'The Myth of the Reluctant Litigant' (1978) 4 *The Journal of Japanese Studies* 359.

[3] For the mechanism of settlements in traffic accident cases see, eg M Ramseyer and M Nakazato, *Japanese Law: An Economic Approach* (Chicago, University of Chicago Press, 1999) 90ff.

[4] This provision has its origin in Art 269 of the German Code of Civil Procedure of 1877, which was adopted by the Japanese legislator as Art 221 of the Code of Civil Procedure of 1890.

[5] This type of procedure was introduced for the first time in 1922 for cases concerning lease of lands and buildings. It was extended to all types of disputes by the Act on Judicial Mediation in Civil Matters in 1951.

[6] For example, experts such as licensed real estate appraisers and licensed architects take part as committee members particularly in cases involving matters such as defective construction.

Table 2: Civil Cases Terminated in District Courts at First Instance

	Cases terminated[a]	Judgments		Compromise in court		Withdrawal of suit		Abandonment of claim		Acknowledgment of claim	
	No	No	%	No	%	No	%	No	%	No	%
1955	59,052	24,012	40.7	10,428	17.7	22,364	37.9	26	0.04	504	0.9
1960	65,157	26,563	40.8	11,597	17.8	24,399	37.4	33	0.05	548	0.8
1965	72,146	29,991	41.6	15,478	21.5	23,552	32.6	43	0.06	700	1.0
1970	83,195	33,765	40.6	21,567	25.9	24,505	29.5	77	0.09	647	0.8
1975	73,809	29,793	40.4	23,525	31.9	17,982	24.4	54	0.07	677	0.9
1980	102,033	43,067	42.2	32,540	31.9	22,239	21.8	118	0.12	1,081	1.1
1985	113,452	52,963	46.7	35,408	31.2	21,097	18.6	101	0.09	1,463	1.3
1990	112,140	48,986	43.7	39,305	35.0	18,906	16.9	131	0.12	1,093	1.0
1995	146,772	69,951	47.7	48,144	32.8	22,532	15.4	166	0.11	1,676	1.1
2000	158,779	80,542	50.7	50,779	32.0	21,823	13.7	173	0.11	1,334	0.8
2005	144,442	67,445	46.7	49,723	34.4	22,317	15.5	171	0.12	963	0.7
2010	238,483	88,632	37.2	77,496	32.5	66,069	27.7	227	0.10	949	0.4

Source: Annual Report of Judicial Statistics.
[a] Including cases concerning personal status (eg divorce), over which family courts have had jurisdiction since 2004.

Table 3: Civil Cases Terminated in Summary Courts at First Instance (Ordinary Procedure)

	Cases terminated	Judgments		Compromise in court		Withdrawal of suit		Abandonment of claim		Acknowledgment of claim	
	No	No	%	No	%	No	%	No	%	No	%
1955	76,265	26,438	34.7	23,575	30.9	22,197	29.1	18	0.02	458	0.6
1960	84,417	29,649	35.1	23,502	27.8	26,897	31.9	16	0.02	359	0.4
1965	60,144	20,016	33.3	16,694	27.8	19,565	32.5	13	0.02	282	0.5
1970	54,750	20,698	37.8	13,595	24.8	17,296	31.6	14	0.03	201	0.4
1975	53,407	21,733	40.7	10,936	20.5	18,472	34.6	11	0.02	221	0.4
1980	72,966	36,465	50.0	13,056	17.9	20,820	28.5	22	0.03	254	0.3
1985	232,059	137,960	59.5	37,409	16.1	50,257	21.7	56	0.02	683	0.3
1990	99,581	48,454	48.7	22,006	22.1	25,001	25.1	45	0.05	210	0.2
1995	243,569	112,446	46.2	68,267	28.0	51,702	21.2	52	0.02	262	0.1
2000	301,185	143,280	47.6	85,392	28.4	63,238	21.0	77	0.03	246	0.1
2005	356,718	150,218	42.1	85,160	23.9	83,177	23.3	110	0.03	167	0.0
2010	624,443	226,286	36.2	78,742	12.6	184,699	29.6	201	0.03	216	0.0

Source: Annual Report of Judicial Statistics.

Court-annexed mediation procedures in civil matters are available for all types of civil disputes except those involving family matters. As a general rule, the proceeding is introduced by a petition from one of the parties to the dispute,[7] though it can also be ordered by the trial court. However, once the pre-trial proceedings for the arrangement of the issues and evidence have been concluded, each party to the lawsuit has the right to refuse the order. The proceeding is not open to the public. Parties are required to appear in person and are normally heard by the mediation committee separately, not in the presence of the other party. The agreement of the parties resulting from successful mediation is recorded by the court and has the same effect as a record of settlement in court, which, in turn, has the same effect as a final and binding judgment. Thus, if a party to a settlement does not fulfil the agreed-upon terms, compulsory execution of the settlement terms is available.

For family cases (eg divorce), the court-annexed mediation procedure in family matters[8] is available. This procedure takes place in family courts. Since an attempt at mediation is a prerequisite to a lawsuit in family cases (Article 257 Act on Procedures in Family Affairs), parties are required to bring the case to the court-annexed mediation before filing a lawsuit. The structure of the proceeding is essentially the same as the normal civil matter mediation.

Tables 4–6 show the number of civil and family court-annexed mediation cases and their results. As Table 6 shows, the rate of success is fairly good in family mediation.

C. ADR Services by Administrative Organs

In addition to these judicial mediation procedures, which take place in courthouses, a number of ADR services are provided by administrative organs. For example, there is the Environmental Dispute Coordination Commission (Kôgai tô Chôsei Iinkai),[9] the Central Labor Relations Commission (Chûô Rôdô Iinkai)[10] and the National Consumer Centre of Japan (Kokumin Seikatsu Centre).[11] Local governments are also involved in dispute resolution services.[12]

In terms of the number of received cases, the National Consumer Centre has been the most important. Its activities consist mainly of consultation services, by which it gives necessary advice to consumers in trouble. In 2011, its network system received 878,598 requests for consultation. Furthermore, it provides mediation services, though on a much smaller scale. It received 150 petitions for mediation in that same year.

It is worth mentioning also that the Dispute Resolution Centre for Nuclear Damage Compensation (Genshi Ryoku Songai Baishô Funsô Kaiketsu Centre) was established in September 2011 as a result of the March 2011 earthquake and the subsequent nuclear accidents. As of 26 July 2013, it has received 7,221 petitions for mediation and 4,616 cases have been terminated, of which 3,494 were terminated by a settlement agreement.

[7] As far as court-annexed mediation in civil matters is concerned, it is not, as a general rule, a precondition for starting proceedings before a court. Exceptionally, it is obligatory in case of an action for increase or decrease in the amount of land or building rent (Art 24-2 Act on Court-annexed Mediation in Civil Matters).

[8] This procedure was introduced in 1947 at the same time as the establishment of family courts.

[9] See <www.soumu.go.jp/kouchoi/english/index.html>.

[10] See <www.mhlw.go.jp/english/org/policy/central-labour.html>.

[11] See <www.kokusen.go.jp/ncac_index_e.html>.

[12] Eg Consumer Life Centre of the City of Tokyo (*Tôkyô-to Shôhi Seikatsu Sôgô Centre*).

Table 4: Judicial Mediation Proceedings per Population

Total population (×1000)		Cases docketed for civil matter mediation[a]	Cases per 1000 persons	Cases docketed for family matter mediation	Cases per 1000 persons
1950	83,200	56,304	0.68	41,412	0.50
1955	89,276	78,955	0.88	43,109	0.48
1960	93,419	64,936	0.70	43,325	0.46
1965	98,275	52,067	0.53	52,528	0.53
1970	103,720	53,377	0.51	64,732	0.62
1975	111,940	45,495	0.41	74,083	0.66
1980	117,060	64,868	0.55	83,064	0.71
1985	121,049	89,209	0.74	85,035	0.70
1990	123,611	61,007	0.49	85,099	0.69
1995	125,570	130,808	1.04	96,099	0.77
2000	126,926	107,120	0.84	114,822	0.90
2005	127,767	48,193	0.38	129,876	1.02
2010	126,382	59,579	0.47	140,557	1.11

Source: Annual Report of Judicial Statistics.
[a] Total of cases docketed in high courts, district courts & summary courts, excluding conciliation proceedings for individuals in insolvency (*Tokutei chotei*) which were introduced in 2000.

D. Private ADR Services

As for private ADR services, a great variety of services are provided in accordance with the type of dispute. They can be grouped into three categories: (i) ADR services sponsored by a specific industry; (ii) ADR services sponsored by a local bar association or an association of experts in a specific field, such as land and building surveyors; and (iii) other ADR services. Since the Act on Promotion of Use of Alternative Dispute Resolution (hereafter ADR Act) entered into force in 2007, some ADR services have obtained certification from the Minister of Justice, which was newly established by this law.[13]

i. ADR Services Sponsored by a Specific Industry

One of the oldest and the most important private ADR organisations, the Centre for Settlement of Traffic Accident Disputes (Kôtsû Jiko Funsô Shori Centre, founded in 1974), belongs to the first category. This centre provides a procedure of semi-mandatory character before its judging committee as the final stage of its ADR services. The award rendered by this committee does not bind the victim of the accident, but it does bind the other party, which is usually an insurance company.[14] This is enabled by

[13] As of 1 June 2013, 124 private ADR services have been certified.
[14] Art 20 of the Centre's rules provides that the insurance company should respect the award of the committee.

Table 5: Civil Matter Mediation Cases Terminated

Year		Cases terminated	Success of mediation		Mediation failed		Withdrawal		Decision in lieu of settlement[a]		Refusal to mediate		Other	
		No	No	%	No	%	No	%	No	%	No	%	No	%
2000	District courts	2,002	1,167	58.3	556	27.8	160	8.0	269	13.4	3	0.1	47	2.3
	Summary courts	296,347	117,847	39.8	26,605	9.0	65,069	22.0	80,599	27.2	5,294	1.8	462	0.2
	Total	298,349	119,014	39.9	27,161	9.1	65,229	21.9	80,868	27.1	5,297	1.8	509	0.2
2005	District courts	1,562	852	54.5	406	26.0	109	7.0	139	8.9	8	0.5	48	3.1
	Summary courts	329,106	28,832	8.8	18,974	5.8	56,214	17.1	215,937	65.6	8,636	2.6	320	0.1
	Total	330,668	29,684	9.0	19,380	5.9	56,323	17.0	216,076	65.3	8,644	2.6	368	0.1
2010	District courts	8,314	726	8.7	386	4.6	51	0.6	7,085	85.2	5	0.1	61	0.7
	Summary courts	51,425	15,932	31.0	13,653	26.5	6,156	12.0	14,947	29.1	221	0.4	516	1.0
	Total	59,739	16,658	27.9	14,039	23.5	6,207	10.4	22,032	36.9	226	0.4	577	1.0

Source: Annual Report of Judicial Statistics.
[a] When parties do not come to a settlement, a court can render a decision representing the content of a possible settlement that it considers to be appropriate. Parties can express their disapproval within two weeks, which makes the decision void. If none of the parties object, the decision has the same effect as a compromise in court. The number of cases includes not only the cases in which the decision took effect, but also those in which the decision became void.

Table 6: Family Matter Mediation Cases Terminated

	Cases terminated	Success of mediation		Mediation failed		Withdrawal		Decision in lieu of settlement[a]		Refusal to mediate		Other	
	No	No	%	No	%	No	%	No	%	No	%	No	%
2000	113,035	52,876	46.8	18,301	16.2	36,323	32.1	2,655	2.3	1,614	1.4	1,277	1.1
2005	129,818	62,326	48.0	23,333	18.0	38,057	29.3	2,839	2.2	1,706	1.3	1,557	1.2
2010	138,917	72,706	52.3	25,174	18.1	35,053	25.2	2,170	1.6	1,614	1.2	2,200	1.6

Source: Annual Report of Judicial Statistics.
[a] See the annotation to Table 5.

the support of the insurance industry for the ADR activities of the centre (the centre was founded under the sponsorship of insurance companies). Similarly, there are also various product liability centres that were founded after the enactment of the Product Liability (hereinafter PL) Law in 1996, eg the PL Centre for Consumer Products[15] (Shôhi Seikatsu Yôhin PL Centre) and the Electric Appliances PL Centre (Kaden Seihin PL Centre). Most of these PL centres are sponsored by a specific industry. In addition,

[15] This centre was established by the Consumer Safety Product Association (Seihin Anzen Kyôkai).

the use of ADR has been strongly promoted in the field of financial business since the amendment of the Financial Instruments and Exchange Act in 2009, which introduced a scheme of mediation procedures conducted by certified investor protection organisations. Such a procedure is provided, for example, by the Financial Instruments Mediation Assistance Centre, which is sponsored by entities such as the Japan Securities Dealers Association and the Investment Trusts Association.

ii. ADR Services Sponsored by a Local Bar Association or Similar Entities

Some local bar associations have their own 'Dispute Resolution Centres' or 'Arbitration Centres'.[16] The procedures offered by these centres consist of mediation and arbitration. However, despite their names, their activities concentrate on mediation, because arbitration requires an arbitration agreement, the existence of which cannot always be expected.

Whereas these centres can accept any type of dispute of a civil law nature, since lawyers are authorised to provide legal services in general, there are ADR centres operated by other types of experts which handle more limited types of disputes corresponding to their area of expertise. This type of service is provided by patent attorneys (*Benri shi*), associations of judicial scriveners (*Shihô shoshi*), administrative scriveners (*Gyôsei shoshi*),[17] labour and social security attorneys (*Shakai hoken rômu shi*), land and building surveyors (*Tochi kaoku chôsa shi*), etc.

iii. Other Private ADR Services

'Other' ADR services, which belong to neither of the two above-mentioned categories, include arbitration and conciliation procedures for maritime affairs of the Japan Shipping Exchange, arbitration and mediation procedures for commercial affairs of the Japan Commercial Arbitration Association and similar procedures of the Japan Sports Arbitration Agency.

There is no statistical data showing the total number of cases received and dealt with by these private ADR services. However, based on each organisation's periodical reports and some available statistics, we can draw a rough picture of the situation.

In terms of the number of received cases, the Centre for Settlement of Traffic Accident Disputes stands out. In 2012, it received 8,478 applications for mediation and there were 6,982 cases terminated by a successful settlement. Some other services receive hundreds of cases per year. For example, the Financial Instruments Mediation Assistance Centre received 334 applications for mediation in 2012. The Dispute Resolution Support Centre of the Sendai Bar Association received 490 applications for mediation in 2011, this number being the largest among ADR centres of local bar associations.[18] In contrast to these rather successful organisations, most private ADR services receive significantly fewer cases. For example, the Japan Shipping Exchange received only 10 applications for arbitration, and the Japan Commercial Arbitration

[16] Eg Arbitration Center of the Daini Tokyo Bar Association. This centre was founded in 1990 as the first organisation of this kind. There are now 34 similar centres.

[17] Administrative scriveners are certified administrative procedure specialists.

[18] The total of 34 centres was 1,370 in 2011.

Association received 17 applications for arbitration and three for mediation, in 2012. The Ministry of Justice reported that the total number of cases that all the 110 certified private mediation organisations received in 2011 was 1,352, with 42 organisations receiving no cases in that year. However, it should be added that, if we take account of their consultation services, the role of such private providers should not be underestimated, for the number of requests they receive for consultation is much larger than applications for mediation.[19] This suggests that it is not mediation by a neutral third party that people in trouble expect primarily from private services. Rather, they want more direct supporters who stand on their side instead of a neutral mediator or arbitrator. If they find themselves in need of intervention by a neutral third party, they seem to prefer going to court.

From these data, we can conclude that the activities of private ADR services vary greatly in quantity and that the number of cases disposed of by these services still remains considerably smaller than the number of lawsuits and court-annexed mediation procedures.

E. Relative Strengths and Weaknesses of Each Dispute Resolution Mechanism

Theoretically, the strength of a lawsuit consists in its compulsory character. The plaintiff can submit a case to the procedure without the defendant's consent. The procedure is equipped with powerful measures to investigate the truth. Thus, it provides a strong device for protecting one's legal rights. Indeed, its rigorous formality and the time required for this create a motive for evading a lawsuit, but these inconveniences are reduced largely by the possibility of a recommendation of settlement by the judge.

According to the common understanding in Japan, mediation conducted by the trial judge has several merits. First, it is efficient because the judge, acting as mediator, does not need to learn the case afresh, since it is his case and he has been already involved as the trial judge. In a similar way, it saves time and energy in case of an inability to reach a settlement: in that event, the judge can simply go back to his original task to render a judgment. Secondly, this method creates a guarantee of quality of the solution. Since it is the trial judge who suggests a solution, parties may expect that it is in accordance with the judge's evaluation on the merits. This is a great advantage of mediation by the trial judge. However, this method has, of course, also problems. First, theoretically, it meets with criticism in terms of the self-determination of parties. In fact, it is questionable whether parties have the full liberty to refuse the judge's proposal because it may result in a similar, or even worse, judgment. Secondly, practically, this mechanism may require a great deal of labour from trial judges. If the increase in the number of lawsuits continues (see above Table 1) and the possibility of increasing the number of judges is quite limited because of financial reasons, judges will one day have no choice but to concentrate their efforts and energy on the rendering of judgments. This is one of the reasons why the Japanese legislator is trying to promote the use of ADR outside courthouses.

The advantages of court-annexed mediation procedures in civil matters are not as

[19] Eg the Ministry of Justice reported that in 2011 the total number of demands for consultation received by all 110 of the certified private mediation organisations was 21,938.

conspicuous as mediation by the trial judge. Enhanced informality and inexpensiveness may be regarded as its main advantages. Furthermore, in cases in which special knowledge is needed, like in medical malpractice or faulty construction cases, experts are readily available as a member of the mediation panel.

In comparison with these court procedures, the strength of dispute resolution centres of bar association is not obvious. Mediation procedures at these centres are conducted by lawyers, but their estimate of the judgment is naturally less reliable than that of the trial judge. The procedure is informal, but is generally no cheaper than court-annexed mediation procedures. There is no means to compel the unwilling opponent to participate in the procedure. The settlement is not immediately enforceable by compulsory execution (see also below III.B.vii). Thus, the competition with court procedures becomes a rather severe one. One possible strategy is to widely introduce the facilitative model of mediation in contrast to the evaluative model primarily encountered in court-annexed mediation, though it is questionable whether lawyers are suited to it. At any rate, to increase the use of these centres, it seems indispensable that lawyers, who are expected to support the activities of their own bar associations, make more effort to persuade clients to use these dispute resolution centres instead of having recourse to lawsuit or court-annexed mediation.

With regard to specialised ADR services, their strength lies basically in the specialty itself. In addition, if ADR services are provided by administrative organs or sponsored by a specific industry, fees can be minimised. Thus, a specialised ADR service can offer a fast and cheap way to resolve disputes, particularly when the disputes it deals with fall into a fixed pattern. Traffic accident cases are typical in this sense. In such cases, individual matters can be reasonably allocated between the court and ADR: regular cases are disposed of by ADR and irregular or difficult ones go to the courts.

F. Conclusion

From the description above, we can conclude that the contrast between highly developed judicial mediation and court-annexed mediation as opposed to still rather inactive private mediation is characteristic of ADR in Japan.[20] In other words, the public sector is predominant in the Japanese ADR landscape.

On the one hand, this can be explained at least partly as a result of market mechanisms. In other words, it is due partly to the relative weakness of private ADR services in comparison with court procedures. In terms of costs and quality, most private providers cannot match courts, though it is not quite fair to compare them on the same terms. Courts are wholly backed by the government and do not have to worry about profitability. They are in every corner of the country and have a strong reputation as a public authority. Besides, most private ADR services focus their activities on B2C or C2C disputes, which are hardly profitable.[21] If their activi-

[20] This is the assessment of mediation in Japan which I offered eight years ago (S Kakiuchi, 'Médiation et droit des contrats: une perspective japonaise' (2004) 17 *Zeitschrift für Japanisches Recht* 97). Notwithstanding the enactment of the ADR Act in 2004, the situation has not essentially changed.

[21] In fact, most of the private organisations are financially in the red. The more they receive cases, the more deficits they incur. Without the financial support of their sponsors (industry, bar association, etc), their activities are not sustainable.

ties improve public welfare nonetheless, it is worth considering giving them public financial support.

On the other hand, since most private ADR services have only recently been started, the shortage of information among potential users is also a serious problem.[22] In other words, the market is far from perfect under the present circumstances. If more information about ADR services were given to the users so as to allow them to consider them as alternatives, it is likely that a number of cases now filed at court would divert to ADR.

In addition, it is problematic that there are at present no provisions of law allowing a court to refer a dispute to an ADR procedure outside the court (see below III.B.iv): judicial mediation and private mediation are currently completely separate in Japan.

II. THE JAPANESE LEGISLATOR'S APPROACH AS REGARDS THE REGULATION OF ADR

The ADR Act, which was enacted in 2004 and entered into force in 2007, is the most important source for understanding the attitude of the Japanese legislator towards ADR.

As its title suggests, the main purpose of the enactment of ADR Act was to promote the use of ADR in Japan. Thus, Article 1 ADR Act provides that its purpose is to enable 'parties to a dispute to choose the most suitable method for resolving a dispute with the aim of appropriate realization of the rights and interests of the people'.[23] For this purpose, the Act declared that

> [t]he government shall, with the objective of promoting the use of alternative dispute resolution, research and analyse the trends, use, and other matters of alternative dispute resolution procedures at home and abroad, provide relevant information, and take other necessary measures, thereby endeavouring to familiarize the public with alternative dispute resolution [Article 4 ADR Act].

A. Promotion of Use of ADR

i. Reasons to Encourage the Use of ADR

As Article 1 ADR Act says, the final objective of the legislator is the 'appropriate realization of the rights and interests of the people'. This idea can be traced back to the beginning of the legislative proceedings on the Act. As a result of the long depression which began in the early 1990s, the 'deregulation' of the Japanese socio-economic system became an important topic in Japan. The idea was to revitalise society by eliminating excessive prior administrative regulation and to instead encourage the judiciary to become the vehicle of necessary *ex post* intervention in order to maintain

[22] In Japan, the abbreviation 'ADR' is quite commonly used without translation. However, some people still take it for 'American Depositary Receipt'.

[23] The English translation of this act is available at <www.japaneselawtranslation.go.jp/law/detail/?id=1958&vm=02&re=02&new=1>.

systemic integrity. This political context led the government to form a special commission for the reform of the justice system in 1999 (Shihô Seido Kaikaku Shingi Kai: Justice System Reform Council), which submitted its final report in 2001.[24] The report pointed out, among other topics, the need for reinforcement and vitalisation of ADR. According to the report, although 'various types of ADR are available in Japan, '[i]n reality . . . with the exception of some organizations, these mechanisms are not fully functioning'. Thus, 'in order to make the justice system more user-friendly', in addition to making special efforts to improve the function of adjudication, 'efforts to reinforce and vitalize ADR should be made so that it will become an equally attractive option to adjudication for the people', because

> [u]nlike the rigid judicial procedures, ADR makes it possible to respond flexibly, with resolutions that give scope to users' autonomy, resolutions behind closed doors to protect privacy and business secrets, simple and prompt resolutions at low cost, fine-tuned resolutions making use of the knowledge of experts in various fields, and resolutions in line with the actual circumstances regardless of legal rights and obligations.[25]

The idea that ADR contributes to realising legal rights is reflected also in other provisions of the ADR Act. For example, Article 3 ADR Act provides that 'ADR procedures shall, *as legal procedures for settling disputes*, be executed in a fair and appropriate manner while respecting the voluntary efforts of the parties to the dispute for dispute resolution' (emphasis added). It is also in accordance with this idea that the ADR Act requires as one of the certification standards for private mediation services that an attorney is always available for consultation when specialised knowledge on the interpretation and application of laws and regulations is required in the process of their services (Article 6(5) ADR Act).

As for the view in academia, it is common to find three viewpoints explaining the value of ADR, these being (i) reduction of the caseloads of courts, (ii) expansion of access to justice and (iii) realisation of values other than justice. Although there are a variety of nuances as regards how to understand the relation between justice and ADR, the prevailing opinion seems to attach importance to ensuring the self-determination of the parties to a dispute by enriching ADR. From this perspective, access to courts should not be restricted without justifiable cause. The reduction of caseloads is hence theoretically expected only as a consequence of the free decisions of users, even if it is practically the main goal of encouraging ADR.[26]

ii. Effectiveness of Promotion of ADR

It is questionable if the ADR Act has been achieving its intended objective. Indeed, the number of certified private mediation services has been increasing. Nevertheless, as

[24] *Recommendations of the Justice System Reform Council* (Shihô Seido Kaikaku Shingi-kai Iken-sho) (issued on 12 June 2001). Its English version is available at <www.kantei.go.jp/foreign/policy/sihou/singikai/990612_e.html>.

[25] Ibid, ch II, part 8.

[26] For an overview of the discussion in Japan see, eg S Kakiuchi, 'Kuni ni yoru ADR no sokushin' [The Promotion of ADR by State] in Y Hayakawa et al, *ADR no Kihonteki Shiza* [ADR: Fundamental viewpoints] (Tokyo, Shinzansha, 2004) 61.

described above in part I.D, as far as *private* ADR services are concerned, the encouraging effect is still not quite conspicuous.

Generally speaking, there is still no particular regulation in the early conflict resolution phase to encourage the use of ADR.[27] However, the legislator is aware that more information about ADR should be given to the public to promote its use. Thus, the ADR Act stipulates as responsibilities of the government that the government and local public entities are to endeavour to provide information on ADR (Article 4 ADR Act). However, as mentioned above, this objective is far from being achieved.

In this regard, the Act on Comprehensive Legal Support enacted in 2004 is worth mentioning. The aim of this law is to provide appropriate legal information and services throughout the nation (Article 2 Legal Support Act). To that end, the Japan Legal Support Centre (Nihon Shihô Shien Centre) was established as the principal vehicle of all the support programs provided by this law.[28] The mission of this Centre, which is nicknamed '*Hô Terasu*',[29] is to provide 'comprehensive legal support' (Article 14 Legal Support Act), which means to offer 'information and data that contribute to the valid use of systems for judicial decisions or other settlements of disputes based on laws' to parties to a dispute (Article 30(1)(i) Legal Support Act). Its information service is carried out mainly by its call centre operators replying to telephone inquiries from parties to a dispute. It is hence expected that the necessary information about ADR will be diffused by activities of the centre. However, this is not actually the case. In 2009, its call centres replied to about 400,000 telephone inquiries, among which information on a specific certified mediation service was offered in only 679 cases. On the one hand, operators themselves do not have enough information about private ADR services. On the other hand, inquirers do not ask for such information because, for most of them, private ADR services still remain out of sight. The situation needs improvement.

Also, there is no general sanction which serves to encourage parties to use ADR services before going to court. Besides, as seen above in part I.E, there are no conspicuous benefits at present as far as private ADR services are concerned. Availability of experts, relative inexpensiveness, speed and a specific mediation method may favour the use of ADR in certain circumstances.

Concerning private ADR services, the competitiveness with court-annexed mediation procedures, rather than with lawsuits, is essential, because court-annexed mediation procedures are their most powerful rivals. As already mentioned above, private ADR services need to appeal to the public through the quality of mediators and their dispute resolution methods, thereby finding niches left for them which are not fully covered by court procedures. This still remains to be achieved.

B. Motives to Regulate ADR Procedures

To a certain extent, the promotion of ADR and its regulation are two sides of the same coin, because regulation aims at ensuring the quality of ADR and, if this is achieved, ADR becomes a more attractive choice for users. However, leaving the pro-

[27] At present, lawyers are not legally required to advise clients as to ADR procedures.
[28] Its services started in October 2006.
[29] Literally, 'Terrace of Law'. 'Terasu' also means 'enlighten'.

motion of ADR out of consideration, there are still at least two other reasons which require the government to control the quality of mediation.

First, the government may have an interest in protecting the users from undue damage caused by a mediation process. For instance, the government has an interest in preventing a mediation process from resulting in an illegitimate agreement, such as one which is against public policy.[30] Agreements induced by any fraud or duress[31] should equally be prevented, even if the content of the agreement is not illegal. In any of these cases, the result of mediation is not legitimate, and thus it seems to be undeniable that these situations should be avoided.

Secondly, concern about the quality of self-determination by the parties may require that they are well informed about their legal situation. If the access to legal information is in fact only limited in Japan as a result of the small number of lawyers and other reasons, one may expect such information to be provided on the occasion of mediation.

In this regard, it is also worth mentioning that the regulation of ADR in Japan has been considerably affected by the existence of an article in the Attorney Act which provides that 'No person other than an attorney . . . may, for the purpose of obtaining compensation, engage in the business of providing legal advice or representation, *handling arbitration matters*, *aiding in conciliation*, . . . or other general legal services'[32] (Article 72 Attorney Act; emphasis added). Thus, it prohibits persons without the qualification of attorney-at-law from engaging in conciliation or mediation on a regular or business basis. Violation of this is punishable as a crime (Article 77 Attorney Act). These provisions have given rise to discussion about whether a mediator or arbitrator without the qualification of attorney at law may receive fees for his or her activities. Theoretically, the prevailing opinion has been that this conduct may be saved from punishment insofar as the mediation or arbitration in question is considered to be unpunishable 'lawful business' in the sense of Article 35 Penal Code. However, notwithstanding this interpretation, the position of mediators or arbitrators remains unsecure because punishability depends on the evaluation of 'lawfulness' in each case. This was one of the problems that the legislator had to cope with in the enactment of ADR Act. According to Article 28 ADR Act, mediators are allowed to receive fees as far as their mediation services have been certified by the Minister of Justice under the scheme established by this Act for carrying out the services of certified dispute resolution. Nevertheless, the problem remains because this exception is not applicable to arbitration and the treatment of uncertified mediators is left untouched.

Consequently, the present position of Japanese law in this regard can be summarised as follows:

(i) On the one hand, if mediation occurs on a purely ad hoc basis, there is no legal regulation. However, Article 3 ADR Act may apply—providing that any ADR procedures, 'as legal procedures for settling disputes, be executed in a fair and appropriate manner' and 'be aimed at achieving prompt dispute resolution based on specialized expertise and in accordance with the actual facts of the dispute'—although no legal sanction is connected to this article.

[30] An agreement which is against public policy is void (Art 90 Civil Code).

[31] Such an agreement may be rescinded (Art 96 Civil Code).

[32] The English translation of this act is available at <http://www.japaneselawtranslation.go.jp/law/detail/?id=1878&vm=02&re=02&new=1>.

(ii) On the other hand, if a mediator carries out his/her services on regular basis, the regulation is different according to whether he/she requires any fees for his/her services. (a) If no fees are intended, the regulation is the same as in case (i). Accordingly the mediator is legally expected to engage in mediation 'in a fair and appropriate manner' and 'based on specialized expertise', etc, but there is no sanction. (b) Conversely, if any compensation is intended, a strict regulation applies. As mentioned above, only attorneys are allowed to engage in such mediation with a few exceptions (Article 72 Attorney Act[33]). One of the major exceptions to this rule was introduced by the ADR Act. Persons who carry out mediation services on a regular basis may obtain certification by the Minister of Justice for their services (Article 5 ADR Act). Mediators of certified ADR providers may receive fees for their certified dispute resolution services notwithstanding Article 72 Attorney Act (Article 28 ADR Act).

As certification standards, the ADR Act imposes diverse conditions. For example, a person who is an organised crime group member is not eligible to obtain certification (Article 7(8) ADR Act). In addition, as mentioned above, in cases where the ADR provider is not qualified as an attorney, the provider has to take 'measures to ensure that an attorney is available for consultation when specialized knowledge on the interpretation and application of laws and regulations is required in the process of providing private dispute resolution' (Article 6(5) ADR Act). According to the guideline issued by the Ministry of Justice for enforcement of the ADR Act[34], 'when specialized knowledge on the interpretation and application of laws and regulations is required' means 'cases where an advanced legal issue, the judgment of which is generally difficult for an ordinary citizen, arises, and its solution would be necessary to determine how to manage the subsequent proceedings'[35] (section 2(5) of the guideline). Furthermore, according to the same guideline, mediators should be capable of determining by themselves whether they stand in need of 'specialized knowledge on the interpretation and application of laws and regulations', namely consultation with an attorney. This determination should not depend on a subjective judgment of the mediator, but it should be made 'in conformity with objective standards based on the type and amount of dispute, nature and substance of the question, etc' (section 2(5) e(a) of the guideline). To meet this requirement, such standards need to be given to the mediator in advance, eg in the form of a manual which explains basic statutes and case law concerning the types of disputes for which the provider is certified, so that the mediator can resort to an attorney when he faces a legal question which is not explained in this manual (ibid).

According to the explanation given by one of the authors of the guideline, the justification for such regulation is found in the idea that 'since private dispute resolution procedures intervene in disputes among other persons, it is natural to require them to be executed in a fair and appropriate manner'.[36]

[33] Punishment by imprisonment with work for not more than two years or a fine of not more than ¥3 million (approximately US$30,000) applies to its violation (Art 77 No 4 Attorney Act).

[34] Only its Japanese version is available at <www.moj.go.jp/content/000004651.pdf>.

[35] Translation by the author.

[36] K Uchibori, 'Saibangai Funso Kaiketsu Tetsuzuki no Riyô no Sokushin ni kansuru Horitsu no Gaiyô' [Outline of the Law on Promotion of Use of Alternative Dispute Resolution] (2005) 4 *Hôritsu no Hiroba* 8 (Translated by the author).

However, it is discussed in academia whether these regulations are not excessive in the way they hinder particular types of mediation, such as mediation based on a purely facilitative approach, in favour of an evaluative, law-oriented approach toward mediation.[37]

C. Constraints as Regards the Regulation of ADR Resulting from Constitutional Law

As regards constraints in the regulation of ADR stemming from constitutional or human rights law, it is worth mentioning the principle of private autonomy as well certain attendant aspects. In Japan, this principle is commonly regarded as the most fundamental principle in the domain of private law, and some argue that it derives from the right of self-determination, which is guaranteed under Article 13 of the Constitution.[38] This principle, which applies basically to all disputes of a private law nature, has several implications concerning the process of dispute resolution.

On the one hand, although the principle leaves the rights and obligations of parties at their own disposition and hence the state has to accept their agreement resolving their dispute, it does not mean that parties are obliged to resolve their disputes by way of settlement. On the contrary, the principle of private autonomy implies parties' freedom *not* to resolve their disputes at all.[39] Moreover, if parties should not be forced to make a concession to resolve their disputes, it implies also that parties are free to claim their substantive rights by way of lawsuit. Thus, the principle of private autonomy is closely connected to the right of access to the courts. This sets a certain limit to the promotive regulation of ADR (see below III).

On the other hand, the principle of private autonomy implies also that if parties wish to resolve their disputes autonomically outside the courts, they are free to decide how. Hence, they may arrange their procedure at their own convenience. This sets a certain limit to the regulation of ADR concerning the details of the procedure.

III. REGULATION OF SPECIFIC ADR INSTRUMENTS

A. Overview

First, judicial mediation procedures and ADR services provided by administrative organs are regulated by law, since these are institutions established by law.

Secondly, as for private mediation procedures, there is the ADR Act, which was enacted in 2004 and entered into force in 2007. In addition, as mentioned above, in

[37] See, eg S Kakiuchi, 'Chôteisha no Shishitsu wo meguru Giron no Igi to Shosô' [Mediator As It Should Be?—Meanings and Aspects of the Question in Current Japanese Context] (2010) 5 *Journal of Japanese Arbitration and ADR* 128.

[38] Art 13 of the Constitution provides that 'All of the people shall be respected as individuals. Their right to life, liberty, and the pursuit of happiness shall, to the extent that it does not interfere with the public welfare, be the supreme consideration in legislation and in other governmental affairs', English translation available at <www.japaneselawtranslation.go.jp/law/detail/?id=174&vm=02&re=02&new=1>.

[39] In the context of the law of civil procedure, this is known as the principle of party disposition (no judgment without action).

the field of financial business there is the Financial Instruments and Exchange Act, amended in 2009.

Thirdly, arbitration is regulated by the Arbitration Law enacted in 2003. This law is based on the UNCITRAL Model Law.[40]

As we have already seen the outline of regulation in respect of judicial mediation in I.B, the explanation here will focus on the regulation of private mediation (part B).[41] The regulation of negotiation and arbitration will be mentioned quite briefly thereafter (parts C and D).[42]

B. Mediation[43]

i. Generality

So far as private mediation is concerned, mediation procedure is widely left to the arrangement between the mediation service provider and its users, who are the parties to a dispute. In other words, the principle of freedom of contract applies entirely. Additionally, since there are no default rules regarding the mediation procedure, it is entirely subject to private regulation by contract.

However, this description needs some additional remarks.

First, except for mediation procedures on a purely ad hoc basis, which are quite exceptional cases, mediation services are provided by certain permanent organisations. In the latter cases, it is common for users to accept the procedural rules provided by these organisations (if users do not like them, they simply decline to use the service). In this sense, rules of these organisations play a role similar to default rules.

Secondly, there is rather strict regulation as regards the qualification of mediators (see above II.B): only the attorneys or mediators of certified ADR providers are allowed to engage in mediation on a regular basis with the intention of receiving fees. Hence, certification standards may well affect the content of private mediation services. In this context, it is worth mentioning that the ADR Act regulates matters such as the neutrality of mediators (Article 6(3) and (4) ADR Act), an appropriate method for giving notification when executing procedures (Article. 6(6) ADR Act) and prompt notification of the request for mediation to the other party (Article 6(9) ADR Act).

Thirdly, as explained below in part III.B viii, provisions of the Consumer Contract Act may apply if a party to the dispute is a consumer.

[40] See S Kakiuchi, 'Uniform Law and Arbitration in Japan' (2010) 7 *University of Tokyo Journal of Law and Politics* 102. See also below III.E.

[41] In Japanese law, there is no distinction between mediation and conciliation in terms of regulation.

[42] In Japanese law, there is no special regulation applicable to expert opinion. If it takes place in a mediation procedure in a broad sense, the same rules apply as in the regulation on mediation. In fact, as seen above in I.E, the competitiveness of private mediation services mainly consists in their speciality in particular fields of disputes. Thus, the role of mediator bears some resemblance to that of an expert, though it seems to be rare that expert opinions as such are asked for independently of a mediation process.

[43] See also H Baum, 'Mediation in Japan: Development, Forms, Regulation and Practice of Out-of-Court Dispute Resolution' in KJ Hopt and F Steffek (eds), *Mediation: Principles and Regulation in Comparative Perspective* (Oxford, Oxford University Press, 2013) 1011.

ii. Influence of the UNCITRAL Model Law on International Commercial Conciliation (2002)

The drafting of the Japanese ADR Law began in February 2002, several months earlier than the enactment of the UNCITRAL Model Law. However, since one of the Japanese representatives on the Working Group on Arbitration—which was in charge of drafting the UNCITRAL Model Law—was a member of the drafting committee of the ADR Act (ADR Kentô-kai) set up within the secretariat of the Headquarters for Judicial System Reform, the legislator was well aware of the discussion in the UNCITRAL Working Group. Thus, the Japanese translation of the Model Law was presented to the committee immediately after its enactment, and was referred to many times during the discussions of the committee.

However, it is hard to find traces of the Model Law in the provisions of the Japanese ADR Act. The main reason for this is that the Japanese legislator abandoned any attempt to incorporate provisions on mediation proceedings, while the regulation of these proceedings is the main topic that the Model Law deals with. Still, some of the topics dealt with by provisions of the Model Law, like the question of confidentiality or enforceability of settlement agreements, have influenced the discussion in Japan and remain as subjects for future legislation.

iii. Effect of a Mediation Clause

While the use of 'good faith negotiation' clauses has been rather common in Japanese contract practice, the use of a clause prescribing mediation remained rare until recently. Consequently, there have been hardly any academic discussions or court decisions on the question.

However, an interesting case was reported quite recently in this regard.[44] In this case, the Tokyo High Court held that a mediation clause does not prevent an action before the state courts and justified this mainly with the following two reasons: (i) unlike an arbitration agreement, in case of which dispute resolution without legal action is guaranteed, a mediation clause cannot replace entirely resort to legal action. Therefore, access to courts should not be readily deprived by its inclusion in a contract; (ii) Article 26 ADR Act, which authorises the court to suspend legal proceedings for four months at the longest when a certified dispute resolution procedure is in progress, presupposes that a mediation clause does not prevent parties from filing a legal action. According to this decision, a mediation clause produces no procedural effect.

As this decision states, it goes too far to conclude that a simple mediation clause provides a reason to dismiss an action brought before a state court. However, it is questionable if this means that such a clause has absolutely no procedural effect. Since it is commonly accepted that an agreement not to bring a legal action before the

[44] Tokyo High Court, Judgment of 22 June 2011, *Hanrei Jihô*, Vol 2116, p 64. In the case at issue, the agreement between the plaintiff and the defendant included the following clause: 'To the extent that any Party disagrees about how to allocate a Shared Resolution Amount . . . under this Agreement, the Parties shall conduct good faith negotiations concerning any such dispute. If such negotiations do not fully resolve the dispute within sixty days of the commencement of such good faith negotiations, any Party may then submit the matter to a neutral Japanese mediator . . . If mediation does not fully resolve the dispute, the Parties agree that any legal action to resolve any remaining issues shall be commenced in the courts of Japan' (translated by the author).

courts (*pactum de non petendo*) is effective, a mediation clause may be interpreted as such an agreement, though its effect should be limited to a certain period, as far as the terms of agreement are precise and reasonable.[45]

As for the question of whether there are any state court procedures aiding the enforcement of a mediation agreement (eg appointing mediators and contesting mediator impartiality), no such procedures currently exist.

iv. Absence of Mechanisms Allowing a Court to Refer a Dispute to a Private Mediation Procedures

As mentioned above in part I.B, a trial court may advise parties to compromise at any stage of the lawsuit (Article 89 Code of Civil Procedure). In addition, a trial court may refer a case to court-annexed mediation. However, once the pre-trial proceedings for arrangement of the issues and evidence have been concluded, each party to the lawsuit has the right to refuse this referral.

As regards private mediation, there is at present no such mechanism. Although the possibility of introducing such an institution was discussed during the legislative proceedings surrounding the ADR Act, it was rejected for the following reasons. First, if this referral is of a compulsory character, it would infringe on the right of access to the courts as guaranteed by the Constitution (Article 32). Secondly, if it means only to recommend to parties that they use ADR on a voluntary basis, it is possible without any express provision of law. Thirdly, under the present state of affairs whereby the performance of extra-judicial ADR procedures remains unsatisfactory and the courts are not well informed about them, such a provision could easily become a dead letter.

Nevertheless, the need for creating a flow of cases from courts to ADR procedures still exists. Thus, recently, the Japan ADR Association, which was founded by private ADR organisations in 2010, submitted to the Minister of Justice its recommendations for the reform of the ADR Act, including a proposal to provide expressly in the Act that courts can recommend to parties that they resort to a private ADR service.[46]

v. Duties of Mediators

a. Duties of Mediators in General. As indicated above in part III.B.i, regulation of private mediation is widely left in the parties' hands, although procedural rules provided by ADR organisations play an important role in practice. This applies equally to the duties of mediators.

However, it is worth mentioning that the ADR Act has several articles regarding the duties of mediators.

First, the Act declares that ADR procedures

> shall . . . be executed in a fair and appropriate manner while respecting the voluntary efforts of the parties to the dispute for dispute resolution, and be aimed at achieving prompt dispute resolution based on specialized expertise and in accordance with the actual facts

[45] See Kakiuchi, 'Médiation et droit des contrats: une perspective japonaise' 104–05.

[46] *Teigen ADR hô no kaisei ni mukete* [Recommendations for the Reform of the ADR Act] recommendation 6-1. Its Japanese version is available at <japan-adr.or.jp/?p=603>. The author participated in the working group preparing the recommendation as its chairperson.

> of the dispute . . . Persons involved in the alternative dispute resolution procedures shall, in compliance with the basic concepts set forth in the preceding paragraph, strive to cooperate and collaborate with one another. [Article 2 ADR Act]

However, this duty is quite abstract and without any sanction.

Secondly, as the certification standards, the Act requires that the applicant should establish

> a method for preserving in an appropriate manner suited to the nature of the information, the communications of the parties to a dispute or other third parties that are contained in opinions stated or materials submitted or presented through private dispute resolution procedures. [Article 6(11) ADR Act]

Thirdly, the Act imposes several duties on certified dispute resolution business operators. For example, certified dispute resolution business operators must, prior to conclusion of a contract for execution of certified dispute resolution procedures, give the parties to a dispute an explanation of certain aspects, including the matters concerning the selection of a dispute resolution provider, matters concerning any fees or expenses payable by the parties to a dispute, and the standard operation process from the commencement to the termination of executing the certified dispute resolution procedures (Article 14 ADR Act).

Generally speaking, it does not make a difference whether the mediator is a lawyer or not. However, while the duty of confidentiality is expressly stipulated for lawyers by the Attorney Act (Article 23[47]) and they are accordingly granted the right to refuse to testify (Article 197 Code of Civil Procedure), the duty of confidentiality of mediators who lack qualification as a lawyer is only indirectly suggested by the above-mentioned certification standards. Consequently, they do not have a right to refuse to testify.

b. Enforcement of the Duties. Theoretically, a client could sue her/his mediator for damages caused by malpractice if the mediator neglected her/his duties. However, no such cases have been reported so far.

c. Mechanisms to Ensure Quality. As for mechanisms to ensure the quality of the service, as mentioned many times, Article 72 Attorney Act and the certification standards of the ADR Act play a certain role (see above II.B and III.B.i). For the certification, it is required that the applicant ADR organisation defines the type of disputes to which it can apply its specialised expertise and that it is capable of selecting as mediator an appropriate person for each case with respect to the nature of the disputes (Article 6(1) and (2) ADR Act). This may give the ADR organisations a motive for improving the quality of mediators.

The most powerful mechanism seems to be the competition with the court-annexed mediation procedures and ADR services provided by administrative organs. As seen above in I.B and C, these public ADR services have been strong competitors to private ADR services. In order to secure more clients, it is essential for the latter to increase their competitiveness in terms of quality.

[47] It provides that '[u]nless otherwise provided by law, an attorney or a former attorney shall have the right and bear the duty to maintain the confidentiality of any facts which he/she may have learned in the course of performing his/her duties'.

vi. Duties of the Parties

As far as private mediation procedures are concerned, the question of under which condition a party may withdraw from an ongoing mediation depends on how the termination of the procedure is regulated by the contract between the service provider and the parties. Normally, rules prepared by the ADR organisation apply to the question, unless otherwise agreed by the parties.[48] For certified private mediation procedures, the ADR Act requires that the conditions and modes for terminating the procedures are determined and that the procedure should be promptly terminated by the mediator when she/he considers it impossible to arrange a settlement between the parties (Article 6(7) and (8) ADR Act).

As regards the remuneration of mediators,[49] mediators with the qualification of attorney and those engaged in certified ADR are expressly authorised to receive fees. The amount is determined by contract, but, again, the rules of the ADR organisations play an important role. For certified private mediation procedures, the ADR Act requires that the organisation should determine the amount or methods of calculation and payment and that they are not extremely unreasonable (Article 6(15) ADR Act).

vii. Enforceability of Mediation Agreements

As explained above in I.B, mediation agreements resulting from judicial mediation are enforceable in the same way as court judgments.

As for private mediation agreements, they remain normal contracts and hence are not enforceable as such. The enforceability of mediation agreements was one of the questions producing the most seriously divergent opinions during the legislative proceedings on the ADR Act. While the opinion in favour of the enforceability was fairly strong, it could not overcome the anxiety over an abuse of such a possibility. However, the debate continues, and the Japan ADR Association proposed the introduction of enforceability recently in its recommendations for the reform of the ADR Act.

Consequently, as a general rule, a party to a mediation agreement needs to file a new lawsuit based on it so as to carry out a compulsory execution if the other party fails to perform her/his obligation. However, it is worth mentioning that there are several ways to facilitate the enforcement of mediation agreements.

[48] For instance, the rules of the Japan Commercial Arbitration Association have the following provision on the question (English version is available at<www.jcaa.or.jp/e/arbitration/docs/e_shouji.pdf>):

Rule 10. Termination of Mediation

1. Unless otherwise agreed by the parties, the mediation proceedings shall be terminated within three (3) months of the date when the mediator was appointed pursuant to Rule 7. At the request of the mediator, the Association may extend this period of time.
2. The mediation proceedings are terminated by any of the following instances:
   (1) The Association has given a notice as provided for in Rule 6 Paragraph 5;
   (2) Settlement has been arrived at by the parties;
   (3) The period of time provided for in the preceding paragraph has expired;
   (4) The mediator, after consultation with the parties, declared in writing to the parties and the Association that there is no hope of resolving disputes by the mediation proceedings; or
   (5) Any of the parties requested termination of the mediation proceedings in writing to the mediator (the Association, if the mediator has not been appointed).
3. When the mediation proceedings are to be terminated, the mediator shall notify the Association to that effect in writing.

[49] Explained above in II.B.

First, if the parties so agree, they can conclude an arbitration agreement and thereby appoint the mediator as their arbitrator. Thus, the arbitral tribunal may record the mediation agreement in the form of an arbitral award, which has the same effect as a normal arbitral award (Article 38(1) and (2) Arbitration Law). A party seeking enforcement based on an arbitral award may apply to a court for a decision authorising such an enforcement against the counterparty (Article 46(1) Arbitration Law). Since this procedure is a simplified one, it can be a useful way to render a mediation agreement enforceable.

Secondly, for the parties who came to a mediation agreement, the institution of 'settlement prior to filing of action' is available. A party may file a petition for settlement with the summary court (Article 275 Code of Civil Procedure) and let the court official record the settlement. Thus, the settlement will have the same effect as a final and binding judgment (Article 267 Code of Civil Procedure).

Thirdly, though the availability is limited to a claim for payment of a certain amount of money or claims concerning any other fungible thing, parties may go to a notary who will accordingly prepare a notarial deed, based on which compulsory execution can be carried out (Article 22(5) Civil Execution Act).

In practice, these three methods (the first one in particular) play a role equivalent to the enforceability of mediation agreements.

viii. Special Rules for Consumer

As regards mediation, the ADR Act provides no special rule for consumers. However, some provisions of Consumer Contract Act may apply to settlement agreements concluded between consumers and business operators.[50] Thus, for example, clauses of such agreements are void if they restrict the rights of consumers or expand the duties of consumers beyond those under the provisions of the Civil Code and other laws, or impair the interests of consumers unilaterally contrary to the principle of good faith (Article 10 Consumer Contract Act).[51]

C. Negotiation

i. Rules Applicable to the Pre-contractual Stage of Negotiation

There is no special procedural rule applicable to the pre-contractual stage of negotiation.

As for rules of a substantive law nature, certain general provisions of the Civil Code concerning the validity of a legal transaction (*Rechtsgeschäft*) have a certain effect on the pre-contractual negotiation. This is the case, for example, with regards

[50] The term 'business operator' as used in this Act means juridical person(s), association(s) and individual(s) who become a party to a contract as a business or for the purpose of business (Art 2(2) Consumer Contract Act).

[51] Commission Recommendation of 4 April 2001 on the principles for out-of-court bodies involved in the consensual resolution of consumer disputes, C(2001) 1016, does not apply to Japan and the Recommendation has not been followed directly. However, the ADR Act has provisions which are analogous to the principles stated in it, although the scope of these provisions is not limited to consumer disputes.

to the provisions on mistake (Article 95 Civil Code), fraud or duress (Article 96 Civil Code).

Furthermore, provisions of the above-mentioned Consumer Contract Act may apply if one party to a negotiation is a consumer and the other a business operator (see above III.B.viii).

ii. Duties to Negotiate

The answer to the question whether duties to negotiate are enforceable depends on the meaning of enforceability.

First, there is the question of whether duties to negotiate are executable in the sense that the procedure of compulsory execution is applicable. Since, on the one hand, it is commonly accepted that specific performance of an obligation of action or inaction cannot be compelled[52] and, on the other hand, execution by substitute is not by nature applicable to an obligation to negotiate, the question comes down to that of the applicability of so-called indirect compulsory execution, namely the method in which the court orders the obligor to pay to the obligee money of a certain amount that is found to be reasonable for securing performance of the obligation, according to the period of the delay or immediately if the obligor fails to perform the obligation within a certain period that is found to be reasonable (Article 172 Civil Execution Act). Presently, the prevailing opinion holds that an obligation is not enforceable even in the way of indirect compulsory execution if its utility consists essentially in voluntary performance.[53] Although there have been practically no discussions on the applicability of indirect compulsory execution to duties to negotiate, it seems difficult to answer the question in the affirmative since spontaneity is essential for a successful negotiation. Besides, it would not make sense to file a lawsuit in order to obtain a title of obligation, which would be necessary for such execution.

Secondly, the question arises whether such duties could be enforced by legal sanction in case of default. This corresponds to the issues discussed below in part iii.

iii. Liability for Breaking Off Negotiation in Bad Faith

So far as a duty to negotiate is agreed, liability can be imposed for its non-performance under the general conditions provided by Article 415 Civil Code.[54] However, it may be hard to prove the existence of damage and the amount thereof.

[52] Art 414 Civil Code provides that the enforcement of specific performance shall not apply to cases where the nature of the obligation does not permit such enforcement. It is commonly accepted that the enforcement of specific performance is not applicable to obligations of action or inaction other than delivery of things because of the nature of obligations.

[53] See, eg T Uchida, *Minpô* [Civil Law], vol III, 3rd edn (Tokyo, The University of Tokyo Press, 2005) 111. For instance, the obligation of a spouse to live together with the other spouse is not enforceable at all.

[54] It provides that if an obligor fails to perform consistent with the purpose of the obligation, the obligee shall be entitled to demand damages arising from such failure.

D. Arbitration

i. The Arbitration Law of 2003

After a long period of inactivity of the legislator dating back to 1890, the new Arbitration Law was enacted in July 2003 and came into force in March 2004. It is based on the UNCITRAL Model Law, and thus Japan became the forty-fifth country to adopt the Model Law.

ii. Minimum Procedural Standard

Since the UNCITRAL Model Law is followed, the structure of regulation is basically the same as Article 19 of the Model Law: parties are free to agree on the procedure, but it may not violate the provisions of the Arbitration Law relating to public policy (Article 26 Arbitration Law). Which provisions of the law belong to those relating to public policy is left to interpretation. The requirement of equal treatment of parties (Article 26 Arbitration Law) can be cited as an example of such provisions.

iii. Arbitration and Mandatory Law

According to the Arbitration Law, the recognition of an arbitration award is to be refused if the content of the arbitral award would be contrary to the public policy of Japan (Article 45(2)(ix) Arbitration Law).

In this regard, it should be noted that the notion of the public policy of Japan is considered more narrowly than the notion of mandatory provisions. Thus, among the mandatory provisions, only those which constitute the fundamental part of the public order of Japan should be considered in this regard. But the question of which mandatory provisions should be considered as constituent of the public order in this sense needs further consideration.[55]

iv. Enforcement of Arbitral Award

As mentioned above in III.B, a party seeking enforcement based on an arbitral award may apply to a court for a decision authorising enforcement based on an arbitral award against the counterparty (Article 46(1) Arbitration Law).

v. Special Rules for Consumers

Arbitration Law has some special provision applicable to consumers. Though it is based on the UNCITRAL Model Law on '*International Commercial* Arbitration', the Japanese Arbitration Law applies as a general rule to all arbitral proceedings regardless of whether they are civil or commercial, international or domestic. However, there is an exception regarding arbitration agreements concluded between consumers and businesses, the subject of which is civil disputes that may arise in the future.

[55] According to some scholars, only the provisions which embody 'superindividual interests' should be considered as such. This understanding might correspond approximately to the French notion of 'lois de police et de sûreté'. See, eg K Miki and K Yamamoto, *Shin chûsai hô no riron to jitsumu* [Theory and Practice of the New Arbitration Law] (Tokyo, Yuhikaku, 2006) 343.

A consumer may cancel such an arbitration agreement unless she/he is the claimant in arbitral proceedings (Article 3(2) Supplementary Provisions to the Arbitration Law). In the case where a business is the claimant in arbitral proceedings, the arbitral tribunal is to carry out an oral hearing prior to any other proceedings (Article 3(3) and (4) Supplementary Provisions to the Arbitration Law). The arbitral tribunal must notify the consumer in advance, by the sending of a document, as well as on the day of the oral hearing, that she/he may cancel the arbitration agreement (Article 3(5) and (6) Supplementary Provisions to the Arbitration Law). If the consumer does not express the intent to waive the right of cancellation on the day of the oral hearing, she/he will be deemed to have cancelled the arbitration agreement (Article 3(6) Supplementary Provisions to the Arbitration Law). She/he will be deemed to have cancelled the arbitration agreement also if she/he fails to appear on the date of the oral hearing (Article 3(7) Supplementary Provisions to the Arbitration Law).

These provisions apply 'for the time being until otherwise enacted' (Article 3(1) Supplementary Provisions to the Arbitration Law).[56] Similar rules apply also to arbitration agreements concerning individual labour-related disputes (Article 4 Supplementary Provisions to the Arbitration Law).

IV. SOME REMARKS ON POLICY QUESTIONS

A. Justifications for the Regulation of ADR

It is not self-evident that the government is concerned with the regulation of ADR, since ADR by nature embodies spontaneous activities of private citizens not depending on public authority. It takes place in the domain of private autonomy. Therefore, as regards the question whether ADR should be regulated at all, the theoretical starting point should be the principle of private autonomy. However, as already discussed above in II.A and B, there seem to be two reasons which may give rise to such concerns by the government, though they are closely related to each other, like two sides of the same coin.

The first reason is the need for the restriction of ADR. If an ADR procedure of poor quality may cause damage to its users, the government may perceive the need to intervene in ADR processes in order to prevent such damage in advance.

The second reason is the need to promote the use of mediation. For this purpose, the government may take a certain interest in improving the quality of ADR procedures.

Although it depends on social conditions if these considerations give sufficient justification for regulating ADR, there seems to be no reason to conclude that ADR should not be regulated at all.

B. Forms and Nature of Regulation

The forms and nature of regulation can vary depending on their purpose and the degree of intervention by public authorities.

[56] English translation available at <www.kantei.go.jp/foreign/policy/sihou/arbitrationlaw.pdf>.

i. General Principles of Civil Law

First, even if we fully admit the parties' autonomy as representing the general rule, it is unavoidable that general principles of civil law, such as conditions for valid agreements, effects of contracts and public order, apply to ADR processes. They provide conditions for a legal system to recognise ADR as a legally relevant phenomenon and set certain limits on private autonomy at the same time.

These rules are of a mandatory nature. It is therefore obvious that these rules can be made only by the legislator, namely the Parliament.

ii. Default Rules for Particular ADR Procedures

As another step forward, certain default rules for particular ADR procedures, from which parties may freely deviate by agreement, may be one of a number of possible options for the legislator.

However, some remarks should be made as to the function of such rules.

First, details of procedure and the content of agreements should, in principle, be left to the parties' hands as far as they remain in the sphere of private autonomy. This means that these aspects are decided through the interaction between the interests of the parties and those of ADR service providers. If ADR consists of spontaneous and autonomous activities of private citizens, this aspect should be considered as being fundamental, and one inherent in the concept of ADR.

In this regard, however, it should be noted that users' needs can vary quite widely and, since a mediation process presupposes at least two parties, it is always necessary to consider the demands of these two (or more) parties, which may differ from one another.

Furthermore, the policies of ADR service providers should be taken into consideration. Here, the provider's aim in its activities and the values to which it commits itself would play an important role. In addition, as far as it wishes to be actually used by people, it would have a certain interest in grasping the demand of users and to make some response thereto. This would be the major concern if the provider considers its activities to be commercial business, whereas there may also be providers attaching only secondary importance to maximising the number of clients. In either case, since parties are often rather indifferent to details of procedure, the policies of providers, as reflected in their procedural rules, normally play a decisive role in this regard. Thus, the parties' role is often limited to choosing the service that looks the most attractive to them or to not using ADR services at all if none meets their actual needs.

From this viewpoint, it is meaningful that the legislator provides certain default rules which, by giving a model of procedural arrangements, indirectly control the interaction between parties and ADR providers and protect the parties' interests. However, on the other hand, for the state aiming to promote the use of ADR, it is essential to develop the diversity of services available so as to cover the various needs of potential users. Therefore, if attempts at default rules or model laws are made, the danger of decreasing the diversity should also be taken into account.

iii. Rules Giving Special Effects to the Use of ADR

If there is a need to promote ADR by giving certain special effects to the use of ADR procedures, such as suspension of prescription and suspension of lawsuits,[57] as is the case in Japan, there should be standards to limit the scope of those effects. These rules are of a mandatory nature and can be made only by the state legislator.

However, again, because such rules will function as a more extensive state intervention into private ADR procedures, the danger of decreasing the diversity of ADR services should be also taken into account.

iv. ADR Procedures Offered by the State

It is also possible that the state could offer some ADR procedures as a component of the state civil justice system.

However, if the state offers such procedures while at the same time supporting private ADR services—as in Japan, where the legislator has, on the one hand, offered some court-annexed mediation procedures yet, on the other hand, is attempting to promote private ADR services by supporting them as an alternative—the question arises if these two approaches are compatible with each other.

Logically, these two approaches seem to be quite compatible with each other. If the objective of the legislator is, for example, the 'realisation of the rights and interests of the people', as the Japanese legislator suggests in Article 1 ADR Act[58] (see above II.A.i), it is natural to consider ADR as part of the justice system. Thus, the question comes down to the choice of the most effective way in which the state achieves the same objective.

However, if the state follows both of these two paths at the same time, it may cause a concern that 'what the right hand gives, the left hand takes away'. As the current situation in Japan suggests, if the state sets up well-equipped public ADR services, they may disturb the development of the private services that the state wishes to promote. Thus, it is necessary to find an effective way for an appropriate case distribution between the public and private sectors, which is not easy, as the current situation in Japan shows.

v. Conclusion

Starting from the principle of private autonomy, it is left to the parties themselves to decide which way is the most appropriate to resolve (or *not* resolve at all) their disputes. Therefore, the essential task of the state should be to ensure the minimum

[57] Regarding the question whether the parties should carry all the costs of the conflict resolution, the answer varies depending on the type of disputes and parties. As regards B2B disputes, there is no reason to give the parties any financial aid. However, the need for such aid may exist in case of B2C or C2C disputes. Considering the function of ADR as part of the justice system (see also below IV.B.iv), it seems to be theoretically justifiable to offer such aid within the scheme of legal aid, though it is not yet the case in Japan. The above-mentioned recommendations of the Japan ADR Association (n 46) also propose the expansion of legal aid in this regard.

[58] English translation available at <www.japaneselawtranslation.go.jp/law/detail/?id=1958&vm=02&re=02&new=1>.

quality of ADR on the one hand and to maximise the available choices and information for its users on the other hand.

From this viewpoint, the measures which the state may take in order to promote the use of ADR procedures are the following.

First, it is essential as the basis of the self-determination of the parties that they are well informed of the characteristics of the available dispute resolution mechanisms. However, we cannot always expect that parties will always be prepared for eventual disputes and be equipped with enough information. Thus, it is desirable to develop easy-to-access information services, which can offer information suitable for actual disputes at the request of parties (see also above II.A.ii).

Secondly, default rules or rules giving the use of ADR procedures certain special effects are worth considering. However, the danger of decreasing the diversity of available procedures should be taken into account in this regard.

Further, more invasive measures should be accepted only as the exception, and need sufficient justification. For example, ADR should not be viewed as a compulsory pre-trial procedure except for in certain specific areas of disputes for which ADR is particularly appropriate, as is the case for family matters in Japan.

BIBLIOGRAPHY

Baum, H, 'Mediation in Japan: Development, Forms, Regulation and Practice of Out-of-Court Dispute Resolution' in KJ Hopt and F Steffek (eds), *Mediation: Principles and Regulation in Comparative Perspective* (Oxford, Oxford University Press, 2013) 1011–1094

Haley, JO, 'The Myth of the Reluctant Litigant' (1978) 4 *The Journal of Japanese Studies* 359

Kakiuchi, S, 'Chôteisha no Shishitsu wo meguru Giron no Igi to Shosô [Mediator As It Should Be?—Meanings and Aspects of the Question in Current Japanese Context]' (2010) 5 *Journal of Japanese Arbitration and ADR* 128

Kakiuchi, S, 'Kuni ni yoru ADR no sokushin' [The Promotion of ADR by State] in Y Hayakawa et al, *ADR no Kihonteki Shiza* [ADR: Fundamental viewpoints] (Tokyo, Shinzansha, 2004) 61–92

Kakiuchi, S, 'Médiation et droit des contrats: une perspective japonaise' (2004) 17 *Zeitschrift für Japanisches Recht* 97

Kakiuchi, S, 'Uniform Law and Arbitration in Japan' (2010) 7 *University of Tokyo Journal of Law and Politics* 102

Miki, K and Yamamoto, K, *Shin chûsai hô no riron to jitsumu* [Theory and Practice of the New Arbitration Law] (Tokyo, Yuhikaku, 2006)

Ramseyer, M and Nakazato, M, *Japanese Law: An Economic Approach* (Chicago, University of Chicago Press, 1999)

Recommendations of the Justice System Reform Council (Shihô Seido Kaikaku Shingi-kai Iken-sho) (issued on 12 June 2001), <www.kantei.go.jp/foreign/policy/sihou/singikai/990612_e.html>

Teigen ADR hô no kaisei ni mukete [Recommendations for the Reform of the ADR Act], <http://japan-adr.or.jp/?p=603>

Uchibori, K, 'Saibangai Funso Kaiketsu Tetsuzuki no Riyô no Sokushin ni kansuru Horitsu no Gaiyô' [Outline of the Law on Promotion of Use of Alternative Dispute Resolution] (2005) 4 *Hôritsu no Hiroba* 4

Uchida, T, *Minpô* [Civil Law], vol III, 3rd edn (Tokyo, The University of Tokyo Press, 2005)

Wollschläger, Ch, 'Historical Trends of Civil Litigation in Japan, Arizona, Sweden and Germany: Japanese Legal Culture in the Light of Judicial Statistics' in H Baum (ed), *Japan: Economic Success and Legal System* (New York, Walter de Gruyter, 1997) 89–142

12

Regulation of Dispute Resolution in the Netherlands: Does Regulation Support or Hinder the Use of ADR?

MACHTELD PEL*

* Many thanks to Willemijn Lont for her research on data for this report; to John Bosnak for his generous contribution to this report and to Hans Fokker, Johan Pel and Frits de Vries for their clarifications on certain points.

I. USE OF DISPUTE RESOLUTION MECHANISMS IN THE NETHERLANDS

A. Characteristics of Netherlands Dispute Resolution Mechanisms and Statistics

THE DUTCH PEOPLE are well known for their 'polder behaviour', which means they are initially inclined to solve any conflict or problem through negotiation or consultation, without involvement of third parties. Mediation fits, so to speak, the Dutch character. This does not detract from the fact that not all problems are addressed by the parties, and that in many cases the conflicting parties call on third parties to assist in solving problems. Only a minority of all problems end in with the civil courts.

Twice, most recently in 2009 and earlier in 2003, the research department of the Dutch Ministry of Security and Justice conducted a survey among Dutch citizens about their experiences with problems that could be solved legally (justiciable problems).[1] The surveys provide a complete quantitative overview of the so-called 'landscape of disputes' as seen from the perspective of Netherlands citizens. This gives us information about the incidence of justiciable problems within the population, the strategies and procedures people choose to solve these problems, and the outcome of the different strategies or procedures for resolving their problems.[2]

Below are some of the results shown in these reports from 2009 (and 2003).

About 60% (67%) of the Dutch population experienced one or more justiciable problems. The average number of problems was 1.9 (2.5). About 6% (9.2%) of the respondents reported having made no attempt to resolve their problems, about 42% (45.3%) handled their problems without professional help and around 52% (45.3%) sought advice to resolve their problems. Lawyers (11.3%), legal expense insurers (10.9%) and various other (non-)professional advisers were asked for their advice.

In 12.7% of the cases an official procedure took place, in 4.9% adjudication and in 7.8% an extra-judicial procedure. Some 6.5% (7%) of the problems were solved by the decision of a third party (judge or other neutral party). About 53% (48%) were settled by agreement (only 3% as a result of mediation). About 40% (35%) of the respondents eventually abandoned their efforts to resolve their problems.

Apart from adjudication, there are many possibilities—of a more or less formal

[1] BCJ van Veldhoven and CM Klein Haarhuis, *Geschilbeslechtingsdelta 2009, Over verloop en afloop van (potentieel) juridische problemen van burgers* (The Hague, WODC, Boom juridische uitgevers, 2009); BCJ van Veldhoven, MJ Ter Voert and M van Gammeren-Soeteweij, *Geschilbeslechtingsdelta 2003, Over verloop en afloop van (potentieel) juridische problemen van burgers* (The Hague, WODC, Boom juridische uitgevers, 2003).

[2] The studies were a replication of the Paths to Justice research done in the UK by H Genn (1999) and in Scotland by H Genn and A Paterson (2001).

Table 1: Extra-judicial Dispute Resolution Procedures, Closed Cases[a]

	2005	2006	2007	2008	2009	2010
Administrative objection procedures	661,244	947,229	1,037,656	920,957	934,595	–
Specific types of conciliation/ binding advice						
Rents commission	58,020	33,491	15,107	11,024	13,839	–
Disputes commission	13,633	12,642	11,204	10,684	10,310	–
Mediation market inclusive of referrals by legal desk and judiciary					47,300	51,690
Mediation referred by						
Legal desk	166	1,413	2,137	2,419	2,758	
Judiciary	830	2,133	3,354	3,708	4,183	4,311
Grievance procedure						
National ombudsman	11,451	14,910	13,096	13,102	12,257	–
Arbitration	1,279	1,056	964	1,192	1,276	–
Other procedures						
Specific legal regulations	1,514	1,703	1,709	1,626	1,515	–

[a] Unfortunately, numbers from all procedures could not be found over the same periods, hence the differences between the data.
Sources: Annual report for the Council for the Judiciary 2010; RJM Vogels, *De stand van Mediation in Nederland 2011 (Zoetermeer, Stratus, 2011)* 11.

character—with regard to dispute resolution in the Netherlands. Preventing unnecessary appeals to the Dutch civil courts is part of the Dutch government's objective for a more efficient administration of justice, where the optimal utilisation of judicial capacity is at the forefront.[3]

Overall, six types of extra-judicial dispute resolution procedures are most commonly used in the Netherlands (see Table 1):

- objection procedure in administrative law;
- dispute committees procedure;
- national ombudsman grievance procedure;
- arbitration;
- mediation; and
- other procedures based on specific legislation, regulations or statutes (eg Commissie Gelijke Behandeling (Equal Treatment Commission), Reclame Code Commissie (Advertising Code Committee)).

It is remarkable that the free mediation market in the Netherlands has developed to

[3] BJ Diephuis, RJJ Eshuis and NE de Heer-de Lange, *Rechtspleging Civiel en Bestuur 2008, Ontwikkelingen en samenhangen* (The Hague, WODC, Boom Juridische uitgevers, 2010).

the extent that mediation sees a far greater use than arbitration. Below are some statistical data about mediation and mediators in the Netherlands.

i. Referral to Mediation and Private Mediation Market

Since April 2005 there have been two structural provisions for referral to mediation: via the legal desk[4] and via the judiciary. Additionally, conflicting parties can start mediation on their own initiative or after referral by other bodies. Other referring bodies comprise, for instance, occupational health and safety services, social services, youth services, the police, social advisors, legal aid insurers and governmental bodies. Recent data on the period from January to April 2011 (Council for the Judiciary) regarding referrals to mediation via the judiciary show that the number of referrals has dropped sharply compared to previous years. The total national decrease is almost 28 per cent, this following a constant increase being witnessed since the time the judiciary began making referrals in 2005. One possible cause of the drop is the scrapping of the incentive contribution (the first 2.5 hours of the mediation for free for the parties) as of 1 January 2011.

At the end of 2011, the Netherlands Mediation Institute (NMI) had a report published[5] on the number of mediators, the number of mediations and the developments over the past five years. At the end of 2011 there were 4,493 registered mediators, of whom 931 were certified. From 2012 the registration system has changed: now there are only registered mediators, of which there are currently about 2,500. A small minority (9.8 per cent) of mediators work exclusively as a mediator; the rest engage in additional professional services. For certified mediators this figure is 21 per cent, and for registered mediators it is 6.8 per cent. In 2011, certified mediators performed 29 mediations on average (14 in 2004) and registered mediators performed seven (three in 2004). The total number of mediations in 2011 is estimated at 51,690 by the NMI (in 2009 it was 47,300).

2011 mediations took place in the following categories:

Family	33%	17,058
Labour	25%	12,922
Community	18%	9,304
Government	8%	4,135
Business to Business	8%	4,135
Other	8%	4,135

The total mediation turnover in 2011 has been estimated at almost €55 million; in 2009 it was €51.1 million. The average mediator fee is €138. The average minimum hourly fee is €111 and the average maximum fee is €160.

On average, 69.8 per cent of the mediations result in full agreement, 13.8 per cent in

[4] Legal desks are providers of primary legal services that answer questions about legal problems and can refer parties who are entitled to legal aid to lawyers and to mediation in order to help them resolve their disputes.

[5] RJM Vogels, *De stand van Mediation in Nederland 2011* (Zoetermeer, Stratus, 2011).

partial agreement and 16.4 per cent in no agreement. These percentages have remained more or less constant over the years.

Enrolment for mediations is mainly through individual channels, ie via referrals within the individual networks or as individual acquisitions. For certified mediators, 21.7 per cent of cases are referrals through the judiciary. This is a decreasing occurrence.[6]

Mediators were also asked what the developments in the market were expected to be. Seventy per cent of the mediators responded that they are expecting (strong) growth. The reasons mentioned most frequently were the increased familiarity with mediation in the general public and the increase in costs of judicial procedures.

Mediation is still not generally known as a method for conflict resolution.[7] However, 21 per cent of the conflicting parties referred by the legal desk were familiar with mediation, whereas this figure was 50 per cent in 2008 among parties referred by the judiciary.

B. Strengths and Weaknesses and Appropriateness of Various Dispute Resolution Mechanisms

i. Objection Procedure in the General Administrative Law Act

Individuals or companies that do not agree with a decision of a government body (varying from decisions on simple licences to complex and large-scale infrastructural plans) first need to make their objections known to the administrative authority before going to court. The General Administrative Law Act regulates the procedure. If the interested party does not agree with the decision on appeal, it can lodge an appeal with the court. The objection procedure is the most frequently used of all the extra-judicial dispute resolution procedures discussed here, mostly because this is a compulsory preliminary stage for an appeal to the Dutch civil court. The costs are relatively low and the duration of the procedure is generally short. Nor is it compulsory to call in judicial assistance. In the case of individual objections, many government bodies use a preliminary stage via informal contacts where problems may be solved or they use mediation, which might even result in avoiding the objection procedure. The latter is an increasing trend and is the result of the mediation projects that were initiated by the government at the beginning of 2000.

ii. Dispute Committees and Their Binding Advices[8]

The law offers the possibility of obtaining a binding advice. In the case of binding

[6] Comparison with van Veldhoven and Klein Haarhuis, *Geschilbeslechtingsdelta 2009* 138: frequent referral via the judicial circuit seems out of the question (as of yet). Most of the involved parties indicate having come to mediation on their own initiative (34%), via the other party (20%), via the employer (12%) or via family members, friends or acquaintances (4%). Only 10% (NB of all mediators: certified and registered) report referrals via the legal aid office, the legal desk, lawyers or judges.

[7] Van Veldhoven and Klein Haarhuis, *Geschilbeslechtingsdelta 2009*; van Veldhoven, Ter Voert and van Gammeren-Soeteweij, *Geschilbeslechtingsdelta 2003*.

[8] Diephuis, Eshuis and Heer-de Lange, *Rechtspleging Civiel en Bestuur 2008, Ontwikkelingen en samenhangen*.

advice, the parties present their dispute to an expert based on an agreement (compromise) in which they bind themselves to the expert's opinion. This variation of conflict resolution is not very often used (see also below III.D).

However, in the Netherlands, calling in one of the 48 *dispute committees* is common and effective. Judicially speaking, here, too, it is a matter of binding advice because the agreements that lead to the disputes include that any potential disputes will be subject to the binding advice of a dispute committee. The committees can refer cases to mediation; in the recent past, this has led to an agreement in only 5 per cent of the entire case load.

There are dispute committees for rental affairs and for consumer affairs; these, in turn, are subdivided into various branches (eg for the legal profession, travel sector or care facilities) which concentrate on consumers. The most common disputes arise in the areas of travel, living arrangements, telecommunications, banking and public utility companies.

Appeals against the decisions of the dispute committee are not possible. Businesses taking part in the scheme have all pledged to abide by these rulings, so in practice the rulings will always be complied with. Parties may, however, present the decision to the courts within two months by issuing a summons to the other party. Research shows that two-thirds of the rents commission clients are satisfied with the quality of the service. Evaluations of the dispute committees show that consumer satisfaction depends to a very large extent on the result of the procedure.

iii. National Ombudsman Grievance Procedure[9]

The national ombudsman is for individuals with grievances about government bodies. The complaint may only be lodged after this has been done with the government body itself and the complaint has not been solved. Ombudsman operations practically cover the entire government. They concern hundreds of institutions, such as the government ministries, the police, the water board, the provinces and councils. The ombudsman's authority covers the execution of government directives, for instance the slow processing of letters or requests, no reactions to the requesting party's statements or the incorrect application of regulations. The national ombudsman can instigate investigations and publish reports that might be made public. Moreover, the ombudsman works hard to have the grievances between the government body and the claimant resolved, and he is well known to be a mediation advocate. National ombudsman services are free. According to research, users are most satisfied with interventions that lead to solutions and less so with resolutions by means of a report.

iv. Arbitration

In the Netherlands, arbitration is mostly used in a professional environment where specific technical or market-related knowledge is essential for dispute resolution particular to conflicts regarding the building industry and to (international) trade disputes. For over 100 years there has been a tradition in the Netherlands to solve problems between professionals in the construction industry by means of two well-known arbi-

[9] Ibid, 93.

tration institutes: the Board of Arbitration for the Building Industry and the Netherlands Arbitration Institute. Most arbitrations take place in the building industry. The power of arbitration lies mostly in the fact that arbitrators are knowledgeable with regard to the subject matter and are able to judge on that basis. The duration of arbitration varies, but is usually more than six months. The costs, compared to adjudication by the state courts, are still usually (very) high. An advantage is that the procedure is not public, which means that company details remain confidential. Another advantage is that the arbitrators are experts in matters of dispute. In my opinion, only these last two aspects regarding arbitration are the real choice-drivers for arbitration, which in other ways does not really differ from adjudication.

v. Mediation

Discussing strengths and weaknesses is not really possible with regard to mediation. Literature often refers to the *advantages and disadvantages of mediation*. I consider these terms to be inaccurate:[10] mediation does not have any objective advantages or disadvantages. A shortcoming of some mediation information material is that it tends to suggest that the mediation method guarantees favourable results. Consequently, no connection is made with the parties' actual choice-drivers or needs, or with the results that would be feasible in that light through mediation or other methods of conflict termination. Specific circumstances determine whether any characteristic or impact of mediation constitutes an advantage or disadvantage in a given case. I therefore prefer to refer to the characteristics and impacts of mediation (see Table 2).[11]

In theory, mediation is suitable for many more cases than it is now used for. I think the problem with expanding mediation on a grand scale is that it presents difficulties in agreeing on the manner of the handling of the conflict for those who have been involved in one, and in the choice of mediator. That is why a good referral system is required. This, in turn, requires the referring parties to be familiar with mediation methods and to be able to provide effective referrals.

vi. Other Procedures

Finally, in the Netherlands there are boards resembling the judiciary which test and/or interpret legislation in certain areas. Examples are the procedures relating to the Commissie Gelijke Behandeling (Equal Treatment Commission) and the Reclame Code Commissie (Advertising Code Committee).

The Commissie Gelijke Behandeling adjudicates grievances about discrimination. According to research, claimants in this area have a greater need for a short and prompt answer or a guided solution than for an extensive judicial judgment. The Reclame Code Commissie judges grievances with regard to whether advertising is misleading or contrary to public order or decency.

[10] M Pel and L Combrink, 'Referral to Mediation by the Netherlands Judiciary' in R Jagtenberg, A De Roo, M Pel, L Combrink, A Klijn and S Verberk (eds), *Customized Conflict Resolution, Court Connected Mediation in the Netherlands 1999–2009*, The Judiciary Quarterly 2011 (The Hague, Netherlands Council for the Judiciary, 2011), available at <www.pelmediation.nl/publications>, 25.

[11] M Pel, *Referral to Mediation, a Practical Guide for an Effective Mediation Proposal* (The Hague, SDU, 2008) 60.

Table 2: The Characteristics and Impacts of Mediation

Characteristics of mediation	Impacts of mediation
• Personal responsibility: conflict to be resolved by the participants themselves based on interests • Mediation is forward looking • Voluntary participation by parties • Confidentiality of the process • Restoration or improvement in communication • Tailored organisation: structure and costs • Opportunity for separate talks (caucus) • Mediation starts by signing a mediation contract • Professional and structured method led by an expert: independent and neutral mediator • The parties determine the pace of the mediation • The agreements reached are set down in a list of agreements or in a settlement agreement	• Prompt solution: limiting costs in terms of time, money and stress • Tailored solution that also serves a party's own interests and a broader solution • Preserve or respectfully terminate the relationship • Final settlement of the conflict or problem • Sustainable solution • Problem-free compliance with agreements

These committees are relatively rarely called upon. Strong points of both committees are that they have specific expertise in their own domains and that their judgments are mostly prompt. A disadvantage is that their ruling is not binding, but merely comprises recommendations.

C. Practical Use and Theoretical Appropriateness Differ—The Market Does Not Really Work

Theoretical appropriateness and practical use do not really match if we consider the statistical data regarding the practical use of all types of dispute resolution mechanism compared to the theoretical strengths and weaknesses of the various dispute resolution mechanisms. The conclusion must therefore be that the market does not really work.

In the Netherlands, the use of dispute committees is well developed and certainly offers adequate practical and observed solutions in many cases of consumer disputes. The use of arbitration is rather limited, but seems to prove satisfactory in the business market in specific branches. In many cases, adjudication suffices, but it only covers a minor part of dispute resolution. Another notable fact is that those who use adjudication are ultimately more satisfied when an agreement is reached than when a verdict is passed. This would argue for an increased use of mediation. Many hold the opinion that, as a newcomer to the market, mediation deserves a much broader use both in the free market through private referrals and through the court-annexed referrals. Theoretically, mediation offers many possibilities for use in both private conflicts and business conflicts, whether or not in combination with a possible prompt determination of concrete judicial disputes. There are a number of supposed reasons for the fact that its use is not as frequent as perhaps it should be. In this subsection, I will quote a number of research reports concerning the use of various dispute resolution methods and will end with some personal remarks.

The WODC[12] report *Paths to Justice in the Netherlands*[13] provides some background on this topic and informs on the use of the various mechanisms in the so-called 'landscape of disputes' as seen from the perspective of Dutch citizens. The following research questions in this study are relevant in answering the question under debate here, namely whether the market functions.

1. To what extent are certain judicial or extra-judicial strategies used, and what circumstances influence this choice?
2. What are the results of the choices made in achieving a solution, and how do they relate to the objectives of the individual seeking justice? (Or: what is decisive with respect to the choice of a solution process?)
3. To what extent do individuals have confidence in the operation of legal provisions?

The theoretical perspective in this study is as follows.

The alternative choices available in specific cases depend to a large extent on the type of problem. This determines which official procedures are available and which are not. It also largely determines to what extent a solution is available in 'the shadow of the law'. The availability of legal aid also plays a role. Subsequently, the issue of which of the available solution strategies is chosen by the person seeking justice is a matter of considering the expected benefits and costs involved in that strategy. The expected benefits are determined by the interests involved in the case, both material and immaterial, and by the estimated chances of success. The anticipated costs depend on the rates and the accessibility of legal aid and official procedures.[14]

Practice is as follows.

The practical applied solution strategy turns out to be more closely related to the type of problem than to general background characteristics. Problems with the purchase of products and services and problems with tenancy are often dealt with personally, whereas legal aid is often used if individuals experience problems related to family relationships or problems with children under 18. The following specific characteristics of the problem and the respondent are much more important: the severity and complexity of the problem and the expected benefits that are at stake; the nature of the other party; and whether or not families are insured for legal expenses.

Objectives of a financial and material nature appear to be important for those seeking justice, but are far from the only objectives.[15] Enforcement of one's own rights and altering the behaviour of the other party also achieve a high score. In the attainment of the main objective, the manner of dealing with the problem, whether as a 'do-it-yourselfer' or as legal aid user, does not appear to make much difference. The

[12] Scientific Research and Documentation Centre of the Ministry of Security and Justice. The WODC is best characterised as an international (criminal) justice knowledge centre. Its purpose is to make a scientific contribution to the development and evaluation of policy set by the Netherlands Ministry of Security and Justice. For more information, see <www.wodc.nl>.

[13] Van Veldhoven and Klein Haarhuis, *Geschilbeslechtingsdelta 2009.*

[14] Ibid, 215

[15] Ibid, 221.

settlement, however, does make a significant difference. In the event of extra-judicial agreement, no less than 89.1 per cent of respondents turn out to have achieved their main objective in the end, while only 65.9 per cent achieve that objective in the event of a final outcome that is settled through a decision in official proceedings. If the content of the agreement or decision does not correspond to the original objectives, this does not necessarily mean that the interested party is severely disappointed. Expectations can, after all, be adjusted in the course of the dispute settlement process. In the event of agreement, 83.3 per cent of those involved consider the result just, while only 58.4 per cent consider this to be the case where a decision resulting from official proceedings constitutes the final outcome. With respect to the respondents' experiences of justice with official proceedings, the outcome seems to carry more weight than procedural aspects.

This conclusion probably does not apply to specialised court procedures. Specialised court procedures sometimes seem to be so successful that the users prefer adjudication over mediation. The '*specialisatie loont*' (specialisation pays off) report[16] presents an analysis of the experiences of big commercial enterprises with specialised adjudication as offered, for instance, by the 'Ondernemingskamer' (Commercial Chamber) of the Amsterdam court of appeal.

The interviewed companies indicate the quality of the specialised courts as good to very good. Alternative forms of dispute resolution are (therefore) found to be less attractive than the procedures at the civil courts. Quality here means a well-reasoned verdict, which takes the necessary decisive action, moving matters forward. Less satisfactory are the turnaround times, including the time needed for the verdict.[17] This report also concludes that, as the lawyers in the researched cases are specialists, they want the judges to be as well. They claim that specialisation comprises asking the appropriate questions and being a good interlocutor. This could also be the reason why arbitration is used in specific cases.

This makes me wonder whether specialised lawyers are aware of the fact that in their cases, too, the underlying conflicts are often the reason why agreements cannot be reached on the substance. Another question is whether this fact of experience concerning the wish for specialisation also argues for the use of technical experts and specialised mediators regarding mediations in commercial conflicts, even if only to meet market demand. There is a niche organisation for mediation in IT conflicts, the SGOA (Foundation Settlement of Automation). It always uses two mediators, one of whom specialises in IT cases.

From 2000, the government policy has been to promote the use of mediation. All courts are familiar with a mediation referral system. This has led to an increasing number of referrals since 2005, an increase which in 2011 has seen a downward adjustment. I will return to the causes for this below. The general policy has anchored mediation as a method in itself and has stimulated the mediation market share. However, the growth is not to the extent that mediation is actually adequately used in appropriate situations. Mediation cases account for only 1.7 per cent of those cases

[16] A Böcker, T Havinga, A Jettinghof, C Klaassen and L Bakker, 'Specialisatie loont?!', see <www.njb.nl>, Actuele Documenten, 2011, week 17.

[17] I Giesen and L Coenraad, 'De toegankelijkheid van de rechtspleging' [2011] *Nederlands Juristenblad* 952, 956.

benefiting from legal aid, and the court-connected referrals only concern about 1 in 1,000 cases.

In a recent publication by Barbara Baarsma[18], '*De mediationmarkt in economisch perspectief*' ('The Mediation Market in an Economic Perspective'), the author states that mediation in the Netherlands is still in a developmental stage and that mediation, because of the unfamiliarity in the public at large, is still used (much more) infrequently than would suit this innovative product—a product which, with exponential growth, could take on work currently done by the legal profession and other advisors. She concludes that the question has not actually been raised and that there is an oversupply. This conclusion fits in with 'Paths to Justice', [19] which also documents that mediation is used in only 2.7 per cent of the cases where parties reach an agreement.

Baarsma calculates a market potential of 62,000 plus 147,000 mediations if, instead of 2.7 per cent, 5–10 per cent of the current sources of mediation cases (dismissal, divorce and guardianship, rent disputes, conflicts with the government, neighbour disputes, commercial disputes, referrals by legal aid insurers, trade unions, dispute committees, government bodies, rents commissions, ombudsman, community mediation and the business market) were solved through mediation.

In her analysis of why there is no potential growth, she mentions the following:

1. Unknown is unloved (40–60 per cent of potential mediation users are insufficiently familiar with mediation).
2. The quality of mediators is insufficiently transparent. Currently, a small group of mediators have made a good name for themselves and thus have built up good practices. This leads to a winner-takes-all market, which may make mediators with fewer noteworthy qualities and a smaller market share pull out.
3. To a certain extent, the advantages of mediation do not directly fall to those who purchase mediation. Moreover (I should add), the subsidy that the government allocated to parties that were referred to mediation by the judiciary, which resulted in the first 2.5 hours of mediation being free of charge, has been cancelled.
4. There is too little repeat demand. According to the 2009 'Paths to Justice' report, only 53 per cent of the mediation participants would opt for mediation again (compared to 70 per cent in 2003).
5. Referrals from the legal profession (judges, lawyers) have fallen in number. This, according to Baarsma, is due to the decrease in their own turnover when they show a preference for mediation. My comment is that this cannot be the case for judges: at most, they might worry about the decrease in their own workload and possibly about future work and income. This hypothesis has not been tested.
6. Finally, Baarsma mentions the insurance paradox as a reason why mediations via trade unions and property insurance companies lag behind. The insurance paradox says that insurers have an incentive to decrease claim levels because this increases the difference between premium-income and expenses, but at the same time they need the incentive to maintain claim levels. If solving a judicial dispute becomes too economical, insurance will no longer be necessary. Consequently, insurers have an incentive not to keep the costs at too low a level.

[18] B Baarsma, 'Blijft mediation de eeuwige belofte of wordt het een volwassen markt?, mediationmarkt vanuit economisch perspectief' [2012] *Nederlands Juristenblad* 14.

[19] Van Veldhoven and Klein Haarhuis, *Geschilbeslechtingsdelta 2009* 138.

I add to this analysis that currently, if one of the parties does not want to comply, mediation clauses in agreements are not considered binding in some court proceedings judgments. The reason is that, according to the corresponding jurisprudence, it is pointless to force parties to go to a mediator when they are not committed to solving their problems. This could also be the reason why such clauses are less prevalent and not observed as much as would be effective. I believe that Baarsma underestimates the significance of referrals, which I consider to be the gateway to mediation.

The sombre mood about the market share or the development in the market with regard to mediation is not shared by the professional body of mediators. The NMI research questioned mediators[20] about the development in the market. Seventy per cent of the mediators expect (strong) growth. The most frequently quoted reason for an expected increase is the greater public familiarity with mediation and the rise in the costs of court procedures.

II. GENERAL APPROACH OF THE LEGISLATOR WITH REGARD TO THE REGULATION OF ADR AND ADJUDICATION

A. Regulation of Various Mechanisms of ADR

Arbitration and binding expert opinion are more or less regulated by law (see III). Specifically, the enforcement of the outcomes of those procedures is regulated, as are (some) procedural rules. The administrative procedures as well as the role and task of the ombudsman are also regulated by law. Mediation as such has not been regulated so far, with the exception of the implementation of the European directive. (See II.A for recent and upcoming regulation.) However, some aspects of the referring faculties within the legal desk and the judiciary are regulated by law.

In 2004 the government established the legal desk.[21] This institution is financed with a subsidy from the Legal Aid Council and the Ministry of Security and Justice. Individuals can obtain legal advice at 30 locations in the Netherlands. Apart from simple advice, the legal professionals at the legal desk may offer referrals to mediation. These cover the following problem areas: labour, family issues, rental disputes and consumer affairs. Those who qualify for legal aid will be given a 'mediation subsidy', which means that mediation costs will be largely paid to the mediator directly by the government. In this case, the participants pay a fee of between €50 and €102 for subsidised mediation.

Additionally, the law regarding legal aid stipulates the necessary requirements for the mediators who perform mediations for the legal desk and the judiciary. The mediators have to be included in a Legal Aid Council register, and the Legal Aid Council has the legal authority to manage this register. The norm for registration comprises specific requirements for the training of the mediator and registration with the NMI, as well as availability requirements.

The law also stipulates the possibility of an enforceable agreement between parties. This is not a specific arrangement with regard to mediation but could be used for

[20] Vogels, *De stand van Mediation in Nederland 2011* 17.

[21] See <www.juridischloket.nl/overhetjuridischloket/organisatie/historie>.

that purpose: mediation agreements can be included in a notarial act and they are then enforceable based on Article 430(1) Law on procedural rules (Rv). Moreover, the law also includes stipulations for the enforcement of agreements attained in mediation after referral by the judge and for settlements attained in a settlement conference before the judge.[22]

In July 2010 a new law was implemented on 'partial dispute procedures' regarding personal injury and death damages. During negotiations, insurance companies and parties who have incurred damage can ask for a decision by the judge on liability or specific issues concerning the damages and then, based on this decision, continue negotiations. This law has subsequently been used in a considerable number of cases[23] and seems to have the expected effect that negations on damages can eventually lead to a quick closure by using decisions on specific issues.

i. Legal Regulation Has Some Effect on the Use of ADR

As a result of the introduction of the possibility for referrals by the legal desk and the judiciary, a (small) influx of referrals has been established. The legal aid arrangements for low-income earners have certainly contributed to their use of mediation. The subsidies, for the initial hours of mediation referred by judges, have, I assume, also contributed to the number of referrals. In any case, the cancellation of this subsidy in 2011 coincides with a significant drop in the number of referrals to mediation. Because of the referrals via the legal desk and the judiciary, the number of referrals in the free market has increased significantly since 2005 (see I.A above). However, it is remarkable that the Netherlands, which is supposed to be at the forefront regarding the judiciary referral system, is not able to present any statistics on the tens of thousands of referred mediation cases, despite the opportunity. On the other hand, there were 52,000 mediations in the free market.

The establishment of the partial dispute procedure regulation also seems to have had a stimulating effect on extra-judicial dispute resolution, as described above, but it does not concern many cases.

There are many publications that ascribe little or no stimulating significance to legal regulations and that consider other methods for the stimulation of the use of ADR as more effective. I will return to that issue. Legislation in itself certainly does not suffice. I personally think that a combination of legislation and promotion by the government, a more decisive approach from suppliers and the integration of the study of conflict in legal training would lead to the most effective use of ADR.

The fact that a regulation in itself does not promote ADR is a valuable conclusion when considering the use of arbitration. In the Netherlands only about 1,300 cases a year are resolved by arbitration (regulated by law) versus 51,690 by mediation (not yet regulated by law).

[22] The possibility of resolving cases in settlement conferences has long since been quite common, and this option is also regulated by law. The judge does *not* act as a mediator; rather, he/she facilitates settlement by hearing the case and discussing the strengths and weaknesses of the case.

[23] Giesen and Coenraad, 'De toegankelijkheid van de rechtspleging' 965.

ii. Reasons Given by the Legislator (Not) to Encourage/Regulate ADR Procedures

Since the end of the 1990s, the promotion of ADR has been an active part of the Dutch judicial policy. The four main goals articulated for promoting ADR were announced as: out-of-court resolution of disputes; attaining the best quality or most effective way of settling disputes; the realisation of various forms of access to justice that make the parties primarily responsible for dispute resolution; and less pressure on the judicial system.[24] One of the hypotheses in setting up the various mediation projects was that, as mediation gains in popularity due to, inter alia, successful referrals by judicial organisations, more people will likely opt for mediation of their own accord, possibly also at an earlier stage. The presence of an organisational referral provision can serve as a stimulus for the use of mediation as large repeat players will deal with their conflicts differently.[25] This has resulted in government bodies using mediation or mediation elements in handling conflicts with individuals.

In the Netherlands, it has been possible for parties to end their conflicts during a settlement conference before a judge, and this is the standard practice in many cases. The agreement thus reached is enforceable. This is why it is justifiable to question the added value of mediation to the judicial system. The answer lies in the predicted impact of mediation: an interest-based final solution to the conflict instead of a rights-based agreement or a rights-based decision by the judge; the opportunity to mend a troubled relationship; restoration of communication between parties; and the ability to retain control of the solution to the conflict.

One of the objectives for supporting referrals to mediation, ie the decrease in the workload of the courts, is possibly no longer very pressing, given the fact that the recent economic crisis has decreased the workload anyway.

Despite the policy of stimulating ADR, the Justice Minister did not support regulation with regard to mediation because he thought it would hamper the further development of mediation. With the exception of the legislatively regulated possibility of legal aid for mediation, the government mediation policy was aimed at allowing mediation as much opportunity for development as possible by issuing as few rules as possible.[26] According to the minister, it was the responsibility of the professional group to develop quality standards. Correspondingly, it has been his position that, until such standards crystallise, it would be premature to support a privilege of non-disclosure. The government has subsequently subsidised the NMI over the years to help them reach these quality-control goals. Nor did mandatory mediation fit into the Dutch mediation policy, according to the minister.

This minimalist approach towards regulation even led to the initial endeavours

[24] B Niemeijer and M Pel, 'Court-based Mediation in the Netherlands: Research, Evaluation and Future Expectations' (2005) 110 *Penn State Law Review* 345.

[25] This became apparent in the tax cases of the Arnhem court and in a parallel mediation project in connection with complaint procedures in the province of Overijssel. See KJ de Graaf, AT Marseille and M Herweijer, *Mediation in Bezwaar: Evaluatie Mediation Project Provincie Overijssel* (Groningen, Vakgroep Bestuursrecht en bestuurskunde, University of Groningen, 2003), see <www.rug.nl/staff/m.herweijer/mediationinbezwaar.pdf>.

[26] Explanatory Memorandum TK bill 32,555 No 3, introduction.

of the Dutch government to block the EC Commission's effort to come up with a European mediation directive.[27]

In 'Frame for a Dutch Portrait of Mediation',[28] Jagtenberg and de Roo comment on the Netherlands legal culture and the promotion of mediation as follows:

> Netherlands legal culture is often described . . . as 'pragmatic', in comparison with that of neighbouring countries such as Germany. Mechanisms for resolving disputes, including legal disputes, relatively quickly and informally have existed in the Netherlands for many decades. The history of mediation is no exception in this respect . . .
>
> The main aims of the upcoming mediation policy were disposing of disputes in the best and most effective way and giving the parties responsibility for resolving disputes.
>
> Naturally, this is not to say that the outcome of mediation is better than that of a court judgment, let alone that judges deliver work of insufficient quality . . . But this does mean that it may be more satisfactory for the parties to some disputes, particularly those in which they have an interest in maintaining an ongoing relationship, to reconcile their differences rather than to seek to be proved right in a court of law at the expense of the other party.
>
> Needless to say, the aims of increasing the parties' own responsibility and not always giving precedence to a strictly legal assessment of a dispute attracted not only support but also criticism from the judiciary. The introduction of mediation could, after all, be interpreted as criticism of the functioning of the judges . . . This is why the term 'effective customized dispute resolution' was introduced. According to this view, decisions of the courts are a method of dispute resolution, alongside mediation, arbitration, negotiation and expert opinions. The aim of court proceedings is now to choose with the parties what would be the most adequate method(s) of resolving the actual dispute, ie to choose between a court judgment, settlement and (referral to) mediation. This choice of words was adopted in the later policy letters and has become accepted in the broader circle of professionals involved in dispute resolution. The typical Netherlands approach is one of pragmatism. This is experimentation through a form of public-private initiative backed by research.

In 2011 the Minister of Security and Justice explained his agenda on innovation (Innovatieagenda 2011) as follows:

One characteristic of a well-functioning judiciary system is that individuals facing a conflict be assisted in solving it in the most satisfactory manner possible. The government would be expected to create and maintain a system that: (i) assists individuals in finding the best possible way in solving the conflict; (ii) provides a variety of well-functioning methods of conflict resolution; (iii) is, as a whole, efficient and effective; and (iv) allows individuals with a judicial problem to count on legal assistance. The minister is convinced[29] that conflict resolution would improve if individuals are given the opportunity to contribute to the resolution if there is sufficient attention to pre-existing, non-judicial problems and if the quality of conflict resolution is guaranteed. These are basic principles and guidelines with regard to innovation.

[27] See J Bosnak, 'The European Mediation Directive: More Questions Than Answers' in A Ingen-Housz (ed), *ADR in Business, Practice and Issues across Countries and Cultures*, vol II (Alphen a/d Rijn, Kluwer Law & Business, 2010) 626.

[28] J Jagtenberg and A De Roo, 'Frame for a Dutch Portrait of Mediation' in R Jagtenberg, A De Roo, M Pel, L Combrink, A Klijn and S Verberk (eds), *Customized Conflict Resolution, Court-connected Mediation in The Netherlands 1999–2009,* The Judiciary Quarterly 2011 (The Hague, Netherlands Council for the Judiciary, 2011), available at <www.pelmediation.nl/publications>, 7.

[29] *Innovatieagenda 2011* (The Hague, Ministerie van Veiligheid en Justitie, 2011), Official Parliamentary Act 33071 nr 5 Den Haag, 2.

Concerning arbitration, it is thought that modernising the regulation of arbitration will make the Netherlands more suitable as a setting for arbitration, which is considered a desirable effect. Therefore, a structural modernisation of the legal framework for arbitration is presently being undertaken. There are no comparable initiatives concerning the regulation of other ADR procedures and there seems no incentive for it.

iii. Implementation of the EU Mediation Directive (Directive 2008/52/EC)

Until recently, mediation had only been regulated on specific topics as described in II.A. The Directive of the European Parliament and of the Council of 21 May 2008 prompted the government to regulate mediation in legislation. The Law (Bill No 32,555) as it was presented by the Ministry of Security and Justice was initially adopted by the House of Representatives in 2011, but subsequently raised a number of concerns in the Senate. The new law comprised:

- New limitation rules, namely that a mediation stops the expiry of limitation and prescription periods (Articles 3:316(4) and (5) and 3:319(3) Burgerlijk Wetboek (BW).
- A new article in the Code of Civil Procedure (Article 22a Rv) which stipulated that the judge could recommend mediation in all cases.
- The privilege of non-disclosure for the mediator, protecting confidentiality. No parties/mediators were to be compelled to give evidence in civil and commercial judicial proceedings or arbitration regarding information arising out of or in connection with a mediation process.
- With regard to enforceability of written agreements, a gap in the law was to be closed: in divorce procedures, too, an agreement in a referred mediation was to be enforceable (Article 279(4) Rv new).

An important issue was, furthermore, that its application was not limited to cross-border mediations. The major changes the law would have brought about concern the mediator's privilege and interruption of prescription periods. Yet as far as privilege was concerned, the problem developed that recently our Supreme Court denied privilege to the mediator.[30]

In an obiter dictum the court held that confidentiality is essential for mediation, and it is also in the interest of society in general that mediation has the possibility of existing as an alternative form of conflict resolution, recognised and encouraged by government. All this speaks in favour of accepting a privilege for the mediator concerning that which is confided to him in this capacity. However, the Court continued:

> An argument against the assumption of privilege is the fact that privilege is an exception, because of the great importance of establishing the truth, which includes that only in extraordinary cases an exception can be made to the obligation to testify of article 165.1 of the code of civil procedure and can only be awarded to a limited group of persons, who, due to the character of their social function, are bound to secrecy about what has been entrusted to them in their capacity. Mediation, however, is a broad notion, not always clearly outlined, and is practised in different forums and under different circumstances, whereas the

[30] Supreme Court 10-4-2009, LJN BG 9470, cited in E Schutte and J Spierdijk, *Juridische aspecten van mediation* (The Hague, SDU, 2011) 93.

group of mediators is hardly well-defined, whereby, apart from mediators who are certified as such by a mediators-organisation on the basis of having fulfilled certain training- and quality requirements, there are also 'ad hoc' mediators for whom no quality guarantees exist. Recognition of a privilege for mediators in general would have as a result that the group of those who are entitled to privilege would be considerably expanded, without sufficient guarantee for the quality of the mediators, which would be incompatible with the exceptional position of privilege. And, in the wake of the necessary limitation of this group, would frequently give rise to disputes about which criteria to apply and the manner how they should be applied. These arguments against privilege must prevail, the court concluded.

In Bill No 32,555, the government attempted to bridge the gap identified by the Supreme Court by trying to limit the number of mediators entitled to privilege. It did so by adding a new subarticle to Article 165, mentioned by the court, granting privilege to the mediator when the confidential character of the mediation has been explicitly agreed upon. It goes beyond the scope of this present submission to describe the discussions which have been triggered by this clause, but the questions it raises are self-evident: who is 'the mediator'? Note, that the term 'mediator' is not protected, unlike 'NMI Mediator', which is a registered collective brand that only a registered NMI mediator is entitled to use. Furthermore, there is a problem of proof concerning the confidentiality agreement because the law does not require such agreements in writing.

All these concerns led the Minister of Security and Justice to withdraw the bill. He introduced a new bill, designed to limit implementation of the Mediation Directive to cross-border dispute and limited to the issues of the directive. This bill, Bill No 33,320, passed the House of Representatives and the Senate unchanged (due to the fact that the Netherlands had surpassed the time limit for implementation to a large extent), and entered into force on 15 November 2012.

iv. More Legislation to be Expected

Moreover, the Minister of Security and Justice has recently announced supplementary legislation regulating, inter alia, quality standards and a national register for mediators to be put into effect in 2014. Also, a private member's bill on mediation was announced by a member of the House of Representatives, so for the first time in history it is to be expected that we will have a considerable amount of legislative activity concerning mediation.

According to the innovation agenda that was drawn up (Innovatieagenda rechtsbestel (2011)), the Minister of Security and Justice wishes to further regulate and stimulate mediation and arbitration with the introduction of the above-mentioned supplementary legislation. Accordingly, he will promote extra-judicial procedures through amendments of the arbitration procedure[31] and through a strengthening of the position of the professional and business disputes commissions. The minister will also campaign for a greater familiarity with mediation, with the aim that mediation will become the norm for individuals, businesses and government bodies.

The determination and ongoing supervision of quality requirements, the conditions for inclusion in the mediators' register, the privilege of non-disclosure and the right of

[31] *Innovatieagenda 2011*, Official Parliamentary Act 33071 nr 5 Den Haag, 9.

individual recourse and/or disciplinary law will be further regulated as well. After the implementation of the supplementary law, the description of concrete mediation rules and their quality assurance will still be left to the self-regulation of professionals practising mediation. This means that the NMI regulations, as described below (III.B.ii and iii), or those of another determinated mediation organisation will concretely determine the quality of mediation.

The minister is also considering creating a differentiated scheme for the contributions to be made by individuals seeking legal aid: required contributions for mediations will be smaller in order to stimulate clients to use mediation. The legal desk will be asked to give more prominence to referrals to mediation, and triage and conflict diagnosis should become normal activities for referring parties.

B. Incentives to Use Certain Types of ADR

At the moment there is, strictly speaking, no regulation concerning the choice between the different mechanisms of conflict resolution. An exception is the objection proceedings in administrative law, which are mandatory and a precondition for starting a procedure before the court.

For people entitled to legal aid, the legal desk offers pro bono advice about how to handle legal problems. Due to the new policy of the Ministry of Security and Justice, the advisers of the legal desk have the task of genuinely referring to mediation all cases that seem suitable. The legal desk also maintains an internet platform offering triage and conflict diagnosis to help people choose the mechanism that suits their problem best.[32] It is also to be expected that the demand for arbitration and mediation will increase, particularly in cases with major financial concerns due to the new regulation of legal costs for adjudication.

Negotiations should be conducted in good faith. A significant body of case law has been developed on this subject (see III.A). This is not seen yet as an incentive to use mediation in general. In labour law, however, the developed case law has an influence in the sense of creating a real incentive to use mediation.

For industrial conflicts that lead to employment incapacity and the absence of employees, the Occupational Health Service regularly recommends mediation. Should an employee or employer refuse to accept this recommendation, it might negatively influence judgment during a later trial concerning dismissal. If the employer or employee refuses to participate, it will often serve to, respectively, increase or decrease the amount of compensation that the Dutch judges may award to the employee in case of dismissal. The same is true for labour conflicts that do not lead to absenteeism and that end up before a judge; in reaching a verdict, the judge will consider whether or not the offer of mediation has been accepted, and a refusal will influence the damages awarded, whether in favour of the employer (higher award) or the employee (lower award).[33]

[32] See <www.rechtwijzer.nl>; rechtwijzer = legal guide.

[33] J Pel, *Arbeidsrecht en mediation* (The Hague, SDU, 2007).

i. Influence of the Legal Culture in the Choice of Dispute Resolution Mechanism

Generally speaking, court procedures are considered to be a last resort in the Netherlands. This point of view applies both to the legislator and to the users of the system. Lawmakers have not openly admitted it, but they were definitely pleased by the cost-reducing effect attributed to mediation. It had hitherto seemed that the legislator had a preference for arbitration and conciliation (binding advice and dispute committees) in civil cases and for the ombudsman and objection procedures in administrative conflicts, as well as for the other procedures mentioned above (I.A). All of these proceedings have been regulated by law for a considerable time. The legislator is now adding mediation to the list of regulated areas of dispute resolution, albeit just for some aspects of mediation.

As mentioned before, people in the Netherlands are inclined to resolve their own conflicts, using many extra-judicial conflict resolution procedures, and will go to court only as a last resort. Generally speaking, the legal culture is also a culture of negotiation and settlement out of court. Lawyers also have an obligation to try to settle cases (see below II.C), and this is standard practice among them. The use of mediation by lawyers is increasing, though there are still different tendencies. Among lawyers, there is still some resistance against advising clients to go to mediation, and some lawyers still see the use of mediation as an attack on their professional pride: 'If our negotiations don't succeed, what could a mediator accomplish?'. Nevertheless, mediation in commercial matters (4,160) has surpassed the use of arbitration (1,300).[34]

In 2006, Van Erp[35] researched the filter effect of extra-judicial procedures. The average filter effect of the extra-judicial dispute procedures appears to exceed 90 per cent. The filter effect hardly varies between the procedures. This means that, once an extra-judicial procedure has started, the percentage of disputes that end up in court is low. Lawyers are required to advise clients with regard to settlement before going to court.

Article 3 of the Code of Conduct of the Dutch Bar Association states that a lawyer should bear in mind that an amicable settlement is often to be preferred over litigation.

Dutch attorneys are also bound to the Code of Conduct of CCBE (the Council of Bars and Law Societies in Europe):

> 3.7.1. The lawyer should at all times strive to achieve the most cost-effective resolution of the client's dispute and should advise the client at appropriate stages as to the desirability of attempting a settlement and/or a reference to alternative dispute resolution.

I am not aware of any disciplinary measures taken against attorneys who disregard this principle. However, from case law established by the disciplinary courts it can be concluded that a general duty rests upon the attorney to provide the client with all relevant information concerning the legal aspects of his/her decisions/behaviour. It can therefore be safely said that, indeed, the attorney has the duty to inform his client about the possibilities of ADR in his/her case.

[34] For statistics see I.A.

[35] JG van Erp and CM Klein, *De filterwerking van buitengerechtelijke procedures* (The Hague, WODC, 2006).

C. Court-annexed Mediation in the Netherlands

The Netherlands judiciary has installed a referral to mediation faculty in all courts of first instance and in all courts of appeal. This means that a system is in place to assure the possibility of referral to mediation in cases that seem suitable for mediation.

i. Development of the Referral Faculty in the Courts since 1999[36]

The question whether mediation, as one form of ADR, could have its own place within the Dutch judicial infrastructure was the most important reason for setting up the pilot scheme, 'Court-annexed Mediation'. The WODC was assigned the task of evaluating this project. The project in the judiciary started in 1999 in five courts of first instance and in one court of appeal; Machteld Pel was the project leader.

The emphasis of the project was on gaining experience with different types of referral. Essentially, this meant that, within the project, not only did an adequate number of mediations have to be realised, but the referrals had to be sufficiently varied as well. In this way, it would be possible to assess the link, if any, between the quality of the referrals and the quality of the mediations and their results. The goal was to be able to draw reliable and valid conclusions. This would enable us to provide better answers concerning the propriety of mediation in the Netherlands judicial system. In 2003 the WODC published the report *Room for Mediation*,[37] based on the research during the project. The conclusion of the research was that there is room for negotiation both before and during court proceedings. Based on these conclusions, the implementation of the referral faculty started in 2005, and from 2007 onwards all courts have had a referral faculty. Since 2007 all courts may refer cases which they consider suitable for mediation, albeit not on a mandatory basis. The pivot and stimulator of all these processes and projects in the aforementioned phases was the Netherlands court-connected mediation agency (LBM). In April 2005, this name was given to the national project agency established in 1999. In October 2009, all the LBM's tasks were taken on by the Council for the Judiciary and the Expert Group for Customized Conflict Resolution.[38]

ii. Referral on Voluntary Basis

Referrals to mediation in the Netherlands' courts are voluntary. This means that parties are free to accept a referral offer by the court. At the start of the project there were financial incentives for the parties to accept the mediation referral.

Until 1 April 2005, taking part in court-referred mediation was free for litigants. Mediators were paid by the courts, which received grants from the Ministry of Security and Justice to promote referrals to mediation. From April 2005 onwards, litigants entitled to legal aid within the framework of regular court proceedings were (and still are) also entitled to legal aid for court-referred mediations. Their sole financial con-

[36] For more details see Niemeijer and Pel, 'Court-based Mediation in the Netherlands'.

[37] Combrink-Kuiters, L and Ter Voert, M, *Ruimte voor Mediation* (The Hague, WODC, Boom juridische uitgevers, 2003).

[38] A group of ADR specialised judges affiliated to the Council for the Judiciary and supported by staff members.

tribution is an income-related client's fee. In order not to create financial obstacles for litigants ineligible for legal aid, the Ministry of Security and Justice subsidised the first 2.5 hours of the mediation. This temporary provision expired on 1 January 2011 and has been replaced by a special low mediator fee, which is implemented by practically all the court-annexed mediators for the first two hours.[39]

iii. Use of External Mediators and Quality of Service

The referral faculty refers cases to external mediators. The external mediators should comply with the quality requirements of the NMI (see III.B.ii and iii), as well as with certain additional conditions required by The Council for the Judiciary. These conditions include a willingness to:

- hold an initial mediation meeting within two weeks of acceptance of the mediation offer by the parties;
- ensure that the monitoring forms are filled out;
- take part in the annual evaluation on the basis of the results reflected in the monitoring forms; and
- have professional liability insurance.

(See III.B ii and iii, regarding quality standards of the NMI.)

Within the courts, the 'mediation officer' is the link between the courts and the mediators and the parties who choose mediation. The mediation officer heads the 'mediation administration office' in the courts and is the contact for litigants with any questions they might have on mediation. He or she also maintains the network of mediators. In the case of oral referral, the judge will appoint the mediation officer once the litigants have agreed to consider the mediation option. The mediation officer is also the contact in the case of written referrals or self-referrals. He or she provides the litigants with information about the mediation process, such as its voluntary nature, the confidentiality of the mediation process, the efforts expected of both parties, and the difference between mediation and a judicial decision. The mediation officer also assists parties in choosing a mediator, and arranges the first appointment between the mediator and the litigants.[40] This intermediary task of the mediation officer is very important since experiences in other countries have shown that litigants often fail to approach a mediator after being referred to mediation by the courts: it commonly proved too difficult for them to choose a mediator together or even to agree on a suitable time for the first session.

iv. The Referral

There are several ways in which legal disputes pending before the courts can end up in mediation: the option can be suggested in a letter to the litigants (written referral), the option can be presented during a court hearing (oral referral) or litigants themselves can opt for mediation (self-referral). In the case of a written referral, the litigants receive a letter prior to the court hearing in which they are encouraged to consider

[39] More information: Pel and Combrink, 'Referral to Mediation by the Netherlands Judiciary', 33.
[40] Pel and Combrink, 'Referral to Mediation by the Netherlands Judiciary', 31.

mediation. A brochure and a so-called 'self-test' accompany this letter. The self-test is a tool to help parties determine whether mediation might be a suitable option. Filling out the self-test has turned out to be the first step for many people towards finding a solution for their problem. Mediation is indicated as a possible option if one of the questions in the test is answered affirmatively. The self-test has proven to be a very important instrument because it appeals to the commitment of litigants—commitment is one of the main success indicators for a successful mediation.[41] Once a case has been referred to mediation, further processing of the case by the court is suspended for a period of three months, ie the maximum processing time of a mediation (though when the mediation takes more time, this period of three months may be extended).

It goes without saying that a properly functioning referral service requires qualified people. To ensure the quality of referrals during court hearings, all judges were offered a referral course. In addition, from 2008 onwards, the training course 'conflict diagnosis' was offered to them as well. To safeguard the future quality of the referral services and to promote 'customised conflict resolution', the referrer's course and the course 'conflict diagnosis' have been included in the programme offered by the Netherlands Centre for Education of Judges (SSR) from 2010 onwards.

v. Description of the Referral, from A (Accepting the Proposal) to Z (Completion of the Procedure)

If the parties opt for mediation at the hearing, the judge will call the mediation officer into the courtroom. The mediation officer will then inform the parties once more about mediation and about specific aspects, such as its voluntary nature, confidentiality, the effort that will be expected of participants in a mediation process and how it differs from a decision by the judge. Because the effort of the parties—their commitment—is one of the main success indicators for a successful mediation in practice,[42] a survey in 2009 asked mediation officers if and how they test whether parties are committed to participating in mediation. In total, 73 per cent of the mediation officers said that they tested commitment after a referral at the hearing. They do this by asking questions and providing information. For example, they ask why the parties opted for mediation and what the dispute is about—and, if people have doubts, where these doubts come from and what can be done about them. According to mediation officers, the most important reasons for a lack of commitment are the costs that mediation entails, a lack of trust in the other party, the feeling that they are being forced into mediation by the lawyer or the judge, and a party's expectation of winning the case. If, after they have received information, the parties still want to solve their dispute by mediation, the mediation officer will help them choose a mediator and will also arrange the first appointment between the mediator and the parties.[43] In principle, this will take place within two weeks of referral. A prompt start may limit further escalation and have a positive effect on the course and outcome of the mediation.

The mediation officer also plays an important role in the case of written referrals. With the written proposal for mediation, the parties receive a sector specific mediation

[41] Pel, *Referral to Mediation* 173.
[42] Internal research report, Netherlands Mediation Office for the Judiciary, 2009.
[43] Ibid.

brochure and a self-test. The self-test helps the parties to decide whether or not to opt for mediation. Contacting the parties after a written proposal for mediation has a very positive effect. If a written offer for referral is accepted, the mediation officer also helps the parties to choose a mediator and arranges the first mediation appointment.

Once the mediation has begun, the mediation officer will monitor the mediation's progress and encourage its timely conclusion. In principle, a case that has been referred to mediation by the judge will be kept on hold for three months—the planned maximum processing time for a mediation. If there are valid reasons, such as a (planned) trial parental contact arrangement or if further talks are still required in a mediation that is progressing positively, the mediation officer may extend the period in consensus with internal agreements and in consultation with the parties.

Naturally, all matters related to the referral will be registered in the mediation administration office and the case administration office. In addition, a mediation file containing all the relevant documents will be kept. The mediation file will always be kept separate from the case file due to the confidentiality of the mediation. The mediation officer will also monitor this.

After the conclusion of mediation, the mediation administration office will (upon request by the mediation officer) inform the referring judge and the court registry if mediation has been completed with full agreement, partial agreement or without agreement. In this way, the judge and the court registry will know whether or not the judicial proceedings will be recommenced, and judges can also gradually learn to assess which cases are suitable for mediation and which are not.

III. APPROACH TOWARDS SPECIFIC ADR INSTRUMENTS

A. Negotiation

There are no specific substantive or procedural rules applicable to the pre-contractual stage of negotiation, but there is an important body of case law from the Supreme Court establishing fair negotiation standards, and especially sanctions for unfair withdrawal from negotiations. There are exceptional cases in which a party that has unfairly/prematurely withdrawn from negotiations is forced by injunction to continue negotiations. Also, there are cases in which damages have been awarded. Liability can be imposed for breaking off negotiations (in bad faith). Until 2005, there was a tendency to limit the possibilities to withdraw. A Supreme Court case in 2005,[44] however, broadened the scope again and put more emphasis on the parties' contractual freedom as long as no contract has been established. Nevertheless, in specific circumstances damages can still be awarded. As the Supreme Court states:

> The criterion that applies to the assessment of liability for compensation for failed negotiations is that each negotiating party—that is obliged to determine its conduct with regard to the other's legitimate interest—is free to break off negotiations, unless this would be unacceptable on the grounds of the other party's justified request in the establishment of the agreement or with regard to the other circumstances of the case.

[44] HR 12-08-05 NJ 2005/467, LJN AT 7337.

B. Mediation

i. Mediation Clauses

Mediation clauses, at present, do not prevent an action before the state courts.

In a divorce case, in the course of which the spouses had orally agreed to try and reach an amicable settlement by means of mediation, a Supreme Court judgment[45] held that, in view of the character of mediation, both parties were at liberty to terminate cooperation at any time. Many writers maintain that, in the case of a well-drafted mediation agreement in a business case, the decision may well turn out differently. Moreover, the Minister of Security and Justice has now announced that a new law will consider making the mediation clause enforceable and compel governing bodies to deploy mediation, or mediation elements, for individual conflict resolution.[46]

ii. Quality Measures and Duties of Mediators?

The Nederlands Mediation Instituut (Netherlands Mediation Institute, NMI)[47] is the national platform for mediation in the Netherlands. The NMI is a private organisation that has been operational since 1995 and operates from within a strictly independent position in society. This independent position as a national mediation platform is possibly unique in Europe.[48] Since 1995, the NMI, in consultation with delegates of professional mediator groups and mediation training institutes, the government and the various mediator organisations, has developed a constantly adjusted qualification system which is now accepted as standard in the Netherlands for all mediators. There are various mediator organisations which have supplementary qualification requirements, but the NMI regulations are considered to be *the* standard regulations by the government. The mediators who work for the judiciary or the legal desk must comply with these standards. The NMI has a standard mediation agreement, regulations, a code of conduct, and complaint- and disciplinary regulations.[49]

The NMI also offers a system of registered mediators. The rules of the NMI do not differentiate as to whether or not a mediator is a lawyer. The code of conduct contains rules about transparency, neutrality, impartiality and the duty to inform the parties about the mediation process. The mediator is bound to these rules, and the parties can use the complaints procedure if the mediator does not comply with them. The complaints procedure is used and the outcomes are published to make it possible for mediators to know what is allowed and what is not.

I have not seen any jurisprudence on malpractice yet. However, mediators are liable, and they all have professional liability insurance. The referral faculties (legal desk and judiciary) have made compliance with the NMI rules and the carrying of insurance mandatory for the mediators who work for them.

[45] HR 20-01-2006, LJN AU3724, NJ 2006,74.

[46] *Innovatieagenda rechtsbestel* 11.

[47] See <www.nmi-mediation.nl>.

[48] Niemeijer and Pel, 'Court-based Mediation in the Netherlands' 376.

[49] See <www.nmi-mediation.nl/english/nmi rules and models/nmi code of conduct.php>.

iii. Duties of the Parties

The NMI mediation rules regulate that each party and the mediator may break off the mediation at any time without any justification. The remuneration is not regulated as such, but the NMI rules prescribe putting the agreed remuneration into the mediation agreement. In cases where parties are entitled to legal aid, the mediators' remuneration is regulated by law (see II.A).

iv. Enforceability of Mediation Agreements (ie Agreements Resulting from Mediation)

Mediation agreements can be enforced. Court-annexed mediation offers this possibility via the minutes of an oral hearing or judgment, in which the agreement may be included. In other mediations, this can be accomplished by notarial deed.

C. Conciliation

The aforementioned dispute committees (see I.B.ii) probably fall under the heading of conciliation as that term is commonly used in the ADR realm. The dispute committees deal with consumer complaints regarding goods and services. They have their own regulations with regard to their procedures (see I.B). The only applicable substantive rules are those regarding the 'constitutive agreement', Civil Code, Book 7, Articles 900–06.[50] For the remainder, the committees have their own regulations governing the procedure and the management of the subject matter addressed. In each case, a consumer representative, a representative of the branch and an independent chairman take part in hearing and deciding the cases.

Calling in one of the 48 *dispute committees* is common and effective. Judicially speaking, it is a matter of binding advice, because the agreements that lead to the disputes include that any possible disputes will be subject to the binding advice of a dispute committee.[51] There are dispute committees for rental affairs and consumer affairs, which are in turn subdivided into various branches (eg for the legal profession, the travel sector and care facilities) that concentrate on consumers. The most common disputes arise in the areas of travel, living arrangements, telecommunications, banking and public utility companies.

Appeals against the decisions of the dispute committee are not possible. The businesses taking part in the scheme have all pledged to abide by these rulings, so in practice the rulings will always be complied with. Parties may, however, present the decision to the courts within two months by issuing a summons to the other party. After that period has lapsed, the decision is irreversible. Research shows that two-thirds of rents commission clients are satisfied with the quality of the service. Evaluations of

[50] Art 900(1):

1. Under a settlement agreement parties bind themselves towards each other, in order to end or to avoid any uncertainty or dispute about what applies to them legally, to the assessment and establishment of a new legal status between them, intended to apply as well as far as it differs from their previously existing legal status.

2. The assessment and establishment of their new legal status can be made by virtue of a joint decision of the involved parties or by virtue of a decision of one of them or of a third party.

[51] In the case of binding advice, the parties present their dispute to an expert based on an agreement (compromise) in which they bind themselves to the expert's opinion.

the dispute committees show that consumer satisfaction depends to a very large extent on the result of the procedure.[52] The committees can refer cases to mediation; in the recent past this led to an agreement in only 5 per cent of cases.

Mini-trials or early neutral evaluation do not find very much in use in the Netherlands, and to my knowledge there are no rulings regarding those instruments. The UNCITRAL (United Nations Committee on International Trade Law) Model Law or the Commission Recommendation 2001 has not been implemented.

D. Expert Opinion

In the Netherlands, the use of an expert opinion will often be required by means of arbitration and, in a few cases, as a binding advice. In the case of binding advice, the parties present their dispute to an expert based on an agreement (compromise) in which they are bound to the expert's opinion. The means of employing this mechanism of third-party ruling is the incidental involvement of a technical specialist in order to render a final expert opinion in contractual disputes. This form of binding advice is not very common, being based on individual compromises in the initial agreement. This does happen in technical disputes between trading parties, but they are exceptions. These procedures provide 'expert binding opinions'.

Conceptually, these opinions are not to be equated with arbitral awards, as there is no procedure for their enforcement. However, in practice it is as difficult to have such an expert opinion overruled as it is to set aside an arbitral award. Legal possibilities exist in order to seek the annulment of the advice, but this path is not commonly pursued. The substantive rules are the same as mentioned earlier (see III.C) in the case of the dispute committees.

E. Arbitration

The UNCITRAL Model Law dates back to December 1985. In the Netherlands, the legislature had been working hard to establish a new arbitration law (to partly replace the current Book IV of Civil Procedure, which was ultimately implemented in 1986). The Netherlands considered the Model Law as at least a provisional draft that had been completed at the time. In principle, there is no essential difference between Model Law and the current Dutch arbitration law, which is, however, much more detailed. A new law is now under construction.

The regulations on arbitration are laid down in the Code of Civil Procedure, Articles 1036–69. These regulations indicate minimum standards for a fair hearing and in respect of evidentiary rules. Most arbitration institutes have their own regulations, in which these matters are described in more detail. The parties may indicate whether the arbitrators must judge according to the rules of the law (and indicate the country whose law is applicable) or whether they judge 'fairly and reasonably'. On the condition that an arbitration award is filed with the court, a writ of execution is obtained with which the ruling can be enforced.

[52] A Klapwijk and M Ter Voert, *Evaluatie de geschillencommissie* (The Hague, WODC, 2009) 82, 93.

IV. POLICY QUESTIONS

A. Should ADR Be Regulated at All?

The first question that arises when thinking about the desirability of legislation or other regulations with regard to ADR is: what purpose does a possible further regulation of ADR serve? The experiences with ADR procedures in the Netherlands and the results of research on the matter have led me to the conclusion that, for the use of the various methods on a large scale, the following are important:

- the method needs to be well known;
- professionals refer to the various procedures;
- the method is cost-effective;
- the users and their professional advisors trust the method;
- the quality standards for the various methods are clear;
- the various methods are accepted officially by the government as an effective method for conflict resolution; and
- the results are adhered to by the parties and parties are satisfied.

Moreover, it should be appreciated that, with the large-scale use of ADR, the relative cost-advantages it presents will increase as the costs of legal procedures rise.

The second question that arises is which ADR procedures in the Netherlands would need further regulations. Currently, in our country, the only discussion is about the necessity of legislation on mediation. The other methods are either used on a grand scale and hardly need further regulation (dispute committees, objection procedures, other specific procedures (see III.A, C and D), or are regulated and used on a limited scale and, I think, there is no need for expansion (eg in arbitration) with regard to the users. Early neutral evaluations or mini-trials are unknown in our country; however, it does not seem likely that they would supplement the methods that are used currently.[53]

My opinion is that mediation is the only ADR method that should be used more frequently because the market for mediation, for the various aforementioned reasons, is not as of yet being used to its full extent, and, moreover, the increasing costs for adjudication prompt the implementation of mediation as a more cost-effective method. In the following considerations on the necessity and the possible content of further regulations for ADR, I will limit myself to regulation of mediation, unless otherwise stated.

Why do people not use mediation more often at present?

Many private persons and professionals are involved in conflicts on a regular basis as advisers, managers and adjudicators. It is a fact that people do not automatically turn to mediation when they find themselves in a conflict situation. There are several reasons for this:[54]

- Mediation is not yet universally accepted as a conflict resolution method. Some parties to conflicts are either unaware that mediation exists, or make inaccurate assumptions about how or when it can be used.

[53] The NAI and the SGOA have offered those methods, but due to non-utilisation these institutes now offer only arbitration and mediation.

[54] Pel, *Referral to Mediation* 13.

- Mediation cannot be initiated unilaterally, unlike other methods for ending a conflict. Once a conflict has escalated to some extent, it can be hard for the parties to agree on mediation and jointly select a mediator, unless they have outside help.
- The parties will sometimes deny that there is a conflict until they are confronted with the urgency of finding a solution, for example by a neutral third party.

Van Erp[55] and Barendrecht[56] also recommend further regulation on particular points: for instance, with regard to opening up the possibility of referral to mediation as a simple procedure for the resolution of partial disputes, or in respect of establishing the binding nature of mediation outcomes in connection with the further implementation of triage and conflict diagnosis methods.

The Minister of Security and Justice wants to regulate mediation and other forms of ADR (the dispute committees, in particular) even further than in the draft law (referred to in III.B.1) with regard to the price increase of court procedures. Additionally, the VVD (liberal political party) has announced an initiative bill in which the following aspects would be regulated:

- mandatory mediation point of access;
- speedy access to deciding judge for subtopics;
- mediation with a possible conclusion of binding advice from the mediator;
- enforceability of the agreement reached during mediation;
- mandatory referrals to mediation; and
- the commitment that the mediator is an expert with regard to content in the field in which he/she offers his/her services.

Barendrecht[57] argues in particular for drawing up final requirements—in consultation with users, the judiciary and ADR providers—which the procedures must meet with regard to various common problem areas. These specific problem areas comprise: family, work, residential matters, consumers and companies. Pricing methods should also be agreed and should take financial capacity into account.

I believe the latter suggestion is a very useful exercise, which should not lead to legislation for all points. I think very detailed regulation in all areas is unnecessary or even counterproductive.

B. Regulation Should Be Limited to Providing a General Legal Framework for Particular ADR Procedures

As far as I am concerned, the regulations concerning mediation could be limited to legally regulated methods of referral and a global regulation of quality standards. The power of mediation lies in the possibility to deliver made-to-measure work, and extremely detailed regulations for procedure, method, quality standards and costs will not contribute to that potential. The fact that people do not find it easy to choose mediation of their own will not change as a result of legal regulations on the

[55] Van Erp and Klein, *De filterwerking van buitengerechtelijke procedures* 69.

[56] JM Barendrecht, 'Innovatie van civiele rechtspleging: de regie naar rechter en gebruiker' [2011] *Nederlands Juristenblad* 293.

[57] Barendrecht, 'Innovatie van civiele rechtspleging'.

quality of mediation unless it results in the referring bodies gaining more confidence in mediation. A comparison between arbitration and mediation is interesting. There are no legal regulations governing the quality of arbitrators. Apparently, the legislator, who has in fact regulated the procedure, assumes that the conflicting parties which choose arbitration can determine whether the arbiter they invite meets the quality standards they require—standards that will be aimed at knowledge in respect of subject matter and method. It seems that arbitration concerns the arbiter's personal qualities in particular, namely experience as an adjudicator and familiarity with the subject-matter.

To what extent would that be different in respect of a mediator? There is a substantial difference between arbitration and mediation: mediation puts more emphasis on method and process, whereas knowledge with regard to subject matter is not a decisive factor, although there is a growing body of opinion that argues for the use of mediators having a base of knowledge as regards the subject matter, particularly concerning evaluative mediation. In fact, this difference makes the personal quality of the mediator even more significant because it is not his or her knowledge of the subject matter that primarily determines success, but the approach and the method. Does this mean there should not be any legal quality standards? I do not think so. Simply because mediation is a new profession, it is important that there are clear guidelines as to what skills and qualifications a mediator should possess. That is why I consider uniform quality standards and an official register for mediators of paramount importance. On the other hand, I consider regulations on the very procedure, other than via regulations from mediators themselves, too limiting for the free interpretation of the mediation process. Moreover, regulations that are too limiting promote mediation to be another form of legal dispute resolution and lead to an undesirable juridification.

C. Triage and Conflict Diagnosis System

Ideally, I would choose a situation where the civil justice system would offer a triage and conflict diagnosis system where a professional conflict diagnostician would assist the conflicting parties in selecting the most effective method of conflict resolution. The multi-door courthouse concept appeals to me very much. This system would also allow easier access to the judge during mediations for decisions on specific points (subrulings). I would prefer that the regulations adopt a more horizontal approach. However, I fear that there is currently little support for this method in the Netherlands.

D. Cost Aspects of Regulation

Basically, it is reasonable that conflicting parties pay their own costs, unless this would hinder access to conflict resolution. Cost is, of course, an important aspect for individual parties in making a selection among the various available means of conflict resolution. Mediation in itself is very cost-effective when compared to arbitration and adjudication. For consumer conflicts, there is access to dispute committees without any costs as such.

The hourly rates for mediation are quite low in the Netherlands. At an average of €160 and an average duration of mediations of about 10 hours, the costs in most cases are affordable for the two parties (each paying 50 per cent). It is only in family cases, neighbour disputes and community-mediations that costs could be an impediment for low-income earners. It is a positive and helpful aspect that in the Netherlands subsidies are available via the legal aid system according to legal regulations.

E. Minimal Regulation, Restricted to Quality Standards and Referral Procedures

My opinion is that all regulations with regard to a mediation register, quality standards, referrals or mandatory preliminary procedures should be mandatory rules, keeping in mind that the content of the quality standards should, I think, be minimum standards where specific groups of mediators could add further quality requirements. In the NMI, the Netherlands has an institute unique in Europe which has developed and maintained good quality standards. I would prefer it if those standards were restructured as general standards, where individual or groups of mediators could present themselves as having higher standards. However, the general register should be accessible to mediators who meet the general minimum standards.

As for the rest, regulations with regard to referrals should be default regulations which could be adjusted by organisations according to their wishes or needs.

F. Set an Example and Stimulate Training and Knowledge of Conflict Management

First, the government should set an example with regard to the choice of mediation. All government bodies should preferably solve their problems within the organisation, or between a government body and a civilian, via mediation. It would have a stimulating effect, as has been proven on a smaller scale (see II.A.ii).

Additionally, the government should force a number of training institutes (universities and other training institutes) to give a prominent place to conflict training, mediation, theory and associated skills within the courses for those professionals who will be confronted with many conflicts during their professional lives (lawyers, judges, managers, HR managers, doctors, accountants, etc).

Finally, a 'triage and conflict diagnosis system' is particularly effective. It has been trialled on a small scale within the judiciary in pilot schemes, and the method proved to be very successful in letting the conflicting parties take as much responsibility as possible for the resolution of their own conflicts. Currently, the legal desks are working with a system of personal online triage and conflict diagnosis. This needs further research and testing before being implemented across the board.

General publicity campaigns on radio, television and modern media could assist in making people more familiar with the use and the results of mediation. In particular, modern media like Twitter and LinkedIn could be very helpful because they resemble word-of-mouth advertising—which up to now has been most effective for choosing mediation—or function as a 'personal referral' by a trusted person.

G. Enforcement and Mediation Clauses

In the project concerning court-annexed mediation, research has shown that enforcement did not stand in the way of successful mediations. Even in cases where the judge's referral was the sole reason for taking part in mediation, the success rate proved to be around 50 per cent or more. This concerned cases where the parties had started a procedure and so had incurred its costs. In cases where the parties go to the mediator first, I believe the success rate would increase. A referral system where the referring parties are forced to refer to mediation, but where mediation does not need to be accepted, would probably have a similar effect.

Mediation clauses should be binding on parties and judges, and should lead to the inadmissibility of court procedures if, contrary to the clause, mediation has not been attempted. Legislation to this effect seems essential to me and is being prepared in the Netherlands.

H. Responsibility for the Choice of a Conflict Resolution Mechanism

Our experiences with various methods of referral show that mediation is most effective when the conflicting parties are themselves motivated to make it a success. This is why specific methods have been developed in the Netherlands whereby the parties are stimulated to choose mediation rather than being convinced (by a third party) as to its merits. In lectures I tend to argue: do not convince, seduce![58]

A written invitation to mediation accompanied by a self-test leads to very high success rates when the invitation is accepted. On the other hand, enforced referrals lead to more acceptances but a somewhat lower success rate. In short, the trick is to find a balance between too much enforcement (yielding too many unsuccessful mediations) and too little (resulting in a high success rate but fewer successful mediations than should be possible).

Training referring bodies in effective choice-drivers and good referral methods has a very positive effect—as has been the case in the Netherlands.

Cost penalties or other methods to 'punish' parties for not using mediation seems most counterproductive to me. Experience in other countries shows that judges and lawyers spend a great deal of (unproductive) time arguing over the consequences of both justified and unjustified refusals to engage in mediation. This creates a legal context which is not conducive to the use of mediation. Moreover, removing the legal context is one of the objectives of mediation, and thus juridification does not suit this purpose.

BIBLIOGRAPHY

Baarsma, B, ' Blijft mediation de eeuwige belofte of wordt het een volwassen markt?, mediationmarkt vanuit economisch perspectief' [2012] *Nederlands Juristenblad* 14

[58] For more details about referral methods see Pel, *Referral to Mediation* 63.

Bauw, E, Dijk, F van and Tulder, F van, 'De angel uit de kostendekkende griffierechten?' [2012] *Nederlands Juristenblad* 6

Barendrecht, JM, 'Innovatie van civiele rechtspleging: de regie naar rechter en gebruiker' [2011] *Nederlands Juristenblad* 293

Böcker, A, Havinga, T, Jettinghof, A, Klaassen, C and Bakker, L, 'Specialisatie loont?!', <www.njb.nl>, Actuele Documenten, 2011, week 17

Bosnak, J, 'The European Mediation Directive: More Questions Than Answers' in A Ingen-Housz (ed), *ADR in Business, Practice and Issues across Countries and Cultures*, vol II (Alphen aan den Rijn, Kluwer Law & Business, 2011) 626–57

Combrink-Kuiters, L, Niemeijer, E and Ter Voert, M, *Ruimte voor mediation* (The Hague, WODC, Boom juridische uitgevers, 2003)

Diephuis, BJ, Eshuis, RJJ and Heer-de Lange, NE de, *Rechtspleging Civiel en Bestuur 2008, Ontwikkelingen en samenhangen* (The Hague, WODC, Boom Juridische uitgevers, 2010)

Erp, JG van and Klein, CM, *De filterwerking van buitengerechtelijke procedures* (The Hague, WODC, 2006)

Giesen, I and Coenraad, L, 'De ketens van en binnen de Nederlandse rechtspleging' [2010] *Nederlands Juristenblad* 963

Giesen, I and Coenraad, L, 'De toegankelijkheid van de rechtspleging' [2011] *Nederlands Juristenblad* 952

Graaf, KJ de, Marseille, AT and Herweijer, M, *Mediation in Bezwaar: Evaluatie Mediation Project Provincie Overijssel* (Groningen, Vakgroep Bestuursrecht en bestuurskunde, University of Groningen, 2003), <www.rug.nl/staff/m.herweijer/mediationinbezwaar.pdf>

Innovatieagenda rechtsbestel (The Hague, Ministerie van Veiligheid en Justitie, 2011)

Jagtenberg, J and De Roo, A, 'Frame for a Dutch Portrait of Mediation' in Jagtenberg, R, De Roo, A, Pel, M, Combrink, L, Klijn, A and Verberk, S (eds), *Customized Conflict Resolution, Court-connected Mediation in The Netherlands 1999–2009*, The Judiciary Quarterly 2011 (The Hague, Netherlands Council for the Judiciary, 2011), <www.pelmediation.nl/publications>, 7–24

Klapwijk, A and Ter Voert, M, *Evaluatie de geschillencommissie* (The Hague, WODC, 2009)

Niemeijer, B and Pel, M, 'Court-based Mediation in the Netherlands: Research, Evaluation and Future Expectations' (2005) 110 *Penn State Law Review* 345

Pel, J, *Arbeidsrecht en mediation* (The Hague, SDU, 2007)

Pel, M, *Referral to Mediation, a Practical Guide for an Effective Mediation Proposal* (The Hague, SDU, 2008)

Pel, M and Combrink, L, 'Referral to Mediation by the Netherlands Judiciary' in Jagtenberg, R, De Roo, A, Pel, M, Combrink, L, Klijn, A and Verberk, S (eds), *Customized Conflict Resolution, Court-connected Mediation in The Netherlands 1999–2009*, The Judiciary Quarterly 2011 (The Hague, Netherlands Council for the Judiciary, 2011), <www.pelmediation.nl/publications>, 25–53

Schutte, E and Spierdijk, J *Juridische aspecten van mediation* (The Hague, SDU, 2011)

Veldhoven, BCJ van, Ter Voert, MJ and Gammeren-Soeteweij, M van, *Geschilbeslechtingsdelta 2003, Over verloop en afloop van (potentieel) juridische problemen van burgers* (The Hague, WODC, Boom juridische uitgevers, 2003)

Veldhoven, BCJ van and Klein Haarhuis, CM, *Geschilbeslechtingsdelta 2009, Over verloop en afloop van (potentieel) juridische problemen van burgers* (The Hague, WODC, Boom juridische uitgevers, 2009)

Vogels, RJM, *De stand van Mediation in Nederland 2011* (Zoetermeer, Stratus, 2011)

13

Regulation of Dispute Resolution in Norway: Vertical and Horizontal Regulatory Strategies

ANNEKEN KARI SPERR

I. INTRODUCTION TO THE CHARACTERISTICS OF ADR IN NORWAY TODAY[1]

A. Most Commonly Deployed ADR Procedures

TODAY THE MOST common understanding of ADR in Norway includes all different methods of conflict resolution that are *alternatives* to ordinary court proceedings.[2] The three methods with the greatest practical importance are bilateral negotiations between the parties, different types of mediation processes and arbitration practices. Other methods include labour dispute negotiations, as well as specialised complaint boards and tribunals such as the Consumer Dispute Commission (Forbrukertvistutvalget) and similar private dispute resolution institutions specific to each industry sector, as, for example, the Insurance Complaint Board (Forsikringsklagenemnda) and the complaint board within the banking sector (Bankklagenemnda), which have since been consolidated into a single dispute board for financial issues (Finansklagenemnda)[3]. With regard to administrative decisions, complaint boards for public law and the institution of the Parliamentary Ombudsman also play a role. With regard to contracts for work and services in certain construction industries we also find specific expert- and 'oppman'-solutions that have proven to be successful resolution methods.[4]

To provide some brief quantitative data, approximately 50 per cent of all civil disputes at the district court level were resolved through ADR mechanisms in the years 2000–06.[5] The same is true for the courts of appeal, while only about 10 per cent of all disputes were resolved at the Supreme Court level.[6] Although there are no general statistics, it seems legitimate to assume that about two-thirds of all civil matters are resolved through ADR (including arbitration processes) and that the total number varies between 5,000 and 10,000 different cases a year.[7]

Added to this is the large number of conflicts that are settled prior to going to court, either as part of the conciliation board process[8] or through other modes of dispute resolution. This clearly shows that a significant majority of all legal conflicts are resolved without ever going to court.[9]

B. Relative Strengths and Weaknesses

The practical benefits of ADR mechanisms are generally valued quite highly. This is

[1] I would like to thank Sverre Blandhol (dr. juris and m. phil. in psychology), mediator and consultant at Palatin AS, for his constructive comments on an earlier version of this text.

[2] A Austbø and G Engebretsen, *Mekling i rettskonflikter,* 2nd edn (Oslo, Cappelen Akademisk Forlag, 2006), 22, and Ot prp no 51 (2004–2005) 60; Innst O no 110 (2004–2005), 17.

[3] See <www.finansklagenemnda.no/vis.asp?id=1>.

[4] PM Ristvedt and OØ Nisja, *Alternative tvisteløsning* (Oslo, Cappelen Akademisk Forlag, 2008) 54ff and 622–29; for more information on 'oppman' solutions, see below section III.D.

[5] It should be noted here that in Norwegian law, as opposed to German law for example, all administrative law disputes are included in civil law. Only criminal law is dealt with separately, by the same courts but according to a separate criminal law procedure.

[6] For more on these numbers see Ristvedt and Nisja, *Alternative tvisteløsning* 33ff.

[7] Ibid, 34.

[8] See below II.B.i and II.C.

[9] For the preparatory legislative materials on this see NOU 2001:32, bind A, 93 and 214.

due to the important advantages that the various alternative dispute resolution instruments provide, compared with a classical court procedure with a binding judgment. Generally speaking, ADR has shown itself to be a faster, cheaper, friendlier and less stressful mode of dispute resolution.[10]

On average, court cases in Norway take six to eight months in the district courts, another six to eight months for trials that go on to the courts of appeal, and six months at the Supreme Court (with an additional 10 weeks for a decision on whether the case should be admitted to the Supreme Court).[11] In comparison with other European jurisdictions, this appears rather unproblematic. However, the use of alternative dispute resolution processes, including arbitration, generally leads to a *faster resolution process*, with the financial and other intangible benefits this brings for the parties. This is particularly true for extra-judicial forms of ADR, for example negotiation or extra-judicial mediation. For judicial mediation and arbitration, a waiting and processing time of at least a few months must be factored in.

ADR involves *lower costs for the parties*, as court fees do not apply and rules of evidence and argumentation are greatly simplified, if they apply at all, reducing the role played by witnesses and legal representation. As the parties carry their own costs as a rule, the risk of having to pay the legal costs of the opposing party is removed. This is not the case, however, for arbitration, where costs may be apportioned as in a traditional court of law, and the costs of paying for the arbitrator and the venue must also be included.[12]

A further advantage of some ADR instruments is that the larger conflict between the parties can be considered, as opposed to merely focusing on the legal aspects of the case at hand; this provides a greater likelihood of *establishing or improving a relationship between the parties*. This is particularly advantageous where the parties need to be able to work together, for example in disputes involving employment, long-term business relationships and family relationships. Mechanisms that help to repair the relationship between the parties, such as negotiation or settlement agreements, are particularly advantageous. The positive effects are less clear, however, where an authoritative decision is given by an oppman.

In some situations there is a further advantage for the parties, in that ADR mechanisms are *not usually subject to the principle of open trial*, so that potential negative publicity can be avoided. Parties wanting to use public interest as a means of placing the opposing party under pressure are more likely to pursue the case through the regular court system.

The biggest *disadvantage* of ADR is that many of its forms are not subject to any kind of monitoring, and this *lack of quality control* may lead to substantially unjust results. This is particularly true for negotiation, where the result is (always)

[10] For the area of judicial mediation, this corresponds to the findings of a comprehensive evaluation of the model project launched in 2000, with the main findings being viewed as still valid today, R Knoff, *Raskere? Billigere? Vennligere? Evaluering av prøveordningen med rettsmekling*, Rapport for Justisdepartementet (Oslo, 2001), see <www.rhknoff.no/Rapporter/R157JD.pdf>.

[11] Although in principle there is a significant lack of accessible and meaningful statistical data, the figures provided here could be taken from the internet pages of the court administration, see <www. domstol.no>; the target of a standard period for a court settlement in the district courts and the courts of appeal has been set at six months.

[12] Compared with regular court resolution of disputes, arbitration may still provide some cost savings, as the costs associated with appeals proceedings and associated legal fees are avoided.

particularly dependent on the negotiating position, capacity and financial resources of the parties. Even mediation, a form of assisted negotiation between the parties, can produce different results for otherwise factually similar cases. In the various mediation processes provided by the courts or within the court system, however, the mediator has a duty to ensure that any imbalances between the parties do not determine the result.[13]

It may also be problematic where parties feel compelled to resort to ADR mechanisms due to financial or other factors, such as time constraints. In this situation, it appears contrary to the *principles of equality and justice* to require the parties to assume the greater individual responsibility for the content and quality of the result involved with most alternative dispute resolution mechanisms.[14] Whether and to what extent this could be true for Norway has not yet been examined; however, the high costs involved with court trials, partly due to the very high legal fees, continue to be a subject of debate.[15] In addition, there are examples in Norway of the six- to eight-month time frame per court process being vastly exceeded; in some areas this may lead the parties to choose alternative dispute resolution mechanisms which are less likely to involve similar commercial or other risks.

A further general disadvantage of ADR is based on the fact that, in contrast with traditional adjudication, it does not contribute to the *clarification or development of the law*. There is a range of opinions on whether and to what extent this is a problem in Norway.[16]

It might be helpful to differentiate more specifically according to the area of law: with this approach, it emerges, for example, that administrative law has a particular problem caused by the fact that the overwhelming majority of all disputes are determined by internal administrative supervisory bodies, while only a small fraction of cases are dealt with by the courts.[17] Although a large number of conflicts are dealt with by the about 50 different kinds of independent complaint boards for public law (*klagenemnder*) that use processes similar to those of a court,[18] these do not

[13] See Tvl, s 1-1(2), point 5, which explicitly states that the outcome of the process should not be influenced by the fact that the parties have unequal access to financial or other resources. For traditional mediation and family mediation (see below III.B.i), this corresponds to the court's duty to give guidance, Tvl, s 11-5. The same applies to mediators, and—despite the greater flexibility of their role and a stronger emphasis on the principles of mediation—even for judicial mediation according to Tvl, s 8-3; see C Bernt, *Meklerrollen ved mekling i domstolene* (Bergen, Fagbokforlaget, 2010) 388–89; see also the comments contained in n 54 below.

[14] Similarly, C Bernt-Hamre, *Rettsmekling* Det Juridiske Fakultets Skriftserie No 97 (Bergen, Det juridiske fakultet, 2004) 25.

[15] See, eg T Nygard-Sture and HK Mjelva, 'Loven skulle kutte kostnadene ved rettssaker betydelig. Men alt tyder på at tusenlappene flagrer like raskt som før', *Bergens Tidende*, 2 February 2012, 1, 6–8.

[16] Although many, including, for example, the former President of the Supreme Court, have spoken out in concern over the number of important decisions being resolved through alternative dispute resolution as opposed to before the Supreme Court, C Smith, 'Voldgift—Domstolenes konkurrent og hjelper' [1993] *Tidsskrift for Rettsvitenskap* 474. Ristvedt and Nisja, *Alternative tvisteløsning* 38, do not view the situation as problematic.

[17] There are approximately 150,000 internal administrative appeals annually, compared to only a few hundred administrative law cases dealt with by the courts each year. In 2011, not untypically, the highest court dealt with only nine administrative law disputes (of a total number of 299 decisions in the field of civil law).

[18] On this point see the report of the government Directorate for Communication, Competence and Administration (Statskonsult) from 2003, Statskonsult, *Klager over alt, Organisering av statlig klagesaksbehandling*, Rapport 2003:19, 1, 13, see <www.difi.no/statskonsult/publik/rapporter/fulltekst/2003-19.pdf>;

contribute to the clarification and development of the law in the same way as traditional adjudication.

At any rate, securing this function of the traditional court process—the clarification and development of the law—was given great attention in the development of the new regulation for civil proceedings (new Dispute Act of 1 January 2008) and in the associated discussions surrounding the regulation of various ADR measures: it set an important goal, to be achieved predominantly through the introduction of a separate small claims procedure for disputes up to NOK 125,000 (about £13,800), the introduction of class actions and the simplification of appeal proceedings, including those before the Supreme Court—in brief, by improving the accessibility of traditional adjudication for all cases, including those dealing with disputes over smaller amounts.[19]

Ultimately, there is a broad consensus that the advantages of ADR instruments in most cases outweigh the disadvantages. This means that the Norwegian approach to ADR is first and foremost a matter of further developing and expanding the various instruments and encouraging their use.

C. Theoretical Appropriateness and Practical Use

Generally, the various alternative dispute resolution instruments are valued not only because of their theoretical advantages, but also because they have very practical benefits for the Norwegian legal system. That said, there is still a need for development and improvement, as seen in the calls for a further expansion of the Arbitration and Dispute Resolution Institute of the Oslo Chamber of Commerce, originally introduced in 1983: this body provides a range of different processes, including a simplified dispute resolution process for smaller disputes (fast-track arbitration), mini-trials and various forms of mediation. However, the Institute is mainly used for international disputes involving one or more foreign parties and usually has only between two and ten proceedings running at a time. At the same time, there are numerous ad hoc proceedings operating outside of the Institute. This has resulted in pressure, not just from the Institute in Oslo itself, but also from the Mediation Committee of the Norwegian Lawyers Association, for a greater consolidation of knowledge and resources, or even for the creation of a new institute.[20]

It has also been correctly noted that the significant advantages that mediation offers are not yet reflected quantitatively in the level of their application—in other words, this alternative to traditional court proceedings has not yet been exhausted. This applies not only to extra-judicial mediation, but also to judicial mediation.[21]

see also the new study on the level of independence shown by this (and other) government administrative bodies and the problems regarding the legal and political legitimisation of this independence, Direktoratet for forvaltning og IKT (Difi), *Uavhengig eller bare uklart? Organisering av statlig myndighetsutøvelse*, Difi raport 2012:7, Oslo, 2012, see <www.difi.no/filearchive/difi-rapport-2012-7-uavhengig-eller-bare-uavklart.pdf>; for more on this see also III.F.ii below).

[19] For the preparatory legislative materials on this see Ot prp no 51 (2004–2005), 43.

[20] See, eg A Rønning, 'Vil ha nytt institutt for mekling' (2011) 91(12) *Advokatbladet* 42.

[21] S Blandhol, 'Hvorfor brukes ikke mekling oftere' (2010) 44(7) *Juristkontakt* 54; B Østgård, 'Hvorfor brukes ikke mekling oftere? Replikk til Sverre Blandhol' (2010) 44(8) *Juristkontakt* 36; S Blandhol, 'Hindringer for forlik kan ramme også den gode advokat' (2010) 44(10) *Juristkontakt* 54; see also various

Finally, it seems to be as necessary as it is important to further the education and training of judicial parties involved in the specific elements of the individual ADR instruments, particularly with regard to negotiation and mediation. This training should cover the relevant considerations for each process, estimating the potential risks and choosing the most appropriate ADR method for resolving the specific case in question.[22] This is particularly true for the area of mediation, which in Norway is set up so that the mediators are allowed broad discretion for tailoring their duties and processes to the individual circumstances of the case. This provides some advantages, but the high level of flexibility also requires a high level of competence from the mediator, in order to be able to establish and maintain a strong dialogue with the parties and to make the right decisions throughout the different phases of the mediation. The high demands placed on mediators require well-thought-out quality assurance mechanisms, including an expansion of the currently barely adequate mediator training, and the introduction of codes of conduct for mediators, ethical principles and *best practice* guidelines.[23]

II. GENERAL APPROACH OF THE LEGISLATOR AS REGARDS THE REGULATION OF ADR AND ADJUDICATION

A. Regulation of ADR

As is characteristic for Norwegian law in general, there is no common systematic national regulation of ADR as such; rather, there are many different rules and pieces of legislation which are not necessarily coordinated. The new Dispute Act of 17 June 2005 (in force since January 2008), however, is founded on a proportionality principle which—together with a generally more active role for the courts, a separate small claims procedure, the introduction of class actions and many other simplifications—aims to achieve a reduction in time and costs as well as a generally more effective legal process. It also includes rules on *traditional mediation* in the sense of ordinary settlement negotiation, a proposed standard agreement for *extra-judicial mediation* and the promotion of an autonomous *judicial mediation process*. It may therefore be regarded as a means of promoting ADR in general, as is indicated by its name alone: Lov om mekling og rettergang i sivile tvister (Law on Mediation and Court Process in Civil Disputes), hereinafter referred to by its Norwegian short form, Tvisteloven (Tvl), or the English name, the Dispute Act.[24]

Particular forms of negotiation are in part specifically regulated by individual fields of law. In labour law conflicts—eg disputes regarding dismissals, suspensions or unfair

newspaper articles such as, for example, R Christophersen and Ø Torvund, 'Ingen vil til megling', *Bergens Tidende*, 10 August 2009, 7.

[22] For more on this see Ristvedt and Nisja, *Alternative tvisteløsning* 59–93; S Blandhol 'Valget mellom forlik og rettssak. Hvor gode er advokater til å bedømme prosessrisiko og hvorfor går det ofte galt?' (2011) 50 *Lov og Rett* 596, and S Blandhol in an interview with A Rønning, 'Advokater er dårlige til å vurdere prosessrisiko' (2011) 91(2) *Advokatbladet* 22.

[23] See AK Sperr, 'Mediation in Norway' in K Hopt and F Steffek (eds), *Mediation—Principles, Regulation and Reform in Comparative Perspective* (Oxford, Oxford University Press, 2012) 1137, 1160–61.

[24] For an English version of the Tvisteloven see <www.ub.uio.no/ujur/ulovdata/lov-20050617-090-eng.pdf>.

time limitations for an employment relationship—negotiations between employees and employers, which also replaced the otherwise compulsory pre-judicial process managed by the conciliation boards, are regulated in sections 17-1 and 17-3 Arbeidsmiljøloven.[25]

Provisions for *arbitration* were previously to be found in the former Dispute Act; however, a specific law—the Voldgiftsloven (Arbitration Act)[26]—was introduced in January 2005. This legislation provides for the regulation of international as well as national disputes.

There are countless other dispute resolution instruments, including specialised complaint boards and tribunals such as the Consumer Dispute Commission (Forbrukertvistutvalget), and similar private dispute resolution institutions specific to each industry sector—for example, the common dispute board for financial issues (Finansklagenemnda). These boards and tribunals are each regulated by specific laws and regulations,[27] or by agreements, statutes and procedural rules developed independently and voluntarily by the private sector parties themselves.[28] The regulation for the (very) numerous public law dispute resolution- and complaint boards is drawn from a similarly broad base. The list includes the Institution of the Parliamentary Ombudsman[29] as well as the Trygderetten—the most prominent example of an administrative body using a process similar to that of the courts to resolve disputes involving administrative decisions in the field of social security law.[30]

B. Incentives to use ADR

i. General Incentives and Legal Culture

Generally speaking, the most important incentives to use ADR may be identified by comparing the main *characteristics* of ADR with ordinary court proceedings. Despite many individual differences, the various ADR procedures are generally viewed as a faster, cheaper, friendlier and less stressful mode of conflict resolution with a satisfactory level of success. For example, mediation proceedings are successfully settled in 70–80 per cent of all attempts, reducing duration and costs as compared with traditional legal proceedings. Settlements are generally viewed as balanced and fair, and even where no settlement is reached the attempt does not prolong the trial process.[31]

In addition, it should be stressed that alternative dispute resolution mechanisms have a long tradition in Norwegian legal culture. They trace back to the Middle Ages, when conflicts were primarily resolved by local arbitral boards, Skiladom, that were appointed by the disputing parties. In the event that these boards failed to reach a mutually acceptable solution, the matter was brought before a general local people's

[25] Arbeidsmiljøloven of 17 June 2005 no 62.

[26] Voldgiftloven of 14 Mai 2004 no 25 (Lov om voldgift, Vogl).

[27] Eg the Consumer Disputes Act (Forbrukertvistloven) of 28 April 1978 no 18.

[28] See, eg <www.finansklagenemnda.no/dllvis5.asp?id=1575>.

[29] Parliamentary Ombudsman Act of 22 June 1962 no 8 (Sivilombudsmannsloven).

[30] Tygderettsloven of 16 December 1966 no 9.

[31] See the final report of a comprehensive evaluation of the model project on judicial mediation procedures in Norway launched in 2000, with the main findings being viewed as still valid today, R Knoff, *Raskere? Billigere? Vennligere? Evaluering av prøveordningen med rettsmekling.*

assembly, a Ting, under traditional Germanic law. For its part, the Ting sought to resolve the majority of conflicts through mutually acceptable settlements.[32] The tradition of using local lay judges as intermediaries between parties prior to a court trial began later with the institution of Forligelseskommisjonene, today known as Forliksrådene (conciliation boards).[33] These boards had limited powers and functioned as a preliminary dispute resolution stage prior to entering the three-tier court system. Members were (and still are) appointed by the municipal council for a period of four years, and worked to achieve a negotiated settlement between the parties to civil law disputes.[34] Originally, they were only granted powers to mediate between parties; however, these powers were broadened to provide a limited power of adjudication. This is now a compulsory part of preliminary proceedings, although some areas of law have been exempted and in some cases given their own dispute resolution processes. This tradition may be regarded as one of the different factors that until the present day have led to a general reluctance to use traditional court processes. Parties to a dispute can avail themselves of a wide range of resolution alternatives in most areas of the law and even the courts are obliged—throughout the proceeding—to consider whether, at any stage, the dispute can be settled amicably through *Mekling*, ie traditional settlement negotiations, or through *Rettsmekling*, ie an independent mediation process, which, according to new regulations, may be instigated by mutual agreement between the parties provided nothing in the nature of the matter or other circumstances argues against it.[35]

ii. Legal and Institutional Incentives

As regards *preliminary obligations before bringing an action*, Chapter 5 of the Dispute Act includes an obligation for the parties to try to achieve a sustainable, mutually acceptable settlement before going to court.[36] As this does not mean that the parties must always agree to an interim solution regardless of the costs, this obligation seems

[32] G Sandvik, 'Rettshistorie—førelesninger' [1990] *Jussens Venner* 229, 287–88.

[33] The first compulsory dispute resolution or mediation requirement was introduced through the Regulations for creating Conciliation Boards from 10 July 1795 (Forordning om Forligelses-Commissioners Stiftelse overalt i Danmark, samt i kjøbstæderne i Norge) and from 20 January 1797 (Forordning om Forligelses-Indretninger paa Landet i Norge).

[34] For more on these institutions see H Næss, *Vel forlikt. Forliksrådene i Norge 200 år 1795–1995* (Stavanger, Kulturkonsult/Justisdepartementet, 1995); Austbø and Engebretsen, *Mekling i rettskonflikter*, 25, 181ff; D Hareide, *Konfliktmegling—et nordisk perspektiv* (Oslo, Scandinavian Academic Press, 2006) 209–22; and D Hareide, *Conflict Mediation—A Nordic Perspective*, translated by LE Kjerland for the Helsinki Conference on Mediation and Conflict Management (Oslo, The Board of Nordic Forum for Mediation and Conflict Management, 2006) 157–67. For current regulations see T Schei, A Bårdsen, DB Nordén, CHP Reusch and TM Øie, *Lov av 17 juni 2005 no 90 om mekling og rettergang i sivile tvister (Tvisteloven), Kommentarutgave*, Bind I, II (Oslo, Universitetsforlaget, 2007), 245–341.

[35] As explicitly provided in Tvl, s 8-1, which states in the original Norwegian: 'Retten skal på ethvert trinn av saken vurdere muligheten for å få rettstvisten helt eller delvis løst i minnelighet gjennom mekling eller rettsmekling, om ikke sakens karakter eller forholdene for øvrig taler imot en slik løsning' (The court shall at each stage of the case consider the possibility of a full or partial amicable settlement to the legal dispute through mediation or judicial mediation, unless the nature of the case or other circumstances suggest otherwise).

[36] See Tvl, s 5-4 (Attempt to reach amicable settlement): the parties shall investigate whether it is possible to reach an amicable settlement of the dispute before action is brought, and shall make a strong attempt at settlement, if necessary through conciliation before a conciliation board, non-judicial mediation or by bringing the dispute before a non-judicial dispute resolution board.

to be a given. However, a judge may use his or her discretion in making a cost allocation determination where it appears *ex post* that a party has deliberately or maliciously rejected an otherwise acceptable offer of settlement. This apparent refusal to accept alternative dispute resolution approaches is not, however, a sufficient ground for the court to reject the case.[37] It can be safely assumed that the same rule also applies in the rare case that a specific law requires pre-trial *negotiations*, as seen, for example, in the Act Relating to Working Hours and Employment Protection (Working Environment Act).[38]

A similar rule applies for extra-judicial mediation based on a previous agreement between the parties. By including legal requirements for extra-judicial mediation in the Dispute Act, the Norwegian legislator took a clear stance in favour of this form of dispute resolution. The purpose of this decision was to strengthen the legitimacy of extra-judicial mediation and to provide a level of quality assurance.[39] Specifically, the relevant sections set forth regulations for the conclusion and contents of a mediation agreement, provisions regulating the selection and remuneration of mediators, and instructions governing the procedure to be followed for extra-judicial mediation. Extra-judicial mediation is usually commenced when deemed necessary by at least one of the parties. An attempt by the other party, in breach of their obligations under the mediation agreement and the relevant sections of the Dispute Act, to prevent an out-of-court dispute resolution and hinder the commencement of the mediation process will result in the applicable fines being levied as a sanction.[40] Additionally, the basic rule requiring that a hearing before a court be preceded by a compulsory dispute resolution process before the Conciliation Board also applies.[41] It must be emphasised, however, that the parties may end the mediation at any time,[42] and that an agreement to mediate made prior to a conflict arising has no binding effect on a consumer.[43]

Judicial mediation is initiated by a court decision. The Norwegian courts have a duty to assess, at every stage of the proceedings, if, and to what extent, a dispute can be settled amicably.[44] They are to ensure that legal proceedings are conducted rapidly, economically and responsibly. They must actively and systematically guide the court process[45] and, in particular, schedule court proceedings after the defendant has lodged his or her statement and discuss with the parties how best to proceed. This involves setting appropriate deadlines and determining whether a conventional settlement negotiation (traditional mediation) or a judicial mediation process should be carried out.[46] While a simple mediation can be initiated without first conducting a formal hearing,[47] judicial mediation requires a formal decision prior to its commencement.[48] In deciding whether to conduct judicial mediation, the court should first consider the

[37] See Tvl, ss 20-2(3)(b) and 20-4(c) and Ristvedt and Nisja, *Alternative tvisteløsning* 404ff.
[38] For more on this see III.B.
[39] See Ot prp no 51 (2004–2005), 111; NOU 2001:32, Rett på sak, Bind A, 211; Innst O no 110 (2004–2005), tvisteloven, 24; and Schei et al, *Tvisteloven* 342.
[40] See Tvl, ss 20-2(3)(b) and s 20-4(c); see also Schei et al, *Tvisteloven* 343ff.
[41] See Tvl, s 6-2(2)(b).
[42] See Tvl, s 7-1(2).
[43] See Tvl, s 7-1(1), sentence 3.
[44] See Tvl, s 8-1; Schei et al, *Tvisteloven* 359ff.
[45] See Tvl, ss 11-6 and 9-4(1).
[46] Tvl, s 9-4(2)(a).
[47] Tvl, s 8-2(1); Schei et al, *Tvisteloven*, 361ff.
[48] Tvl, s 8-3(1).

stated positions and preferences of the parties involved.[49] Although it is possible to decide for mediation in contravention of the parties' stated positions, there must be specific elements in place justifying an attempt at this kind of dispute resolution.[50] Another consideration relevant to the judge's decision on whether to conduct judicial mediation is the likely success of mediation,[51] ie the likelihood of achieving a settlement or successfully utilising other simplified means of settling the dispute. There are also other considerations relating to the balance of power between the parties,[52] such as an imbalance of power, eg the use of legal representation by only one side in the dispute, which argue against the initiation of mediation.[53] Where a decision to proceed with mediation is made despite such an imbalance, the mediator is obliged to assume greater responsibility to protect the weaker party.[54]

iii. The Role of the Lawyer

Lawyers are generally required to advise their clients of relevant ADR procedures before going to court. However, this principle is not generally regulated by legislation—with the exception of a specific provision in the Children Act. The principle can, however, be derived indirectly from Tvl, section 5-4, according to which the parties are generally obligated to investigate whether it is possible to reach an amicable settlement of the dispute before action is brought and to make a serious attempt at settlement, if necessary through conciliation in the sense of traditional mediation before a Conciliation Board, extra-judicial mediation or by bringing the dispute before an extra-judicial dispute resolution board (eg the Consumer Dispute Commission, Forbrukertvistutvalget, FTU). According to section 3.1.3 of the Code of Conduct and Ethical Principles for lawyers, promulgated by the Norwegian Bar Association, lawyers are required to seek a mutually acceptable solution insofar as it serves the interests of their client;[55] and it is, of course, always in the interests of the client (independent of the circumstances of the current dispute) to honour the obligations imposed by Tvl, section 5-4. Section 3.1.3 of the Code of Conduct and Ethical Principles for lawyers details the general regulation in section 1.2(2) of the Code that requires the lawyer to represent the client's best interests, thus complementing the legislative provision in Tvl, section 5-4, which is aimed solely at the parties.

It is only in legislation having in mind the interests of children where an amendment was made in 2003 (in force since April 2004) to include a clear legal obligation addressed directly at lawyers. Section 49 of the Children Act (Barneloven) requires that lawyers must determine the likelihood of a mutually acceptable agreement between

[49] See Tvl, s 8-3(2), sentence 1; s 9-6(1).

[50] See Tvl, s 8-3(2), sentence 3; in the preparatory legislative materials, Ot prp no 51 (2004–2005), 389, disputes between close relatives are cited as an example where a court decision would ultimately only perpetuate the conflict; see also Schei et al, *Tvisteloven* 365.

[51] See Tvl, s 8-3(2), sentence 1.

[52] See Tvl, s 8-3(2), sentence 2.

[53] Ot prp no 51 (2004–2005), 390.

[54] See Schei et al, *Tvisteloven* 366, 371f, and Tvl, s 1-1(2), point 5, which explicitly states that the outcome of the process should not be influenced by the fact that the parties have unequal access to financial or other resources.

[55] See <www.advokatforeningen.no/Etiske-regler/God-advokatskikk/kommentarutgaven/3-Forhold-til-klienten/>; this regulation effectively covers the provision in point 3.7.1 CCBE Code of Conduct (Charter of core principles of the European legal profession and Code of Conduct for European Lawyers), available at <www.ccbe.eu/fileadmin/user_upload/NTCdocument/EN_Code_of_conductp1_1306748215.pdf>.

the parties in disputes regarding parental responsibility, custody or care rights. The lawyers are also required to inform the parties of the possibility of mediation.[56]

It is worth mentioning that the evaluation of process risks and a weighing up of the economic considerations involved in efforts to come to an agreement as opposed to traditional court proceedings has been insufficiently covered in lawyers' education. This lack clearly demonstrates a need for further development, with current discussions centring on whether negotiation should be introduced as a recognised legal specialisation.[57]

C. ADR as a Restriction of Access to Courts

i. ADR Procedures as a Pre-condition for Starting Proceedings

Chapter 6 of the Dispute Act regulates the compulsory preliminary hearing process before a Conciliation Board (Forliksråd) (Tvl, section 6-2).[58] Originally these boards were only granted powers to mediate between the parties, that is, to assist in conciliation between the parties in the sense of a traditional settlement negotiation; today, their authority includes a limited power of adjudication. Some areas of law have been exempted from this preliminary obligation and in some cases have been given their own dispute resolution processes, eg cases involving rental properties, family and custody disputes, disputes arising from dismissal from employment and public law disputes.[59] In addition, the claimant may elect to exclude disputes involving an amount of more than NOK 125,000 (about £13,800) from an attempt at dispute resolution, provided both parties have legal representation.[60] The parties may also agree to make use of an extra-judicial mediation process (*Utenrettslig Mekling*) instead of appearing before the Conciliation Board.[61] Where a case is brought to court without going through the preliminary (obligatory) negotiation before a Conciliation Board (Forliksråd), the court must send the case to the relevant Forliksråd (Tvl, sections 4-2 and 6-2).

ii. Legal Mechanisms for Referring a Dispute to an Alternative Dispute Resolution Mechanism

When action has already been brought to court (either following an unsuccessful hearing before a Conciliation Board or under the exception where a 'preliminary process' was not required), the presiding judge, as already mentioned, has the opportunity to refer the case to judicial mediation against the stated positions of the parties

[56] For more on this see K Sandberg, *Kommentar til barneloven*, Gyldental rettsdata, Norsk Lovkommentar, available at <www.rettsdata.no>, § 49, notes 145 and 146; and K Rønbeck and R Lilleberg, 'Advokatrollen i barnefordelingssaker' (2006) 45 *Lov og Rett* 170.

[57] For more on this see Blandhol, 'Valget mellom forlik og rettssak'; S Blandhol in an interview with A Rønning, 'Advokater er dårlige til å vurdere prosessrisiko' 22; P Ristvedt, 'Advokater og prosessrisiko' (2012) 92(4) *Advokatbladet* 46; and S Blandhol, 'Hvordan kan advokater bli bedre rådgivere i tvisteløsning?' (2012) 92(4) *Advokatbladet* 47.

[58] For the historical background see above II.B.i.

[59] For the latest developments in the institution of the Conciliation Boards see AR Høyer and JB Høyer, 'Forliksrådet—fra lekmannsdomstol til kvalifisert tvisteløsningsorgan?' (2008) 47 *Lov og Rett* 326.

[60] For more on this see Tvl, s 6-2 and the commentary in Schei et al, *Tvisteloven* 259ff.

[61] See Tvl, s 6-2(2)(b).

(Tvl, section 8-3[2], sentence 3). This should, of course, remain an exception and not the rule, and should only occur where specific circumstances indicate that a (further) attempt at mutually acceptable settlement may be successful.[62]

For family law, the Norwegian Barneloven (Children Act) provides a mandatory requirement in sections 51ff for mediation in all legal disputes regarding custody and visitation rights.[63] This requirement also applies in the granting of a divorce settlement that involves children from the marriage who are under 16 years of age; further, the establishment of an increased child allowance from the state also requires the parties to agree to an extra-judicial mediation process.[64] This requirement was intended to assist parents in reaching an amicable solution and, most importantly, to protect the interests and well-being of the children. A mandatory time period of one hour of mediation was introduced in 2007, although this may be extended to a total of seven cost-free hours of mediation if it seems likely to produce a successful outcome.[65] For couples with a higher level of conflict, ie individuals who have not managed to reach an agreement before or during the hour of mandatory mediation, it may not be surprising to find that a failure to reach successful settlement is more of a rule than an exception at this early stage, with the result that most disputes do in fact end up before a court.[66] However, an important legislative amendment from 2004 placed an obligation on the court to assess at every stage of the trial process whether and to what extent an amicable solution might be achieved, and to undertake the necessary measures to achieve it.[67] The first attempt at (judicial) settlement is generally conducted as part of one or more preliminary hearings. The court possesses a comparatively broad discretion with regard to further legal action:[68] it can appoint expert advisors not only to participate in the preliminary discussions, but also to conduct separate discussions with the parties and/or the child(ren) or to investigate the actual circumstances; it can meet with the child(ren) separately or, where necessary, with the assistance of an additional expert or another appropriate person; and it may also have separate communications with the experts involved.[69] In addition to these powers, the

[62] In the preparatory legislative materials, Ot prp no 51 (2004–2005), 389, disputes between close relatives are cited as an example where a court decision would ultimately only perpetuate the conflict; see also Schei et al, *Tvisteloven* 365.

[63] See Austbø and Engebretsen, *Mekling i rettskonflikter* 26ff, 201ff.

[64] See Ekteskapsloven (Marriage Act), s 26, Barneloven (Children Act), s 51 and Barnetrygdeloven, s 9(5).

[65] See Barneloven (Children Act), s 54.

[66] For a comprehensive 2011 report evaluating mediation under the Marriage and Children's Act (with an English summary) see SINTEF Teknologi og samfunn, Rapport A20162, Evaluering av mekling etter ekteskapslov og barnelov, Trondheim 2011, see <www.regjeringen.no/upload/BLD/mekling_ekteskapslov.pdf>.

[67] See Barneloven (Children Act), s 59(2); for the historical background of this section see the detailed Evaluation of the Management of Custody Disputes in the Legal System in NOU 1998:17 (Barnefordelingssaker—avgjørelsesorgan, saksbehandlingsregler og delt bosted), as well as the official explanation provided by the Ministry of Family and Children on the different fundamental changes in barnevernloven (Children Protection Act) from 2004, in *Veileder Q-15/2004, Om saksbehandlingsregler i barnefordelingssaker for domstolene og høring av barn*, see <www.regjeringen.no/upload/kilde/bfd/bro/2004/0005/ddd/pdfv/203406-veiledning_q15-041.pdf>.

[68] See Barneloven (Children Act), s 61(1).

[69] Critical of this kind of break with the *Kontradiktionsprinsippet* (a fundamental Norwegian procedural principle that includes the right to be heard and the adversary principle)is Bernt, *Meklerrollen ved mekling i domstolene* 485–86, who suggests a general rule whereby the judge/mediator in unsuccessful mediations is to have no further participation in a later judicial procedure of the matter where an expert was involved in a preceding attempt at mediation. This suggestion is reminiscent of the solution the legislator has provided for judicial mediation in general, even including the same exceptions, see Tvl, s 8-7(2).

court may also order a new extra-judicial mediation process. Finally, the court may give the parties the opportunity to test out a preliminary settlement for a specified period of time—where necessary, with the participation of an advisor with appropriate expertise—while at all times granting the parties the right to discontinue the trial period and recommence legal proceedings.[70]

D. Special Rules for Consumer Disputes

Consumer disputes are governed by a range of specific regulations and institutions. The most important of these is the FTU, an administrative tribunal subordinate to the Ministry of Children and Equality, whose main purpose is to provide swift, free and reliable decisions in consumer disputes.[71] The Commission handles cases regarding consumer purchases, including credit purchases and tradesmen services. The Commission also handles purchase disputes between two private parties. The FTU procedure represents the second stage of a two-step procedure. The first step consists of an obligatory effort to resolve the dispute through mediation by the local offices of the Consumer Council. Where the first mediation attempt(s) remains unsuccessful, and one or both parties submit a petition no later than four weeks from the time the case was closed, the case is passed on to the secretariat of the Commission. It is then scheduled for the first available meeting after the petition. At the time of writing, a Commission decision takes about four months. Once handed down, the decision becomes binding and enforceable four weeks from the time it is served, unless one or both parties file a suit at the district court within the appeal time frame.

It is worth noting that the number of conflicts being handled by the FTU has doubled in the last decade, to around 1,300 cases in 2011. A third of these cases were decided entirely in favour of the consumer; in another 30 per cent of the cases the judgments were partially in favour of the consumer, with the remainder being dismissed or dropped.[72] The increase in disputes can be explained by the fact that the Consumer Protection Act (Forbrukerkjøpsloven[73]), passed in 2002, adopted explicit consumer rights, and that the focus on consumer rights (across Europe) has been generally increasing.

In addition, there are countless other dispute boards which handle specific consumer-law-related disputes that are outside the ambit of the Consumer Dispute Commission.[74] This includes the common dispute board for financial issues such as banking and insurance matters (Finansklagenemnda), the board for train and air travel complaints or disputes (Transportklagenemnda), the complaints board for disputes regarding the disclosure of information by private companies under the environmental information act (Klagenemnda for miljøinformasjon etter miljøinformasjonsloven) and the board for disputes concerning the erection and purchase of new dwellings (Boligtvistnemnda), as well as specialist boards for disputes concerning the use of mobile

[70] For a critical analysis of this, see below IV.F.
[71] See <www.forbrukertvistutvalget.no/xp/pub/hoved/forside/489332>.
[72] See <www.forbrukertvistutvalget.no/xp/pub/hoved/statistikk/486666>.
[73] Forbrukerkjøpslov of 21 June 2002 no 34.
[74] See <www.forbrukerportalen.no/Emner/klagenemnder >.

telephones, car hire, package tours, the use of private parking spaces, private electricity provision, privately owned debt collection agencies, etc.

Against this background, it is hardly surprising that the Commission Recommendation of 4 April 2001 on the principles for out-of-court bodies involved in the consensual resolution of consumer disputes, C(2001) 1016, has not had any specific additional influence in Norwegian consumer dispute resolution regulation.

III. APPROACH TOWARDS SPECIFIC ADR INSTRUMENTS

A. Negotiation

Norwegian law has only a few individual and very specific regulations for negotiation as an alternative to traditional court proceedings. This is the case for individual labour law disputes, including those concerning dismissal, suspension, unfair time limitation for the employment relationship and employee claims for damages. In this situation, negotiations between the employee and employer replace the preliminary hearing of these disputes before a Conciliation Board (Forliksrådet). The core regulation is contained in sections 17-1 and 17-3 of the Working Environment Act,[75] which regulates matters such as working hours and employment protection. The parties to a dispute must respond to a demand to negotiate, and section 17-3(3) requires the employer to set a date for the negotiations within two weeks of receiving notification. Section 17-3(4) imposes the same duty on the employee where the employer has sent notification of a demand to negotiate. There is no appeal process against this duty, and the dispute may be brought before a court even without negotiations having taken place. Where a party has refused to negotiate prior to going to court, however, it can be safely assumed that this will be reflected in the determination of costs at trial in the same way as will a failure of a party to observe the obligation to try to achieve a sustainable, mutually acceptable settlement before going to court as prescribed by Chapter 5 Tvl.[76]

Negotiations between unions and employers or employers' associations regarding collective agreements are regulated according to the Act of 27 January 2012 no 9, which specifically deals with collective labour disputes (Arbeidstvistloven). According to section 3 of the Act, failure to negotiate or a failed negotiation may provide the basis for a lawful strike or lockout.

Where there are no specific requirements, negotiations between parties conducted without the assistance of a neutral third party are governed by the general rules of contract law. This also applies to determining both at which stage of the negotiation parties become contractually bound and the preconditions necessary to establish a pre-contractual liability for breaking off negotiations.[77] This liability differs for civil and commercial disputes. For ordinary civil disputes, the costs of an unsuccessful negotiation prior to or during a trial proceeding are considered part of the necessary expenses, and are paid via the standard cost allocation according to section 20-51(1)

[75] Arbeidsmiljøloven of 17 June 2005 no 62.

[76] See Tvl, ss 20-2(3)(b) and 20-4(c), and II.B.ii above.

[77] Generally L Simonsen, *Prekontraktuelt ansvar* (Oslo, Universitetsforlaget, 1997).

Dispute Act, provided the full amount of the costs to be repaid does not seem disproportionately high. Where this is the case, the court will reduce the amount to be reimbursed by the unsuccessful party to a more appropriate amount.[78]

For commercial relationships, negotiations are often of a larger scale; they do not end the relationship between the parties but should regulate the relationship in both the near and long-term future. They cover all aspects of commercial negotiations, spanning business transfers, shares and property transactions, rental and supply agreements, etc. The costs of unsuccessful negotiations—ie negative interest in the performance of a contract, here seen as a loss due to frustration of an expectation on reaching an agreement—are not compensated. As a principle, these losses represent a regular business risk for the parties and are therefore not protected by any laws governing the compensation of damages. However, where a party is at fault or has acted culpably or dishonestly during the negotiation in breach of the duty of loyalty owed to the other party, the situation is quite different. Norwegian legal literature indicates that there is a stand-alone preliminary right to damages which is based on general principles of compensation, current legal policy considerations and academic legal opinion.[79] Specific evidence must be provided to justify a comprehensive analysis of the situation, although various aspects, including standard business practices in the industry in question, the duration of the negotiation and the likelihood of concluding a contract, also play a role.[80] The conduct giving rise to a claim of compensation must be clearly unacceptable and culpable.[81] Although the Supreme Court has yet to issue a decision on these matters, an evaluation of relevant decisions in this area suggests a judgment consistent with that put forward in legal literature.[82]

B. Mediation

i. General Information on the Regulation of Different Forms and Areas of Mediation

The Norwegian Dispute Act distinguishes between traditional mediation (section 8 2), judicial mediation (sections 8-3ff) and extra-judicial mediation (sections 7ff).

Traditional mediation refers to a traditional settlement negotiation between parties as a form of conciliation, either as part of dispute resolution through the Conciliation Board (Forliksrådsmekling)[83] or through the courts (originally known as Ordinær Mekling). These extra-judicial means of settlement often occur at the same time as the trial process, though they are not restricted to that time frame. Individual parties are not permitted to meet separately with the court (Caucus) or to have a one-sided confidential exchange of information, and the court (or the Forliksrådet) may not submit suggested solutions, recommendations or other assessments that may undermine its impartiality.[84] This is because the composition of the court (or the Forliksrådet), ie the

[78] Ristvedt and Nisja, *Alternative tvisteløsning* 362–63.
[79] See Ristvedt and Nisja, *Alternative tvisteløsning* 363ff.
[80] Simonsen, *Prekontraktuelt ansvar* 241ff.
[81] Simonsen, *Prekontraktuelt ansvar* 157, 239.
[82] Ristvedt and Nisja, *Alternative tvisteløsning* 363ff.
[83] See above II.C.i.
[84] See Tvl, s 8-2, and for the Forliksrådene Tvl, s 6-8; see also Schei et al, *Tvisteloven* 359ff.

judge(s) and officials that constitute the court, will remain the same and must go on to decide the matter where no settlement is reached.[85]

Judicial mediation is an autonomous mediation process based on the principles and experience gained from a model project, later codified in Tvl, sections 8-3–8-7. The mediator assists the parties in reaching a mutually acceptable solution that is consistent with their interests; as part of this, the mediator may carefully put forward proposed solutions and explain strengths or weaknesses in the legal or factual argumentation of the parties.[86] It was noted during the preparatory stages of the legislation that it was very difficult to define *interest-based mediation* precisely and comprehensively; nonetheless, it was agreed that the process should be defined so as to optimally assist the finding of a solution to the dispute based on the parties' own proposals.[87] In contrast to *traditional mediation*, separate meetings between the parties and the mediator are permitted, as is the one-sided exchange of information. The requirement for impartiality is lower than for traditional mediation as the mediator generally does not decide the matter in the event of a later adjudication.[88]

Additionally, the Norwegian Dispute Act provides a specific form of *extra-judicial mediation*. This process is wholly voluntary, based on a written agreement between the parties, and is conducted under the rules contained in Tvl, Chapter 7; it can be suspended or broken off at any time.[89] The mediator is chosen by the parties, or may be appointed by the district court from the list of court-approved mediators, should the parties so request.[90] Although the mediator is bound by the approach chosen by the parties, he may follow the principles of judicial mediation to supply the parties' approach, when necessary.[91] While the mediator should be impartial and independent in the pursuit of a resolution, in contrast to judicial mediation, the mediator may 'submit' solutions or 'point out' strengths and weaknesses in the parties' arguments.[92] In this sense, the mediator has a somewhat more active role, making this form of mediation more evaluative than judicial mediation.[93]

In addition, Norwegian law recognises mediation through the Konfliktrådene (conciliation boards for criminal law), which mainly provide an alternative to traditional *criminal law procedures for minor offenders*, provided both the accused and the victim agree to the process.[94]

Family law also provides for compulsory mediation according to the Barneloven

[85] Austbø and Engebretsen, *Mekling i rettskonflikter* 44–45; Schei et al, *Tvisteloven* 363.

[86] See Tvl, s 8-5.

[87] See also Ot prp no 51 (2004–2005), s 10.4.8.5.

[88] See Tvl, s 8-7(2); exceptions are, however, possible, where requested by both parties and not considered imprudent by the mediator/judge himself. This may be appropriate when the judge/mediator and the parties have developed a particularly trusting relationship or the judge possesses specialised knowledge or expertise relevant to the matter, see Sperr, 'Mediation in Norway', 1148–49.

[89] Tvl, s 7-1.

[90] Tvl, s 7-2.

[91] Tvl, s 7-3.

[92] Tvl, s 7-3(3).

[93] As argued by Austbø and Engebretsen, *Mekling i rettskonflikter* 43 and 177–78, pointing out the similarities between mediation conducted according to the guidelines developed under the International Bar Association; see also Schei et al, *Tvisteloven* 342–54 for more detail.

[94] See Austbø and Engebretsen, *Mekling i rettskonflikter* 26, 194ff.

(Children Act) and for optional mediation under the provisions of the Ekteskapsloven (Marriage Act).[95]

Of the available forms of *private mediation*, a prime example is the Institutt for Voldgift og Alternativ Tvisteløsning (Institute for Arbitration and Alternative Dispute Resolution), formed by the Oslo Chamber of Commerce in 1984. In 1995 this group added to its traditional dispute resolution mechanisms *mediation*, as a simplified resolution instrument, as well as a more active version of *conciliation* and the *mini-trial*.[96] It must again be noted, however, that the mediation services offered by the Chamber of Commerce are rarely used in practice; it appears not to be a widely used alternative to traditional settlement approaches in the commercial context.[97]

In a similar manner, the mediation procedure offered by the Forsikringsklagekontoret (Insurance Complaints Bureau)[98] since 2000 appears to have a limited relevance for disputes between insurance providers and policy holders. This procedure is predominantly based on the same principles as judicial mediation, but with the added requirement of legal representation for both sides, which makes it more expensive than the better known and evolving court-based service, limiting its potential to make an impact on the market.[99]

ii. Legal Framework

The fundamental reform of the Norwegian Dispute Act in 2008 established the legal framework for mediation in Norwegian law. While Part I (Chapters 1–4) of the Act provides the general requirements and responsibilities regulating civil proceedings, alternative methods of dispute resolution are mostly dealt with in Part II (Chapters 5–8). Here, Chapter 5 (Preliminary Obligations) and Chapter 7 (Out-of-Court Mediation) are directly related to the preliminary phase prior to legal proceedings. Chapter 6 deals with arbitration proceedings in Forliksrådene (Conciliation Boards), and Chapter 8 lays out traditional mediation and judicial mediation procedures (*Mekling* and *Rettsmekling*).

In addition to this legal foundation, important supplementary regulations for judicial and extra-judicial mediation are provided by the Forskrift til Tvisteloven (Tvistelovsforskriften) of 28 December 2007 (Supplementary Regulations to the Dispute Act).[100] Its provisions deal with the compensation of parties' expenses, financial guarantees and the selection of and necessary qualifications for mediators.[101]

The area of family law also includes the Guidelines for Mediation under the Marriage Act and the Children Act, released by the Ministry of Children and Equality,

[95] For more details on mediation in family law matters see above II.B.iii and II.B.ii; see also Sperr, 'Mediation in Norway' 1154–56.

[96] See the relevant regulation guideline in *Regler for Oslos Handelskammers Institutt for Voldgift og Alternativ Tvisteløsning*, available from Regelverk at <www.chamber.no/no/tvistelosning/>.

[97] Austbø and Engebretsen, *Mekling i rettskonflikter* 29–30.

[98] This office provides a form of preliminary assessment for the common dispute board for financial issues (Finansklagenemnda), see <www.forbrukerportalen.no/temaer/forsikring/viewNG?section=innboforsikring_forsikringsklagekontoret#forsikringsklagekontoret>.

[99] Ibid, 30–31.

[100] Forskrift til Tvisteloven (Tvistelovforskriften), FOR-2007-12-21-1605, <www.lovdata.no/cgi-wift/ldles?doc=/sf/sf/sf-20071221-1605.html>.

[101] See Tvistelovforskriften, Chapter 2, ss 4–9.

which details the content and goal of mediation in family matters, the qualifications of mediators, the location of mediation, mediation procedure, costs, etc.[102]

Further sources of law can be found in the preparatory legislative materials,[103] which play a significant role in legislative interpretation and argumentation in Norwegian law.

It should also be mentioned that section 1 of the Domstolloven (Act relating to the Courts of Justice) provides that the Conciliation Boards (Forliksrådene) serve as one of the preliminary dispute resolution bodies for the three tiers of the court system, with a limited adjudicatory authority as set down in Tvl, section 6-10.[104]

Ultimately, it should be noted that, under the Agreement on the European Economic Area, Directive 2008/52/EG of the European Parliament and Council from 21 May 2008 has no direct effect on specific aspects of mediation in civil and commercial disputes in Norway. The current rules for EU countries do, however, play an indirect role in cross-border conflicts for Norway.[105]

iii. The Duties of the Mediators

Mediators' duties are formulated quite generally in the Norwegian Dispute Act. It stipulates that mediators should possess the required expert and personal qualifications to carry out a judicial or extra-judicial mediation.[106] They should be independent and impartial, and they should be able to satisfactorily clarify all potential issues that may lead to doubts about their neutrality and impartiality. Court-appointed mediators may be rejected for a lack of impartiality.[107] All mediators should set out and explain the process and the approach to be used for mediation and follow the guidelines for documentation, recording all important data in a mediation process and specific documentation requirements.[108] They are bound by a general duty of confidentiality.[109] Mediator liability in the event of breaches of these duties is not explicitly regulated, making it subject to the general provisions of national law.

With regard to quality assurance in mediation, it must be stated that there is no national certification system in place and that mediator training appears fairly modest, compared to Scandinavian neighbours such as Denmark and Finland. Particularly in light of the fact that the different types of mediation regulations provide Norwegian mediators with a broad discretion for tailoring their duties and processes to the indi-

[102] See Forskrift om mekling etter ekteskapsloven og barneloven, FOR-2006-12-18-1478, available at <www.lovdata.no/for/sf/bl/xl-20061218-1478.html>.

[103] Ot prp no 51 (2004–2005), Om lov om mekling og rettergang i sivile tvister (Tvisteloven), see <www.regjeringen.no/nb/dep/jd/dok/regpubl/otprp/20042005/Otprp-nr-51-2004-2005-.html?id=397198>, and NOU 2001:32, Rett på sak. Lov om tvisteløsning (Tvisteloven), see <www.regjeringen.no/nb/dep/jd/dok/NOUer/2001/NOU-2001-32.html?id=378579>.

[104] Domstolloven (Dl) of 13 August 1915 no 5, see <www.lovdata.no/cgi-wift/wiftldles?doc=/usr/www/lovdata/all/nl-19150813-005.html&emne=domstollov*&&>.

[105] A Nylund, 'Europeisering av sivilprosessen' in J Rui (ed), *Rettshjelp fra kyst til vidde. Festskrift til jusshjelpa i Nord-Norge 20 år* (Oslo, Gyldendal Akademisk, 2009) 209, 224.

[106] For more on this see Tvl, s 7-2(2), sentence 1; Schei et al, *Tvisteloven* 349; and Tvl, s 8-4(1), sentence 1 and (4), sentence 5.

[107] For extra-judicial mediation see Tvl, s 7-3(2); for judicial mediation see Tvl, s 8-4(2) and Dl, ss 106ff.

[108] See Tvl, ss 7-3(4) and 8-5(5).

[109] See Tvl, s 8-6 for judicial mediation. See Tvl, s 7-3(6) for extra-judicial mediation and for the general confidentiality requirements as set down in Dl, s 63a.

vidual circumstances of the case, this modest level of training is quite remarkable. This is a strong argument in favour of an extension of the existing mediator training, and for the introduction of mediator codes of conduct, ethical principles and *best practice* guidelines.[110]

iv. Parties' Duties

The attempt to reach a mutually acceptable solution through mediation obviously carries a risk of failure. The parties are therefore not required to reach an agreement. For judicial mediation, a case will continue to proceed according to the normal judicial process and according to the hearing dates set before the mediation process commenced.[111] There are no restrictions as regards ending an attempt at mediation.

For extra-judicial mediation, the parties must agree to undergo mediation. This agreement, however, only requires the parties to seriously attempt to find a mutually acceptable solution; they are not forced to actually reach agreement. The Dispute Act states very clearly that the parties may end the mediation at any time (section 7-1[2]).

According to Tvl, section 8-6(1), the parties are bound by the principle of confidentiality in the sense that they may not testify as a party or a witness as to what emerged at judicial mediation, nor may they disclose matters that were conveyed to them under the rule of confidentiality. This principle applies to both judicial and extra-judicial mediation (Tvl, section 7-3[6]).

In judicial mediation, both the mediator and, where necessary, another person functioning as an assistant are entitled to payment—unless the mediator is a judge, as mediation forms part of a judge's regular duties.[112] The rate of remuneration is determined by the court.[113] This is usually based on the hourly rate for legal aid providers[114] unless the court, the parties and the mediator have agreed on an alternative rate.[115] In this situation, the parties are responsible for any additional costs, including costs incurred by the involvement of a second assistant; generally, however, the court bears any additional costs incurred.[116]

The parties must pay court costs, any costs for legal representation, and costs for expert witnesses and eye-witnesses. In the absence of specific regulations for court-based mediation, general judicial rules for the allocation of costs apply.[117] This is clearly the case where mediation is unsuccessful, and the costs incurred are allocated

[110] See Sperr, 'Mediation in Norway' 1160–61; for more about the need of mediator training see KA Ipsen, *Trenger meklere opplæring? En studie av mekling, meklingstilnærminger og opplæring i mekling* (Bergen, 2008), available at <http://brage.bibsys.no/nla/bitstream/URN:NBN:no-bibsys_brage_9401/1/Master_Ipsen_h08.pdf>.

[111] Tvl, s 8-7(1).

[112] See Tvl, s 8-4(3), sentence 1.

[113] Ibid.

[114] Forskrift om salær fra det offentlige til advokater mv, FOR-1997-12-03-1441, see <www.lovdata.no/cgi-wift/ldles?doc=/sf/sf/sf-19971203-1441.html>; the hourly rate is currently ca NOK 900 (about £100) not including VAT, see Ministry of Justice and Police Information Paper G-14/2010, see <websir.lovdata.no/cgi-lex/wiftzsok?bas=sf+stv+del+ins+bv+fv+nb+jb+sj+mv+pv+ov&emne1=Forskrift+om+sal%E6r+fra+det+offentlige+til+advokater&button=S%F8k&sok=fast>.

[115] See Tvl, s 8-4(3), sentence 2.

[116] See C Bernt-Hamre, *Rettsmekling*, Det Juridiske Fakultets Skriftserie No 97 (Bergen, Det juridiske fakultet, 2004) 79, 133; NOU 2001:32, *Rett på sak*, Bind A, 229.

[117] See also Tvl, ss 20-1ff.

as part of the cost ruling in the general proceeding.[118] Where judicial mediation successfully results in a settlement between the parties, Tvl, section 19-11(4) contains a special provision that requires the parties to determine the allocation of costs and include this in the settlement agreement, although this may be delegated to the court on the request of both parties. Where the parties are unable to reach agreement in this matter but do not apply for a discretionary decision from the court, they must each bear their own costs. The legislator did not intend for the general regulations on cost allocation contained in Tvl, Chapter 20 to apply in such a case.[119]

For extra-judicial mediation—unless otherwise agreed—the parties must share the costs of remuneration for the mediator and assistant (should one be engaged).[120] The costs of the mediation depend on the mediation agreement itself. Where the parties have agreed to appoint a mediator from the list of judicial mediators,[121] the parties and the mediator may request the court to formally set the level of remuneration.[122]

v. Enforceability of Mediation Agreements

A successful judicial mediation culminates in an agreement which partially or completely resolves the dispute to the satisfaction of the parties. There is a difference between the outcome of a simple *Utenrettslig Forlik* (extra-judicial settlement) and a *Rettsforlik* (judicial settlement): the former has the general effect of a contractual agreement, while the latter is an enforceable agreement with full legal effect.[123] For this reason, most parties to a dispute opt for a *Rettsforlik*.[124]

Originally, a *Rettsforlik* could only be challenged by legal appeal.[125] As these general regulations and time frames were seen as being too strict, the current Law on Mediation and Court Process in Civil Disputes (Tvisteloven) contains a variation in this respect, allowing judicial settlements to now be challenged by means of an *Ugyldighetssøksmål* (claim of invalidity) under the provisions of contract law.[126] This should, first and foremost, ensure that information coming to light subsequent to the mediation process, eg wilful deception perpetrated by one party during the mediation, can later be taken into account.[127]

[118] See Bernt-Hamre, *Rettsmekling* 134ff.

[119] For detailed information see Ot prp no 51 (2004–2005), 438–39.

[120] See Tvl, s 7-4, additionally, Ot prp no 51 (2004–2005), 387, as well as ss 4ff of the Tvistelovforskrift, FOR-2007-12-21-1605, see <www.lovdata.no/cgi-wift/ldles?doc=/ sf/sf/sf-20071221-1605.html>.

[121] See Tvl, s 7-2(1), sentence 2.

[122] Tvl, s 7-4(2).

[123] For more see Tvl, ss 8-5(6), 19-12(1) and 19-13(1). However, this does not in general apply for agreements in family law matters, see Barneloven (Children Act), s 65 and Tvistelovforskriften, s 1(5); for detailed information see also Bernt, *Meklerrollen ved mekling i domstolene* 124.

[124] See, with further annotation, C Bernt-Hamre, 'Hvor aktiv kan rettmekler være under meklingen?—Noen sentrale problemstillinger' in J Giertsen and HF Marthinussen, *Festskrift til Det juridiske fakultet ved Universitetet i Bergen i anledning 25 års jubileet*, Det Jurisdike Fakutets Skriftserie No 108 (Bergen, Det juridiske fakultet, 2005) 75.

[125] See the former Civil Procedures Act (Tvistemålsloven, Tvml), s 286(2).

[126] Tvl, s 19-12(2) and Chapter 3 of the Act relating to the conclusion of agreements (Avtaleloven, Avtl), particularly Avtl, s 36, according to which a settlement may be partially or completely withdrawn or changed to the extent that it would be inappropriate or against principles of good faith were it to be invoked.

[127] See also Bernt-Hamre, 'Hvor aktiv kan rettmekler være under meklingen?', 75, as well as Ot prp no 51 (2004–2005), 133ff and NOU 2001:32, *Rett på sak*, Bind A, 592ff for more detail.

Extra-judicial mediation also concludes with a settlement, the *Utenrettslig Forlik*, although this is limited to the effect of a general contractual agreement.[128]

C. Conciliation

In Norwegian law there is no strict separation between conciliation and mediation: it is therefore not surprising that the United Nations Commission on International Trade Law (UNCITRAL) Model Law on International Commercial Conciliation (2002) has not influenced the Norwegian legislature.

In fact, the somewhat more active role of the mediator in extra-judicial mediation as regulated by Chapter 7 of the Dispute Act has some parallels to conciliation as defined for this analysis.[129] This is because the mediator—in contrast with judicial mediation—may 'submit' solutions or 'point out' strengths and weaknesses in the parties' arguments, making it a more evaluative form of mediation than the judicial variant (as regulated by Chapter 8 Dispute Act).[130] Against this, traditional mediation, as conducted by the Conciliation Boards (Forliksrådene) or through the courts as part of ordinary settlement negotiation, is not truly viewed as conciliation in the sense of this analysis, as the court (or the Forliksrådet) may not submit suggested solutions, recommendations or other assessments that may undermine its impartiality.[131] This is due, as mentioned above, to the fact that the composition of the court (or the Forliksrådet) does not change to decide the matter where no settlement is reached in a preliminary mediation process.[132]

The Institute for Arbitration and Alternative Dispute Resolution, formed by the Oslo Chamber of Commerce, added a range of instruments to its traditional dispute resolution mechanisms in 1995. It now also includes mediation as a simplified resolution instrument, as well as a more active version of conciliation and the mini-trial.[133] These services, however, are rarely used in practice.[134]

D. Expert Opinion

One ADR method currently experiencing a marked global increase is the use of expert opinions or oppmen, ie expert third parties, who are able to quickly deliver independent judgments regarding specific elements of contractual relationships based on their technical and/or legal expertise.[135] These methods have gained particular popularity in the construction industry as part of standard contracts for building construction, ship

[128] Tvl, s 7-3(5) and Schei et al, *Tvisteloven* 354.

[129] The term conciliation is used here for all procedures that result in a non-binding recommendation of the conflict manager regarding the dispute as a whole. The term therefore may cover, for instance, the instruments of early neutral evaluation or mini-trial.

[130] See above III.B.i.

[131] See Tvl, s 8-2, for the Forliksrådene Tvl, s 6-8; see also Schei et al, *Tvisteloven* 359ff.

[132] Austbø and Engebretsen, *Mekling i rettskonflikter* 44–45; Schei et al, *Tvisteloven* 363.

[133] See the relevant regulation guideline in *Regler for Oslos Handelskammers Institutt for Voldgift og Alternativ Tvisteløsning*, available from *Regelverk* at <www.chamber.no/no/tvistelosning/>.

[134] Austbø and Engebretsen, *Mekling i rettskonflikter* 29–30.

[135] See Ristvedt and Nisja, *Alternative tvisteløsning* 54–55.

building and large sections of the oil industry. Generally the parties in these cases have decided against adjudication through the courts, opting instead for dispute resolution through experts. This dispute resolution most commonly takes the form of arbitration, although the standard contracts NS 8405 (Norsk bygge- og anleggskontrakt), NF 05 (Norwegian Fabrication Contract 2005) and NTK 05 (Norwegian Total Contract 2005) also contain provisions on the use of experts. These 'judgments' may be distinguished between those expert decisions which have a binding effect as long as they are not challenged, as used in the standard off-shore contracts NF 05 and NKT 05[136], and non-binding decisions, as seen in the standard Norwegian building contract NS 8405.[137] Although the nature of the conflicts may differ, in most cases the main task of the expert/oppman is effectively the same—to make a decision relating to changes in the contractual relationship.[138] Binding judgments made by an expert or oppman may have the same effect as arbitral decisions, ie they carry the force of law and are enforceable. This clearly shows that the borders between mediation, particularly evaluative mediation, expert opinion and arbitration, are quite porous in nature.

In some cases, oppmen decisions from the construction industry are publicised; the expert legal advice provided by the construction body headquartered in Bergen (BFJR) is particularly significant in this respect. A wide range of expert decisions for cases dealing with offshore contracts have been published in a collection of decisions released by the Nordic Institute for Maritime Law at the University of Oslo. These publications have a high practical significance for their legal areas.[139]

E. Arbitration

Arbitration is a well-known and often-used method of conflict resolution in Norway. The Arbitration and Dispute Resolution Institute of the Oslo Chamber of Commerce, introduced in 1983, has already been mentioned above. The Institute covers national and international disputes within industry, commerce, shipping, offshore/onshore activities and other fields of business activity; it offers arbitration, fast-track arbitration, mediation and mini-trial, or any combination of these. For parties who so wish, the Institute can act as an appointing authority and provide administrative assistance under the rules of UNCITRAL. In practice, however, the most common form of arbitration is ad hoc arbitration, which means that the parties themselves determine central aspects of the arbitration (as, for example, the composition and authority of the tribunal). The Institute in Oslo is mainly used for international disputes involving one or more foreign parties; usually it has only two to ten proceedings running at a time.[140]

[136] K Kaasen, *Petroliumskontrakter—med kommentarer til NF 05 og NTK 05* (Oslo, Universitetsforlaget, 2006) 460–2 and 875–81.

[137] NS 8405, s 43.2; K Marthinussen, H Gieverholt and HJ Arvesen, *NS 8405: kommentarutgave til Norsk standard 8405, Norsk bygge- og anleggskontrakt* (Oslo, Gyldendal Akademisk, 2010) 725–30.

[138] See Ristvedt and Nisja, *Alternative tvisteløsning* 623–26.

[139] Ibid; see K Kaasen, 'Project Integrated Mediation (PRIME)', *Marlus 414—SIMPLY 2011, The Scandinavian Institute's Maritime and Petroleum Law Yearbook 2011* (Oslo, Scandinavian Institute's Maritime and Petroleum Law, 2012) 67–92, about a new (hybrid) alternative to the oppmen resolution, called PRIME (Project Integrated Mediation), which is now used in some standard contracts in the petroleum industry.

[140] See above I.C.

Previously, arbitration was regulated in the former Dispute Act; in 2005 a specific Voldgiftsloven (Arbitration Act) was introduced. This Arbitration Act of 2005[141] fully implemented the UNCITRAL Model Law for *both* international and national disputes. For smaller, national disputes there were—according to the Ministry of Justice and Police—valuable reasons for providing a stricter and more detailed regulation. This dealt, first and foremost, with ad hoc resolution processes in consumer disputes, between private parties or in smaller commercial relationships, ie those relationships for which the parties had not developed a detailed dispute resolution agreement; from the legislator's point of view, regulation and observance of legal certainty aspects were considered more important in these smaller cases than for international and large national dispute proceedings. It is, however, of central importance that the parties are able to derogate from the regulations put forward in the Act, thus creating a customised resolution process. This is especially true where the parties derogate from separate national regulations in order to agree on the application of the Model Law. The simplifications consist mainly of a swifter process, the receipt of a decision within a maximum of six months after the appointment of the judge and cost savings. There is no need for a specific mode of dispute resolution to be chosen in advance; the parties may agree to this approach after a conflict has arisen.

It should be noted that the legislator was aware that putting national and international arbitration together in one piece of legislation may produce regulations that appear more alien to international parties than they in fact are. This potential uncertainty may adversely affect the perception of Norway as being an appropriate jurisdiction for international arbitration; there were, however, practical reasons behind this decision.[142]

The Arbitration Act of 2005 harmonises the regulations for the recognition of Norwegian and international decisions (see section 45(1) Arbitration Act). Reasons against the recognition and enforcement of a judgment are exhaustively detailed in section 46. According to section 45(3), compulsory enforcement of decisions takes place under the general provisions of the Compulsory Enforcement Act (Tvangsfullbyrdelsesloven),[143] as long as there are no specific requirements to the contrary in Chapter 10 Arbitration Act. According to section 47 Arbitration Act, courts may suspend enforcement under specific conditions and demand the payment of some form of security—where requested by the claimant.[144]

F. Hybrid Methods

In addition to the classical forms of ADR, Norwegian law has a large number of ADR forms and procedures for alternative conflict resolution that can be described as hybrid methods as they combine their elements with other basic dispute resolution mechanisms.[145]

[141] Voldgiftloven of 14 May 2004 no 25 (Lov om voldgift, Vogl).
[142] For the preparatory material see Ot prp no 27 (2003–2004), 23–25.
[143] Act of 26 June 1992 no 86.
[144] Ristvedt and Nisja, *Alternative tvisteløsning* 580–81.
[145] For an overview, see the preparatory materials for the Dispute Act, Ot prp no 51 (2004–2005), 63–70.

i. Ombudsman

Perhaps the best known hybrid form of ADR is the institution of the ombudsman. The term ombudsman derives from the Norse terms *ombud*, meaning representative, and *man* (man). An ombudsman is a person appointed to conduct alternative and out-of-court dispute resolution by directing the resolution process and making recommendations, rather than a final decision. The appointment of *Parliamentary Ombudsmen*—to supplement the existing mechanisms protecting individual rights in the area of administrative law—originated in the Nordic countries. However, even the Scandinavian original version does not allow for a uniform definition of the position, as the individual provisions regulating the role differ significantly. In short, however, the primary function of the Scandinavian ombudsman model is to establish a free, *parliamentary*, out-of-court agency independent of the executive to supervise the *executive branch* ex officio, as well as to review claims made from inside the branch.[146]

In Norway, the work of the Parliamentary Ombudsman (Stortingets Ombudsmann) is regulated by the Act concerning the Stortingets Ombudsmann for public administration of 22 June 1962 no 3 (Ombudsmannsloven), which, due to a shared legal tradition and strong similarities in the system of legal protection with regard to administrative law, is closely aligned to its prominent 1953 Danish predecessor.[147] According to section 3, the main task of the Sivilombudsmannen, as the Parliament's representative, is to endeavour to prevent injustice against individual citizens by the public administration and to help ensure that human rights are respected. These duties are undertaken independently, and without reliance on parliamentary or government approval. According to section 4 Ombudsmannsloven, the range of the Ombudsman's activities is almost equal to that of the entire administration. The Ombudsman becomes involved either on application or on his or her own initiative, and must decide whether or not an application justifies further action (see sections 5 and 6[4] Ombudsmannsloven). Although the ombudsman does not have the authority to make a final determination, his recommendations usually shape the final outcome and may lead the administration to change its decision without necessarily requiring court intervention. The Ombudsman therefore has a very strong influence on the resolution of individual disputes and also makes a significant contribution to the further development of administrative law. This influence is justified by the position's institutional base in Parliament (Stortinget).[148] According to section 75(1) of the Norwegian Constitution (Grunnloven) and section 1 Ombudsmannsloven, the civil ombudsman is directly elected by the Stortinget but is not obliged to personally be a member of it; the funding for the position comes from the parliamentary budget, and, as such, the Ombudsman must report to and be answerable to the Parliament. In addition, the holder of the position should have legal qualifications and be eligible to serve as a judge in the Supreme Court. In this way, the civil ombudsman expands upon and provides an alternative to court supervision of administrative decisions—to a certain extent filling the gap (at least in Norway and

[146] AK Sperr, 'Ombudsman' in J Basedow, K Hopt and P Zimmermann (eds), *The Max Planck Encyclopedia of European Private Law* (Oxford, Oxford University Press, 2012) 1221–26.

[147] AK Sperr, *Verwaltungsrechtsschutz in Deutschland und Norwegen. Eine vergleichende Studie zur gerichtlichen Kontrolle von Verwaltungsentscheidungen* (Baden-Baden, Nomos Verlag, 2009) 93ff.

[148] See Ø Rasmussen in JF Bernt and Ø Rasmussen, *Forvaltningsrett I* (Bergen, Fakbokforlaget, 2010) 350.

Denmark) of an otherwise lacking independent court dealing solely with matters of administrative law.

It appears worth mentioning that, by 2005, the institution of a public law ombudsman had been adopted by more than 100 nations worldwide. Indeed, in Norway it was seen as being so successful that it led to the development of a whole range of institutions based on that model, many with a similar name even where they predominantly dealt with structurally different functions and regulations.[149] Since the 1970s, the institution of the ombudsman has also been taken up in many Western states in the area of *consumer protection*.[150] In particular, nations where litigation in state courts has proven very expensive have made a great effort to introduce realistic alternatives to traditional dispute resolution. In addition to arbitration and mediation proceedings, and the creation of special courts and fast-track procedures for small claims,[151] these new different remedies include various ombudsman institutions which are of great importance when it comes to strengthening the consumer's position in consumer-to-business disputes and supporting the individual enforcement of consumer rights. There are two main types of ombudsmen. The first category includes *public* supervisory agencies, such as the Scandinavian consumer ombudsman institutions.[152] Ombudsmen of the second category are, for the most part, *private* dispute resolution agencies, specific to a particular industry sector and established by the suppliers themselves. As an example, the *Insurance Ombudsman Bureau*, since 2001 under the *Financial Ombudsman Service*, was introduced in Great Britain in 1981; in Germany, private banks and the insurance industry established ombudsmen as well (in the years 1992 and 2001, respectively). Ombudsmen of the first category (Scandinavian model with a state-appointed consumer ombudsman) rarely conduct specific arbitrational processes, mostly concentrating instead on the protection of *collective consumer interests*, particularly in cases of misleading commercial practices and unfair competition. For ombudsmen of the second category (private sector ombudsman institutions), however, the resolution of disputes between individual consumers and businesses is their main objective. Compared to the traditional ombudsman for public law and the Scandinavian consumer ombudsmen, the introduction of private ombudsman institutions has brought about a certain degree of innovation in dispute resolution. These private institutions are not confined to merely offering suggestions when resolving a dispute, but are often conferred decision-making authority. In most cases this decision is only binding on the business (up to a specific amount in dispute) while the consumer remains free to go to court. In Norway, as in the other Scandinavian countries, this

[149] The Consumer Ombudsman, the Equality Ombudsman and the Children's Ombudsman are examples of institutions taking on the family name of 'ombudsman' although they differ structurally in that they pursue different duties which are implemented and monitored differently, see A Fliflet, 'Noen frimodige ytringer om domstoler og dommere', Justisdepartementets småskriftserie no 2/1998 (Oslo, Justisdepartementet, Domstolsavdelingen, 1998) 1–12.

[150] See for the subsequent sections Sperr, 'Ombudsman' 1221–26.

[151] Eg the United States Small Claims Courts and the special *Småkravsprosess* in the Norwegian Civil Procedure Code.

[152] Eg the Swedish Konsumentombudsmannen (KO, Consumer Ombudsman), introduced in 1971, who today is a public official of high repute and, at the same time, the Director General of the Konsumentverket (KOV, Swedish Consumer Agency); likewise Denmark (Forbrugerombudsman), Norway (Forbrukerombudet) and Finland introduced institutions whose main objective is to protect collective consumer interests and to ensure compliance with the requirements of the Markedsføringsloven (Marketing Practices Act)—where applicable in connection with further consumer-oriented legislation.

function of resolving disputes between individual consumers and businesses has been taken over by specific public entities (eg the FTU) and private tribunals and complaint boards (eg the common dispute board for financial issues as banking and insurance).[153]

ii. Complaint Boards and Tribunals

The dispute boards based on Norwegian consumer protection law mentioned above, together with numerous other complaint boards and tribunals, make up a further hybrid category of the available Norwegian alternative dispute resolution mechanisms. As chiefly collegial appeal committees, these boards and tribunals function either as private institutions or as public bodies that operate almost completely independently from the traditional administrative hierarchy. They have specialised knowledge and follow a process that closely mirrors that of the courts, which is why they are often referred to as quasi-judicial administrative bodies.[154] One particularly noteworthy example of these kinds of government-based boards and tribunals is the Trygderetten, a quasi-judicial administrative body dealing with social matters in appeals against administrative decisions in social insurance law.[155] Also of practical significance is the Utlendingsnemnd, which provides an appeals committee for decisions made by the Directorate of Immigration. The Appeals Committee Dealing with Disputes over Public Purchases as part of the general competition regulator (Klagenemnda for offentlige anskaffelser) enjoys a positive reputation. Other important committees include those dealing with data privacy protection matters (Personvernnemnda), the Committee for Disputes Regarding the Disclosure of Information by Private Companies under the Environmental Information Act (Klagenemnda for miljøinformasjon etter miljøinformasjonsloven) and the Appeals Committee for Disputes over the Refusal of an Abortion after the 12th Week of Pregnancy (Abortklagenemnd).[156] In 2003, there were approximately 230 of these specific appeals tribunals established at the different administrative levels (ie state administration and (*fylkes-*) communal level), not including the 870 local committees for disputes regarding tax assessment.[157] As there have not been significant changes since then, it can be safely assumed that this number still holds. The tendency to establish specific administrative bodies has been increasing—more than half were established during the last 20 years without necessarily conducting a broad-reaching (systematic) adaptation or integration into the system of judicial protection across the whole field of administrative law.[158]

Although there are a variety of reasons behind the establishment of the different individual bodies, their methods and processes are largely similar: they mostly have an exclusively written process and provide a decision that is based on the current legal

[153] For more on the regulation of these boards see above II.A and particularly II.D.

[154] These kinds of bodies can principally serve a supervisory function for legal relationships between private and public law organisations, and also for conflicts arising between private entities in those individual areas, which are regulated by specific administrative laws (eg competition regulations, consumer protection act).

[155] Tygderettsloven of 16 December 1966 no 9.

[156] Other quasi-judicial administrative appeals bodies are dealt with by T Sletten, *Domstollignende forvaltningsorganer*, Institutt for offentlig retts skriftserie no 3/1990 (Oslo, Institutt for Offentlig Rett, 1990), among others.

[157] See Statskonsult, Rapport 2003:19, 1, 13.

[158] See Statskonsult, Rapport 2003:19, 13, 24, 27f.

situation. Most importantly, their high levels of independence and expertise mean they provide a high level of legal certainty (compared to the general administrative bodies as such). Efficiency is also a very important consideration: the establishment of specific bodies and the outsourcing of dispute resolution is intended to reduce the burden on the administrative apparatus and on the courts; at the same time, it should provide an effective, swift and significantly cost-reduced dispute resolution process.[159]

On a critical note, the establishment of a massive number of independent appeal committees in the area of administrative law has led to a significant watering down of the constitutional principle of government and ministerial instructional competence (and political responsibility). In most cases, important aspects are not sufficiently clarified or systematically set out, including, for example, the distribution of instructional competence and authority to withdraw or revoke administrative decisions, the guarantee of an orderly administrative process, the organisation of internal decision-making processes within the appeal committees and the composition of their secretariats. Exceptions to this include the largest governmental appeal committees, such as the Trygderetten, the Utlendingsnemnd, the Fylkesnemndene for sosiale saker (county social welfare boards) and the Pasientklagenemnd (Patient Appeals Board regarding health services); despite many differences in detail, these bodies generally deal with a great number of claims. and have large and professional secretariats. For most of the other appeal committees the independence from the administrative hierarchy is inadequately regulated, and the organisation of their performance is subject to a great deal of variation, reduced transparency and inconsistency.[160] For this reason, future fundamental reforms are required for public appeal committees, including a stronger foundation in constitutional law, a greater legitimisation of their independence and a systematic regulation of and uniform approach to the performance of their duties.[161]

From the ADR perspective, one could say that complaint boards and tribunals constitute a real alternative to traditional court-based adjudication, institutionally and with regard to staffing issues, although not in terms of substance, as conflicts—similar to court proceedings—are resolved through the provision of an authoritative decision based squarely on up-to-date legal considerations.

IV. POLICY QUESTIONS

A. ADR Regulation—The Discussion so Far

Up to the present date, Norway has had exclusively positive experiences with the regulation of ADR, as most recently seen in the comprehensive provisions regulating the various forms of mediation in the Dispute Act of 2005, which entered into force on 1 January 2008. This regulation not only finally legitimised the previous model

[159] For more details see Sletten, *Domstollignende forvaltningsorganer*; see also Statskonsult, Rapport 2003:19, 13–16.

[160] According to a recent study by the State Directorate for Administration and Information Technology (Difi) on a total of 48 government-based appeal committees, see Direktoratet for forvaltning og IKT (Difi), *Uavhengig eller bare uklart? Organisering av statlig myndighetsutøvelse*, Difi raport 2012:7, Oslo 2012, see <http://www.difi.no/filearchive/difi-rapport-2012-7-uavhengig-eller-bare-uavklart.pdf>.

[161] Ibid, 45–47 for individual proposals.

project for judicial mediation, but also resulted in a fundamental level of quality assurance. There are further benefits in that different actors can more easily be informed or inform themselves about the different procedures, their duties and roles, and other alternatives that may be available, an effect that also provides a certain level of transparency. Additionally, the legislation has motivated parties to use mediation/ADR in resolving disputes. With regard to the numerous substantial advantages of ADR in comparison with traditional court proceedings, this is a welcome change. Looking at the Norwegian experience, it would appear that regulating ADR generally provides a clear advantage.

B. Scope of Regulation for Specific ADR Procedures

ADR as such is not suited to regulation through a single general legal framework. Practical experience has shown that most institutions, methods, regulations and processes in this area are well suited to their purpose, and that the approach taken in Norway allows for individual methods to be adapted to the specifics of individual questions and the interests of the parties involved. However, the introduction of a moderate level of uniformity, particularly with regard to quasi-judicial conflict boards and tribunals in Norway, could lead to greater transparency, making them more user-friendly.

At the international level, the regulation of individual ADR methods is not only possible, but also desirable, using model laws such as those for arbitration. They could lead to an increased development in ADR mechanisms internationally, as, for example, is and was the case with the regulation of mediation at the national level in Norway. This regulation must, however, remain comparatively general and concentrate on the significant characteristics of the individual methods to ensure that any suggestions can be adapted to the individual national requirements and existing conflict resolution systems.

C. Level of State Engagement—ADR as Alternative Resolution or as an Element of the State Civil Justice System

With regard to mediateon and encouraging its use, Norway has had positive experiences so far in not deciding on a particular (vertical or horizontal) strategy. By creating regulation for extra-judicial mediation *and* regulating and institutionalising judicial mediation, they have achieved more in both regards, providing state intervention by merely actively supporting mediation *and* a state offer of mediation as part of the state civil justice system. This approach has delivered good results. The same is true for the area of consumer law, with the approach in Norway consisting of both state (eg the Consumer Dispute Commission, Forbrukertvistutvalget) and privately organised ADR mechanisms and institutions (eg the common dispute board for financial issues such as banking and insurance matters, Finansklagenemnda) which operate successfully. These industry-based, private devices show that alternative dispute resolution is not necessarily better placed within the state civil justice system. The state should not, however, seek to avoid its responsibility of providing an adequate and affordable justice system. Government must take care to ensure that the principles of equality and justice are observed also in private ADR mechanisms, while also continuing to provide an attractive and accessible state civil justice system in terms of time and financial considerations, and still contributing to the further development of the law.

D. Appropriate Allocation of Costs

The fact that ADR traditionally played an important role in Norway, and that it is still being taken up positively today, is partly due to the costs in the traditional court system being so high as to only make it 'worth' using for matters involving large sums of money. In light of this, it is problematic for alternatives to the court system to also impose upon the parties significant cost hurdles. With regard to the considerable economic savings provided by an early alternative dispute resolution (where necessary even a far-reaching and long-term conflict resolution in the broadest sense of the word), it seems appropriate and sensible to provide financial incentives to encourage parties to attempt this resolution. Considering this, ADR instruments should therefore continue to be offered largely free of charge.

E. Effective Approaches for Clarifying Conflicts and their Most Appropriate Resolution Forum

Appropriate training in the assessment of a conflict is essential for early recognition and implementation of the most appropriate dispute resolution strategy. At the time of writing, this has not formed a part of legal education in Norway, although in recent times disciplines such as conflict analysis and process tactics have been increasingly the subject of study, and encouraged as part of legal education and professional development.[162] Studies from the US show a clear correlation between the quality of process-related decisions and lawyer training in alternative dispute resolution.[163] Against this background, the increased focus on alternative dispute resolution seen in Norway in recent years, particularly on mediation, leads us to expect that the quality of risk analysis will continue to improve with the various economic and psychological aspects being better taken into account.

F. ADR as a Compulsory Pre-trial Procedure versus Less Invasive Measures

As shown above, Norway has a long tradition of obligatory settlement negotiation between parties, as part of dispute resolution through the Conciliation Board (*Forliksrådsmekling*) or through the courts (originally known as *Ordinær Mekling*). Today this has become a compulsory part of preliminary proceedings, although some areas of law have been exempted and in some cases given their own dispute resolution pro-

[162] See, eg Ristvedt, 'Advokater og prosessrisiko'.

[163] See Blandhol, 'Hvordan kan advokater bli bedre rådgivere i tvisteløsning?', referring to R Kiser, M Asher und B Mc Shane, 'Let's Not Make a Deal: An Empirical Study of Decision Making in Unsuccessful Settlement Negotiations' (2008) 5(3) *Journal of Empirical Legal Studies* 551.

cesses.[164] Attempts at pre-trial settlement of this kind, even though obligatory, have in general been positively viewed without criticism, due to the time and cost savings for the parties, and the reduced burden on the court system when they are successful. The negative consequences, for example, the slight delay in the commencement of trials generally, do not outweigh the positives.

In the field of family law, an attempt at mediation is compulsory for all legal disputes regarding custody and visitation rights, as well as for divorce settlements that involve children from the marriage who are under 16 years of age.[165] In principle, alternative—and more friendly—dispute resolution strategies, in contrast to classic adjudication, are seen as desirable, particularly with regard to parental care for children, who regularly suffer from the disputes between parents. It is regarded as an aim in itself for the children to preserve as much (positive) contact as possible with both parents. To this end, in order to retain or create functional communication and cooperation between the parents in all questions regarding the well-being of the children, a settlement reached between the parents themselves seems to be more effective than an imposed, authoritative third-party (court) decision. This goes a long way to explaining the numerous court powers to order subsequent mediation attempts where the obligatory mediation attempt failed—even during the trial—to obtain a mutually agreeable settlement wherever possible.[166]

Recently, this approach has received some justified criticism: the clear preference for settlements and the court's powers in this regard require a significant level of mediation training and competence in precisely these sorts of conflict for the judge or the experts appointed to mediate. This competence, however, is not guaranteed in practice.[167] A bad mediation process can contribute to a failure to recognise or prevent serious encroachments, such as violence or manipulation by one parent against the children or the other parent.[168] The experts appointed to the mediation are also often charged with a range of roles and duties that do not fit together well; they must advise the court in making its decision, but at the same time they are often responsible for mediation between the parties or for advising the parents. For the parties, mediation conducted in this way is not necessarily viable for obtaining the best outcome. This is because a future court decision may be more weighted toward the parent who appeared the most cooperative and flexible in the eyes of the mediator.[169] Another systemic problem arises when judges frequently use the same experts for various stages (pre-trial, trial, appeal) of the same case. Additionally, civil procedural law permits experts from the court of first instance to appear as witnesses for a party at subsequent appeals. All this grants the expert a very high level of influence, while not necessarily ensuring the required level of specialist knowledge, expertise or awareness of their own influence.

Judges, experts and lawyers in family law disputes are often regarded as a signifi-

[164] On this see above II.C.i and III.B.i.

[165] See above II.B.ii.

[166] Ibid.

[167] A Nylund, 'Mekling i barnefordelingssaker på godt og ondt' (2011) No 4 *Tidsskrift for familierett, arverett og barnevernrettslige spørsmål* 303.

[168] See G Nordhelle, *Manipulation* (Oslo, Gyldendal Akademisk, 2009) 148–50; see also FL Breivik and K Mevik, *Barnefordeling i Domstolen, Når barnets beste blir barnets verste* (Oslo, Universitetsforlaget, 2012) 125–30.

[169] A Nylund, 'Mekling i barnefordelingssaker på godt og ondt'.

cant authority or powerful group in determining custody and alimony arrangements between the parties with a genuine preference for mutually agreed settlements. In practice, this perception (combined with the relatively high costs incurred in traditional court proceedings) tends to lead to the unacceptable consequence that a parent who is financially, psychologically, socially or otherwise disadvantaged may agree to a settlement that negatively affects the children—or even him- or herself—so as to avoid appearing combative and incapable of also guaranteeing the child the most positive contact possible with the other parent. The seeming risk of creating such a perception is, for many parents, associated with too great a risk of losing the case.[170]

For the future, it is both desirable and very important that the professional parties involved have received a thorough education and training in ascertaining which cases are suited to alternative conflict resolution and which are not. For the well-being of the children, cases with a high level of conflict, where there is a clear power imbalance between the parties or where there are signs of physical or psychological violence or manipulation, must be sufficiently resourced to allow the conflict between the parents to be investigated and handled by well-trained legal and child services staff.

Despite all the fundamental advantages provided by alternative dispute resolution, it does not appear appropriate to favour out-of-court settlement over all other resolution methods as the more ideologically sound approach. Particularly for family law cases with a high level of conflict, the pressure put on a parent to reach settlement can result in inappropriate and harmful outcomes. The interests of the children require an (affordable) public law system, equipped with judges with sufficient expertise and competence and adequate court resources to ensure a thorough handling of the case and a fundamentally sound resolution of the conflict; for many of the above-mentioned cases, traditional authoritative court decisions seem to be necessary.

BIBLIOGRAPHY

Austbø, A and Engebretsen, G, *Mekling i rettskonflikter*, 2nd edn (Oslo, Cappelen Akademisk Forlag, 2006)

Bernt-Hamre, C, *Rettsmekling*, Det Juridiske Fakultets Skriftserie Nr 97 (Bergen, Det juridiske fakultet, 2004)

Bernt-Hamre, C, 'Hvor aktiv kan rettmekler være under meklingen?—Noen sentrale problemstillinger' in J Giertsen and HF Marthinussen (eds), *Festskrift til Det juridiske fakultet ved Universitetet i Bergen i anledning 25 års jubileet*, Det Juridiske Fakultets Skriftserie Nr 108 (Bergen, Det juridiske fakultet, 2005) 75–86

Bernt, C, *Meklerrollen ved mekling i domstolene* (Bergen, Fagbokforlaget, 2011)

Bernt, JF and Rasmussen, Ø, *Frihagens Forvaltningsrett I* (Bergen, Fagbokforlaget, 2010)

Blandhol, S, 'Hvordan kan advokater bli bedre rådgivere i tvisteløsning?' (2012) 92(4) *Advokatbladet* 47

Blandhol, S, 'Valget mellom forlik og rettssak. Hvor gode er advokater til å bedømme prosessrisiko og hvorfor går det ofte galt?' (2011) 50 *Lov og Rett* 596

Blandhol, S, 'Hvorfor brukes ikke mekling oftere' (2010) 44(7) *Juristkontakt* 54

Blandhol, S, 'Hindringer for forlik kan ramme også den gode advokat' (2010) 44(9) *Juristkontakt* 54

[170] For more on this see Breivik and Mevik, *Barnefordeling i Domstolen* 127.

Breivik, FL and Mevik, K, *Barnefordeling i Domstolen, Når barnets beste blir barnets verste* (Oslo, Universitetsforlaget, 2012)

Christophersen, R and Torvund, Ø, 'Ingen vil til megling', *Bergens Tidende*, 10 August 2009, 7

Dalseide, N, 'Saksbehandlingreglene for tvister om foreldreansvar, barnets faste bosted og samvær etter endringslov 20 juni 2003—noen utvalgte problemstillinger' [2004] *Tidsskrift for familierett, arverett og barnevernrettslige spørsmål* 172–216

Fliflet, A, 'Noen frimodige ytringer om domstoler og dommere', Justisdepartementets småskriftserie Nr 2/1998 (Oslo, Justisdepartementet, Domstolsavdelingen, 1998) 1–12

Hareide, D (ed), *Konfliktmegling—et nordisk perspektiv* (Oslo, Scandinavian Academic Press, 2006)

Hareide, D, *Conflict Mediation—A Nordic Perspective*, translated by LE Kjerland for the Helsinki Conference on Mediation and Conflict Management (Oslo, The Board of Nordic Forum for Mediation and Conflict Management, 2006)

Høyer, RA and Høyer, JB, 'Forliksrådet—fra lekmannsdomstol til kvalifisert tvisteløsningsorgan?' (2008) 47 *Lov og Rett* 326

Ipsen, KA, *Trenger meklere opplæring? En studie av mekling, meklingstilnærminger og opplæring i mekling* (Bergen, 2008), <http://brage.bibsys.no/nla/bitstream/URN:NBN:no-bibsys_brage_9401/1/Master_Ipsen_h08.pdf>

Kaasen, K, *Petroliumskontrakter—med kommentarer til NF 05 og NTK 05* (Oslo, Universitetsforlaget, 2006)

Kaasen, K, 'Project integrated mediation (PRIME)', *MarIus 414—SIMPLY 2011, The Scandinavian Institute's Maritime and Petroleum Law Yearbook 2011* (Oslo, Scandinavian Institute's Maritime and Petroleum Law, 2012) 67–92.

Knoff, RH, *Raskere? Billigere? Vennligere? Evaluering av prøveordningen med rettsmekling*, Rapport for Justisdepartementet (Oslo, 2001), <www.rhknoff.no/Rapporter/R157JD.pdf>

Marthinussen, K, Giverholt, H and Arvesen, HJ, *NS 8405: kommentarutgave til Norsk standard 8405, Norsk bygge- og anleggskontrakt* (Oslo, Gyldendal Akademisk, 2010)

Nordhelle, G, *Manipulation* (Oslo, Gyldendal Akademisk, 2009)

Nygard-Sture, T and Mjelva, HK, 'Loven skulle kutte kostnadene ved rettssaker betydelig. Men alt tyder på at tusenlappene flagrer like raskt som før', *Bergens Tidende*, 2 February 2012, 1, 6–8

Nylund, A, 'Europeisering av sivilprosessen' in JP Rui (ed), *Rettshjelp fra kyst til vidde. Festskrift til jusshjelpa i Nord-Norge 20 år* (Oslo, Gyldendal Akademisk, 2009) 209–24

Nylund, A, 'Meklingsmodeller i tvisteloven: terapi, tvekamp eller kreativ problemløsning?' (2010) 49 *Lov og Rett* 272

Nylund, A, 'Mekling i barnefordelingssaker på godt og ondt' (2011) No 4 *Tidsskrift for familierett, arverett og barnevernrettslige spørsmål* 303

Næss, HE, *Vel forlikt. Forliksrådene i Norge 200 år 1795–1995* (Stavanger, Kulturkonsult/Justisdepartementet, 1995)

Ristvedt, PM and Nisja, OØ, *Alternativ Tvisteløsning* (Oslo, Cappelen Akademisk Forlag, 2008)

Ristvedt, PM, 'Advokater og prosessrisiko' (2012) 92(4) *Advokatbladet* 46

Rønbeck, K and Lilleberg, RK, 'Advokatrollen i barnefordelingssaker' (2006) 45 *Lov og Rett* 170

Rønning, A, 'Vil ha nytt institutt for mekling' (2011) 91(12) *Advokatbladet* 42

Rønning, A, 'Advokater er dårlige til å vurdere prosessrisiko' (2011) 91(2) *Advokatbladet* 22

Sandberg, K, *Kommentar til barneloven*, Gyldendal rettsdata, Norsk Lovkommentar, <www.rettsdata.no>

Sandvik, G, 'Rettshistorie—førelesninger' [1990] *Jussens Venner* 229

Schei, T, Bårdsen, A, Nordén, DB, Reusch, CHP and Øie, TM, *Lov av 17 juni 2005 Nr 90 om mekling og rettergang i sivile tvister (Tvisteloven), Kommentarutgave*, Bind I, II (Oslo, Universitetsforlaget, 2007)

Schei, T, 'Norsk sivilprosess moderniseres' in T Andersson and B Lindell (eds), *Festskrift til Per Henrik Lindblom* (Uppsala, Iustus Föelag, 2004) 589–600

Simonsen, L, *Prekontraktuelt ansvar* (Oslo, Universitetsforlaget, 1997)

Sletten, T, *Domstollignende forvaltningsorganer*, Institutt for offentlig retts skriftserie Nr 3/1990 (Oslo, Institutt for Offentlig Rett, 1990)

Smith, C, 'Voldgift—Domstolenes konkurrent og hjelper, T' [1993] *Tidsskrift for Rettsvitenskap* 474

Sperr, AK, 'Mediation in Norway' in K Hopt and F Steffek (eds), *Mediation—Principles, Regulation and Reform in Comparative Perspective* (Oxford, Oxford University Press, 2012) 1111–38

Sperr, AK, 'Ombudsman' in J Basedow, K Hopt and P Zimmermann (eds), *The Max Planck Encyclopedia of European Private Law* (Oxford, Oxford University Press, 2012) 1221–26

Sperr, AK, *Verwaltungsrechtsschutz in Deutschland und Norwegen. Eine vergleichende Studie zur gerichtlichen Kontrolle von Verwaltungsentscheidungen* (Baden-Baden, Nomos Verlag, 2009)

Østgård, B, 'Hvorfor brukes ikke mekling oftere? Replikk til Sverre Blandhol' (2010) 44(8) *Juristkontakt* 36

Additional public documents

Statskonsult, *Klager over alt, Organisering av statlig klagesaksbehandling*, Rapport 2003:19, Oslo 2003, <www.difi.no/statskonsult/publik/rapporter/fulltekst/2003–19.pdf>

Direktoratet for forvaltning og IKT (Difi), *Uavhengig eller bare uklart? Organisering av statlig myndighetsutøvelse*, Difi raport 2012:7, Oslo 2012, <www.difi.no/filearchive/difi-rapport-2012–7-uavhengig-eller-bare-uavklart.pdf>

SINTEF Teknologi og samfunn, Rapport A20162, Evaluering av mekling etter ekteskapslov og barnelov, Trondheim 2011, www.regjeringen.no/upload/BLD/mekling_ekteskapslov.pdf>

14

Regulation of Dispute Resolution in Switzerland: Mediation, Conciliation and Other Forms of ADR in Switzerland

ISAAK MEIER IN COOPERATION WITH MIGUEL SOGO, SOTIRIOS KOTRONIS, SARAH SCHEIWILLER, DAVID SIEGWART, CLAUDIA WYSS, DHEDEN ZOTSANG AND CARLO HAMBURGER

I. DIFFERENT FORMS OF ADR IN SWITZERLAND AND THEIR SIGNIFICANCE

A. Introduction

i. Subject of the Report

THIS REPORT DEALS with ADR procedures in Switzerland.[1] In the first part, we present the very different forms of ADR procedures which are established and used in this country. The second part focuses on the main subject, which is the legal framework of ADR.

The present report offers a look at the ADR procedure in private/civil law matters. The ADR forms in public law and criminal law will not be discussed, although these forms are also of significant importance in Switzerland.[2]

Amongst the ADR forms for civil law disputes, the ADR forms in insolvency proceedings will not be mentioned. As is the case in many other countries, in Swiss law there are different forms of insolvency proceedings which aim at a voluntary arrangement between the debtor and her/his creditors.[3] However, to provide an overview of all these forms of ADR procedures, it would be necessary to launch a special project.

In my opinion, arbitration is definitely not an ADR procedure the way it is meant in this chapter. Rather, it is a (private) form of adjudication. Therefore, it will only be addressed very briefly.[4]

ii. Glossary

In Switzerland one has to draw a distinction between mediation and conciliation. Furthermore, the widespread 'Ombuds-procedures', as well as the so-called 'judgment proposal' procedures, which have a long tradition in Switzerland, need to be defined.

[1] Any exact citation of articles of the Swiss Code of Civil Procedure follows the translation provided by SV Berti (ed), *ZPO, Schweizerische Zivilprozessordnung* (Basel, Helbing Lichtenhahn Verlag, 2009) 523ff.

[2] For mediation in criminal matters see generally C Schwarzenegger, U Thalmann and V Zanolini, *Mediation im Strafrecht: Erfahrungen im Kanton Zürich* (Zurich, Kriminologisches Institut—Universität Zürich, 2006) and in public law T Pfisterer, 'Über Konsens- und Mediationslösungen im öffentlichen Recht (konferieren statt prozessieren)' [2002] *Zeitschrift für schweizerisches Recht* 169 (see also Art 33b VwVG = Federal Act of December 20th 1968 on Administrative Procedure).

[3] See, eg Arts 333ff IC (Insolvency Code [SchKG]); see also K Amonn and F Walther, *Grundriss des Schuldbetreibungs- und Konkursrechts*, 8th edn (Bern, Stämpfli Verlag, 2008) s 53 comments 5ff and s 57 comments 1ff.

[4] See III.F.

Conciliation in Switzerland mainly means all manners of procedures to resolve a legal dispute which are led by a third person (conciliator).[5] The term does not set further limits. It can either be a private out-of-court procedure or an official part of the court procedure operated by a justice of the peace or another official. If conciliation takes place while a legal action is pending and is led by a judge, this conciliation procedure would be called a 'settlement conference'. In each procedure, the conciliator may act in a very different way. He can be very active and make proposals to settle the dispute or take a more passive role.

Mediation is regarded in public discussions in Switzerland—and hence in this chapter—as a special form of conciliation with high ethical standards. Mediation is typically a structured procedure which aims at providing a deeper and more profound look at the conflict.[6] Normally, a mediator is a competent and skilled person with respect to his task. Instead of supporting a negotiation according to the positions of the parties, the mediator inquires after their specific interests (the Harvard Concept). He would be reluctant to make proposals to resolve the conflict. His main goal is to empower the parties to find their own solution which best meets the interests of both parties.[7]

If the term 'mediation' is used in this narrow sense, it has to be taken into account that the law itself perceives mediation more in the sense of conciliation.[8] Although the legislator probably had this above-described ethical procedure in mind, the law does not say what 'mediation' means (see Articles 213ff Swiss Code of Civil Procedure, CCP). Therefore, a traditional conciliation narrowly led by a (private or public) conciliator would be embraced by this legal notion.[9]

The procedure conducted by an '*ombudsman*' is a special form of ADR in Switzerland. It is introduced to resolve all sorts of consumer disputes. The ombudsman is a neutral person who examines the claim of a consumer after hearing the suppliers' standpoint on the case. If she/he arrives at the result that the supplier did not act according to the law and/or contract, she/he negotiates a solution with the supplier on behalf of the consumer.

Finally, in Switzerland, we find an important ADR form which in this chapter is called a 'judgment proposal procedure' (see Articles 210ff CCP). It is a mixture between a (legally binding) judgment and a voluntary arrangement (settlement).[10] The court renders a provisional judgment based on a somewhat restricted examination of

[5] I Meier, *Schweizerisches Zivilprozessrecht* (Zurich/Basel/Geneva, Schulthess Juristische Medien, 2010) 585.

[6] D Mürner, *Gerichtsnahe Zivilmediation*, Diss Zurich (Zurich/Basel/Geneva, Schulthess Juristische Medien, 2005) 60f; see also Meier, *Schweizerisches Zivilprozessrecht* 584.

[7] U Gloor and B Umbricht Lukas in P Oberhammer (ed), *Kurzkommentar, Schweizerische Zivilprozessordnung* (Basel, Helbing Lichtenhahn Verlag, 2010) Vor Arts 213–218 comment 10; see also PS Gelzer and P Ruggle in K Spühler, L Tenchio and D Infanger (eds), *Basler Kommentar, Schweizerische Zivilprozessordnung* (Basel, Helbing Lichtenhahn Verlag, 2010) Vor Arts 213–218 comment 2.

[8] Meier, *Schweizerisches Zivilprozessrecht* 593; Gelzer and Ruggle in Spühler, Tenchio and Infanger (eds), *Basler Kommentar, Schweizerische Zivilprozessordnung* Vor Arts 213–218 comment 1.

[9] Meier, *Schweizerisches Zivilprozessrecht* 593.

[10] D Infanger in Spühler, Tenchio and Infanger (eds), *Basler Kommentar, Schweizerische Zivilprozessordnung* Art 210 comment 1; Gloor and Umbricht Lukas in Oberhammer (ed), *Kurzkommentar, Schweizerische Zivilprozessordnung* Art 210 comment 1; see generally C Leuenberger and B Uffer-Tobler, *Schweizerisches Zivilprozessrecht* (Bern, Stämpfli Verlag, 2010) comments 11.28ff.

the facts and/or the law. The judgment is deemed to be final and/or enforceable if the losing party does not file an ordinary proceeding (Article 211(3) CCP).

iii. Overall View of the Different Forms of ADR in Switzerland

In Switzerland, only a very small number of legal disputes are decided by adjudication (binding judgment). In most cases, the involved parties agree on a settlement.

The vast majority of legal disputes in Switzerland are solved by bilateral negotiation, with or without the help of lawyers. However, of great importance are also ADR procedures which are led by a neutral person (conciliator, mediator).

Court-related conciliation is based on a long and well-established tradition. In almost every case, the parties have to undergo a mandatory settlement conference led by a justice of the peace before an action can be brought to court (Article 197 CCP). After filing the legal action, at least one settlement conference managed by the court and normally presided over by a judge will take place (Article 124(3) CCP). Later—if a settlement cannot be reached—the judge will be part of the decision-making body. In general, these settlement conferences are very successful. Whereas justices of the peace resolve about 40 per cent of all the cases, the percentage of settlements in court is more than 60 per cent of all the cases.[11]

For the majority of consumer disputes, suppliers of a branch of industry (banks, insurance companies, car dealers) have established a variety of ombudsman procedures.[12] This ADR procedure absorbs almost every consumer dispute; only very few cases are still handled by the court.

Furthermore, Swiss law provides special fast-track procedures in which the court renders a provisional judgment based on a somewhat restricted examination of the facts and/or the law. As mentioned above, the judgment becomes final and/or enforceable if the losing party does not file an ordinary proceeding. In Switzerland, these 'judgment proposal procedures' exist in very different forms. This chapter deals only with the judgment proposal proceeding according to Articles 210ff of the new Code of Civil Procedure and the so-called '*Rechtsöffnungsverfahren*' according to Article 82 IC.[13]

Despite Switzerland's own independent and rich tradition of ADR,[14] the mediation movement which arose approximately 20 years ago had a great impact on the country. Today, mediation is of significant importance mainly in the fields of divorce disputes and disputes in all sorts of organisations. Because there was no need for conciliation to a greater extent, mediation always was and still is understood in the sense of a comprehensive and sophisticated dispute resolution procedure. As long as procedural law was cantonal law, only a few (cantonal) codes of civil procedure enacted any rules on mediation.[15] Meanwhile, the new national Code of Civil Procedure has its own section on mediation (Articles 213ff CCP).

[11] See I.C.iv.

[12] See I.F.ii.

[13] This will be briefly mentioned below, see I.D.

[14] O Schneider, 'Grundlegendes zu Einigung und Mediation' (2010/4) '*Justice—Justiz—Giustizia*': *Die Schweizer Richterzeitung*, available at <www.richterzeitung.ch> nos 1ff; B Umbricht Lukas and U Gloor, 'Die Mediation in der Zivilprozessordnung' [2010] *FamPra.ch: Die Praxis des Familienrechts* 819.

[15] See, eg canton of Geneva (Arts 71aff CCP Geneva). See also Explanatory Report ('Message') to the Swiss Code of Civil Procedure (Botschaft zur Schweizerischen Zivilprozessordnung) of 28 June 2006, 7335; Gelzer and Ruggle in Spühler, Tenchio and Infanger (eds), *Basler Kommentar, Schweizerische Zivilprozes-*

iv. The New Swiss Code of Civil Procedure and the Legal Sources of Mediation and Other Forms of ADR

Since the beginning of the year 2011, Swiss procedural law is unified. The new Swiss Code of Civil Procedure (CCP) replaced the 24 different cantonal laws. Even if the code adopted some new constructions, such as in the field of mediation, the principal purpose is still to continue the tradition of Swiss procedural law, especially concerning the mandatory pre-trial conciliation procedure (Article 197ff CCP) and the importance of the settlement conferences during the court proceeding (Articles 91, 124(3), 226(2) and 273(3) CCP). The unification only concerns civil procedural law in a narrower sense. The organisation of the court in regard to the lower level courts is still governed by cantonal law (Article 122(2) Federal Constitution). Furthermore, cantonal law applies to the legal costs (Article 96 CCP).

A difficult question is whether and to what extent federal or cantonal law is competent to establish rules about ADR. Federal law is certainly competent to answer all the ADR questions which are connected to a rule of procedural law (for example, the question whether the mediator can testify as a witness in a trial; see Article 166(1) lit d CCP). In the same way, the cantons can legislate in the few areas which are still governed by cantonal law. Therefore, they can define the qualifications required of a mediator who wants to be paid by the state. Furthermore, the cantons may offer mediation free of charge, as some cantons do in certain fields.[16] In my opinion, all the other questions concerning ADR are to be answered by federal law. The competence to rule on procedural law also entails the power to set up rules regarding ADR as far as such rules are generally appropriate, eg regarding minimal standards for an ombudsman procedure.

B. Out-of-court or Court Settlement through Negotiation between the Parties

i. The Legal Nature of an Out-of-court or a Court Settlement

A contract in which the parties agree to settle a dispute by means of negotiation is an ordinary contract of private law (CO = Code of Obligations).[17]

If a court proceeding is already pending and the parties inform the court about this agreement, it will be a court settlement according to Article 217 CCP.[18] The agreement remains a contract of private law, but it also has procedural effects: the agreement itself completes the procedure and is enforceable in the same manner as a judgment (Article 241(2) CCP).

sordnung Vor Arts 213–218 comments 5f; C Kumpan and C Bauer, 'Kapitel 18, Mediation in der Schweiz' in KJ Hopt and F Steffek (eds), *Mediation* (Tübingen, Mohr Siebeck Verlag, 2008) 853, 862ff; Meier, *Schweizerisches Zivilprozessrecht* 583f; Umbricht Lukas and Gloor, 'Die Mediation in der Zivilprozessordnung', 819.

[16] See III.B.iv.b.

[17] BGE 124 II 8 (p 12, con 3b); BGE 110 II 44 (p 46, con 4); BGE 105 II 273 (p 277, con 3a); see generally M Guldener, *Schweizerisches Zivilprozessrecht*, 3rd edn (Zurich, Schulthess Polygraphischer Verlag, 1979) 394; Meier, *Schweizerisches Zivilprozessrecht* 233.

[18] SV Berti, *Einführung in die schweizerische Zivilprozessordnung* (Basel, Helbing Lichtenhahn Verlag, 2011) 116; Leuenberger and Uffer-Tobler, *Schweizerisches Zivilprozessrecht* no 11.45; Meier, *Schweizerisches Zivilprozessrecht* 595.

ii. Rules Concerning Negotiation

According to private law, there is no duty to negotiate an out-of-court solution to a legal dispute before going to trial. Only the legal conduct rules contain an obligation to negotiate (see Article 9 Swiss Conduct Rules). However, the parties can agree on such a duty, even though the nature and effects of this kind of contractual clause are not completely clear.[19] In general, it is regarded as void by law, and a party can go to court at any time despite the existence of such a clause.[20] She/he will only be liable for breach of contract (Article 97ff CO).[21]

C. Pre-trial Conciliation and Settlement Conferences at Court

i. In General

Conciliation and adjudication are equivalent goals of Swiss civil procedure. Although conciliation chronologically occurs first,[22] there is no priority for this form of dispute resolution. Adjudication comes second simply because there is no room for a settlement after the rendering of a judgment.

Conciliation and adjudication complement and influence each other; they are combined in one procedure. As mentioned above, in almost every case the parties have to undergo a mandatory settlement conference led by a justice of the peace before an action can be brought to the court (Article 197 CCP). After filing the legal action, at least one settlement conference will thus take place.

Conciliation as it is typically handled by Swiss courts or justices of the peace is mainly based on an analysis of the facts and the law, and the risks of the parties going to court. The risks of a legal action are determined by the probability of winning and the estimated costs in the event of losing the case. The interests of the parties in their legal positions are rarely the subject of negotiation.

[19] According to Schütz, this contractual clause is a condition for rendering a judgment on the merits (GJ Schütz, *Mediation und Schiedsgerichtsbarkeit in der Schweizerischen Zivilprozessordnung*, Diss Bern (Bern, Stämpfli Verlag, 2009) nos 476ff). The same opinion is held by E Bucher, 'Was macht den Schiedsrichter? Abschied vom "Schiedsrichtervertrag"—und Weiteres zu Prozessverträgen' in Bachmann et al (eds), *Grenzüberschreitungen, Beiträge zum Internationalen Verfahrensrecht und zur Schiedsgerichtsbarkeit, Festschrift für Peter Schlosser zum 70. Geburtstag* (Tübingen, Mohr Siebeck, 2005) 97, 99; N Voser, 'Sanktion bei Nichterfüllung einer Schlichtungsklausel, Kommentar zum Urteil des Kassationsgerichts vom 15 März 1999' [2002] *ASA Bulletin* 380; criticising the substantive qualification is I Meier, 'Mediation und Schlichtung in der Schweiz, unter besonderer Berücksichtigung der gesetzlichen Rahmenbedingungen für Mediation' in Veröffentlichungen des Schweizerischen Instituts für Rechtsvergleichung (ed), *'Mediation' als alternative Konfliktlösungsmöglichkeit?* (Zurich/Basel/Geneva, Schulthess Juristische Medien, 2002) 295ff, 314. Against Guldener, *Schweizerisches Zivilprozessrecht* 51 (fn 4), 224 (fn 25), 259f (fn 8); H Eiholzer, *Die Streitbeilegungsabrede*, Diss Freiburg (Freiburg, Universitätsverlag Freiburg, 1998) 62f and 180ff, especially 185 (no 673). See also KassGer. ZH 15 March 1999 (*Blätter für Zürcherische Rechtsprechung (ZR)* 99, 2000, no 29, pp 86f); OG ZH 11 September 2001 (*Blätter für Zürcherische Rechtsprechung (ZR)* 101, 2002, no 21, pp 77ff con 3).

[20] Schütz, *Mediation und Schiedsgerichtsbarkeit in der Schweizerischen Zivilprozessordnung* no 479.

[21] As actual delivery is not enforceable in this case, liability only occurs for damages (Schütz, *Mediation und Schiedsgerichtsbarkeit in der Schweizerischen Zivilprozessordnung* no 473 and 500); see also KassGer ZH 15 March 1999 (*Blätter für Zürcherische Rechtsprechung (ZR)* 99, 2000, no 29, pp 86f).

[22] Explanatory Report ('Message') to the Swiss Code of Civil Procedure (Botschaft zur Schweizerischen Zivilprozessordnung) of 28 June 2006, 7328.

Conciliation in this sense is not a proceeding conflicting with adjudication. Furthermore, conciliation in this sense is a sort of device for enforcing the law. In a settlement conference during trial or in a pre-trial conciliation meeting, the parties want to secure their 'rights' to the greatest extent possible. In a legal dispute over a contract, the parties normally seek performance. But they do not want to renegotiate their contractual rights based on the interests of the parties as is typical in mediation. They are only ready to adjust their rights to the risk of costs and the length of trial.

As the enormous success of conciliations shows,[23] this form of dispute resolution fulfils the needs of the great majority of the parties. The parties prefer conciliation over adjudication for several reasons: instead of having a chance to obtain everything in a judgment in the future, they can obtain part of it now with certainty. Instead of depending on the unpredictable judgment in adjudication, the parties themselves can handle the dispute in a way they can approve of. In this respect, conciliation serves the need of the parties for self-determination.

ii. Combining and Interweaving of Conciliation and Adjudication in Swiss Procedural Law

Swiss procedural law is characterised by combining conciliation and adjudication in the same procedure. Conciliation in the view of Swiss procedural law is not an alternative to adjudication but is a part of the same procedure which aims at solving the dispute in either way.

Obviously conciliation plays an important role in many judiciary systems. But, to my knowledge, there is no other country in which conciliation is such a central point of the proceedings. More or less each step of the procedure serves at the same time as adjudication and conciliation (see the table overleaf).

iii. Conciliation Hearing Led by a Justice of the Peace

In more or less every case, most cantons require the parties to participate in a conciliation hearing led by a justice of the peace (Article 197 CCP).[24]

The conciliation hearing is characterised as follows.

- Most justices of the peace are laymen/laywomen.[25] They have little information about the case. They only know what the parties disclose at the hearing. The conciliation hearing takes about half an hour on average. Therefore they are not able to give an in-depth legal assessment of the case. Instead of an assessment, they

[23] See I.C.iii and I.C.iv.

[24] According to Art 198 CCP, there is no conciliation attempt, for instance, in case of actions under the Debt Enforcement and Bankruptcy Act or actions before the commercial court (especially commercial matters between persons who are registered in the Swiss commercial register with a litigation value of more than CHF 30,000).

[25] Leuenberger and Uffer-Tobler, *Schweizerisches Zivilprozessrecht* no 11.5; Meier, *Schweizerisches Zivilprozessrecht* 48; K Spühler, A Dolge and M Gehri, *Schweizerisches Zivilprozessrecht* (Bern, Stämpfli Verlag, 2010) s 48 comment 8.

Table: Adjudication and Conciliation

Adjudication	**Conciliation**
Conciliation proceedings (Articles 197ff CCP)	
Conciliation proceedings are the first step of the adjudication proceedings (procedural condition of admissibility).	The mandatory conciliation hearing led by a justice of the peace aims at settling the case at this early stage of the procedure.
Adjudication proceedings	
Exchange of pleadings and preparation of main hearing (Articles 220ff CCP)	
In the statements of claim and defence, the parties offer their alleged facts and their evidence as a part of the proceedings on the merits.	With their statements the parties also try to create a basis for a successful negotiation at the subsequent preparatory hearing.
Preparatory hearing (Articles 226 CCP)	
In the formal part of the preparatory hearing the parties have the opportunity to complete their statements of facts and evidence.	The main goal of the preparatory hearing is a settlement conference led by the judge who later—if the parties do not settle—writes a proposal for the decision on the merits.
Main hearing	
The main hearing contains an exchange of arguments, taking evidence and closing statements.	In most cases in the main hearing or in a special meeting the court again encourages the parties to settle the case.
Decision on the merits	
The court decides the dispute on the merits.	What the parties have disclosed in the settlement conferences and how they have behaved influences the court's decision.

emphasise the general risks of a trial (costs, burden of proof, duration and psychological stress of a procedure).[26]

- The justices of the peace in most cantons are not part of the court that later decides the case if the parties do not settle. They therefore concentrate on settling the case and do not feel or behave like real judges. Nevertheless, for the inexperienced parties the conciliation hearing has a quite formal atmosphere and makes them feel as if they are at court.
- At the conciliation meeting, the parties have to appear in person. However, unlike in most former cantonal laws, they can be accompanied by their lawyers or by another person (Article 204(2) CCP). In the district of Zurich, in 2011, the parties were accompanied by a lawyer and/or another person in around 50 per cent of the cases. One the one hand, the presence of an additional person led to longer conciliation proceedings (1.5 hours and more) and more administrative work, especially due to the time-consuming arrangement of appointments. On the other hand, the presence

[26] Meier, *Schweizerisches Zivilprozessrecht* 235; Spühler, Dolge and Gehri, *Schweizerisches Zivilprozessrecht* s 48 comment 4.

of a lawyer and/or another person was regarded as helpful in a large number of cases, especially in cases with a higher level of complexity.[27]

The pre-trial conciliation hearings have been a success story under the cantonal law and are under the new law so far as well.[28] On average, more than 40 per cent of all the cases are settled.[29] The main reasons are:

- In Switzerland, the costs of litigation (court costs and attorney's fees) are very high, and, since legal aid especially for the middle class is not satisfactory,[30] many parties have to settle the case as a practical matter.
- A very important reason is also that the parties get a first impression of how it 'feels' to go to court. They can then decide whether they really want to proceed further. Some of them may already have fulfilled their need by being able to narrate their dispute to a justice of the peace as a judge-like person.
- Finally, the reason for the settlement may simply be because the compulsory conciliation hearing allows the parties to meet again after communication has been interrupted by the dispute.[31]

iv. Preparatory Hearing (Settlement Conferences at Court)

Article 226 CCP says, in respect of the preparatory hearing:

> The court can conduct preparatory hearings at any time (sec 1). Preparatory hearings allow a free discussion of the matter in dispute, the pleading of additional facts, an attempt to reach a settlement and the preparation of the main hearing (sec 2). The court may take evidence (sec 3).

The preparatory hearing usually takes place after the exchange of the first pleadings.[32] But it is also possible to conduct it before they are exchanged or at the later stage of the procedure.[33]

The preparatory hearing expresses very clearly the dual system of adjudication and conciliation. The main part of the preparatory hearing is a settlement conference. But the formal first part of the hearing (pleading of additional facts, preparation of the main hearing) serves to continue with the proceeding which finally ends in a decision.

The preparatory hearings are led by the judge who later decides the case as a

[27] *Annual Report 2011 of the Justice of the Peace Organisation of the District of Zurich*, 10f, available at <www.stadt-zuerich.ch/content/dam/stzh/portal/Deutsch/Friedensrichteramt/Formulare%20und%20Merkblaetter/FR_Jahresbericht_2011.pdf>.

[28] I Staubli, 'Der Friedensrichter in der Schweiz' in PG Mayr (ed), *Öffentliche Einrichtungen zur aussergerichtlichen Vermittlung von Streitigkeiten* (Wien, MANZ'sche Verlags- und Universitätsbuchhandlung, 1999) 191.

[29] In 2010, for instance, about 45% of the terminations in the canton of Zurich were concluded as a result of a settlement, about 35% in the canton of Schwyz, about 27% in the canton of Grisons and about 48% in the canton of Zug.

[30] Meier, *Schweizerisches Zivilprozessrecht* 425f.

[31] Meier, *Schweizerisches Zivilprozessrecht* 235.

[32] C Leuenberger in T Sutter-Somm, F Hasenböhler and C Leuenberger (eds), *Kommentar zur Schweizerischen Zivilprozessordnung (ZPO)* (Zurich/Basel/Geneva, Schulthess Juristische Medien, 2010) Art 226 comment 17; Meier, *Schweizerisches Zivilprozessrecht* 339; G Naegeli in Oberhammer (ed), *Kurzkommentar, Schweizerische Zivilprozessordnung* Art 226 comment 7; E Pahud in A Brunner, D Gasser and I Schwander (eds), *Schweizerische Zivilprozessordnung (ZPO)* (Zurich/St Gallen, Dike Verlag, 2011) Art 226 comment 2.

[33] See Art 226(1) CCP.

single judge or as a member of a panel of judges. According to the Swiss legal tradition, a judge's involvement in a conciliation hearing is not itself a ground for recusal (Article 47(2) lit b CCP).[34]

The judge in most cases has a strong practical incentive to settle the case because writing a judgment proposal is a very time-consuming task. Therefore she/he will commonly make a great effort to help or sometimes even push[35] the parties to settle.

The negotiation of the parties is mainly based on a settlement proposal of the judge. She/he assesses the parties' chances to win the case based on their first statements and the documents presented. The settlement proposal mirrors this assessment expressed in percentages. For example, if the plaintiff asks for CHF 100,000, the judge may suggest settling for CHF 70,000, because the plaintiff has the law on her/his side but will have difficulty in proving some of her/his allegations.

This settlement proceeding has nothing to do with mediation. The parties do not disclose their interests and how they themselves assess their chances of winning. It is a hidden negotiation, as is typical in a market place.

Both parties hold to their statements, and try to convince the other party and the judge that their chances of winning are better than the judge's assessment. The parties cannot confess that their standpoints may have some weaker points, because they always have in mind that the procedure could go on. Nevertheless, after haggling for maybe one or more hours, on average more than 40 per cent of all the cases are settled (see Figure 1). The main reasons are the following:

- Because the settlement proposal is made by the judge who would later decide the case, the parties assume that the content of a later judgement would be about the same. Therefore, relying on the judgment instead of accepting the settlement proposal is in most cases not a real choice in the parties' view.
- For the same reason, the lawyers in most cases also advise their clients to settle, because they do not want to be blamed by them if they ultimately receive less in the judgment than they could have had in a settlement earlier on. Furthermore, the lawyers have an incentive to settle because they have already earned most of the fee they can expect out of this case with the first statement and the preparatory hearing.
- As noted above in respect of conciliation meetings, additional incentives for settlement are the length of a trial and the costs of litigation. In order to encourage the parties to settle, the court only asks for the minimum court costs if they settle. A judgment would be at least twice as expensive as a settlement.
- Finally, a very important point is the culture in Switzerland. There is a long and strong tradition in the legal and political culture of resolving a dispute with a compromise which gives both parties a chance of saving face.

v. Assessment of the Dual System of Conciliation and Adjudication

Can this dual system be recommended for other countries or is it a system which is

[34] This could only be a ground if a judge does not treat both parties equally in the settlement conference.

[35] U Egli, *Vergleichsdruck im Zivilprozess, eine rechtstatsächliche Untersuchung*, Diss Zurich 1995 (Berlin, Duncker und Humblot, 1996) 43ff; Meier, *Schweizerisches Zivilprozessrecht* 235.

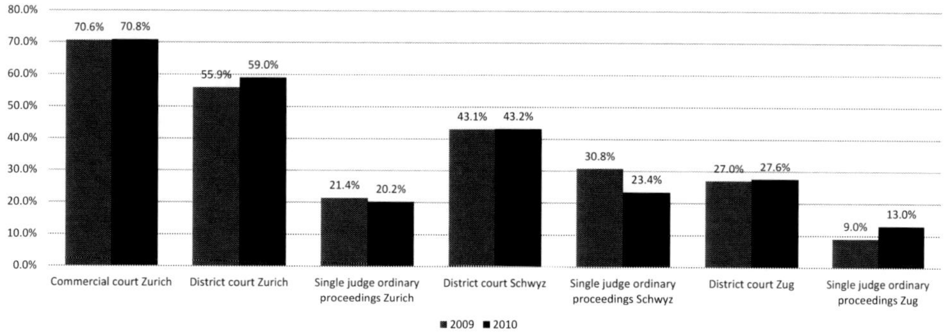

Figure 1. Settlements (in %) in all of the cases terminated.

well suited only to Switzerland? In my opinion, this system could fulfil the needs of the parties in every country. My reasons for this are as follows.

- Most parties in most countries primarily want 'justice' in the sense they want what the law offers. They are not ready to renegotiate their claims. In a dual system according to the Swiss model, both a judgment and a settlement are based on the parties' rights. In the vast majority of cases, the parties prefer a settlement to a judgment because they want—based on an assessment of their chances of winning the case—the certainty of less now rather than the unknown risks of a judgment.
- Another important point is that this dual system gives the parties a chance to choose whether they want to rely on a third person's decision in the judgment or participate in 'finding the law' in a settlement conference. In short, they can choose between self-determination, co-determination and heteronomy. Not surprisingly, most parties opt for self-determination in a settlement.
- Finally, the combination of adjudication and conciliation in one procedure serves the need of the parties for a fair procedure according to the rule of law. *Conciliation can be considered as being part of the process of reaching a judgment*. This means that all the fundamental principles of fairness, the right to be heard, principles of equal treatment and so on are also applicable in the conciliation meetings and settlement conferences. In my opinion, the fact that the judge who led these settlement attempts later participates in the making of a decision does not conflict with the guarantee of an independent judge. Working out a settlement proposal can be seen as a part of the decision-making process.

D. Judgment Proposal

With the 'judgment proposal' (*Urteilsvorschlag*), the new Swiss code offers a special form of ADR (Articles 210ff CCP), which already existed in the former codes of the cantons of St Gallen,[36] Aargau and Schwyz.

[36] C Leuenberger, 'Streiterledigung zwischen Vergleich und Urteil: Modell eines einfachen und raschen Verfahrens' in I Schwander and WA Stoffel (eds), *Beiträge zum schweizerischen und internationalen Zivilprozessrecht, Festschrift für Oscar Vogel* (Freiburg, Universitätsverlag Freiburg Schweiz, 1991) 54ff.

A justice of the peace can, if the conciliation fails or if one of the parties does not show up, in cases with the amount in dispute up to CHF 5,000, render a judgment proposal based on the statements of the parties at the conciliation meeting and their produced documents (Article 210 CCP). The justice of the peace applies the law, but can also consider equity aspects.[37]

Article 211(1) CCP describes the meanings and effects of the judgment proposal: 'The judgment proposal is deemed accepted, and has a *res iudicata* effect, unless one of the parties declines it within 20 days of written notification. No grounds need be given for the rejection.' In case of a rejection, the justice of the peace normally grants leave to the claimant to bring the action before the ordinary court.[38]

The same form of ADR in the former law of the canton of St Gallen was reasonably successful.[39] As the first experiences in practice with the new law show, the judgment proposal serves as a sort of a default judgment if one of the parties does not show up.

In my opinion, this institution makes sense, especially in clear or nearly clear-cut cases. Whereas a defendant may not be willing to recognise the validity of a claim during the conciliation meeting and a plaintiff may, likewise, not be prepared at that time to withdraw an unfounded action, each may be ready to accept the judgment proposal after being able to discuss it with friends and/or having it checked by a lawyer. Also, the function of this institution as a default judgment is a convincing area of application.

The problems with the judgment proposal are mainly based on the fact that the parties very often are not represented by lawyers at this early stage of the procedure. If the parties do not take legal advice because they cannot afford it or erroneously do not deem it necessary, they can easily mistake the judgment proposal for a real judgment. One also has to question whether the justices of the peace, who are typically laymen or laywomen, are able to render a legitimate judgment proposal.[40]

In 2011, in the district of Zurich, 134 judgment proposals were rendered; they were rejected in 21 cases. Even though the law does not contain a rule stating the obligation to include a reasoning in the judgment proposal, experience has shown that including a statement of reasons will lead to more acceptance on behalf of the parties.[41]

Types of ADR which are similar to the judgment proposal include the order for payment and the summary proceeding for money claims according to Article 82 IC (Insolvency Code = SchKG).

In order to enforce a money claim that has not yet been brought to court, the creditor can file an enforcement request for the issue of an order for payment

[37] Meier, *Schweizerisches Zivilprozessrecht* 238; I Meier, *Rechtsschutz im summarischen Verfahren als Alternative zum ordentlichen Zivilprozess im schweizerischen Recht* (Cologne, Bundesanzeiger, 1997) 210f.

[38] Infanger in Spühler, Tenchio and Infanger (eds), *Basler Kommentar, Schweizerische Zivilprozessordnung* Art 212 comment 8.

[39] Meier, *Rechtsschutz im summarischen Verfahren* 212.

[40] Meier, *Rechtsschutz im summarischen Verfahren* 214.

[41] *Annual Report 2011 of the Justice of the Peace Organisation of the District of Zurich*, 11f, available at <www.stadt-zuerich.ch/content/dam/stzh/portal/Deutsch/Friedensrichteramt/Formulare%20und%20Merkblaetter/FR_Jahresbericht_2011.pdf>.

(summons to pay) at the enforcement office (Article 69 IC).[42] The creditor only has to specify the claim (eg CHF 10,000 according to the contract of XYZ); he does not have to give any grounds.[43]

Within 10 days from receipt, the debtor can object to the summons to pay (Article 74 IC). If she/he does not reject it, the creditor can go on with the enforcement procedure (seizing the debtor's assets or starting bankruptcy proceedings).

In the case of an objection, the creditor can set it aside by filing a legal action in an ordinary proceeding or in a summary proceeding according to Article 82 IC. The latter requires that the debtor has signed recognition of debt or that the claim is based on a contract signed by the debtor.[44] The court sets the objection aside in a provisional decision unless the debtor is able to make a prima facie showing that he has a defence against the existence of the debt (Article 82(2) IC). The provisional decision becomes final if the debtor does not bring an action in ordinary proceedings for a declaration that the claim is not founded according to Article 83(2) IC (*Aberkennungsklage*).

This summary proceeding in combination with the order for payment is an extremely successful procedure. Less than 12 per cent of the orders for payment are objected to by the debtors, and an estimated percentage of less than 10 per cent of the debtors file a claim against the creditors according to Article 83 IC.[45]

The summary proceeding according to Article 82 IC and also the summons to pay can be characterised as follows: the former is a formalised summary judgment, but it also has elements of a settlement, because—as mentioned above—it only becomes final if the debtor accepts it by not filing a legal action. The latter can be seen as an offer of the creditor to the debtor for a settlement. The 'offer' is accepted if the debtor does not reject it within 10 days.

These two forms of ADR cannot be discussed here in full. The order for payment in particular is a well-known traditional form of ADR that exists in many European countries and was recently introduced in European law.[46] Their mention in this chapter is warranted to show the great variety of forms of alternative dispute resolutions apart from rendering an ordinary judgment. In Switzerland, this kind of fast-track proceeding for money claims is of great importance.

E. Mediation

i. In General

a. Introduction. As mentioned above, conciliation has a long and well-established tradition in Switzerland. Mediation, conversely, is quite a new institution. Approximately

[42] H Fritzsche and HU Walder-Bohner, *Schuldbetreibung und Konkurs nach schweizerischem Recht*, Band I (Zurich, Schulthess Polygraphischer Verlag, 1984) s 17 comment 1.

[43] Amonn and Walther, *Grundriss des Schuldbetreibungs- und Konkursrechts* s 17 comment 1.

[44] D Vock in D Hunkeler (ed), *Kurzkommentar, Schuldbetreibungs- und Konkursgesetz* (Basel, Helbing Lichtenhahn Verlag, 2009) Art 82 comment 3.

[45] I Meier, 'Die dogmatische Situation des Vollstreckungsrechts aus der Sicht des schweizerischen Rechts' [2008] *Zeitschrift für Zivilprozess* 295, 321.

[46] Meier, 'Die dogmatische Situation des Vollstreckungsrechts' 319f.

25 years ago, mediation came across from the US either directly or via Germany.[47] In 1989, the Groupe romand pour la médiation familiale was founded. In 1992, the association Schweizerischer Verein für Familienmediation (today Schweizerischer Verein für Mediation) was established. Currently, mediation is of significant importance especially in divorce disputes, neighbourhood disputes and employment conflicts.[48]

b. Overview of the Legal Rules on Mediation. Whereas few former cantonal procedural laws had any rules about mediation,[49] the new code provides a special section with regard to mediation (Articles 213–18 CCP). The mediation rules in several European countries served as models for the new law.[50] The law more or less follows the guidelines of the EU Mediation Directive of 2008.[51] The most important points are:[52]

- The parties can request before or during the conciliation meeting that mediation takes the place of conciliation (Article 213(1) CCP). In contentious proceedings, the parties can apply to the court for mediation and the court can also recommend it (Article 214 CCP). During mediation, the proceedings remain suspended (Article 214(3) CCP).
- The parties can jointly request the court to ratify the agreement reached during the mediation. The ratified agreement has a *res iudicata* effect (Article 217 CCP).
- Several rules guarantee the confidentiality of the mediation proceeding. The mediator has the right to refuse to cooperate in providing evidence concerning facts learned in mediation (Article 166(1) lit d CCP). He is not allowed to report on the mediation to the justice of the peace or to the judge of contentious proceedings (compare Article 216 CCP). The mediator is not allowed to act in the same case as another mediator, a justice of the peace or a trial judge (Article 47(1) lit b CCP). Finally, a party is not allowed to use the opponent's statement if the mediation fails (Article 216(2) CCP).
- The new limitation rules in Article 135 CO ensure the limitation period is interrupted when mediation instead of conciliation or contentious proceedings is used.

[47] See also on the origins of mediation in Switzerland M Galli-Widmer, '§ 52 Mediation in der Schweiz' in F Haft and K Gräfin von Schlieffen (eds), *Handbuch Mediation* (München, CH Beck Verlag, 2009); Gelzer and Ruggle in Spühler, Tenchio and Infanger (eds), *Basler Kommentar, Schweizerische Zivilprozessordnung* Vor Arts 213–218 comments 5f; P Liatowitsch, 'Anhang Mediation' in I Schwenzer (ed), *FamKommentar Scheidung, Band II: Anhänge*, 2nd edn (Bern, Stämpfli Verlag, 2011) comments 10ff; I Meier and C Duve, 'Vom Friedensrichter zum Mediator. Einführung von Mediation in bestehende Institutionen der Streitschlichtung' (1999) 95 *Schweizerische Juristenzeitung* 157; E Mertens Senn, *Vermittlung im Sühnverfahren vor dem Hintergrund der Mediation*, Diss Lucerne (Zurich/Basel/Geneva, Schulthess Juristische Medien, 2007) 11ff.

[48] See also Explanatory Report ('Message') to the Swiss Code of Civil Procedure (Botschaft zur Schweizerischen Zivilprozessordnung) of 28 June 2006, 7243 and 7335.

[49] See, eg canton of Geneva (Arts 71a ff CCP Geneva). See also Explanatory Report ('Message') to the Swiss Code of Civil Procedure (Botschaft zur Schweizerischen Zivilprozessordnung) of 28 June, 2006, 7335; Kumpan and Bauer, 'Mediation in der Schweiz', 862ff.

[50] Explanatory Report ('Message') to the Swiss Code of Civil Procedure (Botschaft zur Schweizerischen Zivilprozessordnung) of 28 June 2006, 7252ff and 7256; see, eg Austria: Zivilrechts-Mediations-Gesetz, BGBl I Nr 29/2003 and Zivilrechts-Mediations-Ausbildungsverordnung, BGBl II Nr 47/2004.

[51] Directive 2008/52/EC of the European Parliament and of the Council of 21 May 2008 on certain aspects of mediation in civil and commercial matters, OJ L136/3.

[52] See also Meier, *Schweizerisches Zivilprozessrecht* 593ff; JA Mirimanoff, 'Feasibility of Mediation Systems in Switzerland' [2009] *ASA Bulletin* 473ff; JT Peter, *Gerichtsnahe Mediation. Kommentar zur Mediation in der ZPO* (Bern, Stämpfli Verlag, 2011) 53ff; P Ruggle in Spühler, Tenchio and Infanger (eds), *Basler Kommentar, Schweizerische Zivilprozessordnung* Arts 213ff; Umbricht Lukas and Gloor, 'Die Mediation in der Zivilprozessordnung', 820ff.

Unlike in Germany,[53] '*gerichtsinterne Mediation*' (court internal mediation), which is led by a judge not acting as a trial judge, is not provided by the unified procedural law as the organisation of the judiciary is still regulated by cantonal law.[54] As far as I am aware, none of the cantonal laws have enacted such rules so far.[55] In the canton of Zurich, the High Court, as the supervisory body of the district courts in administrative questions, refused to allow such an attempt mainly due to the lack of a legal basis.

It would also fall under cantonal law to set up rules and standards for someone who would like to work as a mediator and/or to protect the title of a mediator. None of the cantons have taken such measures so far. Therefore, with regard to cantonal law, the mediation market is completely self-regulated. A more indirect quality assurance takes place through the fact that the courts regularly refer to lists of mediators with recognised qualifications when recommending mediation.[56] Another indirect way of setting quality specifications is that mediation paid for by the state can only be provided by attorneys who are registered in the cantonal attorney's register.[57]

c. Mediation According to Article 213ff CCP. As has been explained earlier in this chapter, the concept of mediation according to Article 213ff CCP is to be understood in a very broad sense, since the law itself does not provide a definition of mediation.[58] Therefore, all kinds of negotiations supported and/or led by a third person, such as a traditional out-of-court conciliation based on legal assessments of the claim, are deemed to be covered by these rules.

However, in the ADR landscape in Switzerland, the institution of mediation has the meaning of a specific dispute resolution proceeding characterised by (i) being mainly based on the interests of the parties, (ii) being led by a trained/professional mediator

[53] The federal states of Germany have implemented numerous model projects on court internal mediation (Baden-Württemberg, Bavaria, Berlin, Hamburg, Hesse, Mecklenburg-West Pomerania, Lower Saxony, North Rhine-Westphalia, Rhineland-Palatinate); see R Greger, 'Regelungsempfehlungen vor dem Hintergrund der Pilotprojekte an deutschen Gerichten' [2010] *Rabels Zeitschrift für ausländisches und internationales Privatrecht* 781ff; L Löer, 'Richterliche Mediation. Möglichkeiten der Einbindung von Mediation in das Gerichtsverfahren am Beispiel des Zivilprozesses' [2006] *Zeitschrift für Zivilprozessrecht* 199ff; AR Moltmann Willisch, AM Kraus and F von Hammerstein, 'Richterliche Mediation an Berliner Zivilgerichten. Ein Erfahrungsbericht' [2011] *Zeitschrift für Rechtspolitik* 58f. Among these projects the model project of Lower Saxony received considerable attention throughout Germany, see *Projektabschlussbericht, Projekt Gerichtsnahe Mediation in Niedersachsen Februar 2005*, Niedersächsisches Justizministerium und Konsens eV, see <www.mediation-in-niedersachsen.de/Abschlussbericht.pdf>; see also W Gottwald, '§ 39 Gerichtsnahe Mediation—Erfahrungen und Lehren aus dem Modellprojekt in Niedersachsen' in F Haft and K Gräfin von Schlieffen (eds), *Handbuch Mediation* (München, CH Beck Verlag, 2009).

[54] Ruggle in Spühler, Tenchio and Infanger (eds), *Basler Kommentar, Schweizerische Zivilprozessordnung* Art 214 comment 5.

[55] See the implementation of the federal mediation rules into cantonal regulations, available at <www.mediationschweiz.ch/cms/dokumente>.

[56] For instance, the information sheet 'Merkblatt Mediation für Parteien' (see <www.gerichte-zh.ch/themen/zivilprozess/mediation.html>) refers to a cantonal webpage which contains a register of mediators in Zurich, see <www.mediatoren-zh.ch/>. See also the guide 'médiation' of the high court of Geneva, available at <ge.ch/justice/guide-mediation#a%20qui%20s%27adresser> and Art 40 of the Code of Private Judicial Law of the canton of Vaud.

[57] See, eg s 23(2) lit d of the Introductory Act to the Code of Civil Procedure (EG ZPO) of the canton of Aargau.

[58] See I.A.ii.

and (iii) involving the application of psychological knowledge, communication theory, etc.[59]

d. Questions to be Answered in Order to Understand Mediation in Switzerland. The world of mediation in Switzerland can be described by answering the following questions:

- Which legal rules apply to mediation? We have already provided a relevant overview.[60]
- Who is entitled to offer mediation? As we will attest, these are mainly private people: lawyers, psychologists and a small handful of full-time mediators. Nevertheless, to a lesser extent, mediation is also provided by public and semi-public institutions.[61]
- How is education and training with regard to mediation organised? What kind of institutions and organisations exist to support their members and mediation in general?[62]
- Which are the areas of application of mediation?[63]
- What statistical data exist in Switzerland that would help us understand the role and scope of mediation? As will be explained shortly, there is an extended survey of 2008 which was made by the SDM (Schweizerischer Dachverband für Mediation), the Swiss umbrella organisation of mediation.[64]

ii. Statistical Data and Surveys

In most cases, mediation in civil matters takes place in private. Therefore, it is very difficult to evaluate how much mediation occurs in Switzerland. Fortunately, the SDM, which is the Swiss umbrella organisation of mediation, recently (2008) carried out a large survey regarding mediation in Switzerland (see Figures 2 and 3).[65] One thousand mediators—more or less all of whom were members of the organisations which were themselves members of the SDM—were asked to fill in a detailed questionnaire. In total, 354 mediators responded to the survey. The most important results are the following.

a. Extension of Mediation in Switzerland. The survey lists 3,513 mediations concerning civil matters. In general, it is difficult to provide an estimate of the exact percentage of the disputes resolved through mediation instead of adjudication. With regard to mediations related to family matters, we are aware of the total amount of divorces (19,321). According to the survey, most of the 1,547 reported family mediations were divorce cases. If the several hundred mediation cases not included in the survey were added in, it could be assumed that approximately 10 per cent of all divorce disputes are resolved through mediation.

59 Meier, *Schweizerisches Zivilprozessrecht* 592.
60 See I.E.i.b and more detailed in III.B.
61 See I.E.iv.
62 See I.E.iii.
63 See I.E.v.
64 See I.E.ii.
65 See <www.infomediation.ch/cms/index.php?id=145>. For all the results of the survey see especially 'Detailergebnisse der Umfrage Mediation Schweiz 2008', available at <www.infomediation.ch/cms/uploads/media/Umfrage_Detailbericht_Alle_Graph_5nov09_d.pdf>.

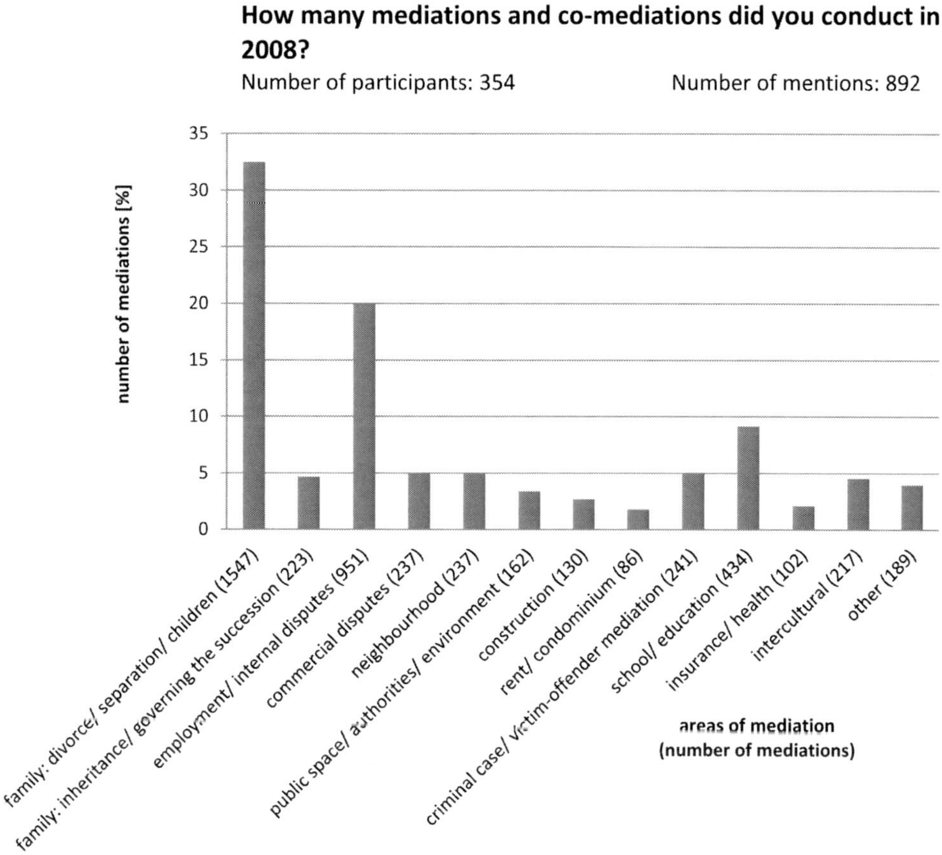

Figure 2. Number of mediations conducted in 2008 by field.

b. Main Fields of Mediation. The survey allows us to discern quite accurately just which fields of mediation are the main ones. The sole uncertainty relates to the number of employment-related mediations, since a number of psychologists tend to mediate in the frame of management consultancies without calling their procedures mediations and without being a member of a mediation organisation.

Not surprisingly, family mediation is the most important field of mediation (1,547, in comparison to 1,966 mediations in other civil matter fields). The next most important field of mediation is employment-related mediation. As mentioned above, in my opinion, the figure of 951 does not reflect reality. It would be fair to assume that mediations concerning work disputes are nearly as frequent as in family matters. The percentage of commercial mediation compared to all mediations concerning civil matters is quite small (237). It is less important than neighbourhood disputes (237). A

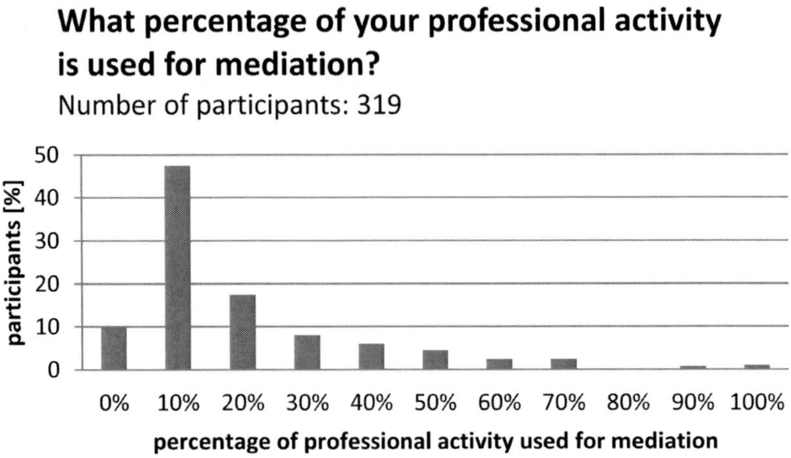

Figure 3. Mediation as a percentage of professional activity.

significant part of mediations with regard to civil matters are those concerning inheritance and governing succession (223).

c. Mediation as a (Small) Part-time Job of Several Professions. The survey also highlights that mediation in Switzerland is mainly a part-time area of employment in several professional branches (lawyers, psychologists, management consultants and social workers). For a significant part of them (more than 60 per cent), mediations comprise less than 20 per cent of their overall workload. Only very few can make a living out of mediation. The percentage of those mediators that devote 70 per cent of their professional activity to mediation-related activities is less than 10 per cent.

iii. Institutions, Titles and Standards

a. In General. In Switzerland, mediation is mainly self-regulated. As mentioned above, the Swiss confederation enacted some rules concerning court-related mediation.[66] The agreements between the parties themselves and between the parties and the mediator are mostly governed by contract law.[67] There are no rules about protecting the title of a mediator, qualifications for mediators or standards for pursuing the profession of mediator.[68] I would suggest that, at least for mediations paid for by the state, the cantonal laws could set up some standards. So far, though, none of the cantons have enacted such rules.

This regulatory gap is filled by private organisations, institutions and societies.

[66] See I.E.i.b.

[67] ML Goetz, '"Anwaltliche Mediation"—eine originär anwaltliche Tätigkeit' (2005) 14 *Aktuelle Juristische Praxis* 282f; Meier, *Schweizerisches Zivilprozessrecht* 586f; Ruggle in Spühler, Tenchio and Infanger (eds), *Basler Kommentar, Schweizerische Zivilprozessordnung* Art 215 comment 3.

[68] Explanatory Report ('Message') to the Swiss Code of Civil Procedure (Botschaft zur Schweizerischen Zivilprozessordnung) of 28 June 2006, 7335; see also Meier, *Schweizerisches Zivilprozessrecht* 590.

b. Organisations of Self-regulation and Titles. In Switzerland mediators are organised in various societies, groups and other institutions. National organisations include:[69] SDM, Schweizerischer Verein für Mediation (SVM), Schweizerische Kammer für Wirtschaftsmediation (SKWM), Mediationsforum Schweiz, Institut für Mediation and Verein Mediation im Strafrecht. Regional institutions include: Groupement pro Médiation in Geneva, Centro Coppia e Famiglia in Mendrisio, Association vaudoise pour la médiation familiale, Mediation Center Zürich, Verein Mediation Region Basel, Arbeitskreis Mediation Schwyz and finally the SAV (Swiss Bar Association).

Both the national and regional institutions have the same aims. Their goal is to promote mediation amongst members of the public and to ensure a high standard in mediation as a profession.[70] In order to become a member of one of these organisations, mediators have to fulfil high standards and, particularly, have received training of at least 120 contact hours. Also, some of these organisations require that their members prove that they work as mediators on a regular basis.[71]

Several of them grant a special title to their members. A member of the SAV is entitled to obtain the title of 'mediator SAV' if she/he can provide evidence of attendance at a recognised school of at least 120 contact hours.[72] Furthermore, in order to maintain this title, the mediator shall attend seminars on mediation of several hours length.[73] Very respected titles are also those of the SDM–FSM and the SVM, for which participants are required to attend at least 200 contact hours of training and coursework.[74]

All the aforementioned organisations offer further education to their members and continue to create a network for contacts between mediation professionals.

c. Education and Training. There is a wide range of education and training offers throughout Switzerland.

Several private and public institutions offer a complete programme of education in mediation. The most important are:[75] Nachdiplomkurs Mediation in Wirtschaft, Umwelt und Verwaltung at the Fachhochschule Aargau; Nachdiplomkurs Mediation, Verhandeln und Konfliktmanagement at the Hochschule für Soziale Arbeit Luzern; Ausbildung in Wirtschaftsmediation at the Institut für Rechtswissenschaft und Rechtspraxis, University of St Gallen and the Zentrum für Wirtschaftsmediation; Basisausbildung in Mediation und Ausbildung in Familienmediation, organised by

[69] See also I Meier, 'Mediation and Conciliation in Switzerland' in N Alexander (ed), *Global Trends in Mediation*, 2nd edn (Alphen aan den Rijn, Kluwer Law International, 2006) 371, 379.

[70] See, eg Art 3 of the statutes of the Schweizerischer Dachverband für Mediation (SDM), available at <www.infomediation.ch/cms/fileadmin/dokumente/de/gesetze/sdm_fsm_statuten.pdf> and Art 3 of the statutes of the Schweizerischer Verein für Mediation (SVM), available at <www.mediation-svm.ch/svm_statut.php>.

[71] See the regulations concerning the recognition of the title 'Mediator SVM', point 1.4, available at <www.mediation-svm.ch/svm_st_reglement.php>.

[72] See the regulations concerning the recognition of the title 'Mediator SAV', point 3.2, available at <mediation.sav-fsa.ch/Reglemente.1394.0.html>.

[73] See the regulations concerning the recognition of the title 'Mediator SAV', point 6.1, available at <mediation.sav-fsa.ch/Reglemente.1394.0.html>.

[74] See, eg the regulations concerning the recognition of the title 'Mediator SDM-FSM', point 8, available at <www.infomediation.ch/cms/uploads/media/Anerkennungsreglement2011_03.pdf>.

[75] See also a list of institutions which provide recognised courses, available at <www.infomediation.ch/cms/index.php?id=188&L=0%27%20and%201%3D1%20> and Meier, 'Mediation and Conciliation in Switzerland'.

the Institut für systemische Entwicklung und Fortbildung in Zurich; Ausbildung in Familienmediation at the Zentrum für Agogik in Basel; mediation education at the Fachhochschule für Soziale Arbeit in Berne; the European Master in Mediation degree programme at the Institut Universitaire Kurt Bösch in Sion; mediation education at the Institut d'études Sociales in Geneva; and mediation training with the law firm Egger, Philipps + Partner AG.

Subject to a few exceptions, all of these programmes entail intensive education and training in mediation, with an average of 200 contact hours. The content of most of these programmes and the topics addressed are based on the European Charter for the Training of Family Mediators in the Areas of Separation and Divorce.[76] Egger, Philipps + Partner AG in Zurich provides a shorter training programme (approximately 80 hours) focusing on the needs of lawyers.

Unlike the law schools in the US and Australia, Swiss law faculties have not embraced either the theory or the skills of mediation as part of the general law curriculum. To the author's knowledge, only the law faculty of the University of Zurich has been offering mediation seminars for students, this occurring since 1998.

iv. Who Offers Mediation?

a. Lawyers. Initially, Swiss lawyers were not very enthusiastic about mediation. Nowadays, this attitude has changed radically. Nowadays, lawyers are competing aggressively for their share of the so far rather modest market for resolving disputes through mediation. The following facts provide adequate information to substantiate this claim.

The SAV created the title of Mediator SAV in order to give its members an advantage in the mediation market. The requirements for this title are completion of a training course of at least 120 hours and attendance at a one-day seminar specifically for lawyer mediators. In order to retain this title, several hours of further education are required in a certain period of time (16 hours within 3 years).[77] The first accredited titles were granted in the summer of 2003. Today (2011), 319 out of the 8,423 (2010) members of SAV are 'mediators SAV'.[78]

In all cantons of Switzerland, there are family/divorce lawyers who offer mediation, often in cooperation with psychologists.[79] A number of lawyers are more focused on business mediation. Accordingly, a group of lawyers founded the Swiss Chamber of Commercial Mediation in Zurich in 1997.[80]

The majority of participants in mediation training programmes across the board are drawn from the legal profession.

[76] C Bono-Hörler, *Familienmediation im Bereiche von Ehetrennung und Ehescheidung, Eine interdisziplinäre Betrachtung unter besonderer Berücksichtigung der Rolle des Rechts und der Rechtsanwälte*, Diss Zurich (Zurich, Schulthess Polygraphischer Verlag, 1999) 122.

[77] See the regulations concerning the recognition of the title 'Mediator SAV', point 6.1, available at <mediation.sav-fsa.ch/Reglemente.1394.0>.

[78] See the register of mediators SAV at <mediation.sav-fsa.ch/Verzeichnis-Mediatoren.1402.0.html> and the total number of SAV members in 2010 at <www.sav-fsa.ch/Mitgliederstatistik.793.0.html>. So far no statistical data for 2011 exists.

[79] Bono-Hörler, *Familienmediation im Bereiche von Ehetrennung und Ehescheidung* 171f; Liatowitsch, 'Anhang Mediation' comments 89 and 120.

[80] Schweizerische Kammer für Wirtschaftsmediation (SKWM), see <www.skwm.ch/index-en.php?frameset=1>.

b. Psychologists and Other Professional Backgrounds of Mediators. Psychologists are the other professionals who have a major stake in the mediation market. At the beginning of the mediation movement, the majority of mediators had an educational background in psychology. Nowadays, lawyers are equally important.

A mediator with an education in psychology would mostly mediate in family matters. However, mediation in employment disputes, especially conflicts in teams and departments at work, are handled by these individuals as well. In these fields, mediation is often integrated into management consultancies and/or team coaching.

Psychologists working as mediators are typically members of the SVM (the Swiss Organisation of Mediators), and also have the highly respected title of a 'mediator SVM'. In order to obtain this title, a member needs not only an education of more than 240 hours but also two years of experience as a mediator.[81]

The third group of mediators comes from other professions such as social workers and people from all sorts of backgrounds. Social workers mediate mostly as employees of a public or semi-public mediation institution.

c. Public and Semi-public Institutions. Mediation in Switzerland is mainly offered by private individuals with the same background as described above. However, in most cantons, as well as in many cities and communities, mediation is also provided by public and semi-public institutions, mainly in the area of family mediation.[82]

Most of these institutions are private organisations maintained by the catholic and protestant churches and subsidised by the state. The costs and expenses that parties have to bear are limited and calculated according to their income.

Mediations are typically conducted by a team of (employed) social workers and/or external lawyers and psychologists. The structure of the compensation of these private sector participants is mainly defined by the amount of hours spent on a case.

The quality of these mediations is usually very high. It can be assumed that these institutions probably attract about a third of all mediations. The problem with these institutions is that they dry up and undercut the mediation market for private mediators.

v. Fields of Application

a. Family Disputes. In Switzerland, mediation is mostly used in the field of family law (divorce cases).[83] However, the exact number of mediation procedures in divorce cases is difficult to calculate. As already mentioned, a recent survey suggests that the percentage of mediated cases is about 10 per cent of all divorce cases in Switzerland.

There are mediators who are specialised in family mediation in all Swiss cantons. As already mentioned,[84] family mediations are often conducted as co-mediations, involving both a lawyer and a psychologist as co-mediators. In the canton of Zurich

[81] See the regulations concerning the recognition of the title 'Mediator SVM', point 2.1, available at <www.mediation-svm.ch/svm_st_reglement.php> and the regulatory statutes of the regulations, point 2.1, available at <www.mediation-svm.ch/svm_st_ausfuhrungs.php>.

[82] See, eg 'Paarberatung Zürich', available at <www.paarberatung-zh.ch> and 'Zentralstelle für Ehe- und Familienberatung Zürich', available at <www.zefzh.ch/index.html>.

[83] Liatowitsch, 'Anhang Mediation' comments 43 and 86. Concerning family mediation see especially Bono-Hörler, *Familienmediation im Bereiche von Ehetrennung und Ehescheidung.*

[84] See I.E.iv.a.

there are also public agencies which offer pro bono family mediation services for low income disputants.[85]

Several special educational programmes are also offered with regard to family mediation.[86]

b. Commercial Disputes.[87] In the last 20 years, considerable efforts have been made to introduce mediation in the resolution of commercial disputes. There are several mediation training programmes available which are specialised in training commercial mediators.[88] As already mentioned, the Swiss Chamber of Commercial Mediation was founded in 1997. Today, the Chamber works together with the Swiss Chamber of Commerce, which in 2007 formulated mediation rules—in addition to the arbitration rules.[89] The Swiss Chamber of Commerce supports a mediation proceeding by appointing a mediator if the parties themselves cannot agree. The Swiss Chamber of Commercial Mediation awards the title of 'Mediator SKWM'. Mediation clauses are gradually replacing or supplementing arbitration clauses in commercial contracts.

Despite these efforts, the practice of mediation has not yet had a major impact on the business world. Hardly any mediator in Switzerland can claim to have a broad and extensive experience in commercial mediation.

The 2008 survey of the SDM documents 237 business-related mediations. The estimated number of non-reported cases is probably not much higher. Swiss Chamber of Commerce statistics document only eight mediations in 2008 and seven in 2009.

c. Conflicts at Work and in the Office. The mediation of disputes between employees of private companies or public agencies is another significant area of practice.[90] Several factors favour mediation in this sector. Typically, workplace disputes involve many personal and psychological factors; the disputing parties often cannot solve the problem without acting together because the dispute involves negotiating a working relationship for the future. Another incentive to participate is that failure to take part in mediation may be frowned upon by the employer and thus could result in unfavourable treatment by the employer towards the *uncooperative employee*.

Resolving conflicts in a public or private organisation is a task not only for mediators but also for many other professionals, such as organisational psychologists, coaches and other business advisers. Therefore, mediators in this specific field typically offer other business services as well as mediation.

vi. Summary

In Switzerland, mediation in its narrower sense, as it is understood and defined in this chapter, is mainly restricted to disputes where personal and psychological aspects are dominant, such as family disputes and conflicts at work. For disputes where commer-

[85] Ibid. See also Meier, 'Mediation and Conciliation in Switzerland' 375.

[86] See I.E.iii.c.

[87] Concerning commercial mediation see especially S Dekker, 'Wirtschaftsmediation' in GG Zindel, PR Peyer and B Schott (eds), *Wirtschaftsrecht in Bewegung. Festgabe zum 65. Geburtstag von Peter Forstmoser* (Zurich/St Gallen, Dike Verlag, Zurich/Basel/Geneva, Schulthess Juristische Medien, 2008), 557ff.

[88] See also Meier, 'Mediation and Conciliation in Switzerland', 378.

[89] See <www.sccam.org/sm/download/swiss_mediation_rules_version_2006_deutsch.pdf>.

[90] See <www.infomediation.ch/cms/uploads/media/Umfrage_Detailbericht_Alle_Graph_5nov09_d.pdf>.

cial and financial interests are at stake, such as in business disputes, the parties clearly prefer conciliation to mediation.

F. ADR Procedures for Consumer Disputes

i. Introduction

In Switzerland, there are special forms of ADR proceedings for consumer disputes. The main branches are: banks, insurance companies, travel agencies and the telecommunications industry.

Most of these ADR proceedings are not provided for by law. An exception in this regard is in the telecommunications industry.[91] All the other conciliation institutions that are described in the following sections are completely self-regulated. They are usually implemented by a branch of industry, such as the banking, insurance or travel sector.

There are two main types of ADR forms for consumer disputes: the ombudsman model[92] and conciliation bodies with equal representation.[93] In the latter case, the targeted branches and consumer organisations are equally represented in the conciliation proceedings in question.

ii. Ombudsman Institutions

a. In General. The ombudsman idea, originally a public institution of the Scandinavian countries,[94] spread across Europe in the 1960s, similar to the American mediation movement that has spread throughout the world since the 1980s. In Switzerland, the ombudsman procedure initially became important in the public sector. However, in the last 20 years it has become even more significant in the private sector, mainly in the field of consumer disputes.

The most important ombudsman institutions are those of the banking industry, the insurance business,[95] the travel industry and the telecommunications sector.[96] Other ombudsman proceedings have been established in, for instance, the following areas: funeral services, hearing aid providers, hotel industry, public transportation and financial service providers.[97] In this chapter we only take into deeper consideration

[91] See I.F.ii.e.

[92] See I.F.ii.

[93] See I.F.iii.

[94] See, eg I Jent-Sørensen, *Der dänische Ombudsmann,* Diss Zurich (Zurich, Schulthess Polygraphischer Verlag, 1985) 27ff.

[95] In the insurance industry, there are two ombudsman institutions, one that is responsible for the health insurance sector (hereinafter called 'health insurance ombudsman') and one that is competent to deal with other insurance disputes, as far as they do not concern social insurance issues (hereinafter called 'private insurance ombudsman'). See the explanation on Switzerland's Official Web Portal (sub-chapter State and Law, Mediation Services, Ombudsmen, available at <www.ch.ch/private/00093/00106/00534/00535/index.html?lang=en>).

[96] Regarding the number of inquiries treated by these institutions in 2010 see I.F.ii.e and I.F.ii.f.

[97] The website of the Federal Consumer Affairs Bureau (sub-chapter Themen, Aussergerichtliche Streitbeilegung) provides a list of the above-mentioned ombudsman institutions and other conciliation bodies, which is directly linked to the homepages of these institutions, see <www.konsum.admin.ch/themen/00113/index.html?lang=de>. Therefore see also the English language ombudsmen list provided

the ombudsman institutions of the banking, insurance, travel and telecommunications sectors.

The ombudsman typically has a dual role: as a neutral third person, he works out a solution proposal after having heard both parties. Subsequently, he sends this proposal to the parties. Should the industry supplier not fully accept it, the ombudsman tries to negotiate a reasonable compromise with him. In this regard, the ombudsman acts to a certain extent as an 'advocate' of the consumer.

In the subsequent sections the ombudsman institutions are discussed mainly regarding the following issues: access to proceedings, independency, structure of proceedings, importance as ADR institution and assessment.

b. Access to Proceedings. Ombudsman proceedings are easily accessible to all affected parties. In general, the consumers either do not have to pay anything or pay only a very small amount.[98] Regarding their concerns, consumers can consult the ombudsman in either oral or written form.[99]

The only—albeit serious—problem is that most ombudsmen refuse or are reluctant to deal with claims if the affected consumers are already represented by a lawyer.[100] In practice, this leads to the consumer having to choose between a cheap and fast procedure without the support of a lawyer or the filing of a suit in an ordinary court proceeding, in which he is represented by a lawyer.

c. Independency. All ombudsmen are legally independent. They are employed by an independent foundation, and from a legal point of view no one can give them any instructions on how to deal with their cases.

In terms of fact, however, there are some aspects that limit this independency. On the foundation boards, the branches in question are always represented by two or more people. The other board members are usually politicians. or sometimes representatives of consumer organisations. Even if the representatives of these branches of industry hold the minority of seats on the boards, they have a disproportionately high influence in these institutions, especially with regard to the nomination and selection of an ombudsman.

Furthermore, the fact that an ombudsman always has to negotiate with essentially the same set of individuals representing large suppliers decreases the prospects of achieving the best solutions for the consumer in any particular case.[101]

by Switzerland's Official Web Portal (sub-chapter State and Law, Mediation Services, available at <www.ch.ch/private/00093/00106/index.html?lang=en>). See also M Krampf, 'Zum Schlichter statt zum Richter' (2011) No 3 *Beobachter*, available at <www.beobachter.ch/justiz-behoerde/buerger-verwaltung/artikel/ombudsstellen_zum-schlichter-statt-zum-richter/>.

[98] According to the regulation on fees (Art 4) of the telecommunications ombudsman institution the supplier is charged CHF 20 for the procedure, see <www.ombudscom.ch/media/file/23.Gebuehrenreglement_dt_01_08_2011.pdf>. The other ombudsman proceedings that are described more closely in this chapter are free of charge. See also M Krampf, 'Zum Schlichter statt zum Richter'.

[99] See I.F.ii.d.

[100] M Krampf, 'Zum Schlichter statt zum Richter'.

[101] See I.F.ii.g.

d. Proceedings. The ombudsman usually handles a specific case in the following manner:[102] the consumer who wants to complain about a supplier (insurance company, bank, travel agency or telecommunications service provider) contacts the ombudsman office either by telephone, e-mail or letter. The vast majority of cases can already be settled or dismissed at this stage because most complaints are evidently unfounded or the ombudsman is not competent to deal with them.[103]

In a minority of cases, the ombudsman arrives at the conclusion that a claim may be justified. In this event, the consumer has to submit the complaint in writing, containing statements of the facts and the documents and pieces of evidence required to intervene effectually with the corresponding providers.[104] Thereafter, the ombudsman asks the supplier to describe his point of view on the matter in dispute. At this point, the ombudsman reviews the claim and the statements of the supplier. A personal meeting between the two parties seldom takes place. If he reaches the decision that the complaint is at least partly founded, he works out a proposed solution, which is based not only on legal criteria but also on reasons of equity.

Afterwards, the ombudsman sends this proposal to the parties. Should the supplier not fully accept it, the ombudsman tries to negotiate a reasonable compromise with him. In most cases, the consumer accepts whatever the ombudsman can get from the supplier because going to court for most consumers does not constitute a genuine alternative. In the event of disputes with banks, this may be different because in these cases the value of the claim is often much higher than in normal consumer disputes.

The ombudsman's proposal can be accepted or rejected by each party, but in certain cases of the travel industry the suppliers declare in advance that they will accept the outcome of the ombudsman proceedings.[105] In these cases, the ombudsman proceeding is no longer a special type of conciliation procedure, but is instead a (binding) arbitration.[106]

[102] On this see <www.ombudsman-assurance.ch>; <secure.om-kv.ch>; <www.bankingombudsman.ch>; and <www.ombudsman-touristik.ch>. Regarding the special procedure of the telecommunications ombudsman institution see below I.F.ii.e.

[103] In 2010, the private insurance ombudsman had to deal with 3,983 inquiries. Of these, 511 cases (13%) were dismissed due to a lack of jurisdiction. Of the remaining 3,472 cases, 3,072 (89%) could be settled already at this stage because they were obviously unfounded. See *Annual Report 2010 of the Private Insurance Ombudsman* 1, available at <www.ombudsman-assurance.ch/html/downloads/Jahresbericht_2010_Dt.pdf>. The Swiss banking Ombudsman concluded 1,984 cases in 2010, of which 1,615 cases (81%) could be settled at the beginning of the procedure. See *Annual Report 2010 of the Swiss Banking Ombudsman* 10 and 16, available at <www.bankingombudsman.ch/fileadmin/download/pdf/jahresberichte/bom_jb_2010_de.pdf>.

[104] In 2010, the private insurance ombudsman requested a supplier's statement in 400 (11%) out of 3,472 cases that fell within his jurisdiction. See *Annual Report 2010 of the Private Insurance Ombudsman* 1. The banking Ombudsman intervened in 369 (19%) out of the 1,984 cases considered in 2010. See *Annual Report 2010 of the Swiss Banking Ombudsman* 10 and 16.

[105] In Germany, for instance, this is the case with the banking and insurance ombudsman. The suppliers of the banking and insurance sector have undertaken to accept all decisions of the ombudsman, provided that the sum in dispute does not exceed a certain amount. On this see the respective websites, available at <www.bankenverband.de/themen/geldinfos-finanzen/schlichtungsstelle/ombudsstelle-ablauf-des-verfahrens> and <www.versicherungsombudsmann.de/Navigationsbaum/IhreBeschwerde/Verfahrensende/index.html>.

[106] The Swiss Financial Market Supervisory Authority (FINMA) has recently made the proposal to prescribe by law a binding effect for all decisions of the banking Ombudsman in which the sum in dispute does not exceed a certain amount. On this see the reluctant position of the Swiss banking Ombudsman, available at <www.bankingombudsman.ch/fileadmin/download/pdf/sonstiges/Vernehmlassung_zum_FINMA_Vertriebsbericht_2010.pdf>.

e. 'Ombudscom', the Only Ombudsman Institution Provided by Law. The ombudsman institutions of the private sector are usually completely self-regulated by the branches in question. An exception to this is made in the telecommunications industry.[107]

In Article 12c(1) of the Telecommunications Act (TCA), the Federal Office of Communications (OFCOM) has been given the duty of establishing a conciliation body for disputes between consumers and providers of telecommunications and value-added services or to entrust a third party with this task. The OFCOM has opted for the second variation and therefore mandated the 'Ombudscom' foundation. Although 'Ombudscom' is an independent institution, it is different from the other ombudsman bodies of the private sector, under supervision of the OFCOM.

'Ombudscom' has decided to set up an ombudsman procedure which is structured similar to court proceedings. After submitting the complaint form to 'Ombudscom', there is a first and, if needed, a second exchange of letters between the consumer and the supplier. In case the parties do not reach a settlement, the ombudsman renders a decision, which has, however, no binding legal effect.[108]

In order to seek guidance, 'Ombudscom' was consulted by 3,050 persons in 2010. This led to 1,165 cases.[109] Of these, 850 cases were concluded in 2010. In 164 cases the consumer withdrew his complaint after having read the supplier's statement; in 354 cases the parties reached a self-contained settlement; and in 332 cases the ombudsman authored a decision, 234 of which were accepted by both parties.[110]

f. Importance of Ombudsman Proceedings. The above-mentioned ombudsman proceedings are of great importance to the branches of the industry in question.[111] It can be assumed that these ADR institutions absorb the vast majority of consumer disputes in these branches. Ombudsman proceedings are also very efficient. Most cases can somehow be settled, even though the consumer often gets nothing or only little.

In 2010, the private insurance ombudsman requested a supplier's statement (intervention) in only 400 (11%) out of 3,472 cases. A total of 348 'intervention cases' could be concluded in 2010, with the insurer making concessions to the injured persons in 231 of those cases (66%). The other 3,072 cases could be settled without the need of an intervention because they were obviously unfounded.[112] The banking ombudsman intervened with the suppliers in 369 (19%) out of the 1,984 cases completed in 2010. From this number, the banks made concessions to its consumers in 87 cases (23%). The

[107] For details see below III.D.

[108] Concerning the procedure see the rules of procedure of the 'Ombudscom' foundation, see <www.ombudscom.ch/media/file/26.2011_1_1_Verfahrensreglement_deutsch.pdf>.

[109] According to the terminology of 'Ombudscom', a case is established if the consumer has submitted the complaint form under the conditions set out in Art 5(1) rules of procedure of the 'Ombudscom' foundation, ibid.

[110] On this see *Annual Report 2010 of the Telecommunications Ombudsman Institution* 10ff, available at <www.ombudscom.ch/media/file/16.2010_Jahresbericht_deutsch.pdf>.

[111] In 2009/2010, the ombudsman institutions of the insurance, banking and travel sectors treated the following number of inquiries: private insurance ombudsman, 4,210/3,983 (requests received); health insurance ombudsman, 5,523/6,303 (requests received); banking ombudsman, 4,198/1,984 (cases concluded); travel ombudsman, 1,863/1,746 (requests received). On these statistical values see *Annual Report 2010 of the Private Insurance Ombudsman* 1; *Annual Report 2010 of the Health Insurance Ombudsman* 4, <secure.om-kv.ch/2010/Taetigkeitsbericht_2010.pdf>; *Annual Report 2010 of the Swiss Banking Ombudsman* 10; and *Annual Reports 2009 and 2010 of the Travel Ombudsman* 3 respectively 2, <www.ombudsman-touristik.ch/unsere-tipps/archiv-downloads/>.

[112] See *Annual Report 2010 of the Private Insurance Ombudsman* 1 and 8.

other 1,615 cases could be settled, due to their obviously unfounded nature, without the need of an intervention.[113] In those cases where the ombudsman, after having heard the supplier's statement (intervention), reached a decision that the consumer complaint was at least partly founded, the success rate, ie the decision meeting with acceptance of both parties, was around 90%.[114]

g. Assessment. Ombudsmen proceedings are suitable to meet the needs of both parties (consumers and suppliers).

It is exactly this kind of procedure that an angry consumer, who feels 'cheated' by a supplier, is looking for. For consumers, it is either free of charge or very inexpensive; the ombudsman office can be contacted by telephone, e-mail or letter; there is not much paperwork to complete; additional documents can be handed in anytime during proceedings; hearings, which can be very exhausting and time-consuming, take place in only very few cases; normally, it is the ombudsman and not the consumer who tries to negotiate a compromise with the supplier; the procedure is conducted within a very short time; and if the complaint is founded, the consumer usually gets at least a part of what he has been asking for. The average consumer would not go to court unless either the sum in dispute runs to at least several thousand Swiss francs or other very important legal interests are affected. Therefore, contacting an ombudsman institution often represents the only practicable way for consumers to resolve a dispute. In any event, the consumer is free to go to court anytime.

Settling a dispute in an ombudsman procedure is also in the supplier's interest (short duration of proceedings, low costs and minimal paperwork to complete). It ties up far fewer resources than a court proceeding would. Furthermore, compared to court rulings, the ombudsman's 'decision' does not set a kind of precedent for similar cases, which could be unfavourable for the supplier. This is due to the fact that, on the one hand, ombudsmen normally do not deliver a binding decision and, on the other, most cases do not result in any sort of publication.

The annual reports of the different ombudsman institutions, which are usually presented at a press conference, may outline some complaints the ombudsman had to deal with frequently. However, the criticism of certain suppliers is always moderate and well balanced. Harsher criticism is only expressed against the 'black sheep' of the branches in question. In this respect, there is a quality check, though it is narrowly restricted. All these advantages have led to the fact that most ombudsman proceedings have been implemented by branches of industry and not by government or consumer organisations.

The problems of these proceedings lie in the outcome. It can be assumed or, alternatively, has to be feared that the proposed solution grants only a part of what the consumer could have obtained under a court judgment or conventional settlement.

There are several reasons for this: the election procedure for ombudsmen, in which the representatives of the suppliers always have a disproportionately high influence, favours people who are not overly consumer-friendly. Furthermore, the ombudsman can only work efficiently if the cases can be solved within a short time. This is only possible if he does not insist on the full amount to which the consumer would be oth-

[113] See *Annual Report 2010 of the Swiss Banking Ombudsman* 10 and 16.
[114] M Krampf, 'Zum Schlichter statt zum Richter'.

erwise entitled, but, instead, provides a solution he knows will most likely be accepted by the supplier. Because ombudsmen always have to deal with more or less the same customer agents of a few large suppliers, they become attuned to one another. On average, this may lead to a rather moderate settlement level. All in all, this means that ombudsmen who are too consumer-friendly cannot survive in the long run.

iii. Conciliation Institutions with Equal Representation

a. In General. Apart from the different ombudsman proceedings, there are ADR procedures of private conciliation institutions in which consumer organisations and representatives of the branches in question are equally represented. This form of ADR can be found, for instance, in the textile sector and in the more important area of the advertising industry.

The Textile Industry Conciliation Board provides a normal ADR procedure, which has the goal of resolving bilateral conflicts between a consumer and a supplier.[115] The conciliation procedure of the advertising industry is conducted by the Swiss Fair Trading Commission. This self-regulatory organisation aims to guarantee a high standard of integrity in the whole advertising industry.[116] Apart from resolving individual disputes, these proceedings also serve to develop general principles for the advertising sector.[117] Therefore, complaints are only treated if they are of general importance.[118]

b. Proceedings and Decision-making. Both procedures are easily accessible to all affected parties. They are free of charge[119] or quite affordable,[120] and are usually conducted within a short time. Although consumers need to submit their complaints in writing, including their statements of the facts and the documents and pieces of evidence required to judge the cases, the proceedings are very informal and consumer friendly. Personal meetings between the two parties do not take place.[121]

Unlike the Textile Industry Conciliation Board, the Swiss Fair Trading Commission

[115] The Textile Industry Conciliation Board of the Swiss Dry Cleaners Association, the Swiss Fashion Stores Association and Swiss consumer organisations tries to resolve disputes that have either arisen between consumers and dry cleaners or consumers and textile retailers. For this see Switzerland's Official Web Portal (sub-chapter State and Law, Mediation Services, Ombudsmen, available at <www.ch.ch/private/00093/00106/00534/00535/index.html?lang=en>), see also the information sheet of the Textile Industry Conciliation Board, available at <www.textilpflege.ch/nc/verband/schadenfaelle.html?cid=166&did=262&sechash=b550e9ea>.

[116] This includes 'any form of advertising, direct marketing, sponsorship, sales promotion and public relations'. See Switzerland's Official Web Portal (sub-chapter State and law, Mediation services, Ombudsmen, available at <www.ch.ch/private/00093/00106/00534/00535/index.html?lang=en>).

[117] Principles of integrity in commercial communications, see <www.lauterkeit.ch/pdf/grundsaetze.pdf>.

[118] Art 10 rules of organisation of the Swiss Fair Trading Commission, see <www.lauterkeit.ch/pdf/reglement.pdf>.

[119] The Swiss Fair Trading Commission only charges a handling fee (CHF 500) if the complaint is directed against a competitor (Art 18 rules of organisation of the Swiss Fair Trading Commission, ibid).

[120] The Textile Industry Conciliation Board normally charges a handling fee of CHF 100 for both, consumers and suppliers. If the consumer prevails, the supplier has to refund the handling fee to him. See the information sheet of the Textile Industry Conciliation Board, available at <www.textilpflege.ch/nc/verband/schadenfaelle.html?cid=166&did=262&sechash=b550e9ea>.

[121] Regarding these explanations see the rules of organisation of the Swiss Fair Trading Commission, <www.lauterkeit.ch/pdf/reglement.pdf>, and the information sheet of the Textile Industry Conciliation Board, <www.textilpflege.ch/nc/verband/schadenfaelle.html?cid=166&did=262&sechash=b550e9ea>. The founder's agreement of the Textile Industry Conciliation Board, which, among other things, sets out the procedure, has not been published.

decides claims not only based on the law, but also on the above-mentioned (I.F.iii.a) self-developed general principles and on guidelines of the ICC (International Chamber of Commerce) Code of Advertising Practice.[122]

The effects of the decisions in the procedures respectively used are very different.

- The decisions of the Textile Industry Conciliation Board are not binding on the parties and therefore 'only' have the character of a conciliation proposal.[123]
- The decisions of the Swiss Fair Trading Commission are binding in the sense that the Commission, where the supplier continues to conduct himself unfairly, can impose, among others penalties, the following sanctions against him: publication of the decision, recommendation to industry organisations to exclude the supplier from membership, and a request made to newspapers and other advertising media to suspend the disputed publication.[124] However, for state courts such decisions are not binding. Therefore, both parties still have the possibility of challenging the outcome of the conciliation procedure at court.

c. Importance, Effectiveness and Assessment of Conciliation Institutions with Equal Representation. The Textile Industry Conciliation Board does not have many cases to decide because the procedure provided by this Board is probably not well enough known, but the few complaints filed with this conciliation body are handled very effectively.[125]

The Swiss Fair Trading Commission is a very important and effective self-regulatory organisation. In the last few years the commission handled, on average, 300 complaints per annum.[126] It can be assumed that this well-known procedure attracts the vast majority of all advertising disputes; in other words, this procedure almost completely replaces state court proceedings.

In my opinion, these conciliation institutions with equal representation constitute an almost perfect form of ADR procedure for solving consumer disputes. The equal representation of consumer organisations and representatives of the branches in question in the decision-making body guarantees a well-balanced outcome of the procedure. The proceeding itself is very informal and consumer-friendly.[127] The decisions are not binding (without *res iudicata* effect) like an arbitration award. I consider this to be an advantage rather than a disadvantage because it keeps the procedure simple and quick.

[122] See Principles of integrity in commercial communications p 2, available at <www.lauterkeit.ch/pdf/grundsaetze.pdf>, and Art 1(3) rules of organisation of the Swiss Fair Trading Commission, available at <www.lauterkeit.ch/pdf/reglement.pdf>. Regarding the ICC Code of Advertising Practice, see <www.lauterkeit.ch/pdf/ICC_CC2011E.pdf>.

[123] Founder's agreement of the Textile Industry Conciliation Board, 2.9 (not published).

[124] Art 20 rules of organisation of the Swiss Fair Trading Commission, see <www.lauterkeit.ch/pdf/reglement.pdf>.

[125] In 2010/2011, the Textile Industry Conciliation Board had to deal with 60 cases, of which 24 cases (40%) resulted in decisions in favour of the complainant (*Annual Report 2010/2011 of the Textile Industry Conciliation Board*, not published).

[126] See *Annual Report 2010 of the Swiss Fair Trading Commission* 32, available at <www.lauterkeit.ch/pdf/taetigkeit10.pdf>.

[127] However, compared to the value of clothing articles, the handling fee of CHF 100 charged by the Textile Industry Conciliation Board is too high.

II. GENERAL APPROACH OF THE LEGISLATOR AS REGARDS THE REGULATION OF ADR AND ADJUDICATION

A. In General

i. The Effect of Legal Regulation on the Use of ADR

As already seen, in Switzerland we find legal rules about ADR mainly for court-annexed mediation and conciliation.[128]

With the new regulation on mediation in the CCP, the legislator wanted to promote mediation in civil matters.[129] In my opinion, we can assume that the new rules in fact have this expected effect and that the amount of mediations in civil matters will increase for several reasons.

As I will discuss later, the rules foster mediation. But the legislative action itself has a fostering effect. A statutory regulation of mediation is an excellent form of advertising. It makes mediation a recognised institution of the legislator. Therefore, it has definitely challenged its still widespread image as a more esoteric form of dispute resolution with which serious lawyers do not deal.

Because mediation is now an official part of civil procedural law, it is part of the curriculum at every Swiss university. University textbooks have to dedicate at least a short chapter to it. Also, it can no longer be ignored in the commentaries for practitioners. The new legislation in procedural law has led to a growing number of articles on mediation in law journals and anthologies.[130]

Most, if not all, Swiss courts now have at least a leaflet about mediation on their web pages, with references to the web pages of mediation organisations and/or information on them.

The Swiss umbrella organisation of mediation (SDM), the Swiss Bar Association, the Swiss Chamber of Commerce and the Swiss association of judges for conciliation and mediation founded the working group KMS (Koordination Mediation Schweiz = coordination of mediation in Switzerland). Each canton has a cantonal working group. These groups collect information on cantonal legislation in this area and try to coordinate it.

Whether all these efforts will lead to more mediation and, if so, to what extent remains to be seen over the next few years.

ii. Reasons Given by the Legislator for Regulating ADR Procedures and the View in Academia

As regards the rules on conciliation in the new CCP, the legislator did not give any special reasons, since conciliation has always been part of the civil procedure.[131] Only the new rules concerning mediation need some explanation.

[128] See I.C and I.E.

[129] Explanatory Report ('Message') to the Swiss Code of Civil Procedure (Botschaft zur Schweizerischen Zivilprozessordnung) of 28 June 2006, 7335ff.

[130] For a detailed list see Meier, *Schweizerisches Zivilprozessrecht* 583.

[131] See Explanatory Report ('Message') to the Swiss Code of Civil Procedure (Botschaft zur Schweizerischen Zivilprozessordnung) of 28 June 2006, 7328.

In general, the new law follows the tradition of the former cantonal procedural laws, but the legislator also wanted to take into account important developments which had occurred in civil procedure abroad. One of them was ADR, and especially mediation. The legislator noticed that ADR was becoming increasingly important in European countries and worldwide.[132] In the government's explanatory report of 2006 to the draft of the new law, the EU regulations and green books concerning this topic were explicitly mentioned.[133] With the regulation of mediation, the Swiss legislator wanted to promote an institution which was obviously successfully applied in other countries.

A more profound regulation of mediation was also demanded by scholars and practitioners. They criticised a former draft of the new law, authored in 2003 by a commission of experts (mainly judges and lawyers), which mentioned mediation only incidentally in the rules on adjournment and in provisions concerning the right to refuse to give evidence.[134]

B. Incentives to Use Certain Types of ADR

i. The Regulation of ADR Procedures in the Early Conflict Resolution Phase

The Swiss legislator does not prefer conciliation to adjudication or vice versa. Both are equivalent goals of civil procedure. Although conciliation is held earlier,[135] there is no priority for this form of dispute resolution.

The parties cannot choose between conciliation and adjudication. The first step of a legal action is a mandatory conciliation led by a justice of the peace (Article 197 CCP). If the dispute cannot be settled, the parties can go to court (Article 209 CCP). After the first statements of the parties, another form of conciliation takes place—a settlement conference led by a trial judge (Article 226 CCP).

In the new CCP, mediation was added to conciliation and adjudication. However, unlike conciliation and adjudication, mediation is not designed as a further service of the court. The parties who want to mediate have to go to a mediator outside the court.[136] Despite this, one cannot say that mediation is less appreciated than adjudication and conciliation; the legislator simply thought that this represents the best solution for mediation.

[132] Explanatory Report ('Message') to the Swiss Code of Civil Procedure (Botschaft zur Schweizerischen Zivilprozessordnung) of 28 June 2006, 7252ff.

[133] Explanatory Report ('Message') to the Swiss Code of Civil Procedure (Botschaft zur Schweizerischen Zivilprozessordnung) of 28 June 2006, 7253; Green Paper on alternative dispute resolution in civil and commercial law, 19 April 2002, COM(2002) 196 final; Proposal for a directive of the European Parliament and the Council on certain aspects of mediation in civil and commercial matters, 22 October 2004, COM(2004) 718 final.

[134] I Meier, *Vorentwurf für eine Schweizerische Zivilprozessordnung* (Zurich/Basel/Geneva, Schulthess Juristische Medien, 2003) 53f.

[135] Explanatory Report ('Message') to the Swiss Code of Civil Procedure (Botschaft zur Schweizerischen Zivilprozessordnung) of 28 June 2006, 7328.

[136] See Art 215 CCP; Explanatory Report ('Message') to the Swiss Code of Civil Procedure (Botschaft zur Schweizerischen Zivilprozessordnung) of 28 June 2006, 7336; Meier, *Schweizerisches Zivilprozessrecht* 594.

In sum, Swiss procedural law combines adjudication and conciliation in one procedure and gives the parties the possibility, as a third option, to choose mediation instead of conciliation at every step of the procedure. The court can foster mediation by recommending it to the parties (Article 214(1) CCP) and/or—concerning the children's care in family disputes—by urging the parties to go to mediation (Article 297(2) CCP).

In general, the advantages and disadvantages of the three options lie in the special character and nature of each. Consequently, the parties can be expected to choose the one or the other, according to their preferences. It is only regarding the costs that the legislator has given preferential treatment to conciliation and adjudication. Whereas the Swiss legislator offers legal aid for conciliation and adjudication,[137] it is not generally provided for mediation, except in non-pecuniary matters concerning children (Article 218(1) and (2) CCP).[138] It should be noted that federal law does, however, explicitly give the cantons the power to offer legal aid in every case (Article 218(3) CCP).

ii. The Role of Legal Culture Regarding the Choice of ADR Procedures

As shown in the first part of this chapter, conciliation is extremely successful in Switzerland.[139] But mediation also plays a significant role, especially in disputes where psychological aspects are predominant.[140]

a. Conciliation. A very interesting but difficult question to answer is whether and to what extent the successes of conciliation are based on tradition or on objective factors such as the cost and length of adjudications, or on the special form of these institutions.

In Switzerland, there is a long and strong tradition in the legal culture of resolving disputes by a settlement and thus giving both parties a chance to save face.[141] This is certainly an important reason why conciliation is so successful, but one should not overestimate this reason. I am convinced that the Swiss model of intermingling conciliation and adjudication would also work in a completely different cultural environment.

b. Mediation. For Swiss culture, mediation in the sense described above[142] was and is a rather strange form of ADR. Openness towards a mostly strange opponent and a willingness to disclose one's real interests and wishes—traits which are needed in mediation—are not generally encountered in the Swiss culture. This might be the reason why media-

[137] See Art 118(1) lit b in conjunction with Art 95(2) CCP.

[138] F Emmel in Sutter-Somm, Hasenböhler and Leuenberger (eds), *Kommentar zur Schweizerischen Zivilprozessordnung (ZPO)* Art 117 comment 3; L Huber in Brunner, Gasser and Schwander (eds), *Schweizerische Zivilprozessordnung (ZPO)* Art 117 comment 6; V Rüegg in Spühler, Tenchio and Infanger (eds), *Basler Kommentar, Schweizerische Zivilprozessordnung* Art 118 comment 6.

[139] See I.C.iii and I.C.iv.

[140] See I.E.vi.

[141] See I.C.iv.

[142] See I.A.ii.

tion is mainly restricted to cases where an obvious solution cannot be found without looking at the psychological background of the dispute.[143]

iii. The Role of Lawyers Regarding ADR Procedures

In Switzerland, the conduct and duties of the attorneys are governed by federal law (mainly Article 12 Federal Act on the Freedom of Movement for Lawyers, FAFML) and the rules of conduct of the Swiss Bar Association.

Article 12 FAFML does not explicitly say that the lawyers have to point out to their clients the available ADR procedures, nor that they have to try to resolve a dispute amicably before going to court. However, there is no doubt that these duties lie in the general duty of an attorney to carefully advise his clients (Article 12 lit a FAFML) if an ADR procedure and/or a settlement would be in their best interests.

Unlike the FAFML, the conduct rules and standards of the Swiss Bar Association say in Article 9 specifically:

> Lawyers foster the amicable solution of disputes if this lies in the interest of the clients. In representing or advising a party, they support mediation if the parties already are involved in it or they take into account mediation if the parties are interested in it.

C. Restriction of Access to Court with a View to ADR

i. ADR Procedures as a Precondition for Starting Proceedings Before a State Court

As has been a feature of Swiss procedural law, the parties have to attend a conciliation meeting, normally led by a justice of the peace, before being allowed to take legal action at the trial court (Article 197 CCP). Therefore, attending a conciliation meeting is a precondition for starting proceedings before the court which ultimately decides the case.[144]

Exceptionally, in some cases (eg divorce cases) and for some procedures there is no conciliation meeting and a legal action has to be filed directly at the trial court.

ii. Mechanisms That Allow a Court to Refer a Dispute to an Alternative Dispute Resolution Mechanism

a. Conciliation. At any stage of a procedure, the court can invite the parties to a settle ment hearing (Article 124 (3) CCP). If they do not appear, they have to pay the additional costs for the conciliation procedure to the opposing party.

b. Mediation. The court can suggest mediation to the parties at any time during trial (Article 214(1) CCP). In family disputes concerning children, the court can even urge the parties to a mediation attempt (Article 297(2) CCP).[145] If the parties do not cooperate

[143] See I.E.i.c.
[144] See I.C.i.
[145] See also L Staub, 'Die Pflichtmediation als scheidungsbezogene Kindschutzmassnahme' [2009] *Zeitschrift des Bernischen Juristenvereins* 404ff; B Umbricht Lukas and U Gloor, 'Arbeitskreis 6: Angeordnete

in this case, apart from having to bear the additional costs for the mediation procedure, there are no sanctions.[146]

iii. The Competences of the Court Regarding Alternative Procedures

Conciliation in the frame of a settlement conference is always led by the judge who later decides the case, whether as a single judge or as a member of a panel of judges.[147]

On the other hand, mediation is not (yet) provided by the court.[148]

iv. Guarantee of the Quality of the Service with Regard to External Neutrals

In Switzerland, there are no legal rules to ensure the quality of a mediation recommended or ordered by the court.[149] The whole mediation industry is more or less based on self-regulation.[150]

A certain quality assurance takes place if and insofar as federal (Article 218(2) CCP, non-pecuniary matters concerning children under certain circumstances) or cantonal law provides legal aid for mediation or provides for mediation at no cost. A mediator who wants to be paid by the state needs to have recognised qualifications.[151]

Furthermore, the courts foster the quality of the mediators insofar as they distribute lists of mediators with recognised qualifications to the parties interested in mediation.

D. The Influence of Constitutional/Human Rights Law on ADR Regulations

Influences of the constitution and the human rights convention on ADR regulations are not discussed in Switzerland. In my opinion, this question should be answered as follows.

i. Conciliation

Conciliation in the context of a meeting at the conciliation authority or in a settlement conference during trial is part of the official court procedure. Therefore, all the constitutional and human rights principles also apply to the conciliation as far they are relevant to this procedure (Articles 29, 29a and 30 Federal Constitution; Article 6 European Convention on Human Rights). That includes the right of equal treatment, the right to be heard, the right to legal aid and principle of fairness.

The (in most cases) mandatory conciliation meeting hinders access to the court

Mediation' in I Schwenzer and A Büchler (eds), *Fünfte Schweizer Familienrecht§Tage* (Bern, Stämpfli Verlag, 2010) 161ff.

[146] D Steck in Spühler, Tenchio and Infanger (eds), *Basler Kommentar, Schweizerische Zivilprozessordnung* Art 297 comment 17. See also Art 213(3) CCP; Explanatory Report ('Message') to the Swiss Code of Civil Procedure (Botschaft zur Schweizerischen Zivilprozessordnung) of 28 June 2006, 7336.

[147] See I.C.iv.

[148] See I.E.i.b.

[149] See I.E.iii.a.

[150] See I.E.iii.

[151] See, eg canton of Aargau, s 23(2) Introductory Act to the Code of Civil Procedure (EG ZPO); canton of Fribourg, Art 126(3) Court Organisation Act; canton of Geneva, Art 67 Court Organisation Act.

for a short period of time. However, in my opinion, this does not violate the right of access to justice. A settlement reached in a pre-trial conciliation meeting is also a form of 'law enforcement' which cannot be seen as inferior to a judgment. Therefore, if the parties are invited to such a meeting in every case, one cannot say that 'access to justice' is not guaranteed. The invitation of the parties to a settlement conference is part of this constitutional guarantee of access to justice.

The right of access to justice would only be violated if the sanctions for not appearing or not cooperating at the meeting were too harsh. This is certainly not the case according to the new Swiss CCP. If the defendant does not show up, the conciliation authority proceeds in the same manner as when no settlement has been reached (Article 206(2) CCP).

ii. Mediation

Mediation is more or less completely governed by private law (Code of Obligations). There is a private law contract between the parties and the mediator to carry out the mediation.[152] The mediation itself is based on a special mediation agreement or on a mediation clause in a contract.[153]

Constitutional principles in general do not apply to private law.[154] However, they may influence the private law in a more indirect way. An example of this is the question whether the parties can agree in a contract to mediate in the event of a dispute before being allowed to go to court. According to the prevailing opinion in literature and practice, such an agreement would not preclude a party from taking legal action immediately.[155] This opinion is based on the view that the constitutional principle of access to justice is stronger than a contractual agreement on mediation.[156]

Furthermore, rules which are similar to constitutional principles can be derived from contract law and the protection of legal personality in private law (Article 27 Swiss Civil Code, CC). A mediator who does not treat the parties equally and/or acts unfairly violates the mediation contract. Besides that, an agreement in which a party agrees to accept the result of an unfair mediation and/or a mediator who is biased towards one party could be void according to Article 27(2) CC (unmoral restriction of personal rights).

E. The Influence of the UNCITRAL Model Law on International Commercial Conciliation (2002) on the Drafting of Legislation

It is highly unlikely that this UNCITRAL Model Law has somehow influenced the legal rules on mediation and conciliation.

[152] Meier, *Schweizerisches Zivilprozessrecht* 586f; Peter, *Gerichtsnahe Mediation* 17.

[153] Eiholzer, *Die Streitbeilegungsabrede* 74ff (nos 283ff); Peter, *Gerichtsnahe Mediation* 17ff; Schütz, *Mediation und Schiedsgerichtsbarkeit in der Schweizerischen Zivilprozessordnung* nos 429ff.

[154] T Gächter in G Biaggini, T Gächter and R Kiener (eds), *Staatsrecht* (Zurich/St Gallen, Dike Verlag, 2011), s 30 comments 59ff.

[155] KassGer ZH 15 March 1999 (*Blätter für Zürcherische Rechtsprechung (ZR)* 99, 2000, no 29, pp 86f); Meier, *Schweizerisches Zivilprozessrecht* 598f.

[156] See III.B.v.

The whole system of conciliation before or in connection with a trial is very old, going back to the era immediately following the French revolution.[157] Most of the cantonal laws had already adopted this institution. Therefore, conciliation developed independently and was not influenced by foreign and international law.

The UNCITRAL Model Law is not an example of the new mediation rules, either. According to the Explanatory Report to the Swiss Code of Civil Procedure, this source of law was not taken into consideration.[158] The Report only mentions laws of foreign states (US, Austria, France, UK, Germany, Canada etc) and the legal sources of the EU.[159]

F. Special Rules for Consumers and Their Development

As shown in the first part of this chapter, ADR procedures play an increasingly important role in consumer disputes in Switzerland.[160] Mainly these are through established ombudsman institutions, though in a few cases conciliation institutions with equal representation have also been implemented.[161]

These forms of ADR seem to be a more or less autonomous development of the Swiss legal culture. The Swiss banking ombudsman, for example, has been conducting conciliation proceedings since 1993.[162] Therefore, it is much more likely that the newer ombudsman institutions have been influenced by the older ones, and/or that the different bodies mutually have influenced each other, than that foreign law sources—such as the Commission Recommendation of 4 April 2001 on the principles for out-of-court bodies involved in the consensual resolution of consumer disputes—have served as models.

III. REGULATION OF SPECIFIC ADR INSTRUMENTS

A. Resolving Disputes by Negotiation

Most disputes are resolved by negotiations between the involved parties, with or without involving lawyers. In Switzerland, negotiation is completely governed by private law.

The general principle of 'acting in good faith' also applies in negotiation, even if the parties do not reach an agreement. Article 2(2) CC says that 'Every person must act in good faith in the exercise of his or her rights and in the performance of his or her obligations'. If a party violates this duty, she or he can become liable according

[157] HU Walder-Richli and B Grob-Andermacher, *Zivilprozessrecht,* 5th edn (Zurich/Basel/Geneva, Schulthess Juristische Medien, 2009) nos 13ff; Gelzer and Ruggle in Spühler, Tenchio and Infanger (eds), *Basler Kommentar, Schweizerische Zivilprozessordnung* Vor Arts 213–218 comment 5.

[158] Explanatory Report ('Message') to the Swiss Code of Civil Procedure (Botschaft zur Schweizerischen Zivilprozessordnung) of 28 June 2006, 7252ff.

[159] Ibid.

[160] See above I.F.ii.e ff and I.F.iii.c.

[161] See above I.F.ii and I.F.iii.

[162] See the website of the Swiss banking Ombudsman, available at <www.bankingombudsman.ch/en/association/the-banking-ombudsman>.

to the liability of *culpa in contrahendo*. The nature of this liability is much disputed. According to the prevailing scholarly opinion, it is a quasi-contractual duty, which means a mixture of duties under tort and contract law.[163]

The contracting parties can agree to resolve a possible dispute initially by negotiations and not directly in court. The violator of this clause can be held liable, but it does not prevent a party from taking legal action immediately.[164]

B. Mediation

i. In General

Due to the new CCP, which came into force in 2011, quite detailed rules for mediation connected to a court procedure have been introduced. The very precisely and compactly formulated rules read as follows:[165]

Article 213 Mediation instead of conciliation proceedings
[1] Where the parties jointly so request, mediation takes the place of conciliation proceedings.
[2] Such request must be contained in the application for conciliation proceedings or made at the conciliation hearing.
[3] If one of the parties informs the conciliation authority that mediation has failed, the authority grants leave to bring the action.

Article 214 Mediation in contentious proceedings
[1] The court can recommend mediation to the parties at any time.
[2] The parties can jointly apply to the court for mediation at any time.
[3] The court proceedings are stayed until one of the parties revokes the application or informs the court that the mediation has been terminated.

Article 215 Organisation and conduct of the mediation
The organisation and conduct of the mediation is left to the parties.

Article 216 Mediation and court proceedings
[1] The mediation is independent of the court proceedings and confidential.
[2] The parties' statements cannot be used in the court proceedings.

Article 217 Ratification of an agreement between the parties
The parties can jointly request that the court ratify their agreement reached in the mediation. The ratified agreement has *res iudicata* effect.

Article 218 Costs of the mediation
[1] The parties bear the costs of the mediation.
[2] In non-pecuniary matters relating to children, the parties are entitled to free mediation where:

a. they lack the necessary means; and
b. the court recommends mediation.

[3] Cantonal law may provide for further cost assistance.

[163] See, eg P Gauch and WR Schluep, *Schweizerisches Obligationenrecht Allgemeiner Teil*, 9th edn (Zurich/Basel/Geneva, Schulthess Juristische Medien, 2008) nos 975ff and for further literature no 962a.

[164] See III.B.v.

[165] With minor adjustments, in accord with the translation provided by SV Berti (ed), *ZPO, Schweizerische Zivilprozessordnung*, 523ff, especially 578.

In addition to these rules, which are mostly binding, Article 297(2) CCP says that a court in family matters concerning orders relating to a child can direct the parents to make an attempt at mediation. Furthermore, concerning the impartiality of a judge, Article 47(1) lit d CCP specifies that a person cannot be a judge in a case if she/he has already acted as a mediator in the same case. Finally, a mediator has the right to refuse to testify as a witness with regard to facts learned during mediation (Article 166(1) lit d CCP).

According to the explanatory report to the governmental draft of the new CCP, the legislator has taken into consideration Directive 2008/52/EC of the European Parliament and of the Council of 21 May 2008 on certain aspects of mediation in civil and commercial matters in the form of the draft of 2004.[166] The above quoted rules in fact appear as a (somewhat incomplete) transformation of the EU directive in Swiss law, although Switzerland is not a Member State. The major differences are:

- The Swiss rules only deal with mediation which has taken take place instead of a conciliation meeting or during a court proceeding. Out-of-court mediations are not included.
- So far in Switzerland, there are no legal rules to assure the quality of mediation.[167] Furthermore, there is no rule which interrupts the limitation period during an out-of-court mediation.

ii. Mechanisms That Ensure the Quality of the Service

As already mentioned elsewhere, there are no legal mechanisms to assure the quality of mediation and/or the qualification of a mediator.[168]

iii. The Duties of a Mediator

The duties of a mediator are primarily determined by the (private law) contract between the mediator and the parties. In this contract, the parties have to/may say how the mediator should conduct the mediation (for instance, whether the mediator should engage in caucuses, when and where the mediation takes place).[169] The parties could naturally also lay the whole process of mediation in the hands of the mediator.

As already mentioned, the contractual duties of mediators are supplemented by rules in the CCP. The mediator is not allowed to act as a trial judge in subsequent proceedings (Article 47(1) lit b CCP). She/he has the right to refuse to cooperate where she/he would have to testify with regard to facts learned while acting as a mediator (Article 166(1) lit d CCP). Finally, the mediator has to keep all the information concerning the mediation strictly confidential from the trial judge (compare Article 216(1) CCP).

A mediator registered as an attorney has additional duties. Acting as a mediator

[166] Explanatory Report ('Message') to the Swiss Code of Civil Procedure (Botschaft zur Schweizerischen Zivilprozessordnung) of 28 June 2006, 7253.

[167] See I.E.iii.a.

[168] See I.E.iii.a.

[169] S Gabriel, *Die Haftung des Mediators im schweizerischen Rechtssystem*, Diss Lucerne (Bern, Stämpfli Verlag, 2008) 75ff; see also Eiholzer, *Die Streitbeilegungsabrede* 204ff (nos 728ff); Meier, *Schweizerisches Zivilprozessrecht* 586f.

in Switzerland is regarded as a part of the activity as an attorney. Therefore the legal rules of conduct according to Article 12 FAFML also apply in this respect. For example, an attorney is only allowed to work simultaneously for two people with conflicting interests if she/he treats them equally and impartially (compare Article 12 lit b FAFML), which means that the mediator's duty of neutrality is also covered by the attorney's duties. The general duty of an attorney to act carefully and professionally (Article 12 lit a FAFML) means, for example, that a lawyer may act as a mediator only if he is sufficiently qualified and trained. Furthermore, an attorney has a strong duty of confidentiality which also applies in mediation (Article 13(1) FAFML).

A mediator who violates her/his (contractual or legal) duties is liable according to Article 97 CO (contractual liability).[170] In Switzerland, however, to date, no case has been seen in which a mediator was found liable for breaching her/his duties. If a mediator violates her/his duties as an attorney, disciplinary sanctions can be imposed (Article 17 FAFML).

iv. The Duties of the Parties and the Remuneration of the Mediators

a. In General. The duties of the parties in mediation are based on the contract between the mediator and the parties, as well as the mediation agreement between the parties themselves. Both agreements could also be combined in a single contract between the mediator and both parties.

The contractual agreement between the parties normally obliges them to participate in a mediation and to act in good faith. Furthermore, in addition to the legal rules, the parties could agree on rules concerning confidentiality. For example, the parties could agree to not call the mediator as a witness or to not use any documents produced during the mediation. Article 216 CCP provides only that the parties' 'statements' cannot be used in court proceedings.

The parties may terminate the mediation at any time without giving any specific justification, although the parties have to act in good faith. In my opinion, a contractual clause which stipulates the opposite violates the right of personal freedom according to Article 27(2) CC ('No person may surrender her or his freedom or restrict the use of it to a degree which violates the law or public moral').[171]

b. Cost of Mediation. Generally, the parties have to bear the costs of mediation, even if it is recommended by the court (Article 218(1) CCP). The parties normally agree on the costs in the contract between the mediator and the parties. Neither the federation nor the cantons have yet enacted guidelines for the remuneration of mediators.

Mediation paid for by the state is provided for in federal law as regards non-pecuniary matters concerning children if the parties do not have the financial means to pay for it, and in every case if the mediation was ordered by the court (Article 218(2) CCP).

According to Article 218(3) CCP, the cantons can also provide cost-free mediation in other disputes. Some cantons provide mediation in matters concerning children

[170] Gabriel, *Die Haftung des Mediators im schweizerischen Rechtssystem* 106ff.

[171] According to the translation provided by the Federal Chancellery, see <www.admin.ch/ch/e/rs/2/210.en.pdf>.

and family, but also generally if the parties do not have the financial means to pay for it.[172]

v. Mediation Clause

Due to the increasing importance of mediation with regard to business contracts, more and more mediation clauses can be found. In these clauses the parties agree not to take legal action in the case of a dispute for a certain period of time, and to try and reach an out-of-court solution in mediation.

According to the prevailing opinion in literature and practice, such an agreement is valid.[173] A party who violates this duty could become liable.[174] However, this clause does not bind a court because the right of access to justice is not at the disposition to the parties. Each party could proceed to court at any time.[175]

vi. Enforceability and Review of Mediation Agreements

a. Enforceability of Agreements Reached during Mediation. If the parties go through mediation instead of holding a pre-trial conciliation meeting according to Article 197ff CCP, or attend mediation while the dispute is already pending at a court, an agreement reached during mediation could be easily enforced. The parties could jointly request the ratification of their agreement by the court or, alternatively, by the conciliation authority. The ratified agreement has *res iudicata* effect (Article 217 CCP) and therefore can be enforced like a judgment.

If a party wants to challenge the agreement due to a defect of legal intent or an error, etc, she/he has to apply to the court for reopening of the proceeding (Article 328(1) lit c CCP).

An agreement reached during a mediation which is not related to conciliation meetings or court proceedings is regarded as an ordinary contract. If this contract is not fulfilled by a party, the other party would have to take legal action in an ordinary proceeding.

b. Review of the Mediation Agreement. A mediation agreement has to be inspected before it may be ratified by the court. However, Article 217 CCP does not give any standards for this examination. In my opinion, the review should be restricted to invalidity, inconsistency and incompleteness.[176] However, according to the prevailing scholarly

[172] See, eg s 23(2) of the Introductory Act to the Code of Civil Procedure (EG ZPO) of the canton of Aargau, Art 66 of the Court Organisation Act of the canton of Appenzell Ausserrhoden, Art 127 of the Court Organisation Act of the canton of Fribourg and Art 12 of the Introductory Act to the Code of Civil Procedure (EG ZPO) of the canton of Grisons.

[173] Gelzer and Ruggle in Spühler, Tenchio and Infanger (eds), *Basler Kommentar, Schweizerische Zivilprozessordnung* Vor Arts 213–218 comment 15; Meier, *Schweizerisches Zivilprozessrecht* 598.

[174] Ibid.

[175] KassGer. ZH 15 March 1999 (*Blätter für Zürcherische Rechtsprechung [ZR]* 99, 2000, no 29, pp 86f); on the legal sanctions for violating such an agreement see Eiholzer, *Die Streitbeilegungsabrede* 147ff (nos 541ff).

[176] Meier, *Schweizerisches Zivilprozessrecht* 588 and 595f. See also Gelzer and Ruggle in Spühler, Tenchio and Infanger (eds), *Basler Kommentar, Schweizerische Zivilprozessordnung* Art 217 comment 14; Peter, *Gerichtsnahe Mediation* Art 217 comment 15.

opinion, the court also has to check whether the agreement is highly inappropriate and/or unfair for one of the parties.[177]

vii. Court-based Mediation Programmes

Whereas the procedural law has been unified since the beginning of 2011, the organisation of the courts is still governed by cantonal law. Therefore, court-based mediation programmes would have to be introduced by the cantons.[178]

C. Conciliation

i. In General

For conciliation, three areas of application have to be distinguished:

- conciliation as part of the court proceeding;[179]
- conciliation in the sense of mediation according to Article 213ff CCP; and
- conciliation not related to a court proceeding.

ii. Form and Content of Regulation of Pre-trial Conciliation and Conciliation during a Court Proceeding

a. Pre-trial Conciliation According to Articles 197ff CCP. Conciliation by a state conciliation authority is regulated in detail in Articles 197ff CCP. The most important points of this regulation are:

- The claimant can file a motion for conciliation in writing or orally (Article 202(1) CCP).
- The conciliation authority can request production of the relevant documents and may carry out an inspection (Article 203(2) CCP).
- The parties must appear in person at the conciliation hearing, but they can be accompanied by a legal representative or by some other person they trust (Article 204(1) and (2) CCP).
- Statements of the parties may neither be recorded nor used in subsequent contentious proceedings at court (Article 205(1) CCP).
- If conciliation fails, in general the conciliation authority grants leave to the plaintiff to bring the action at court (Article 209(1) lit b CCP). However, in a case with a litigious value of up to CHF 2,000, the conciliator can render a judgment provided the claimant so requests (Article 212(1) CCP). If the litigious value is no higher than CHF 5,000, the conciliator can submit a judgment proposal to the parties (Article 210(1) lit c CCP).[180]

[177] Explanatory Report ('Message') to the Swiss Code of Civil Procedure (Botschaft zur Schweizerischen Zivilprozessordnung) of 28 June 2006, 7337.

[178] See I.E.i.b.

[179] See III.C.ii.

[180] See I.D.

A very interesting feature of conciliation is that, unlike a mediator (Article 47(1) lit b CCP), the conciliator is, in general, allowed to act as a judge in the same case (Article 47(2) lit b CCP).[181] This shows that the legislator has made a clear distinction between mediation and conciliation.

b. Conciliation in the Frame of a Settlement Conference. Conciliation in a settlement conference is completely embedded in the court proceedings. Therefore its regulation can be kept brief. Article 226(2) CCP mentions an attempt to reach a settlement as one of the goals of the preparatory hearings. Furthermore, as one of the general principles of the procedure, Article 124(3) CCP says that the court 'can attempt at any time to bring the parties to an agreement'.

D. ADR Procedures for Consumer Disputes

i. In General

As shown in the first part of this chapter, ombudsman institutions have been established in Switzerland in most branches of industry relevant to consumers.[182] Furthermore, different conciliation bodies with equal representation have been implemented in the recent past to resolve consumer disputes.[183] It is typical that these conciliation institutions are completely self-regulated. Usually there are no legal rules addressing them, and they are not under the supervision of any state authority. The CCP only mentions this form of dispute resolution insofar as it gives ombudspersons the right not to testify with respect to the facts learned while acting as ombudsman (Article 166(1) 1 lit d CCP).

An exception to this is made in the telecommunications industry. Quite recently, the (federal) legislator enacted detailed rules regarding the implementation of a conciliation procedure to resolve disputes between consumers and providers of telecommunications and value-added services. Unexpectedly, these provisions were not introduced because a private conciliation organisation was seen to be not functioning well. The reason for this was simply that the telecommunications industry hesitated to establish such a procedure whereas the legislator wanted to provide it because the Federal Office of Communications (OFCOM) itself had to deal with many consumer complaints, despite not being the most appropriate body for this effort.[184] The legislator also argued that EU Directive 2002/22/EC on universal service and users' rights relating to electronic communications networks and services (Universal Service Directive) already demands a similar ADR procedure.[185]

In Article 12c(1) TCA, the OFCOM has been given the duty to establish a conciliation body or to entrust a third party with this task. The OFCOM has opted for the second alternative because the telecommunications industry, as a result of the

[181] See I.C.iv and I.E.i.b.
[182] See above I.F.ii, especially I.F.ii.a.
[183] See above I.F.iii, especially I.F.iii.a.
[184] Explanatory Report ('Message') on the amendment of the Telecommunications Act (TCA) (Botschaft zur Änderung des Fernmeldegesetzes (FMG)) of 12 November 2003, 7973f.
[185] Ibid, 7973.

introduction of legal regulations, is now ready to implement such a procedure. It therefore mandated the 'Ombudscom' foundation, which, since 2008, has been conducting conciliation procedures on its behalf.[186]

The relatively detailed legal guidelines for this ADR procedure are set down in the TCA and in the Ordinance on Telecommunications Services (OTS).[187]

ii. Federal Regulations on the Conciliation Procedure of the Telecommunications Sector

Concerning the conciliation procedure of the telecommunications sector, the TCA and the OTS mainly provide the following rules and principles:

- The parties are not bound by the dispute resolution decision (Article 12c(3) TCA).
- The party invoking the dispute resolution service shall pay a handling fee. The provider of telecommunications services or value-added services shall bear the costs of the procedure minus the handling fee (Article 12c(2) TCA).
- It (the dispute resolution service) shall fulfil its dispute resolution mission independently, objectively, transparently and efficiently. It is not subject to any general or particular instruction regarding the resolution of disputes (Article 43(2) OTS).
- The dispute resolution service shall issue procedural rules (Article 44(1) OTS). The agent shall submit its procedural rules and its rules on charges and amendments thereto to OFCOM (Federal Office of Communications) for approval (Article 44(2) OTS).
- The dispute resolution service must be fair, expeditious and affordable for customers (Article 45(1) OTS).
- An application for resolution of a dispute is permitted only if:
  a) the party making the application has previously tried to reach an agreement with the other party to the dispute;
  b) it is submitted under the conditions laid down in the procedural rules of the dispute resolution service;
  c) it is not obviously abusive;
  d) no court or arbitration court is dealing with the matter (Article 45(2) OTS).
- The dispute resolution procedure ends with the withdrawal of the application, agreement between the parties, the resolution proposal or the rejection of the application as clearly abusive (Article 45(5) OTS).
- The submission of an application for resolution of a dispute does not prevent a civil action (Article 46(1) OTS).
- The dispute resolution service shall terminate the procedure as soon as a court or arbitration court begins dealing with the matter (Article 46(2) OTS).
- Any provider of telecommunications or value-added services which is involved in a dispute resolution application must take part in the dispute resolution procedure. It shall comply with the dispute resolution service's requests for information (Article 47(1) OTS).
- Providers of telecommunications or value-added services shall on request provide

[186] *Annual Report 2010 of the Telecommunications Ombudsman Institution* 5; for details see I.F.ii.e.
[187] See <www.admin.ch/ch/e/rs/7.html>.

the dispute resolution service with the telecommunications traffic data necessary for resolution of the dispute and the other personal data of their customers provided they hold such data (Article 47(2) OTS).

E. Expert Opinion (*Schiedsgutachten*)

As part of the evidence rules, Article 189 CCP lays down the principles of the arbitrator's expert opinion. This article has the following wording:[188]

> [1] The parties can agree to obtain an arbitrator's expert opinion relating to disputed facts.
> [2] The form of such agreement is governed by article 17 sec 2.[189]
> [3] The arbitrator's expert opinion is binding on the court with regard to the facts established therein, provided:
> a. the parties had liberty of disposition with regard to the legal relationship in question;
> b. no grounds for recusal existed against the expert arbitrator; and
> c. the arbitrator's expert opinion is without bias and is not manifestly incorrect.

The expert opinion according to Article 189 CCP replaces the court's ruling insofar as it determines a relevant fact. The expert opinion binds the court if the requirements cited above are met. Article 189 CCP only expressly mentions the disputed facts. But, as has always been acknowledged in practice, related questions of law can also be decided by such an expert opinion (eg the amount of liability, which includes factual questions and questions of law).

Whereas the federal court has decided that the arbitrator's expert opinion is governed by private law,[190] the prevailing opinion as to the new CCP regards it as an institute of procedural law.[191] In my opinion, the latter is in fact the correct view. The arbitrator's expert opinion has its main effect in trial; it somehow anticipates the judgment. Furthermore, several procedural principles apply to the process of drawing up an arbitrator's expert opinion. Article 189(3) lit b CCP requires that the expert be as independent as a judge. In my opinion, the expert also has to comply with constitutional principles of fairness, the right to be heard and equal treatment of the parties.[192]

The main areas of application of arbitrators' expert opinions are the building and construction industry, disputes about liability and insurance, winding up of companies and other fields where complicated factual determinations are relevant to resolving a

[188] With minor adjustments, in accord with the translation provided by SV Berti (ed), *ZPO, Schweizerische Zivilprozessordnung* 570.

[189] Form for a jurisdiction agreement.

[190] BGE 129 III 535 (p 538, con 2); BGE 67 II 146 (p 148, con 2).

[191] Explanatory Report ('Message') to the Swiss Code of Civil Procedure (Botschaft zur Schweizerischen Zivilprozessordnung) of 28 June 2006, 7325; Meier, *Schweizerisches Zivilprozessrecht* 325; HA Müller in Brunner, Gasser and Schwander (eds), *Schweizerische Zivilprozessordnung (ZPO)* Art 189 comment 13; K Perroulaz in Baker and McKenzie (eds), *Schweizerische Zivilprozessordnung (ZPO)* (Bern, Stämpfli Verlag, 2010) Art 189 comment 7; different Guldener, *Schweizerisches Zivilprozessrecht* 598 (fn 16 lit a); A Dolge in Spühler, Tenchio and Infanger (eds), *Basler Kommentar, Schweizerische Zivilprozessordnung* Art 189 comment 3.

[192] Meier, *Schweizerisches Zivilprozessrecht* 327.

dispute. The arbitrator's expert opinions are seen as being of a certain importance,[193] but statistical data do not exist.

F. Arbitration

i. The Influence of the UNCITRAL Model Law on International Commercial Arbitration on National Legislation

Swiss law distinguishes between national and international arbitration. National arbitration is governed by the Swiss Code of Civil Procedure whereas international arbitration is governed by the Code on Private International Law.

The rules on arbitration in the Swiss Code of Civil Procedure were modelled on the Inter-Cantonal Concordat on Arbitration of 1969 that governed arbitration between the Cantons before it was unified in the Swiss Code of Civil Procedure in 2011. The UNCITRAL Model Law was also consulted, but merely secondarily.

The same has to be said for the rules on arbitration in the Code on Private International Law. They do not follow the UNCITRAL Model Law. However, they do not follow the Inter-Cantonal Concordat on Arbitration of 1969 either. Instead, they are based on an independent conception.

Although Switzerland did not adopt the UNCITRAL Model Law, there are no fundamental differences between both sets of rules.[194] Further, different Swiss provisions reflect some of the concepts of the UNCITRAL Model Law.

ii. Minimum Procedural Standard

Swiss law does not explicitly state which provisions of the arbitration rules in the Swiss Code of Civil Procedure and in the Code on Private International Law (CPIL) are mandatory. Pursuant to Article 373(4) CCP, the following minimum standard applies: 'The arbitral tribunal must guarantee the equal treatment of the parties and their right to be heard in adversarial proceedings'. Apart from that, the mandatory character of a procedural provision on arbitration has to be determined by construction. In general, the following provisions are considered to be part of the minimum procedural standard: the determination of arbitrability, the minimum form of the arbitration agreement, the observance of the equality of the parties in respect of the appointment of the arbitrators, the right to challenge an arbitrator, the exclusion of the free administration of justice, the minimum contents of the arbitral award, the rules of challenging an arbitral award and the competences of state courts related to arbitration.

[193] B Carl, *Aussergerichtliche Formen der Streitbehandlung im Bauvertragsrecht*, Diss Zurich (Zurich/Basel/Geneva, Schulthess Juristische Medien, 2010) nos 11ff, 199ff and 330.

[194] D Hochstrasser and M Blessing in H Honsell, NP Vogt and AK Schnyder (eds), *Basler Kommentar, Internationales Privatrecht*, 2nd edn (Basel, Helbing Lichtenhahn Verlag, 2007) Einleitung zum Zwölften Kapitel comment 190.

iii. The Abrogation of Mandatory Law in Arbitration

In arbitration, the parties may choose the applicable law by agreement. They may also authorise the arbitral tribunal to decide the case *ex aequo et bono*. The abrogation of the intrinsically applicable law encompasses in either case its mandatory provisions.[195] Thus, mandatory law may principally be abrogated. But there is a limit. So-called interventionist norms cannot be abrogated due to public policy reasons. It is highly controversial, however, which provisions qualify as interventionist norms in which constellations.[196] The observation of interventionist norms is guided by Articles 18 and 19 CPIL, which apply in arbitration by analogy. Article 18 states, as to the application of Swiss interventionist norms, that: 'Imperative provisions of Swiss law which, by reason of their particular purpose, must be observed regardless of the law designated by this Statute are reserved'. Article 19 CPIL similarly determines the application of imperative norms of foreign law.

Mandatory venues that would apply in state court proceedings do not principally hinder arbitration. National arbitration is allowed even if as a consequence a mandatory forum is abrogated. The prevailing view is of the same opinion with regard to international arbitration. Consequently, arbitration is in principal also possible in subject matters that are typically governed by mandatory venues—as, for instance, in consumer law, in employment law and in landlord–tenant law.

iv. Rules of Enforcement

Arbitral awards are equivalent to state court decisions. They particularly have the same effects in regard to legal force and enforceability. Accordingly, arbitral awards are enforced in the same way as state court decisions. However, there is a distinction between domestic arbitral awards and arbitral awards from abroad.

Domestic arbitral awards are enforced in exactly the same manner as domestic state court decisions. Because an appeal does not suspend their legal effect or enforceability, arbitral awards are immediately enforceable after their announcement. The parties may, but do not have to, request a certificate of enforceability from the state court. The enforcement proceeding depends on whether there is a monetary or a non-monetary arbitral award. However, the state courts are the competent authority for enforcement in either case.

The enforcement of foreign arbitral awards begins with the recognition and declaration of enforceability of the arbitral award pursuant to the New York Convention of 1958. Switzerland applies the New York Convention even if the arbitral award was rendered in a state that is not a member of the convention. After recognition and declaration of enforceability, the arbitral award is enforced in the same way as a domestic arbitral award. Thus, the same rules of enforcement apply as for state court decisions.

[195] T Rüede and R Hadenfeldt, *Schweizerisches Schiedsgerichtsrecht*, 2nd edn (Zurich, Schulthess Polygraphischer Verlag, 1993) 277; G Walter, W Bosch and J Brönnimann, *Internationale Schiedsgerichtsbarkeit in der Schweiz* (Bern, Stämpfli Verlag, 1991) 194.

[196] B Berger and F Kellerhals, *Internationale und interne Schiedsgerichtsbarkeit in der Schweiz* (Bern, Stämpfli Verlag, 2006) nos 1300ff; PA Karrer in Honsell, Vogt and Schnyder (eds), *Basler Kommentar, Internationales Privatrecht* Art 187 comments 229ff.

IV. POLICY RECOMMENDATIONS

A. Introduction

Before answering the questions whether and how ADR should be regulated by the state, we have to illustrate which forms of ADR should be supported by the state in the first instance.[197]

Furthermore, although the question of regulation of ADR cannot be answered generally, it can be answered for the different types and forms of ADR. A general question at this point is whether there is a right to a fair ADR procedure in addition to the constitutional right of access to justice.[198]

B. Which Forms of ADR Should Be Supported by the Legislator?

In my opinion, based on the Swiss experience and tradition in ADR, the state should favour the following proceedings.

i. Conciliation Integrated in the Process of Adjudication

For disputes in civil matters in general, conciliation should be offered as a part of the process of adjudication. Integrated in the decision-making process, the parties should have the possibility to settle the case at an early stage of the procedure based on an assessment of the probability to win the case and according to the related risks.

ii. Mediation as an Alternative to Conciliation

Mediation after filing a legal action or outside of a court proceeding should be supported by the legislator as an alternative to conciliation. Mediation in the sense it is understood in this chapter is a professional and well-established dispute resolution procedure, which typically focuses on the interests of the parties and the psychological aspects of the disputes. Another issue is the legal situation: even though it is only one of a number of aspects, mediation takes place, as phrased by Robert Mnookin, in the 'shadow' of the law.[199]

iii. Ombudsman Proceedings for Consumer Disputes

Ombudsman proceedings constitute a suitable and adequate form of ADR for resolving consumer disputes. They are easily accessible to all affected parties. For consumers, the procedure is either free of charge or very inexpensive. Neither consumers nor suppliers

[197] See IV.B.

[198] See IV.C.

[199] R Cooter, S Marks and R Mnookin, 'Bargaining in the Shadows of the Law: A Testable Model of Strategic Behaviour' [1982] *The Journal of Legal Studies* 225ff.

have to complete much paperwork, and the vast majority of cases can be conducted within a short time to the satisfaction of both parties.[200]

C. From the Right of Access to Justice to the Right of Access to a Fair Dispute Resolution

As mentioned above in I, in Switzerland, conciliation and adjudication are equivalent goals of civil procedure. Both are integrated in the same procedure determined by principles of a state under the rule of law. In the same sense, the fundamental right of access to justice should be understood in a broader sense as a right of *access to a fair dispute resolution*.

A state under the rule of law has to guarantee access not only to an adjudication procedure but also to consensual forms of dispute resolution. Yet this does not mean that a state has to provide ADR mechanisms or to regulate them. Providing and regulating ADR mechanisms is only necessary if, and insofar as, the free market itself does not provide such procedures and/or the provided procedures are insufficient and unfair.

In order to guarantee the right of access to a fair dispute resolution, the legislator has to follow several principles.

In addition to adjudication, the state has to provide, support and/or foster the most important adequate forms of consensual dispute resolution procedures.

The parties have the right to choose which procedure they want to initiate. If the legislator wants to support a special form of dispute resolution, the restrictions related to other forms of dispute resolutions should be moderate.

Adjudication must always be a real alternative to consensual forms of dispute resolution. Therefore, the state should never foster ADR rather than repairing deficiencies of the ordinary court proceeding.

A difficult question is whether the right to a fair dispute resolution (adjudication and ADR) can be derived from the constitution today or whether the legislator would have to provide for it specifically. In Switzerland, the existence of unwritten constitutional rights has always been acknowledged.[201] In my opinion, apart from adjudication, such a right certainly exists for conciliation. A court procedure which neither allows the parties to settle the case nor supports them in settling it cannot be regarded as a fair and effective procedure.[202] The same must be assumed for mediation.

[200] See I.F, especially I.F.ii.g. Conciliation procedures with equal representation also constitute an appropriate form of ADR for resolving consumer disputes and should therefore be supported by the legislator in the same way (see I.F.iii).

[201] See, eg BGE 121 I 367 (p 370, con 2a); Biaggini in Biaggini, Gächter and Kiener (eds), *Staatsrecht* s 9 no 6; U Häfelin, W Haller and H Keller, *Schweizerisches Bundesstaatsrecht*, 7th edn (Zurich/Basel/Geneva, Schulthess Juristische Medien, 2008) nos 226ff; P Tschannen, *Staatsrecht der Schweizerischen Eidgenossenschaft*, 3rd edn (Bern, Stämpfli Verlag, 2011) s 3 nos 19ff.

[202] *Cf* Art 29(2) of the Federal Constitution.

D. Regulation of Conciliation as a Part of the Process of Adjudication

i. In General

Conciliation should be integrated into the process of adjudication, and therefore offered and regulated by the state.

This is obvious for the settlement conference during the court proceeding. It being completely integrated in the court proceeding and thus led by a judge who later decides the case as a single judge or as a member of a panel of judges is one of the reasons why conciliation in the frame of a settlement conference is as successful as it is.[203]

Furthermore, pre-trial conciliation should be organised and regulated by the state as well. As in the Swiss CCP, it makes sense to give the conciliator additional areas of responsibilities, such as deciding cases with minimal litigious value or rendering a judgment proposal. Also for conciliation, issues have to be taken care of by the conciliator that should be done by a state institution, including granting leave to bring the action (Article 209 CCP), requesting production of the relevant documents by the parties (Article 203(2) CCP) and concluding the proceeding after reaching a settlement (*cf* Article 241 CCP).

ii. Should the Conciliation Meeting be Mandatory?

a. Regulation in Switzerland. The new Swiss CCP generally provides that a conciliation attempt has to take place in every case (Article 197 CCP). In cases with a litigious value of at least CHF 100,000, the parties can jointly waive conciliation proceedings (Article 199(2) CCP). The 2003 draft of the new code provided that the claimant her/himself could have waived the pre-trial conciliation in every pecuniary matter with a litigious value of greater than CHF 20,000. However, because of harsh criticism of voluntary conciliation in the draft, this rule was replaced by the current solution.[204]

In addition to the question whether conciliation should be voluntary or mandatory, the legislator has to lay down the consequences of a party's not showing up, or not participating and/or negotiating in good faith.

In Switzerland, there are no consequences at all if the defendant does not participate. If the defendant is in default, the conciliation authority proceeds in the same way as if no settlement has been reached (according to Article 206(2) CCP).

b. Assessment of the Different Regulations. In my opinion, the current solution of the Swiss CCP is the most preferable one. As the practice in Switzerland indicates, it makes sense to provide a mandatory conciliation at the beginning of a trial (see Article 197 CCP). It can be assumed that significantly fewer conciliations will take place and corresponding settlements reached if the defendant can choose whether he wants to attempt conciliation or go directly to the trial court. However, the consequences if the defendant does not appear have to be moderate, as they are in the CCP. Otherwise it would violate the constitutional right of access to justice.

[203] See I.C.iv.

[204] Explanatory Report ('Message') to the Swiss Code of Civil Procedure (Botschaft zur Schweizerischen Zivilprozessordnung) of 28 June 2006, 7329; *Consultation Report to the Preliminary Draft of the Swiss Code of Civil Procedure (Bericht zum Vorentwurf der Schweizerischen Zivilprozessordnung) of June 2003* 472; Meier, *Vorentwurf für eine Schweizerische Zivilprozessordnung* 50f.

E. Regulation of Mediation

i. In General

According to mediation, three forms of regulations have to be taken into consideration:

- The most intensive form of regulation is necessary if the state itself wants to offer mediation by special agencies or by the court (*gerichtsinterne Mediation*).
- The legislator could regulate the profession of a mediator or provide other rules to safeguard the quality of mediation.
- The third form of regulation concerns the civil procedural questions related to mediation, such as adjourning the procedure during mediation and mediators' rights to cooperate in taking evidence.

ii. Offering Mediation by State Authorities

a. Introduction. There are mainly two reasons for the state to offer mediation:

- The free market does not offer enough mediation, or
- For some reason, mediation organised by the state is more suitable than mediation by private individuals.

b. Court Internal Mediation. It could be argued that mediation should be offered together with adjudication, and probably also conciliation, under one roof according to the famous multi-door court house originally proposed by Frank Sander.[205] Therefore, the best solution would be if judges who work in this facility anyway would also deal with this kind of dispute resolution.

In my opinion, there is no reason at all to assume that the judges are better suited to this job than separate institutions if the state has to offer mediation. On the contrary, court internal mediation has several disadvantages: a judge who acts as a mediator in one case and as a trial judge in another case has an incentive to solve as many cases in mediation as possible in order to reduce the general workload of the court. Therefore, she/he may tend to push the parties to settle. Furthermore, if a court offers mediation in addition to traditional conciliation by a trial judge, it might be difficult for the parties to distinguish between these different forms of dispute resolution.

c. Special State Institutions for Mediation. In my opinion, if the state has to offer mediation at all, it would have to establish special institutions for the process. At least in Switzerland, establishing a special institution is not necessary because the private sector offers enough.[206]

iii. Guarantee of the Quality of Mediation

In order to guarantee the (constitutional) right to fair dispute resolution procedures, the state has to make sure that enough qualified mediators are available and people

[205] FEA Sander, 'Varieties of Dispute Processing' in LA Levin and RR Wheeler (eds), *The Pound Conference: Perspectives on Justice in the Future* (St Paul, MN, West Publishing Co, 1979) 65ff, 83f.
[206] See I.E.iii.

are not harmed by unqualified mediators. Therefore, if necessary, the legislator has to intervene by providing regulations. In Switzerland, there are enough qualified mediators and hence there does not seem to be a serious problem of unqualified mediators. Therefore, in this respect, the need for regulations is not urgent.

iv. Rules Concerning Procedural Questions Related to Mediation

The indisputable centrepiece of regulation in mediation is the body of rules which have the dual task of (i) determining the relationship and tension between mediation and adjudication/conciliation and (ii) preserving mediation's equality with these forms of dispute resolution. As seen in Swiss law, these rules primarily entail: the possibility of the parties going through mediation instead of pre-trial conciliation; the possibility of mediation during a court proceeding; ratification of a mediation agreement in order to make it enforceable; and rules to guarantee confidentiality of mediation.[207]

F. Regulation of ADR Procedures for Consumer Disputes

i. In General

In Switzerland, several very successful ombudsman procedures have been established, as well as other forms of ADR to resolve consumer disputes.[208] Most of them are completely self-regulated by the branches of industry in question. An exception to this is made in the telecommunications industry.[209]

In my opinion, the legislator should generally regulate ombudsman and other conciliation proceedings for the following reasons:

- As the Swiss experiences have shown, ADR forms for consumer disputes actually replace state court proceedings to a great extent.[210] Especially if only little money is at stake, going to state courts does not represent a real alternative for consumers.[211] In most branches of industry there is only one ADR procedure available. Therefore conciliation bodies have a kind of monopoly status within their fields of activity.
- In my opinion, completely self-regulated ADR proceedings always suffer from a lack of credibility. Even if the ombudsman or conciliation body is formally independent, this issue remains a problem.[212]

ii. Content of Regulation

The regulation should contain standards and principles which have to be observed by all ADR institutions dealing with consumer disputes. The legal provisions on the conciliation procedure of the telecommunications sector give a good example of how to

[207] See I.E.i.b and III.B.i.
[208] See I.F.ii and I.F.iii.
[209] See I.F.ii.e and III.D.
[210] See I.F.ii.e ff and I.F.iii.c.
[211] See I.F.ii.g.
[212] See I.F.ii.g.

introduce such state regulation.[213] In addition, the legislator could also take into consideration the convincing principles of the 'Commission recommendation of 4 April 2001 on the principles for out-of-court bodies involved in the consensual resolution of consumer disputes'.[214]

Furthermore, these ADR procedures should be supervised by state authorities.[215] Within the framework of this surveillance, the supervisory authority would also have to carefully control the election process of ombudsmen and other conciliators.

G. Costs of ADR

i. In General

An additional important policy question associated with ADR is who is to bear the costs (of the procedure). As seen in Switzerland, the following rules apply:

- Cost rules applicable to adjudication apply equally for conciliation occurring either according to Articles 197ff CCP or during a court proceeding. If necessary, a party could obtain legal aid (Article 118(1) lit b in conjunction with Article 95(2) lit a CCP).[216]
- In general, mediation has to be paid for by the parties. Legal aid is only provided in family disputes concerning children.[217] For other disputes, the cantonal law can offer mediation at no cost.[218]
- The ADR forms for consumer disputes are available at no or only minimal cost for the consumer.[219]

ii. Policy Question of Costs of ADR

ADR procedures normally are cheaper than a court proceeding simply because they are typically much less time-consuming. Additionally, the question has to be answered whether the state should provide ADR at no cost or only a fraction of the real cost for everyone or, at a minimum, for the people who cannot afford it.

Adjudication and ADR procedures are equally valid forms of dispute resolution. The decision which one should take place is up to the parties. Therefore, it is not appropriate if the legislator favours ADR by providing them at no or little cost. On the other hand, legal aid should exist not only for adjudication and court-annexed conciliation, but also for mediation. The concept of legal aid according to Article 29

[213] See I.F.ii.e, III.D.i and III.D.ii.

[214] Available at <eur-lex.europa.eu>; see also II.F.

[215] This is already the case with the conciliation body of the telecommunications sector ('Ombudscom' foundation), which is under the supervision of the Federal Office of Communications (OFCOM), see Art 50 Ordinance on Telecommunications Services (OTS).

[216] See BGE 119 Ia 264 (p 267 f, con 4b); U Egli in Brunner, Gasser and Schwander (eds), *Schweizerische Zivilprozessordnung (ZPO)* Art 207 comment 10.

[217] See III.B.iv.b.

[218] Ibid.

[219] See I.F.ii.b.

of the Federal Constitution in my opinion includes not only adjudications but also ADR in general.[220]

H. 'Triage' for Adjudication, Conciliation and Mediation

Who should carry the responsibility of seeing that disputes are channelled to the (most) adequate procedure? In my opinion, this is mainly the task of the lawyers and the other individuals giving counsel to the parties. Secondly, all the authorities, agencies and bodies which handle a dispute have the duty to inform the parties about feasible alternatives.

Attorneys have the duty to inform their clients of all the various manners of dispute resolutions. This is part of their general duty of care in advising their clients.[221] As for the court, the CCP expressly allows the judges to recommend mediation to the parties at any time (Article 214(2) CCP). In my opinion, it is a mediator's (contractual) duty to make sure the parties know of all legal alternatives to mediation.[222]

At least in Switzerland, it would be regarded as completely exaggerated to establish a special office at court or an agency by the state or a private institution for the selection of the disputes for the different respective forms of dispute resolution.

BIBLIOGRAPHY

Amonn, K and Walther, F, *Grundriss des Schuldbetreibungs- und Konkursrechts*, 8th edn (Bern, Stämpfli Verlag, 2008)

Baker and McKenzie (eds), *Schweizerische Zivilprozessordnung (ZPO)* (Bern, Stämpfli Verlag, 2010)

Berger, B and Kellerhals, F, *Internationale und interne Schiedsgerichtsbarkeit in der Schweiz* (Bern, Stämpfli Verlag, 2006)

Berti, SV (ed), *ZPO, Schweizerische Zivilprozessordnung* (Basel, Helbing Lichtenhahn Verlag, 2009)

Berti, SV, *Einführung in die schweizerische Zivilprozessordnung* (Basel, Helbing Lichtenhahn Verlag, 2011)

Biaggini, G, Gächter, T and Kiener, R (eds), *Staatsrecht* (Zurich/St Gallen, Dike Verlag, 2011)

Bono-Hörler C, *Familienmediation im Bereiche von Ehetrennung und Ehescheidung, Eine interdisziplinäre Betrachtung unter besonderer Berücksichtigung der Rolle des Rechts und der Rechtsanwälte*, Diss Zurich (Zurich, Schulthess Polygraphischer Verlag, 1999)

Brunner, A, Gasser, D and Schwander, I (eds), *Schweizerische Zivilprozessordnung (ZPO)* (Zurich/St Gallen, Dike Verlag, 2011)

[220] Which does not correspond to the prevailing scholarly opinion in Switzerland: I Jent-Sørensen in Oberhammer (ed), *Kurzkommentar, Schweizerische Zivilprozessordnung* Art 117 comment 12; JP Müller and M Schefer, *Grundrechte in der Schweiz*, 4th edn (Bern, Stämpfli Verlag, 2008) 899 and fn 42f; Rüeggin in Spühler, Tenchio and Infanger (eds), *Basler Kommentar, Schweizerische Zivilprozessordnung* Art 117 comment 6; G Steinmann in B Ehrenzeller, P Mastronardi, RJ Schweizer and KA Vallender (eds), *Die schweizerische Bundesverfassung, Kommentar*, 2nd edn (Zurich/St Gallen, Dike Verlag, Zurich/Basel/Geneva, Schulthess Juristische Medien, 2008) Art 29 comment 36.

[221] See III.B.iii.

[222] Meier, *Schweizerisches Zivilprozessrecht* 587; see also Gloor and Umbricht Lukas in Oberhammer (ed), *Kurzkommentar, Schweizerische Zivilprozessordnung* Art 213 comment 11.

Bucher, E, 'Was macht den Schiedsrichter? Abschied vom "Schiedsrichtervertrag"—und Weiteres zu Prozessverträgen' in B Bachmann et al (eds), *Grenzüberschreitungen, Beiträge zum Internationalen Verfahrensrecht und zur Schiedsgerichtsbarkeit, Festschrift für Peter Schlosser zum 70 Geburtstag* (Tübingen, Mohr Siebeck, 2005) 97–118

Carl, B, *Aussergerichtliche Formen der Streitbehandlung im Bauvertragsrecht*, Diss Zurich (Zurich/Basel/Geneva, Schulthess Juristische Medien, 2010)

Cooter, R, Marks, S and Mnookin, R, 'Bargaining in the Shadows of the Law: A Testable Model of Strategic Behaviour' [1982] *The Journal of Legal Studies* 225

Dekker, S, 'Wirtschaftsmediation' in GG Zindel, PR Peyer and B Schott (eds), *Wirtschaftsrecht in Bewegung. Festgabe zum 65. Geburtstag von Peter Forstmoser* (Zurich/St Gallen, Dike Verlag, Zurich/Basel/Geneva, Schulthess Juristische Medien, 2008) 557–78

Egli, U, *Vergleichsdruck im Zivilprozess, eine rechtstatsächliche Untersuchung*, Diss Zurich 1995 (Berlin, Duncker und Humblot, 1996)

Ehrenzeller, B, Mastronardi, P, Schweizer, RJ and Vallender KA (eds), *Die schweizerische Bundesverfassung, Kommentar*, 2nd edn (Zurich/St Gallen, Dike Verlag, Zurich/Basel/Geneva, Schulthess Juristische Medien, 2008)

Eiholzer, H, *Die Streitbeilegungsabrede*, Diss Freiburg (Freiburg, Universitätsverlag Freiburg, 1998)

Fritzsche, H and Walder-Bohner, HU, *Schuldbetreibung und Konkurs nach schweizerischem Recht*, Band I (Zurich, Schulthess Polygraphischer Verlag, 1984)

Gabriel, S, *Die Haftung des Mediators im schweizerischen Rechtssystem*, Diss Lucerne (Bern, Stämpfli Verlag, 2008)

Galli-Widmer, M, '§ 52 Mediation in der Schweiz' in F Haft and K Gräfin von Schlieffen (eds), *Handbuch Mediation* (München, CH Beck Verlag, 2009)

Gauch, P and Schluep, WR, *Schweizerisches Obligationenrecht Allgemeiner Teil*, 9th edn (Zurich/Basel/Geneva, Schulthess Juristische Medien, 2008)

Goetz, ML, '"Anwaltliche Mediation"—eine originär anwaltliche Tätigkeit' (2005) 14 *Aktuelle Juristische Praxis* 282

Gottwald, W, '§ 39 Gerichtsnahe Mediation—Erfahrungen und Lehren aus dem Modellprojekt in Niedersachsen' in F Haft and K Gräfin von Schlieffen (eds), *Handbuch Mediation* (München, CH Beck Verlag, 2009)

Greger, R, 'Regelungsempfehlungen vor dem Hintergrund der Pilotprojekte an deutschen Gerichten' [2010] *Rabels Zeitschrift für ausländisches und internationales Privatrecht* 781

Guldener, M, *Schweizerisches Zivilprozessrecht*, 3rd edn (Zurich, Schulthess Polygraphischer Verlag, 1979)

Häfelin, U, Haller, W and Keller, H, *Schweizerisches Bundesstaatsrecht*, 7th edn (Zurich/Basel/Geneva, Schulthess Juristische Medien, 2008)

Honsell, H, Vogt NP and Schnyder AK (eds), *Basler Kommentar, Internationales Privatrecht*, 2nd edn (Basel, Helbing Lichtenhahn Verlag, 2007)

Hunkeler, D (ed), *Kurzkommentar, Schuldbetreibungs- und Konkursgesetz* (Basel, Helbing Lichtenhahn Verlag, 2009)

Jent-Sørensen, I, *Der dänische Ombudsmann*, Diss Zurich (Zurich, Schulthess Polygraphischer Verlag, 1985)

Kumpan, C and Bauer C, 'Kapitel 18, Mediation in der Schweiz' in KJ Hopt and F Steffek (eds), *Mediation* (Tübingen, Mohr Siebeck Verlag, 2008), 853–84

Leuenberger, C, 'Streiterledigung zwischen Vergleich und Urteil: Modell eines einfachen und raschen Verfahrens' in I Schwander and WA Stoffel (eds), *Beiträge zum schweizerischen und internationalen Zivilprozessrecht, Festschrift für Oscar Vogel* (Freiburg, Universitätsverlag Freiburg Schweiz, 1991) 54–66

Leuenberger, C and Uffer-Tobler, B, *Schweizerisches Zivilprozessrecht* (Bern, Stämpfli Verlag, 2010)

Löer, L, 'Richterliche Mediation. Möglichkeiten der Einbindung von Mediation in das Gerichtsverfahren am Beispiel des Zivilprozesses' [2006] *Zeitschrift für Zivilprozessrecht* 199

Meier, I, *Rechtsschutz im summarischen Verfahren als Alternative zum ordentlichen Zivilprozess im schweizerischen Recht* (Cologne, Bundesanzeiger, 1997)

Meier, I, 'Mediation und Schlichtung in der Schweiz, unter besonderer Berücksichtigung der gesetzlichen Rahmenbedingungen für Mediation' in Veröffentlichungen des Schweizerischen Instituts für Rechtsvergleichung (ed), *'Mediation' als alternative Konfliktlösungsmöglichkeit?* (Zurich/Basel/Geneva, Schulthess Juristische Medien, 2002) 295–324

Meier, I, *Vorentwurf für eine Schweizerische Zivilprozessordnung* (Zurich/Basel/Geneva, Schulthess Juristische Medien, 2003)

Meier, I, 'Mediation and Conciliation in Switzerland' in N Alexander (ed), *Global Trends in Mediation*, 2nd edn (Alphen aan den Rijn, Kluwer Law International, 2006) 371–88

Meier, I, 'Die dogmatische Situation des Vollstreckungsrechts aus der Sicht des schweizerischen Rechts' [2008] *Zeitschrift für Zivilprozess 295*

Meier, I, *Schweizerisches Zivilprozessrecht* (Zurich/Basel/Geneva, Schulthess Juristische Medien, 2010)

Meier, I and Duve, C, 'Vom Friedensrichter zum Mediator. Einführung von Mediation in bestehende Institutionen der Streitschlichtung' (1999) 95 *Schweizerische Juristenzeitung* 157

Mertens Senn, E, *Vermittlung im Sühnverfahren vor dem Hintergrund der Mediation*, Diss Lucerne (Zurich/Basel/Geneva, Schulthess Juristische Medien, 2007)

Mirimanoff, JA, 'Feasibility of Mediation Systems in Switzerland' [2009] *ASA Bulletin* 473

Moltmann-Willisch, AR, Kraus, AM and von Hammerstein, F, 'Richterliche Mediation an Berliner Zivilgerichten. Ein Erfahrungsbericht' [2011] *Zeitschrift für Rechtspolitik* 58

Müller, JP and Schefer, M, *Grundrechte in der Schweiz*, 4th edn (Bern, Stämpfli Verlag, 2008)

Mürner, D, *Gerichtsnahe Zivilmediation*, Diss Zurich (Zurich/Basel/Geneva, Schulthess Juristische Medien, 2005)

Oberhammer, P (ed), *Kurzkommentar, Schweizerische Zivilprozessordnung* (Basel, Helbing Lichtenhahn Verlag, 2010)

Peter, JT, *Gerichtsnahe Mediation. Kommentar zur Mediation in der ZPO* (Bern, Stämpfli Verlag, 2011)

Pfisterer, T, 'Über Konsens- und Mediationslösungen im öffentlichen Recht (konferieren statt prozessieren)' [2002] *Zeitschrift für schweizerisches Recht* 169

Rüede, T and Hadenfeldt, R, *Schweizerisches Schiedsgerichtsrecht*, 2nd edn (Zurich, Schulthess Polygraphischer Verlag, 1993)

Sander, FEA, 'Varieties of Dispute Processing' in LA Levin and RR Wheeler (eds), *The Pound Conference: Perspectives on Justice in the Future* (St Paul, MN, West Publishing Co, 1979) 65–87

Schneider, O, 'Grundlegendes zu Einigung und Mediation' (2010/4) *'Justice—Justiz—Giustizia': Die Schweizer Richterzeitung* no 1

Schütz, GJ, *Mediation und Schiedsgerichtsbarkeit in der Schweizerischen Zivilprozessordnung*, Diss Bern (Bern, Stämpfli Verlag, 2009)

Schwarzenegger, C, Thalmann, U and Zanolini, V, *Mediation im Strafrecht: Erfahrungen im Kanton Zürich* (Zurich, Kriminologisches Institut—Universität Zürich, 2006)

Schwenzer, Ingeborg (ed), *FamKommentar Scheidung, Band II: Anhänge*, 2nd edn (Bern, Stämpfli Verlag, 2011)

Spühler, K, Dolge, A and Gehri, M, *Schweizerisches Zivilprozessrecht* (Bern, Stämpfli Verlag, 2010)

Spühler, K, Tenchio, Luca and Infanger, D (eds), *Basler Kommentar, Schweizerische Zivilprozessordnung* (Basel, Helbing Lichtenhahn Verlag, 2010)

Staub, L, 'Die Pflichtmediation als scheidungsbezogene Kindschutzmassnahme' [2009] *Zeitschrift des Bernischen Juristenvereins* 404

Staubli, I, 'Der Friedensrichter in der Schweiz' in PG Mayr (ed), *Öffentliche Einrichtungen zur aussergerichtlichen Vermittlung von Streitigkeiten* (Wien, MANZ'sche Verlags- und Universitätsbuchhandlung, 1999) 175–191

Sutter-Somm, T, Hasenböhler, F and Leuenberger, C (eds), *Kommentar zur Schweizerischen Zivilprozessordnung (ZPO)* (Zurich/Basel/Geneva, Schulthess Juristische Medien, 2010)

Tschannen, P, *Staatsrecht der Schweizerischen Eidgenossenschaft*, 3rd edn (Bern, Stämpfli Verlag, 2011)

Umbricht Lukas, B and Gloor, U, 'Arbeitskreis 6: Angeordnete Mediation' in I Schwenzer and A Büchler (eds), *Fünfte Schweizer Familienrecht§Tage* (Bern, Stämpfli Verlag, 2010) 161–181

Umbricht Lukas, B and Gloor, U, 'Die Mediation in der Zivilprozessordnung' [2010] *FamPra.ch: Die Praxis des Familienrechts 819*

Voser, N, 'Sanktion bei Nichterfüllung einer Schlichtungsklausel, Kommentar zum Urteil des Kassationsgerichts vom 15 März 1999' [2002] *ASA Bulletin* 380

Walder-Richli, HU and Grob-Andermacher, B, *Zivilprozessrecht*, 5th edn (Zurich/Basel/Geneva, Schulthess Juristische Medien, 2009)

Walter, G, Bosch, W and Brönnimann, J, *Internationale Schiedsgerichtsbarkeit in der Schweiz* (Bern, Stämpfli Verlag, 1991)

15

Regulation of Dispute Resolution in the United States of America: From the Formal to the Informal to the 'Semi-formal'

CARRIE MENKEL-MEADOW

I. INTRODUCTION: HISTORY AND CHARACTERISTICS OF DISPUTE RESOLUTION IN THE US: FORMALISM, INFORMALISM AND 'SEMI-FORMALISM' WITH AND WITHOUT REGULATION

THE STORY OF ADR in the US is one of '*co-optation*' of what was to be a *serious challenge to formalistic and legalistic approaches* to legal and social problem solving and is now highly institutionalised by its more formal use in courts.[1] At the same time, use of private forms of dispute resolution in mediation, arbitration and newly hybridised forms of dispute resolution among disputants who can choose (and afford) to leave the formal justice system (in both large commercial matters and private family matters) has resulted in claims of increased *privatisation of justice*, with consequences for access to justice in different areas of legal dispute resolution. These consequences include difficulty of access to some forms of private dispute resolution for those who cannot afford them and claims that, with mass exits from the formal system by those who can afford to 'litigate' elsewhere, there is less interest in

[1] See C Menkel-Meadow, 'Pursuing Settlement in an Adversary Culture: The Law of ADR' (1991) 19 *Florida State Law Review* 1.

judicial service and reform. In addition, in recent years consumers and employees have been subjected to contractual commitments to mandatory arbitration, sustained by the US Supreme Court, which has all but eliminated choice about where to resolve certain kinds of disputes. All of these claims are highly contested by practitioners, judges and scholars of the American legal system.[2]

The uses of various forms of ADR are difficult to assess as much occurs in private, non-reportable settings and there is no national or centralised form of 'regulation' of dispute resolution in the US. As reported below, there are many sources of regulation in case law, statutes and local procedural rules at both federal and state levels, but much dispute resolution activity in the US remains private and market based, as parties may choose contractually before, during or after a dispute has arisen, how to manage their disputes—through private negotiation and settlement, mediation, arbitration, fact-finding, neutral evaluation or a variety of newly hybridised forms of dispute resolution. There is no formal reporting requirement of such processes or their outcomes, so much remains unknown about the actual dimensions of private dispute resolution, now often fully approved of and sanctioned by public institutions. As this paper will describe, dispute resolution in the US is now formal, informal and 'semi-formal'.

The watershed years for regulation of formal dispute resolution in the US might be considered to be both *1938* (the year that both the Federal Rules of Civil Procedure were drafted by a stellar committee of lawyers, judges and academics, and enacted (by passive approval of the US Congress) and *Erie v Tompkins*[3] was decided (ruling that procedural rules were federal (national) and substantive rules would be state law in diversity cases in American federal courts, thus overturning the prior practice of the reverse, state procedural law in all federal courts with enforcement of 'federal common law' for substantive decisions) and *1976* (when the Pound Conference on the Causes of Popular Dissatisfaction with the Administration of Justice included a paper by Harvard Professor Frank Sander[4] which heralded the beginning of consideration for formal judicial policy 'varieties of dispute processing', including mediation, arbitration, neutral evaluation, fact-finding and ombuds as 'alternatives' to formal adjudication).

The juxtaposition of these important historical events in a single paragraph should give one the sense that dispute resolution and its regulation in the US is inherently complex, involving both national (what we call federal) and state regulation (with 50 different states), and a great variety of informal and private processes that remain largely unregulated in the public sphere (though sometimes scrutinised in public litigation when constitutional, contractual or other challenges are made). This chapter attempts to describe this complex legal landscape and, in the end, concludes that, at least in the US, 'model laws of ADR' are unlikely to succeed at the national level. Current efforts to create 'uniform state laws' (a separate process for making uniform those subjects that transcend state boundaries, as in the Uniform Commercial Code[5])

[2] See, eg J Resnik, 'Many Doors? Closing Doors? Alternative Dispute Resolution and Adjudication' (1995) 10 *Ohio State Journal on Dispute Resolution* 211.

[3] 304 US 64 (1938).

[4] FEA Sander, 'Varieties of Dispute Processing' in A Levin and R Wheeler (eds), *The Pound Conference: Perspectives on Justice in the Future* (St Paul, MN, West Publishing Co, 1979) 111.

[5] The National Conference on Commissioners for Uniform State Laws (NCCUSL) has successfully drafted and promoted the Uniform Commercial Code for contract law, family law (adoption measures) and many other subjects, but has been less successful in dispute resolution matters. At the time of writing, the Uniform

have been largely unsuccessful in dispute resolution. The formal regulatory landscape in dispute resolution in the US now consists of at least the following legal sources:

- The US Constitution (what process is 'due' in what (public) procedures and what governmental bodies are assigned what dispute resolution functions, eg separation of powers?)
- Federal legislation (eg Civil Justice Reform Act of 1990,[6] Administrative Dispute Resolution Act of 1996,[7] Alternative Dispute Resolution Act of 1998[8])
- Federal rules of civil procedure (and criminal procedure for plea bargaining rules), including
  - Local rules for each federal district (94)
  - Circuit Court of Appeals rules and practices for mediation and other forms of settlement and ADR procedures (11 circuits and two specialty appeals bodies, for trade and patents[9])
- Common law jurisprudence and many precedents from US Supreme Court and appellate federal courts on many ADR issues (including mandatory arbitration (see below), confidentiality, privileges, enforceability and 'good faith' participation requirements, among others)
- Administrative agency rules and practices in a variety of subject areas, including securities regulation, civil litigation, energy and environment, education, business and commerce, labour and military procurement (and including a federal governmental coordinating body for ADR efforts in federal agencies[10])
- State legislation (50 states and several territories, eg Puerto Rico)
- State common and decisional law[11]
- Uniform Mediation Act/ Uniform Arbitration Act (efforts to create common state law regulation in different aspects of dispute resolution)
- Private contracts (specifying conditions and rules for dispute resolution, often enforced by courts, making common law rulings (with precedential effects) and including mass, trade association, institutional and organisational forms of 'internal' dispute resolution)
- Private decisional law (eg arbitration awards, some public (eg investment and labour) and most private (eg commercial arbitration) awards
- Private organisational rule systems (eg American Arbitration Association rules for arbitration, mediation; International Institute for Conflict Prevention and Resolution (CPR), Association of Conflict Resolution (ACR), including
  - Substantive
  - Procedural and
  - Ethical Rules

Mediation Act (2001) (specifying rules for confidentiality in mediation) has been adopted in only 11 states, making it hardly a 'uniform' regulation.

[6] 28 USC § 471.

[7] 5 USC § 571.

[8] 28 USC § 651.

[9] RJ Niemic, *Mediation and Conference Programs in the Federal Appeals Courts* (Washington, DC, Federal Judicial Center, 1997).

[10] Office of Dispute Resolution, Department of Justice, Interagency Working Group on ADR, see <www.usdoj.gov>.

[11] See, eg J Coben and P Thompson, 'Disputing Irony: a Systematic Look at Litigation about Mediation' (2006) 11 *Harvard Negotiation Law Review* 43.

At the level of procedural rules, little was said in 1938 about anything other than formal trials, though innovations in information sharing and American-style discovery, class actions, simplicity of pleading rules, and a rule (Rule 16) about pre-trial settlement conferences with judges introduced some new processes for dispute resolution outside of a full-blown trial. Over the years, those rules have been amended many times to include complex rules about settlement offers (Rule 68), the use of court appointed special masters to facilitate discovery and settlement (Rule 53), limits on discovery, and increased participation of both judges and court adjuncts to 'intervene' and promote settlement activity,[12] among other relevant rule amendments, the most important being the role that the Rules of Civil Procedure (Rule 83) allocates to each individual federal trial (district) court (94 of them in 50 states) to make its own 'local rules', which has turned out to be a major source for ADR regulation in federal courts.[13] Over the years, most states have conformed their formal procedural rules to look much like the federal rules, though with respect to 'ADR' some states took the lead in promoting (and regulating) the use of court-adjunct processes to encourage settlement (eg Massachusetts, Florida, Ohio, New York, Texas and California).[14]

After the procedural 'revolution' in 1938, American formal law turned most of its attention to creating new substantive rights, through the activism of a variety of social and legal movements, civil (and now human) rights, consumer rights, women's rights, environmental protection, gay rights and anti-poverty activism, using both legislation and litigation to create, establish and litigate about these new legal rights and entitlements. At the same time, the procedural innovation of class actions led to many more law suits to efficiently claim on behalf of discriminated individuals and groups, securities and consumer frauds, mass tort victims and other aggregated claims. All of this led to an expansive increase in litigation and to the somewhat contested claim that the US was the most litigious nation in the world.[15]

The movement for more 'informal' justice in the US in the late 1970s and early 1980s[16] drew its inspirations from a variety of sources, including the desire for qualitatively better options and solutions for dispute resolution problem solving in substance,[17] and more party participation and empowerment in procedure and process, as part of larger political movements seeking democratic participation in the polity and the legal system. The impetus for much procedural reform, however, came from courts and judicial officials, including then Chief Justice Warren Burger, who sought to decrease court dockets and case processing time, reduce litigation cost and complexity, and for the cynics among us, move cases away from federal courts to other fora, including state courts, small claims venues, and other processes outside of the

[12] See, eg C Menkel-Meadow, 'For and Against Settlement: Uses and Abuses of the Mandatory Settlement Conference' (1985) 33 *UCLA Law Review* 485.

[13] E Plapinger and D Stienstra, *ADR and Settlement in the Federal District Courts* (Washington, DC, Federal Judicial Center, 1996).

[14] See N Rogers, C McEwen, S Cole, J Coben and P Thompson *Mediation, Law Policy and Practice*, 3rd edn (St Paul, MN, Thomson Reuters, 2011).

[15] M Galanter, 'Reading the Landscape of Our Disputes: What We Know, Don't Know (and Think We Know) about Our Allegedly Contentious and Litigious Society' (1983) 31 *UCLA Law Review* 4.

[16] RL Abel (ed), *The Politics of Informal Justice: The American Experience* (New York, Academic Press, 1982).

[17] C Menkel-Meadow, 'Toward another View of Legal Negotiation: The Structure of Problem Solving' (1984) 31 *UCLA Law Review* 754.

courts, tied together in the nomenclature of 'alternative' dispute resolution. Thus, from the beginning, at least two different motivations for alternative or less formal processes were present—the '*quantitative-efficiency*' concerns to make justice more accessible, cheaper, faster and efficient, and the more '*qualitative-party empowering*' ideas that, with greater and more direct party participation, and identification of underlying needs and interests, parties might identify more tailored solutions to their problems that would be less brittle and binary than the win/lose outcomes of formal courts, with 'limited remedial imaginations'.[18]

In recent years, the progress of dispute resolution variations has been labeled, by this author, as '*process pluralism*',[19] and by others as '*appropriate*' (not alternative) *dispute resolution*, connoting recognition that not all matters should be subjected to the same treatment—'one size of legal process does not fit all'. Different kinds and numbers of parties, issues, structures of disputes and legal matters might dictate different formats of dispute processing.[20] This is a serious questioning of the American procedural ideal of 'transsubstantive' procedure,[21] and such claims invoke both notions of 'technocratic' assignment of cases to efficient or appropriate fora,[22] as well as more deeply jurisprudential concerns about whether different processes are necessary to ensure different kinds of justice in different situations. Must 'all cases' be treated 'alike' or, if 'like cases' are to be treated 'alike', how do we know which cases are 'like enough' each other to be treated with the same process and procedure?

Debates about 'the vanishing trial'[23] and the loss of formal procedures, as fewer and fewer cases make it all the way to full adjudication in the US (only about 2 per cent of cases filed in a wide variety of courts, both federal and state, general and specialised, now go on to full trial), have raged among scholars, judges and lawyers, as there is now concern, on the part of some, that not enough cases are available to generate the precedents we need in a common law, stare decisis legal regime to transparently produce reasoned rules and principles for the governance of our society.[24] As I argued some years ago, this is a question of 'Whose Dispute Is It Anyway?'[25]—the parties seeking dispute resolution or the larger society that needs transparent and certain kinds of (adversarial?) processes to produce law and justice for the 'many' out of the disputes of the 'few'.

The relationship of process to assessments of justice is a serious jurisprudential question, considered by many procedural theorists. A separate field of 'procedural justice' or 'the social psychology of justice' has claimed for decades, through empirical study,

[18] Ibid.

[19] C Menkel-Meadow, 'Peace and Justice: Notes on the Evolution and Purposes of Legal Processes' (2006) 94 *Georgetown Law Journal* 553.

[20] C Menkel-Meadow, *Dispute Processing and Conflict Resolution: Theory, Practice, and Policy* (Burlington, Ashgate Press, 2003).

[21] SN Subrin, 'The Limitations of Transsubstantive Procedure: An Essay on Adjusting the "One Size Fits All" Assumption' (2010) 87 *Denver University Law Review* 377.

[22] The idea that the 'forum should fit the fuss' was originally Professor Maurice Rosenberg's (Columbia University) is now captured by FEA Sander and SB Goldberg, 'Fitting the Forum to the Fuss: A User Friendly Guide to Selecting an ADR Procedure' (1994) 10 *Negotiation Journal* 49.

[23] M Galanter, 'The Vanishing Trial: An Examination of Trials and Related Matters in Federal and State Courts' (2004) 1 *Journal of Empirical Legal Studies*, 459.

[24] SN Subrin, 'Litigation and Democracy: Restoring a Reasonable Prospect of Trial' (2011) 46 *Harvard Civil Rights-Civil Liberties Law Review* 399; O Fiss, 'Against Settlement' (1984) 93 *Yale Law Journal* 1073.

[25] C Menkel-Meadow, 'Whose Dispute Is It Anyway? A Philosophical and Democratic Defense of Settlement (in Some Cases)' (1995) 83 *Georgetown Law Journal* 2663.

that users of dispute resolution process assess the 'justice' and 'fairness' of processes independently from the outcomes parties achieve.[26] From the American side, I have long claimed that Lon Fuller is our 'jurisprudent of process',[27] for in a series of articles Fuller has argued that each different process, whether adjudication, arbitration, mediation, legislation or regulation (and other processes, such as voting) has its own 'integrity'—that is, its own norms, ethics and types of outcomes produced, each requiring its own philosophical justification, as well as the possibility of its own set of 'rules'.[28]

In the modern-day experience of so many varied processes used for dispute resolution (reviewed below), I often ask if Lon Fuller would approve of the great *hybridisation* of process that has occurred in recent decades, with such new forms as mediation and arbitration combined to form *med-arb* or *arb-med*[29] (in labour, family, commercial disputes), '*early neutral evaluation*'[30] or '*settlement conferences*', a process comprising both judges and lawyers, giving evaluative feedback to counsel and parties in pre-trial settings,[31] '*summary jury trials*'[32] (jury advisory opinions in public courts for settlement purposes), '*mini-trials*'[33] (private hybrid processes using witness testimony, argument, negotiation, mediation and sometimes arbitration) and '*private judging*',[34] where private parties hire judges to adjudicate matters in secrecy, with full appellate processes and protection of the courts (as is authorised by state constitutions and statutes, such as in California)—and now even *private juries*[35] are hired to resolve disputes outside of the courts, so there is independent lay fact-finding, but no public record of the outcome or deliberations. What would Lon Fuller, and what should we, scholars and practitioners of procedural law, make of all these various processes? How do we know if these processes are fair, just and appropriate for either the parties themselves or the larger system of legal dispute resolution?

In this chapter I will address these questions by suggesting that, in the US, we now have more than 'formal' or 'informal' processes—we have many 'semi-formal' (hybrids or mixtures of processes), and the question is how shall we evaluate the efficacy, efficiency and legitimacy of so many different kinds of process. In the US, we have

[26] EA Lind and T Tyler, *The Social Psychology of Procedural Justice* (New York, Plenum Press, 1988); N Welsh, 'Remembering the Role of Justice in Resolution: Insights from Procedural and Social Justice Theories' (2004) 54 *Journal of Legal Education* 49.

[27] C Menkel-Meadow, 'Mothers and Fathers of Invention; The Intellectual Founders of ADR' (2000) 16 *Ohio State Journal of Dispute Resolution* 13.

[28] K Winston (ed), *The Principles of Social Order: Selected Essays of Lon Fuller*, revised edn (Oxford and Portland Oregon, Hart Publishing, 2001).

[29] C Menkel-Meadow, L Love, A Kupfer Schneider, J Sternlight, *Dispute Resolution: Beyond the Adversarial Model*, 2nd edn (New York, Wolters Kluwer, 2011) 526–29; C Menkel-Meadow (ed), *Complex Dispute Resolution: Vol 1 Foundational Processes* and *Vol 2, Multi-Party Dispute Processes, Decision Making and Democracy* (Farnham, Ashgate Press, 2012).

[30] W Brazil, 'A Close Look at Three Court-Sponsored ADR Programs: Why They Exist, How They Operate, What They Deliver, and Whether They Threaten Important Values' [1990] *University of Chicago Legal Forum* 303.

[31] C Menkel-Meadow, 'For and Against Settlement: The Uses and Abuses of the Pre-Trial Settlement Conference' (1985) 33 *UCLA Law Review* 485.

[32] J Alfini, 'Summary Jury Trials in State and Federal Courts: A Comparative Analysis of the Perceptions of Participating Lawyers' (1989) 4 *Ohio State Journal of Dispute Resolution* 213.

[33] ED Green, *The CPR Legal Program Mini-Trial Handbook* (New York, Matthew Bender & Co, 1982).

[34] Cal Civ Proc Code §§ 638-645 (West Supp 2004); Fla Stat Ann § 44.104 (West 2003 & Supp 2004); A Kim, 'Rent-a-Judges and the Cost of Selling Justice' (1994) 44 *Duke Law Journal* 166.

[35] M Jacobs, 'Legal Beat: Private Jury Trials: Cheap, Quick and Controversial', *Wall Street Journal*, 7 July 1997.

a very elaborate *formal justice system of federal and state rules of procedure (both civil and criminal)*, as well as countless specialised tribunals with their own procedural rules, such as in bankruptcy, labour, family law, securities, technology, trade, patent and trademark, and taxes.

We also have many *informal fora* for dispute resolution, including private uses of mediation, arbitration and related processes, religious courts and mediation agencies, specialised business and industry panels of dispute resolution (eg banking, insurance, franchise, construction, technology, sports and energy), using both mediation and arbitration techniques,[36] community and neighbourhood dispute resolution processes,[37] online consumer forms of dispute resolution,[38] internal organisational forms of dispute resolution (ombuds or 'IDR' (internal dispute resolution[39]), including grievance processes in large corporations, universities, trade unions, government agencies and non-governmental institutions[40]), as well as dispute resolution fora even in illegitimate enterprises—gangs[41] and organised crime.

We now also have a more hybrid set of processes which can be called '*semi-formal*' *forms of dispute resolution*, which utilise both private and public processes with increasingly structured and formal aspects of process, even if there is little to no recourse to more formal adjudication or appellate review. These include the 'ADR' programmes 'annexed' to courts, with a great deal of federal and state variations in rules, and access to courts after use, mandatory arbitration clauses found in many consumer and business contracts, which obligate parties to use structured out of court arbitration tribunals, some with very detailed procedural rules, but little to no appeal to courts (under the Federal Arbitration Act's limited grounds for vacatur of an arbitration award[42]), as well as the elaborate structure of international commercial arbitration which is now quite 'formal' in its conduct, if still mostly unattached to formal courts.[43] Thus, the notion of any omnibus 'regulation' of ADR is simply

[36] CPR Industry Panels Dispute Resolution.

[37] S Merry and N Milner, *The Possibility of Popular Justice: A Case Study of Community Mediation in the United States* (Ann Arbor, University of Michigan Press, 1993).

[38] E Katsh and J Rifkin, *Online Dispute Resolution: Resolving Conflicts in Cyberspace* (San Francisco, Jossey Bass, 2001); MSA Wahab, E Katsh and D Rainey (eds), *Online Dispute Resolution: Theory and Practice* (The Hague, Eleven International Publishing, 2012).

[39] L Edelman, H Erlanger and J Lande, 'Internal Dispute Resolution: The Transformation of Civil Rights in the Workplace' (1993) 27 *Law & Society Review* 497.

[40] W Ury, J Brett and S Goldberg, *Getting Disputes Resolved: Designing Systems to Cut Costs of Conflict* (San Francisco, Jossey Bass, 1988).

[41] S Venkatesh, *Gang Leader for a Day* (New York, Penguin, 2008).

[42] 9 USC § 10; *Hall Street Associates v Mattel*, 552 US 576 (2008).

[43] Y Dezalay and B Garth, *Dealing in Virtue: International Commercial Arbitration and the Construction of a Transnational Legal Order* (Chicago, University of Chicago Press, 1996). But see A Stone Sweet, 'Arbitration and Judicialization' (2011) 1(9) *Onati Socio-Legal Series 1*, who argues that some forms of international arbitration (state–investor arbitration) are becoming increasingly judicialised by explicitly publishing rulings, giving reasons in opinions and decisions, which include common legal doctrines like proportionality and balancing, allowing *amicus curiae* briefs, treating past decisions as precedential and arguing for appellate processes. Some scholars (I am among them, see C Menkel-Meadow, 'Are Cross-Cultural Ethics Standards Possible or Desirable in International Arbitration?' in P Gauch, F Werro, P Pichonnaz (eds), *Melangés en l'honneur de Pierre Tercier* (Geneva, Schulthess, 2008)) think that even international commercial arbitration, a creature of private contract, is in fact, dependent on the state—national courts for enforcement and recognition of awards, pursuant to a public international law treaty (the New York Convention for the Recognition and Enforcement of Foreign Arbitral Awards, 1958) and that international commercial arbitration is, in fact, creating a common law of modern *lex mercatoria*, T Carbonneau, *Lex Mercatoria and Arbitration: A Discussion of the New Law Merchant*, (Huntington, NY, Juris Net, 1997).

impossible to imagine in the US with this great variety of types of process and locations of process in both public and private, and now 'hybrid' spheres.[44]

Years ago, in an effort such as the present one, I imagined that a 'core' set of ethical guidelines for conducting mediation could be designed,[45] and I spent five years chairing a commission to write uniform ethical rules for lawyers serving as third-party neutrals (arbitrators and mediators) in alternative processes[46] (a subject that had never been regulated by American ethical and professional responsibility rules for lawyers in general).[47] Though many private organisations have now followed with rules of ethics (confidentiality, conflicts of interest, etc) for third parties and advocates in ADR proceedings, there are in fact not that many 'core' principles upon which everyone can agree. Even within the US, conflicts of interest, ex parte communications with arbitrators, practice with non-legal professionals, methods of fee payment,[48] and a host of other issues remain variable and contested.

As I have written before, when ADR is taken to multi-national or international contexts, the issues become even more complicated, as different systems impose different rules with respect to such issues as whether witnesses may be prepared before testimony (malpractice if not done in the US, unethical in England and Germany), discovery, cross-examination, written versus oral testimony, conflicts of interest[49] and many other procedural differences. The European Directive on Mediation (2008/58/EC) has an ethics code appended to it (European Code of Conduct for Mediators[50]), but I predict that these principles will have many difficult legal and social cultural issues in application, and they already fail to deal with all the issues that might arise in a multi-national mediation setting.

For purposes of this chapter, I use the term 'semi-formal' from American etiquette dressing requirements ('smart casual' is the British equivalent) to connote the attempt to locate dispute processes half way between formal tuxedos or 'black tie' and evening gowns of the bygone days of formal gatherings (and formal regulation), and the totally

[44] American Bar Association, Section of Dispute Resolution, 'Considering Regulation of ADR' (2013) 19(3) *Dispute Resolution Magazine* 4–44.

[45] C Menkel-Meadow, 'Professional Responsibility for Third Party Neutrals' [July 2009] *Alternatives to the High Cost of Litigation* 129; C Menkel-Meadow, 'Ancillary Practice and Conflicts of Interest: When Lawyer Ethics Rules Are Not Enough' [February 1995] *Alternatives to the High Cost of Litigation* 15.

[46] CPR-Georgetown Commission on Ethics and Standards in ADR, Model Rule for the Lawyer as Third Party Neutral (2002), available at <www.cpradr.org/Resources/ALLCPRArticles/tabid/265/ID/622/Model-Rule-for-The-Lawyer-as-Third-Party-Neutral.aspx>.

[47] There is now some minimal regulation in the American Bar Association Model Rules of Professional Conduct which recognises that lawyers may serve in these capacities, MRPC Rule 2.2, but 'tribunals' to which a lawyer owes a duty of candor includes arbitration, but excludes mediation (Rule 1.1 definition (o)), which has been assimilated to include a slightly different set of ethics for negotiation found in Model Rule 4.2 (allowing some forms of 'puffing' (exaggeration), no duty to disclose true 'opinions' or one's real principal).

[48] Whether ADR should permit 'contingent fees' (or a percentage of the settlement amount for the mediator or award for the arbitrator), as is permitted in American litigation, remains a hotly contested subject. Some private mediators and arbitrators also charge very large (and unregulated) daily or hourly fees as well, rising to as much as tens of thousands of dollars a day or many thousands of dollars an hour in high stakes matters. For lawyers in more traditional practice, the ethics rules now require at least some written disclosures of 'reasonable' fees, and in some settings (eg class actions, bankruptcy, and statutory fee cases) there is some judicial review of fees in some matters.

[49] C Rogers, *Ethics in International Arbitration* (Oxford, Oxford University Press, 2013).

[50] The new International Mediation Institute (based in the The Hague) has also been promulgating suggested standards and rules for mediators, both for competence and ethics, and for cultural competency as well, see <www.IMImediation.org>.

informal or casual dress more common in today's variety of professional, family and entertainment gatherings. To request 'semi-formal' dress is to ask the gentlemen to wear ties and jackets, if not tuxedos, and to hope that the women will wear, if not dresses and skirts, than at least 'fancy pants'. The idea is to preserve some notion of order, elegance, solemnity and seriousness to the social event. Thus, 'semi-formal' uses of mediation and arbitration in the courts suggest (sometimes falsely) that someone is looking over or supervising the choice of mediators or arbitrators and ensuring their competence and ethics, and, in some cases, permitting a further appeal to the black-robed (and formal) adjudicator. What level of regulation is appropriate for formal, informal and now 'semi-formal' dispute resolution remains, for me, somewhat problematic, as I report below on a wide variety of regulatory differences in both federal and state courts in the US, as well as some private settings in which dispute resolution occurs. More problematic is the assumption that 'regulation' will be effective and can guarantee some measure of both quality of process and access to process in such a variegated environment.

For example, the elaborate rules of the American Arbitration Association, if not full-on Federal Rules of Civil Procedure, still provide for some discovery and mandatory information exchange, that old American practice of document production and factual inquiries of the other side, in person (depositions) and through detailed (and costly) document and now computer searches, preliminary relief, and in some cases the same relief (punitive damages) as courts would provide in the US. Though virtually all of this occurs without full public transparency or appellate review, at least (in theory) everyone knows the rules they have selected (usually through contract or selection of a particular arbitral administering institution). Recently in the US, many efforts to challenge the true 'voluntariness' of these now 'mandatory' clauses to arbitrate contract, consumer, business and employment disputes have failed, as the formal courts, including the US Supreme Court, have sustained contracts which require certain forms of dispute resolution (usually arbitration), even where consumers and employees do not really know or understand what they are signing.[51]

Totally casual or informal forms of dispute resolution are now called 'litigation-lite' (arbitration) or 'mediation-heavy' (evaluative mediation where third party neutrals decide or strongly suggest solutions to parties, rather than simply facilitating party negotiation[52]), and occur without formal clarity about the procedural rules applied or what can happen if the process fails. The question here is whether 'semi formal' processes can legitimately operate in a space between the transparency and presumed consistency of formal justice, and the confidentiality, flexibility and self-determination of informal processes. Should we be subjecting different kinds of process to different

[51] See, eg *Gilmer v Interstate/Johnson Lane Corp* 500 US 20 (1991); J Sternlight, 'Fixing the Mandatory Arbitration Problem: We Need the Arbitration Fairness Act of 2009' (2009) 16 *Dispute Resolution Magazine* 5; J Sternlight, 'Is the US Out on a Limb? Comparing the US Approach to Mandatory Consumer and Employment Arbitration to That of the Rest of the World' (2002) 56 *University of Miami Law Review* 831.

[52] L Love, 'The Top Ten Reasons Why Mediators Should Not Evaluate' (1997) 24 *Florida State Law Review* 937. Some commentators have called this healthy 'intra-process pluralism', where parties can choose variations of forms of mediation or arbitration or negotiation approaches; others are more concerned that processes lose their purity or integrity when they depart from a central 'core'. See, eg L Riskin and NA Welsh, 'Is That All There Is? The Problem in Court-Oriented Mediation' (2008) 15 *George Mason Law Review* 863-932; LL Riskin, 'Decision-Making in Mediation: The New Old Grid and New New Grid System' (2003) 79 *Notre Dame Law Review* 1.

kinds of evaluative criteria and rules or should all process be judged by the same criteria?

This increasing complexification, segmentation and differentiation of process, which was intended to express and be justified by such important justice values as *party choice*, *consent*, *self-determination* and *party-tailored solutions to problems*, now potentially threatens other justice notions of *consistency*, *transparency*, *true consent and knowledge*, as well as *equity*, *equal treatment*, *clarity*, and *socially* '*uniform*' and *just solutions.*

By describing and reviewing some of the more interesting current developments in modern American process pluralism here, I hope to expose the difficulties, paradoxes and contradictions of processes that have different goals and purposes (especially if parties have different goals and purposes within the same dispute), especially when 'semi-formal' is neither formal nor informal. Consider, as reviewed below, the paradox of enforcing private arbitral awards in public courts, the absence of clear enforcement rules for private mediation, the conflicts of private religious 'courts' with public values expressed in formal state courts,[53] the role conflation of judges who mediate or manage settlement conferences rather than adjudicate, and the absence of records by which to judge any of this when parties choose to take their informal or semi-formal dispute resolution processes to entirely private settings. To what extent do we need 'formalism' in the form of public or transparent, uniform rules of process and procedure to judge the legitimacy, fairness or justice of any particular dispute resolution process? To what extent should different processes be permitted to have different forms of legitimacy or justification? Are values of '*party control*' and '*consent*' contradictory to the needs of the state to provide '*public justice*' and both *procedural and substantive* '*transparency*'? Is '*process pluralism*' itself a 'just' good?

II. THE CHARACTERISTICS OF 'FORMAL' JUSTICE

Conceptions of formal justice in modern American jurisprudence include, in a trial or formal hearing setting, transparency or publicity of proceedings, reasoned legal arguments based on legal precedent and 'proven' facts, including witness examination and testimony, and discovery of facts, documents and information, even from adverse parties and sources, public officials (whether elected or appointed in both state and federal variations) as judges who advise fact finders (juries) about the law or engage in fact-finding themselves, as well as make legal rulings, write formal, reasoned opinions that have precedential or *stare decisis* impact on other, like, cases, and most importantly, are governed by formal rules (Federal (or state) Rules of Civil or Criminal Procedure), and are subject to appellate and other review procedures.[54] For Lon Fuller, adjudica-

[53] MA Helfand, 'Religious Arbitration and the New Multi-culturalism: Negotiating Conflicting Legal Orders' (2011) 86 *New York University Law Review* 1231; E Waldman, *Mediation Ethics* (San Francisco, Jossey-Bass, 2011) ch 9.

[54] L Fuller, 'The Forms and Limits of Adjudication' in Winston (ed), *The Principles of Social Order* and (1978) 92 *Harvard Law Review* 353; Fiss, 'Against Settlement'; M Shapiro, *Courts: A Comparative and Political Analysis* (Chicago, University of Chicago Press, 1981); D Luban, 'Settlements and the Erosion of the Public Realm' (1995) 83 *Georgetown Law Journal* 2619; J Resnik, 'Managerial Judges' (1982) 96 *Harvard Law Review* 374.

tion or 'formal justice' is warranted when there is a need for reasoned argument to decide disputes, not only for the immediate disputants, but also to elucidate rules for the larger society, especially when *rights* (and especially competing rights) are at issue. Adjudication requires the decision of 'authoritative' and 'neutral' decision makers who *explain their reasons* (assumed to be agreed to or binding on the disputants and the larger society in which they are embedded), which are derived from what we now commonly call '*the rule of law*', or properly enacted law (legal positivism) or common law interpretive law.

The third party neutral judge or 'universal third' (as historian Martin Shapiro describes the role) is expected to be detached from the parties and the issues, and to 'rule' on the basis of agreed to substantive and procedural rules. This assumes the foundational principle of 'consent' to the juridical form and 'jurisdiction' (power to speak) of the tribunal. Many Anglo-American writers on formal justice also assume a particular kind of process—adversary argument, with assumptions that 'truth', as well as justice, will be produced by hearty and contested, if 'policed', production of evidence, and arguments from 'both' (assuming two) sides.[55] The neutrality and disinterestedness of the 'decider' or 'arbiter' in formal justice is so important to many jurisprudes of formal process that any departure from the distinctive adjudicative role (such as to 'manage' or mediate cases) is regarded as sullying the basic process.[56]

In summary, conceptions of the core aspects of formal justice include:

- Formal and clear *rules of procedures*, known to or consented to by the parties, including allocation of tasks of production of proof and *evidence rules*
- Transparency/*publicity of hearing*
- *Neutrality and disinterestedness of deciders* of both fact (sometimes juries) and law (judges)
- *Access to information* from all parties (under oaths of truth telling), with limited confidentiality or other policy protections
- *Rights or 'rule of law' based outcomes and decisions*
- With appropriate and authorised *legal remedies* ordered by
- *Public officials* (judges) or their delegates (juries), with
- *Public and reasoned decisions* explaining outcomes and legal basis of outcomes for
- *Clarification of rules and basis of decision* for the parties, and guidance for others in similar situations
- *Possibility of review of decisions* for error or other faulty process or substantive reasons

All of these elements define various aspects of the content of the American (and Anglo) conception of 'due process'. Unfortunately (for formal justice and the parties), even some of the strongest proponents of the need for 'adjudication' in some circumstances (eg when 'rights' are necessary to make 'right') acknowledge that some situations call for different elements of dispute resolution or decision making both at the individual (eg family or workplace) and societal (the polity) level. Lon Fuller acknowledged that some relationships (family, workplace, repeat commercial customers) and some matters (the 'polycentric' dispute with many intersecting and mutually affecting

[55] See S Hampshire, *Justice is Conflict* (Princeton, Princeton University Press, 2000).

[56] See, eg Resnik, 'Managerial Judges' and Luban, 'Settlements and the Erosion of the Public Realm'.

issues) were better handled in other forms of resolution (mediation with trades, in some settings, votes of aggregate masses in democratic legislatures, arbitration when privacy, speed and consistency are desired). Rights sometimes conflict with each other, without a clear or single allocation to 'right' (eg consider rights of privacy and public rights to know; parental 'rights' in custody matters, and various conflicts in religious and secular rights in modern constitutional orders). And even some important public matters (eg domestic violence, child abuse, drug use) might be better handled with less public adjudication (and shame) and more private and caring solutions (as in modern problem-solving courts or private restorative justice settings). Categories of case types and proper process treatments do not always neatly converge.

Thus, for Lon Fuller, 'other' processes are themselves morally, politically, socially and legally legitimated by what parties might want or need, or the situation requires. Fuller's (and my own[57]) claims for other processes are based on the 'integrity of process differences' themselves, not just the need for faster, cheaper or more efficient forms of traditional adjudication. Parties might want to preserve relationships or communities or workplaces without brittle, rigid or binary decisions (which could lead to desires for revenge or retribution in repeat play settings). Parties might want to 'share' (eg children in divorce) or preserve, rather than divide, resources. Rules of law might give both or 'all' sides to a particular dispute similar or non-dispositive claims of right. Coordinated, rather than competitive, action could lead to creative new outcomes and solutions to new or unlegislated for problems or issues.[58] Some communities might prefer to resolve their disputes or solve their problems within their own community norms.[59]

III. INFORMAL JUSTICE IN THE US

Although there is a long history of informal justice in the US, with religious, local community and business groups negotiating, mediating or arbitrating their own disputes since the early colonial period and continuing to the present,[60] modern informal dispute resolution in the US is derived from several different substantive fields (labour,[61] commercial law, civil rights,[62] environmental[63] and family law[64]), a judicial

[57] See, eg C Menkel-Meadow, 'Peace and Justice: Notes on the Evolution and Purposes of Process' (2006) 94 *Georgetown Law Journal* 553 and C Menkel-Meadow, 'The Trouble with the Adversary System in a Post-Modern, Multicultural World' (1996) 38 *William & Mary Law Review* 5.

[58] C Menkel-Meadow, 'Aha! Is Creativity Possible in Legal Problem Solving and Teachable in Legal Education' (2001) 6 *Harvard Negotiation Law Review* 97.

[59] O Chase, *Law, Culture and Ritual: Disputing Systems in Cross-Cultural Context* (New York, NYU Press, 2005); PH Gulliver, *Disputes and Negotiations: A Cross Cultural Perspective* (New York, Academic Press, 1979); L Nader and H Todd (eds), *The Disputing Process—Law in Ten Societies* (New York, Columbia University Press, 1978); C Freshman, 'Privatizing Same-Sex Marriage through Alternative Dispute Resolution: Community Enhancing Versus Community Enabling Mediation' (1997) 44 *UCLA Law Review* 1687.

[60] JS Auerbach, *Justice without Law? Resolving Disputes without Lawyers* (Oxford, Oxford University Press, 1983).

[61] JT Barrett, *A History of Alternative Dispute Resolution: The Story of a Political, Social and Cultural Movement* (San Francisco, Jossey Bass, 2004).

[62] A Pfund (ed), *From Conflict Resolution to Social Justice: The Work and Legacy of Wallace Warfield* (New York, Bloomsbury Press, 2013).

[63] L Bacow and M Wheeler, *Environmental Dispute Resolution* (New York, Springer, 1984).

[64] G Friedman, *A Guide to Divorce Mediation* (New York, Workman, 1993).

movement (docket clearing efficiency[65]) and a social movement (party empowerment, consumer[66] and civil rights accountability and more tailored solutions to social and legal problems) of the 1970s and 1980s, which together produced a turn to private negotiation, mediation,[67] community consensus building,[68] and commercial arbitration processes.[69]

Modern American dispute resolution has a strong intellectual grounding[70] in decision sciences,[71] game theory,[72] international relations, economics, social and cognitive psychology,[73] anthropology,[74] sociology[75] and political science, as claims for 'better' solutions to legal and social problems were articulated with reference to 'interest and needs'-based negotiations,[76] pie-expanding, not dividing, resource allocation,[77] efficient information sharing and processing,[78] and a move away from purely 'competitive' processes to collaborative and coordinated decision making.[79]

In the 1970s and 1980s, theorists of better problem solving, combined with judicial and political activists, called attention to many processes 'alternative' to court- and formal-based dispute resolution, including dyadic and multi-party negotiation, mediation, arbitration and hybrid processes like community consensus building, ombuds within organisations and victim–offender mediation in criminal matters.[80] What was formerly under the radar screen (negotiation as the most common form of dispute resolution, through settlements prior to, during or even after trial) became the subject of formal instruction in law schools, empirical and social science study,[81] and policy

[65] W Burger, 'Isn't There a Better Way?' (1982) 68 *American Bar Association Journal* 274.

[66] C Harrington, *Shadow Justice: The Ideology and Institutionalization of Alternatives to Court* (Westport, Greenwood Press, 1985).

[67] C Menkel-Meadow, L Love and A Schneider, *Mediation: Practice, Policy, and Ethics* (New York, Wolters Kluwer, 2nd edn, 2013); C Menkel-Meadow (ed), *Mediation: Theory, Policy and Practice* (Aldershot, Ashgate, 2000).

[68] See, eg L Susskind, S McKernan and J Thomas-Lermer, *The Consensus Building Handbook: A Comprehensive Guide to Reaching Agreement* (Thousand Oaks, Sage Publications, 1999); R Schoenholtz, 'Neighborhood Justice Systems: Work Structure and Guiding Principles' (1984) 5 *Mediation* Quarterly 3.

[69] S Mentschikoff, 'Commercial Arbitration' (1961) 61 *Columbia Law Review* 846.

[70] C Menkel-Meadow, 'Roots and Inspirations: A Brief History of the Foundations of Dispute Resolution' in M Moffitt and R Bordone (eds), *Handbook of Dispute Resolution* (San Francisco, Jossey Bass, 2005).

[71] R Zeckhauser, R Keeney and J Sebenius (eds), *Wise Choices: Decisions, Games and Negotiations* (Boston, MA, Harvard Business Press, 1996)

[72] D Luce and H Raiffa, *Games and Decisions: An Introduction and Critical Survey* (New York, John Wiley, reproduced by Dover, 1987).

[73] K Arrow et al, *Barriers to Conflict Resolution* (New York, WW Norton, 1995); D Pruitt and SH Kim, *Social Conflict: Escalation, Stalemate and Settlement* (New York, McGraw Hill, 2004).

[74] K Avruch, *Culture and Conflict Resolution* (Washington DC, USIP Press, 1998).

[75] L Coser, *The Functions of Social Conflict* (New York, Free Press, 1956).

[76] C Menkel-Meadow, 'Chronicling the Complexification of Negotiation Theory and Practice' (2009) 25 *Negotiation Journal* 415.

[77] R Fisher, W Ury and B Patton, *Getting to YES*, 3rd edn (New York, Penguin, 2011).

[78] C Menkel-Meadow, 'Know When To Show Your Hand' (2007) 10(6) *Negotiation Newsletter, Program on Negotiation Harvard*.

[79] J Nash, 'Two Person Cooperative Games' (1953) 21 *Econometrica* 129; R Walton and R McKersie, *A Behavioral Theory of Labor Negotiations* (New York, McGraw-Hill, 1965); M Deutsch, *The Resolution of Conflict: Constructive and Destructive Processes* (New Haven, Yale University Press, 1973).

[80] C Menkel-Meadow, 'Restorative Justice: What Is It and Does it Work?' 3 *Annual Review of Law and Social Science* 10:1 (Annual Reviews, Stanford, 2007).

[81] C Menkel-Meadow, 'Dispute Resolution' in P Cane and H Kritzer (eds), *Oxford Handbook of Empirical Legal Research* (Oxford, Oxford Press, 2010).

making by courts.[82] Judges like Chief Justice Warren Burger, who wanted to reduce case loads in the courts, touted the advantages of more responsive, private forms of dispute resolution in out of court negotiation, mediation and other forms of dispute resolution. The US Congress appropriated money for 'neighborhood justice centers' which were to deal with 'minor disputes', using both lawyers and non-lawyer mediators for such matters as neighbourhood disputes, minor (misdemeanour) crimes, small commercial disputes, landlord–tenant disputes and a variety of other matters. Restorative justice, in the form of victim–offender mediation, 'healing' and 'sentencing circles', were derived from American (and Canadian and Australian) indigenous ('Indian') groups to provide community-based alternatives to criminal punishment, especially, but not exclusively, used for juvenile offenders. Such efforts at community-based restorative justice are now used even in felony and serious crimes in a few pioneering states (eg Wisconsin).[83] National level processes, in other countries, are now used for restorative justice in the form of truth and reconciliation commissions, supplemental to or substitutionary for formal adjudication in post-conflict, post-civil war and acknowledgement of national wrongs (eg Canada Indian Residential Schools Truth and Reconciliation Process[84]), but so far have been rejected with respect to the American experience of slavery, destruction of indigenous communities and other national or government supported harms.

Specialised areas of law, like family law and labour law,[85] had long used informal processes, like negotiation and mediation, for dispute resolution, but the practices of both family and labour mediation began to be applied and opened out to a greater variety of legal (class actions, torts and contracts claims), political (resource allocation, environmental disputes, local government disputes) and social disputes (community policing, racial tensions, ethnic tensions, educational institutions). Lawyers and law students, as well as other professionals, began to seek training in mediation and the 'healing arts', as well as continuing study of more conventional litigation skills. To date, however, there is virtually no official licensing or credentialing for mediators or other dispute resolution professionals.[86]

Perhaps most interestingly, various forms of 'informal' dispute resolution have been used to great effect in 'extra-, non- or il-' legal enterprises. The film *The Godfather* dramatised the use of 'elder' mediation in resolving disputes within the '*cosa nostra*' (Mafia) and, more recently, sociologist Sudhir Venkatesh gained access to both internal gang mediation and informal 'community policing' mediation of gang-related disputes in Chicago, within gangs and in relations that gang members have with the larger community.[87] I have come to call this form of informal dispute resolution A^2 (*alternative*

[82] C Menkel-Meadow and B Garth, 'Civil Procedure: Policy, Politics and People' in P Cane and H Kritzer (eds), *Oxford Handbook of Empirical Legal Research* (Oxford, Oxford Press, 2010).

[83] J Geske, 'Why Do I Teach Restorative Justice to Law Students' (2005) 89 *Marquette Law Review* 327.

[84] P Regan, *Unsettling the Settler Within: Indian Residential Schools, Truth Telling and Reconciliation in Canada* (Vancouver, University of British Columbia Press, 2010).

[85] C Menkel-Meadow, 'The National Labor Relations Act Legacy: Collective or Individual Dispute Resolution or Not?' (2011) 26 *ABA Labor & Employment Journal* 249.

[86] A few states (eg Florida, Texas, Massachusetts, California) require some limited training and certification to perform mediation or other dispute resolution services in the courts, but not in private practice.

[87] Venkatesh, *Gang Leader for a Day* 96–111, 158–63.

alternative) Dispute Resolution, having learned some years ago about the effectiveness of gang leaders in mediating disputes in the *favellas* of Rio de Janeiro.[88]

Those who were dissatisfied with the 'limited remedial imaginations' of courts' limited power to order creative relief[89] or the 'adversarial culture' of legal problem solving,[90] and others who wanted to encourage more direct party participation without the need for professionals (lawyers and judges) in dispute resolution, combined to form what was later called the 'informal justice movement'.[91] This social movement encouraged individuals and communities to seek resolution of social, political, economic and even legal problems outside of the courts, using community mediation, consensus building, group organising and strategies that allowed more than two parties to seek resolution of problems by negotiated and 'consensual', not court-commanded, solutions. In the private corporate sector, hundreds of Fortune 500 companies and their large law firms signed the 'Center for Public Resources Pledge' to pursue out of court dispute resolution procedures with each other before continuing or initiating litigation. Over time, these 'informal' processes were criticised for 'privatising' justice that many thought should remain in the public and formal sector[92] for transparency of process, generation of public precedential rulings and equalisation of unequal power or economic endowments. Others, including this author, continued to maintain that some aspects of 'informal' dispute resolution (absence of some formal rules, confidentiality, 'trading of preferences', creation of new party-specific norms and tailored solutions to problems) produced better 'justice' for some, if not all, disputants. Thus, core claims of value for 'informal' justice included:

- Direct *party empowerment and participation* in case 'presentation' and resolution
- *Self-determination*
- *Consent*
- *Tailored solutions*, based on party needs and interests, not necessarily 'rights' and claims of law (utilising tailored individual, religious, ethical or communitarian principles for resolution, eg 'joint custody' in divorce and children's custody)
- *Non-monetised outcomes* and solutions (apologies, trades, in-kind, other forms of 'relief')
- *Future*, not just past, *oriented problem solving*, without need necessarily of fact finding or assessment of blame
- *Confidentiality*, producing the opportunity for changed 'positions', trades and non-precedential accommodations or solutions, as well as *privacy* protection for disputants of all kinds, individuals and organisations
- Inclusion of more than two litigant 'parties in interest' (*multi-party dispute resolution*)
- *Reduction of elite and professional decision makers* in parties' lives and disputes, utilisation of party 'consent', not command, as legitimating value
- *Flexible, situation specific, rules* and practices of proceedings

[88] First National Congress of Mediation, Brasília, Brazil, March 2008.

[89] See C Menkel-Meadow, 'Toward another View of Legal Negotiation'.

[90] R Kagan, *Adversarial Legalism: The American Way of Life* (Cambridge, MA, Harvard Press, 2001); D Tannen, *The Argument Culture: Moving from Debate to Dialogue* (New York, Random House, 1998).

[91] See Abel, *The Politics of Informal Justice*; Harrington, *Shadow Justice*.

[92] See, eg Abel, *The Politics of Informal Justice*; Resnik, 'Managerial Judges'; Luban, 'Settlements and the Erosion of the Public Realm'; Fiss, 'Against Settlement'.

- *Contingent solutions* (capable of being revisited with changing conditions) without precedential force or rigidity
- *'Reorientation' of the parties to each other*[93]—promoting *healing relationships*, not rupture and continued conflict and resentment of formal litigation or punitive results in criminal matters[94]
- Potentially *faster and cheaper dispute resolution* ('efficiency')
- Greater *legitimacy of and compliance with* party-chosen outcomes

The relative success and power of some forms of informal processes led, beginning in the 1980s, to adaptations and transformations of private informal processes like negotiation, mediation and arbitration, and their hybrids, to use in more public settings—thus courts began to 'annex' mediation and arbitration processes (and in some cases to make them mandatory), business began to formalise, in contracts, uses of mandatory arbitration, and a variety of organisations began to 'internalise' and mandate the use of informal grievance processes as a condition precedent of any recourse to public and formal litigation processes. At the same time, even formal public court processes began to use and transform themselves into more 'informal' processes such as 'problem-solving courts' in drug, youth, family, mental health and vice courts,[95] the pre-trial settlement conference morphed into a mediation session,[96] and multi-party participatory consensus building fora turned into public 'negotiated rule-making' proceedings in administrative and regulatory law and proceedings,[97] all of which eventually received legal recognition in formal rules and legislative authorisations.[98] Uses of informal negotiation and dispute resolution processes (hybrids of mediation and arbitration) were increasingly used to settle mass class actions in tort, consumer law, securities, employment and other matters,[99] and even single dramatic mass disasters like the deaths arising out of the 11 September 2001 terror attack on New York[100] were dealt with by use of informal settlement processes with public funds and public recognition. The 'informal' has become 'semi-formal'.

IV. 'SEMI-FORMAL' JUSTICE IN THE US

With the expansion and acceptance of ideas of informal consensual problem solving and dispute resolution in the early 1990s, all branches of the US government responded.

[93] See, eg L Fuller, 'Mediation: Its Form and Its Functions' (1971) 44 *Southern California Law Review* 305.

[94] M Umbreit, *The Handbook of Victim–Offender Mediation* (San Francisco, Jossey Bass, 2000).

[95] Center for Court Innovation, *2011 Annual Report* (New York, 2011); G Berman and J Feinblatt, *Good Courts; The Case for Problem Solving Justice* (New York, New Press, 2005).

[96] R Wissler, 'Court-Connected Settlement Procedures: Mediation and Judicial Settlement Conferences' (2011) 26 *Ohio State Journal on Dispute Resolution* 271; P Robinson, 'Judicial Settlement Conference Practices and Techniques' (2009) 33 *American Journal of Trial Advocacy* 113.

[97] P Harter, 'Negotiating Regulations: A Cure for the Malaise?' (1982) 71 *Georgetown Law Journal* 1; J Freeman, 'Collaborative Governance in the Administrative State' (1997) 45 *UCLA Law Review* 1.

[98] See Menkel-Meadow, Love, Kupfer Schneider and Sternlight, *Dispute Resolution* ch 12 and 13.

[99] D Hensler, 'A Glass Half Full, a Glass Half Empty: The Use of Alternative Dispute Resolution in Mass Personal Injury Litigation' (1995) 73 *Texas Law Review* 1587; C Menkel-Meadow, 'Ethics and the Settlement of Mass Torts: When the Rules Meet the Road' (1995) 80 *Cornell Law Review* 1159.

[100] K Feinberg, *What's A Life Worth? The Unprecedented Effort to Compensate the Victims of 9/11* (New York, Public Affairs, 2006).

Courts began, at both federal and state levels, to offer, at first voluntary, then later mandatory, programmes of court-annexed mediation and arbitration processes, and later included such processes as 'early neutral evaluation' (a process in which counsel in a case meet with a volunteer or paid lawyer to review claims, schedule discovery and information exchange, pursue settlement and get an informal 'evaluation' of the merits of the case). A few innovative judges, like Thomas Lambros in Ohio and Jack Weinstein in New York, began to adapt private settlement techniques for public cases. Lambros originated the 'summary jury trial', in which lawyers (and witnesses) presented shortened versions of their cases (usually in no more than one day) to those in the jury *venire* for an 'advisory opinion' by the jurors for use in further case settlement negotiations. This practice was criticised as conflating the public function of the jury,[101] whose members came to court expecting to find facts in a litigated case, and instead were used to assist private negotiation discussions. Summary jury trials were often used in high-value fact disputes (asbestos and other mass claims) in order to set baseline lay fact evaluations of the quality of formal proof and evidence. When some judges ordered the use of this process in individual cases (eg civil rights) against the will of the parties, litigants began to appeal to higher courts and the process has declined in usage in recent years. Legal questions also were raised about whether there could be public access to these proceedings, which were a hybrid of private negotiations, but conducted in a public courtroom.[102]

Federal District Judge Jack Weinstein, among others, used the formal Civil Procedure Rule permitting the use of Special Masters (Fed R Civ Proc 53) to organise discovery and case evaluation in complex cases (also asbestos and other mass claims and class actions, as in the famous *Agent Orange* case[103]) and then permitted special masters (such as the now similarly famous Ken Feinberg, special master of the 9/11 Fund) to act as mediators in settling such cases, with some controversial imprimatur of the judicial office.[104]

The 1980s and 1990s saw modification of the Federal Rules of Civil Procedure to allow the use of some of these settlement practices (Rule 16 was amended to make negotiation of settlement an explicit part of the pre-trial conference and many federal courts used the local rule power of Fed R Civ Proc 83 to craft local rules for the use of ADR in 'court annexed' programmes).[105] The federal courts in New York City, San Francisco, Boston and Washington, DC were among the early pioneers of complex menus of ADR choices and requirements to use some form of ADR.[106] Now, by virtue of federal legislation, the Civil Justice Reform Act of 1990 (requiring all federal courts to implement some cost and delay ameliorative programmes), the Judicial Improvements and Access to Justice Act of 1988 (allowing experimentation with mandatory arbitration in federal courts), the Administrative Dispute Resolution Act of 1990 (authorising the use of negotiated rulemaking processes in administrative regulation)

[101] R Posner, 'The Summary Jury Trial and Other Methods of Alternative Dispute Resolution: Some Cautionary Observations' (1986) 53 *University of Chicago Law Review* 366.

[102] *Cincinnati Gas & Elect Co v General Electric Co*, 854 F 2nd 900 (6th Cir 1988).

[103] P Schuck, *Agent Orange On Trial* (Cambridge, MA, Harvard Press, 1988).

[104] J Weinstein, *Individual Justice in Mass Tort Litigation* (Evanston, Northwestern Press, 1995).

[105] J Maull, 'ADR in the Federal Courts: Would Uniformity Be Better?' (1996) 34 *Duquesne Law Review* 245.

[106] See, eg ND California Rules of ADR.

and, finally, the Alternative Dispute Resolution Act of 1998 (requiring all federal courts to implement some programme of ADR, while allowing each district court to decide what is best for its region), virtually every federal court in the US has some form of ADR. These courts report on the usage rates of mediation, arbitration, and settlement programmes in a non-uniform manner. Statistical reports available from many of the most populous states (including New York, California, Texas and Michigan; see below) demonstrate high usage of a variety of non-trial forms of dispute resolution, within the formal court, with 'settlement rates' ranging from 30 per cent to over 70 per cent in some courts. Virtually all of the federal courts of appeals now have formal mediation programmes, most with full-time staffs, a few relying on volunteer mediators[107] (this author has been a mediator in the District of Columbia Circuit Court of Appeals and has also trained the staff and volunteer mediators, as well as judges, in many federal courts).

Even the executive branch of the US government strongly encouraged use of ADR. During President Clinton's presidential term, Attorney General Janet Reno required mediation training of herself and her senior staff (I performed this training), authorised an 'ADR czar' position in the Justice Department, currently the Program of Dispute Resolution in the Justice Department, allocated funds for the settlement of cases involving the federal government, and changed policies having to do with federal government participation in arbitration and mediation programmes. In addition, an Interagency ADR Working Group representing all the major federal agencies began to meet regularly to discuss dispute resolution programmes throughout the federal government. Many agencies now provide for 'collateral duty' in which employees in one agency act as mediators or dispute resolution consultants to other agencies in the government (thus providing some neutrality and lack of conflict of interest in internal agency matters). An awards programme honoured such branches of the government as the Army Corps of Engineers and the Navy for instituting non-litigation dispute resolution processes in procurement contracts, and later even in dispute resolution issues in war zones.[108] In addition, many federal agencies now have internal dispute resolution programmes, including ombuds to resolve internal conflicts[109] (employment, policy), as well as to deal with disputes with clients or customers of particular agencies (eg Environmental Protection Agency, Securities and Exchange Commission, National Institutes of Health, Department of Energy).

These uses of 'informal' dispute processes within the formal government are one form of 'semi-formal' dispute resolution, sometimes, but not always, authorised by regulation, at other times just by agreed-to practices or recommendations. Practices can change with the change of political administration. To what extent should formal rules of procedure, requirements of transparency, publicity, rule of law, appeals from decisions or mediation or negotiated agreements be applied to such processes? To what extent are such processes really 'consensual'? And if, instead, they are 'mandated', what redress is there to formal courts? Finally, questions have been raised about whether these processes really do live up to their promises and intended goals.

[107] SP Davidson, 'Privatization and Self-Determination in the Circuits: Utilizing the Private Sector within the Evolving Framework of Federal Appellate Mediation' (2006) 21 *Ohio Journal of Dispute Resolution* 1.

[108] J Joseph, 'Mediation in War: Winning Hearts and Minds Using Mediated Condolence Payments' (2007) 23 *Negotiation Journal* 219.

[109] H Gadlin, 'The Ombudsman—What's In a Name?' (2000) 16 *Negotiation Journal* 37.

In the middle of the 1990s, the federal government supported a major $5 million research programme (fielded by the RAND Corp) to determine if ADR in the courts really did 'reduce cost and delay'. The results were decidedly mixed and controversial. RAND found that there was little actual reduction in cost and delay in courts that used mediation, arbitration or early neutral evaluation processes,[110] but the RAND study itself was criticised for studying a moving target. Many of the courts in the study were changing their policies to conform to the legislation discussed above as the study was ongoing. Courts in the federal system that were 'matched' because of similar caseloads for comparison and 'control' purposes were, in fact, quite different, geographically, culturally and in terms of their caseloads.[111] At the same time as the RAND study was conducted, a smaller study, also funded by the federal government (by the Federal Judicial Center), did find that certain ADR practices in the courts were effective in reducing time to trial and total costs for final dispute resolution.[112] Both studies found considerable user satisfaction with different court-based dispute resolution options, even where respondents had no comparison base because they could not take their single dispute to different or controlled treatments for comparison.[113] Thus, the effectiveness, efficiency and efficacy of ADR in the courts, as compared to an ever-shrinking number of cases actually tried in courts (what is an appropriate 'baseline' measure of 'normed' dispute resolution?), continues to be vociferously contested and debated among legal practitioners and scholars.

As the courts and formal governments have made more use of informal processes, there has also been a growth and extension of informal processes becoming more 'semi-formal' in the private sector. With the modern growth of ADR in the 1980s, the prime movers were actually large American corporations which, in 1979, founded the Center for Public Resources to promote the uses of mediation, arbitration and other private consensual processes in American business.[114] Commercial arbitration has always been a common way to resolve disputes among and within participants in the same industry,[115] but in the 1980s large corporations, through CPR, signed a 'pledge' to pursue ADR first when disputing with each other (within and across industries). Though not all members were compliant—many corporations continued to use

[110] J Kakalik, T Dunworth, L Hill, D McCaffrey, M Oshiro, N Pace and M Vaiana, *An Evaluation of Mediation and Early Neutral Evaluation Under the Civil Justice Reform Act* (Santa Monica, RAND, 1996)

[111] C Menkel-Meadow, 'When Dispute Resolution Begets Disputes of its Own Conflicts among Dispute Professionals' (1997) 44 *UCLA Law Review* 1871; E Plapinger and D Stienstra, *ADR and Settlement in the District Courts* (Washington, DC, Federal Judicial Center, 1996); C McEwen and E Plapinger, 'RAND Report Points Way to Next Generation of ADR Research' (1996–1997) 3 *Dispute Resolution Magazine* 10.

[112] D Stienstra, M Johnson, P Lombard and M Pecherski, *Report to the Judicial Conference Committee on Court Administration and Case Management: A Study of Five Demonstration Programs Established Under the Civil Justice Reform Act of 1990* (Washington, DC, Federal Judicial Center, 1997).

[113] EA Lind, R MacCoun, P Ebener, W Felstiner, D Hensler, J Resnik and T Tyler, *The Perception of Justice: Tort Litigants' Views of Trial, Court-Annexed Arbitration and Judicial Settlement Conferences* (Santa Monica, RAND, 1989).

[114] CPR's private corporate strategy was picked up in the UK with Karl Mackie's founding of CEDR (Center for Effective Dispute Resolution, see <www.cedr.com>) in London, and now the International Mediation Institute, see <www.imimediation.org>, headquartered in the Netherlands, as an attempt to promote and certify commercial and 'cultural' competence in mediation (encouraged by the passage of the European Directive on Mediation 2008/52/EC Directive of the European Parliament and Council, 21 May 2008).

[115] See, eg L Bernstein, 'Opting Out of the Legal System: Extralegal Contractual Relations in the Diamond Industry' (1992) 21 *Journal of Legal Studies* 115.

traditional lawsuits—CPR used its bully pulpit and private funds to promote the use of both traditional forms of 'A'DR and help develop new ones—such as the 'mini-trial'. The mini-trial allowed private companies (the first big case was *TRW v Telecredit* in a patent infringement dispute) to privatise their dispute (protecting confidentiality of evidence, trade secrets, customer lists, experts), choose the decision makers (expert arbitrators or facilitative mediators) and the form of process (negotiation, mediation and witness examination), and control costs and evidence presented. Mini-trials were used in a wide variety of large cases in the 1980s and 1990s, concurrent with continued use of courts in cases where large companies were sued by customers or in class action securities, mass torts, consumer or employment matters. Most recently CPR has developed a new pledge for the twenty-first century, encouraging corporations, in times of economic downturns, to develop more 'systematic approaches' to dispute resolution management, as a good business management principle—encouraging more system design of iterative dispute resolution, more early dispute settlement, and recognition that there are many possible ways to resolve corporate disputes outside of costly litigation, including internal conflict audits, accountability for dispute costs to functional, not legal units, and other business management devices.[116]

Thus, private ADR was often combined with public ADR and different processes are selected for use against and with different classes of parties. In general, many courts allowed stays of public litigation while parties pursued various forms of private ADR. CPR, as well as the American Arbitration Association, another private provider of dispute resolution services, also developed formal protocols for industry-wide and specific forms of dispute resolution—thus, oil and gas, franchise, construction, health care and hospital, labour management, mass disasters, environmental, pharmaceutical and other industry-specific 'model rules and clauses' for dispute resolution were drafted and disseminated. In some industries, the success of these private protocols and 'model rules' provides a fully formalised alternative to the public justice system.

In addition to these private tribunals serving industry, several new providers of dispute resolution services emerged in the 1980s. The Judicial Arbitration and Mediation Service (now known solely by its acronym JAMS) was founded by a state court judge in California who retired from the bench to found one of the most successful purveyors of private dispute resolution services, now serving all the major commercial centres in the US (and now including offices in many world capitals) and beginning to compete with the international tribunals (the International Chamber of Commerce in Paris, the London Court of International Arbitration, the AAA's Center for International Dispute Resolution, the Hong Kong, Cairo and Stockholm tribunals for international dispute resolution) for arbitration and mediation services. Former judges and private attorneys now earn upwards of $5,000 per day for private dispute resolution services.

In international settings, arbitration may be enforced in national courts where countries have signed on to the UN New York Convention for the Recognition and Enforcement of Foreign Arbitral Awards (1958); domestically enforcement is through the Federal Arbitration Act, as if a court judgment has been rendered (with a limited number of grounds for vacatur). In contrast, mediation agreements in the US have no more formal legal force than a contract and must be sued on for enforcement as with any private contract. This is in contrast to some other countries (eg Israel) which now

[116] 'CPR Launches 21st Century Corporate ADR Pledge', *National Law Journal*, 21 January 2013.

treat mediation agreements, in some settings, as if they were arbitration awards, with relatively easy enforcement in courts.

As commercial arbitration has emerged as an important (but still not the only preferred) form of dispute resolution[117] between and among commercial parties, large companies, in fields ranging from telecommunications to health and hospitals, banks, car rentals and computers, etc, have now imposed mandatory 'private' arbitration on consumers and employees, a practice that has been sustained against many legal attacks, by the US Supreme Court.[118] The US is an outlier in permitting this form of private dispute resolution to be mandated in private contracts, without, so far, guaranteed recourse to a public court challenge, except in a few limited instances. Even claims of unconscionability or other coerced contract defences have been rejected in this context. Thus, 'informal' private contractual arbitration (often dictated by the terms of a form contract written by a powerful corporation) has become the 'norm' for many kinds of disputes. Recently a courageous (former lawyer) individual complainant tried to use a small claims court as a way around some of the contractual limits of arbitration and class action litigation. Her victory in the small claims court was reversed on appeal taken by the losing company (Honda).[119] There have been increasing efforts to attempt to regulate private consumer and employment arbitration (so far through unsuccessful efforts to pass federal legislation, the Arbitration Fairness Act, prohibiting the use of mandatory pre-dispute contractual arbitration in consumer, employment and franchise disputes). A few states (like California) have managed to add a few protections for consumers (conflicts of interest of arbitrators) through civil procedure rules or other state legislation (which is now often invalidated in federal court as pre-empted by the Federal Arbitration Act). This attempt to 'regulate' consumer arbitration has, however, also led to some efforts in the private sector to make consumer or employment arbitration subject to some basic 'due process protocols'.[120]

In addition to private contracting, both at the industry and individual level, smaller communities have also continued to use informal out of court processes in a variety of contexts. Religious and ethnic groups have long offered their own courts, mediation and arbitration services for disputes within their own communities. Recently, tensions have been exposed when, as in family law, the formal court must still be the final authority on divorce or spousal or child support, when one party asks for acceptance of the agreement of a religious court, or when one party seeks public court orders to require another party to satisfy legal requirements of the religious court for secular benefit.[121] The interplay of private religious courts and doctrines for dispute

[117] T Eisenberg and G Miller, 'The Flight from Arbitration: An Empirical Study of Ex Ante Arbitration Clauses in the Contracts of Publicly Held Companies' (2007) 56 *DePaul Law Review* 3335 (finding that many large companies are not using arbitration clauses in their contracts with each other, though they are often imposing such clauses on their contracts with individual consumers).

[118] See J Sternlight, 'Creeping Mandatory Arbitration: Is It Just?' (2005) 57 *Stanford Law Review* 1631. See, eg *AT&T v Concepcion,* 131 Sup Ct 1740 (2011).

[119] J Hirsh, 'Honda Civic Loses Unusual Small Claims Suit (to Heather Peters)', *Los Angeles Times*, 1 February 2012, Business Section, 1.

[120] See, eg Employment Due Process Protocol; J Dunlop and A Zack, *Mediation and Arbitration of Employment Disputes* (San Francisco, Jossey Bass, 1997); C Drahozal and S Zyontz, 'Private Regulation of Consumer Arbitration' (2011), <ssrn.com/abstract=1904545>.

[121] See, eg Helfand, 'Religious Arbitration and the New Multi-culturalism'; M Grossman, 'Is This Arbitration? Religious Tribunals, Judicial Review and Due Process' (2007) 107 *Columbia Law Review* 169; CL Wolfe, 'Faith Based Arbitration: Friend or Foe?' (2006) 75 *Fordham Law Review* 427.

resolution has become a legal issue in a variety of multi-cultural nations, including the US, Canada,[122] the UK and Australia in the common law world and France and other legal regimes in Asia and Europe. Recently, several states in the US (Oklahoma, Arizona and Nebraska) famously used their 'democratic' referenda and legislative processes to ban the use of 'foreign, international or *Shar'ia* law' in their state courts.[123] Many other states (eg Alabama, Texas, South Carolina, Wyoming and South Dakota) are attempting in one form or other to do the same thing. Most of us in the legal academy and many, but not all, of those on the bench (the judiciary) believe these laws are unconstitutional, but they represent a strong sentiment to police the use of communitarian, religious and ethnic enclaves' use of their own formal rules and laws, as well as processes. Religious courts or arbitration or mediation centres in family matters are used by Jews (Bet Din[124]), Christians[125] and Muslims,[126] and for the most part have had their outcomes confirmed by courts which apply the regular standards for enforcing arbitration awards under the Federal Arbitration Act.

Local communities have also used informal processes (consensus building, deliberative democracy, public policy mediation[127]) to resolve land use, environmental, cultural and ethnic conflict, budget allocation and other disputes, outside of formal processes. With a new cadre of professionals specifically trained to engage complex communities in such disputes and group decision making, complex multi-party disputes may be resolved with agreements, often contingent, and monitoring programmes (such as in resource management, land use and zoning, waste siting) which straddle public and private decision making rules and bodies.[128] The legal issue often then involves whether a public body, such as a regional zoning land-use or federal resource agency, must participate and approve agreements reached in private settings, outside of formal court, legislative or administrative hearings. These processes may themselves now be quite 'formal', adhering to community developed rules of engagement, delegation of state, federal or local authority, but such negotiated agreements still often require formal governmental approval, and what was accomplished through these creative informal processes may unravel when returned to more formal and adversary proceedings.[129]

Thus, the conundrums, paradoxes and issues in these 'semi-formal' forms of dispute resolution include the relation of the private form of dispute resolution and its 'outputs' or agreements to the state—when and if one party seeks to move dispute

[122] The Premier of the province of Ontario in Canada sought to ban the use of faith-based family arbitration in his jurisdiction, see Helfand, 'Religious Arbitration and the New Multi-culturalism' fn 30, while the Archbishop of the UK called for the inclusion of Shar'ia law in British family law determinations. Ibid.

[123] This referendum has been held to be unconstitutional, see *Awad v Ziriax* No CIV-10-1186-M 2010 WL 4814077 (WD Oklahoma).

[124] See, eg *Kingsbridge Ctr of Israel v Turk*, 469 NYS 2d 732 (App Div 1983); *Kovacs v Kovacs*, 633 A 2d 425 (Md 1993).

[125] G Waddell and J Keegan, 'Christian Conciliation: An Alternative to "Ordinary" ADR' (1999) 29 *Cumberland Law Review* 583.

[126] *Abd Alla v Mourssi*, 680 NW 2d 569 (Minn Ct of App 2004).

[127] S Carpenter and WL Kennedy, *Managing Public Disputes: A Practical Guide for Professionals In Government, Business and Citizen Groups* (San Francisco, Jossey Bass, 2001); SL Podziba, *Civic Fusion: Mediating Polarized Public Disputes* (Chicago, ABA Press, 2012).

[128] C Menkel-Meadow, 'Getting to Let's Talk: Commentary on Collaborative Processes in Environmental Dispute Resolution' (2008) 8 *Nevada Law Journal* 835.

[129] See, eg A Camacho, 'Mustering the Missing Voices: A Collaborative Model for Fostering Equality, Community Involvement and Adaptive Planning in Land Use Decisions, Installment Two' (2005) 24 *Stanford Environmental Law Journal* 269.

resolution from one sector to the other—for appellate review, appeal to public or state values, or to get state enforcement of relief or to reverse what was accomplished in the more informal process.

V. WHAT LITTLE WE KNOW ABOUT DISPUTE RESOLUTION USE AND REGULATION

Since the beginning of the modern ADR movement in the US, scholars have called for the ability to empirically study and assess claims made about the relative uses and satisfaction with such processes. Evaluation research (such as in the RAND studies reported above) has sought to look at comparisons between different processes. Social scientists at the Federal Judicial Center have long urged uniform reporting requirements and uniformity of case types and categories on case dockets for comparisons between cases and types of process and for accurate time series to study developments over time. Alas, such uniformity of data reporting does not, for the most part, exist, even within the federal system. Much like the US Census, which has changed its categories of 'nationality' in almost every decennial census,[130] case categories, dispositions and other reported information are ever changing. Below, I report on some of the available data from both court (public) and a few private sources.[131]

I reviewed a sample of federal and state court ADR systems for whatever data were available on cases actually referred to ADR and whatever data were available on dispositions. The data available are scanty (it appears the Administrative Office of the Courts at the federal level is not keeping track of ADR statistics by court on a regular basis). Courts vary on their requirements to use some form of ADR (based on local rules, local legal cultures and interpretations of the requirements to provide some form of ADR in all federal cases, as now required by the Alternative Dispute Resolution Act of 1998—which 'required' use of some form of ADR in every federal court, but provided no funding appropriation for this purpose). Examples of the kind of information that has been collected are the rates of mediation success in some courts. For example, the Eastern District of New York (including two counties of New York City and the rest of Long Island) tracks mediation success rates by case type. Successful mediations resulting in settlement vary by case type, ranging (for a seven-year reporting period from 2003 to 2010) from 38.5% in employment discrimination, 36% in other civil rights, 43% in personal injury matters, 32% in contract disputes and 51% in insurance matters to a much lower rate for intellectual property matters (22% in trademark, 30% in copyright and a low of 13% in patent cases). The Western District of Missouri (another relatively active district in ADR) offers voluntary facilitative mediation, early neutral evaluation, case evaluation and settlement conferences with most usage of settlement conferences (54%); followed by mediation (34%) and lower rates of utilisation of neutral case evaluation.

Over time, use of (voluntary) mediation has increased somewhat in federal courts

[130] N Mezey, 'Erasure and Recognition: The Census, Race and the National Imagination' (2003) 97 *Northwestern University Law Review* 1701.

[131] An earlier paper of mine reports summarily on empirical research to date on dispute resolution, Menkel-Meadow, 'Dispute Resolution'.

offering such processes; early neutral evaluation practices are used, though only in a few courts, and are the least used in courts that provide a fuller menu of choice (the Northern District of California (federal) and state courts in Michigan were primary innovators in this evaluative form of ADR), and settlement conferences (with judges or magistrate judges) remain the most common form of ADR in the federal courts. A few courts (a federal statute provided legal support for experimental, now permanent, arbitration programmes for five federal districts) require mandatory arbitration of civil cases below a certain value. The arbitrators are volunteer panel lawyers and 'appeals' from those arbitrations are de novo to trial, with a 'penalty' of costs if the appellant does not do better at trial than in the arbitration. These practices have been challenged in the US as violating the constitutional 'right to jury' in civil cases under the Seventh Amendment, but these challenges have failed as long as some ability to go to trial *after* arbitration is still permitted, even if it is 'taxed' with a bond or penalty payment.[132] Offers of settlement under Rule 68 of the Federal Rules also 'tax' refusals to settle by requiring any party to whom a settlement offer is made and refused to pay legal fees and costs if that party does not do better than the settlement offer at trial.

All federal courts of appeal now offer mediation before argument; all but one circuit now employs paid staff mediators. The District of Columbia (in the nation's capital) still relies on volunteer lawyers. It is difficult to compare numbers and practices in particular districts because processes vary so much. Virtually all federal courts rely on unpaid lawyers to conduct ADR sessions, with the exception of mandatory settlement conferences which are conducted either by full Article III (life-time appointed) judges or statutory magistrate judges. Whether such court adjunct personnel should be paid from public funds remains a controversial issue. A few district court rules provide for the parties to pay fees for mediators beyond a certain minimal period of mediation (usually one day or more than five hours). Different courts provide for different forms of training and assessment of such court adjuncts, and there has been concern about addition to or removal from the 'rolls' of this prestigious 'federal' listing, often used for career enhancement.

What should be clear from this simple report is that there is a profound irony in federal ADR—when the 1938 federal rules of procedure were enacted the idea was for some uniformity of federal procedural rules in civil matters; the reality with respect to ADR practice is that it varies enormously by local rule, local legal culture and practice.[133]

At the state level, most states do provide some statistical summaries of the uses of various forms of ADR, but methods of data collection, categories about which data are collected and outcome measures vary considerably. For example, Florida, which is another state which pioneered use of ADR (and provides rules for training and credentialising of its court mediators), reports extensive data by district (circuit) within the state (documenting great local variations in use of ADR) on case types ordered to

[132] See D Golann, 'Making Alternative Dispute Resolution Mandatory: The Constitutional Issues' (1989) 68 *Oregon Law Review* 487; L Bernstein, 'Understanding the Limits of Court-Connected ADR: A Critique of Federal Court-Annexed Arbitration Programs' (1993) 141 *University of Pennsylvania Law Review* 2169. These rulings of American courts are analogous to recent European courts rejecting claims that mandatory ADR referrals might violate Art 6 of the European Convention on Human Rights.

[133] See J Maull, 'ADR in the Federal Courts: Would Uniformity be Better?' (1996) 34 *Duquesne Law Review* 245.

ADR (mediation primarily with some arbitration and abandonment of another form of ADR, summary jury trial formerly used in Florida[134]) and ratios of cases ordered to ADR with ADR actually conducted, ranging by case type and locale from a low of about 33% to close to 100%, evidencing great variations in the acceptance of ADR local 'cultures'. New York reports that, for a seven-year reporting period (2002–09), close to 300,000 cases in the state were submitted to some form of ADR, also with great variations by city and county (eg 80,000 for New York City and less than 100 for Hamilton County, a more rural county). The percentage of cases resolved by some form of ADR in this same period ranged from 45% for the whole state to 41% for New York City and a low of 16% in Saratoga, with highs as much as 60–70% in some counties (including Westchester, a suburban county just north of New York City, which has been an active locale for training mediators). Massachusetts, another state active in promoting ADR reports high settlement rates of cases, without allocating reports to particular ADR processes.

States vary considerably in the rules and regulations promulgated for use of ADR, ranging from mandatory assignments for all cases under a particular monetary amount, particular case types, exceptions for some case types (eg common exclusions for constitutional cases, prisoner's rights, social security cases), to court informal referrals or compelled order to ADR after settlement conferences, voluntary selection or mandated referral in particular matters (eg in medical malpractice, some form of ADR is often required as a condition precedent for bringing a lawsuit). States vary in their practices as to whether they use '*opt-out*' rules (all cases under certain values automatically subjected to some form of mediation or ADR, unless the parties have a good reason for opting out) or '*opt-in*' systems in which parties choose to use some form of ADR. There is at present a very robust debate in court practice and the academic literature about which is 'better' for the parties (where party choice is the primary value) or the 'system' (higher settlement rates and reduced costs). Many states have subject-specific statutes requiring informal dispute resolution mechanisms for particular kinds of disputes, often medical malpractice, certain kinds of consumer disputes (eg 'lemon laws' for defective cars or products[135]). As a result of the 2008 economic downturn, it was predicted that there would be an increase in use of various form of ADR as parties could less afford expensive litigation. In 2012, the state of California announced it would close hundreds of local courts in a multi-million dollar budget cut for governmental expenditures. Although many predicted that this would increase the use of mediation, many local jurisdictions, including my own in Los Angeles, also terminated the local court mediation programme to reduce additional court costs.[136]

Many consumer and employment contracts now contain mandatory arbitration clauses, challenges to which have been denied as 'pre-empted' under federal law by the Federal Arbitration Act. A few states, concerned about claimed abuses in some

[134] J Alfini, 'Summary Jury Trials in State and Federal Courts: A Comparative Analysis of the Perceptions of Participating Lawyers' (1989) 4 *Ohio State Journal on Dispute Resolution* 213.

[135] S Talesh, 'The Privatization of Public Legal Rights: How Manufacturers Construct the Meaning of Consumer Law' (2009) 43 *Law & Society Review* 527.

[136] Although many decried this action, some private mediators I know think this is a good result as there was little quality control of the state-operated 'volunteer' mediator programme. Private mediators hope that, at least in bigger cases, the parties will now choose the more expensive, but allegedly better quality, private mediation services they provide.

forms of ADR (conflicts of interests of mediators or arbitrators, coerced settlements in some court-annexed mediation programmes), have attempted regulation of ADR practice through special rules of procedure (California has conflicts of interests rules for arbitrators in its rules of civil procedure), or in lawyer or other professional ethics codes. The status of state regulation of arbitration is now clouded by a US Supreme Court case which held that the Federal Arbitration Act pre-empts, at the federal level, any effort at state interference with or regulation of arbitration.[137]

Although the use of contractual arbitration has now been federally 'legitimated' by a series of Supreme Court cases sustaining such clauses, how those arbitrations are actually conducted remains essentially private, determined by contractual provisions or by the private rule systems of the leading arbitral tribunals and administering organisations, such as the American Arbitration Association and JAMS. Although some states have attempted to regulate some aspects of arbitration, such as by restricting and limiting its use in some contexts (consumer, employment or other matters), most of those statutes have now been rendered void by the US Supreme court's recent decision in *AT&T Mobility v Concepcion* (holding that a state ruling that class actions in arbitration were permissible was 'pre-empted' by federal arbitration law). In the mediation area there is very little state legislation, except for those states which have provided for confidentiality protections and in some cases, evidentiary privileges for mediators (and/or arbitrators)[138] (who cannot be called to testify in later formal legal proceedings).

The US does not, at either the federal or state level, regulate who may be an ADR professional—there are no certification or licensing requirements for mediators, arbitrators or others who attempt to resolve disputes 'informally', though, increasingly, some states, eg Florida, Massachusetts and California, do attempt to regulate training and standards for court-adjunct ADR professionals. Mediators and arbitrators in private settings often are non-lawyer professionals such as engineers and architects in construction disputes, accountants in financial and contractual cases, social workers and psychologists in family matters.

Mediation is increasingly used in more and more settings (internal family issues without dissolution, education matters, probate, internal business relationships without lawsuits, organisational dispute resolution) that are far removed from courts and not subject to any reporting or regulatory schemes. Thus, the ability to generate any accurate accounting of just how much mediation or ADR there is is virtually impossible.[139]

Whatever data and formal rules may be available from the formal and 'semi-formal' arenas, the largest sector of 'ADR' is clearly private (involving voluntary and now contractually mandated mediation, arbitration or choices to use some of the newer hybrids), and the private sector remains fiercely private. I have served on various study committees which have attempted to gather data on the use, outcomes and other

[137] See *AT&T Mobility v Concepcion*, 131 Sup Ct 1740 (2011).

[138] See, eg Cal Evidence Code §§ 703.5 and 1115–28 (requirements for privilege of mediators and arbitrators not to testify in subsequent litigation and requirements for preserving confidentiality of mediation proceedings).

[139] See T Stipanowich, 'The Vanishing Trial: The Growth and Impact of Alternative Dispute Resolution' (2004) 1 *Journal of Empirical Legal Studies* 843 (reporting on difficulty of obtaining data on private ADR and reporting a limited set of data sets from a variety of private providers of ADR services such as the American Arbitration Association, etc).

information on private dispute resolution. Although a few studies have now appeared in some sectors (comparative employment arbitral data from the American Arbitration Association and the US Postal Service,[140] and some data on consumer arbitration),[141] analysing whether employees and consumers fare equitably when disputing with larger companies or 'repeat players'[142] (the results are decidedly mixed), most information from the largest private providers of dispute resolution services remains relatively obscure, with no formal requirements to report information. One ADR provider sought to become publicly traded on the New York Stock Exchange, which would have required public disclosures, but that effort proved unsuccessful.[143] Having had some access to some informal data from one of the largest providers of private arbitration and mediation services in the country (JAMS and another private 'firm' providing mediation services) I have seen first hand one aspect of the 'repeat player effect'. Large companies with multiple disputes (in California, the major banks, the major supermarkets, Kaiser Permanente Health Care, Toyota car dealerships, etc) tend to use the same providers over and over again. Thus the providers have some incentive to 'please' their repeat player clients with awards that favour them to continue to receive business. Since all kinds of contracts now provide for arbitration or mediation by some of these major private providers, the 'one-shotters' (consumers, tenants, employees) may not even know how often a provider works for a particular company and will therefore be ignorant of possible biases, incentives, etc. (My own home rental agreement some years ago included a form requiring arbitration with JAMS for any dispute arising under the lease. As a dispute resolution professional, I struck the clause from the contract.[144])

Thus, to the extent that we know so little about how much arbitration actually occurs and how it is in fact conducted in the private sphere, it is difficult to assess how it should and could be regulated. In the last 15 years a wide variety of consumer and employee representative groups have attempted to pass federal legislation, the Arbitration Fairness Act, to limit uses of mandatory arbitration in a wide variety of contexts, so far to no avail (with the exception of one statute that prevents mandatory arbitration of dealer-franchisee disputes among car manufacturers and dealers; this special statute does not restrict the use of mandatory arbitration for consumer purchases of automobiles!).[145]

[140] See L Bingham, *Mediation at Work. Transforming Workplace Conflict at the United States Postal Service* (Washington, DC, IBM Center for The Business of Government, 2003); L Bingham, 'Employment Arbitration: The Repeat Player Effect' (1997) 1 *Employment Rights and Employment Policy Journal* 189.

[141] Searle Civil Justice Institute, *Consumer Arbitration before the American Arbitration Association* (Chicago, Searle Center on Law, Regulation, and Economic Growth, Northwestern University School of Law, 2009).

[142] C Menkel-Meadow, 'Do the Haves Come Out Ahead in Alternative Justice Systems? Repeat Players in ADR' (1999) 15 *Ohio State Journal Dispute Resolution* 19.

[143] Judicate, originally based in Philadelphia, sought to become a publicly traded company in the late 1980s. JAMS, the most successful of private ADR providers remains a private corporation.

[144] W Glaberson, 'Misuse of Arbitration?', *New York Times*, 1996, 1.

[145] Congress has provided that pre-dispute arbitration agreements are not valid in two instances. The Motor Vehicle Franchise Contract Arbitration Fairness Act of 2001 protects car dealers from arbitration imposed by car manufacturers, but interestingly does nothing to prohibit car dealers from requiring their customers to arbitrate future disputes, as has become common. Another piece of legislation protects members of the military from arbitration imposed by payday lenders. It is 'unlawful for any creditor to extend consumer credit to a covered member or a dependent of such member with respect to which . . . the creditor requires the borrower to submit to arbitration or imposes onerous legal notice provisions in the case of a dispute' (10 USC § 987(e)(3) (2000)).

VI. ASSESSING JUSTICE IN PLURAL PROCEDURAL PRACTICES

Dispute resolution in the US is now characterised by multiple or parallel tracks, what I and others have called 'process pluralism'. Parties, depending on their economic and legal circumstances, may often choose between formal legal proceedings or less formal forms of dispute resolution. On the other hand, some parties may have no choice at all (such as the 'helpless' consumers and employees who are required to agree to mandatory arbitration processes in their form (adhesion) contracts). In many matters, well-endowed disputants may switch from one form of dispute resolution to another—starting with litigation and then shifting to either court-mandated or chosen mediation, negotiation or arbitration, using private or publicly paid-for third-party neutrals. In other cases, parties may choose informal forms of dispute resolution and then seek enforcement of mediation or negotiated agreements or arbitral awards in public courts for enforcement (injunctive relief or execution on assets). The terrain is diverse, uphill, downhill and often rocky for the uninitiated or not so well endowed. Although the 'ADR' movement was originally formed to make access to justice easier and to reduce the reliance on legal or other professionals, the truth is that the landscape of disputing has indeed become more and more complex, with the predictions of outcomes, costs and strategies harder and harder to produce with any degree of accuracy.

The field of dispute resolution and litigation in the US now contains both scholars and practitioners who urge the return to courts and trials for more transparency, equalisation of rules and process and general monitoring of both processes and outcomes, many claiming that a trial rate (in civil matters) of less than 2 per cent of all matters filed is an inadequate number for a democratic society to produce legal precedents and fair process. For these commentators, informal or even 'semi-formal' process may be considered to be 'empty suits' (no visibility or accountability to those outside of the dispute resolution process), to continue the social dressing metaphor. Or, as another critique, one form of dispute resolution may seem to be 'masquerading' as another—seeming to have court formality or approval when, in reality, there is little to no (not even 'informal') review of what occurs in the dispute resolution process. Others among us, and I am one of those, still prefer to see process pluralism as offering the opportunity for party choice, both about process and about the kinds of outcomes that might be possible (trades, new creative solutions, shared commitments to agreements). I have always preferred a full closet from which to select my clothes for a particular event!

Yet, I remain haunted or affected by Lon Fuller's claims that each process has its own 'integrity' or purpose—one set of values (privacy, on-going relationships, spider web-like intertwined issues in a single problem) for one kind of problem may dictate one kind of process (mediation) that would be inappropriate for another kind of problem (the elimination of injustice in a public institution like education: *Brown v Board of Education*). Thus, Lon Fuller and others would suggest that we should be clear about both the purposes and uses of each process. Attempts to specify in advance particular processes for particular kinds of disputes have not been particularly successful in the US (some courts prohibit the use of ADR in constitutional cases, prisoner's cases, civil rights matters, *pro se* (self-representation); others do not), in part because, in the hands of skilled parties, lawyers and third-party neutrals, almost any informal or semi-formal process can be made more flexible, cheaper, faster and more creative than formal processes, so process choice and effectiveness often turns on the particular actors in the process, not on the structure itself. Fuller's attempts to uncover the jurisprudential bases for process choice is now being applied to international or transnational disputing too, where 'the formal' has been even less effective, in public, if not private dispute resolution.[146] Yet, it remains unclear whether it is structure and function or personality[147] that determines how fair, just and effective a particular process is.

Some years ago, when I was consulting for a major international organization, I was asked to develop a formula for assessing the 'success' of any system of dispute resolution. The exercise was instructive for me because I realised that we need both qualitative and quantitative measures of effective dispute resolution, and also that 'measures' of success for a 'system'[148] may be different from measures of 'justice' or 'satisfaction' for disputants or users of any process. I offered the following set of criteria, variables and factors in the assessment of dispute processes (a combination of 'objective' and 'subjective' measures), while recognising that no single study could ever hope to include measures of them all.

Quantitative or "Objective" Measures

- Number of conflicts or disputes in relevant 'universe' (which and how many form into formal claim or complaint)
- Number of contacts or cases (in a particular process, as compared to the full 'universe' of possible cases or comparable cases in another process)
- Numbers of issues
- Number of cases resolved/settled/closed/disposed of ('settlement rates')
- Number of cases referred to another process
- Number of cases dropped
- Case types (categories within systems, eg employment promotion, dismissal, communication, etc)
- Numbers of parties
- Types of agreements, resolutions, outcomes
- Time to process case
- Cost of processing case—to complainant, to third-party neutral, to programme or system
- Comparisons (where possible) of all of the above comparable cases in different systems
- Comparisons of pre-conflict resolution programme claiming (grievance systems, litigation) or violence with post-programmatic claiming
- Comparisons of rates of compliance with agreements, judgments or orders

[146] R Michaels, 'A Fuller Concept of Law beyond the State? Thoughts on Lon Fuller's Contributions to the Jurisprudence of Transnational Dispute Resolution' (2011) 2(2) *Journal of International Dispute Settlement* 417.

[147] D Curran, J Sebenius and M Watkins, 'Two Paths to Peace: Contrasting George Mitchell in Northern Ireland with Richard Holbrooke in Bosnia-Herzegovina' (2004) 20 *Negotiation Journal* 513.

[148] The new field of 'dispute system design' in the US (and other countries) is tasked with both developing and evaluating 'systems' of dispute resolution in both public and private settings where there are iterative disputes, see (2009) 14 *Harvard Negotiation Law Review* special issue 'Dispute System Design'.

- Durability/longevity of outcomes
- Longitudinal comparisons of changes in usage, time for processing, case types, etc
- Demographic data on users, third-party neutrals, and other facilitators or professionals
- Variations in usage, outcomes, solutions by demographics, and differential characteristics of disputants and third-party neutrals, eg 'experience' ratings
- Awareness of ability to choose different processes (an attitudinal measure)

Qualitative or Subjective Measures

- Criteria for selecting particular processes
- Client satisfaction
- Improved relationships (post-conflict societies (eg Rwanda), families, workplaces, commercial relations)
- Improved communication
- Enhanced workplace productivity
- Learned conflict resolution/communication/relational skills ('transformative' mutual intersubjective understandings or learned use of new processes, eg lawyers using mediation and other forms of problem solving)
- 'Better' outcomes (more creative, individually tailored, deeper solutions)
- Perceived self-determination/autonomy/control over decision making
- Compliance with national, systemic, family, company, workplace and contractual norms/rules when legitimacy is less questioned
- Perceptions of fairness, justice and legitimacy of process
- Trust in institutions, both dispute processing and others
- Resolution of systemic issues (proactive conflict resolution, policy changes)
- 'Value added' to organisation or institution

But this list, whether exhaustive or not, cannot quantify, combine or 'equalise' measures of 'justice' with measures of 'efficiency', and disputants cannot subject themselves either simultaneously or sequentially to formal, semi-formal or informal processes to determine which works best for them in a particular matter. Yet, I worry that, while formal processes produce some modicum of review through formal procedures, court scrutiny, and published decisions and data, and informal processes promise only that the parties can do what they want 'if they agree' (consent based), then 'semi-formal' processes are perhaps the most problematic processes. Informal processes are those we believe the parties have consented to—are they? 'Semi-formal' processes may be monitored ('court annexed' or use of private arbitration tribunal rules of procedure) or made more formal by accessing state power (whether judicial or otherwise) for enforcement, but often, they are not. Court annexed programmes do not necessarily get reviewed by judges or other government officials. Private mediation and arbitration agreements and awards are not generally available to parties outside of the processes. Those who choose private processes, even with elaborate internal rule systems, may also have no recourse to subsequent review, especially when agreements are confidential. (Perhaps this explains why so many of the newer international dispute resolution organisations are now using or proposing appellate processes, eg the World Trade

Organization Appellate Body, ICSID, both for review and for transparency and consistency of results.)[149]

Is process pluralism always a good thing (is there a time when too many choices may be a bad idea?[150]), and how are we to know? When we have so many choices, and so many different possible measures of what constitutes a fair, just or good process, it may be virtually impossible to specify a uniform and universally satisfying dress code. So, in the US, for the near future, it may be 'come as you are'—formal, informal or 'semi-formal'. Perhaps in a country this diverse the choice of dispute process should be similarly diverse, but it makes one wonder, along with Lon Fuller, whether each process choice must or should have its own integrity (and policed rules?). I would not wear a ballgown to a barbecue and I would not wear a bathing suit to the courthouse. Do we need a dress code or forms of regulation for different kinds of dispute resolution? If so, how should we 'dress' for different kinds of disputes and processes? What rules of transparency, confidentiality or publicity, fairness, ethics, conflicts of interests, disclosures, procedures and accountability can be applied across all these different forms of process? I have more questions than I have answers (as I stand before my closet and try to decide what to wear to court, a negotiation session, a mediation, arbitration or session with my organisation's ombuds).

BIBLIOGRAPHY

Abel, RL (ed), *The Politics of Informal Justice: The American Experience* (New York, Academic Press, 1982)

Alfini, J, 'Summary Jury Trials in State and Federal Courts: A Comparative Analysis of the Perceptions of Participating Lawyers' (1989) 4 *Ohio State Journal of Dispute Resolution* 213

American Bar Association, Section of Dispute Resolution, 'Considering Regulation of ADR' (2013) 19(3) *Dispute Resolution Magazine* 4.

Arrow, K et al, *Barriers to Conflict Resolution* (New York, WW Norton, 1995)

Auerbach, JS, *Justice without Law? Resolving Disputes without Lawyers* (Oxford, Oxford University Press, 1983)

Avruch, K, *Culture and Conflict Resolution* (Washington, DC, USIP Press, 1998)

Bacow, L and Wheeler, M, *Environmental Dispute Resolution* (New York, Springer, 1984)

Barrett, JT, *A History of Alternative Dispute Resolution: The Story of a Political, Social and Cultural Movement* (San Francisco, Jossey Bass, 2004)

Berman, G and Feinblatt, J, *Good Courts; The Case for Problem Solving Justice* (New York, New Press, 2005)

Bernstein, L, 'Opting Out of the Legal System: Extralegal Contractual Relations in the Diamond Industry' (1992) 21 *Journal of Legal Studies* 115

Bernstein, L, 'Understanding the Limits of Court-Connected ADR: A Critique of Federal Court-Annexed Arbitration Programs' (1993) 141 *University of Pennsylvania Law Review* 2169

Bingham, L, 'Employment Arbitration: The Repeat Player Effect' (1997) 1 *Employment Rights and Employment Policy Journal* 189

[149] See Stone Sweet, 'Arbitration and Judicialization'.

[150] C Guthrie, 'Panacea or Pandora's Box? The Costs of Options in Negotiation' (2003) 88 *Iowa Law Review* 601—is a rosé a good choice when some of the dinner guests want red wine and the others want white?

Bingham, L, *Mediation at Work: Transforming Workplace Conflict at the United States Postal Service* (Washington, DC, IBM Center for the Business of Government, 2003)
Brazil, W, 'A Close Look at Three Court-Sponsored ADR Programs: Why They Exist, How They Operate, What They Deliver, and Whether They Threaten Important Values' [1990] *University of Chicago Legal Forum* 303
Burger, W, 'Isn't There a Better Way?' (1982) 68 *American Bar Association Journal* 274
Carbonneau, T, *Lex Mercatoria and Arbitration: A Discussion of the New Law Merchant* (Huntington, NY, JurisNet, 1997)
Camacho, A, 'Mustering the Missing Voices: A Collaborative Model for Fostering Equality, Community Involvement and Adaptive Planning in Land Use Decisions, Installment Two' (2005) 24 *Stanford Environmental Law Journal* 269
Carpenter, S and Kennedy, WL, *Managing Public Disputes: A Practical Guide for Professionals In Government, Business and Citizen Groups* (San Francisco, Jossey Bass, 2001)
Center for Court Innovation, *2011 Annual Report* (New York, 2011)
Chase, O, *Law, Culture and Ritual: Disputing Systems in Cross-Cultural Context* (New York, NYU Press, 2005)
Coben, J and Thompson, P, 'Disputing Irony: a Systematic Look at Litigation about Mediation' (2006) 11 *Harvard Negotiation Law Review* 43
Coser, L, *The Functions of Social Conflict* (New York, Free Press, 1956)
Curran, D, Sebenius, J and Watkins, M, 'Two Paths to Peace: Contrasting George Mitchell in Northern Ireland with Richard Holbrooke in Bosnia-Herzegovina' (2004) 20 *Negotiation Journal* 513
Davidson, SP, 'Privatization and Self-Determination in the Circuits: Utilizing the Private Sector within the Evolving Framework of Federal Appellate Mediation' (2006) 21 *Ohio Journal of Dispute Resolution* 1
Deutsch, M, *The Resolution of Conflict: Constructive and Destructive Processes* (New Haven, Yale University Press, 1973)
Dezalay, Y and Garth, B, *Dealing in Virtue: International Commercial Arbitration and the Construction of a Transnational Legal Order* (Chicago, University of Chicago Press, 1996)
Dunlop, J and Zack, A, *Mediation and Arbitration of Employment Disputes* (San Francisco, Jossey Bass, 1997)
Edelman, L, Erlanger, H and Lande, J, 'Internal Dispute Resolution: The Transformation of Civil Rights in the Workplace' (1993) 27 *Law & Society Review* 497
Eisenberg, T and Miller, G, 'The Flight from Arbitration: An Empirical Study of Ex Ante Arbitration Clauses in the Contracts of Publicly Held Companies' (2007) 56 *DePaul Law Review* 3335
Feinberg, K, *What's A Life Worth? The Unprecedented Effort to Compensate the Victims of 9/11* (New York, Public Affairs, 2006)
Fisher, R, Ury, W and Patton, B, *Getting to YES*, 3rd edn (New York, Penguin, 2011)
Fiss, O, 'Against Settlement' (1984) 93 *Yale Law Journal* 1073
Freeman, J, 'Collaborative Governance in the Administrative State'(1997) 45 *UCLA Law Review* 1
Freshman, C, 'Privatizing Same-Sex Marriage through Alternative Dispute Resolution: Community Enhancing Versus Community Enabling Mediation' (1997) 44 *UCLA Law Review* 1687
Friedman, G, *A Guide to Divorce Mediation* (New York, Workman, 1993)
Fuller, L, 'Mediation: Its Form and Its Functions' (1971) 44 *Southern California Law Review* 305
Fuller L, 'The Forms and Limits of Adjudication' (1978) 92 *Harvard Law Review* 353
Fuller, L, 'The Forms and Limits of Adjudication' in K Winston (ed), *The Principles of Social Order: Selected Essays of Lon Fuller*, revised edn (Oxford and Portland, Oregon, Hart Publishing, 2001)

Gadlin, H, 'The Ombudsman—What's in a Name?' (2000) 16 *Negotiation Journal* 37
Galanter, M, 'Reading the Landscape of Our Disputes: What We Know, Don't Know (and Think We Know) about Our Allegedly Contentious and Litigious Society' (1983) 31 *UCLA Law Review* 4
Galanter, M, 'The Vanishing Trial: An Examination of Trials and Related Matters in Federal and State Courts' (2004) 1 *Journal of Empirical Legal Studies* 459
Geske, J, 'Why Do I Teach Restorative Justice to Law Students' (2005) 89 *Marquette Law Review* 327
Glaberson, W, 'Misuse of Arbitration?', *New York Times,* 1996, 1
Golann, D, 'Making Alternative Dispute Resolution Mandatory: The Constitutional Issues' (1989) 68 *Oregon Law Review* 487
Green, ED, *The CPR Legal Program Mini-Trial Handbook* (New York, Matthew Bender & Co, 1982)
Grossman, M, 'Is This Arbitration? Religious Tribunals, Judicial Review and Due Process' (2007) 107 *Columbia Law Review* 169
Gulliver, PH, *Disputes and Negotiations: A Cross Cultural Perspective* (New York, Academic Press, 1979)
Guthrie, C, 'Panacea or Pandora's Box? The Costs of Options in Negotiation' (2003) 88 *Iowa Law Review* 601
Hampshire, S, *Justice is Conflict* (Princeton, Princeton University Press, 2000)
Harrington, C, *Shadow Justice: The Ideology and Institutionalization of Alternatives to Court* (Westport, Greenwood Press, 1985)
Harter, P, 'Negotiating Regulations: A Cure for the Malaise?' (1982) 71 *Georgetown Law Journal* 1
Helfand, MA, 'Religious Arbitration and the New Multi-culturalism: Negotiating Conflicting Legal Orders' (2011) 86 *New York University Law Review* 1231
Hensler, D, 'A Glass Half Full, a Glass Half Empty: The Use of Alternative Dispute Resolution in Mass Personal Injury Litigation' (1995) 73 *Texas Law Review* 1587
Hirsh, J, 'Honda Civic Loses Unusual Small Claims Suit (to Heather Peters)', *Los Angeles Times*, 1 February 2012, Business Section, 1
Jacobs, M, 'Legal Beat: Private Jury Trials: Cheap, Quick and Controversial', *Wall Street Journal*, 7 July 1997, B-1
Joseph, J, 'Mediation in War: Winning Hearts and Minds Using Mediated Condolence Payments' (2007) 23 *Negotiation Journal* 219
Katsh, E and Rifkin, J, *Online Dispute Resolution: Resolving Conflicts in Cyberspace* (San Francisco, Jossey Bass, 2001)
Kagan, R, *Adversarial Legalism: The American Way of Life* (Cambridge, MA, Harvard Press, 2001)
Kakalik, J, Dunworth, T, Hill, L, McCaffrey, D, Oshiro, M, Pace, N and Vaiana, M, *An Evaluation of Mediation and Early Neutral Evaluation Under the Civil Justice Reform Act* (Santa Monica, RAND, 1996)
Kim, A, 'Rent-a-Judges and the Cost of Selling Justice' (1994) 44 *Duke Law Journal* 166
Lind, EA, MacCoun, R, Ebener, P, Felstiner, W, Hensler, D, Resnik, J and Tyler, T, *The Perception of Justice: Tort Litigants' Views of Trial, Court-Annexed Arbitration and Judicial Settlement Conferences* (Santa Monica, RAND, 1989)
Lind, EA and Tyler, T, *The Social Psychology of Procedural Justice* (New York, Plenum Press, 1988)
Luce, D and Raiffa, H, *Games and Decisions: An Introduction and Critical Survey* (New York, John Wiley, reproduced by Dover, 1987)
Love, L, 'The Top Ten Reasons Why Mediators Should Not Evaluate' (1997) 24 *Florida State Law Review* 937

Luban, D, 'Settlements and the Erosion of the Public Realm' (1995) 83 *Georgetown Law Journal* 2619

Maull, J, 'ADR in the Federal Courts: Would Uniformity Be Better?' (1996) 34 *Duquesne Law Review* 245

McEwen, C and Plapinger, E, 'RAND Report Points Way to Next Generation of ADR Research' (1996–1997) 3 *Dispute Resolution Magazine* 10

Menkel-Meadow, C, 'Aha! Is Creativity Possible in Legal Problem Solving and Teachable in Legal Education' (2001) 6 *Harvard Negotiation Law Review* 97

Menkel-Meadow, C, 'Ancillary Practice and Conflicts of Interest: When Lawyer Ethics Rules Are Not Enough' [February 1995] *Alternatives to the High Cost of Litigation* 15

Menkel-Meadow, C, 'Are Cross-Cultural Ethics Standards Possible or Desirable in International Arbitration?' in P Gauch, F Werro and P Pichonnaz (eds), *Melangés en l'honneur de Pierre Tercier* (Geneva, Switzerland, Schulthess, 2008) 1–22

Menkel-Meadow, C, 'Chronicling the Complexification of Negotiation Theory and Practice' (2009) 25 *Negotiation Journal* 415

Menkel-Meadow, C (ed), *Complex Dispute Resolution: Vol 1 Foundational Processes and Vol 2, Multi-Party Dispute Processes, Decision Making and Democracy* (Farnham, Ashgate Press, 2012)

Menkel-Meadow, C, *Dispute Processing and Conflict Resolution: Theory, Practice and Policy* (Burlington, Ashgate Press, 2003)

Menkel-Meadow, C, 'Dispute Resolution' in P Cane and P Kritzer (eds), *Oxford Handbook of Empirical Legal Research* (Oxford, Oxford Press, 2010) 596–624

Menkel-Meadow, C, 'Do the Haves Come Out Ahead in Alternative Justice Systems? Repeat Players in ADR' (1999) 15 *Ohio State Journal Dispute Resolution* 19

Menkel-Meadow, C, 'Ethics and the Settlement of Mass Torts: When the Rules Meet the Road' (1995) 80 *Cornell Law Review* 1159

Menkel-Meadow, C, 'For and Against Settlement: Uses and Abuses of the Mandatory Settlement Conference' (1985) 33 *UCLA Law Review* 485

Menkel-Meadow, C, 'Getting to Let's Talk: Commentary on Collaborative Processes in Environmental Dispute Resolution' (2008) 8 *Nevada Law Journal* 835

Menkel-Meadow, C, 'Know When To Show Your Hand' (2007) 10(6) *Negotiation Newsletter, Program on Negotiation* 1

Menkel-Meadow, C (ed), *Mediation: Theory, Policy, and Practice* (Aldershot, UK, Ashgate, 2000)

Menkel-Meadow, C, 'Mothers and Fathers of Invention; The Intellectual Founders of ADR' (2000) 16 *Ohio State Journal of Dispute Resolution* 13

Menkel-Meadow, C, 'Peace and Justice: Notes on the Evolution and Purposes of Legal Processes' (2006) 94 *Georgetown Law Journal* 553

Menkel-Meadow, C, 'Professional Responsibility for Third Party Neutrals' [July 2009] *Alternatives to the High Cost of Litigation* 129

Menkel-Meadow, M, 'Pursuing Settlement in an Adversary Culture: The Law of ADR' (1991) 19 *Florida State Law Review* 1

Menkel-Meadow, C, 'Restorative Justice: What Is It and Does it Work?' 3 *Annual Review of Law and Social Science* 10:1 (Annual Reviews, Stanford, 2007)

Menkel-Meadow, C, 'Roots and Inspirations: A Brief History of the Foundations of Dispute Resolution' in M Moffitt and R Bordone (eds), *Handbook of Dispute Resolution* (San Francisco, Jossey Bass, 2005) 13–31

Menkel-Meadow, C, 'The National Labor Relations Act Legacy: Collective or Individual Dispute Resolution or Not?' (2011) 26 *ABA Labor & Employment Journal* 249

Menkel-Meadow, C, 'The Trouble with the Adversary System in a Post-Modern, Multicultural World' (1996) 38 *William & Mary Law Review* 5

Menkel-Meadow, C, 'Toward another View of Legal Negotiation: The Structure of Problem Solving' (1984) 31 *UCLA Law Review* 754

Menkel-Meadow, C, 'When Dispute Resolution Begets Disputes of its Own Conflicts among Dispute Professionals' (1997) 44 *UCLA Law Review* 1871

Menkel-Meadow, C, 'Whose Dispute Is It Anyway? A Philosophical and Democratic Defense of Settlement (in Some Cases)' (1995) 83 *Georgetown Law Journal* 2663

Menkel-Meadow, C and Garth, B, 'Civil Procedure: Policy, Politics and People' in P Cane and H Kritzer (eds), *Oxford Handbook of Empirical Legal Research* (Oxford, Oxford Press, 2010) 679–704

Menkel-Meadow, C, Love, L and Kupfer Schneider, A, *Mediation: Practice, Policy and Ethics* (New York, WoltersKluwer, 2nd edn, 2013)

Menkel-Meadow, C, Love, L, Kupfer Schneider, A and Sternlight, J, *Dispute Resolution: Beyond the Adversarial Model*, 2nd edn (New York, Wolters Kluwer, 2011)

Mentschikoff, S, 'Commercial Arbitration' (1961) 61 *Columbia Law Review* 846

Merry, S and Milner, N, *The Possibility of Popular Justice: A Case Study of Community Mediation in the United States* (Ann Arbor, University of Michigan Press, 1993)

Mezey, N, 'Erasure and Recognition: The Census, Race and the National Imagination' (2003) 97 *Northwestern University Law Review* 1701

Michaels, R, 'A Fuller Concept of Law Beyond the State? Thoughts on Lon Fuller's Contributions to the Jurisprudence of Transnational Dispute Resolution' (2011) 2(2) *Journal of International Dispute Settlement* 417

Nader, L and Todd, H (eds), *The Disputing Process—Law in Ten Societies* (New York, Columbia University Press, 1978)

Nash, J, 'Two Person Cooperative Games' (1953) 21 *Econometrica* 129

Niemic, RJ, *Mediation and Conference Programs in the Federal Appeals Courts* (Washington, DC, Federal Judicial Center, 1997)

Pfund, A (ed), *From Conflict Resolution to Social Justice: The Work and Legacy of Wallace Warfield* (New York, Bloomsbury Press, 2013)

Plapinger, E and Stienstra, D, *ADR and Settlement in the Federal District Courts* (Washington, DC, Federal Judicial Center, 1996)

Podziba, SL, *Civic Fusion: Mediating Polarized Public Disputes* (Chicago, ABA Press, 2012)

Posner, R, 'The Summary Jury Trial and Other Methods of Alternative Dispute Resolution: Some Cautionary Observations' (1986) 53 *University of Chicago Law Review* 366

Pruitt, D and Kim, SH, *Social Conflict: Escalation, Stalemate and Settlement* (New York, McGraw Hill, 2004)

Regan, P, *Unsettling the Settler Within: Indian Residential Schools, Truth Telling and Reconciliation in Canada* (Vancouver, University of British Columbia Press, 2010)

Resnik, J, 'Managerial Judges' (1982) 96 *Harvard Law Review* 374

Resnik, J, 'Many Doors? Closing Doors? Alternative Dispute Resolution and Adjudication' (1995) 10 *Ohio State Journal on Dispute Resolution* 211

Riskin, L, 'Decision-Making in Mediation: The New Old Grid and New New Grid System' (2003) 79 *Notre Dame Law Review* 1

Riskin, L and Welsh, NA, 'Is That All There Is? The Problem in Court-Oriented Mediation' (2008) 15 *George Mason Law Review* 863

Robinson, P, 'Judicial Settlement Conference Practices and Techniques' (2009) 33 *American Journal of Trial Advocacy* 113

Rogers, C, *Ethics in International Arbitration* (Oxford, Oxford University Press, 2013)

Rogers, N, McEwen, C, Cole, S, Coben, J and Thompson, P, *Mediation, Law Policy and Practice*, 3nd edn (St Paul, MN, Thompson Reuters, 2011)

Sander, FEA and Goldberg, SB, 'Fitting the Forum to the Fuss: A User Friendly Guide to Selecting an ADR Procedure' (1994) 10 *Negotiation Journal* 49

Sander, FEA, 'Varieties of Dispute Processing' in A Levin and R Wheeler (eds), *The Pound Conference: Perspectives on Justice in the Future* (St Paul, MN, West Publishing Co, 1979) 111–32

Schoenholtz, R, 'Neighborhood Justice Systems: Work Structure and Guiding Principles' (1984) 5 *Mediation Quarterly* 3

Schuck, P, *Agent Orange On Trial* (Cambridge, MA, Harvard Press, 1988)

Searle Civil Justice Institute, *Consumer Arbitration before the American Arbitration Association* (Chicago, Searle Center on Law, Regulation, and Economic Growth, Northwestern University School of Law, 2009)

Shapiro, M, *Courts: A Comparative and Political Analysis* (Chicago, University of Chicago Press, 1981)

Sternlight, J, 'Creeping Mandatory Arbitration: Is It Just?' (2005) 57 *Stanford Law Review* 1631

Sternlight, J, 'Fixing the Mandatory Arbitration Problem: We Need the Arbitration Fairness Act of 2009' (2009) 16 *Dispute Resolution Magazine* 5

Sternlight, J, 'Is the US Out on a Limb? Comparing the US Approach to Mandatory Consumer and Employment Arbitration to That of the Rest of the World' (2002) 56 *University of Miami Law Review* 831

Stienstra, D, Johnson, M, Lombard, P, and Pecherski, M, *Report to the Judicial Conference Committee on Court Administration and Case Management: A Study of Five Demonstration Programs Established Under the Civil Justice Reform Act of 1990* (Washington, DC, Federal Judicial Center, 1997)

Stipanowich, T, 'The Vanishing Trial: The Growth and Impact of Alternative Dispute Resolution' (2004) 1 *Journal of Empirical Legal Studies* 843

Stone Sweet, A, 'Arbitration and Judicialization' (2011) 1(9) *Onati Socio-Legal Series* 1

Subrin, SN, 'Litigation and Democracy: Restoring a Reasonable Prospect of Trial' (2011) 46 *Harvard Civil Rights-Civil Liberties Law Review* 399

Subrin, SN, 'The Limitations of Transsubstantive Procedure: An Essay on Adjusting the 'One Size Fits All' Assumption' (2010) 87 *Denver University Law Review* 377

Susskind, L, McKernan, S and Thomas-Lermer, J, *The Consensus Building Handbook: A Comprehensive Guide to Reaching Agreement* (Thousand Oaks, Sage Publications, 1999)

Talesh, S, 'The Privatization of Public Legal Rights: How Manufacturers Construct the Meaning of Consumer Law' (2009) 43 *Law & Society Review* 527

Tannen, D, *The Argument Culture: Moving from Debate to Dialogue* (New York, Random House, 1998)

Umbreit, M, *The Handbook of Victim-Offender Mediation* (San Francisco, Jossey Bass, 2000)

Ury, W, Brett, J and Goldberg, S, *Getting Disputes Resolved: Designing Systems to Cut Costs of Conflict* (San Francisco, Jossey Bass, 1988)

Venkatesh, S, *Gang Leader for a Day* (New York, Penguin, 2008)

Waddell, G and Keegan, J, 'Christian Conciliation: An Alternative to "Ordinary" ADR' (1999) 29 *Cumberland Law Review* 583

Wahab, MSA, Katsh, E and Rainey, D (eds), *Online Dispute Resolution: Theory and Practice* (The Hague, Eleven International Publishing, 2012)

Waldman, E, *Mediation Ethics* (San Francisco, Jossey-Bass, 2011)

Walton, R and McKersie, R, *A Behavioral Theory of Labor Negotiations* (New York, McGraw-Hill, 1965)

Weinstein, J, *Individual Justice in Mass Tort Litigation* (Evanston, Northwestern Press, 1995)

Welsh, N, 'Remembering the Role of Justice in Resolution: Insights from Procedural and Social Justice Theories' (2004) 54 *Journal of Legal Education* 49

Winston, K (ed), *The Principles of Social Order: Selected Essays of Lon Fuller*, revised edn (Oxford and Portland Oregon, Hart Publishing, 2001)

Wissler, R, 'Court-Connected Settlement Procedures: Mediation and Judicial Settlement Conferences' (2011) 26 *Ohio State Journal on Dispute Resolution* 271

Wolfe, CL, 'Faith Based Arbitration: Friend or Foe?' (2006) 75 *Fordham Law Review* 427

Zeckhauser, R, Keeney, R and Sebenius, J (eds), *Wise Choices: Decisions, Games and Negotiations* (Boston, MA, Harvard Business Press, 1996)